PRIVATE PRESS

and

Fine Printing

Hill's *Berwell* II 238

CATALOGUE 234

Oak Knoll Books

THUCYDIDES AN ATHENIAN

wrote the history of the war in which the Peloponnesians & the Athenians fought against one another. He began to write when they first took up 1. *Greatness of the war.* arms, believing that it would be great and memorable above any previous war. For he argued that both states were then at the full height of their military power, and he saw the rest of the Hellenes either siding or intending to side with one or other of them. No movement ever stirred Hellas more deeply than this; it was shared by many of the Barbarians, and might be said even to affect the world at large. The character of the events which preceded, whether immediately or in more remote antiquity, owing to the lapse of time cannot be made out with certainty. But, judging from the evidence which I am able to trust after most careful enquiry, I should imagine that former ages were not great either in their wars or in anything else.

THE country which is now called Hellas was not regularly settled in 2. *Weakness of an-cient Hellas: readi-ness of the early tribes to migrate: the richer districts the more unsettled; some of the poorer, like Attica, in reality the more prosperous.* ancient times. The people were migratory, and readily left their homes whenever they were overpowered by numbers. There was no com-merce, & they could not safely hold intercourse with one another either by land or sea: The several tribes cultivated their own soil just enough to obtain a maintenance from it. But they had no accumulations of wealth, & did not plant the ground; for, being without walls, they were never sure that an invader might not come & despoil them. Living in this manner and knowing that they could anywhere obtain a bare subsistence, they were always ready to migrate; so that they had neither great cities nor any considerable resources. The richest districts were most constantly changing their inhabitants; for example, the countries which are now called Thessaly and Boeotia, the greater part of the Peloponnesus with the exception of Arcadia, and all the best parts of Hellas. For the productiveness of the land increased the power of individuals; this in turn was a source of quarrels by which communities were ruined, while at the same time they were more exposed to attacks from without. Certainly Attica, of which the soil was poor and thin, enjoyed a long freedom from civil strife, and therefore retained its original inhabitants. And a striking confirmation of my argument is afforded by the fact that Attica through immigration increased in population more than any other region. For the leading men of Hellas, when driven out of their own country by war or revolution, sought an asylum at Athens; and from the very earliest times, being admitted to rights of citizen-ship, so greatly increased the number of inhabitants that Attica became incapable of containing them, and was at last obliged to send out colonies to Ionia.

THE feebleness of antiquity is further proved to me by the circumstance 3. *No unity among the early inhabitants: no common name of Hellenes or Barbar-ians; or common ac-tion in Hellos before the Trojan War.* that there appears to have been no common action in Hellas before the Trojan War. And I am inclined to think that the very name was not as yet given to the whole country, and in fact did not exist at all before the time of Hellen, the son of Deucalion; the different tribes, of which the Pelasgian was the most widely spread, gave their own names to different districts. But when Hellen & his sons became powerful in Phthiotis, their aid was invoked by other

b 1   1

Item 74

Private Press and Fine Printing

1. (Acorn Press) Peckham, Howard H.(editor). MEMOIRS OF THE LIFE OF JOHN ADLUM IN THE REVOLUTIONARY WAR. Chicago: The Caxton Club, 1968, large 12mo., cloth with paper cover label. xii, 143, (3) pages. $ 45.00
First edition, printed in an edition of 1100 copies of which this is one of 500 bound in cloth for the members of the Caxton Club. Printed by the Acorn Press. Unique account of the war through the eyes of a prisoner of British-held New York City. Introduction by the editor. Spine faded.

2. (Adagio Press) THE ADAGIO PRESS PAMPHLETS. Harper Woods, MI: The Adagio Press, 1967–1968 and 1970, two pamphlets contained in a printed 7.5″ x 10.5″ envelope. (24); 15+(1) pages. $ 45.00
"Typographic Embellishers" is one in an edition limited to 248 numbered copies printed in the winter of 1967–1968. Displays a collection of decorative prints in five colors. The second pamphlet, "A Gathering of Typographic Odds & Ends Rescued From Sundry Sources and Now Protected in the Cases at The Adagio Press," is one in an edition of 200 copies, originally printed as a supplement to "Typographic Embellishers" in 1970. Continues the collection of decorative prints found in the first volume, printed in black on a brown paper.

3. (Adagio Press) Bahr, Leonard F. MISCELLANEA TYPOGRAPHICA, NOTES ON BOOKS AND PRINTING, NUMBER THREE. (Grosse Pointe, MI: The Private Press of Leonard F. Bahr), 1957, large 12mo., stapled booklet in envelope. 15+(1) pages. $ 25.00
Printed in an edition limited to 475 copies by Leonard F. Bahr at his Adagio Press, for distribution among members of the National Amateur Press Association (Tanner, no. 1). With the essay *Some Trends in Recent Trade Book Design*. Printed in Weiss roman and italic on white Eagle A Text paper.

4. (Adagio Press) Bahr, Leonard. EXPERIMENTS WITH THE BRADLEY COMBINATION ORNAMENTS. Harper Woods, MI: The Adagio Press, 1967, 8vo., original paper wrappers, printed mailing envelope. (16) pages. $ 45.00
Limited to 473 numbered copies and hand-set by Leonard Bahr. Printed on different colored papers. Small tear along front hinge at top of spine.

5. (Adagio Press) THE COLLECTED EPHEMERA OF THE ADAGIO PRESS. Harper Woods, MI: The Adagio Press, n.d., six loose folded sheets in a 7. 5″ x 10.5″ printed envelope. $ 35.00
One in a series of numbered sets of ephemera. Includes type specimens, typographic exercises, and announcements for various times and reasons. Each item is printed in two to five colors. One small tear at edge of envelope.

6. (Adagio Press) Polscher, Andrew. THE EVOLUTION OF PRINTING PRESSES FROM WOOD TO METAL. Harper Woods, MI: Adagio Press, n.d., large 12mo., stiff paper wrappers. (7) pages. $ 25.00
Privately printed by Leonard Bahr. An examination of the printing press from 1800 to 1820 when they went from wood to metal. Illustrated.

7. (Adagio Press) PRINTING IN PRIVACY, A REVIEW OF RECENT ACTIVITY AMONG AMERICAN PRIVATE PRESSES. Grosse Pointe Park: Adagio Press, 1960, 8vo., stiff paper wrappers. 24 pages. $ 20.00
Limited to 550 copies. Surveys by Levenson and Lieberman, notes on the colophons of various private presses, an article by Steve Watts on 19th century typefaces and a discussion of work in progress. Handprinted.

8. (Adagio Press) Ruskin, John. CONTEMPTIBLE HORSE, THE TEXT OF JOHN RUSKIN'S LETTER TO 'MY DEAR TINIE' WRITTEN FROM THE BRIDGE OF ALLAN ON 31 AUGUST 1857. WITH AN INTRODUCTORY ESSAY BY NORMAN H. STROUSE AND FIVE PEN-AND-INK ILLUSTRATIONS BY ADELE BICHAN. Harper Woods, MI: Adagio: the Private Press of Leonard F. Bahr, 1962, 8vo., quarter cloth with marbled paper covered boards. xix, 23-43, (3) pages.

$ 95.00

First edition, limited to 365 copies. Second production of this private press. The text of John Ruskin's letter to 'My Dear Tinie'. Sharp satire on British industrialization.

9. (Adagio Press) TYPOGRAPHIA 1. Harper Woods, MI: The Adagio Press, 1976, 8vo., paper wrappers, mailing envelope. 27 pages. $ 45.00

Printed in an edition limited to 325 numbered and signed copies. This is a commonplace book of typographic exercises interspersed with notes on printing, typography and the private press.

10. (Adagio Press) TYPOGRAPHIA TWO. Harper Woods, MI: The Adagio Press, 1979, 8vo., stiff paper wrappers. pp.29-60. $ 45.00

Printed in an edition limited to 325 numbered copies. A continuation of the work presented as Typographia 1. This copy is signed by the private press owner, Leonard Bahr. This is a commonplace book of typographic exercises interspersed with notes on printing, typography and the private press.

11. (Alembic Press) Bolton, Claire. A BORDER SPECIMEN. Marcham: The Alembic Press, 2000, small 4to., quarter cloth, decorated paper covered boards. 108 pages.

$ 250.00

Printed in an edition limited to 180 numbered copies, this being one of the 160 trade edition. A specimen book of typographic borders held by the Alembic Press. The Press was given a collection of Monotype casting equipment that belonged to W.H. Heffer of Cambridge, and then added a small amount from Hive Printers in Letchworth. After some time the equipment was made operational and a considerable number of matrices for casting flowers and ornaments were found. The finished book is illustrated with specimens of 380 Monotype borders, 33 founders borders, each displayed in almost 580 different squares. Chapter headings are used to demonstrate border styles, from Baskerville to Victorian gothic. Some specimens are tipped-in and some are printed in a variety of colors. The text was written and keyboarded by Claire Bolton in Bembo and the type and borders were cast by David Bolton. Includes a bibliography and a chronology of Monotype border designs. An encyclopedic production.

12. (Alembic Press) Bolton, Claire. ALEMBIC PRESS GUIDE TO SUNDRY PRINTING PLACES & SOURCES THAT MIGHT BE OF INTEREST TO OTHER PRIVATE PRESS PRINTERS. Illustrated by John Smith. Oxford: The Alembic Press, 1991, 12mo., cloth-backed marbled paper covered boards. 85 pages.

$ 68.00

Third edition, revised and enlarged, limited to 180 numbered copies. A guide to printing places, suppliers, museums, bookdealers, papermakers, etc. Contains over 300 entries and covers the whole world.

13. (Alembic Press) Bolton, Claire. UP MILL; A HAMPSHIRE PAPERMILL IN 1696. Winchester: The Alembic Press, 1984, 8vo., quarter calf. (36) pages. $ 65.00

Limited to 120 numbered copies of which this is one of the ten special copies bound in quarter leather and printed on hand-made paper. Introductory text followed by a reprint of the detailed inventory of a papermill that was made in 1696. Text is illustrated.

14. (Alembic Press) Bolton, Claire. THE WINCHESTER BOOKSHOP & BINDERY. Oxford: The Alembic Press, 1991, 8vo., quarter cloth. 77 pages. $ 125.00
First edition, limited to 250 copies. An interesting account of the history of the P & G Wells bookshop and bindery and its evolution from the bindery - bookselling firm of Thomas and John Burdon in 1757, through James Robbins (1806–1844) and David Nutt (1844–1862). Well illustrated with line blocks and photographs, some showing 19th century binding tools.

15. (Alembic Press) CAXTON'S INDULGENCE OF 1476. Abingdon: The Alembic Press, 1995, 25 x 33 cm., sewn into red card covers. $ 50.00
Limited to 150 copies. Facsimile reproduction of the first item of printing in England by William Caxton, an indulgence printed for the Abbot of Abingdon Abbey. With English translation and printed on various papers with calligraphy by Carolyn Blackmore.

16. (Alembic Press) COMPTON MARBLING PORTFOLIO OF PATTERNS. Oxford: The Alembic Press, 1992, small 4to., portfolio tied with ribbon. 18 sections loosely inserted. $ 150.00
First edition, limited to 150 numbered copies. Contains 17 examples of Compton Marbling's paper, each developed especially for an individual customer, or for themselves for a particular market. Each sample is tipped into a folded leaf with descriptive text. Some of the sheets contain other samples, such as an original that was used by the company for matching. Portfolio is covered with Compton marbled paper. Text is hand set in Kennerley and printed on 120 gsm Rivoli paper.

17. (Alembic Press) DELITTLE, 1888–1988, THE FIRST TEN YEARS IN A CENTURY OF WOOD LETTER MANUFACTURE, 1888–1895. Oxford: The Alembic Press, 1988, small 4to., cloth-backed boards. 63 pages. $ 82.50
Limited to 155 numbered copies. Issued on the centenary of the firm of DeLittle, the only surviving firm in England cutting wood- letter. Extracts from the actual day book of the firm for the period 1888 to 1895 showing the daily running of a business devoted to the production of wood-letter. Enhanced by 2 tipped-in specimens mostly printed from the actual letters used to print DeLittle specimen books and 17 illustrations in black and white. Printed by hand by Claire Bolton at her private press.

18. (Alembic Press) Gerard, John. FLAX PAPERS. Marcham: The Alembic Press, 1996, small 8vo., stiff paper wrappers, cloth folder. 30 pages. $ 125.00
Limited to 100 numbered copies. Printed by hand on paper made from a flax cellulose half-stuff. History, manual on producing paper and actual samples of "dew-retted flax fiber before cooking and beating," six different samples of paper made from flax taken after various times of beating and other variations, a sample of "water-retted flax fiber before cooking and beating" and three samples of paper made from this type of flax. Interesting booklet.

19. (Alembic Press) A GRANJON ARABESQUE. Hyde Farm House, Marcham, Oxford: Alembic Press, 1998, miniature book (2.75 x 2.5 in./ 7.25 x 6.5 cm), sewn, printed paper over stiff self paper wrappers. 71 pages. $ 60.00
Limited to 140 numbered copies. Sixteenth-century book ornaments revisited. Fifty-plus compositions using six Monotype Granjon arabesque ornaments, nos. 310 to 315. Designed, printed and bound by Claire Bolton. Gatherings are sewn into sleeves formed by an accordion-folded strip attached in turn to the covers.

20. (Alembic Press) Laver-Gibbs, Christine. THE EARLY YEARS OF GRIFFEN MILL 1986–1998. Marcham, Oxfordshire: Alembic Press, 1999, large 8vo., quarter cloth, patterned paper-covered boards, paper spine label. 42 pages, with 4 additional leaves of paper samples. $ 140.00
Limited to 120 numbered copies, including 100 in this edition. The Griffen Mill in Somerset makes papers for conservation and reproduction, that is, papers with a high degree of permanency and matching the appearance and handling characteristics of the paper of the original which is to be restored, repaired, or reproduced. Among the special papers which it has made to date are papers for restoration of some

damaged Tudor account books, Islamic endpaper for conservation work at the India Office, lining paper for conservation of historic wallpapers, and paper for the reproduction of a 16th-century map. Some of the papers designed at Griffen Mill have also become available commercially. This Alembic Press imprint, designed and produced by Claire Bolton and written by C. Laver-Gibbs, proprietor and operator of the Mill, recounts the history of Griffen Mill and discusses selected papers produced there, with samples. There are 4 bound-in sheets of samples, and 8 smaller tipped-in specimens, plus reproductions of two watermarks and a woodcut showing the processes of hand-papermaking. The book itself is printed on Griffen paper, and the cover pattern is printed on Griffen Mill ledger paper.

21. (Alembic Press) Macfarlane, Nigel. HANDMADE PAPERS OF THE HI-MALAYAS. Winchester: The Alembic Press, 1986, oblong 12mo. (5.5 x 13.5 inches), enclosed in a cloth-backed board portfolio. 44 pages. $ 225.00
Limited to 108 numbered copies. Handprinted on sheets of nine different papers from Nepal and Bhutan. Describes the making of paper in this region and includes illustrations, some of which are printed in a second color.

22. (Alembic Press) SPECIMENS OF WOOD TYPE HELD AT THE ALEMBIC PRESS. Oxford: The Alembic Press, 1993, oblong folio bound at top, quarter cloth, three metal tabs. Five preliminary leaves followed by 43 leaves of specimens. $ 160.00
Limited to 100 numbered copies. The large woodtype specimens are printed in different colors. Includes a two page introduction by Claire Bolton and a table of contents listing the different type faces used.

23. (Alembic Press) A TALE OF TWO BENCHES. Marcham: The Alembic Press, 2000, 8vo., quarter cloth with paper covered boards. 19, (3) pages. $ 50.00
Printed in an edition limited to 120 numbered copies. A reprint of a chapter from Robert Gibbings' book "Till I End my Song," along with his original wood engraving. Included is an introduction describing how Gibbings came to be in Marcham, a history of the Pointer family and Simon Brett's engraving of one of Bill Pointer's benches, who to this day still lives in Marcham and makes benches.

24. (Alembic Press) TE DEUM LAUDAMUS, SOLEMN TONE FROM THE SARUM PSALTER. Marcham, (England): The Alembic Press, 1995, miniature book (3 x 2.75 inches), quarter cloth with gold paste-paper covered boards, paper spine label. (26) pages. $ 60.00
Printed in an edition limited to 110 copies by Claire Bolton at the Alembic Press at the Hyde Farm House in Marcham, England. Includes a two-color wood engraving by Simon Brett. The musical type used to print this volume is from St. Mary's Press who printed the first edition of this score in 1942.

25. (Alembic Press) TO MARBLE THE EDGES OF BOOKS OR PAPER. Marcham: The Alembic Press, 1994, 12mo., self paper wrappers. 4 pages printed French fold and enclosed in an envelope. $ 20.00
Limited to 100 copies, of which this is one of 40 copies printed on 18th century paper. Reprint of a note from "The Artists Vade Mecum," Peterhead, 1819, printed by P. Buchan.

26. (Alexandria Press & Print) Albert, Marvin Howard. THE END GAME, A POEM AND DESIGN FOR CHESS. Seattle: Alexandria Press & Print, 1966, small 8vo., stapled stiff paper wrappers. (12 pages). $ 25.00
Author's edition, printed in typescript and limited to 22 numbered copies. Some yellowing to pages and front cover. Facsimile of chess board and pieces on title page.

27. (Alexandria Press & Print) Albert, Marvin Howard. THE MAGIC CLOWN. San Francisco: Alexandria Press & Print, (1964), 16mo., loose leaves laid in stiff wrappers. (34) pages. $ 30.00
Hand-set by the author in an edition limited to 24 numbered copies and printed at the Little (One-Man) Print Shop by Don P. Little. Photograph pasted on title page and two others in text, including one of the printer in his shop. Title page creased and others unpaginated and in no certain order.

28. (Alexandria Press & Print) Albert, Marvin Howard. SIFTING OF INFINITY. San Francisco: Alexandria Press & Print, (1962), small 4to., plastic ring binder. (52) pages.
$ 30.00

This edition, hand-set and hand-printed by the author, is limited to 24 numbered copies. Poetry. Pages starting to brown. A later edition, published in 1963 by Colonial Press, Northport, Alabama, in wrappers, is also enclosed. Hand-written letter from the author loosely laid in.

29. (Alexandria Press & Print) Albert, Marvin Howard. SOMEWHERE COMING SOMEWHERE GOING. San Francisco: Alexandria Press & Print, (1964), 4to., loose signatures in self paper wrappers. (24) pages.
$ 45.00

Hand-set , printed, and illustrated with twenty linocuts by the author in an edition limited to 24 numbered copies.

30. (Alexandria Press & Print) Albert, Marvin Howard. THE TEMPEST MYTH. San Francisco: Alexandria Press & Print, (1963), large 4to., loose signatures laid in stiff paper wrappers. (24) pages.
$ 55.00

Hand-set and printed by the author in an edition limited to 24 numbered copies. Illustrated by the author with eight linocuts in text and one pasted on front cover. Poetry.

31. (Alexandria Press & Print) Albert, Marvin. THIS FACT OF MAN. Seattle: Alexandria Press & Print, (1966), 4to., self-paper wrappers. (8) pages.
$ 25.00

The author's proof edition limited to 15 numbered copies. Some yellowing to title page and text.

32. (Allen Press) Euripides. THE BACCHAE, DIONYSUS, THE GOD. Kentfield: The Allen Press, 1972, large 4to., quarter cloth with wood veneer covered boards and a cloth slipcase. unpaginated.
$ 650.00

Printed in an edition limited to 130 copies. (Allen Press 38). The Bacchae is considered one of the great dramas of all times, the masterpiece of Euripides. Dionysus (Bacchus), God of wine and fertility is the chief character. Three full-page color etchings, one for each of the three acts are by French artist, Michele Forgeois, which are signed and numbered. The etchings were registered in Paris, and the plates cancelled. The all-rag paper was made by hand especially for The Allen Press, and so watermarked. Printed damp on a Columbian handpress, model 1846. The title is in orange, olive and black, and the colors orange, blue, olive and blue-green highlights are printed throughout the text. Each page has a border (head and side only) of Greek letters, one section of the borders (both head and side) is printed in a series of six colors. The Greek lettering was accomplished by James MacDonald, a nationally known calligrapher. Slipcase has some fraying of cloth along edges.

33. (Allen Press) Flaubert, Gustave. THE TEMPTATION OF ST ANTHONY. Kentfield: Allen Press, 1974, small folio, cloth. (vi), 83, (iii) pages.
$ 600.00

Printed in an edition limited to 140 copies handset and printed by hand on Michelangelo mould-made rag paper. (Allen no.40). Titles and marginal notes printed in red. Ornaments printed in black and light blue. Twenty four illustrations taken from Francis Carmody's (the editor and author of the introduction) personal collection of original source material used by Flaubert. A portrait of Saint Anthony reproduced from a block print by Odilon Redon. Translation by Lafcadio Hearn. Bound in a Fortuny cloth based on a fifteenth century Persian design: blue background fabric stamped with an overall stylized Egyptian palm tree pattern. Yellowing in gutters.

34. (Ampersand Press) Powell, Lawrence Clark. GIACOMO GIRALAMO CASANOVA, CHEVALIER DE SEINGALT, 1725–1798. Pasadena, CA: Ampersand Press, 1948, small 12mo., stiff paper wrappers. (iv), 23+(1) pages.
$ 35.00

Printed by Grant Dahlstrom at the Ampersand Press for members of the Zamorano Club of Los Angeles and other friends of the author and the printer. In a somewhat different form this essay was originally read at a meeting of the Zamorano Club in March, 1947. Powell was later to be Head Librarian at UCLA.

35. (Amphora Press) Spencer, Eleanor P. THE PRINTER'S RELICT, AN EXAMPLE TO HER SEX. Baltimore: Amphora Press, 1937, large 12mo., cloth. (12) pages. $ 45.00

Printed in a limited edition, but unstated edition, for the Amphora Press of Elizabeth Mann and Mary T. Williams, by E.L. Hildreth & Company. The author was a professor at Goucher College. Brief survey of female printers in 18th century America, most of whom had taken over their late spouse's business, including Anne Catharine Green, publisher of the *Maryland Gazette*, and Printer to the Province from 1767 to her death in 1775.

36. (Anchor & Acorn Press) Balzac, Honore De. BALZAC ON PAPERMAKING. Los Angeles: Anchor & Acorn Press, 1994, large oblong 12mo., stiff paper wrappers. 11+(1) pages. $ 17.50

Printed in an edition limited to two hundred copies by Anchor & Acorn Press, composed in Baskerville and Granjon types, in celebration of the Twenty-First Biennial Meeting of the Zamorano Club of Los Angeles and the Roxburghe Club of San Francisco, 1994, as a keepsake for their members and friends. Translated by Joanne Sonnichsen, with original French text on facing pages, being an extract from the third chapter of *Illusions Perdues: Les Deux Poetes*, 1837.

37. (Anderson, Caroline) Cleland, Robert G. AS A WATCH IN THE NIGHT. (N.P.: printed for the author, 1954), 8vo., cord-tied stiff paper wrappers. (3+1 pages). $ 17.50

Printed for the author by Caroline Anderson in an edition limited to 300 copies. Originally broadcast over the Columbia Broadcasting System on Edward R. Murrow's program, *This I Believe*. A presentation copy from the author, signed with his initials on the front free endpaper.

38. (Anderson, Gregg) Baughman, Orvil. ONE HUNDRED QUATRAINS AND TWENTY QUATRAINS FROM THE STYLUS OF CURTIUS SOREDD THE ELDER NOW FOR THE FIRST TIME RENDERED OUT OF THE ORIGINAL SANSWIT INTO ENGLISH VERSE. Pasadena, CA: Gregg Anderson, 1927, small 8vo., fold-out pamphlet. (4) pages. $ 25.00

Invitation to subscribe to *One Hundred Quatrains and Twenty Quatrains* which appeared in 1928 under the title *One Hundred and Thirty Quatrains*. Anderson and Baughman together operated the California-based Grey Bow Press whose heyday ran from the mid-20s until World War II. Page (1) subtitle within border of blue sectional type ornaments; ornament vignette on page (3).

39. (Anderson, Gregg) TO REMEMBER GREGG ANDERSON, TRIBUTES BY MEMBERS OF THE COLUMIAD CLUB. N.P.: Privately printed, 1949, 8vo., cloth. Various paginations for the different articles. $ 85.00

First edition, no limitation given but definitely printed in a small edition. Articles by Keith Anderson, Roland Baughman, Oscar Lewis, Harold Hugo, Ward Ritchie and the bibliography by Powell. Each of the articles was printed by a different printer. With *Bibliography of Gregg Anderson*. by Lawrence Clark Powell. Wear along front hinge.

40. (Angelica Press) Carroll, Lewis. WASP IN A WIG, A "SUPPRESSED" EPISODE OF THROUGH THE LOOKING-GLASS AND WHAT ALICE FOUND THERE. With a Preface, Introduction and Notes by Martin Gardner. New York: The Lewis Carroll Society of North America, 1977, 8vo., cloth. xiv, 11 pages followed by the facsimile. $ 45.00

First edition, limited to 750 copies and printed by Dennis Grastorf at his Angelica Press. This copy is not numbered and is a "Reviewer's copy."

41. (Angelica Press) THE DESIGNER'S GOURMET. New York: The Angelica Studio, 1979, 8vo., paper wrappers. (iv), 14, (2) pages. $ 15.00

A book of holiday recipes contributed by designers, and compiled by Paul Chevannes and Dennis Grastorf. Printed in an edition of 250 copies, illustrated by Paul Chevannes.

42. (Angelica Press) Grastorf, Dennis. 5 LINE W-49 FROM WOOD 2, MORGAN PRESS. A type specimen leaf printed in New York at the Angelica Press, 1976, one folio leaf (13 x 20 inches). $ 25.00

A single specimen leaf from Dennis Grastorf's *Wood Type of the Angelica Press*. Printed directly from wood type onto fine Tweedweave paper. Specimen includes full upper and lowercase alphabets, numbers, and some punctuation. This is a stylized, angular, early twentieth century specimen of wood type from the Morgan Press Typographers. Title printed in red at lower edge. A fine leaf suitable for framing.

43. (Angelica Press) Grastorf, Dennis. 6 LINE AETNA EXTRA CONDENSED NO.1. A type specimen leaf printed in New York at the Angelica Press, 1976, one folio leaf (13 x 20 inches). $ 20.00

A single specimen leaf from Dennis Grastorf's *Wood Type of the Angelica Press*. Printed directly from wood type onto fine Tweedweave paper. Specimen includes full upper and lowercase alphabets and numbers and some punctuation and symbols. Title printed in red at lower edge. A fine leaf suitable for framing.

44. (Angelica Press) Grastorf, Dennis. 6 LINE GOTHIC TUSCAN CONDENSED. A type specimen leaf printed in New York at the Angelica Press, 1976, one folio leaf (13 x 20 inches). $ 20.00

A single specimen leaf from Dennis Grastorf's *Wood Type of the Angelica Press*. Printed directly from wood type onto fine Tweedweave paper. Specimen includes full uppercase alphabet and punctuation. Title printed in red at lower edge. A fine leaf suitable for framing.

45. (Angelica Press) Grastorf, Dennis. 8 LINE NO. 189 FROM HAMILTON'S WOOD TYPE BOOK, 1899–1900. A type specimen leaf. (New York: Angelica Press, 1976), one folio leaf (13 x 20 inches). $ 25.00

A single specimen leaf from Dennis Grastorf's *Wood Type of the Angelica Press*. Printed directly from wood type onto fine Tweedweave paper. Specimen includes full upper and lowercase alphabets, numbers, and four ligatures. Title printed in red at lower edge. An attractive leaf suitable for framing.

46. (Angelica Press) Grastorf, Dennis. THIS FONT CUT BY HAND - NAME UN-KNOWN. A type specimen leaf printed in New York at the Angelica Press, 1976, one folio leaf (13 x 20 inches). $ 20.00

A single specimen leaf from Dennis Grastorf's *Wood Type of the Angelica Press*. Printed directly from wood type onto fine Tweedweave paper. Specimen includes uppercase alphabet and some numbers. Title printed in red at lower edge. A fine leaf suitable for framing.

47. (Angelica Press) Irving, Washington. CHRISTMAS AT BRACEBRIDGE HALL. Brooklyn: The Angelica Press, (1974), tall 8vo., cloth-backed boards, paper spine label. (x), 70, (4) pages. $ 45.00

Limited to 2000 copies. With preface by Dennis and Marilyn Grastorf, the printers.

48. (Angelica Press) Lerner, Abe. FORM & CONTENT, THE BOOKS OF THE AMERICAN PRIVATE PRESSES TODAY. New York: The Angelica Press, 1979, 8vo., stiff paper wrappers, cord-tied. (iv), 9+(1) pages. $ 25.00

Limited to 500 numbered copies. Designed by Dennis J. Grastorf with printing by Gary R. Wightman at the Amity Press.

49. (Angelica Press) Mattingly, John R. WHEN MEN WERE ANIMALS AND AN-
IMALS WERE MEN, A STUDY OF THE GRAPHIC WORK OF DAVID
ITCHKAWICH. New York: The Angelica Press, 1976, oblong small 4to., quarter
leather, slipcase. xviii, 92, (4) pages. $ 125.00
Limited to 520 copies signed by the printer, Dennis Grastorf and the author. Printed letterpress on
Ragston paper in 12 pt. Kennerley Old Style. Preface by M.C. Lang. With illustrations throughout text.
Slipcase shows wear. Book is very fine.

50. (Angelica Press) Morley, Christopher. THE CURIOUS CASE OF KENELM
DIGBY. N.P.: The Universal Coterie of Pipe Smokers, 1975, 8vo., marbled stiff paper
wrappers, paper cover label. (vi), 23, (5) pages. $ 40.00
Limited to 500 numbered copies printed at The Angelica Press signed by the printer and illustrator. Con-
tains the first publication of a Morley caricature as frontispiece and a brief foreword and afterword by
Herman Abromson.

51. (Angelica Press) Swift, Jonathan. VOYAGE TO LAPUTA. New York: The Angelica Press, 1976, 8vo., two toned cloth, top edge stained green, slipcase. xii, 99, (2) pages.
                                                                                           $ 45.00
Letterpress printed in an edition limited to 1000 numbered copies by Dennis Grastorf at the Angelica
Press. Signed by Warren Chappell, who was responsible for the book's overall design and profuse illustrations. Included in addition to the text are passages entitled "About this edition" and About the Author" by the printer Dennis Grastorf. An attractive publication that is the result of the collaboration between a well known press and a celebrated illustrator.

52. (Anthoensen Press) IN TRIBUTE TO FRED ANTHOENSEN, MASTER
PRINTER. Portland, ME: Anthoensen Press, 1952, small 8vo., cloth- backed boards. x,
142 pages. $ 125.00
Limited to 300 copies. Contains essays by Carl Weber on the Portland Printer, Walter Whitehill on The
Iconographic Society, Rudolph Ruzicka on My Anthology, Harold Hugo on The Columbiad Club of
Connecticut, With a Bibliography, Lawrence Wroth on The Thomas Johnston Maps of the Kennebeck
Purchase, Paul Bennett on Typographic Debut and others. Loosely inserted is a broadside (folded) which
is a printed letter from Anthoensen thanking the people that participated in producing the book (this
broadside is limited to 100 copies). The remnants of the envelope that held this broadside (addressed to
Paul Bennett) is stapled to the broadside. Book is slightly rubbed around the edges.

53. (Anthoensen Press) Barrett, Clifton Waller (editor). THE WALPOLE SOCIETY
NOTE BOOK. (Portland, ME): Walpole Society, 1981, 8vo., quarter cloth with paper-
covered boards, paper spine label. 75, (3) pages. $ 17.50
Printed for the Walpole Society in an edition limited to 50 copies at the Anthoensen Press, in Bell and
Monticello types. Proceedings of the 71st Annual Meeting held at Natchez, Ms. With *Footnotes on Book
Collecting* by the editor, described by him as "a baker's dozen of collecting tales." Photographs.

54. (Anthoensen Press) Goudy, Frederic W. FRED GOUDY'S LAST LETTER. With
a Note by Sol Hess. N.P.: The Typophiles, n.d., 12mo., self paper wrappers. (4) pages.
                                                                                           $ 10.00
Monograph 30. Suggested by P.K. Thomajan and printed by Fred Anthoensen. When folded out,
Goudy's last letter is reproduced.

55. (Anthoensen Press) Dwiggins, W.A. MSS. BY WAD, BEING A COLLECTION
OF THE WRITINGS OF DWIGGINS ON VARIOUS SUBJECTS, SOME
CRITICAL, SOME PHILOSOPHICAL, SOME WHIMSICAL. New York: The
Typophiles, 1947, 12mo., cloth, slipcase. xiv, 152, (3) pages. $ 65.00
First edition, limited to 900 copies. Chapbook XVII. With many illustrations. Printed at the Anthoensen
Press. Slipcase rubbed. Bookplate.

56. (Anthoensen Press) Schubert, Leland. A BIBLIOGRAPHY OF THE PUBLICA-
TIONS OF THE ROWFANT CLUB, PART TWO 1925–1961. Cleveland: Row-
fant Club, 1962, 8vo., quarter cloth with paper-covered boards, paper spine label. 78
pages. $ 150.00
Printed in an edition limited to 175 numbered copies at The Anthoensen Press, Portland, Maine, on Curtis Ragston paper. The Rowfant Club published two or three books per year, frequently by a private press
such as Marchbanks, Grabhorn, Lakeside, Caxton, or Bruce Rogers (1926). Titles printed include *The
Preface to Samuel Johnson's Dictionary of the English Language, Before Life Began,* by Dard Hunter,
and *On Dry-Cow Fishing as a Fine Art,* by Kipling, as well as annual Yearbooks and articles.

57. (Anthoensen Press) Whitehill, Walter Muir. A BOSTON ATHENAEUM AN-
THOLOGY, 1807–1972. Boston: Boston Athenaeum, 1973, small 8vo., stiff paper
wrappers. 48 pages. $ 15.00
Selections from the Annual Reports of the author, who was director of the Athenaeum from 1966–1972,
a private library and club, which included John Quincy Adams among its members. Printed by the Anthoensen Press with illustrations by Rudolph Ruzicka.

58. (Anthoensen Press) Wilde, Oscar. THE IMPORTANCE OF BEING EARNEST,
A TRIVIAL COMEDY FOR SERIOUS PEOPLE IN FOUR ACTS AS ORIGI-
NALLY WRITTEN. New York: The New York Public Library, 1956, small 4to., paper-
covered boards in slipcase. xxxii, (6), 184 (4) pages; (vi), facsimiles of the typescripts of
Acts I, III and IV and manuscript of Act II. $ 250.00
Printed in an edition limited to 500 numbered copies on Lee paper at the Anthoensen Press. Illustrations
and collotype facsimiles by the Meriden Gravure Company. Issued as Publication No. 6 in the Arents Tobacco Collection. *The Importance of being Earnest* was originally written in four acts, but for reasons
made clear in Sarah Dickson's introduction, it was "materially shortened by the author and produced
and printed in England and the United States in three acts." Yet the complete manuscript and several
typescripts of the four acts in various stages of composition survive. In this edition all the play as originally written is printed. One act in manuscript, the second and third corrected typescripts of the three
other acts are reproduced in collotype facsimile. With reproduction of program from first performance
in England, sketches from scenes in *The Illustrated London News,* etc. Slipcase worn.

59. (Apha) EIGHTH ANNUAL CONFERENCE KEEPSAKE. N.P.: (American
Printing History Association, 1983), 4to., stiff paper portfolio, paper cover label.
$ 35.00
Printed folder containing 15 private press Keepsakes produced for the conference, a four page brochure
giving an agenda and various other pieces of ephemera. Includes privately printed keepsakes of all sizes
and typographic designs.

60. (Apha) A TYPE MISCELLANY, TWENTIETH ANNIVERSARY BROAD-
SIDE PORTFOLIO. N.P.: American Printing History Association, 1994, folio, clam-
shell box with paper cover label containing a four page printed introduction by Michael
Peich, a printed broadside listing participants and 29 poster contributions by different
private presses. $ 250.00
Limited to 200 sets. Designed by Jerry Kelly with preliminary pages printed by The Stinehour Press.
Contributions by Dwight Agner, Mark Argetsinger, Lowell Bodger, John DePol, Morris Gelfand, Darrell
Hyder, Steve Miller, Henry Morris, David Pankow, Gaylord Schanilec, Neil Shaver, Michael Tarachow
and others. Bookplate.

61. (Aralia Press) Mason, David. ARALIA PRESS: POETRY AND FINE PRINT-
ING. N.P.: (Aralia Press, 2000), small 8vo., stiff paper wrappers. 29, (3) pages. $ 15.00
Printed in an limited to 1000 copies. A catalogue which accompanied the exhibition of books by the Aralia Press held from September to November in 2000. It describes the books the have published from
1983 to 2000. It was designed by Jerry Kelly and is illustrated.

62. (Archtype Press) Bentley, Wilder (Editor). N'EN PARLONS PLUS!, EXCERPTS FROM DIVERS PAPERS & CHRONICLES OF THE ARTS CLUB, 1937–1938. Berkeley: Archetype Press, 1939, folio, cloth with printed design on front cover. 19+(1) pages. $ 250.00
Limited to 105 copies, set up and printed on a handpress by Wilder Bentley ("and his faithful spouse, Ellen") on dampened Strathmore Wayside Text for at The Archetype Press in Euclid Court, Berkeley, Ca and issued for private distribution among members of The Arts Club & their friends. Printed in "a bastard version" of Caslon Oldface italic and Goudy Modern roman. Wood-engraved abstraction of the initial I for the Prolegomena, vignette on the title-page, and design for the front cover by John C. Haley. Excerpts from chronicles of The Arts Club's past season. "It is not primarily designed to explain to the world in general what we are, what we do, how well we reason, or how badly we sing. Rather it is a souvenir, intended to revive some of our very happy memories." Finely printed.

63. (Arif Press) Horace (Flaccus, Quintus Horatius). QUINTI HORATI FLACCI ARS POETICA. (Berkeley, CA: Arif Press), 1989, large 8vo., stiff paper wrappers. (33) pages. $ 65.00
Elegantly printed and designed by Wesley B. Tanner in an edition of 150 copies. One of the Rounce & Coffin Club's Western Books of 1990. First section *Ars Poetica* taken from C.O. Brink's 1971 *Horace On Poetry*; second section *Vita Horati* from John Carew Rolfe's 1914 *Suetonius*.

64. (Arion Press) THE ARION PRESS: FALL 1985. San Francisco: The Arion Press, 1985, small 8vo., paper wrappers. (6) pages. $ 15.00
A pamphlet printed by The Arion Press with news of the press, such as their new location, upcoming books, book fairs they attended, etc.

65. (Arion Press) Fleet, William Henry. HOW I CAME TO BE GOVERNOR OF THE ISLAND OF CACONA. San Francisco: The Arion Press, 1989, 8vo., quarter cloth with paper covered boards and paper spine label. xiv, 204, (2) pages. $ 135.00
Limited to 325 copies printed by hand at the Arion Press. The text is a reprint of the rare original edition which was printed in Montreal in 1852. The text is a satire of colonial government which was originally printed in Montreal. Illustrated with photo-engraved vignettes by the publisher, Andrew Hoyem and containing a new introduction by the Canadian author, Robertson Davies. Includes prospectus.

66. (Arion Press) HARRIET MARTINEAU AND AMERICA, SELECTED LETTERS FROM THE REINHARD S. SPECK COLLECTION. Edited with an Introduction by R.A. Burchell. Berkeley: The Friends of The Bancroft Library, 1995, 8vo., stiff paper wrappers, paper cover label. 119 pages. $ 17.50
Finely printed by the Arion Press in an unstated number of copies. With a biographical sketch of Speck.

67. (Arion Press) JACK GANNON, JACK OF ALL TRADES AND MASTER OF ONE. N.P.: The Arion Press, 1986, oblong 12mo., cloth-backed boards. (56) pages.
                                                                                        $ 75.00

Limited to 300 copies, printed for subscribers of Arion Press and members of the Roxburghe and Zamorano Clubs. Introduction by Oscar Lewis, and the memoir, "The Master Apprentice" by David Greenhood. Also includes reprints of Gannon's yearbook and collection of poems. Illustrated with woodcuts and frontispiece portrait.

68. (Arion Press) Koch, Rudolf. TYPEFOUNDRY IN SILHOUETTE, HOW PRINTING TYPE IS DEVELOPED AT KLINGSPOR BROS. IN OFFENBACH ON THE RIVER MAIN. San Francisco: The Arion Press, 1982, 4to., loose broadsides in limp cloth portfolio. 28 leaves. $ 100.00
Silhouettes of all facets of this German type producer. Prospectus loosely inserted. Front cover shows light wear along outer edge.

69. (Arion Press) Zinman, Michael. THE AMERICAN BIBLE. Four volumes. Ardsley: The Haydn Foundation for the Cultural Arts, 1992, large 4to., fawn cloth portfolio boxes, gilt red morocco labels on spines and upper covers. 38 original leaves from American Bibles, matted with letterpress tilting to each mount. $ 4,750.00

First edition, limited to 100 numbered sets of four portfolios finely printed by Andrew Hoyem at the Arion Press. This landmark publication presents for the first time the history of the Bible in America through a display of thirty-eight original leaves from the most significant editions of the Scriptures printed in the present geographical area of the United States. The Bibles span a period of over 200 years, from 1663 to 1878. The leaves are from the collection of the noted Americanist Michael Zinman, who has selected them and written an explanatory text for each, and who provides a preface as well. Also included is an essay by Professor Mark A. Noll. The original leaves are boxed according to four distinct groupings: Bibles in the languages of the natives of America, Bibles in English from the 18th and 19th centuries (two portfolios), and Bibles in other languages. The first portfolio contains eight leaves, including one from the first Bible printed in America, translated in Massachusetts (1663), usually called the Eliot Indian Bible, and another from the second edition of 1685, as well as significant appearances in Mohawk, Hawaiian, Cherokee, and other languages. The second and third portfolios are comprised of ten leaves each, including one from the first Bible in English printed in America (1782), one from the first illustrated Bible printed in America (1791), one from Noah Webster's modernization of the Bible in English (1883), one from the first Catholic Bible (1790), and one from the first publication of the New Testament in the Confederacy (1862). This section also contains many other important firsts relative to the appearance of the Holy Writ in America. The fourth portfolio contains ten leaves, including one from the first Bible in German printed in America by Christopher Saur (1743), and one from the first Bible printed on paper manufactured in America (1763). Also represented here are the first American Bibles printed in Hebrew, French, Greek, Spanish, Portuguese, Dutch, and Swedish. A duplication of this collection on one's own would involve great effort and expense. The leaves, some of them containing illustrations, are suitable for framing or display, and are already appropriately matted.

70. (Artichoke Press) Shasky, Florian J., Ed. HAND BOOKBINDING IN CALIFORNIA, A KEEPSAKE IN TWELVE PARTS FOR THE MEMBERS OF THE BOOK CLUB OF CALIFORNIA MDCCCCXCIV. (Mountain View, California: Artichoke Press, 1994), small 4to., stiff paper portfolio. (48) pages. $ 55.00

A collection of twelve folders made for the members of the Book Club of California by Jonathan Clark. Co-edited by Shasky and Joanne Sonnichsen. Each folder is a leaf folded into four pages, containing an essay on a different facet of either bookbinding or collecting. Various colors used for the leaves. The gilt decorated cover is adapted from the Founding Statement of The Bookbinders' Guild of California, 1902. Typeface is Adobe Jenson, a multiple-master design by Robert Slimbach used here for the first time in publication, courtesy of Adobe Systems, Inc. Illustrations throughout. Folders loose in stiff paper portfolio.

71. (Ascensius Press) [MAILING ENVELOPE FILLED WITH EPHEMERAL MATERIAL PRODUCED BY SCOTT VILE AT HIS ASCENSIUS PRESS]. $ 30.00

Includes everything from hand-printed calling cards to broadsides announcing events. Interesting group.

72. (Ascensius Press) Edwards, George (editor). GROLIER CLUB ITER HIBERNICUM. New York: The Grolier Club, 1998, 8vo., quarter cloth, with paper covered boards. xiv, 153+(1) pages. $ 65.00

Printed in an edition limited to 350 copies at the Ascensius Press. The Grolier Club's trip to Ireland in 1997. The Irish harp and calligraphy for the special edition was done by Timothy O'Neill and the type designs originated with William Caslon for the text and with Victor Hammer for the uncial title. The Grolier Club device on the title page is by Bruce Rogers.

73. (Ashendene Press) Longus. AMOURS PASTORALES DE DAPHNIS ET CHLOE. Traduction de Messire J. Amyot éditée et corrigée par Paul-Louis Courier. Chelsea: The Ashendene Press, 1933, large 8vo., publisher's green pigskin by W.H. Smith & Son stamp-signed in gilt on the rear turn-ins, covers ruled in gilt, front cover with central gilt vignette, spine paneled and lettered in gilt in compartments, board edges and turn-ins ruled in gilt, all edges gilt, quarter black morocco clamshell case. [iv], iv, 163, [2] pages. $ 22,500.00

One of 20 copies printed on vellum, out of a total edition of 310 copies. (Ashendene no. XXXIX) "The printing of an edition of Amyot's translation of 'Daphnis et Chloé' was first referred to in the Notice which I issued to subscribers in February, 1931. It was then described as being printed on Japanese paper. This edition was actually printed during the year 1931. Unfortunately the ink used was very slow in drying and the sheets were packed before it had sufficiently hardened. The mistake was not discovered until the sheets were unpacked at the binders when it was found that very bad 'set-off' had occurred on many of them. As the book would have been unworthy of the Press I reluctantly decided to destroy the whole edition with the exception of 10 copies, which I had made up from the least spoiled sheets, and some odd specimen pages... I greatly regret the mishap to this edition, as it was a pretty book... the second edition is practically a line for line reprint of the first, though there are slight differences in the collation of the two volumes" (StJohn Hornby, Ashendene Bibliography p.94). With twenty-six illustrations (four full-page) drawn and cut on wood by Gwendolen Raverat. Printed in Ptolemy type, with marginal notes in red. Initials filled in by hand in gold and blue by Graily Hewitt and his assistants. Printer's mark C in red. Minimal darkening to spine, otherwise a fine copy.

74. (Ashendene Press) Thucydides. HISTORY OF THE PELOPONNESIAN WAR. Chelsea: Ashendene Press, 1930, small folio, full pigskin. (viii), 363, (vii) pages. $ 3,500.00

Printed in an edition limited to 260 copies on paper. (Bibliography no.37). Printed in Ptolemy type on hand-made paper with the Ashendene Press knight-in-armor watermark. Printed in black with red initials and marginal notes. Hornby states that the three-line red initial beginning each chapter and the opening lines of each of the eight books were designed by Graily Hewitt. (Note: Franklin says the initials are from Gill's Utopia alphabet.) The design once again demonstrates Hornby's great skill in typography, and his penchant for printing books where he could be creative with the format, including the elaborate marginal notes. Hornby expected this to be one of the last two books from the press, except for the Bibliography, but he subsequently decided to do the Book of Ecclesiasticus. Bound in full white pigskin, with gold lettering on spine. Binding signed by W.H. Smith and Sons, which Hornby indicated in his Bibliography meant that it was probably designed and/or bound by Sidney Cockerel. Slight rubbing and soiling of white pigskin.

75. (Ashendene Press) WISDOM OF JESUS THE SON OF SIRACH COMMONLY CALLED ECCLESIASTICUS. Shelley House, Chelsea: The Ashendene Press, 1932, tall 4to., original full limp orange vellum with matching silk ties, spine lettered in gilt, original marbled board slipcase. (iv), 182 pages. $ 3,000.00

Finely printed in an edition limited to 353 copies of which this is one of 328 copies printed on specially made paper by Batchelor & Sons. (Bibliography no. XXXVIII; Franklin pp.186–197,242). Printed in Subiaco type. This was one of the last items to be issued by the press, and the last to bear the hand colored initials of Graily Hewitt and his assistants Ida D. Henstock and Helen E. Hinckley. These initials appear throughout in green and blue and are an attractive compliment to the text which is printed in red and black throughout. Two colors of hand colored initials were only used on one other occasion by the press in 1902 for Dante's Inferno. The bookseller James Bain found this book "one of the most beautiful books that has ever come from the Ashendene Press; it is quite perfect in every way" (Franklin p.195). With an autograph note from the collator A.D. Power, dated 11 April 1933, loosely inserted: "With acknowledgments and apologies for the word 'Syndics' being omitted." St. John Hornby wrote in the Bibliography that "The printing of this book was due to the fact that my friend and partner, A.D. Power, had with the help of one or two Hebrew scholars compiled from the various versions of 'Ecclesiasticus' a text which he subsequently caused to be written out on vellum and illuminated by A.J. Fairbank and Louise

Powell respectively in a volume of great beauty. One day he happened to tell me that he thought of having the version printed, as many of his friends wished to possess it. The temptation to add yet one more book to my list was too strong for me to resist and I there and then offered to print a small edition. I have never regretted having done so, as in my humble judgment it is one of the most satisfactory of the books of the Press." Bookplate of Cambridge University Press: Syndics Library on Front pastedown. Well preserved copy.

76. (Ashendene Press) THE XI. BOOKES OF THE GOLDEN ASSE OF LUCIUS APULEIUS. Chelsea: Ashendene Press, 1924, small 4to., original quarter cloth with paper covered boards, paper spine label. vii, (i), 230, (2) pages. $ 2,000.00
Printed in an edition limited to 181 copies, this being one of 165 copies printed on paper. (Franklin p. 241; Ashendene Press no.33). This was first published at London in Fleet Streate at the sign of the Oliphante by Henry Wykes, Anno 1566. This story in archetypal Pre-Raphaelite taste, appeared time and again in various forms from the private presses. The shoulder notes are printed in red and the chapter initials are mostly printed in red, but the larger initials at the beginning of each of the eleven books are in blue. Well preserved copy.

77. (Avon Old Farms School Press) March, Frederic. SOLOLOQUY WHILE WAITING FOR THE KING AND QUEEN TO COME TO THE PREMIERE OF "HAMLET." Avon, CT: Avon Old Farms School Press, 1982, large 12mo., stiff wrappers. unpaginated, but (i), 2+(1). $ 17.50
Printed in an edition limited to 100 copies, composed and printed by Andrew Iverson at the Avon Old Farms School Press. Issued as a keepsake on the occasion of a previous owner's visit to the school. A note from John DePol loosely inserted, with his signature on the front endpaper. From a "Soliloquy" given by the American actor Frederic March at the Odeon Theatre, London, 7 May 1948.

78. (Barbarian Press) Brender A Brandis, Gerard. ENDGRAIN EDITIONS ONE: GERARD BRENDER A BRANDIS. Mission, BC: Barbarian Press, 2000, small 4to., quarter cloth with paper covered boards, with a paper spine label. not paginated.
$ 160.00
Printed in an edition limited to 200 copies this being one of the 150 regular edition. This is the first in a projected series of Endgrain Editions, each of which will feature a contemporary artist and their wood-engravings. Brandis is widely admired in Canada and abroad, particularly for his superb botanical studies, which are found in many of his books, pamphlets, and prints for framing. The type is Joanna, with Libra and Augustea for display and the papers are Book White Wove and Siluiran both made by the Zerkall Mill. The printing of the engravings are all from the wood by Jan Elseted.

79. (Barbarian Press) Busza, Andrzej and Czaykowski, Bogdan (editors). GATHERING TIME: FIVE MODERN POLISH ELEGIES. Mission, BC: Barbarian Press, 1983, large 8vo., quarter cloth with printed paper covered boards, dust jacket. x, 11-63, (5) pages. $ 150.00
Printed in an edition limited to 200 copies. Five Polish poems written between 1948 and 1977: Iwaszkiewicz; Wierzynski; Jastrun; Milosz; Bialoszewski. Binding by Charlotte Bagshawe. Curtis Rag paper. Presswork by Jan Elsted. Design and handset by Crispin Elsted.

80. (Barbarian Press) Carroll, John. RUMOUR OF A SHARK. Mission, BC: Barbarian Press, 1999, large 8vo., handmade paper over stiff paper wrappers, paper cover label, top and bottom edges cut, some fore edges deckled. (ii), 55, (3) pages. $ 53.50
First edition, limited to 125 copies, signed by the author. A collection of poems by John Carroll. Titles include Rumour of a Shark, Another Fall, Snow of You, I will Tell You This, White Wall, and more. Handset in Garamont type by Goudy and printed on Somerset Text Laid paper. Bound in green handmade paper with author and title printed in green on white cover label. Title page decorated with a tipped-in illustration from a design by Janet Downey.

81. (Barbarian Press) Grey, Edward. GIBLINGS & GREY AND THE CHARM OF BIRDS. Toronto: Friends of the Thomas Fischer Rare Book Library, 1998. (But Mission, BC: Barbarian Press, 1998), small 8vo., quarter cloth, with decorated paper covered boards, and a paper spine label. (66) pages. $ 100.00
Printed in an edition limited to 300 copies. Twenty wood engravings of birds are printed from the original blocks engraved by Robert Giblings which are accompanied by the appropriate text by Lord Grey. Includes and introduction by Richard Landon.

82. (Barbarian Press) Kishkan, Theresa. INISHBREAM. Mission, BC: Barbarian Press, 1999, tall 8vo., quarter Japanese silk with printed patterned paper covered boards, paper spine label, top edge cut, fore and bottom edges deckled. 84 pages followed by 3 leaves. $ 175.00
Printed in an edition limited to 240 numbered and signed copies, this copy being from a series of 175 finely printed on Zerkall Silurian paper. Illustrated throughout with twenty-one wood engravings by John DePol. A fictional account of the authors experience of a year spent in the 1970s on a small island off the coast of Ireland. A lively novella that tells its story through conversations, scraps of song and storytelling.

83. (Barbarian Press) Lu Chi. WEN FU, THE ART OF WRITING. (Mission, BC): Barbarian Press, 1986, large 12mo., cloth. 38, (4) pages. $ 75.00
Printed in an edition limited to 200 numbered copies by Crispin & Jan Elsted at Barbarian Press, on Mohawk Superfine paper, handset on pica Joanna (Elsted, A15). The calligraphy is by Yim Tse. Translation and afterward by Sam Hamill. A classic work discussing the use of language and composition, originally published around 300 A.D.

84. (Basilike Press) Abercrombie, Lascelles. A PERSONAL NOTE. Toronto: Basilike, 1974, 8vo., marbled paper covers, paper cover label. (12) pages. $ 20.00
Limited to 125 copies printed by John Paul Davies at his private press. This essay originally appeared in THE EIGHTEEN-SIXTIES ESSAYS published in 1932.

85. (Baskerville, John) Juvenal and Persius. D. JUNII JUVENALIS ET AULI PERSII FLACCI SATYRAE. Birmingham: John Baskerville, 1761, 4to., full contemporary red Turkey morocco, triple gilt border on covers, dentelles, gilt-tooled spine, all edges gilt. 240 pages. $ 750.00
Gaskell no.15. With the following suppressed leaves at E2, K4, U4 and Z3 rather than the canceled pages. Two types of paper were used in printing this book, good quality and medium quality. This copy was printed on medium quality which has "purplish patches" in places. (Gaskell). Mild spotting throughout, minor dampstaining on the last five leaves. Wear at extremities.

86. (Baskerville, John) Lucretius. DE RERUM NATURA LIBRI SEX. Birminghamae: Johannis Baskerville, 1772, 4to., contemporary brown polished calf, five raised bands, red leather spine label. (ii), 280 pages. $ 750.00
First Baskerville edition. (Gaskell 43, OCD 516). Lucretius' only known work in which the ancient poet expounds the physical theory of Epicurus. Arranged in six sections all in Latin. Finely printed on good quality Writing Royal laid paper. Book label of the Scottish estate of Auchincruive (South Ayrshire) on front pastedown. Wear at tips; split along front hinge at top. Well preserved copy.

87. (Baskerville, John) Walker, Benjamin. RESTING PLACES OF THE REMAINS OF JOHN BASKERVILLE, THE THRICE-BURIED PRINTER. Birmingham: Birmingham School of Printing, 1944, small 4to., stiff paper wrappers, cord-tied. 13+(1) pages. $ 55.00
Wallis p.98. Printed by hand by the students. With four illustrations.

88. (Baskerville, John) HOLY BIBLE. CONTAINING THE OLD TESTAMENT AND THE NEW: TRANSLATED OUT THE OF THE ORIGINAL TONGUES, AND WITH THE FORMER TRANSLATIONS DILIGENTLY COMPARED AND REVISED, BY HIS MAJESTY'S SPECIAL COMMAND. APPOINTED TO BE READ IN CHURCHES. Cambridge: Printed by John Baskerville, 1763, large folio (19 1/4 x 12 1/2 inches; 485 x 320 mm.), contemporary diced calf, tooled in blind and gilt, marbled endpapers, all edges gilt. [573] leaves. $ 9,500.00

First edition, first issue, with the list of subscribers ending with Winwood. (Darlow & Moule 857, Gaskell 26, Herbert 1146, Huntington Library Great Books in Great Editions, 6) Originally priced four guineas in sheets, for subscribers, "[t]he edition consisted of 1250 copies, of which 556 were remaindered in 1768 and bought by the London bookseller R. Baldwin at 36s. each. Baldwin was offering copies at three guineas in sheets in 1771" (Gaskell). "Aesthetically, the highest point in English Bible printing so far was John Baskerville's folio printed at Cambridge in 1763. To achieve his ambition to print a folio Bible, Baskerville had to become University Printer, on not very advantageous terms. The Bible uses his types, paper and ink, and shows his characteristic 'machine-made' finish: very smooth and even in colour and impression, with glossy black ink on smooth paper. The design is traditional, but the quality of material and workmanship is so high, and the conventions are so delicately modified and consistently applied that the result is extremely impressive" (The Cambridge History of the Bible: The West from the Reformation to the Present Day, p. 464). "One of the most beautifully printed books in the world" (Dibdin). This edition "has always been regarded as Baskerville's magnum opus, and is his most magnificent as well as his most characteristic specimen" (T.B. Reed, A History of the Old English Letter Foundries, p. 279.) Text in double columns. Rubbed at extremities. Hinges cracked but strong. Occasional very light foxing. Short (1/2 inch) tear at fore-margin of title. Bookplate and old description mounted on front pastedown. Overall, a lovely copy of the first issue of this masterpiece of Bible printing.

89. (Baughman, Roger) Nichols, John. OBITUARY NOTICE OF ROGER PAYNE, BOOKBINDER, REPRINTED FROM THE GENTLEMEN'S MAGAZINE FOR DECEMBER, 1797. (Pasadena, CA: Roger Baughman, 1935), 12mo., stiff paper wrappers. (ii), 2 pages. $ 20.00

Printed by Roland Baughman in an edition limited to 100 copies at his press in Pasadena. "Nichols' notice is given here in the belief that it never before has been reprinted in full."

90. (Bayberry Hill Press) Hooke, Deborah Johnson. NATURE'S CHANGES. Meriden, CT: Bayberry Hill Press, 1978, large 8vo., quarter cloth with paper-covered boards. (vi), 23, (3). $ 85.00

Printed by Foster Macy Johnson in an edition limited to "about" 75 numbered copies on mold-made Arches paper. "This little book of Debe's poems has been printed (without editing) by her loving grandfather." The type used is 12 point Caslon with 24 point Caslon Italic for the poem's titles and for the folios. "This may well be the very last book that I shall print at Bayberry Hill Press."

91. (Bayberry Hill Press) Johnson, Ruth and Foster. KELMSCOTT REVISITED. Meriden, CT: Bayberry Hill Press, 1966, 4to., quarter leather with patterned paper covered boards, paper cover label, slipcase. viii, 25, (3) pages. $ 125.00

A monograph written and printed primarily as a keepsake for the Columbiad Club of Connecticut. Tells of a trip to England by the authors to visit the sites of Doves Press, Kelmscott Press, Ashendene Press, William Morris' home and other important places in the history of fine printing. Examples of printing using Doves, Kelmscott Golden and Troy types and the Ashendene Ptolemy type are shown. Printed using Bookman type on Arches paper, deckle edges. Initial letters reproduced from the great Kelmscott Chaucher. The "Acorn" pattern wallpaper used in binding was designed by William Morris. Boards chipped at edges and corners. Presentation from Johnson on free endpaper. Wear at bottom of slipcase.

92. (Baynard Press) Merrick, Leonard. FOUR STORIES. London: The Baynard Press, 1925, large 8vo., original limp vellum with title in gilt on spine. 101, (3) pages. $ 250.00
Limited to 200 copies numbered and signed by the author. Printed by hand in two colors on Kelmscott handmade paper. Four stories by Merrick. The 6th in the Vine Books series, produced by Wilfred Pardington, and issued to subscribers from the office of The Bookman's Journal. The two small woodcuts are by Norman Janes. Covers slightly age yellowed.

93. (Beaumont Press) Blunden, Edmund. TO NATURE. Westminster: Beaumont press, (1923), 8vo., quarter buckram with patterned paper covered boards, fore and bottom edges deckled. (xii), 50, (2) pages. $ 75.00
Limited to 390 numbered copies(Beaumont, pp.70–72). The cover decorations, endpapers. and 34 Initial Letters designed by Randolph Schwabe, The typography and binding arranged by Cyril William Beaumont on his Press at 75 Charing Cross Road, Westminster. An advance copy of the book was acknowledged by Edmund Blunden: "It is a book which almost topples over my stern faith in the art of earlier printers as compared with the modern, and will stand in honor on my shelves...Mr. Schwabe's little pictures have my warm praise and gratitude."

94. (Beaumont Press) Blunden, Edmund. MASKS OF TIME, A NEW COLLECTION OF POEMS ... PRINCIPALLY MEDITATIVE. Westminster: Beaumont Press, 1925, 8vo., quarter cream buckram, decorated paper covered boards. xvi, 58, (2) pages. $ 95.00
Limited to 310 numbered copies on handmade paper (Beaumont, 19). The author notes that the second part of these poems "brings together some verses relating to war experiences and its reverberations...which should be a comprehensive view of their great and strange subject." Cover decorations and initial letters designed by Randolph Schwabe. Typography and binding arranged by Cyril William Beaumont and printed on his press at 75 Charing Cross Road.

THE FIRST BOOK OF THE PRESS

95. (Beaumont Press) Drinkwater, John. TIDES. (Westminster: Beaumont Press, 1917), 8vo., quarter cloth and paper-covered boards, paper spine and cover labels. 36 (2) pages. $ 125.00
Printed in an edition limited to 270 copies of which this is one of 250 numbered copies printed on Head's hand-made paper. (Beaumont, 1). This is the first book issued by the Beaumont Press. Designed and set in 14-point Caslon Old Face by Cyril William Beaumont on his Press at 75 Charing Cross Road. Bound by F. Sangorski and G. Sutcliffe on quarter rough-surfaced buckram in decorated boards. The label on the front cover was written by Miss M. Coleman "in green and violet on a pale stone-colored paper." The first copies were sent to Drinkwater, who remarked "I congratulate you upon an extremely beautiful piece of book production. I have no criticism to make...nothing but admiration (Beaumont, p.8)." Bookplate of previous owner on front pastedown

96. (Beaumont Press) Flecker, J.E. LETTERS OF J.E. FLECKER TO FRANK SAVERY. (Westminster: Beaumont Press, 1926), 8vo., quarter vellum with illustrated paper covered boards. 125+(1) pages. $ 100.00
Printed in an edition limited to 390 numbered copies of which this is one of 310 printed on handmade paper. The twenty-first book issued by the Beaumont Press. The typography and binding produced by Cyril William Beaumont on his press at 75 Charing Cross Road, the decorated cover designed by B. Claudia Guercio, and the title page by Randolph Schwabe. These letters include the author's service in World War I, ending with his death circa 1915. "I'm damned frightened the Germans are going to win and steal a third of France...the world will be hell if they do."

97. (Beaumont Press) Lloyd, Robert. THE ACTOR. Westminster: Beaumont Press, 1926, 8vo., quarter cloth with decorated paper covered boards. xix, 23, (3) pages. $ 85.00
Limited to 270 numbered copies. Prefatory essay by Edmund Blunden. The cover, title-page embellishments and theatrical figures in text are designed and drawn by Randolph Schwabe. Typography and binding arranged and produced by Cyril W. Beaumont, 75 Charing Cross Road, London. Lloyd was an

eighteenth century poet of light verse who died in 1764. According to Edmund Blunden, he feared nothing, not even the critics " Who like scarecrows stand Upon the poet's common land, And with the severity of sense Drive all imagination thence."

98. (Beaumont Press) Nichols, Robert. THE SMILE OF THE SPHINX. (London: Beaumont Press, 1920), small 8vo., quarter fawn buckram with decorative paper-covered boards. 58 (2) pages. $ 95.00

Printed by Cyril William Beaumont in an edition limited to 260 numbered copies. (Beaumont, 11). Set in 12-point Caslon Old Face and printed on hand-made paper. Text printed in black, with a cover-design, title-page decoration (in 3 colors) 4 other decorations and end-papers by Ethelbert White. The first book issued by Beaumont with a new staff, that included S.R. Minns as pressman and W. Smith as compositor. A few small ink stains on covers.

99. (Beaver School Press) THE SUN'S GIFT. Chestnut Hill: Beaver School Press, 1930, small 8vo., cloth, paper cover label. (x), 25, (iv) pages. $ 35.00

First edition, limited to 125 copies. A collection of poems which was the work of grades four, five, and six at the Beaver School Press. The printing was done by the Printers Guild and the five linocuts were done by the art group. Covers faded.

100. (Bennett, Paul A.) PAUL A. BENNETT PRIVATE PRESS KEEPSAKE (1897–1966), GATHERED TOGETHER BY FRIENDS AND TYPOPHILES. New York: The Typophiles, n.d. (circa 1967), 59 pamphlets loosely inserted in a box with a wrap-around paper label. $ 150.00

Limited to about 200 copies. With contributions by 60 (59 present in this copy) different private presses including Valenti Angelo, Leonard Bahr, Edna Beilenson, Joe Blumenthal, Jane Grabhorn, the Grovers, Emerson Wulling and Ward Ritchie. Contains the title section and the section listing all 60 participants. The contribution entitled "J. Johnson, Typ. Oddments from his Typographia" is missing .

101. (Berliner, Harold) Corbiere, Tristan. POEMS. Nevada City, CA: Harold Berliner, (1988), large 4to., quarter cloth with marbled paper covered boards, slipcase. 105, (3) pages. $ 200.00

Printed in an edition limited to 150 numbered copies on handmade green Charter Oak paper manufactured by J. Barcham Green. Presentation from the publisher to John and Thelma DePol on first blank. Design and frontispiece illustration by Wolfgang Lederer. Selected and introduced by William A. Newsom and translated by C.F. MacIntyre. Bookplate and signature of John DePol on front pastedown. prospectus loosely inserted.

102. (Berliner, Harold) Dickens, Charles. CHRISTMAS CAROL. Nevada City, CA: Harold Berliner, (1976), 4to., two-toned cloth. 117+(3) pages. $ 100.00

Printed in an edition limited to 750 copies signed by the illustrator, Wolfgang Lederer. Illustrations printed in color. Title page printed in red and black.

103. (Berliner, Harold) Gregory, Susan Myra. WHEN WE BELONGED TO SPAIN OLD CALIFORNIA TALES. Nevada City, CA: Harold Berliner, (1983), 8vo., two-tone cloth. xxii, 50, (4) pages. $ 85.00

Printed in an edition limited to 375 numbered copies. Designed and ornamented by Wolfgang Lederer. Edited with a foreword and notes by John D. Short, Jr.

104. (Berliner, Harold) Knight, Max (Translator). KNIGHTS AND VALENTINES. FRENCH LOVE SONGS OF THE FIFTEENTH CENTURY. Nevada City, CA: Harold Berliner, (1989), small 4to., cloth. 119, (5) pages. $ 95.00

Printed in an edition limited to 285 numbered copies. Originally created by A Florentine Chansonnier from the Time of Lorenzo the Magnificent. the poems in this volume were translated by Max Knight from Manuscript Banco Rari 229 held by the Biblioteca Nazionale Centrale in Florence. The foreword by Howard M. Brown establishes the history of the verses, each of which is illustrated by Wolfgang Lederer with colored line drawings. Presentation copy signed "For John From Howard 10–26–92" on front pastedown along with John DePol signature and bookplate, additional DePol bookplate on back pastedown.

105. (Berliner, Harold) Lee, Brian North. THE BOOKPLATE DESIGNS OF CLAUD LOVAT FRASER. Nevada City, CA: Harold Berliner, Printer, 1985, 8vo., cloth, paper cover and spine labels. 85, (3) pages. $ 80.00
Limited to 650 numbered copies printed by hand by Berliner with the assistance of Elton Foote. With illustrations of Fraser's bookplates throughout often reproduced in color. Includes a list of his bookplates, unused bookplate designs, and a select bibliography.

106. (Berliner, Harold) Long, Haniel. THE POWER WITHIN US. Nevada City: Harold Berliner, (1975), large 8vo., cloth. 47, (3) pages. $ 75.00
Printed in an edition limited to 750 numbered copies. The story of a handful of Spaniards, which were washed ashore in the Gulf of Mexico in 1528, and traveled across the entire continent, barefoot and naked for eight years led by Nunez Cabeza de Vaca. It was designed by Wolfgang Lederer and printed on Curtis Ray paper in Lutetia types. A prospectus is loosely inserted.

107. (Between-Hours Press) White, Lewis F. BRIEF ACCOUNT OF THE BETWEEN-HOURS PRESS, BEN GRAUER PROPRIETOR. Engravings by John DePol. New York: The Privy Council Press, 1952, small 8vo., paper wrappers. (18) pages. $ 20.00
First edition, limited to 1200 copies of which this is one of the 350 numbered copies printed for the Typophiles.

108. (Bibliophile Society) FOURTH ANNUAL BANQUET OF THE BIBLIOPHILE SOCIETY (1906) OF BOSTON. Boston: The Bibliophile Society, 1906, 8vo., stiff paper wrappers, slipcase. (18) pages. $ 30.00
Presentation of a punch bowl and tray of sterling silver and gold "valued at nearly $4000" to William K. Bixby of St. Louis, in recognition of his having collected and turned over to the society nearly $150,000 of books and manuscripts. With remarks, menu, engraving of Bixby as frontis, and photograph and description of the punch bowl. Cord missing from wrappers. Newspaper clipping from "The Boston Herald," January 12, 1906, laid in.

109. (Bibliophile Society) Lamb, Charles. THE LETTERS OF CHARLES LAMB, IN WHICH MANY MUTILATED WORDS AND PASSAG. With an introduction by Henry H. Harper. Five volumes. Boston: Issued by the Bibliophile Society (printed at the Riverside Press), 1905, folio (vol. I)/8vo., (vols. II-V), paper-covered boards (vol. I: paper-covered limp boards in an unattached casing of paper-covered boards). x,(ii),78,(86); (viii),348; 7-337+1); 349+(1); 358,(2) pages, with an additional 4 pages and 29 leaves various volumes. $ 350.00
Limited to 470 copies, for members only. Texts of 762 letters of Charles Lamb (a few from Mary Lamb) from 1796 through 1834, to Coleridge, Wordsworth, Southey, Hazlitt, Godwin, et al., arranged in chronological order, occasionally with notes. The introductory volume contains Harper's discussion of earlier editions of Lamb's correspondence and of the liberties taken/mistakes made by previous editors, several posthumous accounts of Lamb by contemporaries, and 20 facsimiles of Lamb letters, each with a brief introduction by Richard Garnett. Volume II contains an index to the letters. Vol. I has a portrait engraving in two states (one signed by the artist) and several additional illustrations; vols. II, III and V each contain a frontispiece engraving. Several volumes partly unopened. Paper covering of boards shows infrequent superficial damage, front hinge of vol. V is splitting.

110. (Bieler Press) Gallo, Philip. A PRINTER'S DOZEN. Los Angeles: The Bieler Press, 1992, 8vo., stiff paper wrappers. (19) pages. $ 120.00

Limited to 200 numbered copies, signed by the author and the artist. Handset using ATF Garamond Bold & Trump Medieval Bold and printed on Invicta English mould made paper. Contains 12 poems dealing with the printer and the printshop. Featuring a five color engraving by Gaylord Schanilec.

111. (Binnacle Press) Levy, Robert E. LOG: FIVE DAYS ABOARD THE SCHOONER "STEPHEN TABER." Oyster Bay, NY: Binnacle Press, 1962, 8vo., stiff paper wrappers, paper cover label. (ii), 18, (4) pages. $ 20.00

Printed in an edition limited to 600 copies printed for friends of the Binnacle Press. Designed and illustrated by John DePol. The text type is Linotype Times Roman with Bulmer display on Strathmore Text and Ivory Wove Paper. With centerfold chart of the route of the schooner "Stephen Taber" 10 to 15 July, 1961.

112. (Bird & Bull Press) Abercrombie, Lascelles. TOWER IN ITALY A LEGEND, BEING A ROMANTIC PLAY IN ONE ACT. Toronto: Basilike, 1976, 8vo., paper wrappers. 31 pages. $ 45.00

First edition, one of 175 numbered copies. (Taylor B5). Designed and printed by Henry Morris at the Bird & Bull Press.

113. (Bird & Bull Press) Adams, John W. INDIAN PEACE MEDALS OF GEORGE III OR HIS MAJESTY'S SOMETIME ALLIES. Crestline: George Frederick Kolbe, 1999, 8vo., cloth, leather spine label. 263, (3) pages. $ 165.00

Limited to 500 numbered copies printed letterpress by Henry Morris at his Bird & Bull Press for George Kolbe. Printed on Frankfurt mouldmade paper using Dante types composed by Michael and Winifred Bixler. With the duotones printed by Stinehour Press. Bound by Cambpell-Logan Bindery. With a history of the medals which itself is a good course in early Americana accompanied by a number of illustrations. Also includes a bibliography of the medals. With design obviously by Henry Morris and having chapter vignettes printed in red. This book was printed by Mr. Morris as a commission for George Kolbe and was not issued to his standing order customers.

114. (Bird & Bull Press) Adelman, Seymour. CHANGING PATTERNS IN THE FUNCTION OF TRAVEL AGENCIES. Philadelphia: Taylor & Hessey, 1981, 8vo., paper wrappers. 31 pages. $ 35.00

Printed in an edition limited to 400 numbered copies. Printed by Henry Morris at the Bird & Bull Press. Text is based on a speech by the noted collector, Seymour Adelman, about an imaginary trip to London in 1817 when it would have been possible to meet William Wordsworth, Coleridge, Blake, Shelley, Keats and Edgar Allan Poe. Mr. Morris has illustrated the book with his own typographical whimsy including a "to let" classified ad for Keat's apartment printed on type hammered dull by Mr. Morris to add to its realism.

115. (Bird & Bull Press) ANTHOLOGY OF DELAWARE PAPERMAKING. With an introduction by Gordon A. Pfeiffer and four wood engravings by John DePol. New Castle, DE: The Delaware Bibliophiles and Oak Knoll Books, 1991, 8vo., quarter cloth, printed paper over boards, leather spine label. Approx. 96 pages. $ 195.00

Limited to 200 numbered copies. Set in Bell and printed on mouldmade paper by Henry Morris at his Bird & Bull Press. This work is based on an original article written by Barbara Benson about the general history of papermaking in Delaware. To this has been added two previously published articles - "The Gilpins and their Endless Papermaking Machine" by H.B. Hancock and N.B. Wilkinson; and "Papermaker Joshua Gilpin introduces the Chemical Approach to Papermaking in the U.S." by Sidney M. Edelstein. Finally there is a previously unpublished thesis written by Patricia M. Brown outlining the history of the Curtis Paper Company in Newark, Delaware. This is an important article as little has previously been published about the history of this mill which eventually supplied paper to so many of America's fine book producers. The four original wood engravings by John DePol beautifully illustrate a number of the mills and a papermaking scene.

116. (Bird & Bull Press) Atkyns. PAIR ON PRINTING. Introductions by Carey S. Bliss. North Hills: Bird & Bull Press, 1982, 8vo., cloth, paper spine label. 141 pages.
$ 60.00

One of 500 copies. This is the first reprinting in facsimile of two important first books on printing in English. The first is Atkyns' *The Origin and Growth of Printing* (1664) which is the first book devoted to the subject of printing; the second is William Caslon's first type specimen book, also the first English type specimen book. Carey Bliss, the curator of rare books at the Huntington Library, has written introductions for both books.

117. (Bird & Bull Press) Bachaus, Theodore. THE BOOKSELLERS OF SAN SER-RIFFE. Port Clarendon: San Serriffe Publishing Company, 2001, 8vo., quarter leather with green leather spine label, slipcase. 89, (10) pages with various leaves with tipped-in plates.
$ 300.00

First edition, limited to 200 numbered copies. Those of you who were impressed by Dr. Bauhaus's earlier book on the Private Presses of San Serriffe will be absolutely shattered by this in-depth survey of the booksellers of San Serriffe. The book has an historical introduction by Dr Bauhaus which is followed by chapters on Hobart Flock of Hoki-Nol Books (hmm!), Ki-flongian Booksellers, Ltd., Grandiloquent Bookshop, Cloacina Books, St. Luke's Paper Mill and Bookshop, Contre Kook Mail Order Books and Exterminator Books. Contains tipped-in photographs, a foldout broadside and three woodcuts by Wesley Bates (including one showing Robert and Mildred Flederbach in front of Hoki-Nol Press Books). The book is accompanied by a prospectus and a letter from Dr. Bachaus to the purchaser of the book talking about the book and enclosing four commemorative stamps from the Republic of San Serriffe inserted in an envelope with a canceled stamp.

118. (Bird & Bull Press) Berger, Sid. ANATOMY OF A LITERARY HOAX. New Castle, DE: Oak Knoll Books, 1994, 8vo., cloth, paper cover label. 17, (3) pages. $ 75.00
First edition, limited to 300 copies of which this is one of 50 bound in cloth.

119. (Bird & Bull Press) BIBLIOPHILIC, TYPOGRAPHIC AND POLITICALLY CORRECT WRAPPING PAPER. one leaf printed letterpress describing this packet of material and accompanied by six sets of four different examples of wrapping paper, all enclosed in a manila envelope.
$ 20.00

Henry Morris produced this packet of material for his standing order customers. The wrapping paper was produced on an old offset press. The wrapping paper reproduces old advertisements for printing businesses taken from 19th century Philadelphia directories with additions by Henry of some of his thoughts on the current political climate and other whimsical thoughts. What a fun project. And you can even use the paper if you wish!

120. (Bird & Bull Press) BIBLIOPHILIC EXTRAVAGANZA! N.P.: Bird & Bull Press, 1989, (14.5 x 10 inches), broadside.
$ 25.00

A humorous poster printed in red and black issued to celebrate a dinner with Henry and Pearl Morris, Bob Fleck, Tanya Schmoller, and Lili and Erich Wronker.

121. (Bird & Bull Press) Bidwell, John (editor). EARLY AMERICAN PAPERMAK-ING: TWO TREATISES ON MANUFACTURING TECHNIQUES REPRINT-ED FROM JAMES CUTBUSH'S AMERICAN ARTIST'S MANUAL (1814). New Castle, DE: Oak Knoll Books, 1990, 8vo., cloth, printed paper over boards, leather spine label. 90, (2) pages.
$ 250.00

First edition, limited to 180 copies of which this is one of the trade copies bound thus. The editor, John Bidwell, has located the first known account of hand papermaking to define American practice in relation to its European heritage. This text first appeared in James Cutbush's *The American Artist's Manual* (Philadelphia: 1814) and is reprinted in full. There is also a lengthy and well-researched introduction - written by John Bidwell - that examines the early history of papermaking in America, the English and French sources used by Cutbush, and the specific American papermaking techniques. Each copy contains an original sample of Gilpin machine-made paper. The introduction has been printed by Henry Morris of the Bird & Bull Press on Frankfurt paper. The facsimile reprint has been printed by lithography and the book has been bound by Campbell-Logan Bindery.

ONE OF 10 COPIES

122. (Bird & Bull Press) Bidwell, John (editor). EARLY AMERICAN PAPERMAK-ING: TWO TREATISES ON MANUFACTURING TECHNIQUES REPRINT-ED FROM JAMES CUTBUSH'S AMERICAN ARTIST'S MANUAL (1814). New Castle, DE: Oak Knoll Books, 1990, 8vo., quarter leather, printed paper over boards, in a larger slipcase with a separate portfolio containing two pieces of Robeson handmade paper and two pieces of Gilpin handmade paper. 90, (2) pages. $ 750.00

First edition, limited to 180 copies of which this is one of the 10 extra-special copies bound thus and containing two pieces of original Robeson handmade paper and two pieces of original Gilpin handmade paper. The sheets of Gilpin handmade paper display perfectly what the instructions of Cutbush's MANUAL were expected to achieve, while the tipped-in leaf of Gilpin machine-made paper in the text reveals the advantages of new technology that in time would render those instructions obsolete. Not often can one compare two succeeding technologies so vividly and conveniently. The Robeson handmade paper is referred to in the text as "exhibiting the typical characteristics of handmade stock produced in the middle or late 1830s, when many American mills had already adopted mass production methods." All the watermarks in these four sheets of paper are reproduced as illustrations in the text. Introduction printed by Henry Morris at his Bird & Bull Press.

123. (Bird & Bull Press) Blades, William. NUMISMATA TYPOGRAPHICA, THE MEDALLIAC HISTORY OF PRINTING. Newtown, PA: Bird & Bull Press, 1992, 4to., cloth, paper spine label. (xxviii), 144 pages, xxiv plates. $ 40.00

Reprint, limited to 300 copies. Foreword by Henry Morris. The rarest work by this great 19th century scholar-printer. It took over eight years for Blades to research and write this book, which first appeared in monthly installments in *The Printers' Register,* then published as a book in 1883. Anyone who collects printing medals will be amazed at the accuracy and depth of Blades' research in this area, as this is probably the best book on the subject. Lists 259 medals. Illustrated with 24 plates describing the medals.

124. (Bird & Bull Press) CHARLES MEUNIER'S PLAQUETTE, 1900. LA RE-LIEUSE, A RARE AND BEAUTIFUL DEPICTION OF THE BOOKBINDER IN MEDALLIC ART. Newtown: Bird & Bull Press, n.d. (but 1996), cloth case with cameo die cut in which is loosely inserted the facsimile medal. Accompanied by a hand-printed four page brochure describing this item. $ 60.00

Meunier issued this plaquette showing a women at a bookbinding sewing frame in 1900. Henry Morris owns a copy of the original and thought it worth reproducing. He gives a short historical sketch of Meunier in the brochure. This also discussed in Marianne Tidcombe's new book WOMEN BOOK-BINDERS.

125. (Bird & Bull Press) Craig, Gordon. GORDON CRAIG'S PARIS DIARY 1932–1933. Edited with a Prologue by Colin Franklin. North Hills: Bird & Bull Press, 1982, 8vo., quarter leather with leather tips and leather spine label and Japanese paper sides. 154, (2) pages. $ 185.00

First edition, limited to 350 numbered copies printed by Henry Morris at his Bird & Bull Press. Prospectus is loosely inserted. Includes a number of reproductions of pages of the manuscript. This diary, previously unpublished, covers the period October 16, 1932 to November 11, 1933, and relates a period of Craig's life during which his fortunes were at a low ebb. The diary tells of his friends Beerbohm, Isadora Duncan, Lovat Fraser and Maillol.

126. (Bird & Bull Press) EAST-WEST HAND PAPERMAKING TRADITIONS AND INNOVATIONS EXHIBITION. Newtown: Bird & Bull Press, 1988, broadside. $50.00

Limited to 30 copies. Printed on one side only in two colors, with an illustration from *Chinese Handmade Paper*. Printed by Henry Morris to announce an exhibition of books on papermaking staged by the University of Delaware. Morris printed a limited number of the exhibition catalogue as well.

127. (Bird & Bull Press) Evelyn, John. ACETARIA, A DISCOURSE OF SALLETS. With an Introduction by Kit Currie. Dallas, TX: Still Point Press, 1985, 8vo., set of unbound signatures. 149, (3) pages. $50.00

First edition thus, limited to 300 numbered copies printed by Henry Morris at his Bird & Bull Press on mouldmade Arches text paper. Illustrated by Tottoroto. This set of signatures is not numbered. Evelyn's essay on salads originally appeared in 1699 and is, as Kit Currie describes it, "a delight to read." This edition contains a number of full color illustrations of the vegetables that Evelyn is describing and printed with the usual high quality expected of Henry Morris.

128. (Bird & Bull Press) Feather, John. ENGLISH BOOK PROSPECTUSES, AN ILLUSTRATED HISTORY. Newtown: Bird & Bull Press and Minneapolis: Daedalus Press, 1984, 8vo., quarter morocco with tips, Dutch Gilt sides reproduced from an 18th century German decorated paper, plus 14 larger facsimiles in a separate accompanying portfolio. 109 pages. $300.00

Limited to 325 copies. The history of this important piece of publishing ephemera from its beginning in 1610 up through the 19th century and accompanied by 24 facsimile prospectuses from 2 to 10 pages in length. As the exact size was maintained, it was necessary to place 4 of the facsimiles in a separate portfolio. All but one of the prospectus done in facsimile come from the Bodleian Library. This book is the kind of private press book that Oak Knoll likes to handle; an important new text presented in a superb format. Prospectus loosely inserted.

129. (Bird & Bull Press) Franklin, Colin (editor). DOVES PRESS: THE START OF A WORRY. Edited with an Introduction by Colin Franklin. Foreword by Michael Hornby. Dallas, TX: The Bridwell Library, 1983, small 8vo., cloth-backed boards. 31, (3) pages. $95.00

First edition, limited to 275 copies and printed by Henry Morris at his Bird & Bull Press. Reprints of a number of letters between Cobden-Sanderson, Hornby, Sydney Cockerell and Emery Walker concerning the last days of the Doves Press.

130. (Bird & Bull Press) Harlan, Robert D. CHAPTER NINE THE VULGATE BIBLE & OTHER UNFINISHED PROJECTS OF JOHN HENRY NASH. New York: The Typophiles, 1982, 12mo., paper over boards. 79 pages. $46.50

Printed in an edition limited to 1000 copies, 500 for the Book Club of California and 500 for the Typophiles. This copy has the Typophiles on the title page. It concerns Nash's never-to-be completed Vulgate Bible that was going to be his Magnus opus. This book was printed by Henry Morris at the Bird & Bull Press. With a large, foldout sample of a Nash text page pasted to the inside rear cover. Presentation from Harlan on free endpaper.

131. (Bird & Bull Press) Harris, Elizabeth M. THE ART OF MEDAL ENGRAVING. Newtown, PA: Bird & Bull Press, 1991, 4to., Japanese cloth with leather spine label. 56 pages. $175.00

First edition, limited to 230 numbered copies. With introduction by Henry Morris. Discusses the history and invention of one the lesser-known graphic processes. Includes an original complete folio leaf from Achille Collas' "Tresor de numismatique," which demonstrates the process, and reproductions of medal-engraved American works. Printed on Johannot mouldmade paper. Henry Morris printed only 160 book. Signed and dated by John DePol and with his bookplate.

132. (Bird & Bull Press) Heaney, Howell J. THIRTY YEARS OF BIRD & BULL A BIBLIOGRAPHY, 1958–1988. With a foreword and commentary by Henry Morris. Newtown: Bird & Bull Press, 1988, 8vo., quarter morocco and tips, with Bird & Bull Press paste-paper over boards and a morocco spine label. Accompanied by a cloth folder containing various text pages and ephemera; both inserted in a cloth-covered and lined clamshell box with a morocco spine label. 104 pages. $ 550.00

First edition, limited to 300 numbered copies, of which 275 are for sale. Contains a complete bibliographical description of all books and selected ephemera printed by and for the press plus books printed by the press for others, since 1980. There is also a short-title list of all the entries from the 1979 bibliography, making this the definitive work on this fine private press. Each entry lists the collation, reprints the colophon and in most cases has a fascinating and enlightening commentary written from the heart by Henry Morris. All the humor is there, along with thoughts and beliefs that can probably only really be appreciated by a fellow letterpress printer who feels the anxiety, frustration and total commitment that goes into a private press production! Mention must be made of the type specimen list, contained within the folder of ephemera, which must be one of the most innovative and unique type specimens ever produced. Amazingly the book itself also has tipped-in samples and facsimile pages. Henry Morris took over two years to produce this book making all his own paper, writing, hand typesetting, printing in two colors, folding, pasting, etc. It certainly is a fitting tribute to the press's 30th anniversary.

133. (Bird & Bull Press) Hunter II, Dard. DARD HUNTER & SON. N.P. (but Newtown, PA): Bird & Bull Press, 1998, 4to., quarter black morocco, leather spine label, Japanese cloth-covered boards, cloth-covered clamshell box with leather spine label. 152, (6) pages, with 30 additional pages and 6 additional leaves of paper & printing samples, and reproductions. $ 675.00

Finely letterpress printed in an edition limited to only 225 numbered copies, of which 180 are presubscribed. Henry Morris' Bird & Bull Press has now published a new Dard Hunter book, which aims in part to "provide a reasonable taste of the original [The Life Work], sufficient perhaps to appreciate the unstinting quality of the artistry and uncommon skill that was lavished on this work," and in part to provide additional material, including some on Dard Hunter II. The introduction by Mr. Morris is followed by Dard Hunter II's account of the writing of his father's biography, followed in turn by Dard Hunter III's short account of the life of Dard II, with color plates. Dard Hunter & Son documents Hunter's early Roycroft days, studies in Vienna, stained-glass windows, first paper mill in Marlborough NY, early watermarks, typefounding experiments, the move to "Mountain House," brief venture into large-scale hand papermaking, later moulds and watermarks, and his publications. Each topic is complimented by appropriate illustrations. There are three tipped-in-plates with 55 color reproductions of swatches of marbled and paste papers done by Hunter in his Vienna days, three samples (reprintings by Bird & Bull) of 2-color page or cover designs done for the Roycrofters, photos of the Marlborough Mill and a reduced-size reprint of a Dard Hunter poster drawing of the mill, original leaves from various publications, a bound-in sample of paper made by Dard Hunter and two by his son, tipped-in photos of Dard Hunter demonstrating papermaking at MIT in 1946, and a tipped-in facsimile of a page of notes made by Dard Hunter while visiting an English paper mill. The book concludes with a ten-page facsimile of the journal kept by Dard Hunter II while writing the Life Work. In all, there are about seventy individual text illustrations or facsimiles, twenty or so tipped-in-plates, and sixteen printings or reprintings by the Hunters and print reproductions by Bird & Bull. Set in Ehrhardt type and printed on Frankfurt mould made paper at Bird & Bull. The multitalented Dard Hunter (1883–1966), who eventually settled upon papermaking and the history of paper as his life's work, is a person of considerable interest in the recent history of the book arts. Relatively little, however, of a biographical nature has been published about him: chiefly his own autobiography of 1958, and the Life Work of Dard Hunter by his son, Dard Hunter II (1917–1989), itself an impressive work printed in Dard Hunter II's own type, and produced in a very limited edition in the early 80's.

134. (Bird & Bull Press) Macfarlane, Nigel. PAPER JOURNEY, TRAVELS AMONG THE VILLAGE PAPERMAKERS OF INDIA AND NEPAL. New Castle, DE: Oak Knoll Books, 1993, 8vo., quarter cloth, paper over boards, leather spine label. 103, (i) pages. $ 240.00

First edition, limited to 210 numbered copies. This book is a fascinating and entertaining account of contemporary hand papermaking in India and Nepal. The reader is led on a journey from Rajasthan in the north west of India to Pondicherry in the south, from the cotton growing country of Gujarat to the boulder strewn plateau of the Deccan, from the Katmandu valley in Nepal to the foothills of the Himalayas. Hand papermaking in India and Nepal is steeped in history and interwoven with village life. Along this journey we learn many interesting details, not only of the techniques and methods of making paper, but also of everyday life in India and Nepal. We experience a ride in the second class carriage of an Indian train; an eight-hour car journey through the night in an Indian version of a 1950s Morris Oxford, with a retired army driver at the wheel; and a treacherous walk up the Nepalese mountains while being overtaken by barefoot porters carrying seventy kilo loads! There are also, of course, detailed descriptions of the techniques used to make paper. In Sanganer we learn the papermakers use a "mould" made of hollow grass stems called a chapri, and we experience the making of a chapri while sitting on a charpoy (a string bed) sipping tea. At the Kalam Kush paper mill we watch rags being sorted, hollander beaters disintegrating fibre, and paper being made on European style moulds by papermakers who work from a standing position and pour the pulp onto the mould. It is an enjoyable way to learn about the different techniques used and the reasons why they were developed. Before commencing this journey, we are informed that a sheet of paper made by hand contains in the pattern of its fibers, in the texture of its surface, in its imperfections, the story of its own origin. The surface of a sheet of Nepalese handmade paper is full of tiny specks, which reflect and glitter in the sunlight, because it is made at three thousand meters in the mountains where the fast-flowing mountain stream contains mica, worn away from the rocks. A paper's origin is an underlying theme of this book, and it is a feature which is visually represented by 20 full-page, tipped-in samples of actual handmade papers from India and Nepal gathered by the author during his visits. These colorful papers provide the reader with a real appreciation of how a sheet of paper contains a message and reveals its own journey on the paper road. A fine book on paper history would not be complete unless it was produced by Henry Morris of the Bird & Bull Press. He has designed this book and printed it by letterpress on imported Arches mouldmade paper. As well as the 20 paper samples this book contains 31 black and white illustrations, a chronology of papermaking in India and Nepal, and a select bibliography.

135. (Bird & Bull Press) Morris, Henry. NICOLAS LOUIS ROBERT AND HIS ENDLESS WIRE PAPERMAKING MACHINE. Newton: Bird & Bull Press, 2000, folio, cloth covered portfolio with paper cover label and accompanied by small 4to. cloth covered book with a paper cover label. Both inserted in a folio clamshell box with a leather spine label. 41, (3) pages and additional plates. $ 400.00

Printed in an edition limited to 150 numbered copies. The actual inventor of the paper machine was a 33 year old former artilleryman named Nicolas Louis Robert, 1761–1828. The existence of five of his own ink and watercolor patent drawings was not previously known until Leonard Schlosser bought the set at auction and reproduced them. His reproductions have now been lost except for a very few copies, one of which was given to Schlosser's friend, Henry Morris. These drawings are of historical significance because they describe in detail the very beginning of the paper machine, a machine which had almost as much impact as Gutenberg's printing press. The cheap production of paper and the resultant dissemination of knowledge and information would not have taken place without this invention. The five drawings are reproduced full size on 12" x 16 3/4 card stock and held in a separate board portfolio. With an accompanying book which provides background material on the inventor and his machine and a chapter on the paper collector and historian, Leonard Schlosser.

136. (Bird & Bull Press) Morris, Henry. VIGNETTES, AN ECLECTIC ASSEM-
BLAGE OF ANECDOTES ABOUT PAPERMAKING. Newtown, PA: Bird and
Bull Press, 1999, large 4to., cloth with leather spine label, in special cloth solander case
with leather spine. 72, (5) pages, with additional pages of color illustrations. $ 400.00
First edition, limited to 150 numbered copies printed at The Bird & Bull Press. Includes chapters on Bird
& Bull Incunabula, 19th Century Security Papers, Lessing J. Rosenwald, *Numismata Typographica*,
Farewell to Papermaking, A History of Die Cutting, The Wurzburg Lithography and more. Includes a
tipped in sample of the first Bird & Bull handmade paper (1958). The portfolio case includes two remov-
able cylinder seal impressions. These clay impressions, attributions to the article "Better Late Than
Never," bear images of people and inscriptions from ancient cylinder seals in Babylonia. Full of illustrations in both black and white and color, many tipped-in. Text in Ehrhardt types on Arches Mouldmade
paper. Several pages printed in two colors. The smaller format of this volume of *Vignettes*, with a solu-
tion to the problem of storage encountered with volume one, *Broadside Vignettes*. Prospectus inserted.

137. (Bird & Bull Press) Morris, Henry. BON MOT. N.P.: Bird & Bull Press, n.d., 4to.,
outer cardboard frame with title and Bird & Bull insignia printed at the bottom and 12
broadsides printed on different colored paper. $ 35.00
Each broadside shows a different example of typography and is printed in two colors. Meant as a gift for
standing order customers of his fine private press. Displays Henry Morris's design work and sense of
humor.

138. (Bird & Bull Press) Morris, Henry. FIRST FINE SILVER COINAGE OF THE
REPUBLIC OF SAN SERRIFFE: THE BIRD & BULL PRESS COMMEMORA-
TIVE 100 CORONAS. Including an account of this legendary republic and its connection with the Bird & Bull Press. With a description of similar numismatic rarities and
a 30–year checklist of work produced by the Press, 1958–1988. Newtown: Bird & Bull
Press, 1988, 8vo., quarter morocco with paper-covered sides with a silver coin design on
the front cover. Accompanied by a special holder for the silver proof coin; both inserted
in a slipcase. 57 pages. $ 100.00
First edition, limited to 350 numbered copies. Full of Henry Morris humor about his mythical kingdom
of San Serriffe, a tipped-in numbered stock certificate for 1000 shares of Bird & Bull stock, printed currency of San Serriffe, and even a map of the kingdom. The coin itself is sure to be a numismatic rarity, a
beautifully minted proof silver coin of San Serriffe. Also of interest is the chapter on other privately
minted coins.

139. (Bird & Bull Press) Morris, Henry. GUILFORD & GREEN. North Hills: The Bird
& Bull Press, 1970, 8vo., quarter morocco over patterned paper covered boards. (ii), 88,
(4) pages. $ 525.00
Limited to 210 numbered copies. (Taylor A9). The first part of the book describes a visit made by Henry
Morris to J. Barcham Green, the famous hand papermaking firm in England. Gives a history of the firm
and reproduces correspondence between William Morris and Joseph Batchelor regarding production of
paper. The second section of the book reprints a number of letters written by Nathan Guilford during a
trip to Kentucky in the early part of the 19th century. The interesting series of letters provide real insight into life in the states. Loosely inserted is a dust jacket made up of paper that was not used for the
cover with a piece of the paper folded and inserted in a pocket in the back of this jacket .

140. (Bird & Bull Press) Morris, Henry. NO. V–109, THE BIOGRAPHY OF A
PRINTING PRESS. N.P.: Anne and David Bromer, 1978, miniature book (6.1 x 4.7
cm.), full vellum with "V 109" stamped in silver on front cover, a variant binding. 30, (4)
pages. $ 150.00
First edition, limited to 150 numbered copies; this copy is not numbered. Printed by hand by Henry
Morris at his private press and the only miniature book produced (or ever will be produced) by this fine
press. Includes a bibliography of books printed at the Bird & Bull Press through 1978. This copy was
made up from an extra copy run off at the press.

141. (Bird & Bull Press) Morris, Henry. OMNIBUS, INSTRUCTIONS FOR AMA-
TEUR PAPERMAKERS WITH NOTES AND OBSERVATIONS OF PRIVATE
PRESSES, BOOK PRINTING AND SOME PEOPLE WHO ARE INVOLVED
IN THESE ACTIVITIES. (North Hills, PA): The Bird & Bull Press, 1967, large 8vo.,
quarter leather over decorated paper covered boards. 121 pages. $ 375.00
Limited to 500 numbered copies. Chapters on The Mould, The Beater, Other Necessary Equipment and
Beating Pulp, Some Observations on Private Presses, Making, Drying and Sizing Paper, Notes on Print-
ing and Binding. Includes six samples of paper used by Morris for his books. Loosely inserted is the
prospectus to this book and a printed paper specimen with text referring to page 120 of the book. Bookplate.

142. (Bird & Bull Press) Morris, Henry. PEPPERPOT: INGREDIENTS, CHOICE
BITS OF UNCOMMON PAPERMAKING PUBLISHING AND PRINTING
HISTORY SIMMERED IN A TASTY BROTH OF POETRY, CURRENT
EVENTS AND AMUSING ANECDOTES. LIGHTLY SEASONED WITH A
DASH OF OBSCENITY, AND WITH SELECTED PORTIONS OF TRIPE
ADDED AS IN THE OLD ORIGINAL RECIPE. North Hills: Bird & Bull Press,
1977, 4to., leather spine, paste paper over boards. 86, (4) pages. $ 375.00
Taylor A17. Being the second commonplace book issued by the press. Limited to "approximately 250
copies." Printed by hand by Morris on Green's handmade Bird & Bull paper. Seven articles including an
autobiographical sketch and the first English translation of sections of Jacob Christian Schaeffer's famous 18th century text on papermaking. The later contains four tinted plates showing raw material for
papers. One specimen inserted.

143. (Bird & Bull Press) Morris, Henry. PRINTED PASTE-PAPERS FOR THREE-
PIECE BOOKBINDINGS. Newtown, PA: Bird & Bull Press, n.d. (1990), 12mo., stiff
paper wrappers. 2 leaves of text followed by the specimen sheets. $ 25.00
Limited to 200 copies. Henry Morris spent time during the Spring of 1990 producing paste-paper for sale
to the public. This specimen book shows examples of these papers which he produced based on 18th and
19th century Italian and French woodcut papers. Loosely inserted is a note from the printer concerning
this booklet.

144. (Bird & Bull Press) Morris, Henry. PRIVATE PRESS-MAN'S TALE. With illustrations by Lili Wronker. Newtown, PA: Bird & Bull Press, 1990, 4to., paste paper
over cloth-backed boards, leather spine label. 61, (2) pages. $ 350.00
First edition, limited to 230 numbered copies. Letterpress printed with Van Dijck types on Arches
mouldmade paper and bound by Barbara Blumenthal. A humorous collection of satire and prose, inspired by Chaucer's Canterbury Tales. All the text is related to the book arts - book-collecting, bookselling, printing, papermaking, etc. It includes an imaginary interview with William Morris, a great
poem about the attitude of FINE PRINT magazine, Henry's explanation of the Handmade Paper Today
incident and a review of the antics in Fine Print's book reviews. There are also two excellent articles by
Sidney Berger on Book Fair's and Book Scouts. The illustrations have been very well executed and express all the humour of the text. An essential for anybody who is known in the books about books field,
because they are bound to have been mentioned!

145. (Bird & Bull Press) Morris, Henry. BROADSIDE VIGNETTES. Newtown, PA:
Bird & Bull Press, 1997, giant folio, 10 page introductory booklet, 27 poster/broadsides
(each 19 x 25 inches) in 21 folders, gathered in a cloth clamshell box with paper cover
label. $ 475.00
Printed in an edition limited to only 145 numbered copies by Henry Morris. Broadside Vignettes joins
the typographic aspect of the poster/broadside format with the contextual character of the book, creating a hybrid with some of the best qualities of both. Each of the twenty-one folders holds a complete and
different "short story," almost all of which are on subjects dear to the hearts of the book collector, Private Press connoisseur, or hand-papermaking enthusiast. Two of the twenty-one folders consist of two

sheets, and one include four sheets. Each is printed in two or more colors on a wide variety of imported and domestic papers, with an even wider variety of uncommon type faces. All but two of the vignettes are generously illustrated. Henry Morris has worked steadily on this for the past eight months and has told us that he has never spent so much time, worked harder, or found more satisfaction and pleasure in any previous undertaking. He issues this volume with the goal of producing a new volume each year. And don't worry about how to shelve this giant folio, for Henry has included a simple and practical suggestion regarding the convenient storage of this large case. All but 15 copies have already gone to his standing order customers. Surly to be a most sought-after item.

146. (Bird & Bull Press) Murray, John. PRACTICAL REMARKS ON MODERN PAPER. WITH AN INTRODUCTORY ESSAY BY LEONARD B. SCHLOSS-ER. North Hills, Pennsylvania: Bird & Bull Press, 1981, 8vo., leather spine, decorative paper over boards. 120, (3) pages. $ 300.00

Printed in an edition limited to 300 copies. Being a reprint of a book by John Murray in 1829 on the state of papermaking at that time and the impact on the usefulness and longevity of paper of some of the practices used by the industry. The book is prophetic in tone in light of what has occurred during the 150 years. Schlosser has added an excellent introduction explaining Murray's concerns with using shorter paper fibers in mechanical papermaking machinery, the increased use of minerals in the pulp, the introduction of chemical bleaching, and the introduction of sizing into the pulp. Mr. Morris has added his own introductory remarks about other aspects of John Murray's life. He has also reprinted several abstracts on other Murray discoveries such as a "New Method of saving Lives in cases of Shipwreck and of Fire," a "New Shower Bath" and a respirator for breathing aid.

147. (Bird & Bull Press) Nevins, Iris. VARIETIES OF SPANISH MARBLING, A HANDBOOK OF PRACTICAL INSTRUCTION WITH TWELVE ORIGINAL MARBLED SAMPLES. N.P.: Bird & Bull Press and Iris Nevins, 1991, 8vo., quarter cloth, Spanish marbled sides, leather spine label. 79 pages. $ 250.00

First edition, limited to 250 numbered copies. Composed in Cochin types and printed on Johannot mouldmade paper. Of all the marbled patterns, the Spanish is the most difficult to achieve. This book contains detailed instructions for making twelve different patterns, as well as original 5 x 8 inch specimens. No literature or documentation on the origin or practice of marbling in Spain has thus far been discovered. This book is the first to concern itself exclusively with the technique of Spanish marbling.

148. (Bird & Bull Press) PROCEEDINGS AT A MEETING OF THE VAT PAPER MAKERS HELD AT THE BELL HOTEL, MAIDSTONE ON TUESDAY 8TH, MARCH 1853. North Hills: Bird & Bull Press, 1970, 4to., hand-sewn paper wrappers in a stiff blue paper box. 54 pages. $ 60.00

Taylor A10. Printed in an edition limited to 300 copies. Copied from a hand-written manuscript, this account of a meeting of workers in a hand-made paper mill accurately depicts the working conditions of the day. Social problems brought along by mechanical paper making and allowing women to do certain jobs are discussed. Outer folder is foxed.

149. (Bird & Bull Press) Schlosser, Leonard B. PAIR ON PAPER, TWO ESSAYS ON PAPER HISTORY AND RELATED MATTERS. North Hills, PA: Bird & Bull Press, 1976, small 4to., quarter brown morocco over paper covered boards. 70, (2) pages.
                                                                              $ 300.00

First edition, limited to 220 numbered copies, and printed on paper made by hand by Henry Morris. This interesting book contains a essay by Morris on his discovery of a number of books printed on French paper made from assignats, those pieces of currency used in France during the French Revolution. Includes a number of illustrations and two actual specimens of this currency inserted in a pocket opposite page 29. Schlosser writes on "Some Early Milanese Paper Wrappers," i.e. ream wrappers, with reproductions of a number of them. Prospectus loosely inserted.

Item 150

150. (Bird & Bull Press) Schmoller, Hans, Tanya Schmoller, Henry Morris. CHINESE DECORATED PAPERS, CHINOISERIE FOR THREE. Newtown: Bird & Bull Press, 1987, oblong 8vo. (7.75 x 10 inches), quarter morocco with tips in leather and leather spine label and a reproduction in gold of one of the ream wrappers on the front cover. 77, (3) pages followed by the 24 actual samples of Chinese decorated paper (mostly 6 x 8.5 inches). $ 300.00
First edition, limited to 325 numbered copies. Printed on mouldmade Hahnemuhle paper. Hans and Tanya Schmoller found a cache of Chinese tea chest (or tinsel) paper in England that had been in storage for 50 years. This very colorful paper is no longer being manufactured. The book reprints much of the correspondence between Morris and Schmoller on the production of this book that occurred before Schmoller's death. His wife, Tanya, took the notes that he had written and produced the essay on the paper which follows the correspondence. The samples are the best of the large lot and have been treated by Morris to keep them from further oxidation or degradation.

151. (Bird & Bull Press) Schmoller, Hans. MR. GLADSTONE'S WASHI, A SURVEY OF REPORTS ON THE MANUFACTURE OF PAPER IN JAPAN, THE PARKES REPORT OF 1871. Newtown: Bird & Bull Press, 1984, 8vo., quarter morocco with sides based on a fine decorated paper in the Parkes Collection. 134 pages plus 3 fold-out illustration and a separate suite of color prints in a portfolio, all enclosed in a slipcase. $ 300.00
Limited to 450 copies. Sir Harry Parks was sent to Japan by W.E. Gladstone, the English Prime Minister, to gather information on Japanese papermaking. His report, along with a large selection of handmade paper were sent to England in 1871, there soon buried. Hans Schmoller was told about this important cache of historical information in 1970s and has put together a fascinating history of Parkes, the German

scientist, Engelbert Kaempfer, and has accompanied the history with reprints of both the Parkes report and Kaempfer's description of Japanese papermaking, the first such report. Also reproduced are 20 full size color reproductions of Japanese watercolors depicting papermaking. Each copy of this book also has an extra suite of these plates in a separate portfolio. This book will surely become one of Henry Morris' most important productions.

152. (Bird & Bull Press) Schmoller, Tanya. REMONDINI AND RIZZI, A CHAP-TER IN ITALIAN DECORATED PAPER HISTORY. New Castle, DE: Oak Knoll Books, 1990, 8vo., cloth-backed boards covered with patterned paper, in facsimile of an original Remondini pattern specially executed by Henry Morris, leather spine label. 55, (5) pages. $ 295.00
First edition, limited to 215 numbered copies. Set in Perpetua and printed by letterpress on Johannot mould made paper by Henry Morris at the Bird & Bull Press. Italian block-printed papers were the start of the collection of decorated papers that Tanya Schmolller, and her husband Hans, gathered together for over twenty years. The use of woodblocks to transfer designs to cloth and paper can be traced back in Europe to the fourteenth century. In the region of what is now Italy there were several firms supplying these colorful papers, the most eminent being the firm of Remondini which was established in 1650. This work traces the history of the Remondini enterprise and also that of Giuseppe Rizzi who took over the Remondini woodblocks after 1861. It examines the sales techniques and production methods of these two firms and contains actual specimens of Rizzi decorated paper. Today such samples are rarely found and they are usually very expensive. The illustrations include a three-color facsimile of a Remondini woodblock and a fold-out reproduction of a decree authorizing the sale of gilt paper. There are also four pages of genuine Rizzi paper samples.

153. (Bird & Bull Press) Schulz, Ernst. STUDY OF INCUNABLES, PROBLEMS AND AIMS. Philadelphia: The Philobiblon Club, 1977, 8vo., stiff paper wrappers, paper cover label. vii, 29 pages. $ 45.00
First edition, limited to 500 copies printed by Henry Morris at the Bird & Bull Press.

154. (Bird & Bull Press) Simpson, Henry I. EMIGRANT'S GUIDE TO THE GOLD MINES. Haverford: Headframe Publishing Co., 1978, 8vo., leather spine, marbled paper covered boards. 81 pages, foldout map. $ 200.00
Limited to 250 numbered copies. (Taylor B11). A reprint of this early example of Gold Rush literature with a Prologue and Epilogue by Franz R. Dykstra explaining the significance and true value of this early guide book. Designed and printed by Henry Morris at the Bird & Bull Press and printed on Bird & Bull paper. Bound by E.G. Parrot.

155. (Bird & Bull Press) Stewart-Murphy, Charlotte A. HISTORY OF BRITISH CIRCULATING LIBRARIES, THE BOOK LABELS AND EPHEMERA OF THE PAPANTONIO COLLECTION. Newton, PA: Bird & Bull Press, 1992, tall 8vo., quarter leather, decorated paper over boards. 153, (2) pages. $ 295.00
Limited to 185 numbered copies. Printed on Arches mouldmade paper by Henry Morris at The Bird & Bull Press. Gives a history of British circulating libraries through the use of the Papantonio collection of library book labels and book related ephemera of the eighteenth and nineteenth century by the noted English collector Sir Ambrose Heal. The author has thoroughly researched the subject and has produced an interesting account of the libraries and the increase of literacy among the poorer classes. With related information on the printers, booksellers, engravers and bookbinders of the period. Illustrations of sixty-four labels, trade cards and prints are included.

156. (Bird & Bull Press) Stoneback, H.R. CARTOGRAPHERS OF THE DEUS LOCI THE MILL HOUSE. North Hills: Bird & Bull Press, 1982, 8vo., calf vellum spine and Morris' paste-paper sides. Printed on a limited supply of Dard Hunter's own paper. (24) pages. $ 125.00

First edition, limited to 240 numbered copies. Loosely inserted is a "note to standing order customers." A poem written to help raise funds to preserve Dard Hunter's mill giving a history of the house including Hunter's stay. Dard Hunter produced his first paper in this building; the book is printed on some of Hunter's Lime Rock handmade paper that survived. With illustrations by William Osborne.

157. (Bird & Bull Press) Taylor, W. Thomas and Henry Morris. TWENTY-ONE YEARS OF BIRD & BULL A BIBLIOGRAPHY, 1958–1979. North Hills: W. Thomas Taylor and Bird & Bull Press, 1980, large 8vo., leather spine, paper covered boards. 108+(1) pages. $ 350.00

Limited to 350 numbered copies and oversubscribed on publication. A well produced guide to the printing of one of the finest of private presses in operation today.

158. (Bird & Bull Press) Taylor, W. Thomas and Henry Morris. TWENTY-ONE YEARS OF BIRD & BULL A BIBLIOGRAPHY, 1958–1979. North Hills: W. Thomas Taylor and Bird & Bull Press, 1980, large 8vo., leather spine, paper covered boards with a separate cloth folder containing 13 pieces of ephemera, all enclosed in a cloth box with a leather spine label. 108+(1) pages. $ 600.00

Limited to 350 numbered copies and oversubscribed on publication, this is one of only 140 copies that were issued with the extra portfolio of ephemera and inserted in the box. This copy contains prospectuses to Roller-Printed Paste Papers for Bookbindings, The Paper Maker, the Commonplace Book, a broadside entitled "An Ode to S. & T.," an issue of Swine Print and parts of different books. A well produced guide to the printing of one of the finest of private presses in operation today.

159. (Bird & Bull Press) Twain, Mark. MARK TWAIN. CATALOGUE 130. Los Angeles: Heritage Bookshop, n.d. (1975), 8vo., stiff paper wrappers. 99 pages. $ 30.00

Printed by the Bird & Bull Press. 468 items and an index.

160. (Bird & Bull Press) Valls, Oriol. LIVELY LOOK AT PAPERMAKING. North Hills: Bird & Bull Press, 1980, 8vo., decorated paper covered boards, paper spine label. (45) pages. $ 95.00

Printed in an edition limited to 300 copies. This booklet reproduces 24 advertising cards from the late 18th century which show the various steps involved in papermaking from the rag picker to delivery. The cards were discovered by Valls in the print collection of the Historical Archives of Barcelona. They were originally advertising inducements on packets of cigarette paper to encourage buying.

161. (Bird & Bull Press) Voorn, Henk. OLD REAM WRAPPERS, AN ESSAY ON EARLY REAM WRAPPERS OF ANTIQUARIAN INTEREST. North Hills: Bird & Bull Press, 1969, small 4to., leather spine, marbled paper over boards. 111 pages.
$ 450.00

Taylor A8. Printed in an edition limited to 375 numbered copies. This was by far the largest Bird & Bull edition to date. It took Mr. Morris 30 weeks to make the paper used for it. The book was the result of a trip the Morris's took to Europe in 1967. The separately issued envelope containing two reproductions of a ream wrapper is present. This portfolio reproduces ream wrappers of Honig and is often missing from the book as it is so much larger than the book itself.

162. (Bird & Bull Press) Wilson, Alexander. THE FORESTERS. Newton, PA: Bird & Bull Press, 2000, 8vo., quarter morocco, cloth, cloth-covered slipcase. xx, 112, (3) pages. $ 400.00

Limited to 150 numbered copies. Printed on Arches Mouldmade paper by Henry Morris at the Bird & Bull Press. This book contains Alexander Wilson's long poem The Foresters describing his first "pedestrian journey" with two companions to the Falls of Niagara in the Autumn of 1804. Wilson's work is a wonderfully descriptive account of the spectacular sights of the American wilderness. With engravings by Wesley W. Bates, one of the top-rated wood engravers in North America. Bates works in the classic British style and has produced thirteen full page engravings, plus the title page cartouche, for this book. Composed in Dante types by Michael and Winifred Bixler. Includes a foreword by Henry Morris, a synopsis of the poem by Robert Cantwell, and notes on the text.

163. (Bird & Bull Press) Wolfe, Richard J. and Paul McKenna. LOUIS HERMAN KINDER AND FINE BOOKBINDING IN AMERICA, A CHAPTER IN THE HISTORY OF THE ROYCROFT SHOP. Newtown: Bird & Bull Press, 1985, small 4to., quarter morocco with tips and leather spine-label, gold-decorated paper sides. 161 pages. $ 300.00

S-K 7047. Limited to 325 copies. A history of this German born binder that worked for the Roycrofters from 1897 to 1911. The authors have included much unpublished material relating to Kinder and Hubbard, a rather complete catalogue of impressions of Kinder's bookbinding hand tools and illustrated 14 bindings in full color. Another excellent Bird & Bull production. With prospectus loosely inserted.

164. (Bird & Bull Press) Wolfe, Richard J. ON IMPROVEMENTS IN MARBLING THE EDGES OF BOOKS AND PAPER, A NINETEENTH CENTURY MARBLING ACCOUNT EXPLAINED AND ILLUSTRATED WITH FOURTEEN ORIGINAL MARBLED SAMPLES. Newtown: Bird & Bull Press, 1983, oblong 12mo., quarter leather over marbled paper covered boards, leather tips. 64 pages followed by the tipped-in samples. $ 250.00

First edition, limited to 350 numbered copies. Reprints the first American treatise on marbling, an account which appears in the April, 1829 issue of the Journal of the Franklin Institute, with additional text by Wolfe. Beautifully printed on handmade paper.

165. (Bird & Bull Press) Wolfe, Richard J. THREE EARLY FRENCH ESSAYS ON PAPER MARBLING, 1642–1765. With an Introduction and thirteen original marbled samples. Newton: Bird & Bull Press, 1987, 8vo., quarter bound by E.G. Parrot in morocco and tips with leather spine label, and "snail" pattern marbled paper sides made by Wolfe especially for this edition. 106 pages. $ 350.00

Limited to 310 numbered copies and handprinted by Henry Morris at his Bird & Bull Press on "Umbria" handmade paper. Wolfe has translated an unpublished manuscript from Lyon, circa 1642, containing the earliest known French marbling recipe, an article from Journal Oeconomique, 1758, and an article from the Diderot-D'Alembert *Encyclopedie*, 1765 into English. The Diderot article is especially interesting as it comments on the practical side of marbling, i.e., how much money could be made. The samples were produced by Wolfe using the instructions in the translated manuals. Also included is a four color sequence showing the various steps taken by Wolfe in producing the Placard pattern.

166. (Bird in Hand Press) Bradley, Carol Winifred. ANNE BOLEYN, A GAMBIT WITH FRAGMENTS OF POETRY BY SIR THOMAS WYATT. (San Francisco: Bird in Hand Press, 1972), 12mo., stiff paper wrappers. (22) pages. $ 15.00

Printed in an edition limited to 300 copies. An interesting perspective on the fate of Anne Boleyn accompanied by excerpts from the poetry of Sir Thomas Wyatt. All printing and the linoleum cut illustrations were done in either brown or black by Bruce William Bradley.

167. (Black Archer Press) Saroyan, William. THOSE WHO WRITE THEM AND THOSE WHO COLLECT THEM. Chicago: The Black Archer Press, 1936, 12mo., stiff paper wrappers. (12) pages. $100.00

First edition. Printed in an edition limited 50 copies. Saroyan gives his opinion about the hobby of book-collecting. Prospectus loosely inserted. Covers slightly soiled.

168. (Black Cat Press) Brady, Ernest W. SOLILOQUY OF A POSTAGE STAMP. (Skokie, IL: Black Cat Press, 1978), miniature book (3 x 2 1/4 inches), self paper wrappers. (8) pages. $20.00

First edition. Created as a "Keepsake for Friends," this tiny pamphlet explores the mysterious allure of the humble postage stamp. An uncancelled US postage stamp is affixed to the cover.

169. (Black Cat Press) Forgue, Norman W. POORER RICHARD, AN ALMANACK LONG AFTER FRANKLIN. Chicago: The Black Cat Press, 1954, small 8vo., cloth. 48 pages. $45.00

First edition. Foreword by R. Hunter Middleton. Reminiscences by Forgue on the beginning and early days of his career in printing and publishing. Presentation from "Norman" (Forgue) on first blank page. Bookplate of Doc Leslie.

170. (Black Cat Press) Haas, Irvin. BIBLIOGRAPHY OF MATERIAL RELATING TO PRIVATE PRESSES. Chicago: The Black Cat Press, 1937, 8vo., buckram. xvi, 57 pages. $125.00

Limited to 250 copies. Introduction by Will Ransom. An important book. With the bookplate of Norman Forgue, owner of the Black Cat Press. Prospectus loosely inserted which has the ink inscription of the name and address of Jean Hersholt.

171. (Black Cat Press) Haas, Irvin. BIBLIOGRAPHY OF MODERN AMERICAN PRESSES. Introduction by Will Ransom. Chicago: The Black Cat Press, 1935, 8vo., cloth, paper cover label. 95, (7) pages. $125.00

First edition. Largely an update of Ransom's work on private presses listing new presses and books published after that 1929 work.

172. (Black Cat Press) Middleton, R. Hunter. F.W.G., AN APPRECIATION. Chicago: The Black Cat Press, 1938, 12mo., cloth. 14, (2) pages. $55.00

Limited to 200 copies and printed by Norman W. Forgue at his Black Cat Press. Bookplate of John DePol.

173. (Black Cat Press) Twain, Mark. "1601" OR CONVERSATION AT THE SOCIAL FIRESIDE AS IT WAS IN THE TIME OF THE TUDORS. Chicago: Black Cat Press, 1936, 8vo., cloth. 39+(1) pages. $65.00

Printed in an edition limited to 300 copies, designed and hand-set by Norman W. Forgue in Caslon type on Worthy Coronet paper. Woodcut frontispiece and title page decoration by Ben Albert Benson, printed from the original wood blocks. With introduction and a check-list of various editions and reprints compiled by Irvin Haas. Written in the summer of 1876 after Twain had read Samuel Pepys' diary and been inspired by its "Rabelaisian spirit and lusty vocabulary." Previous owner's signature on front pastedown. Extremities worn.

174. (Black Sparrow Press) Bukowski, Charles. A LOVE POEM. Santa Barbara, CA: Black Sparrow Press, 1979, large 12mo., cord-tied illustrated stiff paper wrappers. (8) pages. $25.00

Printed as a New Year's Greeting to friends of the Black Sparrow Press.

175. (Black Sparrow Press) Cooney, Seamus. CHECKLIST OF THE FIRST ONE HUNDRED PUBLICATIONS OF THE BLACK SPARROW PRESS. With 30 Passing Remarks by Robert Kelly. Los Angeles: Black Sparrow Press, 1971, small 8vo., stiff paper wrappers. 39, (3) pages. $ 20.00
First edition, one of 800 copies in paper.

176. (Black Sparrow Press) Olson, Charles. D. H. LAWRENCE AND THE HIGH TEMPTATION OF THE MIND. Santa Barbara, CA: Black Sparrow Press, 1980, large 12mo., stiff paper wrappers. (13) pages. $ 15.00
Printed in an edition of 176 copies. A handsomely produced New Year's greeting from the publisher of the Black Sparrow Press to its friends. This essay on Lawrence, unpublished during Olson's lifetime, first appeared in the *Chicago Review*.

177. (Black Vine Press) Morison, Stanley. TYPOGRAPHIC DESIGN IN RELA-TION TO PHOTOGRAPHIC COMPOSITION. Introduction by John Carter. San Francisco: The Book Club of California, 1959, 8vo., boards with marbled paper over both covers. (viii), 32, (2) pages. $ 150.00
First edition, limited to 400 copies printed by the Black Vine Press for the Book Club of California (Appleton no.210). Fine.

178. (Blackwells Press) Atkins, Kathleen. A PHYSICS PROBLEM. (Watsonville, Ca): Blackwells Press, 1984, 8vo., stiff paper wrappers. 26, (4) pages. $ 25.00
Designed and printed by Nick Zachreson at Blackwells Press in an edition limited to 250 copies. Set in Lutetia & Arrighi type on Mohawk Letterpress paper. Some of the poems were first printed in *Poetry* and *The Atlantic*. In 1983 the author was awarded the Milliman Award for Poetry and in 1984 a first prize from the Academy of American Poets. This is her first published collection.

179. (Blackwood Press) Macnooder, J Oglethorpe. A COMMON PLACE BOOK. Blackwood Press, 1975, 1983, 4to., stiff paper wrappers. (28); (24) pages. $ 135.00
Volume I has been printed in an edition of 120 numbered copies and Volume II has been printed in an edition of 195 copies. Presentation copies from the printer, Edmund E. Simpson. A commonplace book is one in which are written notable quotations, poems and comments. Hand set Bemo types have been used in this gathering, which is probably the most beautiful of the old-face designs. The lino blocks were drawn and cut by the printer.

180. (Bodoni) Callimachus. CALLIMACO GRECO-ITALIANO ORA PUBBLI-CATO. Parma: Nel Regal palazzoco' tipi Bodoniani, 1792, folio, contemporary half leather, marbled paper covered boards, five raised bands, top edge gilt, spine lettered and tooled in gilt. (14), iv, (6), 74, (6)[lacking one blank leaf], 96, (4) pages. $ 3,500.00
Printed in an edition limited to 160 copies of which this is one of 100 or less printed on this type of paper. This edition has four numbered preliminary pages, no headpiece on page (i), and the type is in all capitals. (Brooks no.441). Includes two versions of the same text printed in one volume. First part with text in Greek, second part with text in Italian. Each with its own separate signatures, pagination, and special title page. Part 1 titled (transliterated) "Hoi tou Kallimachou Kyrenaiou hymnoi te, kai epigrammata"; part 2 titled "Inni di Callimaco cirenesi cogli epigrammi." The book contains the Hymns and Epigrams of the classical Greek poet Callimachus'(305-240 BC). The Hymns are modeled after the Homeric Hymns but are not intended to be recited in public. Instead, they are literary pieces, meant for reading or recitation to a select audience. Italian translation by Giuseppe Maria Pagnini. Also with "Sonnetto" by Vincenzo Jacobacci: (3) pages at end. Four different versions of this book were printed by Bodoni in 1792. The first issue was without a prefatory "Giambatista Bodoni al lettore" and was printed in both capital and lower case types; the second issue contained Bodoni's preface, is printed in all capitals, and occurs in three different states: with five numbered preliminary pages printed with and without an engraved headpiece on page (i) and then this edition with four numbered preliminary pages and no headpiece on page (i). All issues with a headpiece of the Bourbon and Saxon arms on page (7). Marbled paper at edges of boards slightly chipped, minor rubbing to corners. A magnificent example of Bodoni's work.

Item 181

181. (Bodoni) Bodoni, Giambattista. MANUALE TIPOGRAFICO. Two volumes. Parma: Presso la Vedova, 1818, 4to., contemporary quarter mottled sheep over orange paper over boards with vellum tips, smooth spines decoratively tooled in gilt and blind with light brown calf gilt lettering labels, all edges uncut. [14], XXVII, [1, blank], LXXII pp., [2], 265 leaves, pp. 266-267; [2], 275 leaves, pp. 276-279 (leaves 273, 274, and 275 folding). $ 55,000.00

Second edition. (Brooks 1216, Brunet I, col. 1027, Graesse I, p. 460, Updike, Printing Types, II, pp. 169–171.) "The second and final edition of Bodoni's Manuale Tipografico-in two quarto volumes, with a Discorso by his widow and Prefazione by Bodoni-appeared in 1818, five years after his death. It was completed under the care of his widow and Luigi Orsi, who was for twenty years foreman to Bodoni. Signora Bodoni, writing to M. Durand, l'aîné of Metz, from Parma (November 14, 1817), says: 'The Manuale Tipografico in two volumes on papier-vélin-the only kind of paper used for it-is not yet completed, but it will be, without fail, at the beginning of the coming year. I dare to believe that book-lovers will thank me for having published a volume which is so very important to Typography. The reception which it will have, will make up for the trouble it has cost me (although Bodoni has left the blocks or models for it) and the considerable expense which I shall have had to incur before it is finished. Also, in view of the fact that but 290 copies are struck off, I cannot dispose of them at less than 120 francs, without any reduction. M. Rosaspina has engraved au burin the portrait after one which the celebrated Appiani... painted in oils, which is a striking likeness.' The first volume contains, under the title of Serie di Caratteri Latini, Tondi e Corsivi, a series of roman and italic types, which cover 144 pages. These run from parmigianina to papale. Sometimes there are as many as fourteen varieties of the same body in different designs and weights of line... Succeeding pages (145–169) show Serie di Caratteri Cancellereschi, etc... The second volume contains an assemblage of roman and 'italic' Greek capitals, covering sixty-two pages; and exotic types, beginning with Hebrew, run on to the ninety-seventh page. These are followed by German and Russian types, many of great splendour. The book closes with series of borders, mathematical, astronomical, and other signs, musical notation, etc... The work is probably the most elaborate specimen that the world has ever seen-an imposing tour de force" (Updike, Printing Types). A very fine copy.

182. (Bodoni) MEMORIA ED ORAZIONE DEL P. PAOLO M.A PACIAUDI INTORNO LA BIBLIOTECA PARMENSE. Two volumes bound as one. Parma: Co'Tipi Bodoniani, 1815, 8vo., original publishers green paper covered boards, leather spine label, uncut edges. (iv),viii,(ii),97; (v),21+(1)pages. $ 650.00
Printed in an edition of 261 copies. (Gonnelli, p. 202). Text in two sections; first *Memoria Intorno La Reale Biblioteca di Parma*, with index, followed by *Orazione nel Solenne Aprimento della Reale Biblioteca di Parma Presente l'Imperatore Gioseffo II*. A very nice example of printing done by the Bodoni press. Printed two years after Giambatista's death, in 1815, when Luigi Orsi was managing the firm for Bodoni's widow. Collection of works by Father Paolo Maria Paciaudi, renowned antiquarian and prolific author of books on the classics. He was appointed head of Royal Library of Parma at its inception in 1761, and wrote the second section of this volume for the library's official 1769 inauguration, which Emperor Joseph II of Austria attended. Foreword printed in beautiful italic script. Wide margins. Many pages uncut. Minor wear to head and tail of spine.

183. (Book Club of California) Bliss, Carey S. LEAF FROM THE 1583 REMBERT DODOENS HERBAL PRINTED BY PLANTIN. San Francisco: Book Club of California, 1977, small folio, cloth. (xvi), 28, (viii) pages. $ 55.00
Printed in an edition limited to 358 copies. (200th Book of the Book Club of California, no.156). Illustrated with numerous reproductions of herbal engravings from the Herbal and portraits of Plantin and Dodoens. Bliss, at that time Curator of Rare Books at the Huntington Library, considers this herbal to be"...one of the great herbals of history." Included in the Exhibition of Western Books (Rounce and Coffin Club). This copy lacks the leaf but is complete in binding and text.

184. (Book Club of California) BREADBASKET OF THE WORLD, CALIFORNIA'S GREAT WHEAT-GROWING ERA: 1860–1890. San Francisco: The Book Club of California, 1984, oblong 8vo., self paper wrappers. $ 25.00
Designed and produced by Jonathan Clark at The Artichoke Press. Each pamphlet contains text and a photograph of a scene. 10 pamphlets.

185. (Book Club of California) Breen, Patrick. THE DIARY OF PATRICK BREEN, RECOUNTING THE ORDEAL OF THE DONNER PARTY SNOWBOUND IN THE SIERRA 1846-47. (San Francisco): The Book Club of California, (1946), small 8vo., illustrated paper covered boards. 38 pages of text followed by 30 plates of manuscript. $ 125.00
Printed in an edition limited to 300 copies, "the sale of which is restricted to members of The Book Club of California." Hand-set in Bulmer type and printed on an all-rag paper by the L-D Allen Press (Allen, no.5). Engravings and decorative paper used for the binding by Mallette Dean, who did considerable fine work for the Grabhorn Press and others. Introduction & Notes by George R. Stewart. A facsimile of the original manuscript follows the text, reproduced with permission of the Bancroft Library at the University of California, Berkeley. Bookplate of Dwight Lancelot Clarke on front pastedown.

186. (Book Club of California) Browne, Lewis. FINAL STANZA, A HITHERTO UNPUBLISHED CHAPTER OF "THAT MAN HEINE". San Francisco: The Book Club of California, 1929, 8vo., quarter parchment with blue paper covered boards. (vi), viii, 8, (4) pages. $ 45.00
Limited to 400 numbered copies signed by Browne. (Biblio. Book Club of California no.33) Printed by Johnck and Seeger of San Francisco.

187. (Book Club of California) CALIFORNIA GOLD RUSH CAMPS. N.P.: The Book Club of California, 1998, small 4to., stiff paper portfolio. 14 loose signatures.

$ 25.00

A 1998 keepsake which consists of fourteen loose signatures prepared for members of The Book Club of California. It was edited by Robert J. Chandler and designed and printed by Patrick Reagh Printers, Inc. The illustrations and verse for each folder cover are reproduced from the letter sheet, "Life Among the Miners," by Hutchings & Rosenfield in San Francisco.

188. (Book Club of California) THE CALIFORNIA GOVERNMENTAL SEALS. San Francisco: Book Club of California, 1963, small 4to., stiff paper wrappers in two mailing envelopes. $ 25.00

This series of Keepsakes consists of twelve folders, issued during 1963 to its members by The Book Club of California. The series was written by Kenneth M. Johnson, and was edited by Oscar Lewis and John A. Hussey, and printed at the Castle Press. Seals included are the Spanish and Mexican Periods 1769–1846, the California Supreme Court, the City of Santa Barbara etc.

189. (Book Club of California) CALIFORNIA PRINTING A SELECTED LIST OF BOOKS WHICH ARE SIGNIFICANT OR REPRESENTATIVE OF A CALIFORNIA STYLE OF PRINTING. Three volumes, complete. San Francisco: Book Club of California, 1980–87, large square 8vo., paper wrappers. (vi),33,(5); (vi),34,(6); x,55,(3) pages. $ 75.00

Keepsakes from the Book Club of California for the years 1980–1982. (Olmsted p.60.) Part I, edited by Muir Dawson and Carey S. Bliss, describes 30 books from the years 1833–1890. Part II, edited by Bruce L. Johnson and Robert D. Harlan, describes 23 books produced during the years 1890–1925. Part III, edited by Sandra Kirshenbaum and Kenneth Karmiole, describes 30 books that appeared in the years 1925–1975. All three parts give detailed description and commentary on the books included as well as many reproductions. Part III contains an index to the whole. Covers faded.

190. (Book Club of California) Dreyfus, John. WILLIAM CAXTON AND HIS QUINCENTENARY. New York: Typophiles, 1976, 12mo., cloth spine, printed boards. 54, (10) pages. $ 30.00

First edition, limited to 700 copies for the Typophiles and 400 copies for the Book Club of California. Typophile Chapbook 51.

191. (Book Club of California) Dreyfus, John. TYPOGRAPHICAL MASTERPIECE, AN ACCOUNT BY JOHN DREYFUS OF ERIC GILL'S COLLABORATION WITH ROBERT GIBBINGS IN PRODUCING THE GOLDEN COCKEREL PRESS EDITION OF "THE FOUR GOSPELS" IN 1931. San Francisco: The Book Club of California, 1990, 4to., cloth. xiv, 105+(1) pages. $ 275.00

Limited to 450 copies.

193. (Book Club of California) Duncan, Harry. BR, A PANEL DISCUSSION AT THE BRUCE ROGERS CENTENARY HELD AT PURDUE UNIVERSITY BY HARRY DUNCAN, K.K. MERKER AND WARD RITCHIE. N.P.: The Book Club of California, 1981, 12mo., cloth. 65 pages. $ 45.00

First edition, limited to 650 copies. Illustrated.

194. (Book Club of California) EARLY CALIFORNIA TRADE CARDS. San Francisco: Book Club of California, 1966, small 4to., individual folders of four pages each. $ 45.00

Text by William P. Barlow, Jr. and edited by Margot Patterson Doss and John A. Hussey. Printed by Grabhorn-Hoyem for the Club. With a full color reproduction of a trade card in each four page folder. Complete set of 11 folders.

195. (Book Club of California) Franklin, Colin. FOND OF PRINTING, GORDON CRAIG AS TYPOGRAPHER & ILLUSTRATOR. With a Foreword by Edward Craig and an Essay by Gordon Craig on Illustrations in General. San Francisco: The Book Club of California, 1980, tall 12mo., cloth-backed boards. 89, (3) pages. $ 55.00
First edition, printed in an edition limited to 450 copies for The Book Club of California.

196. (Book Club of California) Franklin, Colin. THEMES IN AQUATINT. San Francisco: The Book Club of California, 1978, folio, half red morocco over marbled paper covered boards. viii, 104 pages. $ 325.00
First edition, limited to 500 copies. Printed at Cambridge University Press with color plates printed at the Curwen Press. Designed by John Dreyfus. A history of this form of book illustration and including 16 full color plates. "a handsomely illustrated study of the aquatint by an authority on the subject" - *200th Book of the Book Club of California* no.160.

197. (Book Club of California) GOLD RUSH STEAMERS. San Francisco: The Book Club of California, 1958, 4to., 12 four page folders loosely inserted in mailing envelope. $ 25.00
Each folder describes a different steamer and contains a tipped-in plate showing the steamer. Outer envelope torn.

198. (Book Club of California) Gregory, Joseph W. GREGORY'S GUIDE FOR CALIFORNIA TRAVELERS VIA THE ISTHMUS OF PANAMA, CONTAINING ALL THE REQUISITE INFORMATION NEEDED BY PERSONS TAKING THIS ROUTE. San Francisco: Book Club of California, 1949, 8vo., cloth. (ii), 16, (2) pages. $ 65.00
Printed for the Book Club of California in an edition limited to 300 copies by Harold Seeger and Albert Sperisen at The Black Vine Press (Olmsted, 72). Introduction by Edith M. Coulter. A reprint of the scarce 1850 edition issued as part of the Club's observance of the California centennial year. The author was proprietor of Gregory's California and New York Express from 1850–1853. With map as frontispiece and two facsimile pages.

199. (Book Club of California) Harlan, Robert D. CHAPTER NINE THE VULGATE BIBLE & OTHER UNFINISHED PROJECTS OF JOHN HENRY NASH. New York: The Book Club of California, 1982, 12mo., paper over boards. 79 pages. $ 40.00
Printed in an edition limited to 1000 copies, 500 for the Book Club of California and 500 for the Typophiles. It concerns Nash's never-to-be completed Vulgate Bible that was going to be his Magnus opus. This book was printed by Henry Morris at the Bird & Bull Press. With a large, foldout sample of a Nash text page pasted to the inside rear cover.

200. (Book Club of California) Hart, James D. PRIVATE PRESS VENTURES OF SAMUEL LLOYD OSBOURNE AND R.L.S. WITH FACSIMILES OF THEIR PUBLICATIONS. N.P.: Book Club of California, 1966, tall 8vo., cloth. (ii), 49 pages. $ 65.00
Limited to 500 copies and printed by Alfred and Lawton Kennedy. A history of the amateur press ventures of Stevenson and his son. Nine facsimiles are loosely inserted in a pocket in the back. Bookplate. Slight smudging of free endpaper.

201. (Book Club of California) Jeffers, Una. A BOOK OF GAELIC AIRS FOR UNA'S MELODEON. San Francisco: Book Club of California, 1989, small oblong 8vo., cloth, dust jacket. (xii), 173, (3) pages. $ 125.00
Printed as California Book Club Publication 191 in an edition limited to 500 copies (Harlan, 191). Designed by Ward Ritchie, the text is reproduced in facsimile in Type Centaur monotype on acid-free Mohawk Superfine paper and bound by Bela Blau. This is the first appearance in print of a manuscript of immense importance to collectors of material by and about Una and Robinson Jeffers, begun by her in

1922, and illustrated with more than one hundred original drawings by Robinson Jeffers. An introduction by David Oliphant provides a detailed account of Una Jeffers' abiding interest in Irish music and folklore, noting that the manuscript took three years to complete and that Una used it regularly to play tunes on her small melodeon. Prospectus from Publications Committee laid in. Plain white dust jacket with title written in pencil on spine.

202. (Book Club of California) Kainen, Jacob. GEORGE CLYMER AND THE COLUMBIAN PRESS. New York: The Book Club of California, 1950, small 8vo., cloth. xiv, 60, (2) pages. $ 75.00
Limited to 770 copies of which this is one of the 350 copies printed for the Book Club of California. The others were printed for the Typophiles. Contains much information on this 19th century American printing press inventor. With 8 illustrations of presses. Wear at head of spine.

203. (Book Club of California) Kindersley, David. MR ERIC GILL. New York: The Book Club of California, 1967, 12mo., cloth. 26 pages. $ 40.00
First edition, limited to 400 copies for the Book Club of California out of the total edition. Chapbook 44 of the Typophiles. Prospectus loosely inserted.

204. (Book Club of California) Kostura, William. WILLIAM F LEWIS, A SAN FRANCISCO HOUSE BUILDER. San Francisco: The Book Club of California, 1993, small 4to., stiff paper wrappers. 60, (3) pages. $ 25.00
A story about how houses were built in San Francisco in the 1880's and 1890's. William F. Lewis was one of the hundreds of contractors who built and designed Victorian houses, which failed as did many other builders. Illustrated with photographs of some of the houses designed at that time and the Lewis family.

205. (Book Club of California) Kurutz, Gary F. (editor). CALIFORNIA BOOK ILLUSTRATORS, A KEEPSAKE IN FOURTEEN PARTS FOR THE MEMBERS OF THE BOOK CLUB OF CALIFORNIA. San Francisco: Book Club of California, 1996, 8vo., folders laid in stiff paper portfolio. 14 folders of approximately four pages each. $ 45.00
California Book Illustrators consists of fourteen folders prepared for members of The Book Club of California. The series was edited by Gary F. Kurutz and designed by Michael Osborne Design in San Francisco. Artwork was reproduced in offset lithography in one color, separately as 4-color process tip-ins and in one color as letterpress tip-ins. Introduction by the editor and essays on each artist, several by authors who knew and even patronized them, including Ward Ritchie writing about the wood engraver Paul Landacre (1893–1963), Glen Dawson on Don Percival (1908–1979), illustrator of *Navajo Sketch Book* ,and Harlan Kessel on Valenti Angelo (1897–1982), "Renaissance Man" and illustrator for the Limited Editions Club edition of *The Book of the Thousand Nights and a Night*. Some of the other artists featured are H. Mallette Dean, Grafton Tyler Brown, Maynard Dixon, and Joseph Jacinto Mora.

206. (Book Club of California) Land, Barbara J. (editor). THE 1997 KEEPSAKE, TWELVE TREASURES FROM THE LIBRARY OF THE BOOK CLUB OF CALIFORNIA. (San Francisco): Book Club of California, 1997, 8vo., stiff paper wrappers. unpaginated with folders averaging 4 pages each. $ 45.00
Printed as a 1997 Keepsake for the members of The Book Club of California consisting of thirteen folders loosely inserted in a portfolio. Designed by James Wehlage and printed letterpress in Trajan and Palatino at the Tuscan Press, Novato, CA. The first folder contains a color photograph with a partial view of The Book Club's room and library. Other folders include facsimiles from *The Book of Common Prayer of 1717*, the first George Baxter color print from Robert Mudie's *The Natural History of Birds*, circa 1840, the title-page from the 1850 Dutch edition of Ryan's *Personal Adventures in Upper and Lower California*, the cover from the *Tribune Book of Open Air Sports*, the first book printed from type set on the Mergenthaler Linotype machine, etc. Minor wear to outer portfolio.

207. (Book Club of California) Lewis, Oscar. FIRST 75 YEARS, THE STORY OF THE BOOK CLUB OF CALIFORNIA 1912–1987. San Francisco: The Book Club of California, 1987, slim 8vo., quarter cloth with paper covered boards, gilt decorated front and back covers, gilt lettering on spine. (vi), 54, (2) pages. $ 50.00

Printed in an edition limited to 1200 copies, designed and printed at the Arion Press. A history of the organization, with a list of officers and checklist of the 185 books published from 1914 to 1987. Illustrated with photographs and examples of menus, announcements, postcards, etc. produced by various club members.

208. (Book Club of California) Olmsted, Duncan H. SEVENTY YEARS, A CHECK-LIST OF BOOK CLUB PUBLICATIONS 1914–1983. San Francisco: The Book Club of California, 1984, small 4to., stiff paper wrappers. 60, (2) pages. $ 35.00

Keepsake no.44 issued by this club.

209. (Book Club of California) PORTFOLIO OF BOOK CLUB PRINTERS, 1912–1962. San Francisco: Book Club of California, 1963, small 4to. 12 folders. $ 65.00

Issued in conjunction with the 50th anniversary of the Club. Contributions by Adrian Wilson, Lawton Kennedy, the Plantin Press, the Allen Press, the Grabhorn Press and others. Portfolio shows some wear.

210. (Book Club of California) Ritchie, Ward. FREDERIC GOUDY, JOSEPH FOSTER AND THE PRESS AT SCRIPPS COLLEGE. San Francisco: The Book Club of California, 1978, tall 12mo., cloth-backed marbled paper covered boards, plain paper dust jacket. 38, (2) pages. $ 75.00

First edition, limited to 550 copies. Designed by Ritchie and printed by Richard Hoffman. Ritchie was the first printing instructor at Scripps College. He describes the development of Goudy Scripps and Franciscan by the Grabhorns.

211. (Book Club of California) Sperisen, Albert and John Borden (editors). A PORT-FOLIO OF BOOK CLUB PRINTERS, 1962–1987 (BOOK CLUB OF CALIFORNIA). (San Francisco): Book Club of California, 1987, 8vo., folders loosely inserted in a portfolio. 12 folders of 4 pages each. $ 50.00

Issued as the keepsake for 1987, in an edition limited to 1100 copies, The Club's 75th Anniversary year. The portfolio consists of twelve folders, each printed by or about presses associated with the printing history of The Book Club of California. Introduction by Oscar Lewis, who also supplied copy for a previous portfolio of Club printers on the 50th anniversary of its founding, in 1962. Printers include: The Press in Tuscany Alley, Artichoke Press, Ward Ritchie, Andrew Hoyem , Grabhorn-Hoyem Press, Sherwood Grover & Grace Hoper Press, Arlen and Clara Louise Philpott, Harold Berliner, Patrick Reagh, and The Yolla Bolly Press.

212. (Book Club of California) Teiser, Ruth & Catherine Harroun (editors). PRINTING AS A PERFORMING ART. San Francisco: The Book Club of California, 1970, square 8vo., cloth. 145, (3) pages. $ 95.00

First edition, limited to 450 copies. Contributions by Edwin and Robert Grabhorn, Lawton Kennedy, Lewis & Dorothy Allen, Jack Stauffacher, William Everson, Adrian Wilson and Mallette Dean. Illustrated.

213. (Bookfellows) Haseltine, Burton. GRIFFONAGE. Chicago: The Bookfellows, 1921, 8vo., quarter cloth, paper covered boards. (34) pages. $ 30.00

Printed in an edition limited to 300 copies. A collection of poetry which is illustrated with drawings by Mildred Ross.

214. (Bookman Press) Stevenson, Robert Louis. SELECT ESSAYS OF ROBERT LOUIS STEVENSON: VIRGINIBUS PUERISQUE, CRABBED AGE AND YOUTH, AN APOLOGY FOR IDLERS, AND WALKING TOURS. Bangor (ME): Bookman Press, 1937, large 8vo., quarter cloth, with paper-covered boards, top edge tinted blue, paper-covered slipcase. (iv), 97+(1) pages. $ 65.00
Limited to 200 copies. Essays of R.L. Stevenson (1850–1894): "Virginibus," on relations between the sexes, "Crabbed Age" ["There is a strong feeling in favor of cowardly and prudential proverbs"] on the dubious wisdom of old age, the "Apology" (with a short dialogue in the style of John Bunyan), and "Walking," partly about another essayist, W. Hazlitt. Nicely printed in "Baskerville" (not original Baskerville). Very light browning on top cover edges. Slipcase lacks top & bottom.

215. (Bowne and Co. Stationers) BOWNE & CO., STATIONERS / SOUTH ST. SEAPORT MUSEUM / PRESENTS / THE ART & TECHNIQUE OF / WOOD ENGRAVING / AN INTRODUCTION, TAUGHT... / ...BY / MR. JOHN DE POL [ETC.]. New York: Bowne and Co. Stationers, 1983, broadside (approximately 14.25 x 9.25 inches). $ 15.00
Poster announcing a course in wood engraving by John DePol taught on 5 Wed. evenings beginning on 11/3/82, presumably at Bowne & Co. With a wood engraving showing engraving tools and blocks, various typefaces, and a decoration. Creased.

216. (Boxwood Press) Ratner, Rochelle & B. Solomon. MINHAH. N.P.: The Boxwood Press, 1977, 4to., broadside. $ 7.50
Printed in an edition limited to 13 wood engravings reproduced.

217. (Bradley, Will) Bradley, Will. LEATHER BOTTEL. (Concord, MA: Sign of the Vine, 1903), 16mo., boards, paper cover label. (ii), 9+(1) pages. $ 50.00
First edition. Arranged and put into type by Will Bradley. With frontispiece and designed title page; orange decoration on each page. Distributed by Bradley as a Christmas gift. Front cover spotted.

218. (Bradley, Will) Lamb, Charles. DISSERTATION UPON ROAST PIG BY CHARLES LAMB. (Concord, Ma.: Will Bradley, n.d.), 12mo., original boards, paper cover label. xviii, (4) pages. $ 100.00
First edition thus with designs by Bradley. Spread title page printed in red and black, initial letter and head and tail pieces. Distributed as a Christmas gift.

219. (Bradley, Will) Wither, George. LOVE SONG. Concord: Sign of the Vine, (1903), 16mo., boards, paper cover label. (16) pages. $ 75.00
First edition thus, designed by Will Bradley and containing an art noveau half title and frontispiece. One of four such Christmas booklets issued by Bradley.

220. (Brandywine Press) Degotardi, Johann Nepomuk. THE ART OF PRINTING (SYDNEY, 1861). Two volumes. Sydney: At the Brandywine Press, 1982, small 8vo., stiff paper wrappers. (22); (ii),24,(10) pages. $ 45.00
Limited to 100 numbered and signed copies and printed by hand by Wendy O. Wegner and Jurgen P. Wegner. Biographical sketch of Degotardi by John Fletcher (signed by Fletcher) followed by notes on this history. The second volume is a reprint of the original 1861 pamphlet. The first section of the first volume has underlining.

221. (Brandywine Press) Wegner, J.P. SPLENDID CHAPS. Sydney: Brandywine Press, 1984, 12mo., paper wrappers. (16) pages. $ 35.00
Privately printed and limited to 200 copies including 20 special copies signed and numbered. A Brandywine Press keepsake which gives a brief history of some of the special Australian printers from the eighteenth to the twentieth century.

222. (Bremer Press) Emerson, Ralph Waldo. NATURE. Munich: Bremer Presse for Random House, 1929, 4to., quarter vellum with marbled paper covered boards, top edge cut and gilt, slipcase. 86, (2) pages. $ 350.00

Printed in an edition limited to 530 numbered copies of which this is one of 250 copies numbered I-CCL printed specifically for Random House. This copy is numbered CVII. (Lehnacker et al., no.28). Text in English. Includes a title page and initial letters printed in two colors and designed by Anna Simons. Printed by hand on Zanders watermarked hand-made paper. Slipcase rubbed.

223. (Brewhouse Press) Wakeman, Geoffrey. ASPECTS OF VICTORIAN LITHO-GRAPHY, ANASTATIC PRINTING AND PHOTOZINCOGRAPHY. Wymond-ham: Brewhouse Press, 1970, 4to., half leather over marbled paper covered boards. 64 pages. $ 325.00

First edition, limited to 250 numbered copies. With three actual specimens inserted. An important history of the first commercially successful means of reproducing the printed page. With three mounted specimens demonstrating this method of reproduction. Well printed by this private press. Prospectus and original purchase bill loosely inserted.

224. (Bulmer, William) Goldsmith, Oliver and Thomas Parnell. POEMS. London: William Bulmer and Co., 1795, 4to., contemporary green straight-grain morocco, gilt and blind-tooled, enclosed in quarter leather, paper covered clamshell box. xx, 76 pages. $ 750.00

First Bewick edition. (Hugo 78, Isaac 228). This book, printed by William Bulmer at his Shakespeare Printing Office, contains Goldsmith's poems "The Traveller" and "The Deserted Village," along with Parnell's "The Hermit." Includes twelve woodcuts and vignettes (five full-page). The cuts were drawn by Robert Johnson and John Bewick, and all were engraved by Thomas Bewick except the vignettes on the title pages, one large cut, and the tail-piece, which were done by John Bewick. Also contains Bulmer's famous essay on printing and engraving, and a brief biography of both poets. Tipped to the corner of the first fly-leaf is the signature, "A.G. Byron." With the bookplates of William Menzies and George Dickens Wilkinson, Jr. on front endpapers. Foxing throughout. Boards faded, spine chipped, corners and edges worn. Spine of solander case faded.

225. (Bulmer, William) Dibdin, Thomas Frognall. BIBLIOGRAPHICAL DE-CAMERON; OR, TEN DAYS PLEASANT DISCOURSE UPON ILLUMINAT-ED MANUSCRIPTS, AND SUBJECTS CONNECTED WITH EARLY EN-GRAVING, TYPOGRAPHY, AND BIBLIOGRAPHY. Three volumes. London: W. Bulmer and Co. at the Shakespeare Press, 1817, tall 8vo., 20th century half green morocco over marbled paper covered boards, spine divided into six compartments and heavily gilt, all edges gilt, a signed binding by Hugh Hopkins of Glasgow with his binder's ticket mounted on the verso of the endpaper. (vi),vi,(ii),ccxxv,410,(2); (iv),535,(3); (iv),544,(4) pages. $ 1,950.00

First and only edition. (Windle & Pippin A28; Jackson no.40; Hart no.186). The only edition as Dibdin destroyed the plates to this book at a meeting of the Roxburghe Club. Jackson states that this is perhaps the most lavish of all Dibdin's works, and, especially in the large paper edition, the best printed. Hart calls it "a bibliographer's classic that marks the beginning of the general recognition of bibliomania as a plaything for wealth." The illustrations are spectacular. Complete with all half-titles and printer's imprints.

226. (Bulmer, William) Dibdin, Thomas Frognall. BIBLIOTHECA SPENCERIANA, OR A DESCRIPTIVE CATALOGUE OF THE BOOKS. Four volumes. London: Longman, Hurst, Rees, & Co., 1814–1815, small 4to., slightly later but nineteenth century full polished blue calf with four raised bands, red leather spine labels, all edges marbled. (vi),ix,(iii),lii,383+(1); (iv),503+(1); (ii),509,(5) (two pages loosely inserted in the back); vii,(iii),587+(1); lxxvii,(iii) and plates. $ 1,250.00

Printed in an edition limited 500 copies. (Jackson no.36, Windle no.A25). George John, 2nd Earl Spencer (1758–1834) was one of the great book collectors (De Ricci 72-78), and rather inevitably, one supposes, attracted the services of Thomas Frognall Dibdin (1776–1847), who was Lord Spencer's librarian for a number of years and produced a four-volume catalogue (Bibl. Spenceriana) of the Spencer collection in 1814–15, then "the handsomest and most elaborate catalogue of a private library yet issued" (De Ricci, p.75). Profusely illustrated with additional plates printed in colors and wood engraved illustrations throughout. Vol. I, minor chipping to spine label; vol. III, tail of spine lightly chipped; Vol. IV, corners bumped, front outer hinge cracked, some chipping to head and tail of spine and spine label.

227. (Burke, Marie Louise and Jackson) Burke, Marie Louise. 17 VERSES AND CURSES. N.P.: (Burke Press), 1940, large 12mo., quarter cloth with paper covered boards, paper spine label. (14) pages. $ 50.00

Printed in an edition limited to 50 numbered copies "for the friends of the Press of Marie Louise and Jackson Burke, Christmas, nineteen forty,"

228. (Burke, Marie Louise and Jackson) Burke, Marie Louise. VERSES AND CURSES. San Francisco: (Burke Press), 1941, 12mo., quarter cloth with paper-covered boards, paper spine label. (32) pages. $ 45.00

Printed in an edition limited to 250 copies by the Press of Marie Louise and Jackson Burke, December, 1941. Part of label missing from spine.

229. (Cambridge University Press) Balston, Thomas. JAMES WHATMAN, FATHER & SON. London: Methuen & Co., 1957, 8vo., cloth, dust jacket. xi, 170, (2) pages.
$ 125.00

First edition. Printed at the University Press, Cambridge under the direction of Brooke Crutchley. History of perhaps the most famous papermaker in England. A discovery of business ledgers covering the period 1780 to 1787 led to this book. Also contains information on the importation of Whatman paper to the U.S. Very fine copy.

230. (Cambridge University Press) Barker, Nicolas. PRINTER AND THE POET, AN ACCOUNT OF THE PRINTING OF `THE TAPESTRY' BASED UPON CORRESPONDENCE BETWEEN STANLEY MORISON AND ROBERT BRIDGES. Cambridge: Privately printed, 1970, tall 8vo., cloth-backed boards. (vi), 44 pages. $ 125.00

First edition, limited to 500 copies. Actually a study of type and printing.

231. (Cambridge University Press) Coleman, Roger (editor). JOHN RASTELL. THE FOUR ELEMENTS. Edited by Roger Coleman. Foreword by Brooke Crutchley. Cambridge: University Printing House, 1971, square 8vo., cloth-backed boards. vi, 73 pages.
$ 75.00

First edition, limited to 500 copies. This play was produced as part of the Siberch Celebrations. Coleman discusses Rastell's claim to be the first English printer of a play and gives additional information on this 16th century printer.

232. (Cambridge University Press) Crutchley, Brian. UNIVERSITY PRINTING HOUSES AT CAMBRIDGE FROM THE SIXTEENTH TO THE TWENTIETH CENTURY. Cambridge: University Press, (1962), oblong 8vo., cloth. (ii), 16 pages.
$ 85.00
Limited to 500 copies and issued as the annual Cambridge Christmas book. With an introductory page by Brian Crutchley. Three illustrations in color and a number of tinted illustrations.

233. (Cambridge University Press) Crutchley, Brooke. PRINTER'S CHRISTMAS BOOKS. With a Foreword by Euan Phillips. Cambridge: Cambridge University Press, 1974, square 8vo., half cloth over patterned paper covered boards. 42 pages. $ 125.00
The hardbound version of the Cambridge Christmas Book which describes the other books in the series, a series which started in 1930. With a number of illustrations. Wear at tips.

234. (Cambridge University Press) Crutchley, Brooke. TWO MEN, WALTER LEWIS AND STANLEY MORISON AT CAMBRIDGE. Cambridge: University Press, 1968, small 4to., cloth-backed boards, slipcase. vi, 48 pages followed by seven specimen sheets of fine printing carefully mounted. $ 125.00
Limited to 500 copies. Beautifully printed and containing a title-page opening of the four volume breviary with Reynolds Stone's engravings, printed in red and black.

235. (Cambridge University Press) Davenport, Cyril. ROGER PAYNE, ENGLISH BOOKBINDER OF THE EIGHTEENTH CENTURY. Chicago: Caxton Club, 1929, folio, gilt stamped red cloth, top edge gilt. xx, 79, (3) pages followed by 32 full page plates. $ 700.00
First edition, printed in an edition limited to 250 copies by Walter Lewis at the Cambridge University Press. (Mejer and Herbst no.496, S-K 4999). Not in Brenni. Chapters on Bookbinding in England, Roger Payne's Life and Work and Gold Tooling on Leather. Six plates in color and many in black and white. Also illustrated in the text. Beautifully printed on English handmade paper with the plates executed by Whittingham and Griggs. Covers lightly rubbed.

236. (Cambridge University Press) Dreyfus, John. BRUCE ROGERS AND AMERICAN TYPOGRAPHY A PAPER READ TO THE DOUBLE CROWN BY JOHN DREYFUS. PRINTED TO CELEBRATE THE TENTH ANNIVERSARY OF THE FOUNDATION OF THE AMERICAN BRANCH OF CAMBRIDGE UNIVERSITY PRESS. New York: Cambridge University Press, 1959, 4to., cloth-backed marbled paper covered boards, dust jacket. 23, (3) pages. $ 150.00
First edition, limited to 300 copies. Printed in red and black and reproducing some of Rogers' best known design work, work such as his title page design for *Fra Luca* for the Grolier Club. Very fine copy.

237. (Cambridge University Press) GERMAN INCUNABULA IN THE BRITISH MUSEUM PRINTED IN THE FIFTEENTH CENTURY IN GOTHIC LETTER AND DERIVED FOUNTS. London: Victor Gollancz, 1929, folio, cloth. (iv), 26 pages followed by 152 plates. $ 300.00
First edition, limited to 443 copies of which 398 were printed with the text in English. An important reference book in the study of incunabula. Covers rubbed through on a few places along edges and top of spine bumped. Edge of front cover is spotted. Foxing of preliminary pages and pastedowns. Finely printed at the Cambridge University Press with Collotype plates printed by Charles Whitingham and Griggs.

238. (Cambridge University Press) Hobson, G.D. BINDINGS IN CAMBRIDGE LI-
BRARIES, SEVENTY-TWO PLATES. WITH NOTES BY G.D. HOBSON.
BASED ON RESEARCHES BY N.F. BARWELL, H.M. DAVIES AND THE
LATE CHARLES E. SAYLE. Cambridge: University Press, 1929, folio, cloth stamped
in gilt, top edge gilt, others uncut. xvi, 180 pages. $ 1,500.00

First edition, printed in an edition limited to 230 copies by Walter Lewis at the Cambridge University
Press. (Appleton p.81, S-K 982). With 72 full page plates of bindings including many in full color. Divided into the following groups: A. Preliminary, 1190–1450; B. Gothic, 1470–1520; C. Renaissance,
1520–1590; D. Early Stuart, 1605-55; E. Late Stuart and Early Georgian, 1660–1750. Each binding
shown is accompanied by a long description of the binding, information on previous ownership and historical remarks. Hobson gives indices of owners, binders, booksellers, craftsmen, initials and monograms
of binders and owners, binding centers and subjects of stamps and panels. Of extra interest are the many
other examples that Hobson gives of similar bindings that he knows of in other collections, with information on ownership, pressmark, references to it by other scholars and if any reproductions have occurred. Hobson also describes 45 other Cambridge bindings that have reproduced in other books. According to the former owner of this book, this copy was the property of N.R. Ker and has his notes in
pencil and pen throughout. These notes include additions and corrections. Binding rubbed with wear
along edges. Light foxing.

239. (Cambridge University Press) Hobson, G.D. ENGLISH BINDING BEFORE
1500. Cambridge: Cambridge University Press, 1929, folio, cloth, top edge gilt. (xii), 60
pages followed by 55 full page plates of bindings. $ 650.00

Printed in an edition limited to 500 copies for sale by Walter Lewis at the Cambridge University Press.
(Appleton p.81, S-K 2194). This book is divided into two sections, the Early Bindings, before 1300 and
the Gothic Bindings, c.1450–1500. Given as the Sandars Lecture for 1927. Minor rubbing. A scarce book.

240. (Cambridge University Press) Kendon, Frank. THIRTY-SIX PSALMS, AN
ENGLISH VERSION. Cambridge: Cambridge University Press, 1963, large 8vo.,
cloth. viii (ii), 63+(1) pages. $ 45.00

Printed in an edition limited to 1000 copies. A reworking of the Psalms into appropriate English as part
of the New English Bible. The poet Frank Kendon was invited to take the basic draft provided by a panel
of translators and to adapt it so the qualities of the original Hebrew could be brought out.

241. (Cambridge University Press) Milton, John. PARADISE REGAINED. London:
The Fleuron, 1924, square 8vo., cloth-backed boards. (x), 80 pages. $ 100.00

Limited to 350 numbered copies. With decorations by Thomas Lowinsky including three proofs loosely
inserted in an envelope in a pocket in the back of the book. Finely printed by W. Lewis at the Cambridge
University Press. Spine ends bumped.

242. (Cambridge University Press) Morison, Stanley (editor). FLEURON, A JOUR-
NAL OF TYPOGRAPHY. Vol. V. Edited by Stanley Morison. Cambridge: The University Press, 1926, 4to., cloth. xvi, 205, (21) pages. $ 175.00

Limited to 1370 copies. Article on Karl Klingspor by Julius Rodenberg including a list of books printed
at the Private Press of the Gebr. Klingspor, articles on Laboureur, Bulmer and "Towards an Ideal Italick"
by Stanley Morison. Bookplate.

243. (Cambridge University Press) Morison, Stanley (editor). FLEURON, A JOUR-
NAL OF TYPOGRAPHY. Vol. VI. Edited by Stanley Morison. Cambridge: University Press, 1928, 4to., cloth, dust jacket. xiii, 254, (3) pages. $ 200.00

Limited to 1310 copies. Articles on Rudolf Koch, Geofroey Tory by A.F. Johnson, On Decorative Printing in America by Paul Beaujon (Beatrice Warde), Decorated Types by Stanley Morison and others. Part
of front cover of jacket is lacking.

244. (Cambridge University Press) Heal, Ambrose. THE ENGLISH PENMEN, THEIR PORTRAITS & BIOGRAPHIES. Cambridge: Cambridge University Press, 1945, 4to., half buckram with marbled paper-covered boards. (ii), ix-xl, 209 pages.

$ 550.00

Abridged re-issue of the 1931 first edition, limited to 30 copies (Appleton, 116a), reprinted without the bibliographic section and the calligraphic examples. "With an Introduction on the Development of Handwriting" by Stanley Morison. Hand-writing specimen as frontis and xxiii plates of engraved portraits in text. Very scarce book. Minor cover rubbing and shelf wear.

245. (Cambridge University Press) Morison, Stanley. TALBOT BAINES REED, AUTHOR, BIBLIOGRAPHER, TYPEFOUNDER. Cambridge: University Press, 1960, small 4to., cloth, cameo portrait of Reed on front cover. (x), 80 pages. $ 95.00

First edition, limited to 500 copies. (Appleton no.213). With preface by Brooke Crutchley. This is one in the series of Cambridge Christmas books. Illustrated biography. Covers faded.

246. (Cambridge University Press) Morison, Stanley. TALLY OF TYPES CUT FOR MACHINE COMPOSTION AND INTRODUCED AT THE UNIVERSITY PRESS, CAMBRIDGE, 1922–1932. Cambridge: Privately printed, 1953, tall 8vo., cloth. viii, 102 pages. $ 150.00

First edition, limited to 450 copies (Appleton no.190). Contains a preface and a postscript by Brooke Crutchley, the University Printer. The 17 chapters are all set in a different typeface; with 6 wood engravings by Reynolds Stone. With the bookplate of Geoffrey Ashall Glaister.

247. (Cambridge University Press) Nixon, Howard M. BROXBOURNE LIBRARY, STYLES AND DESIGNS OF BOOKBINDINGS FROM THE TWELFTH TO THE TWENTIETH CENTURY. With an Introduction by Albert Ehrman. London: Maggs Bros., 1956, folio, quarter vellum over blue cloth, blue leather spine label, top edge gilt. x, 251 pages. $ 2,250.00

S-K 1045. Limited to 300 copies printed by Brooke Crutchley at the University Press, Cambridge. (Brenni no.301). An extremely important book and one of the most important authored by Nixon. The 199 books are described in such detail by Nixon that the annotations constitute a history of binding. Each book is illustrated. The binding collection was put together to show the history of binding and hence as many different styles as possible were added to the collection. All but a few of the book described have not been described elsewhere. Minor rubbing of covers and spine label. Scarce book.

248. (Cambridge University Press) REPORT ON THE TYPOGRAPHY OF THE CAMBRIDGE UNIVERSITY PRESS PREPARED IN 1917 AT THE REQUEST OF THE SYNDICS BY BRUCE ROGERS AND NOW PRINTED IN HONOUR OF HIS EIGHTIETH BIRTHDAY. N.P.: The University Printer, 1950, 4to., cloth-backed boards. xii, 36 pages. $ 125.00

Limited to 500 copies as one of the Cambridge Christmas books. Endpapers slightly foxed. Some wear at tip.

249. (Cambridge University Press) ROTHSCHILD LIBRARY, A CATALOGUE OF THE COLLECTION OF EIGHTEENTH -CENTURY BOOKS AND MANUSCRIPTS FORMED BY LORD ROTHSCHILD. Two volumes. Cambridge: Privately printed, 1954, large 8vo., quarter red polished buckram with cloth covers, top edges stained red. 840 pages. $ 250.00

First edition, finely printed by Brooke Crutchley at the Cambridge University Press. Some facsimiles. An important reference book. Pages 65-80 are in facsimile.

250. (Cambridge University Press) Sparrow, John. LAPIDARIA QUARTA. (Cambridge): N.P., (1958), large 8vo., paper wrappers, dust jacket. (46)pages. $ 65.00
Printed in an edition of 160 copies at Cambridge University Press. Fourth in this series, begun by the author in 1943. Anthology of Latin epitaphs and memorial inscriptions from churches, colleges and monuments around the world. English introductory notes for each inscription. Title and colophon designed by Reynolds Stone and printed in red ink. Heavy paper, hand-made. Pages unopened.

251. (Cambridge University Press) Sparrow, John. LINE UPON LINE, AN EPIGRAPHICAL ANTHOLOGY. Cambridge: University Printing House, 1967, 8vo., cloth-backed boards, slipcase. 24 pages followed by 46 examples of inscriptional writing and booklet giving translations inserted in a pocket in the back of the book. $ 125.00
First edition, limited to 500 copies. A study of epigraphy, the art of writing inscriptions. With a presentation from Sparrow on the front free endpaper.

252. (Cambridge University Press) Spenser, Edmund. THE FAERIE QUEENE. Two volumes. Cambridge: University Press, 1909, 4to., quarter cloth with paper covered boards and a paper spine labels. (vi),543+(1); (vi),493+(1) pages. $ 500.00
Printed in an edition limited to 350 copies, this being one of the series of 300 numbered copies. A two volume set which contains several poems. The text here given of Books I to VI of The Faerie Queene is that of the edition of 1596 in two volumes quarto. Of these two volumes, the first contains the second edition of Books I to III, which had already appeared in 1590. Books IV to VI were printed for the first time in 1596. The fragment of Book VII is from the folio edition of 1609. Beautifully printed by John Clay at the University Press and containing a number of typographic ornaments throughout. Light cover wear. Very well preserved set demonstrating University Press printing at its best. Minor spotting of front cover of second volume. Corners bumped.

253. (Cambridge University Press) Swift, William H. JAMES BENNET PEACE, A MODEL EMPLOYER. Cambridge: The University Press, 1923, 12mo., quarter cloth with decorated paper covered boards, paper cover label. (viii), 16 pages. $ 35.00
Printed for "Private circulation only" by Walter Lewis. A tribute to the former Printer to the University of Cambridge by one of his staff. Minor wear to corners.

254. (Cambridge University Press) Voltaire. VOLTAIRE'S ESSAY ON MILTON. Edited by Desmond Flower. Cambridge: Privately printed, 1954, tall 12mo., quarter-cloth with marbled paper covered covers. xvi, 29, (3) pages. $ 150.00
Limited to 400 copies. (Crutchley p.27). The first printing of this essay written by Voltaire in English since his lifetime. Printed on W. & R. Balston handmade paper in type made from copies of the original Baskerville punches by Deberny & Peignot. From the library of John Carter with his booklabel and the following inscription in ink on the free endpaper "John Carter, Washington '55." Loosely inserted is a four page greeting printed in black and red from the University Printer commenting on this book.

255. (Capricorn Press) Everson, William (Brother Antoninus). WHO IS SHE THAT LOOKETH FORTH AS THE MORNING. Santa Barbara, CA: Capricorn Press, 1972, 4to., dark green boards with spine title in gold, and design on front cover in gold, acetate jacket. 19+(1) pages. $ 175.00
Printed in an edition limited to 250 numbered copies signed and numbered by Brother Antoninus. Designed and printed in two colors by Noel Young, title page illustration by Graham Mackintosh in two shades of green and yellow. Hand-bound by Earle Gray. Tear in acetate jacket.

256. (Carriage House Press) Koretsky, Elaine. COLOR FOR THE HAND PAPER-MAKER. Two volumes. Brookline, MA: Carriage House Handmade Paper Works, 1983, 4to., spiral bound stiff paper wrappers with accompanying sheets all enclosed in a cloth drop-leaf box. (iv),85; vi,90 pages. $ 350.00
First edition, this is one of the 100 numbered sets containing extra material and inserted in the box. Nine chapters on the use of color in hand-papermaking followed by summarizes of hundreds of experiments with different pigments each accompanied by a tipped-in sample of the paper produced.

257. (Castle Press) THE ENGRAVER, & THE PRINTER, & THE BOOKBINDER. Pasadena: Ampersand Press, 1947, 12mo., stiff paper wrappers. (16) pages. $ 25.00
Printed in an edition limited to 250 copies by Grant Dahlstrom at his Castle Press in Pasadena. First issued circa 1850 as a chapter in *The Book of Trades* by an unknown author. "It is hoped that his rather casual but pointed descriptions of these three important crafts will be studied and heeded by present day artisans in similar pursuits (Note by Philip S. Brown)."

258. (Castle Press) Austin, Mary. MARY AUSTIN ON THE ART OF WRITING, A LETTER TO HENRY JAMES FORMAN. Los Angeles: Friends of the UCLA Library, 1961, small 8vo., stiff paper wrappers. viii, 5 (3) pages. $ 17.50
Printed by Grant Dahlstrom at the Castle Press, Pasadena, in linotype Aldus and monotype Centaur. First printing of a letter, dated September 17, 1918, of the author's literary methods. Introduction by James E. Phillips.

259. (Castle Press) Carpenter, Edwin H. NATURAL HISTORY OF THE TYPE-STICKERS OF LOS ANGELES COMPILED FROM THE LETTERS OF WM. M. CHENEY. Los Angeles: Rounce & Coffin Club, 1960, square 8vo., cloth-backed boards, dust jacket. xii, 62, (2) pages. $ 50.00
With an introduction by Archer Taylor. Set by Richard Hoffman with printing at the Castle Press. Jacket chipped.

260. (Castle Press) Carpenter, Edwin H. SOME LIBRARIES WE HAVE NOT VIS-ITED, A PAPER READ AT THE ROUNCE & COFFINS CLUB, AUGUST 26, 1947. Pasadena, CA: Ampersand Press, 1947, tall 8vo., stiff marbled paper wrappers, paper cover label. (ii), 8, (2) pages. $ 45.00
Printed by Grant Dahlstrom at his Castle Press. A history of imaginary libraries. With two tipped-in facsimile plates showing books in the Fortsas catalogue.

261. (Castle Press) Dahlstrom, Grant. ALDUS. (Pasadena: Castle Press, 1961), 8vo., single sheet. (4) pages. $ 15.00
Printed by Grant Dahlstrom at the Castle Press. Introduction and samples of ALDUS, a new type design by Hermann Zapf, described as "primarily a linotype face to be used with Palatino display...The Castle Press is the first, and so far, the only source of ALDUS in the United States."

262. (Castle Press) Davies, David W. CLYDE BROWNE, HIS ABBEY & HIS PRESS. Pasadena: Castle Press, 1982, 8vo., stiff paper wrappers. (vi), 38, (2) pages. $ 25.00
Printed in an edition limited to 325 copies for the members of the Roxburghe and Zamorano Clubs on the occasion of their joint meeting in Los Angeles, October 8–10, 1982. Phototypeset in Berthold Bembo and printed by offset lithography on Warren's Olde Style paper by D.W. Davies, Susan Denne and George Kinney at The Castle Press. Clyde Browne designed and built the Abbey San Encino in Los Angeles as his home and a site for the Abbey print shop and press. Starting in 1929, he rented studio space to contemporaries like Larry Powell, Gregg Anderson, and Ward Ritchie, who used the Abbey Press equipment for a dollar on Sundays. Illustrated with photographs and facsimile pages.

263. (Castle Press) Davies, David W. ENQUIRY INTO THE READING OF THE LOWER CLASSES. Pasadena, CA: Grant Dahlstrom, The Castle Press, 1970, tall 8vo., cloth-backed decorated boards, dust jacket. xvi, 92, (2) pages. $ 55.00

First edition, limited to 750 copies. A not-too-serious book about the printed works for the lower classes in England from 1800–185 Chapters on many books, authors and publishers including James Catnach and the Penny Magazine. Bookplate and address label.

264. (Castle Press) Davies, David W. GRANT DAHLSTROM & THE FIRST FIFTY YEARS OF THE CASTLE PRESS. With Memorial Tributes by D.W. Davies, James C. Greene, Ward Ritchie, & Jake Zeitlin. Pasadena: The Castle Press, 1981, 8vo., cloth. (viii), 77, (3) pages. $ 65.00

Limited to 500 copies. With illustrations. Printed at The Castle Press in hour of the 50th Anniversary of the Press. Covers slightly faded, especially along edge of covers.

265. (Castle Press) Endore, Guy. A NETWORK OF SYMBOL. (Pasadena: Castle Press, 1962), 12mo., stiff paper wrappers. 31+(1) pages. $ 15.00

Printed by Grant Dahlstrom at the Castle Press in Pasadena. A lecture, substantially Chapter Eleven, of a novel about the Marquis de Sade, given by the author before the graduating class of the School of Library Service, UCLA, May 25, 1962. Covers slightly soiled with light crease.

266. (Castle Press) Johnson, A.B. LETTER OF A.B. JOHNSON, ESQ. Pasadena: Jacob Zeitlin and Robert Rypinski, 1948, small 12mo., stiff paper wrappers. viii, 34+(1) pages. $ 25.00

Printed in an edition limited to 200 copies for Robert Rypinski and Jacob Zeitlin by Grant Dahlstrom at the Castle Press, Pasadena, of which 60 copies were for distribution to the members of The Rounce & Coffin Club. Reprinted for the first time since its appearance in the *Albany Argus* of Oct. 17, 1834, by the author of *A Treatise on Language or The Relation Which Words Bear to Things*.

267. (Castle Press) Lawrence, D.H. EIGHT LETTERS BY D.H. LAWRENCE TO RACHEL ANNAND TAYLOR. Pasadena: Castle Press, 1956, 8vo., stiff paper wrappers. (14) pages. $ 25.00

Printed by Grant Dahlstrom at the Catle Press, Pasadena. A small collection of early Lawrence letters, purchased in 1955 by the Friends of the UCLA Library, and passing directly from Lawrence's correspondent, Mrs. Rachel Annand Taylor, to the Library. Seven of the eight letters were written in 1910, when his mother was dying of cancer. The letter of December 3, 1910, makes explicit reference to his Oedipal complex and his attempts to escape from it.

268. (Castle Press) [LOT OF SIX PIECES OF PRINTED MATERIAL FROM THE CASTLE PRESS]. Pasadena: Castle Press, n.d. (but circa 1970s). $ 25.00

Lot includes *A Christmas Greeting from The Castle Press*, undated but probably from the mid 1970's, that contains a reprint of *How to Carve a Christmas Goose*, circa 1800, a 1976 12mo. booklet *A Life of Ralph Kettell*, reprinted from *Aubrey's Brief Lives*, several pages of excerpts from the entries on" love" from the 1842 *Encyclopedia Britannica*, a 1974 wedding invitation, and a brochure of selected books designed and printed by Dahlstrom 1948–1974. Grant Dahlstrom (1902–1980) operated the Castle Press from 1943 until he sold it to George Kinney and Susan Denne in 1979, continuing to work as their designer.

269. (Castle Press) LOVE, A DESCRIPTION. Pasadena: The Castle Press, n.d., 12mo., paper wrappers. 13 pages. $ 15.00

Reprinted from the 1842 edition of The Encyclopedia Britannica, several definitions of love were printed in The New Yorker. They are now reprinted here.

270. (Castle Press) LOVE (EXCERPTS FROM THE 1842 EDITION OF THE EN-CYCLOPEDIA BRITANNICA). Pasadena: The Castle Press, n.d., large 12mo., self paper wrappers. 13, (3) pages. $15.00

Printed by Grant Dahlstrom at the Castle Press, undated but probably the 1970's. The *New Yorker* had published this article "with appropriate comment" about ten years earlier, and "Now, without comment, we reprint them."

271. (Castle Press) MacIntyre, C.F. AUTUMN TITHES. (Pasadena, CA: Roxburghe Club of San Francisco, 1949), 8vo., stiff paper wrappers. (4) French fold page. $15.00

Printed by Grant Dahlstrom at the Castle Press, Pasadena, in an edition limited to 100 copies, for members of the Roxburghe Club of San Francisco "and other friends of Larry Powell." A page of verse.

272. (Castle Press) Davies, David W. BRUCE MCCALLISTER, LOS ANGELES' FIRST FINE PRINTER. Pasadena: Castle Press, 1984, 8vo., stiff paper wrappers. x, 38 pages. $25.00

First edition. Bruce McCallister (1881–1945) moved to Los Angeles in 1907 and was soon a partner in the printing firm of Young & McCallister, and mentoring Ward Ritchie, Grant Dahlstrom, and others. He printed several books for the Zamorano Club and later for Dahlstrom at his Castle Press. Photo as frontis and list of McCallister publications with illustrations.

273. (Castle Press) Muir, John. RAMBLES OF A BOTANIST AMONG THE PLANTS AND CLIMATES OF CALIFORNIA. Mariposa, CA: Rocking K Press, 1974, small 8vo., stiff paper wrappers. 43+(1) pages. $17.50

Printed by Grant Dahlstrom at The Castle Press, Pasadena. Presented to the Roxburghe and Zamorano Clubs, September, 1974, by William F. Kimes, with an introduction by him. This is the first reprinting of these essays since their first appearance as a magazine article and newspaper column in 1872 and 1873. Photographs, map, and a chronology of Muir's life (1838–1914).

274. (Castle Press) THE OLD MAID'S LAST PRAYER AND FREE CONFES-SION; WITH THE AUTHOR'S PETITION TO CUPID ON THEIR BEHALF. (Pasadena: Castle Press, 1949), large 8vo., wrappers. 6 pages. $15.00

Attributed to the Castle Press, with the author and number of copies unknown. Done in the style of eighteenth century erotica.

275. (Castle Press) Sadleir, Michael. PASSAGES FROM THE AUTOBIOGRAPHY OF A BIBLIOMANIAC. With an Introduction by Bradford A. Booth. Los Angeles: University of California Library, 1962, tall 8vo., paper wrappers. xiv, 40 pages. $35.00

Limited to 500 copies and printed by Grant Dahlstrom at the Castle Press. Reprinted from Sadlier's *XIX Century Fiction* with the added introduction. Chipped along edges.

276. (Castle Press) Smith, Walter E. CHARLES DICKENS IN THE ORIGINAL CLOTH... PART I. Los Angeles: Heritage Book Shop, 1982, 4to., cloth, dust jacket. xx, 120, (3) pages. $75.00

First edition. Printed at the Castle Press, this bibliography gives comprehensive new details on the bindings and textual data of Dickens' first editions. With facsimiles of title pages and primary bindings.

277. (Castle Press) TO HONOR JAMES RATHWELL PAGE, CHAIRMAN OF THE BOARD, CALIFORNIA INSTITUTE OF TECHNOLOGY, 1943–1954. Los Angeles: California Institute of Technology, (1955), large 8vo., stiff paper wrappers. viii, 15+(1) pages. $15.00

Printed for CalTech by Grant Dahlstrom at the Castle Press in Pasadena. Remarks at a dinner given in James Page's honor at the California Club, Los Angeles, November 17, 1954.

278. (Castle Press) Weber, Jeff and Romaine Ahlstrom (editors). L.A. PUBLIC LI-BRARY SINCE 1872, A BICENTENNIAL EXHIBITION HONORING JOHN D. BRUCKMAN (1928–1979). Los Angeles: Los Angeles Public Library, 1981, 8vo., cloth, paper cover label. x, 44, (2) pages. $ 25.00

Designed and printed by The Castle Press, Pasadena, in an edition limited to 1000 copies. Set in Linotype Aldus and handset Palatino types and printed on Warren's watermarked Antique Olde Style paper. A catalogue of the traveling exhibition from the libraries outstanding collection of materials, mostly on the history of Los Angeles and California, issued in the city's Bicentennial Year. Includes memorial ad-dress for John Bruckman, late Collection Development Manager for the Los Angeles Public Library, by Jake Zeitlin. Illustrated.

279. (Castle Press) Zeitlin, Jake. MORE WHISPERS & CHANTS. Pasadena: Amper-sand Press, 1952, small 8vo., folded sheet. (4) pages. $ 20.00

Advance sample, printed February, 1952, by Grant Dahlstrom at The Castle Press. Folded sheet with title page and a poem.

280. (Castle Press) Zeitlin, Jake. MORE WHISPERS & CHANTS. Pasadena: Amper-sand Press, 1952, small 8vo., quarter cloth with paper-covered boards. (vi), 19, (3) pages. $ 65.00

Printed by Grant Dahlstrom at the Castle Press, Pasadena. Poems written by the author "twenty years ago, when I had more of the urge to sing. I send them out as a friend sends a letter to another." Half-title page lacking.

281. (Catfish Press) Catich, Edward M. REED, PEN, & BRUSH ALPHABETS FOR WRITING AND LETTERING. Two volumes. Davenport, Iowa: The Catfish Press, (1972), 8vo. and 4to., half cloth over marbled paper covered boards, paper cover labels. 32 pages in book and 28 heavy leaves printed on both sides loosely inserted in 4to. port-folio. $ 375.00

Limited to 100 copies though this is not stated in the book. Beautifully printed in red, blue and black. The portfolio contains reproductions of alphabets while the book describes the art of calligraphy and explains the plates.

282. (Cedar Tree Press) Thomas, Martha Banning. POEMS FOR PEOPLE. Boston: The Cedar Tree Press, 1925, 8vo., parchment-backed boards, paper cover label. (viii), 47, (3) pages. $ 20.00

Limited to 150 numbered copies, the first production of the press. (Ranson no.1). "A publishing title used for one book designed and published by Mr. Capon, but printed elsewhere." Cover label rubbed. Front free endpaper lacking.

283. (Celadine Press) Wain, John. MID-WEEK PERIOD RETURN, HOME THOUGHTS OF A NATIVE. Stratford-upon-Avon: Celadine Press, 1982, 8vo., quarter cloth, marbled paper-covered boards. (24) pages. $ 125.00

Limited to 175 numbered copies, signed on colophon by author and illustrator of which this is one of 85 copies hardbound thus. Historical-literary-personal reminiscences and reflections of the author on a train ride from Oxford to Stoke-on-Trent, with drawings by Arthur Keene. Printed for the Celadine Press by Skelton's Press.

284. (Centaur Press) Thomajan, P.K. KIDAZE. Continental: Centaur Press, 1961, small 8vo., cloth with paper cover label. (31) french fold pages. $ 30.00

First edition. Privately printed and limited to 300 numbered and signed copies. A collection of short sto-ries. Illustrations by Walter Kaprielian. Printed by Dwight Agner.

285. (Center for Edition Works) Ruark, Gibbons. SMALL RAIN. Purchase, NY: The Center for Edition Works, 1984, small 4to., portfolio. (15) leaves. $ 75.00
Limited to edition of 100 signed and numbered copies. An early collection from the pen of Ruark, these poems, which explore the joy of exploration combined with the loneliness of separation, provide a firm foundation to his development as one of America's finest poets. Includes presentation note from Carol Sturm and Doug Wolf who designed and printed the leaves in ATF Garamond. The titles, done in red, are set in display selections from the Robinson-Pforzheimer Collection, a permanent typographic research archive within the SUNY-Purchase Visual Arts Department.

286. (Chanter Press) [LOT OF 19 PIECES FROM SENIOR GRAPHIC DESIGN CLASSES IN THE CHANTER PRESS AND NEW LABORATORY PRESS, COLLEGE OF FINE ARTS, AT THE CARNEGIE INSTITUTE OF TECHNOL-OGY, 1961-64]. (Pittsburgh: Chanter Press and New Laboratory Press, 1961–1964), folio to 12mo., stiff portfolio covers with items laid in loosely. $ 125.00
Lot of 19 pieces of senior class projects from the Chanteer Press and New Laboratory Press, under the direction of Jack W. Stauffacher, at the College of Fine Arts, Department of Graphic Arts, Carnegie Institute of Technology, variously dated from 1961 to 1964. The lot includes an illustrated twenty-six page booklet in stiff paper wrappers, *The Privileges of 10 April 1840*, a little-known text of Stendahl, composed towards the end of his life, limited to 185 copies, and first printed in *Les Quatre Vents*, No. 6 (Paris, 1946). Also, *To Face the Real Crisis: Man Himself*, by Archibald MacLeish, a 10–page reprint in loose signatures of a *New York Times Magazine* article, limited to 300 copies, May, 1963. The remaining items are printed single-sheet, in a variety of sizes, paper, type specimens and quotations, some suitable for framing. The portfolio wrappers and three sheets have tears near the bottom right corner, but none of the copy or images are damaged.

287. (Cheloniidae Press) Robinson, Alan J.(editor). H.P.M., HAROLD PATRICK MCGRATH. Easthampton, MA: Cheloniidae Press, 1991, 4to., decorated paper over boards, front cover and spine label. (x), (80), (vi) pages. $ 600.00
First edition, limited to 210 numbered copies of which only 100 are for sale. Printed at Wild Carrot Letterpress by Daniel Keleher using Cheloniidae rag paper. Published to commemorate the 50th anniversary of the printing career of Harold Patrick McGrath, Master Printer for the Gehenna Press, Pennyroyal Press, and Cheloniidae Press. It contains sixty recollections, reminiscences, histories, etc. from friends, family, artists and fellow printers. Also included are four wood engravings by Leonard Baskin, six wood engravings by Barry Moser, an etched portrait, a wood engraving by Fritz Eichenberg, a two-color portrait by Lance Hidy and four wood engravings by Alan James Robinson. The title page and two other pages have hand calligraphy by Suzanne Moore and Elizabeth Curtis. A fine production which is printed in two colors throughout. This copy has the following in the colophon: This is copy number "XLIX Ap" and is signed by McGrath and Robinson.

288. (Cheney, William Murray) Cheney, William M. THE AUK PRESS. (Los Angeles: The Auk Press, 1934), large 12mo., self paper wrappers. (4) pages. $ 50.00
A manifesto for the establishment of The Auk Press in Los Angeles, stamped April, 1934 on the back (Jones, No.3). This was the first item to be completed on Cheney's own press. Brick-red linoleum cut of *The Auk* at his press on the front cover, within a line border. *He is actually able to set type & print , inept as he appears, and different as he is from any other Auk you've seen.* Printed in Caslon Oldstyle type on a Poco proof press. Some creases to paper.

289. (Cheney, William Murray) (Carpenter, Edwin H.). LETTER TO A LEXICOG-RAPHER. San Francisco: n.p., n.d. (but 1960), 12mo., paper wrappers. 12 pages.$ 20.00
Second printing, printed by the Plantin Press. (see Jones no.21) A humorous, if in bad taste, letter written by the fictitious E. de Fumier to the equally fictitious M. Cambronne. Claiming to draw upon his Army experience for his knowledge, the writer elaborates upon the dozens of colorful expressions where a common scatological English word occurs. Two-page postscript added in this edition.

290. (Cheney, William Murray) Carpenter, Edwin H. LETTER TO A LEXICOGRA-PHER. Los Angeles: n.p., n.d. (but 1952), 12mo., stiff paper wrappers. 9 pages. $35.00
First printing, limited to 139 copies. (Jones no.31). A humorous, if in bad taste, letter written by the fictitious E. de Fumier to the equally fictitious M. Cambronne. Claiming to draw upon his Army experience for his knowledge, the writer elaborates upon the dozens of colorful expressions where a common scatological English word occurs. Nicely printed by William Murray Cheney.

291. (Cheney, William Murray) Dahlstrom, Grant. WHO IS WILLIAM CHENEY? In California Librarian, vol. XXIII, no. 1,. January, 1962, 8vo., self paper wrappers. (4) pages inserted between pp. 32 and 33. $10.00
In the early 1960's, the *California Librarian* presented a series of inserts that were designed not only to provide a discussion of a local printer's work but also an illustration of it. Printed and designed by Grant Dahlstrom, this issue presents the work of William Cheney. The front cover features Cheney's printer's mark.

292. (Cheney, William Murray) DE CELEBRATIONE FESTIVEA QUAE DIE GU-LARUM MAJARUM PROPTER EXITUM. N.P.: Will Cheney, n.d., broadside (17 x 11 inches). $30.00
Broadside printed in two colors by Will Cheney which reproduces the original text of the Rounce & Coffin Club's announcement of May 5, 1959.

293. (Cheney, William Murray) Harmsen, Tyrus G. THE PLANTIN PRESS OF SAUL AND LILLIAN MARKS. Los Angeles: Dawson's Book Shop, 1960, large 12mo., paper covered boards. (ii), 21+(1) pages. $85.00
Printed by Wm. M. Cheney in an edition limited to 200 copies. Brief history of The Plantin Press, started by Saul and Lillian Marks in Los Angeles in 1931."Working with a minimum of typefaces, carefully selected, and handled with taste and skill, Saul Marks soon gave evidence of typography that was satisfying and distinctive." Includes a summary of his work grouped by publisher, starting with a catalogue printed for the antiquarian bookseller and amateur printer, Jake Zeitlin, in 1932. Other early imprints were some of the Book Club of California's keepsake series, the 1949 Western Books exhibition catalogue, printed for the Rounce & Coffin Club, and a handsome volume entitled *The Hand of Zamorano*, printed in 1956. Tipped in photo of Saul & Lillian Marks working at their press as frontis.

294. (Cheney, William Murray) [LOT OF 5 MINIATURE ITEMS PRINTED BY WILLIAM M. CHENEY]. (Los Angeles): various publishers, circa 1970 to 1984. $20.00
The lot contains a book label for Peggy Christian, *Bookseller*, Los Angeles; two miniature bookplates for miniature books printed with the owner's name, one being Audrey Arellanes, who edited a volume on miniature bookplates designed by Cheney (*Some Minor Book Plates*, 1975, printed for Dawson's Book Shop) ; a proof sheet of pp.17–18 for an unidentified book printed by Cheney for Dawson's, and 4 pages of commentary on the second edition of *Arkwright's Journey* (Jones, p. 89), by E.H. Carp, Fall, 1977.

295. (Cheney, William Murray) POCKET KNIVES. Napa, CA: Gordon Williams, 1983, small 12mo., cloth. vi, 60, (4) pages. $20.00
Second edition corrected, limited to an unspecified number of copies. Handset in 10 and 12 pt. Bembo types and printed on Warren's Olde Style paper with a Washington hand press. Foreword by Gordon Williams, with 2 line-drawings as illustrations.

296. (Cheney, William Murray) A TREATISE ON POCKET KNIVES. Los Angeles: Wm. M. Cheney, 1964, 16mo., cloth. 36 pages. $25.00
First edition. (Jones no.57). Sometimes referred to as the Gatehouse Edition, as Cheney at that time was resident at the Press at the Gatehouse of the Clark Library, part of the UCLA system. Spoof of scholarly essays. Handset in 10 and 12 pt. Bembo types and printed on Warren's Olde Style paper with a Washington hand press. Illustrated with 2-line drawings.

297. (Chilmark Press) Trypanis, C.A. THE ELEGIES OF A GLASS ADONIS. New York: Chilmark Press, (1967), 4to., paper over boards, slipcase. 31+(1) pages. $ 125.00
Limited to 450 signed and numbered copies. With typographical note by Will Carter. Designed and printed by Will and Sebastian Carter at the Rampant Lions Press. Prospectus loosely inserted.

298. (Chiswick Press) Allnutt, W.H. NOTES ON PRINTERS AND PRINTING IN THE PROVINCIAL TOWNS OF ENGLAND AND WALES. London: Chiswick Press, 1879, small 4to., stiff paper wrappers. 14 pages. $ 55.00
First printing. A paper read at the first annual meeting of the library association of the United Kingdom, October 3, 1878. Includes "Table of Places in England and Wales with their Earliest Specimens of Typography," 1480–1801. Pages looses, minor foxing.

299. (Chiswick Press) Bullen, A.H. (editor). LYRICS FROM THE DRAMATISTS OF THE ELIZABETHAN AGE. London: John C. Nimmo, 1889, small 8vo., cloth, top edge gilt, fore and bottom edges deckled. xxviii, 243 pages. $ 55.00
Printed in an edition limited to 500 numbered copies at the Chiswick Press. A collection of lyrical poetry from several writers including William Shakespeare and John Milton. Includes an index of first lines and a list of authors. Presentation on front free endpaper, "Gilbert Murray-from Cecilia-haworth 1890." Former owner has indicated this as Bullen's wife. Later ink inscription also on front free endpaper.

300. (Chiswick Press) CATALOGUE OF THE LIBRARY OF THE ATHENAEUM, LIVERPOOL. N.P.: Proprietors of the Athenæum, 1864, contemporary pebbled cloth. xxxvi, 589, (3) pages. $ 150.00
The third catalogue of the Liverpool Athenæum, founded in 1798. A classified catalogue with about 90 divisions and subdivisions for roughly 20,000 volumes. Entries are bibliographically rather minimal. With an alphabetical index. Affixed to the inside of the front cover is a bookplate of "G.T. Robert Preston," who is probably the "George T.R. Preston" noted in list of "proprietors" of the library. Printed at the Chiswick Press by Whittingham & Wilkins. Occasional light foxing. Top edge and covers are moderately soiled, with the bottom corners bumped. Generally well-preserved.

301. (Chiswick Press) Cobden-Sanderson, T.J. ECCE MUNDUS, INDUSTRIAL IDEALS AND THE BOOK BEAUTIFUL. Hammersmith: Hammersmith Publishing Society, 1902, 8vo., vellum-backed paper covered boards. (37) pages. $ 95.00
Two separate articles by Cobden-Sanderson. Attractively printed at The Chiswick Press, Charles Whittingham & Co.

302. (Chiswick Press) Hunter, H.L. LEAVES OF GOLD AN ACCOUNT OF THE ANCIENT CRAFT OF GOLDBEATING AND ITS DEVELOPMENT INTO A MODERN INDUSTRY. (London): George M. Whiley, (1951), large 8vo., cloth, leather cover and spine labels. 70, (2) pages. $ 275.00
Printed by the Chiswick Press in an unspecified "limited private edition" of which this is copy 27 signed by Cecil Whiley who collaborated in the preparation of the text. Provides a clear and concise history of this ancient craft by suppliers of gold leaf to the Crown. Black and white illustrations throughout by John Minton. Bibliography. Cover slightly soiled.

303. (Chiswick Press) Jacobi, Charles T. GESTA TYPOGRAPHICA, OR A MEDLEY FOR PRINTERS AND OTHERS. London: Elkin Mathews, 1897, tall 12mo., original cloth-backed boards. x, 132 pages. $ 60.00
First edition. Nicely printed by the Chiswick Press. Includes sections on first facts, printers' errors, humorous incidents and a glossary of terms. Covers slightly age darkened. Endpapers foxed. With the signature of James Moran.

304. (Chiswick Press) Jacobi, Charles T. SOME NOTES ON BOOKS AND PRINT-ING; A GUIDE FOR AUTHORS AND OTHERS. London: Chiswick Press, 1892, 8vo., creme-colored buckram. viii, 54 pages followed by 38 plates of type specimens of the Chiswick Press and 13 paper samples, 6 of which are hand-made. $ 145.00
First edition. (Hart no.136). Actually an expanded version of his *On the Making and Issuing of Books* which was published in 1891. Jacobi was the managing partner of the Chiswick Press. Covers soiled. Also has a section on bookbinding. Presentation copy "à M. Octave Uzanne from the author. July '97."

305. (Chiswick Press) Mackail, J.W. SOCIALISM AND POLITICS: AN ADDRESS AND A PROGRAMME. Hammersmith: Hammersmith Publishing Society, 1903, small 8vo., quarter vellum, paper covered boards. 37, (3) pages. $ 75.00
First edition. This address, given in Clifford's Inn Hall by invitation of the Metropolitan Council of the Independent Labour Party on February 5, 1902, shows William Morris' influence on MacKail's political ideas. Printed at the Chiswick Press for T.J. Cobden-Sanderson. Covers soiled and corners slightly bumped.

306. (Chiswick Press) Mayo, Charles Herbert. BIBLIOTECA DORSETIENSIS, BEING A CAREFULLY COMPILED ACCOUNT OF PRINTED BOOKS AND PAMPHLETS RELATING TO THE HISTORY AND TOPOGRAPHY OF THE COUNTY OF DORSET. London: Privately printed at the Chiswick Press, 1885, 8vo., original cloth, beveled edges. x, 296 pages. $ 125.00
Besterman 1658. About 1,250 entries, arranged by topic and then by date: Histories and Descriptions, Guide Books, Ecclesiastical Literature, Acts of Parliaments, etc. etc., with over half being "Works Relat-ed to Particular Parishes" (subarranged by place). With some annotations; entries for "Newspapers" give brief publishing histories. With a list of Dorset printers and index of author's names. Ex-library copy with paper library label on front cover and library stamp in various places internally. Rebacked with original cloth laid-down on new cloth and with new endpapers.

307. (Chiswick Press) Mackail, J.W. WILLIAM MORRIS, AN ADDRESS DELIV-ERED THE XITH NOVEMBER MDCCCC AT KELMSCOTT HOUSE, HAM-MERSMITH, BEFORE THE HAMMERSMITH SOCIALIST SOCIETY. Ham-mersmith: Hammersmith Publishing Society, 1902, 8vo., vellum-backed boards. (36) pages. $ 85.00
A reprint of the Doves Press edition that has been printed at The Chiswick Press, Charles Whittingham & Co. Covers soiled.

308. (Chiswick Press) Morris, William. STORY OF THE GLITTERING PLAIN WHICH HAS BEEN ALSO CALLED THE LAND OF LIVING MEN OR THE ACRE OF THE UNDYING. London: Reeves and Turner, 1891, small 8vo., cloth, gilt stamped cover and spine, rough-cut pages. (viii), 172 pages. $ 45.00
First ordinary edition, printed at the Chiswick Press. (Forman no. 123) This simple version of *The Glit-tering Plain*, the first book to be published by the Kelmscott Press and one of its most influential, was prepared for the general public after the original was quickly subscribed. Owner's bookplate on front pastedown. Front hinge separated, joint starting to split at front boards, rear inner hinge cracked, wear to head and tail of spine and corners, slight darkening to page edges.

309. (Chiswick Press) Vallance, Aymer. ART OF WILLIAM MORRIS. London: George Bell & Sons, 1897, thick folio, original publisher's quarter cloth with dark blue buckram covered boards, top edge gilt. xii, 167 pages followed by XL leaves of plates and xxx, (2) pages. $ 4,500.00
Printed by the Chiswick Press in an edition limited to 220 numbered copies. Includes chapters devoted to Morris in Oxford, his art and poetry, the firm of Morris and Co., Kelmscott Manor, and on Book dec-oration and the Kelmscott Press. Beautifully illustrated with forty finely chromolithographed plates

printed by W. Griggs and Sons in addition to other illustrations and facsimiles within the text. Includes a bibliography of the Kelmscott Press by Temple Scott. Engraved bookplate on front pastedown. Some internal foxing.

310. (Chiswick Press) Richardson, Benjamin Ward. AT NOVIOMAGUS, A TRIB-UTE OF AFFECTION TO THE LATE SIR BENJAMIN WARD. N.P.: Chiswick Press, n.d. (circa 1897), large 12mo., original half cloth with marbled paper-covered boards. Frontispiece; (xii), 39+(1) pages, with MS letter bound in. $45.00
Privately printed for the members of the Noviomagus society by the Chiswick Press. A fanciful account, by Richardson, of the city of Noviomagus in Roman times. Very slight wear to covers. Bookplate.

311. (Chiswick Press) A CATALOGUE OF AN UNIQUE COLLECTION OF AN-CIENT ENGLISH BROADSIDE BALL. London: n.p. (J.R. Smith-printed at the Chiswick Press), 1856, small 8vo., later quarter leather, with (probably) contemporary marbled paper-covered boards, marbled endpapers, leather spine label. viii, 141, (3) pages. $95.00
The publisher, bookseller, student of English dialects, and bibliographer J.R. Smith (1810–1894) is probably best known as the author of the first complete bibliography of English writers on angling and ichthyology (1856) and as the publisher of the "Library of Old Authors" series. This is a priced catalogue of 408, generally 16th- and 17th-century popular broadsides. Entries indicate place and printer, and sometimes seem to give the full text, but do not indicate date (unless it appears in the text). Woodcuts are enumerated. Headings or opening lines are printed in black letter, the rest in a standard roman face. Printer of this, as for many of Russell's publications, was the Chiswick Press. Boards are rubbed, chipped and worn. The later, utilitarian rebacking is in good condition. Some separation of binding before title page.

312. (Chiswick Press) Strange, Edward F. ALPHABETS, A HANDBOOK OF LET-TERING WITH HISTORICAL CRITICAL. London: George Bell and Sons, 1895, 8vo., original stiff paper wrappers, dust jacket. xix, 294, (2) pages. $150.00
First edition, one of 75 numbered copies printed on Japanese vellum and bound-thus. Printed at the Chiswick Press as part of the Ex-Libris Series edited by Gleeson White. Over 200 illustrations. Outer wrapper is chipped with tear along back hinge. Bookplate on free endpaper. Blank page before half-title missing.

313. (Chiswick Press) Strong, L.A.G. THE BIG MAN. London: Joiner & Steele, 1931, large 8vo., cloth. (ii), 45+(1) pages. $45.00
Printed at the Chiswick Press in an edition limited to 550 numbered copies signed by the author, of which 500 only were for sale. Illustrated with a frontispiece by Tirzah Garwood and a foreword by A.E. Coppard. Issued as No. 6 of the Furnival Books, with a slip tipped in noting that the publisher had changed from William Jackson, but that name was retained on the title-page "in order that the set of twelve books may be typographically uniform." The author is described in the introduction as being part of an informal playreading set at Oxford created by Aldous Huxley, Roy Campbell, and Richard Hugh-es, with occasional visits by W.B. Yeats. Some wear to extremities.

314. (Chiswick Press) Tedder, Henry R. and Ernest C. Thomas (editors). TRANSAC-TIONS AND PROCEEDINGS OF THE FIRST ANNUAL MEETING OF THE LIBRARY ASSOCIATION OF THE UNITED KINGDOM HELD AT OX-FORD, OCTOBER 1,2,3, 1878. London: Chiswick Press, 1878, 4to., original two toned-cloth. viii, 191 pages. $150.00
The Library Association was founded in 1877 with the first Annual Meeting held in 1878. The first 13 pages of this report contain the various committee reports. This is followed by 22 separate chapters on various aspects of library work including Subscription Libraries, On Covering Books in American Cloth, The Filing of Newspapers, Professorships of Bibliography, Is the Printed catalogue of the British Muse-um Practicable?, etc. Well printed by Charles Whittingham. Spotted along fore-edge of covers.

315. (Chiswick Press) Toynbee, Paget. JOURNAL OF THE PRINTING-OFFICE AT STRAWBERRY HILL, NOW FIRST PRINTED FROM THE MS OF HORACE WALPOLE, WITH NOTES. London: Constable and Co. by the Chiswick Press, 1923, 4to., quarter calf. xii, 152 pages. $ 125.00

First edition, limited to 650 copies. With 12 full page illustrations. Important document in the study of the history of Walpole's private printing establishment. Leather is rubbed and covers age darkened. Bookplate.

316. (Clarke & Way) Bennett, Joseph. DECEMBRIST, A BOOK OF POEMS. New York: Clarke & Way, 1951, 8vo., paper covered boards, slipcase. (viii), 61+(1) pages.

$ 20.00

Printed in an edition limited to 440 copies. The designs were made by George Stave and the typography is by David Way. The type was hand-composed in Comstock, Deepdene, and Lutetia Italic by Robert Levy. The sheets were printed by W. Irving Senne at the Centaur Press and bound by Frank Fortney.

317. (Colt Press) Hall, Carroll Douglas. TERRY-BRODERICK DUEL. Woodcuts by Mallette Dean. San Francisco: The Colt Press, (1939), 8vo., cloth-backed boards, paper spine label. 89+(1) pages. $ 65.00

The third production of this press established by William M. Roth, Jane Swinerton and Jane Grabhorn. The presswork was done by Lawton Kennedy. Covers rubbed along edges with spotting. Front endpaper and pastedown yellowed.

318. (Colt Press) [LOT OF 7 PIECES OF EPHEMERA FROM THE COLT PRESS]. San Francisco: Colt Press. $ 35.00

Lot of catalogues, an announcement, checklist, newsheet, and 2 postcards from the early 1940's. This was a fine press, printing first editions of *The wife of Martin Guerre*, by Janet Lewis, and *Ambrose Bierce, The Wickedest Man in San Francisco*, by Franklin Walker, among its titles. Several catalogues in original postmarked envelopes with customers name and address.

319. (Colt Press) Stewart, George R. TAKE YOUR BIBLE IN ONE HAND, THE LIFE OF WILLIAM HENRY THOMES AUTHOR OF A WHALEMAN'S AD-VENTURE ON LAND AND SEA, LEWEY AND I, THE BUSRANGERS, A GOLD HUNTER'S ADVENTURES, ETC. San Francisco: The Colt Press, 1939, small 4to., cloth-backed boards, paper spine label. 66, (4) pages. $ 65.00

First edition, limited to 750 copies printed by Jane Swinerton, William Roth and Jane Grabhorn. (Biblio. no.11). With marginal illustrations by Mallette Dean. Covers soiled and age darkened along edges. With original prospectus loosely inserted which is addressed to Harry Gage and signed by Paul Bennett.

320. (Columbian Chappel 415) Petko, Edward. AT SEVENTY: RICHARD J. HOFF-MAN. Los Angeles: Columbian Press, 1982, oblong 8vo., linen, paper spine and cover label. (ii), 35, (3) pages. $ 150.00

Printed in an edition limited to 100 copies. Issued to celebrate the seventieth birthday of Richard J. Hoffman, printer, and author of " A Gathering of Types" and its sequel "A Decorative Divertissement." Designed and printed by Ethan B. Lipton with typesetting by Jack M. Conway. Illustrated with photographs of Hoffman at work in his shop. With laid in invitations to Hoffman's seventieth birthday in 1982. Presentation on colophon page "This copy for Roger Levenson ex dono authoris."

321. (Columbian Chappel 415) Petko, Edward. AT SEVENTY: RICHARD J. HOFF-MAN. Los Angeles: Columbian Press, 1982, oblong 8vo., linen, paper spine and cover label. (ii), 35, (3) pages. $ 250.00

Printed in an edition limited to 50 copies. Issued to celebrate the seventieth birthday of Richard J. Hoffman, printer, and author of " A Gathering of Types" and its sequel "A Decorative Divertissement." On Urabec-Hoffman all-rag handmade paper, from the Brooks. Bros. Shirts and old linens of his friend, Dr.

John Urabec. Designed and printed by Ethan B. Lipton, typesetting by Jack M. Conway, and signed by them. Illustrated with tipped in photographs of Hoffman at work in his shop. With laid in invitations to Hoffman's seventieth birthday in 1982.

322. (Columbian Chappel 415) Bullen, Henry Lewis, et al. PROJECT '85. Los Angeles: Columbian Chappel 415, 1985, large 12mo., cloth. (x), (163) pages. $ 55.00
First edition, limited to 125 copies. The Chappel is named for the first real American invention in printing, the iron hand-press "Columbian" built by George Clymer in 1829. In this volume, a group design and publishing venture, six well-written and handsomely produced essays discuss the influence and achievements of six masters of printing: Nicolas Jenson; Aldus Manutius; William Morris; Mark Twain; Linn Boyd Benton; Richard Marsh Hoe. The formats of each essay vary, with the content, typography, and often typesetting and presswork the efforts of the individual contributors, such as: Gary Marc Remson; Jack M. Conway; Tom Parker; Richard J. Hoffman. Credits thus at the end of each section. Includes black and white and color illustrations. Binding done by Bela Blau.

323. (Columbian Chappel 415) Wentz, Roby. HAYWOOD HUNT AND HUNT TOWERS. Los Angeles: Columbian 415 Chappel, n.d., small 8vo., cloth. 33, (3) pages, with frontispiece. $ 30.00
Printed in an edition of 250 copies. Memoir of a San Francisco printer. The first book printed by this Chappel according to the colophon which lists the nine members including Richard Hoffman.

324. (Costmary Press) Tourgee, Albion W. GOLDEN WEDDING FANCY, AN UN-PUBLISHED POEM BY ALBION W. TOURGEE, WITH A NOTE BY DEAN H. KELLER. Kent, OH: The Costmary Press, 1971, large 12mo., stapled, self paper wrappers. (8) pages. $ 17.50
Limited to 250 copies. Unpublished poem from a type manuscript by the writer, Civil War veteran, Reconstructionist and diplomat A.W. Tourgée (1838–1905). Disbound (the staple has fallen out).

325. (Covici Friede) Aldington, Richard. LOVE AND THE LUXEMBOURG. New York: Covici, Friede Inc, 1930, 8vo., cloth, top edge gilt, plain paper dust jacket. (iv), 53+(1) pages. $ 75.00
Printed in an edition limited to 475 numbered copies, each signed by the author and designer. Noted as printers copy on the colophon. Designated by AIGA as one of the fifty best designed books for 1930. Blank verse. Former owner has written title - author in pencil on spine of the jacket.

326. (Cowell Press) Wilson, Adrian and Joyce Lancaster Wilson. HIGHEST FORM OF FLATERY WITH A LEAF FROM THE 1497 EDITION OF THE PIRATED NUREMBERG CHRONICLE PRINTED AT AUGSBURG. Santa Cruz: University of California at Santa Cruz, Cowell Press, 1982, 4to., quarter leather over cloth, dust jacket. (14) pages. $ 450.00
First edition, limited to 90 numbered copies of which this is one of the first 60 copies bound in quarter leather. The first publication of The Cowell Press, a private press associated with the University of California. With a history of the press by John Dizikes and acknowledgments by George R. Kane, the press instructor. With an actual leaf from Johann Schoensperger's pirated edition of the Nuremberg Chronicle executed in 1497. Jacket yellowed from acidity of leather on spine with small piece missing, else fine.

327. (Cuala Press) Miller, Liam. DUN EMER PRESS, LATER THE CUALA PRESS, WITH A LIST OF THE BOOKS, BROADSIDES AND OTHER PIECES PRINTED AT THE PRESS. New York: The Typophiles, 1974, 8vo., paper wrappers. 131 pages. $ 45.00
One of 500 copies. Preface by Michael B. Yeats. An excellent study of the press as well as a bibliography.

328. (Cuckoo Hill Press) Beys, Christopher. ACTA CHRISTOPHORI BEISII. Pinner: Cuckoo Hill Press, 1962, 12mo., self paper wrappers. (4) pages. $ 7.50
Monograph 70. Grandson of Plantin.

329. (Cuckoo Hill Press) Chambers, David. THE OFFICE PRESS. (Pinner, Middlesex, England): Cuckoo Hill Press, (1961), large 12mo., stiff paper wrappers. (16) pages.
$ 25.00
Printed in an edition limited to 111 copies by David Chambers at his Cuckoo Hill Press. Printed from Bembo and Castellar type on damped mould-made Fabriano Ingres paper. The Office Press was used for the colophon and title, and an Alexandra for the text. Detailed account of converting an old office letter copying press into a reasonably efficient printing press that would take a chase seven by eleven inches. Illustrated with drawings.

330. (Cummington Press) Bond, Harold. DANCING ON WATER. West Branch: The Cummington Press, 1969, 12mo., cloth, paper spine label. 88 pages. $ 65.00
First edition. Printed in an edition limited to 285 numbered copies, this being one of the 185 printed on Basingwerk parchment paper. A collection of poems by Bond which previously appeared in a number of periodicals.

331. (Cuneo Press) THE CHRISTMAS BOOK. Chicago: The Cuneo Press, 1969, 8vo., simulated leather. (x), 182 pages. $ 25.00
With an introduction by John Cuneo followed by reprints of essays by Edith Wharton, George Randolph Chester, Henry Cuyler Bunner, Arthur Sherburne Hardy and Pope Paul VI. With original Illustrations specially prepared for this volume.

332. (Curwen Press) Best, John. POEMS AND DRAWINGS IN MUD TIME. Leicester: Orpheus Press, (1960), large 8vo., decorated paper covered boards. not paginated. $ 45.00
Printed in an edition limited to 1000 copies, in which 50 are numbered and signed, at The Curwen Press, London. A collection of poems by John Best illustrated with drawings by Rigby Graham. Lines from Robert Frost's 'Two Tramps in Mud Time' in 'A Further Range' are reprinted.

333. (Curwen Press) CURWEN PRESS ALMANACK 1926. London: Published for The Curwen Press At the Office of The Fleuron, n.d., tall 12mo., cloth-backed boards. (x), 39, (17) pages. $ 15.00
Limited to 425 numbered copies. Drawings by Randolph Schwabe and an article by Harold Child. Has a catalogue of the books published by The Fleuron. Covers worn with part of board exposed.

334. (Curwen Press) de la Mare, Walter. A SNOWDROP. London: Curwen Press, 1929, small 8vo., paper-covered boards. (14) pages. $ 85.00
Printed for Faber & Faber by the Curwen Press, limited to 500 numbered copies signed by the author, being No. 20 of the Ariel Poems series, and printed on English hand-made paper. Drawings by Claudia Guercio, who designed many vignettes for Curwen, and was married to the illustrator Barnett Freedman. Minor wear at head and tail of spine.

335. (Curwen Press) Farleigh, John. GRAVEN IMAGE, AN AUTO-BIOGRAPHICAL TEXTBOOK. London: The Macmillan Co., 1940, 8vo., boards, dust jacket. 383 pages. $ 85.00
First edition. Farleigh has combined a textbook on engraving and an auto-biography. The textbook portion of his book is profusely illustrated showing famous engravers at work and examples of their engravings. Beautiful jacket covering an equally beautiful cover. Printed at the Curwen Press. Piece of jacket missing at top of spine.

336. (Curwen Press) Fraser, Claud Lovat. SIXTY-THREE UNPUBLISHED DE-SIGNS. London: First Edition Club, n.d., 12mo., quarter cloth with Lovat Frasier de-signed patterned paper covered boards. xii, 63, (3) pages. $ 125.00
Limited to a numbered edition of 500 copies. The introduction by Holbrook Jackson explains that the de-signs were created for the lyric poem, *A Shropshire Lad*, by A.E. Housman. For unknown reasons, they were refused by Housman and remained unpublished until they were gathered for this volume printed at the Curwen Press.

337. (Curwen Press) A GARLAND OF ELIZABETHAN SONNETS. London: Leonard Parsons, 1923, large 12mo., quarter cloth with paper-covered boards, paper spine label. (viii), 34, (4) pages. $ 25.00
Printed at the Curwen Press in an edition limited to 500 numbered copies on Zanders hand-made paper, in Garamond monotype with Rizzi decorated paper boards (Simon, 238). Sixty-four sonnets selected for subject matter and style, with "those which are lightest and most youthful in thought and spirit coming first."

338. (Curwen Press) Monro, Harold. THE WINTER SOLSTICE. (London: Faber & Gwyer, 1928), 12mo., stiff paper wrappers. (4) pages. $ 35.00
Issued as No. 13 in The Ariel Poems series and printed at The Curwen Press, Plaistow. Harold Monro (1879–1932) devoted himself to the propagation of poetry and founded several magazines, including *The Poetry Bookshop*. Two drawings by David Jones (1895–1974), who also did engravings for St. Dominic's Press and Gregynog Press before eye trouble forced him to give it up in 1930.

339. (Curwen Press) Pierre-Victor. SPLEEN AND OTHER STORIES. Translated from the French ... by H.B.V.. With an Introduction by Havelock Ellis. London: Chap-man & Hall, 1928, 8vo., cloth-backed patterned paper covered boards, dust jacket with paper cover label, top edge gilt, others uncut. xxvi, 178 pages. $ 25.00
Limited to 1000 numbered copies. Jacket has pieces missing at spine ends.

340. (Curwen Press) Simon, Oliver and Julius Rodenberg. PRINTING OF TO-DAY, AN ILLUSTRATED SURVEY OF POST-WAR TYPOGRAPHY IN EUROPE AND THE UNITED STATES. Introduction by Aldous Huxley. London: Peter Davies Limited and New York: Harper and Brothers, 1928, large 4to., cloth-backed boards. xix, 83 pages with 122 reproductions of various examples of typography. $ 65.00
First edition. The facsimiles are often in two colors. Spine faded with wear at spine ends. Printed at The Curwen Press.

341. (Curwen Press) Balston, Thomas. SITWELLIANA, 1915–1927, BEING A HANDLIST OF WORKS BY EDITH, OSBERT, AND SACHEVERELL SITWELL AND OF THEIR CONTRIBUTIONS TO CERTAIN SELECTED PE-RIODICALS. London: Duckworth, 1928, 12mo., original decorated boards, paper cover label. x, 24 pages. $ 60.00
First edition. Printed at the Curwen Press. Has three portraits of the authors by Albert Rutherston. Rubbed spot on front cover. Bookplate.

342. (Curwen Press) Curwen. SPECIMEN BOOK OF PATTERN PAPERS DE-SIGNED FOR AND IN USE AT THE CURWEN PRESS. London: The Fleuron Limited, 1928, 4to., cloth. not paginated. $ 2,250.00
Printed in an edition limited to 145 numbered copies for sale in England and 75 copies for sale in the United States. A specimen book of pattern papers. The papers in the following collection are from designs reproduced by offset printing, the original key pattern being a line block from a drawing, or a wood-en-graving. The designers of these papers are Lovat Fraser, Albert Rutherston, Margaret James, Thomas Lowinsky, E.O. Hoppe, Edward Bawden and Paul Nash. The wood engravers are Paul Nash, Enid Marx, Eric Ravilious and Harry Carter. Covers rubbed.

[61]

Item 342

343. (Curwen Press) Stone, Reynolds. REYNOLDS STONE, ENGRAVINGS. WITH AN INTRODUCTION BY THE AUTHOR. With an Introduction by the Artist and an Appreciation by Kenneth Clark. Brattleboro: The Stephen Greene Press, (1977), small 4to., cloth, dust jacket. xliv, 151, (3) pages. $ 85.00
First U.S. edition though printed by the Curwen Press in England with a new title page. 40 pages of introductory remarks and notes on Stone's engravings followed by 150 pages of reproductions of the engravings done in red, blue and black.

344. (Curwen Press) Symons, A.J.A. EMIN, THE GOVERNOR OF EQUATORIA. London: The Fleuron Ltd., 1928, square 8vo., cloth- backed decorated paper covered boards. (viii), 47 pages. $ 125.00
Limited to 300 numbered copies. Printed by Oliver Simon at The Curwen Press using Van Krimpen's "Lutetia" and with a printed note stating that this was the first use of that type in England. Presentation from the author in calligraphic script on the free endpaper "R.H. Carruthers very amiably from the author." Spine faded.

345. (Curwen Press) Williams, Harold. BOOK CLUBS & PRINTING SOCIETIES OF GREAT BRITAIN AND IRELAND. London: The First Edition Club, 1929, 8vo., decorated cloth. viii, 126 pages. $ 65.00
First edition, limited to 750 copies. (Hart no. 226). Well printed in red and black at the Curwen Press. Discussions of Bibliomania, Scottish Book Clubs, History and Topography, Later Historical and Record Societies, Literary and Text Societies, Collectors, Bibliographical Societies, etc. Pastedowns and endpapers foxed.

346. (Curwen Press) SCENERY OF GREAT BRITAIN AND IRELAND IN AQUATINT AND LITHOGRAPHY 1770–1860, FROM THE LIBRARY OF J.R. ABBEY, A BIBLIOGRAPHICAL CATALOGUE. London: Privately printed at the Curwen Press, 1952, thick 4to., cloth, leather spine label, dust jacket, top edge gilt. xx, 399 pages. $ 850.00

First edition, limited to 500 numbered copies. A magnificent catalogue with 34 colored plates and 54 figures in the text. Full bibliographical descriptions given. The jacket is chipped and spotted. Prospectus loosely inserted.

347. (Cygnet Press) Blake, William. AUGURIES OF INNOCENCE, TOGETHER WITH THE REARRANGEMENT BY DR. JOHN SAMPSON AND A COMMENT BY GEOFFREY KEYNES KT. Burford, Oxfordshire: Cygnet Press, 1975, 8vo., stiff paper wrappers. 18, (4) pages. $ 35.00

Printed in an edition limited to 375 numbered copies by Simon Rendall at the Cygnet Press, in Bell and Union Pearl type on mould-made paper.

348. (Dahlstrom, Grant) Clary, William W. FIFTY YEARS OF BOOK COLLECTING. Los Angeles: The Zamorano Club, 1962, 8vo., cloth-backed boards. 49 pages. $ 60.00

Talk given by William Clary to the Zamorano Club. Illustrations. Printed by Grant Dahlstrom. Spine is age darkened.

349. (Dahlstrom, Grant) Drake, Stillman. THE UNSUNG JOURNALIST AND THE ORIGIN OF THE TELESCOPE. Los Angeles: Zeitlin & Van Brugge, 1976, small 8vo., stapled stiff paper wrappers. 19+(1) pages. $ 20.00

Printed by Grant Dahlstrom, Pasadena, in an edition limited to five hundred & thirty copies for private distribution from Jake & Josephine Zeitlin. Essay about a 1608 newsletter in Holland that noted a patent application for the telescope by Hans Lipperhey, information that quickly resulted in its duplication throughout Europe. Includes facsimile of the original printed newsletter inserted in sleeve.

350. (Dahlstrom, Grant) Dunbar, John R. THE COMBAT AT THE BARRIER. Pasadena: Grant Dahlstrom, 1967, large 4to., stiff wrappers. (vi), 36 (2) pages. $ 45.00

Printed in an edition limited to 300 copies, 100 copies of which are for private distribution. Designed by Grant Dahlstrom and printed by The Castle Press (Davies,52). An account of the extravagant spectacle, le combat a la barriere, that took place in Nancy, seat of the dukes of Lorraine, on the fourteenth of February, 1627. The charm of this occasion has survived over three hundred years, "not because of the splendor of its setting or the nobility of its principals, but rather because it was *enrichy des figures du sieur Jacques Callot.*" Ten plates with commentary follow text.

351. (Dahlstrom, Grant) A HISTORY OF PRINTING TYPES. (Pittsburgh: Grant Dahlstrom, 1927), 4to. 1 leaf. $ 30.00

A facsimile of the title page from *A History of Printing Types* by Daniel B. Updyke, done as a student project by Grant Dahlstrom (1902–1980) during his year as a student at Carnegie Tech in 1927. Crease-marks from folding in middle of page, with closed tears on margins and some foxing. Notation at bottom of page in ink identifying it as Dahlstrom's work.

352. (Dahlstrom, Grant) [ONE PIECE OF EPHEMERA PRINTED IN 1936]. N.P.: (Grant Dahlstrom, 1936), 8vo., self paper wrappers. (4) pages. $ 15.00

An invitation to a birthday celebration and concert on May 29, 1936. Color wood engraving by George J. Cox on cover. This party featured live music by the Coolidge Pro Arte Quartette, a recital by Dorothee Manski of the *Metropolitan Opera,* and the Bruin Bugle Quartette playing a call to a Polonaise through the garden. Dancing afterward.

353. (Dahlstrom, Grant) [STUDENT PROJECT BY GRANT DAHLSTROM WHILE A STUDENT AT CARNEGIE TECH, 1926]. Pittsburgh: n.p., 1926, folio. 1 sheet. $ 45.00

Sheet of Latin text printed on thick paper, with hand colored heading and paragraph markers. Several practice letters drawn on back. A few lines partially underlined or a letter circled and the page folded. Dahlstrom (1902–1980) was a student in the printing department at Carnegie in 1926, associated with the Laboratory Press and its founder, Porter Garnett.

354. (Dahlstrom, Grant) Beef-Eater. ILLUSTRATIONS OF EATING. Pasadena, CA: Grant Dahlstrom, 1971, square 8vo., two-toned paper-covered boards, dust jacket. (xi), 56, (2) pages. $ 85.00

Printed in an edition limited to 250 copies. Reprints an 1847 book describing culinary practices from around the globe. Dust jacket torn near spine and slightly spotted.

355. (Dahlstrom, Grant) Warde, Beatrice. STANLEY MORISON. (Pasadena: Grant Dahlstrom, 1967), 8vo., stiff paper wrappers. (ii), 16 pages. $ 25.00

Limited to edition of 500 copies. Warde delivered this speech at the Paul A. Bennett Memorial Lectures in New York, October 25, 1967. Morison, who had passed away just two weeks earlier, had been scheduled to appear at the meeting. Frontispiece is black and white photograph of Morison.

356. (Dahlstrom, Grant) W. IRVING WAY, 1853–1931, AN AUTOBIOGRAPHICAL FRAGMENT. N.P.: Reprinted from the February 1968 issue of Hoja Volante by Roby Wentz and Grant Dahlstrom for a joint meeting of the Roxburghe and Zamorano Clubs, 1974, 8vo., decorated paper wrappers, paper cover label. vi, 6 pages. $ 35.00

Reprint of this autobiographical sketch by Way. With spread page reproduction of Way's Kelmscott Press commission. Combined with Williams to form Way & Williams. Presentation from Wentz to Kit Currie.

357. (Dahlstrom, Grant) Edelstein, J.M. (editor). GARLAND FOR JAKE ZEITLIN ON THE OCCASION OF HIS 65TH BIRTHDAY & THE ANNIVERSARY OF HIS 40TH YEAR IN THE BOOK TRADE. Los Angeles: Grant Dahlstrom & Saul Marks, 1967, tall 8vo., orange cloth back with patterned cloth sides, paper spine label. (x), 131 pages. $ 95.00

First edition, limited to 800 copies. Typography by Marks and printing by Dahlstrom. With nice presentation from Zeitlin on half-title.

358. (Daniel Press) Jones, Robert. THE MUSES GARDIN FOR DELIGHTS, OR THE FIFT BOOK OF AYRES, ONELY FOR THE LUTE, THE BASE-VYOLL AND THE VOICE. Oxford: Daniel Press, 1901, 8vo., limp vellum, leather ties, deckle edges, bound by Mrs. Daniel. (vi),vi, (4), 44 (4) pages. $ 250.00

Printed in an edition limited to 130 numbered copies. (Warren, pp.127-8). Edited, with an introduction by William Barclay Squire. A reprint, without the music, of the only known copy of the 1610 edition by the composer and poet Robert Jones, from Lord Ellsmere's library at Bridgewater House, London. Bookplate of Sibyl Colefax and Arthur Colefax on front pastedown. One tie lacking and one tie short.

359. (Dawson, Muir) DON SANTIAGO KIRKER (REPRINTED FROM THE SANTA FE REPUBLICAN, NOVEMBER 20, 1847). Los Angeles: Privately Printed, 1948, 12mo., cloth. (iv), 14, (6) pages. $ 45.00

Printed in an edition limited to 200 copies and signed by Muir Dawson on the colophon. Bound by C. Frank Fox. James Kirker was one of the most colorful of the early mountain men. An account of his life was originally published in the St. Louis Post, but no copy of that issue is known to have survived (Introduction by Glen Dawson). Notes by Arthur Woodward follow text. Label of previous owner on front pastedown.

361. (De La More Press) Clarke, Sir Ernest (editor). THE CHRONICLE OF JOCELIN OF BRAKELOND: A PICTURE OF MONASTIC LIFE IN THE DAYS OF ABBOT SAMSON. (London): De La More Press, 1903, 12mo., paper-covered boards. xliv, 285+(1). $ 25.00

Published by Alexander Moring at the De La More Press, London, and printed by Butler & Tanner at The Selwood Printing Works. Edited and with a preface by Sir Ernest Clarke. Twelfth century memoirs of monastic life at Bury Abbey. With the seal of Abbot Samson as frontispiece. Bookplate of previous owner on front pastedown endpaper. Pages uncut.

362. (De Vinne Press) CATALOGUE OF AN EXHIBITION OF SELECTED WORKS OF THE POETS LAUREATE OF ENGLAND. New York: The Grolier Club, 1901, 8vo., paper covered boards paper spine label. xx, 81+(1) pages. $ 45.00

Printed in an edition of 300 copies on hand-made paper at the De Vinne Press. Mezzotint portrait of Ben Johnson by S. Arlent Edwards as frontis. Chart of the poet laureates chronologically arranged, from Chaucer to Alfred Austin (1896). With collations of their books. Spine chipped, worn at extremities.

363. (De Vinne Press) Penfield, Frederick Courtland. THE MOTOR THAT WENT TO COURT, A FACT-STORY, WITH RANDOM ILLUSTRATIONS. N.P.: Privately printed, 1909, 8vo., half vellum with paper covered boards, paper cover label, top edge gilt, fore and bottom edge deckled. (x), 92, (2) pages. $ 45.00

First edition. As a Christmas token, the Penfields had this story, which was written by Mr. Penfield and first appeared in The Century Magazine, printed and bound by the De Vinne Press. The delightful tale of a motor car and how it helped to strengthen "strained international relations" during a trip through Spain is complemented by 26 black and white illustrations. Presentation copy. Cover lightly soiled.

364. (De Vinne Press) SOME ACCOUNT OF THE "GIBBS-CHANNING" PORTRAIT OF GEORGE WASHINGTON PAINTED BY GILBERT STUART. New York: Privately Printed, 1900, 8vo., cloth, leather spine label. (v), 26, (3) pages. $ 75.00

Privately printed in an edition limited to 200 copies by the De Vinne Press. Provenance and discussion of the Gilbert Stuart portrait of Washington painted from life in September, 1795 and sold soon after to the painter's friend Colonel George Gibb. When this book was published in 1900, the painting was owned by Mr. S.P. Avery of New York, who purchased it in 1889. Engraving as frontis and others in text.

365. (Denrich Press) Thorp, Willard Brown. PERSPECTIVES OF THE SPIRIT. Chula Vista, CA: Denrich Press, (1910), large 12mo., paper covered boards. 94 pages. $ 25.00

First edition thus. Inscribed by the author on front free endpaper to May Wise, with her bookplate on front pastedown, signed by Florence England Nosworthy. A book of aphorisms on spiritual themes and daily life. Some stains on covers, worn at extremities. X-Lib, with a few markings on edges.

366. (Ditchling Press) Cammell, Charles Richard. XXI POEMS. Edinburgh: The Poseidon Press, 1943, small 8vo., paper wrappers. (5), 28, (2) pages. $ 75.00

Second edition. Printed in an edition limited to 250 copies. Signed by author, "With the author's compliments Chas Cammell. A collection of 21 poems which have been printed on Batchelor Handmade Paper by H.C.C. Pepler at his Ditchling Press. A letter from Cammell to Mrs. Badger dated April 2nd, 1954 is loosely inserted.

367. (Doomsday Press) Eckman, James. WEEK ENDS WITH TOM CLELAND. Rochester, MN: The Doomsday Press, 1971, stiff paper wrappers, front cover label portrait of Cleland. (vii), 12, (2) pages. $ 20.00

Limited to 150 copies. James Eckman spent week ends with Cleland in designing the Mayo brothers' 100th anniversary official seal. Story of their relationship. The portrait of Cleland on the front cover is by Rockwell Kent.

368. (Doves Press) IN JUNE OR JULY MR. COBDEN-SANDERSON WILL PUBLISH AT THE DOVES PRESS. N.P. (but Hammersmith): The Doves Press, 1914, single leaf 6.5" x 9", printed on both sides, some edges deckled. $ 17.50

Publication notice for a collection of poems by Ann Shelley. Also includes notice of two other works in preparation: a collection of poems by Keats and *The Rape of Lucrece* by Shakespeare.

369. (Doves Press) TORQUATO TASSO. N.P. (but Hammersmith): The Doves Press, 1913, 8vo., single leaf. (4) pages. $ 25.00

Publication notice for *Torquato Tasso* by Ein Schauspiel von Goethe. Printed in two colors. Includes notice of three other recent publications and three works in preparation, all by or relating to the works of William Shakespeare. Also contains information on bindings for the works and how to order.

370. (Doves Press) AMANTIUM IRAE: LETTERS TO TWO FRIENDS 1864–1867. Hammersmith: The Doves Press, 1914, 8vo., original full limp vellum. 141, (2) pages. $ 1,500.00

Printed in an edition limited to 153 copies, this being one of 150 printed on handmade paper. (Doves Press, catalogue Raisonne pg 23). Letters addressed by T. J. Cobden-Sanderson to his dear friends, Lord and Lady (Katherine Stanley) Amberley in the years 1864 to 1867. It has been printed in red and black, and has a gravure portrait frontispiece. This book has the smallest limitation of all the Doves Press Books. Presentation copy "To Maude Stanley in memorium from her old affectionate friend the writer, C.-S. 14 October 1913." One corner bumped.

371. (Doves Press) APRIL. Hammersmith: The Doves Press, 1915, 8vo., self paper wrappers. (4) pages. $ 25.00

Announcement of Goethe's Lieder, Gedichte, & Balladen. With notes of other recent and forthcoming publications.

INSCRIBED

372. (Doves Press) Browning, Robert. DRAMATIS PERSONAE. Hammersmith: The Doves Press, 1910, 8vo., full original limp vellum. 202, (1) pages. $ 950.00

Printed in an edition limited to 265 copies, this being one of 250 on handmade paper. (Doves Press, catalogue Raisonne pg 23). A poem by Robert Browning, in which the text is that of the first edition of 1864, and printed in red and black. Presentation in the hand of T.J. Cobden-Sanderson "To Marie Little with the best of wishes from her ever well-wishing friends, T.J. and Annie Cobden-Sanderson May 1912."

373. (Doves Press) ENGLISH BIBLE CONTAINING THE OLD TESTAMENT & THE NEW. Five volumes. Hammersmith: The Doves Press, (1903–1905], five folio volumes (13 3/16 x 9 3/16 inches; 335 x 234 mm), full levant morocco, gilt-lettered spines with raised bands, board edges and turn-ins ruled in gilt, top edge gilt, others uncut.
                                                          $ 12,500.00

One of 500 copies printed on handmade paper by T.J. Cobden-Sanderson and Emery Walker. (Clark Library, Kelmscott and Doves, pp. 90–92, Huntington Library, Great Books in Great Editions, 7, Ransom, Private Presses, p. 251, no. 6, Tomkinson, p. 54, no. 6, Hutner and Kelly, Century for the Century, 4.) "This edition of the Bible is considered the masterpiece of the Doves Press... The type is a particularly crisp and faithful version of Jenson's fifteenth-century roman. It was cut in only one size, which was used in all of the half-hundred issues of the Press. When the Press was discontinued in 1916, the type and matrices were destroyed by Cobden-Sanderson to prevent their misuse." (Huntington Library, Great Books in Great Editions) The distinctive red initial letters, executed by hand by Edward Johnston, are described by Ransom (Private Presses, p. 56) as "a pattern for all time of complexity reduced to the minimum of simplicity." This copy inscribed on rear fly-leaf of Volume I: "The Magnum Opus of my husband, T.J. Cobden Sanderson's/printing at the Doves Press./Anne Cobden-Sanderson June 22nd 1926/San Francisco." Bound by Sangorski & Sutcliffe (in the mid 1930s?) in full crimson levant morocco. Minimal foxing in Volume I. Bookplate removed from front pastedown of each volume. Laid in is a

Item 372

typed exhibit card stating that this copy (from the collection of John Howell) was exhibited in the Temple of Religion at the 1939 Golden Gate International Exposition. Also laid in is the original Doves Press two-leaf subscription form for the Bible.

374. (Doves Press) Goethe, Johann Wolfgang von. FAUST ERSTER TEIL. Hammersmith: Doves Press, 1906, 8vo., limp vellum. 260 pages. $ 850.00
Limited to 325 copies of which this is one of 300 printed on paper. (catalogue Raisonne, p.20; Tompkinson, Ransom no.10). Printed in black and red. Bookplate.

375. (Doves Press) IN PREPARATION. N.P. (but Hammersmith): The Doves Press, 1911, 8vo., some edges deckled. (4) pages. $ 30.00
Notice of four works in preparation, including works by Wordsworth, Shakespeare, etc. with a list of recently published works, including Goethe's Faust, Shakespeare's Sonnets, and more. Printed in two colors.

376. (Doves Press) MacKail, J.W. WILLIAM MORRIS, AN ADDRESS DELIVERED. Hammersmith: The Doves Press, 1901, 8vo., original limp vellum, with gilt-lettered spine. (ii), 28 pages. $ 450.00
Printed in an edition limited to 315 copies, this being one of the 300 printed on paper. (Doves Press, catalogue Raisonne pg 16; Tomkinson pg 52). An address delivered by J.W. MacKail on November 11, 1900, at Kelmscott House, about the activities and friendships of William Morris. It has been printed in red and black by T.J. Cobden-Sanderson and Emery Walker. This is the third publication of the press.

[67]

377. (Doves Press) McKail, J.W. WILLIAM MORRIS, AN ADDRESS DELIV-ERED. Hammersmith: The Doves Press, 1901, 8vo., original limp vellum, with gilt-lettered spine, in a cloth chemise with a quarter morocco and a cloth covered boards slipcase. (ii), 28 pages. $ 3,750.00

Printed in an edition limited to 315 copies, this being one of the 15 printed on vellum. (Doves Press, catalogue Raisonne pg 16; Tomkinson pg 52). An address delivered by J.W. McKail on November 11, 1900, at Kelmscott House, about the activities and friendships of William Morris. It has been printed in red and black by T.J. Cobden-Sanderson and Emery Walker. This is the third publication of the press. Includes a John Saks bookplate.

378. (Doves Press) NOTICE IN JUNE WILL BE PUBLISHED. Hammersmith: The Doves Press, 1907, (9 x 6.75 inches), single leaf. $ 25.00

Includes the publishing schedule, price, and limitations for the AREOPAGITICA, SARTOR RESARTUS, and APOLOGIA.

379. (Doves Press) RECENT PUBLICATIONS 1907–1909. N.P. (but London): The Doves Press, 1909, 6.5˝ x 9.25˝, single leaf approximately. printed on both sides. $ 15.00

Notice of publication of eight works by the Doves Press from 1907 to 1909, including works on Shakespeare, Caxton, etc. Also includes notice of six works in preparation. Printed in black with titles all in capitals. Some minor spotting and general discoloration due to age.

380. (Doves Press) Tennyson, Alfred Lord. SEVEN POEMS AND TWO TRANS-LATIONS. Hammersmith: Doves Press, 1902, limp vellum. 55 pages. $ 3,750.00

Limited to 325 copies of which this is one of 25 copies to be printed on vellum. (catalogue RAISONNE p.22; Ransom and Tomkinson no.4). The two translations from Homer are printed in red, and Tennyson's poems are printed in black.

381. (Doves Press) TO THE SUBSCRIBERS OF THE DOVES PRESS APOLO-GIA. Hammersmith: The Doves Press, 1914, 8vo., broadside. $ 20.00

Tomkinson p.52. A statement related to the 1914 publication of Amantiun Irae, reaffirming the presses mission to "insist upon and to illustrate, -the Vision of Cosmic Order, Order wrought in rhythm & touched with Beauty and Delight."

382. (Duensing, Paul Hayden) 25, A QUARTER-CENTURY OF TRIUMPHS AND DISASTERS IN THE MICROCOSM OF THE PRIVATE PRESS & TYPEFOUNDRY OF PAUL HAYDEN DUENSING. Kalamazoo: Duensing, 1976, small 4to., stiff paper wrappers. (36) pages. $ 65.00

First edition, limited to 250 copies. Contains a bibliography of books printed by Duensing.

383. (Duensing, Paul Hayden) Hoffmann, Alfred (translator). PROCEEDINGS OF THE MASTER PRINTERS OF BASEL AGAINST JOHANN PISTORIUS, TYPEFOUNDER, BEFORE THE LOWER COUNCIL OF THAT CITY DUR-ING JUNE, 1698. (Vicksburg, MI): privately printed, (1982), small 8vo., stiff paper wrappers. (16) pages. $ 25.00

Printed in an edition limited to 120 copies. 60 copies distributed to attendees of the Oxford Typefounding Conference in July, 1982, and 40 to the Typocrafters meeting in Kalamazoo, October 1-3, 1982. Text set by hand in 14 point Janson and "an experimental casting of a 28 point Fraktur" and printed on Louvaine Supreme paper at The Private Press and Typefoundry of Paul Hayden Duensing, Vicksburg, Michigan.

384. (Duensing, Paul Hayden) Langendijk, Pieter. TWO DUTCH POEMS. N.P.: (Paul Hayden Duensing, 1975), small 8vo., paper wrappers. 8 leaves. $ 20.00
Second, revised edition; limited to 190 copies. Two poems about printing; one claims that Koster invented printing.

385. (Duensing, Paul Hayden) [LOT OF 14 PIECES OF TYPE SPECIMEN EPHEMERA FROM THE PRIVATE PRESS AND TYPEFOUNDRY OF PAUL HAYDEN DUENSING]. Kalamazoo, MI: Paul Hayden Duensing. $ 35.00
A varied lot of types and ornaments, including a broadside on *The Book of Hours*, set and printed as a specimen of the 24pt. XVI Century Roman (No.13003), a brochure as a specimen of 16 point Jessen (9027), a sheet featuring 14 point Rustica, a broadside *To The Art of Lettercasting*, printed in an issue of 200 copies for The Typophiles, a card of *Unciala for Christmas*, and other interesting items.

386. (Duensing, Paul Hayden) Neville, Harry A. GRAPHIC HISTORY OF THE ART OF PRINTING, INK OR WHIM. N.P.: (Private Press of Paul Duensing, 1967), 8vo., stiff paper wrappers. (18) pages. $ 45.00
Limited to 150 copies. With highly decorative title page printed in red and blue.

387. (Duensing, Paul Hayden) PRIVATE PRESS AND TYPEFOUNDRY OF PAUL HAYDEN DUENSING. Kalamazoo, MI: Privately printed, 1967, 8vo., paper wrappers. 10 pages. $ 35.00
Printed in an edition limited to 341 copies. Being a checklist of this private press's work with a biographical essay on the press and specimen sheets of its type and ornaments. Fine.

388. (Duensing, Paul Hayden) A SHELF-LIST OF TYPEFOUNDERS SPECIMEN BOOKS. Kalamazoo, MI: The Private Press and Typefoundry of Paul Hayden Duensing, (1969), 8vo., stiff paper wrappers. (17) pages. $ 35.00
Limited to 200 copies. A bibliography describing 56 typefounders specimen books. With photocopies of articles about Duensing loosely inserted. Signed by John DePol. Small spot on front cover.

389. (Duensing, Paul Hayden) STEREO-TRYPES — 94 DOUBLE-ENTENDRES; SUGGESTIONS FOR NAMES OF TYPEFACES WE CAN DO WITHOUT; NOW ISSUED AS A WARNING TO TYPE-FLOUNDERS EVERYWHERE. Kalamazoo, MI: The Private Press and Typefoundry of Paul Hayden Duensing, 1970, small 8vo., stiff paper wrappers. (8) pages. $ 20.00
Limited to an edition of 250 copies. Created by the authors as a "greeting to their friends and associates...on All Fools' Day, April 1, 1970, a holiday which seems vaguely related to anyone who would be in this field in the first place." Small stains on bottom of front cover.

390. (Edition Tiessen) EDITION TIESSEN, LIEFERBARE BUCHER I / II. Two volumes. Neu Isenburg: Edition Tiessen, n.d. (1996), oblong small 8vo., stapled, stiff paper wrappers. (36); (30) pages. $ 20.00
Two catalogues from Edition Tiessen, the first listing 29 books and 3 "special publications" (items distributed gratis to established customers) from the Ed. Tiessen, plus 2 sets (1962-73 & 1974–1986) of catalogues from the "Versandbuchhandlung Wolfgang Tiessen," with 84 illustrations, an introduction by W. Tiessen, and reprints of two reviews or excerpts of reviews of the Ed. Tiessen. The second lists 20 books with 74 illustrations and reprints of 6 reviews. Book entries include bibliographic and physical description, edition information, and sometimes a quotation from the text. Accompanying illustrations show bindings, covers, title pages, text illustrations, or text specimens. A prospectus for publication no.76, "Zen Stories," and a price list for books still available as of 9/1/96 are loosely inserted under the cover of Cat. no. I.

391. (Edition Tiessen) Tiessen, Wolfgang et al. DIE EDITION TIESSEN. Neu-Isenburg: Edition Tiessen, Verlag Wolfgang Tiessen, 1995, tall 4to., cloth, paper label on spine & front cover. 29, (3), 143, 25, (3) pages. $ 102.00

Signed by Wolfgang Tiessen on the colophon. A retrospective and commemorative publication marking the discontinuation of the Edition Tiessen and the retirement of W. Tiessen from involvement in printing. In three parts: two articles by Tiessen and three articles on the Ed. Tiessen by other authors; 190 illustrations of title pages, book illustrations, bindings and text samples from the Ed. Tiessen; and a catalogue of the 80 regular imprints and the 27 special publications from the Edition Tiessen, along with a list of illustrators with biographical data for each, and bio-bibliographic information on W. Tiessen.

SPECIAL EDITION

392. (Edition Tiessen) Tiessen, Wolfgang et al. DIE EDITION TIESSEN. Two volumes. Neu-Isenburg: Edition Tiessen, Verlag Wolfgang Tiessen, 1995, tall 4to., cloth, paper spine and cover label, slipcase, with a quarter-cloth-&-boards binder containing loose sheets. 29, (3), 143, 25, (3) pages, with 33 sheets in the binder. $ 350.00

Special edition, signed by Wolfgang Tiessen on the colophon, with a extra portfolio of specimens of marbled and printed patterned papers. A retrospective and commemorative publication marking the discontinuation of the Edition Tiessen and the retirement of W. Tiessen from involvement in printing. In three parts: two articles by Tiessen and three articles on the Ed. Tiessen by other authors; 190 illustrations of title pages, book illustrations, bindings and text samples from the Ed. Tiessen; and a catalogue of the 80 regular imprints and the 27 special publications from the Edition Tiessen, along with a list of illustrators with biographical data for each, and bio-bibliographic information on W. Tiessen. The binder accompanying this vol. has a backing of the same fabric and color, with paper colored boards, and contains 32 samples of patterned paper (approx. 5x7 in.) affixed to stiff paper stock, and one sheet identifying their designers, and the books (and bindings) for which they were used. Now out of print.

393. (Editions Petrouchka) Haly, Richard. ESTAMPIDA: A LYRIC FOR DANCING TRANSLATED FROM THE PROVENÇAL OF RAIMBAUT DE VAQUEIRAS. Berkeley: Editions Petrouchka, 1982, 4to., decorated stiff paper wrappers, cord tied, edges deckled. (18) pages. $ 65.00

Limited to an edition of 40 signed copies. Provençal Estampida, the courtly dance of the 12th–14th century, provides the earliest surviving examples of written instrumental music. The famous troubadour song, "Kalenda maia," was written by Raimbaut de Vaqueiras and set to an existing melody. The musical notation for the first verse provides the cover illustration. Printed on Hammer and Anvil paper by Wesley B. Tanner.

394. Ege, Otto F. (Editor). ORIGINAL LEAVES FROM FAMOUS BIBLES NINE CENTURIES 1121–1935 A.D. Cleveland: Otto F. Edge, n.d. (1945?), folio, portfolio containing thirty-eight leaves from Bibles, each mounted and matted separately, with an informational card appended to each. $ 7,500.00

The late Otto F. Ege, Dean of the Cleveland Institute of Art and Lecturer on History of the Book at the School of Library Science, Western Reserve University, over a period of forty years, collected leaves from famous and rare Bibles and Testaments, dating from the twelfth to the twentieth century. In an effort to increase awareness of the history of the book through the dissemination of individual pages to schools, libraries, calligraphers, and printers, he prepared portfolios with each leaf separately mounted and matted and appropriately annotated. Included here are such famous examples as Bruce Rogers' 1935 Oxford Lectern Bible, the 1903–1905 Doves Bible, both the first and second issues of the 1611 King James Bible, the second issue of the Eliot Indian Bible (1685), several early polyglot Bibles, a suppressed Luther Bible (1541), the 1497 Koberger Bible, and others. With the original introductory leaf.

395. (Ellis, Richard) VIGIL OF VENUS. New York: The Cheshire House, 1931, small 4to., parchment-backed boards, top edge gilt. (ii), 31, (3) pages. $ 30.00

Limited to 875 copies printed by Richard Ellis for Cheshire House. Decorations in orange ink. Introduction and translation by Joseph Auslander and reprint of an essay by Walter Pater.

396. (Elm Tree Press) Dana, Charles L. (editor). FRAGMENTS FROM VERMONT'S PARNASSUS. Edited by Charles L. Dana. Woodstock, VT: The Elm Tree Press, 1929, 8vo., cloth spine, paper over boards, paper spine label. viii, 8, 42 pages. $ 25.00
A collection of poetry by Vermont citizens printed at this Vermont private press. With the bookplate of Dana. Soiled covers.

397. (Elm Tree Press) French, Mary M. B. A LITTLE ABOUT A NUMBER OF THINGS. Woodstock, VT: Elm Tree Press, 1948, large 12mo., cloth. (vi), 104 pages.
$ 25.00
Printed at the Elm Tree Press by William Edwin Rudge, III, who was later director of the Yale University Press (Barlow, page 14). With seven illustrations by Helen P. Chalfant. A little about courtesy, eels, grass, a spring harvest (maple sugaring), the ginkgo tree, amber, etc. X-Libris bookplate of William Stone on front pastedown.

398. (Elmete Press) Moran, James. HERALDIC INFLUENCE ON EARLY PRINTERS' DEVICES. Leeds: The Elmete Press, 1978, small 4to., decorated cloth, top edge gilt. xvi, 104 pages. $ 135.00
First edition, limited to 475 numbered copies. An excellent study by Moran, well printed, by this British press in two colors throughout.

399. (Enitharmon Press) Halliwell, Steven. ALAN CLODD AND THE ENITHARMON PRESS, A CHECKLIST OF HIS PUBLICATIONS 1967–1987 AND PRIVATE PRINTINGS 1958–1998, COMPILED BY STEVEN HALLIWELL WITH A TRIBUTE BY JEREMY REED. London: Enitharmom Press, 1998, large 8vo., buckram, paper spine label. 80 pages. $ 41.00
Limited to 265 numbered copies, including 200 in this version. Alan Clodd starting printing in 1958 and founded the E. Press, largely a poetry press, in 1967. In 1987 he turned the Press over to Stephen Stuart-Smith but has continued printing on his own. This checklist, compiled by S. Halliwell with introductions by Clodd and the poet and novelist Jeremy Reed, lists 118 Enitharmon Press titles, 33 ephemera, 37 private printings, 14 "ghosts" (announced, not published), and some catalogues. There are 7 tipped-in black-and-white reproductions of title pages, text, and book illustrations, including one affixed to the front cover, and a photograph of Clodd. With indexes.

400. (Enschedé) Blumenthal, Walter Hart. BOOKMEN'S TRIO VENTURES IN LITERARY PHILANDERING. Worcester: Achille J. St. Onge, 1961, small 8vo., parchment-backed marbled paper covered boards. 86 pages. $ 35.00
First edition, finely printed in an edition limited to 500 copies by Joh. Enschedé. Three books about books stories.

401. (Enschedé) Blumenthal, Walter Hart. CHARM OF BOOKS. Philadelphia: Friends of the Free Library of Philadelphia, 1961, small 8vo., parchment-backed marbled paper covered boards. (viii), 112 pages. $ 35.00
First edition, limited to 500 copies finely printed by Joh. Enschedé. Short biographical essays on the authors behind the world's literary classics and rare books.

402. (Enschedé) Braches, Ernst. STEADFAST TIN SOLDIER OF JOH. ENSCHEDE EN ZONEN, HAARLEM. Amsterdam: Just Enschedé, 1992, large 8vo., paper covered boards made from linen rags with typescript design on front cover. 53, (3) pages. $ 150.00
Standard edition, limited to 175 numbered copies. A history and discussion of Enschedé No. 6 type, with a specimen giving a complete survey available to the printer. Chapters on the appearance and revival of Enschedé No. 6, and its use by various printers, including D.B. Updike and The Stanbrook Abbey Press (1955). Text designed and handset by Bram de Does. Offset illustrations printed by Jan de Jong, Amsterdam.

403. (Enschedé) DIES EST LAETITIAE, HET MIDDELEEUWSCHE GEZANG GEDRUKT MET IN ZAND GEGO TEN LETTERS. Haarlem: Joh. Enschedé en Zonen, n.d., 16mo., stiff paper wrappers, printed envelope. (8) pages followed by the 8 page facsimile. $ 45.00

With text in different languages including English. Enschedé cast the type used to print the facsimile in sand in an attempt to demonstrate that this older method used by early printers could be used successfully.

404. (Enschedé) Lamb, Charles. NEW YEAR'S EVE/OUDEJAARSAVOND. (Haarlem: Joh. Enschedé en Zonen, 1957), large 12mo., paper-covered boards. 33, (2)pages.
$ 17.50

One of the author's essays from Elia, printed in English and Dutch by the publisher as a New Year's greeting for friends. Text type and open capitals on the title belong to the Romulus family; initials are Molé Foliate capitals. Portrait of Lamb by S.L. Hartz. Pastepaper for binding was hand-made in Denmark. Foreword by poet J.C. Bloem. Slip inserted with New Year's greeting from the publisher. Bookplate of John DePol on front pastedown.

405. (Enschedé) Rubens, Maria. 'T IS TOCH VERGEVEN', TWEE BRIEVEN VAN MARIA RUBENS AAN HAAR MAN JAN RUBENS UIT HET JAAR MDLXXI. Haarlen, Netherlands: Joh. Enschedé en Zonen, 1962, 12mo., cloth. 76 pages.
$ 65.00

Booklet produced and sent as a Christmas and New Year's greeting to friends of the printer. Two letters from Maria Rubens to her husband while he was in prison and facing the death penalty for adultery. The couple were the parents of yet unborn artist Peter Paul Rubens. This is a revised reprint of the original 1939 limited edition version prepared by Professor W. G. Hellinga. Reprint in 12 pts. Lutetia roman and italic from presses of Joh. Enschedé en Zonen. Typography by Josephine Holt. Contents divided into three sections: first Dutch, then French and English translations. Leaflet with holiday greeting inserted. Inscription on front inside paste-down by noted British author and type designer Alfred Fairbank.

406. (Enschedé) Schouten, Alet. VIGNETTEN VAN ENSCHEDÉ OP HAARLEMS STRAMIEN. (Haarlem): Joh. Enschedé en Zonen, 1978, small 8vo., paper covered boards. 69+(1) pages. $ 45.00

A handsomely produced book commemorating the 275th jubilee of venerable foundry Joh. Enschedé en Zonen. Co-written and edited by Schouten and Simone Schell. Journal format notes landmark events in Enschedé's history in tandem with those of its hometown of Haarlem. Lavish use of firm's contemporary vignettes in various colors to illustrate text. Printed in Jan van Krimpen's Romulus type. Binding by Brandt-Weesp; typography by B. de Does.

407. (Equinox Press) Lawrence, D.H. WE NEED ONE ANOTHER. New York: Equinox, 1933, large 12mo., cloth. 68 pages. $ 45.00

Two essays by Lawrence, "We Need One Another" and "The Real Thing" on the psychological relationships between the sexes. (Roberts no. A64, Hart pp. 36-41). It is illustrated with drawings by John P. Heins. The four illustrations were criticized for not being appropriate for the book because of their erotic nature, and Equinox received several letters of protest. It was set in Linotype Garamond and no work by hand was done on the physical book. Remnants of dust jacket present.

408. (Esslemont, David) Bewick, Thomas. BIRDS, IMPRESSIONS FROM ORIGINAL WOOD-BLOCKS. Montgomery, Wales: David Esslemont, 1997, large 8vo., paste paper covered boards, paper spine label. 7+(1) pages followed by 17 numbered leaves of prints. $ 180.00

Printed in an edition limited to 100 copies of which this is one of 50 copies bound in boards. 17 illustrations printed by David Esslemont from the original wood blocks, now in the possession of the Central Library of Newcastle upon Tyne, for Bewick's History of British Birds. British Birds was one of the most successful works of the English wood engraver Thomas Bewick (1753–1828) and appeared in 8 editions from 1797 to 1826. The accompanying brochure indicates the date of the edition in which each illustration first appeared, along with the page number and, sometimes, notes from Bewick's own records on the sources of his engravings, e.g. "taken from a drawing presented to the author," "drawn from one shot at Axwell Park, near Newcastle upon Tyne," etc. With some references.

409. (Esslemont, David) THE FALL OF XENOPHON. Montgomery: David Esslemont, n.d., large 8vo., paper covered boards, with a paper spine label. 12, (3) pages.
$ 50.00
Printed in an edition limited to 300 numbered copies. This story was originally published in The Hive of Ancient and Modern Literature, (Solomon Hodgson, Newcastle, 1799). This amusing eighteenth-century tale recounts the disasters and misfortunes that befall a modest man when he dines with his neighbor. The illustrations are adaptations and enlargements of four contemporary wood engravings by Thomas Bewick.

410. (Esslemont, David) Sandford, Lettice. A WOOD ENGRAVING BY LETTICE SANDFORD. Severn Villa, Powys, Wales: Esslemont and Grossman, 1997, small 4to., card portfolio with paper label and print in paper and tissue protector, one folded sheet (8vo., (4) pages) inserted. $ 35.00
Limited to 115 copies. Printed by David Esslemont from the original block by Lettice Sandford, a student of Blair Hughes-Stanton, for the frontispiece to Hero and Leander by Marlowe, originally published by the Golden Hours Press, London, 1933. Sandford also founded the Boar's Head Press with her husband Christopher and provided illustrations for the Golden Cockerell Press, which she and her husband took over in 1933. In the accompanying insert, Carol Grossman mentions the "great delicacy of details of [Sanderson's] work, accomplished with dexterous combinations of deep blacks and extremely fine white lines." Engraving printed on Japan vellum.

411. (Esslemont, David) THE WOOD ENGRAVINGS OF DAVID GENTLEMAN. Montgomery, Powys, Wales: David Esslemont, 2000, 4to., full black buckram, red paper spine label, cloth slipcase. xviii, (ii), 131, (2) pages. $ 450.00
Printed in an edition limited to 350 numbered copies. The first collection of David Gentleman's engravings to be published. The book contains over 300 wood engravings and includes work ranging from book illustrations from early books done while a student at the Royal College of Art to the well-known engravings for Clare's "The Shepherd's Calendar." Also included are designs for postage stamps, press advertisements, book covers, and all the engravings for the Charing Cross Underground mural. With only a few exceptions the engravings are printed directly from the artist's original wood blocks. Fiona MacCarthy contributes an introduction which describes Gentleman's upbringing and training and reveals the influences on his work. She also reviews his work not only as a wood engraver but also as an artist and designer, acknowledging his unique creative skills and sensitivity. With a foreword by Gentleman.

412. (Fahey Press) Juniper, William. THE LAW OF DRINKING. San Francisco: Herbert and Peter Fahey, 1935, large 12mo., cloth, paper cover label. 27+(1) pages. $ 55.00
No stated limitation. Loosely based, according to the author, on that Solemne and Joviall Disputation, Theoreticke and Practicke; briefly Shadowing the Law of Drinking, Together, with the solemnities and controversies occuring: Fully and freely discussed according to the Civill Law, written in Latin by Richard Braithwaite in 1626. "How you may beare your drinke, and so prevaile, That though some fall, your brains may never faile."

413. (Fanfrolica Press) Lindsay, Jack & P.R. Stephensen (editors). LONDON APHRODITE. Six numbers, the complete set of this periodical. London: The Fanfrolica Press, 1928–1929, 8vo., stiff paper wrappers. $ 250.00
Ransom No.22. Cave calls this periodical "a deliberately outrageous and iconoclastic 'little magazine,' whose title was intended to challenge The London Mercury. Like most little magazines it was a complete failure. Only six numbers were planned, and all were published, but they ruined the press." With con-

tributions by a number of well known authors including Liam O'Flaherty, Sacheverell Sitwell, T.F. Powys, Rhys Davies, Aldous Huxley, and Lawrence Powys. With prospectus to series loosely inserted in the first volume. First volume has some yellowing around edges of covers.

414. (Farquhar, Samuel T.) Bacon, Francis. OF STUDIES. San Francisco: (Johnck & Seeger), 1928, large 12mo., paper boards, paper cover label. (9) pages. $ 200.00
Printed in an edition of 50 copies to distribute to friends. Book designed and type hand set by Samuel T. Farquhar, his first work of type composition. Presswork done by well-known printer Lawton Kennedy, and the work completed in the shop of Johnck & Seeger in San Francisco. Bacon's famous brief essay on study and learning, with his famous quotation: "Some books are to be tasted, others to be swallowed, and some few to be chewed and digested...." Minor abrasion to front board.

415. Ferrand, Michel. GERMINAL. New York: George Wittenborn, 1958, 8vo., paper covered boards. Unpaginated (10 double leaves). $ 350.00
Printed in an edition limited to 75 numbered copies. (Artist and the Book 130). A poem by Michel Ferrand illustrated with six etchings by American book artist Terry Haass. Haass' work is "notable for refinement of technique as well as fitness to text." Signed in ink below the colophon by Terry Haass.

416. (Ferriss, Lester R.) DuRee, Vikki (translator). A LETTER FROM GUATEMALA. Berkeley: Bancroft Library Press, 1994, 8vo., stiff paper wrappers. (4) pages. $ 45.00
Printed in an edition limited to 35 copies on an Albion handpress by Lester R. Ferriss, et. al., handset in Frederic Goudy's University of California Old Style on handmade Barcham Green Bodleian paper. The frontispiece was cut in linoleum by Erik Tellander. The paste paper wrappers were made by the printers. This letter offers a perspective on the settlement of Guatemala by two Spaniards who sought & made a fortune there. In contrast to the arid prose of official reports, it gives us a personal view of Guatemala in early 1541 (introduction by Anne Mohr).

417. (Fleece Press) Brett, Simon. MR. DERRICK HARRIS 1919–1960. Denby Dale (England): The Fleece Press, 1998, small 4to., quarter cloth, decorated paper-covered boards / small 4to., sewn, stiff paper wrappers / oblong small 4to., stiff paper folder with paper label on front, loose sheets (about 29 x 38. 5 cm), ALL in a cloth-covered clamshell with a fitted interior. 53, (5) pages with one additional foldout leaf / 3 leaves / 9 sheets. $ 320.00
Limited to 280 copies. Derrick Harris' (1919–1960) wood-engraved images appeared in the late 40's and the 50's in various Folio Society publications and other books, and in a number of BBC publications. His rather graceful and sprightly, decorative and stylized (with elements of folk art and 18th-century illustration), and often implacably cheerful images seem also to have anticipated much commercial art of the following decades, and Harris also designed posters, advertisements, magazine covers, etc. Harris' death by suicide suggests that the cheerfulness was in part an aesthetic phenomenon, and in that respect one of the most interesting illustrations reproduced here is that of an individual, not at all cheerful- or even friendly-looking, about to try on a mask. Harris was largely forgotten in the years following his death, and Garrett's 1978 History of British Wood Engraving makes no mention of him. The book by Simon Brett discusses the life and works of Derrick Harris, with about 50 reproductions large and small of wood engravings by him. The sewn brochure contains three additional large engravings by Harris, and the folder contains a set of nine colored wood engravings done around 1946 for a never-published children's book entitled "Royal Flush" (the text is now lost). The whole is very well printed by Simon Lawrence, a long-time admirer of Harris' work, at the Fleece Press, using original blocks for the engravings.

418. (Fleece Press) Chapman, Hilary. THE WOOD ENGRAVINGS OF ETHELBERT WHITE. Wakefield: The Fleece Press, 1992, tall 4to., stiff paper wrappers, clam shell box, paper label on spine and front cover. 20, (2) pages. $ 250.00
Limited to 200 copies. A short essay, with a checklist of his engravings, and a short bibliography. Illustrated with White's engravings, and two tipped in photographs. The book is accompanied by two larger engravings, matted on acid-free boards.

419. (Fleece Press) Hodgson, Herbert. HERBERT HODGSON PRINTER, WORK FOR T.E. LAWRENCE & AT GREGYNOG. Wakefield, West Yorkshire: The Fleece Press, (1989), 8vo., quarter cloth, paste paper over boards, paper spine label. 43, (2) pages.
$ 80.00

First edition. Limited to 340 copies, printed by letterpress on Hahnemuble mould made paper. A very interesting autobiography of this fine printer's life. The account of the printing of *Seven Pillars of Wisdom* is particularly interesting.

420. (Fleece Press) Lee, Brian North. BOOKPLATES AND LABELS BY LEO WYATT. With an introduction by Will Carter. West Yorkshire: The Fleece Press, 1988, tall 8vo., quarter cloth, paste paper over boards, slipcase. 78 pages followed by 16 examples of copper engraved bookplates.
$ 250.00

First edition, limited to 300 copies. Printed by letterpress using Didot Spectrum type on Zerkall mould-made paper by Simon Lawrence. Contains a biographical essay on this engraver-letterer, plus a full checklist of all his bookplates cut in both wood and copper. Well illustrated with fifty-five wood engravings printed by letterpress and sixteen copper engravings reproduced by offset lithography by Meriden-Stinehour.

SPECIAL EDITION

421. (Fleece Press) Lee, Brian North. DEAREST JOANA. Two volumes. Denby Dale, West Yorkshire: The Fleece Press, (2001), small 4to., quarter natural vellum with marble paper covered boards, slipcase. 160; 160 pages.
$ 700.00

Limited to an edition of 40 copies. The life of artist Joan Hassall is celebrated through the many letters she wrote to family and friends throughout her life. Her attitude toward life, her beliefs, her love of music and art, her frail health and her devotion to cats, all are laid out here in her own inimitable style. Beginning with her days at school and ending just days before her death, the diverse contours of her life and activities are revealed to all who wish to make the acquaintance of this remarkable artist. In addition to sixty wood engravings, a wide range of her other work, dust jacket designs, line drawings, photographs, stamp designs and a variety of ephemeral pieces, are presented, many in full color. This edition contains an additional group of engravings, printed as an extra section to the book.

422. (Fleece Press) Lee, Brian North. DEAREST JOANA. Two volumes. Denby Dale, West Yorkshire: The Fleece Press, (2001), small 4to., quarter cloth with marble paper covered boards, slipcase. 160; 160 pages.
$ 535.00

Limited to an edition of 260 copies. The life of artist Joan Hassall is celebrated through the many letters she wrote to family and friends throughout her life. Her attitude toward life, her beliefs, her love of music and art, her frail health and her devotion to cats, all are laid out here in her own inimitable style. Beginning with her days at school and ending just days before her death, the diverse contours of her life and activities are revealed to all who wish to make the acquaintance of this remarkable artist. In addition to sixty wood engravings, a wide range of her other work, dust jacket designs, line drawings, photographs, stamp designs and a variety of ephemeral pieces, are presented, many in full color.

423. (Fleece Press) Myers, Robin (editor). AUTO-BIOGRAPHY OF LUKE HANSARD, WRITTEN IN 1817. With an Introduction by Robin Myers and wood engravings by John Lawrence. Wakefield: The Fleece Press, 1991, small 4to., printed paper over cloth-backed boards, slipcase. 156, (2) pages.
$ 200.00

First edition, limited to 250 copies. Set in Van Dijck and printed by letterpress on mouldmade Zerkall. Provides a first hand account of the provincial book trade in mid-eighteenth century England and of the London trade and parliamentary printing to 1817. Includes John Rickham's evidence given to the Select Committee on Printing Done for the House, 1828. Well printed and beautifully illustrated. A signed print by John Lawrence is in a separate pocket at the back of each copy of this book. Bookplate.

424. (Fleece Press) Rogerson, Ian. MOODS AND TENSES, THE PORTRAITS AND CHARACTERS OF PETER REDDICK. Huddersfield: The Fleece Press, 1999, large 8vo., quarter cloth with pastepaper covered boards with paper spine label, slipcase. 54, (4) pages with two additional fold-out plates. $ 200.00

First edition, limited to 220 copies printed at the Fleece Press. A look into the life and works of engraver Peter Reddick, from his initial contact with engraving through his great success as renown book illustrator. Illustrated with many of his engravings including several portraits of poets such as Tennyson, Shakespeare, and Wordsworth, and many of his works from the Folio Society Thomas Hardy editions. Set in Scotch Roman and printed on Zerkall paper. Bound in orange quarter cloth with an orange and brown pastepaper made by David Esslemont.

425. (Fleece Press) Selborne, Joanna and Lindsay Newman. GWEN RAVERAT, WOOD ENGRAVER. West Yorkshire: Fleece Press, (1996), large 4to., quarter cloth, marbled paper covered boards, slipcase. 148, (6) pages. $ 500.00

One of an edition of 260 copies. A tribute to a remarkable artist, one whose prints represent some of the most appealing and evocative images of twentieth century graphic art. An accomplished painter, draftsman, lithographer, theater designer, author and critic, she was best known for her wood engravings. Her work in this field was used by commercial publishers when few of them thought of wood engraving as a suitable illustrative medium. The text is divided into two parts, the first concerned primarily with the artist's life and technique, with references and bibliography. The second part documents her works, and give full descriptions of all books she illustrated, as well as individual blocks. Lavishly illustrated with examples of Raverat's work, many plates tipped in, several in color. Bound in gold quarter cloth, boards covered with marbled paper in shades of brown, gold and black, made by Ann Muir. Peter J. Sanderson set the Scotch Roman; the paper used is Zerkall. The slipcase is constructed with gold cloth edges, boards covered with gray-green paper.

426. (Fleece Press) Woolnough, C.W. PRETTY MYSTERIOUS ART, A LECTURE BY C.W. WOOLNOUGH TO THE ROYAL SOCIETY OF ARTS. Introduction by Barry McKay & new marbled samples by Ann Muir. Denby Dale: Fleece Press, 1996, small 8vo., cloth-backed marbled paper covered boards, paper spine label and enclosed in cloth clam-shell box with paper spine label. 51, (5) pages. $ 125.00

Limited to 300 copies. Printed by hand by Simon Lawrence at his Fleece Press. Includes ten tipped-in specimens of marbled paper including variants of Old Dutch and Spanish and progressive plates showing the development of a specimen sheet.

427. (Florence Press) Blake, William. THE MARRIAGE OF HEAVEN AND HELL AND A SONG OF LIBERTY. London: Chatto and Windus, 1911, large 12mo., quarter leather, paper covered boards. 79 pages. $ 95.00

First edition of this transcription. A collection of verse and prose poetry by William Blake. Transcribed and with an introduction by Francis Griffin Stokes. Spine faded.

428. (Florin Press) Bewick, Elizabeth. COMFORT ME WITH APPLES AND OTHER POEMS. Introduced by Kevin Crossley-Holland. (Biddenden): The Florin Press, (1987), tall narrow 4to., Laura Ashley print cloth, leather spine label, paper slipcase. 39+(1) pages. $ 155.00

Printed in an edition limited to 135 numbered and signed copies. This collection of twenty poems deals with the realities of love, relationships and old age with insight and sensitivity. The eight wood engravings by Graham Williams are charming and add just the right touch.

429. (Florin Press) Forge, Andrew. AN APPRECIATION OF NAUM GABO. (Biddenden, Kent): Florin Press, (1985), large 8vo., cloth. 47+(1) pages. $ 75.00
First edition, limited to 500 copies. Published to coincide with the opening of the exhibition tour of Naum Gabo in Dallas, September 1985. A look at the work of the modernist sculptor. Nabo is known for his clean lines and use of membrane-like strings in his metal sculptures. This volume is illustrated with tipped-in color plates. Sir Norman Reid provides a preface.

430. (Florin Press) Hazlitt, William. CHARACTER OF JOHN BULL. Staplehurst: The Florin Press, 1978, 12mo., cloth-backed paper covered boards. (16) pages. $ 45.00
Limited to 200 numbered copies signed by the illustrator, Graham Williams. Printed on handmade paper produced by Barcham Green.

431. (Florin Press) Wyatt, Leo. A SUITE OF LITTLE ALPHABETS ENGRAVED IN WOOD. N.P.: Florin Press, 1988, 8vo., individually matted prints gathered in a plastic perspex box. one introductory leaf, 12 separate matted prints. $ 325.00
Printed in an edition limited to 35 sets. Second printing from the original blocks used in Wyatt's 1986 *Little Book of Alphabets*. Sets contain twelve prints of twelve alphabets: Uncial, Gothic, Lombardic, etc., each one on a differently colored background. Each print numbered, mounted on cream acid-free card. Printed by hand on an Albion Press on specially made paper by Barcham Green with inks mostly made by hand. Press device engraved by Simon Brett. Printed and published by Graham Williams. Introduction by Graham Williams.

432. (FlugBlatt-Presse) Andersen, Hans Christian. DIE STOPFNADEL. (Lahnstein): FlugBlatt-Presse, 1985, 12mo., cloth with darning needle set into front cover. 45, (2) pages. $ 236.00
First edition, limited to 135 numbered and signed copies. Andersen's classic fairy tale, "The Darning Needle" is updated courtesy of Peter Malutzki, a graphic designer/artist. The darning needle's journey from a woman's dress to the kitchen sink is accompanied by Malutzki's prints. The illustrations include photographs, wood type, a piece of German newspaper from 1852 and gold leaf. In German.

433. (FlugBlatt-Presse) Artmann, H.C. DER AERONAUTISCHE SINDTBART ODER SELTSAME LUFTREISE VON NIEDERCALIFORNIEN NACH CRAIN, DREIßIGSTES ABENDTEUR AVT CAPITUL. (Lahnstein): FlugBlatt-Presse, 1987, 8vo., paper covered boards. 67, (2) french fold pages. $ 212.00
First edition, limited to 120 numbered and signed copies. Artmann's 1979 story of opera goers is transformed by Peter Malutzki through his imaginative illustrations. Malutzki takes a single image of an opera-going couple and overprints it with color zinc plates in a new way for each page. Handset and letterpress with Candida kursiv, gewöhnlich and halbfett.

434. (FlugBlatt-Presse) Eich, Günter. UNTER WASSER. EIN MARIONETTEN-SPIEL. (Lahnstein): FlugBlatt-Presse, 1990, tall narrow 4to., paper covered boards. 109, (2) pages. $ 236.00
First edition, limited to 100 numbered and signed copies. Eich provides us with an underwater play for marionettes. His handset text is accompanied by illustrations of brass rules, old woodcuts, feathers and letter forms which act as puppets on the page. The text, along with woodcuts and linocuts, are printed on blue handmade Japanese paper. Printed with Futura schmalmager and schmalhalbfett.

435. (FlugBlatt-Presse) Malutzki, Peter. VON ANTON BIS ZEPPELIN. EIN FIGURENALPHABET. (Lahnstein): FlugBlatt-Presse, 1995, large 8vo., accordion fold with printed cloth covered boards. unpaginated. $ 295.00
First edition, limited to 100 numbered and signed copies. A contemporary alphabet book. Malutzki has photographed a series of sculptures made of concrete and steel which feature a single letter from the alphabet. These are set alongside various texts which speak of that letter. For example, Lewis Carroll's *Alice in Wonderland* accompanies the letter M. Handset and letterpress with Futura. In German and English.

Item 435

436. (FlugBlatt-Presse) Rosei, Peter. UNSER LANDSCHAFTSBERICHT. (Llahn-stein: FlugBlatt-Presse, 1996), small 4to., accordion fold with stiff paper boards. 42, (2) pages. $ 400.00

First edition, limited to 60 signed and numbered copies. The text, by Peter Posei, is printed over 22 original black and white photographs by Ines V. Ketelhodt. The photographs feature a nude body, framed and lit to evoke a day landscape when the accordion folded book is read from one direction and a night landscape when read from the other. Printed over the "landscapes" are figures by the graphic artist Peter Malutzki. These figures are printed with letterpress material, such as plates, brass rules, etc.

437. (Folio Society) Beare, Geraldine (editor). CRIME STORIES FROM THE 'STRAND'. London: The Folio Society, 1991, 8vo., decorated cloth, slipcase. xviii, 350 pages. $ 25.00

First edition, second printing. A collection of mysteries previously printed in the *Strand Magazine*. Includes 20 stories by Arthur Conan Doyle, Agatha Christie, and more. Introduction by H.R.F. Keating. Black and white illustrations by David Eccles. Minor rubbing to case.

438. (Folio Society) Dreyfus, John and John Letts (editors). FOLIO 34, A CHECK-LIST OF THE PUBLICATIONS OF THE FOLIO SOCIETY 1947–1980. London: Folio Press, 1981, 8vo., cloth. 128 pages. $ 30.00

Introduction by John Dreyfus. Books appear in chronological sequence within each year. With illustrations and index. Folio Society booklist of titles laid in.

439. (Folio Society) FOLIO 21, A BIBLIOGRAPHY OF THE FOLIO SOCIETY 1947–1967. With an Appraisal by Sir Francis Meynell, R.D.I. London: The Folio Press, 1968, 4to., cloth, slipcase. 207 pages. $ 60.00
With many reproductions of this press's books, title pages and illustrations.

440. (Folio Society) FOLIO 40, A CHECKLIST OF THE PUBLICATIONS OF THE FOLIO SOCIETY 1947–1987. London: The Folio Press, 1987, 8vo., cloth. 157+(1) pages. $ 35.00
Introduction by Nicolas Barker. Bibliography of Folio Society imprints from 1947–1987, arranged in chronological sequence within each year. With illustrations and index.

441. (Folio Society) Lawrence, David Herbert. WOMEN IN LOVE. London: The Folio Society, 1982, large 8vo., cloth, paper-covered slipcase, top edge stained yellow. Frontispiece; 447 pages, with 17 additional leaves of plates. $ 25.00
Folio Society edition of the Lawrence classic, with twenty lithographic line drawings by Charles Raymond and introduction by Richard Hoggart. Light staining at top of covers.

442. (Folio Society) Trollope, Anthony. BARCHESTER TOWERS. London: Folio Society, 1977 (but 1982), 8vo., quarter cloth with decorated paper covered boards, top edge stained green, slipcase. 462 (2) pages. $ 25.00
Reprint edition. Trollope's original novel of 1857 with an added introduction by Julian Symons (Walsdorf E21 for original edition). Illustrated by Peter Reddick. Front and back end papers decorated with a map based on Trollope's own sketch.

443. (Folio Society) Trollope, Anthony. FRAMLEY PARSONAGE. London: Folio Society, 1979 (but 1983), 8vo., quarter cloth with decorated paper covered boards, top edge stained yellow, slipcase. 472 (2) pages. $ 25.00
Reprint edition. Trollope's original novel of 1861 with an added introduction by Julian Symons (Walsdorf E24 for original edition). Illustrated by Peter Reddick. Front and back end papers decorated with a map based on Trollope's own sketch.

444. (Folio Society) Trollope, Anthony. THE LAST CHRONICLE OF BARSET. London: The Folio Society, 1980, 8vo., quarter cloth, decorated paper-covered boards, decorated endpapers, paper-covered slipcase. 772, (2) pages. $ 25.00
Trollope's last Barsetshire novel, with one of the series' most striking characters. Introduction by Julian Symons, drawings by Peter Reddick. Folio Society publication no. 475, in the series binding design. Endpapers bear a map derived from Trollope's own sketch of "Barsetshire." Some minor spotting of backing.

445. (Folio Society) Trollope, Anthony. THE WARDEN. London: The Folio Society, 1976, 8vo., quarter cloth with decorated paper covered boards, slipcase, top edge stained brown. 234, (2) pages. $ 25.00
Reprint edition. Trollope's original novel of 1855 with an added introduction by Julian Symons (Walsdorf E20 for original edition). Illustrated by Peter Reddick.

446. (Folio Society) Trollope, Anthony. DOCTOR THORNE. London: The Folio Society, 1978, 8vo., quarter cloth, decorated paper-covered boards, paper-covered slipcase. 507 pages. $ 25.00
Folio Society no. 426. 1980 reprint of the Society's 1978 ed. of Trollope's 3rd Barsetshire novel: the Greshams, an old country family, are in dire straits, and young Frank G., who wishes to marry for love, may find it his duty to marry for money. Drawings by Peter Reddick. A few spots on the covers.

447. (Folio Society) Wells, H.G. THE HISTORY OF MR POLLY. London: Folio Society, 1957, 8vo., printed cloth, leather spine label, top edge stained red, paper slipcase. 205+(1) pages. $ 35.00

Folio Society edition. First published in 1910, "Mr. Polly" shows Wells at his most optimistic and assures his place in the history of English comic novelists. Black and white drawings by Ian Ribbons. Minor foxing on edges.

448. (Fortune Press) Harris, Frank. NEW PREFACE TO "THE LIFE AND CONFESSIONS OF OSCAR WILDE." London: Fortune Press, (1925), 8vo., cloth, paper cover label. 55+(1) pages. $ 20.00

First edition. Documents Lord Douglas' attempts to reconcile with Frank Harris and to have a new preface added to later editions of Harris' biography of Oscar Wilde which Douglas claimed wrongfully defamed him. When Harris reneged on the deal, Douglas had the re-written preface printed at his own expense in an effort to clear his name. Spine detached, owner's monogram in ink on title page.

449. (Fortune Press) Summers, Montague. ESSAYS IN PETTO. London: The Fortune Press, n.d. (but 1928), 8vo., quarter cloth with paper-covered boards, fore edges uncut. Frontispiece; x, 183 pages. $ 135.00

First edition, this copy being one of 70 copies printed on handmade paper and "finely bound." (Smith no.526.) This copy however is out of series and not signed by the author as called for in the bibliography. Essays on various literary topics, including Ann Radcliffe, Jane Austen, Byron, Samuel Pepys, and the Marquis de Sade. Frontispiece is a portrait of Summers. Covers rubbed. discolored. Corners and head and tail of spine bumped. Some foxing of pastedowns and free endpapers.

450. (Four Winds Press) Lear, Edward. A LEAR SONG, THE BROOM, THE SHOVEL, THE POKER, AND THE TONGS. N.P.: Four Winds Press, 1977, oblong small 8vo., quarter leather, paste paper-covered boards, loose sheets, cards, in pocket. (14) pages, with 2 additional leaves and 1 card in pocket. $ 85.00

Limited to 150 copies. Printing of an 1868 letter of Edward Lear containing an early form of The Broom, the Shovel, the Poker, and the Tongs (published in Nonsense Songs, 1871). Accompanying the text are three Lear drawings (the published form had two). With a foreword by Philip Hofer and an "informal bibliography of the Hofer-Lear books in the library at the Four Winds Press." The two sheets in the pocket are facsimiles of the letter, and the card is an erratum notice. Light rubbing on bottom edges of covers.

451. (Gallimaufry Press) Hansard, T.C. HAIL COLUMBIA. Bethesda: The Gallimaufry Press, 1970, small 8vo., stiff paper wrappers with a paper cover label. (iii), 9, (2) pages. $ 25.00

Printed in edition limited to 275 copies. Two testimonials, one foreign and one domestic, concerning the capabilities of Mr. George Clymer's iron printing press. The Hansard commentary was taken from his printing manual, Typographia; the Seaton letter is from Rollo Silver's The American Printer, 1787–1825; and the illustration is from a wood engraving in Savage's Practical Hints on Decorative Printing of 1822.

452. (Gehenna Press) Baldwin, James. GYPSY & OTHER POEMS. N.P.: Gehenna Press, 1989, 4to., leather backed decorated paper covered boards with a cloth covered clamshell box with a leather cover and spine label. variously paginated. $ 3,500.00

Printed in an edition limited to 325 numbered and signed copies of which this is one of 50 copies bound thus and containing the six etched portraits numbered and signed by Baskin. (Gehenna 93). A book of unpublished poems by James Baldwin. This was a book that was being discussed by Leonard Baskin and Baldwin when he died unexpectedly and prematurely so instead this volume was published to memorialize him. Baskin had etched six portraits of Baldwin from early manhood to the visage of his last years which are included in this book. The book was printed using a special casting of Centaur type made by Harold Berliner's Typefoundry at Nevada City, California with presswork by Wild Carrot Letterpress of Hadley, Massachusetts. The etchings themselves were printed directly from the copper plates. The trade edition of the book only contains one portrait as the frontispiece. These special 50 copies were bound by Daniel Gehnrich.

453. (Gehenna Press) CATALOG. Rockport, ME: The Gehenna Press, n.d. (but 1992), 4to., self paper wrappers. (8) pages. $ 15.00

First edition. This catalog lists the books available from the Gehenna Press as it celebrated fifty years of fine book-making. Price list dated April 15, 1992 loosely laid in. Includes color woodcuts taken from four of the titles listed. Slightly creased.

454. (Gehenna Press) FLEVRONOLOGIA, DIVERS ETCHINGS FORMED FROM FLEURONS BY LEONARD BASKIN. N.P.: Gehenna Press, 1996, large 8vo., full morocco, clamshell case. (12), (1) pages with 32 additional leaves of plates.
$ 7,000.00

Limited to 26 numbered copies. Signed by the artist (& owner of the Gehenna Press) Leonard Baskin on the colophon, who has also signed each of the 32 leaves of prints. Thirty-five color prints, including 2 on the title page and 1 on the colophon, of etchings derived from "flowers" (a.k.a. "typographical orna-ments," or "printer's flowers," or "fleurons"). Or these etchings themselves understood as page decora-tions. With many motifs associated with Mr. Baskin's art: birds and bird-like figures, insects, plant-life, human-like images and grotesques, often exhibiting some process of transformation. There is little here of Baskin's tormented or ominous figures, care-worn portrait faces, or his prophetic birds or birdmen, perhaps because purpose and scale of the illustrations favor the small (but important) things: what Baskin himself, discussing another artist, refers to as the "radiant realism of insect, flower, and plant" (Baskin: Iconologia, 1988, p.164) or the "mundane" which is made "to glow with obdurate monumen-tality" (Ibid., p.90). Even the grotesques here (many of them bird-like), which actually comprise about half the illustrations, mostly lack threat, and the transformations which they represent seem peaceful or whimsical. The prints have tissue paper protectors. The front cover has a three-color stamped design (unattributed, but undoubtedly by Baskin), the central part of which is repeated in a cut-out on the front of the clamshell case. There is a paper label on the spine of the clamshell. Excellent condition.

455. (Gehenna Press) THE LAST LETTER OF JAMES AGEE TO FATHER FLYE. Boston: Godine, 1969, 8vo., paper wrappers. (12) pages. $ 30.00

Printed in an edition limited to 500 numbered copies by the Gehenna Press. This is the last in a long cor-respondence between James Agee and James Flye, a priest and teacher at St. Andrew's a school in Ten-nessee. Agee died of a heart attack at the age of forty-five and this letter was found unopened by Father Flye. The back cover has a one inch faded spot across the top.

456. (Gehenna Press) Scott, John Anthony (editor). THE DEFENSE OF GRACCHUS BABEUF BEFORE THE HIGH COURT OF VENDOME. Northampton: The Gehenna Press, 1964, 4to., full leather chemise laid in a cloth-covered clamshell box with a leather spine. (ii), 83, (5) pages in addition to 21 etched portraits printed on spe-cial paper and loosely inserted throughout the text. $ 1,500.00

Printed in an edition limited to 300 numbered copies. (Brook 36). Signed by Leonard Baskin. This is one of the numbered 51 to 300 copies, which contains twenty-one etched portraits signed by Thomas Cor-nell on blue Fabriano, enclosed in unbound, uncut signatures. Selected for translation in this volume is the first part of Babeuf's general defense, for it contains the heart of his plea and constitutes in its own right a document of great value for the historian of the French Revolution, for the political scientist, and for the student of Babeuf's life. The paper is Nideggen made in Germany, and the pressman was Harold McGrath. The suite of etchings were printed by Emiliano Sorini in New York and it was designed and produced by Leonard Baskin.

457. (Gentry, Helen) Greenhood, David. POEMS, ET CETERA. San Francisco: Helen & Bruce Gentry, 1934, 8vo., quarter cloth paper-covered boards. 31+(1) pages. $ 45.00

Some of these poems were previously published in the periodicals Measure, Menorah Journal, The Na-tion, The Occident, Palms, Poetry--A Magazine of Verse, This Quarter, and Voices. Some soiling to boards.

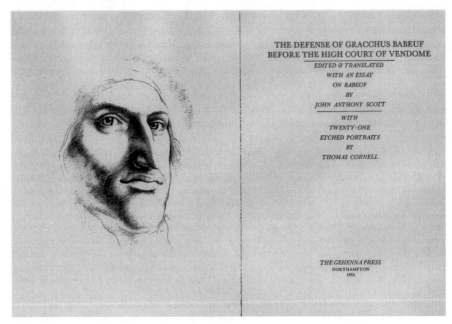

THE DEFENSE OF GRACCHUS BABEUF
BEFORE THE HIGH COURT OF VENDOME
*EDITED & TRANSLATED
WITH AN ESSAY
ON BABEUF
BY
JOHN ANTHONY SCOTT*

*WITH
TWENTY-ONE
ETCHED PORTRAITS
BY
THOMAS CORNELL*

THE GEHENNA PRESS
NORTHAMPTON
1964

Item 456

458. (Gentry, Helen) Andersen, Hans Christian. THE NIGHTINGALE. San Francisco: Helen & Bruce Gentry, 1934, tall 12mo., decorated paper covered boards, paper spine and cover labels. (32) pages. $ 45.00
Decorated by Frank Gregory. With illustrations printed in black and green. Paper covering along front hinge partially cracked.

459. (Gentry, Helen) Foote, Elvira. ASPEN LEAVES. San Francisco: Helen Gentry, 1929, 12mo., paper-covered boards with paper cover label. (40) pages. $ 65.00
Hand-printed for the author by Helen Gentry with Lutetia type and Glaslan paper. The poems were originally published in *Palms* magazine. "This press is established with the conviction that the printer who takes up his task in true aesthetic spirit must answer the stern requirements of sound workmanship (Helen Gentry, *The Leaflet*, Number One, January, 1930)."

460. (Gentry, Helen) THE LEAFLET. Five Issues. (San Francisco: Helen Gentry, 1930–1934), 12mo., paper wrappers. unpaginated. $ 100.00
First editions. Numbers 1-5 of this occasional publication from the Helen Gentry Press. Issue one (January 1930) is devoted to the aims of the press. Issue 2 (November 1930) prints Vance Thompson's "The Two Deaths of Oscar Wilde." Issue 3 (October 1931) features Joachim Gasquet's "Cezanne. What He Said To Me." Issue 4 (December 1932) contains Harry Lyman Koopman's "Exceptions to the Rule of Legibility." Issue 5 (April 1934) discusses John Ira Gannon.

461. (Gilliss Press) Andrews, William Loring. PAUL REVERE AND HIS ENGRAV-ING. New York: Charles Scribner's Sons, 1901, 8vo., white creme colored paper covered boards gilt-stamped on front cover and spine, stiff paper dust jacket, top edge gilt, slip-case. xiv, 171 pages. $ 450.00

Limited to 135 copies, printed at the Gilliss Press. Extraordinarily well produced book with engraved title-page by E.D. French and numerous illustrations including a colored frontispiece. Head and tail-pieces and initials by Sidney L. Smith. Pictorial paste-downs. Jacket is slightly chipped at top of spine; slipcase shows more wear with piece of top missing. Bookplate of Alfred Jerome Brown on free endpa-per.

462. (Gilliss Press) Andrews, William Loring. HEAVENLY JERUSALEM, A MEDI-AEVAL SONG OF THE JOYS OF THE CHURCH TRIUMPHANT, WITH AN-NOTATIONS BY WILLIAM LORING ANDREWS. New York: Charles Scribner's Sons, 1908, 8vo., stiff paper wrappers, top edge gilt, stiff paper chemise, slipcase. xxviii, 78, (2) pages. $ 385.00

First edition, limited to 152 copies of which this is one of the 27 copies to be printed on "Imperial Japan Paper." With engravings by Sidney L. Smith and other illustrations, rubricated initials and an illumi-nated copy of a page from a 15th century musical manuscript. Chemise has a piece missing in the mid-dle of the spine. Book is in very fine condition.

463. (Gilliss Press) Drake, Joseph Rodman. CULPRIT FAY AND OTHER POEMS. New York: The Grolier Club, 1923, tall 8vo., parchment backed boards, top edge gilt, oth-ers uncut. xv, 49 pages. $ 35.00

Limited to 300 copies. One of a series of six books designed by famous printers for the Eminent Ameri-can Printers Series sponsored by the Grolier Club. This book was designed by Walter Gilliss. Minor cover soiling.

464. (Glade Press) Hondius, Jodocus. HONDIUS ON HANDWRITING, THE PREFACE TO THE THEATRUM ARTS SCRIBENDI. Wormley, Great Britain: Glade Press, 1970, large 12mo., cloth, paper cover label. (iv), 13, (3) pages. $ 45.00

Printed in an edition limited to 40 numbered copies printed and bound at the Glade Press, Wormley in 1970. The Writing Book of Jodocus Hondius introduced and translated from the Latin by A.S. Osley, as a follow up to his earlier work *Erasmus on Handwriting*. Hondius (1563–1611) was known primarily as a cartographic engraver, but published his writing book in 1594 as an anthology of specimen pages by contemporary writing masters. This book reproduces his text of rules for learning how to write, with one plate on italic lettering engraved by Hondius.

465. (Gleniffer Press) Kaplan, Edward. MECHOS. Paisley: Gleniffer Press, 1982, tall 8vo., cloth. 13 leaves. $ 20.00

Limited to 150 numbered copies. Originally performed at St. Clement's Poetry Festival in 1981. Distrib-uted by the Swamp Press in the US. Printed and published by Helen and Ian Macdonald of Paisley.

466. (Golden Bib Press) Goldsmith, Arthur. A BIG CROAKER AND A LITTLE BOY. Poughkeepsie, NY: Golden Bib Press, 1964, small 16mo., stiff paper wrappers, paper cover label. (12) pages. $ 17.50

Printed in an edition limited to 100 copies by the noted author-photographer at the AIGA Workshop for the Golden Bib Press.

467. (Golden Cockerel Press) APOLLONIUS OF TYRE. HISTORIA APOLLONII REGIS TYRI. London: The Golden Cockerel Press, 1956, large 8vo., full morocco, gilt tooling, top edge gilt, cloth slipcase. 68 pages. $ 800.00

Limited to 300 numbered copies of which this is one of 75 "special" copies bound in full morocco and containing an extra set of the six engravings (plus one not in the book). (Cock-a-Hoop 203). Printed on mould-made paper in Aldine Bembo type. The *Historia* is a Latin novel of the fifth or sixth century

The Amazon Fleet sails

THE AMAZONS
A NOVEL BY
IVOR BANNET

Engravings by
CLIFFORD WEBB

Printed and published in England by
THE GOLDEN COCKEREL PRESS
1948

Item 468

translated here by Paul Turner. It has been suggested that the *Historia* is an elaboration of a lost Greek novel written either by an imitator of Xenophon or by Xenophon himself. The plot includes all the traditional elements of a Greek novel, such as pirates, dreams, storms at sea, lovers parted and reunited, and chastity preserved under difficulties. Illustrated with a series of six line-engravings in copper by Mark Severin. Includes an introduction by Turner and a prospectus. Previous owner's bookplate on front paste-down endpaper. Slipcase slightly rubbed.

468. (Golden Cockerel Press) Bannet, Ivor. THE AMAZONS. London: Golden Cockerel Press, 1948, small 4to., full leather, tooled in gilt, top edge gilt, cloth covered slipcase. 252, (1) pages. $ 850.00
Printed in an edition limited to 500 copies of which this is one of 80 specially bound by Sangorski and Sutcliffe and signed by the author and engraver. (Cockalorum 181). This book, a retelling of the Amazon conquests, was designed, produced and published by Christopher Sandford at the Golden Cockerel Press, London, in Poliphilus type, with Centaur initials, on Arnold's mould-made paper. With 12 engravings by Clifford Webb and 3 maps by Mina Greenhill. Includes an introduction by the author.

469. (Golden Cockerel Press) Barclay, John. EUPHORMIO'S SATYRICON. N.P.: The Golden Cockerel Press, 1954, small 4to., original full red morocco with the front cover and spine stamped in gilt with a cockerel design, in a slipcase. (iii), 158, with 7 leaves of plates. $ 650.00
First edition in English. Printed in an edition limited to 260 numbered copies this being one of 60 specially bound in full red morocco gilt. (Cock-A-Hoop p196). This novel immediately became a European best-seller and was reprinted in 20 different editions between 1603 and 1773, and translated once into Dutch, once into German, and four times into French. This translation is from the Latin into English for

the first time, from the 1605 edition, by Paul Turner. It has been finely illustrated with ten wood engravings by Derrick Harris with borders in red. Printed in red and black. Slipcase slightly worn and soiled.

470. (Golden Cockerel Press) Bennett, Arnold. THE BRIGHT ISLAND. London: The Golden Cockerel Press, 1924, large 8vo., original full limp vellum. xii, 128+(1) pages. $ 350.00
Limited to 200 copies signed by the author. Printed at The Golden Cockerel Press in two colors on Kelmscott handmade paper. This is the fifth of the Vine Books series issued to subscribers from "The Bookman's Journal" office. A play in which the island characters are the traditional figures of the old Italian comedy, some of them very familiar to the playgoers of all Western countries. It has been printed in red and black. Bookplate of Oliver Brett on the front pastedown. Covers slightly soiled with spine ends bumped.

471. (Golden Cockerel Press) Chaucer, Geoffrey. CANTERBURY TALES WITH WOOD ENGRAVINGS BY ERIC GILL. Four volumes. Waltham Saint Lawrence: Golden Cockerel Press, 1929–1931, narrow 4to. (12 1/2 x 7 1/2 inches), quarter Niger morocco over patterned boards, gilt-lettered spine with raised bands, top edge gilt, others uncut. 152; 190; 198; 220 pages. $ 6,000.00
One of 485 numbered copies on Batchelor handmade paper, out of a total edition of 500 copies. (Chanticleer 63, Gill 281) Chaucer's consummate narrative tales, an unfinished series of stories purporting to be told by a group of pilgrims journeying from London to the shrine of St. Thomas Becket and back, are beautifully enhanced by one full-page illustration, twenty-nine half-page illustrations, 269 decorative borders, tail-pieces, and line-fillers, and sixty-one initial letters printed in black, red, or blue, all engraved on wood by Eric Gill. Bound by Sangorski & Sutcliffe. Spines faintly sunned, very light wear to extremities, small glue stains to endpapers where they touch the leather, bookplates on front pastedowns. A near fine set.

472. (Golden Cockerel Press) COCKALORUM, A SEQUEL TO CHANTICLEER AND PERTELOTE BEING A BIBLIOGRAPHY OF THE GOLDEN COCKEREL PRESS, JUNE 1943 - DECEMBER 1948. London: The Golden Cockerel Press, n.d. (1949), tall 8vo., cloth, dust jacket. 112 pages. $ 135.00
First edition. Presentation from Christopher Sandford to James Moran dated 1953 on free endpaper. Sandford wrote the introduction to this book and was the principal partner in the Golden Cockerel Press. Jacket chipped at head of spine.

473. (Golden Cockerel Press) Hartnoll, Phyllis. THE GRECIAN ENCHANTED. London: Golden Cockerel Press, 1952, small 4to., full two-toned leather, gilt tooling, top edge gilt, cloth covered slipcase. 80 pages. $ 1,350.00
Limited to 360 numbered copies of which this is one of 60 that are specially bound by Sangorski and Sutcliffe in grey and pink morocco and contain, in a gusset, a second set of the eight illustrations along with an extra one, all printed by hand from copper plates. (Cock-a-hoop 189). A simple love tale illustrated with 8 aquatints by John Buckland Wright. Printed on Arnold's mould-made paper in Caslon's Old Face type. Signed by the author and the engraver. Edges of slipcase beginning to fray.

IN A DESIGNER BINDING

474. (Golden Cockerel Press) SONG OF SONGS. N.P.: The Golden Cockerel Press, 1978, folio, crushed levant morocco, gilt-tooled edges and turn-ins, turn-ins with small red morocco floral onlays, top edge gilt, others uncut, handmade paper free endpapers tooled in gilt in snowflake patterns and stamped and embossed with leaf patterns, green velvet doublures, crushed levant morocco slipcase. 59+(1) pages. $ 18,500.00
Printed in an edition limited to 204 copies of which this is one of 65 copies printed on Batchelor handmade paper with six extra signed plates. (Chanticleer no.110). Well illustrated with thirteen full-page line engravings on copper by Lettice Sandford depicting verses from The Song of Songs. New transla-

tion, notes, and introduction by W.O.E. Oesterley. Finely printed in red and black throughout. Specially bound for the Judaica collector Saul Shapiro by Emilio Brugalla in full dark blue crushed levant morocco, stamp-signed and dated (1978) on front turn-in. Covers with elaborate modelled, tooled, and multi-colored onlaid morocco borders in floral patterns, surrounding central sunken panels decoratively tooled in gold and silver around a large figure composed of colored morocco onlays (front cover: a queen with scepter and crown, and Stars of David on her robes; back cover: the head of a stag with leaves and flowers). Gilt-lettered spine, with modelled circular panels, elaborate gold and silver tooling and multicolored morocco floral onlays. A fine copy of this attractive private press book, in a simply magnificent onlaid binding and morocco pull-off case that is probably a joint production by Emilio Brugalla, (1901–1987) the important Spanish bookbinder and his son, Santiago, who was then in the process of taking over his father's practice.

475. (Golden Cockerel Press) Thoreau, Henry David. WHERE I LIVED & WHAT I LIVED FOR. Waltham Saint Lawrence: The Golden Cockerel Press, 1924, small 12mo., quarter parchment, with paper covered boards. 45, (4) pages. $ 250.00
Printed in an edition limited to 380 numbered copies. (Chanticleer 21) An essay taken from Walden, or Life in the Woods, by Thoreau. Printed in black and blue in Caslon type, on Kelmscott hand made paper. It is illustrated with 5 wood-engravings by Robert Gibbings in blue ink. It has the bookplate of the Golden Cockerell Press on the front pastedown indicating that it once was the press copy. Spine age darkened; rubbed along edges.

476. (Golden Cockerel Press) THE TRUE HISTORIE OF LUCIAN THE SAMOSATENIAN. London: The Golden Cockerel Press, 1927, 4to., quarter leather, cloth, top edge gilt, paper covered slipcase. (iv), 43, (2) pages. $ 950.00
Limited to 275 numbered copies. (Chanticleer 53). In his True History, which begins by warning the reader that its events are completely untrue and impossible, Lucian describes a voyage that starts on the sea, continues in the skies, and includes visits to the belly of a whale and to the Elysian fields. The tale is a satirical parody of ancient traveler's tales that strain human credulity. This edition includes a translation from Greek into English by Francis Hickes. Printed together with the Greek and decorated with wood engravings by Robert Gibbings. The text of the Greek, set with the assistance of the Oxford University Press, is that of the Jacobitz edition (1852). The English is taken from the first edition (1634) in the British Museum. With an introduction by J.S. Phillimore. Slipcase chipped with one hinge cracked.

477. (Golden Eagle Press) Honce, Charles. JULIAN HAWTHORNE COLLECTION. New York: Privately printed, 1939, small 4to., cloth, top edge gilt. 59 pages.
$ 275.00
First edition, limited to only 35 copies. 56 page biography and bibliography of the works of the son of Nathaniel Hawthorne and an author in his own right. Honce's second book. Designed by S.A. Jacobs and printed at The Golden Eagle Press of Mount Vernon, NY. With a full page presentation from Charles Honce "For James E. Arnay, who is one of the smartest bookmen I know and who has undoubtedly the greatest collection of Mark Twain in the world ..." and another inscription on the colophon page. This is copy number 2 of this limited edition. Also loosely inserted is a postcard from the Honces to the Arnays.

478. (Golden Eagle Press) Honce, Charles. TALES FROM A BEEKMAN HILL LIBRARY, AND OTHER NEWS STORIES ON TUNES, TRAVELS, TRIBULATIONS AND TRENCHERING. New York: At The Golden Eagle Press, 1952, large 8vo., cloth, top edge stained green. 126+(1) pages. $ 225.00
First edition, limited to 100 numbered copies. The paper is Basingwerk Parchment, the type linotype typography Caledonia designed by William Addison Dwiggins. With a presentation from the Honces on the colophon page and an additional presentation dated 1961 and 1962 on free endpaper. Dedicated to H.L. Mencken. Contains numerous illustrations by Joe Cunningham and Milt Morris. Spine chipped and free endpaper has corners missing.

479. (Golden Hind Press) Smith, Alexander. DREAMTHORP. Madison, NJ: The Golden Hind Press, 1935, 8vo., paste-paper covered boards, paper spine label. (vi), 24, (2) pages. $ 45.00

A Christmas book issued by the Rushmores. Illustrated by Warren Chappell. With colored initial letters. Minor cover rubbing. Two bookplates.

480. (Golden Hind Press) Spencer, Edmunde. SELECTIONS FROM THE AMORETTI WRITTEN BY EDMUNDE SPENCER. Madison, NJ: The Golden Hind Press, 1943, tall 8vo., paper covered boards, paper cover label. 18, (2) pages.

$ 55.00

Limited to 100 copies printed by Arthur Rushmore at his private press. Presentation "For Joe Blumenthal with best wishes for the next twenty years - Arthur Rushmore. 10/16/46." Covers faded with damage to paper covering along hinges.

481. (Golgonooza Letter Foundry & Press) Baudin, Fernand. FROM MECHANICAL TO CYBERNETIC EXERCISES. New York: The Typophiles, 1997, 8vo., stiff paper wrappers, cord-tied. (ii), 18, (4) pages. $ 25.00

Typophile Monograph New Series - Number 14. Limited to 500 copies designed, printed and bound by Dan Carr & Julia Ferrari at Golgonooza Letter Foundry & Press. Preface by Theo Rehak.

482. (Golgonooza Letter Foundry & Press) Brody, Catherine Tyler. JOHN DEPOL AND THE TYPOPHILES, A MEMOIR AND RECORD OF FRIENDSHIPS. New York: The Typophiles, 1998, 8vo., quarter blue cloth with patterned paper covered boards. 101, (3) pages. $ 65.00

Typophile Chap Book - New Series Number Two. Limited to 500 copies designed by Dan Carr and printed in the original metal Monotype Dante on vintage Mohawk Letterpress Text by J. Ferrari & D. Carr at Golgonooza Letter Foundry & Press. Well illustrated with reproductions of John DePol's wood engravings. Distributed for the Typophiles by Oak Knoll Press.

483. (Goodenough Art) Strong, Peggy Heigold. BASED ON A TRUE STORY. Happytown, ME: Goodenough Art, 1995, slim 8vo., self paper wrappers, dust jacket. Unpaginated. $ 45.00

Edition of 100, signed by author/illustrator. Eight separate pieces of conceptual art, the theme being one person's experience in learning to rely on oneself and becoming "goodenough." A two signature pamphlet of 28 pages, bound with five-hole stitch, with stiff paper black dust jacket, screen printed lettering and design in white. Printed on a 1950 Vandercook Model No. 4 proof press using handset type, photoengraving and linocut.

484. (Goodenough Art) Strong, Peggy Heigold. GOOD FRIENDS. (Ellsworth, ME: Goodenough Art, 2000), small 12mo., self paper wrappers, cord tied, paper envelope. (12) pages. $ 17.50

Edition of 150, numbered and signed by the author/illustrator. This delightful 12 page book explores the meaning of being friends with simple text and black, white and blue illustrations.

485. (Goodenough Art) Strong, Peggy Heigold. WAITING FOR FROGS. N.P.: (Goodenough Art, 1995), accordion fold tall slim 12mo., paper covered boards. Unpaginated. $ 45.00

Edition of 100, numbered and signed by the author/illustrator. The author chronicles the arrival of her favorite harbingers of spring, the peepers. This book about hope makes a wonderful and unusual gift. Accordion fold, twelve pages with hard side-covers in Kasugami jade with block print frog design in black, can be displayed free standing. The graphics show an abstract landscape in soft brown/black, with the text in black. Letterpress printed.

486. (Goodman, Julius, Jr.) McCoy, Garnett. PRINTING, PRINTERS AND PRESS-ES IN EARLY DETROIT. Detroit: Book Club of Detroit, 1962, small 8vo., cloth-backed boards. xiv, 33, (3) pages. $ 65.00
First edition, limited to 299 copies, and printed by Julius Goodman, Jr. at his private press, Junto. With drawings by Donald Weeks. History of printing from its beginning in 1796.

487. (Goudy Chapel) GREAT PRESSES OF THE GOUDY CHAPPEL, BEING AN INADVERTENT BICENTENNIAL OBSERVANCE. New York: The Goudy Chapel, 1976, 12mo., cloth, paper cover label. Not paginated. $ 35.00
No limitation given but about 200 copies. Short history of the Goudy Chapel followed by eight sepa-rately printed contributions by members of the Chapel. Includes The Artichoke Press, The Private Press of the Haywoods, Herity Press, Press of the Iron Horse, Powers Private Press, the Pre-Columbian Press, Ron Press and Under the Cellar Steps Press.

488. (Goudy Chapel) CHAPPELBOOK HONORING THE MOXON CHAPPEL (THE VERY FIRST, BORN APRIL 24, 1957, IN MENLO PARK, CALIFOR-NIA) ON ITS 25TH ANNIVERSARY. New York: Goudy Chappel, (1982), 12mo., stiff paper wrappers, paper cover label. $ 20.00
Private press contributions by 11 members printed on different paper and in different type. Includes the Four Penny Press, The Stone House Press, the Ron Press, the Press of the Iron Horse, Under the Cedars Press, the Endgrain Press (John DePol), the Private Press of the Haywoods and the Herity Press. Covers faded.

489. (Goudy Chapel) OUR TWENTIETH ANNIVERSARY. N.P.: Goudy Chappel, 1978, 8vo., loose sheets. (14) pages. $ 20.00
Each month of this calendar keepsake is designed, illustrated and printed by a member firm of the Chap-pel, with paper selected by each. Printers represented include Hy Needleman's Press, the Ron Press, William A. Dwiggins, Herity Press, Four Penny Press, Artichoke Press, Press of the Iron Horse, etc.

490. (Grabhorn-Hoyem) GRABHORN-HOYEM PRESSBOOKS. San Francisco: Andrew Hoyem, n.d., 20 1/2" x 8", broadside. one leaf, folded. $ 15.00
Advertisement listing for sale 13 titles still with the imprint of Grabhorn-Hoyem Press, the partnership of fine printers ended after the death of Robert Grabhorn (1973). Printed by Andrew Hoyem.

491. (Grabhorn-Hoyem) Hart, James D. THE SCHOLAR AND THE BOOK COL-LECTOR, AN ADDRESS DELIVERED ON OCTOBER 29TH, 1970 ON THE 50TH ANNIVERSARY OF THE FOUNDING OF THE ALBERT M. BENDER COLLECTION. Oakland: Mills College Library, 1971, large 8vo., stiff paper wrappers. 29+(1) pages. $ 35.00
First edition. Explores the long-standing relationship between book collectors and scholars which works to preserve and to enhance the life of the mind. Printed in San Francisco by Grabhorn-Hoyem in black with light blue ornaments. Slight wear to edges of cover.

492. (Grabhorn Press) Baer, Warren. THE DUKE OF SACRAMENTO, A COMEDY IN FOUR ACTS. San Francisco: Grabhorn Press, 1934, 8vo., quarter cloth with paper-covered boards, paper spine label, un-printed dust jacket. (xii), 77+(1) pages. $ 55.00
Printed in an edition limited to 550 copies, this being the first volume of the third series of Rare Ameri-cana (Heller, 212). Reprinted from the rare edition of 1856, to which is added a sketch of the Early San Francisco Stage by Jane Bissell Grabhorn, and twelve illustrations in color by Arvilla Parker. Handset in Garamond type on English mold made paper. Set from the only known copy, then in Ed Grabhorn's pos-session, of one of the earliest plays printed in California. Unprinted dust jacket shows wear to extremi-ties and has title hand-printed in ink on spine.

493. (Grabhorn Press) Bennett, Melba Berry. IN REVIEW - POEMS. San Francisco: (The Grabhorn Press), 1946, 8vo., stiff paper wrappers folded over boards, fore edge deckled. 34, (2) pages. $ 45.00

Limited edition of 200 copies printed for the author. (Heller and Magee no. 420) Selection of poems that reflect the concerns of everyday life. Title page is printed in red and black with red decorations and divisional titles throughout. Cover edges worn, spine faded.

494. (Grabhorn Press) Carpenter, Kenneth. COLLECTOR'S CHOICE, AN EXHIB-IT OF REPRESENTATIVE EXAMPLES FROM THE COLLECTIONS OF MEMBERS OF THE ROXBURGHE CLUB OF SAN FRANCISCO HELD IN THE PALACE OF THE LEGION OF HONOR ON THE OCCASION OF THE JOINT MEETING OF THE ZAMORANO CLUB OF LOS ANGELES & ROX-BURGHE CLUB OF SAN FRANCISCO SEPTEMBER 17–18, 1960. San Francisco: Roxburghe Club, 1960, large 12mo., stiff paper wrappers. 48+(1) pages. $ 30.00

Printed in an edition limited to 150 copies by the Grabhorn Press. (Harlan no.617). Distributed as keepsakes for Club member. In his foreword Oscar Lewis notes that Roxburghe Club members assembled their favorite books from their own collections for this unconventional exhibit. Carpenter includes a brief quote from each member explaining their selections.

495. (Grabhorn Press) Case, Alexander T. A SOLDIER AND MR. LINCOLN...THE FIFTY-SIXTH GROVE PLAY OF THE BOHEMIA. San Francisco: The Bohemian Club, 1961, 8vo., decorated paper-covered boards, paper spine label. (vi), 70 pages.
$ 40.00

Limited to 2,250 copies. Bibliography of the Grabhorn Press 1957–1966 and of Grabhorn/Hoyem 1966–1973, no. 627. With "music notes" by the composer, loosely inserted notice of casting changes. Corners, tail of spine rubbed; bumped on one bottom corner, tail of spine.

496. (Grabhorn Press) Dobie, Charles Caldwell. GOLDEN TALISMAN. San Francisco: (printed by the Grabhorn Press) for the Bohemian Club, 1941, small 8vo., quarter cloth with paper spine label and decorated paper covered boards, top edge cut, fore and bottom edges deckled. (iv), 47, (9) pages. $ 35.00

First edition. Limited to 1300 copies printed for the Bohemian Club of San Francisco (Magee 356). A Grove play by Dobie. Includes six illustrations by Albert J. Camille, printed in black, green, and yellow. Title printed in yellow and decorated with a black and yellow tree. Includes music by Alec Templeton. Set in Centaur monotype on mold made paper. Name in ink on first free end paper.

497. (Grabhorn Press) Erskine, Charles. THE BEAUTIFUL WEDDING. San Francisco: Grabhorn Press, 1929, small 8vo., paper covered boards, paper cover label. 89, (2) pages. $ 175.00

Printed in an edition limited to 200 copies. (Magee no. 123). Presentation copy "To Jeanne with great love-Katherine, Note: The text was written by my step-father Charles Erskine sent word and the addenda by my mother, Sara Bird Field." A keepsake distributed to guests and friends of Colonel Wood and Sara Bard Field to commemorate the marriage of Katherine Field and James Caldwell. The headpiece illustration is by Ray Boynton.

498. (Grabhorn Press) Field, Sara Bard. DARKLING PLAIN. New York: Random House, 1936, 8vo., cloth, dust jacket. (xii), 92, (2) pages. $ 55.00

First edition; printed by the Grabhorn Press. (Magee no.247). Magee says that 1500 copies were printed. Presentation from the author "For Jake, Josephine and Judy Zeitlin with faith - not in this poetry - but in the friendship that prompts the giving. Sara Bard Field. The Cats, Los Gales, Calif. July 29, 1940." With the small booklabel of Jake Zeitlin. Jacket spine age darkened and with small tear at top of spine.

499. (Grabhorn Press) FINE BOOKBINDINGS EXHIBITED AT THE GOLDEN GATE INTERNATIONAL EXPOSITION, SAN FRANCISCO; MXMXXXIX. San Francisco: Privately printed, 1939, 4to., stiff paper wrappers, paper spine label. (vi), 33 pages. $ 65.00

Limited to 400 copies printed by the Grabhorn Press in black and red. No illustrations but a list of book-binders and the books exhibited. With a foreword by Morgan Gunst. Chipped around edges.

500. (Grabhorn Press) GRABHORN PRESS THIRD SERIES OF RARE AMERI-CANA 1934-35. San Francisco: The Grabhorn Press, 1934, small 4to., paper wrappers. (8) pages. $ 25.00

Notices of the five books constituting the third series.

501. (Grabhorn Press) Howell, John. THE FRIENDSHIP OF BOOKS, A CALI-FORNIA BOOKMAN. San Francisco: (Grabhorn Press), 1954, large 8vo., stiff paper wrappers. 12 pages. $ 35.00

Reprinted for the author in an edition limited to 250 copies from the *Quarterly News-Letter* of The Book Club of California by the Grabhorn Press (Heller, 555). Anecdotes about the author's experiences as a rare book dealer in early twentieth century San Francisco, including the destruction of his store by the 1906 earthquake, and a visit by A. Edward Newton in 1931, when he bought a silver teapot which had belonged to Charles Dickens, with his monogram engraved on the side.

502. (Grabhorn Press) Lewis, Oscar. THE GRABHORN PRESS: A MOVING TALE. Orinda, CA: (Press of the Golden Key), 1982, large 4to., stiff paper wrappers, cord tied, deckled edges. (18) pages. $ 45.00

Limited to an edition of 120 copies. This essay on the early days of the Grabhorn Press first appeared in the *New York Herald Tribune*. Caricatures by Jane Grabhorn. Printed by Kathi & Don Fleming for the 1982 joint meeting of the Roxburghe and Zamorano Clubs.

503. (Grabhorn Press) Lyman, George D. THE BOOK AND THE DOCTOR. San Francisco: Privately printed by the author, 1933, 8vo., paper-covered boards with title pasted around spine and covers. 29, (5) pages. $ 75.00

Privately printed for the author by the Grabhorn Press in an edition limited to 50 copies. Inscribed by the author on front free endpaper (Heller, 198). Twenty-five copies presented to members of the Rox-burghe Club and twenty-five copies to members of the Vicious Circle. Set in Caslon monotype italic. The text was printed from the original plates, similarly numbered, of *California As It Is, by F.R. Wierzbicki, First Series of Rare Americana, No. 8.*Corners bumped, small pieces missing from head and tail of spine, small closed tear at bottom edge of front cover. Title page illustration & headpiece by Valenti Angelo.

504. (Grabhorn Press) Magee, Dorothy. BIBLIOGRAPHY OF THE GRABHORN PRESS. San Francisco: Grabhorn Press, 1957, large 4to., quarter morocco with decorat-ed paper covered board. xxix, (iii), 119+(1) pages, with reproductions, facsimiles, etc. in-serted. $ 950.00

Printed in an edition limited to 225 copies. The second volume of the Grabhorn bibliography which in-cludes a checklist of titles, 1916–1940, bibliography of books, 1940–1956, bibliography of ephemera and Christmas greetings, 1940–1956, and an index of titles, authors, and types. Finely illustrated throughout with original leaves of various sizes and from various books described. Many of theses are elaborately printed in color. An interesting association item as loosely inserted is a typed note of appreciation by var-ious colleagues of James D. Hart which has been signed by 32 of them and was meant to accompany this gift to Hart. Spine slightly faded.

505. (Grabhorn Press) Mandeville, Johns. VOIAGE AND TRAVAILE OF SIR JOHN MAUNDEVILE, Kt., WHICH TREATETH OF THE WAY TO HIERUSALEM, AND OF MARVAYLES OF INDE, WITH OTHER ILANDS

AND COUNTRYES. New York: Random House, 1928, small folio, brown morocco over original mahogany boards by William Wheeler, original morocco-edged slipcase. (iv), 156, (2) pages. $ 1,500.00

First edition limited to 150 copies. (Heller & Magee 107, Wagner, pp. 21-22, Barr, pp. 30–31) One of Grabhorn's most impressive works, this volume was selected as one of the Fifty Books of the Year. The text is that of the English edition of 1725 (a reprint of a 300 year old manuscript), collated with seven other manuscripts (several produced during Mandeville's life, 1300–1372) and four early printed editions, in Latin, French, English, and Italian. "The Grabhorns have brought to book work a freshness, a newness, a complete departure from any traditional school. . . The boldness of occasional illustrations, combined with vigorous arrangements of type, gives to Grabhorn books their principal charm. One need only examine . . . *Sir John Mandeville*. . . to realize the strength and beauty of a bold type arrangement. . . . one eminent authority says it is the finest book printed in English. Difficult as it is to compare books, such a statement at least indicates the high regard held for some Pacific Coast printing" (Dana Jones, *The West's Fine Printing is Worth Knowing*, quoted by Barr, p. 10.) With thirty-four decorative initials hand illuminated in red, blue, and gold, and thirty-one illustrations after those in early editions and manuscripts, by Valenti Angelo. Printed on unbleached Arnold paper, with presswork by Edwin Grabhorn. Bibel Gotisch type designed by Rudolph Koch, here used for the first time in America; type set by Robert Grabhorn and John Gannon. Slight abrasions to spine, two leaves faintly discolored from inserted clipping on inferior paper, else fine in publisher's original morocco-edged slipcase. With the original prospectus laid in.

506. (Grabhorn Press) Rapp, Albert. THE ANCIENT GREEKS AND JOE MILLER WITH A PROLEGOMENON BY NAT SCHMULOWITZ. N.P.: Privately Printed for Members of the Roxburghe Club of San Francisco, 1958, 4to., stiff paper wrappers, cord-tied. 32, (2) pages. $ 45.00

Printed in an edition limited to 300 copies. (Harlan no. 594) Anecdota Scowah Number Three. This study of the wit and humor of the ancient Greeks clearly shows that they were a gelastic—laughter loving—people. Long praised for its wisdom, now comes this paean to the humor of ancient Greece.

507. (Grabhorn Press) Rapp, Albert. JOE MILLER OF THE NEAR EAST ONSOZ. BY NAT SCHMULOWITZ. N.P.: Privately printed for Members of the Roxburghe Club of California, 1960, 4to., stiff paper wrappers. 38, (2) pages. $ 45.00

Limited to 300 copies. Anecdota Scowah Number Four. A study of the humor of the Turk, Nasreddin Hojah.

508. (Grabhorn Press) Ridgely, Laurence Butler. SANTA FRANCESCA, OUR LADY OF THE GOLDEN GATE. San Francisco: (The Grabhorn Press), 1935, 8vo., quarter parchment, paper covered boards. 49+(1) pages. $ 65.00

Printed in an edition limited to 250 copies. (Heller and Magee no. 231) Book of inspirational verse pays tribute to both natural and man-made wonders. The title page and table of contents are printed in red and black with the section titles, decorative initials and colophon also printed in red.

509. (Grabhorn Press) THE ROSTER ZAMORANO CLUB LOS ANGELES AND ROXBURGHE CLUB OF SAN FRANCISCO 1955. San Francisco and Los Angeles: Roxburghe Club and the Zamorano Club, 1955, 8vo., paper covered limp boards, cord-tied. 31+(1) pages. $ 35.00

First edition. Listing of all the members of both the Zamorano and Roxburghe Clubs prepared by the San Francisco organization as a token of friendship. Corners bumped, top edge creased.

510. (Grabhorn Press) Saddlebags, Jeremiah. JOURNEY TO THE GOLD DIGGINS. Illustrated by J.A. & D.F. Read. A Collotype Facsimile of the Original Edition of 1849. With an Introduction by Joseph Henry Jackson. Burlington, CA: William P. Wreden, 1950, oblong small 8vo., cloth-backed boards, paper spine label. x, 63 pages. $ 100.00

Limited to 390 copies. (Magee no.494). Illustrated in color.

511. (Grabhorn Press) THE SERMON ON THE MOUNT. (San Francisco: Grabhorn Press, 1924), folio, quarter cloth with paper boards, pictorial paper cover label, deckled edges. (10) pages. $ 450.00

Edition limited to 190 copies. (Grabhorn Bibliography no. 63) The colored title page illustration, which was repeated on the front cover label, was created by Stafford Duncan. Head and tail of spine and edges of cover chipped.

512. Grabhorn, Robert. SHORT ACCOUNT OF THE LIFE AND WORK OF WYNKYN DE WORDE WITH A LEAF FROM THE GOLDEN LEGEND PRINTED BY HIM AT THE SIGN OF THE SUN IN FLEET STREET, LONDON, THE YEAR 1527. San Francisco: The Book Club of California, 1949, tall 4to., cloth-backed decorated paper covered boards, paper cover and spine label. (iv), 14, (4) pages. $ 750.00

Limited to 375 copies and printed for the Book Club of California by the Grabhorn Press. (Borden, Magee & Olmsted no.37; Grabhorn Bibliography 486). Text printed in red and black throughout. Text was written by Robert Grabhorn. This copy does not contain the 1527 leaf but rather an incunabula leaf from William Caxton's translation of St. Jerome's *Vitas Patrum* (STC 14507), printed by Wynkyn de Worde in 1495, being leaf y3, folio clxxi, from *The Lyfe of Saynt Appollynare*.

513. (Grabhorn Press) Watson, Douglas S. NEIGHBORS OF YESTERDAY. (San Francisco: Roxburghe Club, 1934), 8vo., glazed paper-covered boards. (ii), 10, (2) pages. $ 65.00

Printed in an edition limited to approximately 100 copies for complimentary distribution to members of the Roxburghe Club of San Francisco (Heller, 206). Story of early printing in San Francisco. With colored drawing of the Grabhorn Press building by Arvilla Parker on title page, three reproductions of early San Francisco lithographs and two full-page facsimiles. Printed label with colored drawing by Arvilla Parker on front cover. Hand-set in Janson type on machine made paper. Bookplate of previous owner on front pastedown and another with Grabhorn Press logo laid in. Parts of spine missing but binding tight.

514. (Grace Hoper Press) COMMON-PLACE BOOK, WITH SOMETHING FOR EVERYBODY. Aptos: Grace Hoper Press, 1969, tall 4to., quarter cloth with decorated paper covered boards. 54 pages. $ 200.00

Limited to 200 copies; printed on mould made paper from W.S. Hodgkinson. Compiled by Sherwood Grover and James D. Hammond, this Grace Hoper Book expands again the tradition of the common-place book into the realm of the finest of art forms practiced by the private press. The designs are printed in red, black and blue.

515. (Grace Hoper Press) Grover, Sherwood. COMMON PLACE BOOK SIX. N.P.: Aptos & Woodside, 1983, 4to., quarter cloth, with decorated paper covered boards. (iv), 47+(1) pages. $ 195.00

Printed in an edition limited to 200 copies. This is the sixth Commonplace Book which was an off-again on-again project of James Hammond and Sherwood Grover. A collection of quotes by famous people from various sources and ages, printed in a variety of types. Beautifully illustrated with notes on the types included.

516. (Grace Hoper Press) Grover, Sherwood. FRAGMENT FROM COMMON-PLACE BOOK SEVEN. San Francisco: The Roxburghe Club, 1987, 4to., stiff paper wrappers. (iv), 26+(1) pages. $ 175.00

First edition, printed in an edition limited to 225 copies. Published posthumously by the Roxburghe Club and printed by Felicia Rice at her Moving Parts Press. Printed in red and black throughout with some pages bearing the additional blue.

517. (Grace Hoper Press) Hart, James D. E & RG, THE GRABHORN BROTHERS. (Los Angeles: Roxburghe-Zamorano Clubs, 1978), large 4to., single folded sheet. (4) pages. $45.00

Printed in an edition limited to 225 copies by Sherwood Grover. Hart's essay focuses on the honorary degree bestowed on the Edwin and Robert Grabhorn by the University of California in 1963. Keepsake presented at the 1978 joint meeting of the Roxburghe and Zamorano Clubs in Los Angeles. Black and white photograph of Edwin by Ansel Adams taken in 1960 was reproduced here for the first time. Back cover faded.

518. (Grace Hoper Press) Sowers, Roy Vernon. MY FRIEND ARISTIDE. San Francisco: Roxburghe-Zamorano Clubs, 1984, large 8vo., stiff paper wrappers, cord tied. (14) pages. $25.00

Limited to an edition of 200 copies. Tells the tale of an unwitting accomplice to a literary hoax that appeared in newspapers in 1923. Printing by the Grace Hoper Press for the Roxburghe and Zamorano Clubs was sponsored by Dorothy Whitnah and Sherwood Grover.

519. (Grain-ag Press) PRIVATE PRESS, HANDBOOK TO AN EXHIBITION. Loughborough: Loughborough Technical College, 1968, 8vo., cloth. (iv), 30 pages. $45.00

Of the 600 copies, this is one of the 150 numbered hardbound copies. Printed by Thomas Rae at the Grain-ag Press. Rae had printed the Plough Press's first book, *Anaglyptography*. With information on the Plough Press.

520. (Gravesend Press) THE SONG-STORY OF AUCASSIN & NICOLETTE. Lexington: The Gravesend Press, n.d., small 8vo., paper wrappers. pages 41 to 48, unopened. $25.00

A prospectus which includes an actual leaf from the production of The Song-Story of Aucassin & Nicolette. The text is hand-set in Rudolph Koch's Jenssen type, and is printed on dampened Hayle hand-made paper.

521. (Greenwood Press) Spiegelberg, Frederic. SPIRITUAL PRACTICES OF INDIA. San Francisco: Greenwood Press, 1951, 8vo., quarter buckram with decorated paper covered boards, paper spine label. xvi, 68, (2) pages. $65.00

Printed in an edition limited to 500 copies. Translated from the German by Edith E. King-Fisher. Introduction by Alan W. Watts. Designed by Jack Werner Stauffacher. Includes chapters on "The Task & Aim of Spiritual Discipline," "The Technique of Respiration," and "The Laying-out of the Mandala." Illustrated with line cuts and halftones. Advertisment pasted on front pastedown, small tear on front free endpaper.

WITH TRIAL SHEETS

522. (Gregynog Press) Bridges, Robert. EROS AND PSYCHE. N.P.: Gregynog Press, 1935, 4to., original cream pigskin blocked gold with a circular flower and butterfly device in gold on front cover, with top edge gilt, in an original buckram slipcase, with a paper spine label. 5 pieces of ephemera in various sizes included. (viii), 141, (3) pages. $1,700.00

Printed in an edition limited to 300 copies, this being one of the 285 copies bound in white pigskin. (Harrop 33). A poem by Robert Bridges which was printed in red and black with initials in green on Batchelor's Gregynog hand-made paper. It is beautifully illustrated with 24 wood engravings, engraved from the designs of Edward Burne-Jones' drawings. These were prepared for engraving by Dorothy Hawksley, five of which were cut by Haberly, and the others by R. John Beedham. The green wood-engraved initials are by Graily Hewitt. This is the only book produced in the new Gregynog type at the Press. Laid in are; a bifolium specimen of the new type in letter pairs with penciled marginal note 'extra color' on hmp; a specimen of six decorated initials which are not used in the book; and a 4 page prospectus of specimen leaves from the book. Also included is a single leaf Monotype specimen of "Gwendoline," the orig-

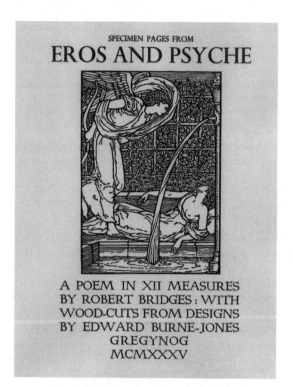

SPECIMEN PAGES FROM

EROS AND PSYCHE

A POEM IN XII MEASURES
BY ROBERT BRIDGES : WITH
WOOD-CUTS FROM DESIGNS
BY EDWARD BURNE-JONES
GREGYNOG
MCMXXXV

Item 522

inal working name for the type, titled Trial No. 2. There is a single leaf typescript account of the book from Haberly's papers for which he was presumably responsible. The book and buckram box are slightly foxed with the slipcase soiled. All together an unusual copy.

523. (Gregynog Press) Thomas, Edward. CHOSEN ESSAYS. Montgomeryshire, Wales: Gregynog Press, 1926, large 8vo., blue buckram, deckled edges, gilt-blocked outline vase of flowers on front cover. (viii), 102+(2) pages. $ 250.00
Printed in an edition limited to 350 copies. (Harrop, pp. 31-33). Wood engravings throughout by Robert Ashwin Maynard and Horace Walter Bray. Engraved portrait of author on title page from a photograph by Frederick Evans. Pages 1–10 lightly foxed and previous owner's signature on front free endpaper. Spine faded with minor wear to head and tail of spine. Essays on Welsh countryside selected by Ernest Rhys.

524. (Grey Bow Press) Benet, William Rose. MAD BLAKE. (Los Angeles: Grey Bow Press), 1937, 8vo., stiff paper wrappers. (4) pages. $ 17.50
Printed at the Grey Bow Press, (originally founded by Gregg Anderson in 1926), Los Angeles, by E.G. Davies. A 16-line poem by a winner of the Pulitzer prize.

525. (Grian-Aig Press) Prince, Joan. POEMS BY JOAN PRINCE. Greenock, Scotland: Grain-aig Press, 1969, small 8vo., stiff paper wrappers, stiff paper dust jacket. (ii), 23+(1) pages. $ 25.00
Limited to 240 copies, 40 of which for the Society of Private Printers. A book of poems on a Scottish theme, which were first published in "The Weekly Scotsman" and "Breakthru," set in 12 point Perpetua types and printed by Thomas Rae at his Grian-aig Press. Signed by the author.

526. (Guthrie, Stuart) Chesshire, May. AN ANTHOLOGY. Horsham: Stuart Guthrie, (1937), small 4to., quarter cloth with paper covered boards, paper cover label. (vi), 23+(1) pages. $ 95.00

Printed in an edition limited to 250 copies. A collection of poems written by May Chesshire, selected from letters to her brother Llewelyn. They were selected and arranged by Diana Harding, with a preface by John Cowper Powys. It is illustrated with a woodcut frontispiece. Minor discoloration of the spine and the corners are slightly rubbed.

527. (Gwasg Gregynog) Goethe, Johann Wolfgang von. POEMS. Tregynon, Newton, Powys: Gwasg Gregynog, 2000, 4to., quarter leather, paper covered boards, slipcase. viii, (ii), 51+(3) pages. $ 300.00

Printed in an edition limited to 200 numbered copies of which this one of fifty specially bound in quarter leather. This book was published by Gwasg Gregynog to celebrate the 600th anniversary of the birth of Johann Gutenberg and the 250th of Johann Wolfgang Goethe. This collection of some forty recent English translations of Goethe's poetry, edited and introduced by T.J. Reed, represents the breadth of the artistic and intellectual interests of Goethe as they developed throughout his lifetime. Illustrated with a title-page silhouette of Goethe and typographical decoration to some of the poems. Neil Holland has also illustrated the covers with two woodcuts of the author, which are printed in pastel colors typical of those chosen by Goethe for his house in Weimar. Set in Monotype Ehrhardt and printed in two colors on mouldmade paper from the Hahnemuhle mill at Dassel.

528. (Gwasg Gregynog) Goethe, Johann Wolfgang von. POEMS. Tregynon, Newton, Powys: Gwasg Gregynog, 2000, 4to., quarter cloth, paper covered boards, paper slipcase. viii, (ii), 51+(3) pages. $ 170.00

Printed in an edition limited to 200 copies of which this one of 150 bound in quarter cloth. This book was published by Gwasg Gregynog to celebrate the 600th anniversary of the birth of Johann Gutenberg and the 250th of Johann Wolfgang Goethe. This collection of some forty recent English translations of Goethe's poetry, edited and introduced by T.J. Reed, represents the breadth of the artistic and intellectual interests of Goethe as they developed throughout his lifetime. Illustrated with a title-page silhouette of Goethe and typographical decoration to some of the poems. Neil Holland has also illustrated the covers with two woodcuts of the author, which are printed in pastel colors typical of those chosen by Goethe for his house in Weimar. Set in Monotype Ehrhardt and printed in two colors on mouldmade paper from the Hahnemuhle mill at Dassel.

529. (Gwasg Gregynog) Jones, Glyn and T.J. Morgan. THE STORY OF HELEDD. Newtown, Wales: Gwasg Gregynog, 1994, 4to., quarter cloth, decorated paper covered boards. 39, (15) pages. $ 150.00

Edition of 400 copies, 330 of which in this form and numbered. This is a retelling of the ancient Welsh saga of Princess Heledd, with an introduction and new material by Jenny Rowland. The narrative has been reconstructed by the authors, and the poetry translated from surviving manuscripts. The poetry is also presented in a modernized Welsh version. Beautifully illustrated by the engravings of Harry Brockway, printed in russet and black from the original blocks. Designed and printed by David Esslemont on Hahnemuhle and Zerkall paper, bound by Smith Settle.

530. (Gwasg Gregynog) Olivers, Thomas. THOMAS OLIVERS OF TREGYNON, THE LIFE OF AN EARLY METHODIST PREACHER WRITTEN BY HIM-SELF. Tregynon, Newtown, Powys: Gwasg Gregynog, 1979, large 8vo., cloth, paper spine label. 56 pages. $ 75.00

Limited to 375 numbered copies. The third imprint of Gwasg Gregynog (Gwasg G., Descriptive Cat. of Printing, 1970–1990, p.4--according to which edition size is 400 and the date of publ. Jan. 1980). Published for the 200th anniversary of the printing of the autobiography of the Methodist preacher and Tregynon native T. Olivers (1725–1799), an associate of John Wesley. Oliver's early life, his conversion, and experiences as an itinerant preacher, with a portrait engraving and a short bibliography of his works. A facsimile of Oliver's signature is blind-stamped on the front cover, and an extra spine label is tipped in before the back cover.

531. (Gwasg Gregynog) PLEASANT HISTORY OF LAZARILLO DE TORMES, DRAWN OUT OF SPANISH BY DAVID ROWLAND OF ANGLESY. Newtown (Powys): Gwasg Gregynog, 1991, tall 8vo., quarter cloth, pictorial paper over boards. 116 pages. $ 140.00
Limited to 300 numbered copies, this being one of 200 copies bound thus. Edited by Gareth Alban Davies. Designed and printed by David Esslemont using Monotype Garamond type on Zerkall mould-made paper. Illustrated with woodcuts and wood engravings by Frank Martin from the original blocks, some in two colors. The story is the first of the Spanish picaresque romances, and gives the history of the rogue son of a miller who goes through a series of jobs and disadvantaged or rascally employers.

532. (Gwasg Gregynog) Rogerson, Ian. AGNES MILLER PARKER WOOD EN-GRAVINGS FROM XXI WELSH GYPSY FOLK-TALES JOHN SAMPSON AND THE GYPSIES OF WALES. Powys, Wales: Gwasg Gregynog, 1997, folio, quar-ter red cloth with paper covered boards, slipcase. 54, (2), followed by 17 plates, (4) pages.
$ 425.00
Limited to 200 numbered copies, 185 thus bound. A history of the publication of the monumental 1933 work from Gwasg Gregynog, *XXI Welsh Gypsy Folk-Tales*. It begins with a touching description of the funeral of John Sampson, arguably the foremost scholar in the field of Welsh Gypsy folklore, and covers the life of Sampson, the gestation of the Gregynog Press book, and the making of the book. The contri-butions of Agnes Miller Parker, and her wood engravings which illustrated it, are discussed. Printed and bound at Gregynog Press by David Esslemont, David Vickers and Alan Wood using Monotype Bembo on Zerkell mouldmade paper. Seventeen wood engravings by Parker from XXI WELSH GYPSY TALES and Gregynog's 1931 edition of THE FABLES OF ESOPE, printed by hand on hand-made Japanese Gampi Vellum from the original blocks lent by the National Library of Wales, follow the text. Issued as the second volume of Agnes Miller Parker Wood Engravings.

533. (Gwasg Gregynog) Ryder, John. INTIMATE LEAVES FROM A DESIGNER'S NOTEBOOK. Newtown: Gwasg Gregynog, 1993, 8vo., cloth-backed decorated paper covered boards. 149, (5) pages. $ 150.00
Limited to 400 numbered copies designed by Ryder and printed by David Esslemont at Gregynog on Zerkall mould-made paper. With a foreword by Jan Morris. Eleven chapters including a number giving Ryder's thoughts on book design, one on Pablo Neruda as a typographer and information on copybooks of lettering and calligraphy. Some illustrations.

534. (Haberly Press) Haberly, Loyd. CITY OF THE SAINTED KING AND OTHER POEMS WRITTEN & PRINTED BY LOYD HABERLY. St. Louis: The Haberly Press, 1941, 8vo., cloth-backed boards, dust jacket. (ii), 120+(1) pages. $ 65.00
Limited to 1250 copies. Jacket chipped with wear along edges and is price clipped; name in ink on free endpaper.

535. (Hague & Gill) Malory, Sir Thomas. LANCELOT AND ELAINE BEING THE EIGHTH TO THE TWENTIETH CHAPTERS OF THE EIGHTEENTH BOOK OF SIR THOMAS MALORY'S LE MORTE DARTHUR WITH ENGRAV-INGS BY JOAN HASSALL. Pigotts: Hague & Gill, 1948, 12mo., quarter black mo-rocco, Cockerell marbled paper covered boards. (viii), 75, (2) pages. $ 1,500.00
Limited to two hundred copies of which only twenty five or so were issued, and of these none were bound at the press. (Chambers 29, Davis 30). James Davis in his "Printed by Hague and Gill" quotes from a G.F. Sims catalogue, "this book was not in fact completed or published. A series of accidents led to many copies being destroyed and the project abandoned. We purchased the surviving complete sets of sheets and they have been bound by Sangorski and Sutcliffe in Curwen Press coloured wrappers." But, the boards of this copy are covered in what appears to be Cockerell marbled paper, so perhaps this is the "one copy bound by Rene Hague" which Davis notes quoting from another G.F. Sims catalogue. The text is set in Joanna (on uncut, handmade paper) and follows exactly that printed by William Caxton in 1485, as given in the edition of H. Oskar Sommer (London, 1889). Caxton's misprints have not been correct-

ed. Le Morte d'Arthur is the first account of the Arthurian legend in modern English prose. It retells the adventures of the knights of the Round Table in chronological sequence from the birth of Arthur. Includes five wood engravings by Joan Hassall. Certainly the scarcest Hague & Gill title published.

536. (Hague & Gill) Gill, Eric. UNHOLY TRINITY. London: J.M. Dent for Hague and Gill Ltd., 1938, 8vo., stiff paper wrappers, paper slipcase. (12 leaves). $ 175.00
First edition. (Gill 37). This book contains 11 short essays written by Eric Gill, each with an accompanying illustration by Denis Tegetmeier. These essays express Gill's strong anti-war opinions and thoughts on obtaining peace.

537. (Halcyon Press) Shelley, Percey Byshe (translator). SIX HYMNS OF HOMER. Maastricht, Holland: The Halcyon Press, 1928, 8vo., cloth. 19, (4) pages. $ 125.00
Limited to 450 numbered copies. This book contains six of Homer's hymns with the English translation by Percy Bysshe Shelley facing the original Greek. Composed in Antigone Greek (Bowman 226) and Lutetia Roman type both designed by Jan van Krimpen. Printed on Pannekoek Dutch mouldmade paper. Edited by Paul van de Woestijne.

538. (Hammer, Victor) IN COMMEMORATION OF THE 60TH ANNIVER-SARY OF THE FRONTIER NURSING SERVICE, THE UNIVERSITY OF KENTUCKY LIBRARY. Lexington: University of Kentucky, 1985, four page foldout invitation in mailing envelope with two other pieces. $ 20.00
Printed by hand. With notes in pencil on the mailing envelope concerning the printing of this invitation.

539. (Hammer, Victor) ANDROMACHE: A TRAGEDY, FREELY TRANSLATED INTO ENGLISH IN 1674 FROM JEAN RACINE'S "ANDROMAQUE" BY A YOUNG GENTLEMAN & JOHN CROWNE. Lexington: Anvil Press, 1986, small 4to., unbound sheets. (12) pages only of this book. $ 25.00
Title page and foreword by Desmond Flower of this book which was limited to 100 numbered copies printed by Carolyn Hammer and W. Gay Reading at the Anvil Press in Victor Hammer's American and Andromaque uncial types. The foreword by Desmond Flower is complete.

540. (Hammer, Victor) Cassidorus. OF SCRIBES. Lexington: Stamperia del Santuccio, 1958, small 4to., paper covered boards. (8) pages. $ 950.00
Printed in an edition limited to 50 copies. (Holbrook pg. 147 Opus XIV). The text was written circa 562 for the scriptorium at the Monastery of Vivarium founded by Cassidorus in the sixth century. The Latin text is set in all capital letters, and the English translation is by Friar Augustine Wolff of the Abbey of Gethsemani. A two-color initial "E" with a scribal monk in the background, is cut from brass by Victor Hammer, and is printed in red and blue at the beginning of the text. It was designed and printed by Carolyn Hammer. Two very small abrasions on the spine.

541. (Hammer, Victor) De Alarcon, Pedro Antonio. THE THREE-CORNERED HAT. New York: H. Bittner, 1944, 8vo., cloth. 151+(1) pages. $ 95.00
Printed in an edition limited to 500 copies, set and printed by hand by Victor & Jacob Hammer at the Wells College Press, Aurora, NY. *El Sombrero de Tres Picos* was first published in 1874, and here translated into English by Lawrence M. Levin, with 21 woodcuts in color by Fritz Kredel. A picaresque tale originally called *The Corregidor and The Miller's Wife*.

542. (Hammer, Victor) Fiedler, Conrad. CONRAD FIEDLER'S ESSAY ON ARCHI-TECTURE. Berkeley: University of California Press, (1951), large 8vo., paper covered boards, paper spine label. v, (iii), 56 pages. $ 300.00
Printed in an edition limited to 100 copies at The Press of Carolyn Reading in Lexington, Kentucky. (Holbrook, Introduction, no.1). Finely letterpress printed on Arnold Unbleached paper in red and black in Victor Hammer's American Uncial type. Introduction by Victor Hammer. Translated from the original German by Edgar Kaufmann Jr., Victor Hammer, and Alvina Brower. Presentation from Carolyn Reading dated 1954 on free endpaper. Part of spine covering rubbed away.

Item 540

543. (Hammer, Victor) Hebel, Johann Peter. FRANCISCA AND OTHER STORIES. Lexington: Anvil Press, 1957, 12mo., cloth, dust jacket. (i), xii, (ii), 106, (2) pages. un-opened. $ 250.00

Printed in an edition limited to 175 numbered copies. A collection of stories by Johann Peter Hebel, a German poet from the 1800's who was also considered one of Germany's rare talents. This was translated by Clavia Goodman and Bayard Quincy Morgan. It was printed on Japanese Hosho paper, and the woodcut on the wrapper is by Victor Hammer from a drawing by Leo Delitz. Very fine condition.

544. (Hammer, Victor) MEMORY AND HER NINE DAUGHTERS THE MUSES. New York: George Wittenborn, Inc., 1957, large 8vo., printed paper covered boards, dust jacket. (ii), 107+(1) pages. $ 950.00

Printed in an edition limited to 252 numbered copies, this being copy "one." (Hammer 14, Holbrook 21). The dust wrapper is printed with a woodcut by Victor Hammer showing a diagram of measurements and auxiliary lines of the front wall of his Chapel in Kolbsheim. (See also: Opus xiii.) It was printed by Carolyn Hammer and case bound in unused printed sheets from Opus XIII by Lucy Crump. This particular copy is case bound with the opening page of text of the Opus XIII which has a large blue and red brass-cut initial "G." Jacket soiled.

545. (Hammer, Victor) MESA. N.P. (various places): Herbert Steiner, 1945/46/55, small 4to., cloth, paper label on front cover. 45,(5); 45,(5); 46,(5) pages. $ 150.00

Mesa, a limited edition literary periodical (ULS 2615). We offer three issues (No.1 of Autumn, 1945; no.2, Autumn, 1946, and no.5, Autumn, 1955), of which the first two had a run of 300 copies and the last a run of 280 copies. The first two issues were printed by Victor and Jacob Hammer at the Wells College Press, and the last issue by Jacob Hammer in Lexington, KY, in association with the Anvil Press. The editor and copyright holder of Mesa was Herbert Steiner, who was first at Wheaton College and later at Penn State at State College. Mesa was an eclectic but certainly not avant-garde literary journal which printed short literary works, excerpts, letters, and criticism, either in the original language or in translation. Many items were previously unpublished or excerpted from publications then in preparation. Some contents: An English translation of an ancient South American Indian play of Rabinal, letters of Hugo von Hofmannsthal in German, an article in French on an unknown rough draft by Valery, and poems in Spanish by Miguel de Unamuno. With notes and one or two advertisements per issue. No. two has two-tone cloth. No.2 has some faint scratches on the covers, otherwise these are in excellent condition.

546. (Hammer, Victor) Tyndale, William (translator). THE GOSPELL OFF S. LUKE. (THE NEW TESTAMENTE M.D. XXVI.). (Lexington, KY: Anvil Press, 1955), 12mo., paper-covered boards with wrap around spine label. (ii), 93, (2) leaves. $ 250.00
Limited to 300 copies (Holbrook, 15). One of four volumes issued separately as *The New Testament*, 1954-55, from Tyndale's 1526 translation (he was strangled and burnt as a heretic in 1536). Wooducts of the Evangelists and their symbols are by Victor Hammer, after the Holkham Bible drawings. Designed by Victor Hammer and printed in red and black by Jacob Hammer on Arnold unbleached paper with deckle edges and unopened paper. Light foxing on front cover and endpapers.

547. (Hammer, Victor) Tyndale, William (translator). THE GOSPELL OFF S. MATHEW. (THE NEW TESTAMENTE M.D. XXVI.). (Lexington, KY: Anvil Press, 1955), 12mo., paper-covered boards with wrap around paper spine label. (ii), 85, (2) leaves. $ 250.00
Printed in an edition limited to 300 copies (Holbrook, 15). One of four volumes issued separately as *The Newe Testamente*, 1954-55, from Tyndale's 1526 translation (he was strangled and burnt as a heretic in 1536). Woodcuts of the Evangelists and their symbols are by Victor Hammer, after the Holkham Bible drawings. Designed by Victor Hammer and printed in red and black by Jacob Hammer on Arnold unbleached paper with deckle edges and unopened pages.

548. (Hammer, Victor) VICTOR HAMMER, ARTIST AND PRINTER. Lexington: The Anvil Press, 1981, small 4to., cloth, cardboard slipcase. (x), 213, (2) pages. $ 150.00
One of 500 numbered copies of a total edition of 550 copies. The book was designed by Martino Mardersteig in Dante type and printed at the Stamperia Valdonega in Verona. The book contains an essay "Who is Victor Hammer?" by Rudolf Koch; a review of Hammer's mezzotints by Ulrich Middledorf; chapters on "Engraving and Woodcuts" and "Inscriptions & Symbols" by Carolyn Hammer; a chapter on uncial type faces by R. Hunter Middleton and other essays by such people as Hermann Zapf and a bibliography by David Farrell. Illustrated. Very small spot on front cover.

549. (Hammer Creek Press) ALONG THE HAMMER CREEK AND THE HAMMER CREEK PRESS WITH SOME DATA. N.P.: The Hammer Creek Press, 1952, 12mo., stiff paper wrappers, cord-tied. (12) pages. $ 100.00
Two woodcuts by John DePol depict the Hammer Creek and the press used by John Fass at his Hammer Creek Press. This press was originally owned by Bruce Rogers while he was at the Riverside Press.

550. (Hammer Creek Press) HAMMER CREEK PRESS TYPE SPECIMEN BOOK. New York: The Hammer Creek Press, 1954, 12mo., paper covered boards, paper cover label. 51+(1) pages. $ 650.00
Printed in an edition limited to 122 copies of which this is one of 100 printed on handmade paper. (Cohen no.31; Burke, pp.24-25). One of the most substantial productions of John Fass printed on the small handpress of Bruce Rogers. Includes sections devoted to typefaces, borders and decorative material, and turtles by various artists. These include turtles by John DePol, Burton Carnes, Valenti Angelo. Some pages printed in color. Presentation by John Fass in pencil on front free endpaper.

552. (Hampshire Typothetae) HAMPSHIRE TYPOTHETAE. (Northampton, MA): The Hampshire Typothetae, (1977), 8vo., stiff paper wrappers. (4) pages. $ 10.00
Limited to 1500 copies. Statement of purpose of this press established by Harold McGrath and Barry Moser.

554. (Har-Ma Press) Smith, Harold and Alma. THE FRIENDS SPEAK. (Sacramento): Har-ma Press, (1981), 8vo., cloth. 55+(1) pages. $ 35.00
Printed by the Har-ma Press in an edition limited to 160 numbered copies by Harold F. Smith, type set by Alma Smith, and inscribed by the authors on the first blank. A sample of information received by the authors from a Source they called "Friends," elicited verbally from meditation.

555. (Har-Ma Press) Smith, Harold and Alma. LISTENING TO LIFE. Sacramento: Har-ma Press, (1985), 8vo., cloth. 75 (3) pages. $ 65.00
Printed in an edition limited to 140 numbered copies on a handpress made by Harold F. Smith, type set by Alma Smith, inscribed on the front flyleaf in ink and printed and bound by them in Centaur 18 point on Mohawk Letter Press paper. Wood engravings by Harold Smith. Information from "a higher realm" received by the authors.

556. (Har-Ma Press) Smith, Harold and Alma. QUOTE. (Sacramento): Har-ma Press, (1983), 8vo., cloth. 59+(1) pages. $ 55.00
Printed in an edition limited to 125 numbered copies and inscribed by the authors on the front flyleaf. Printed on a Har-ma handpress, with type hand set in 18 Point Centaur by Alma Smith, and printed and bound by them on Mohawk Letter Press paper. With wood engravings by Harold Smith. Guidance and instructions received by the authors from a "Force we call Friends"

557. (Har-Ma Press) Smith, Harold and Alma. THE WISE MAN STORIES. Har-Ma Press, (1978), small 8vo., cloth. 41+(1) pages. $ 17.50
Printed in an edition limited to 100 numbered copies on 12 Point Centaur, "in a corner of the garage, on a minipress made by Harold F. Smith; type set by Alma Smith. Inscribed by the authors to previous owner on front free endpaper, with a personal bookmark laid in.

558. (Har-Ma Press) Smith, Harold and Alma. THE WISE MAN STORIES AND TEACHINGS, FRIENDS ANONYMOUS. N.P.: Har-Ma Press, (1979), small 8vo., cloth. 72, (2) pages. $ 35.00
Printed in an edition limited to 125 numbered copies. Inscribed by the authors to Roger Levenson on front free endpaper, with a Christmas card and personal letter laid in. Printed in blue with two illustrations. Spine faded.

559. (Harrison of Paris) Byron, Lord. CHILDE HAROLD'S PILGRIMAGE, A RO-MAUNT. With illustrations by Sir Francis Cyril Rose, Bart. New York: Harrison of Paris, (1931), small 4to., pink cloth stamped in black and with beveled edges, slipcase with paper cover label. Slipcase partially detached on bottom. 236, (2) pages. $ 65.00
Limited to 700 numbered copies of which this is one of 660 printed on Montgolfier vellum. The ninth publication of the press (Ransom no.9). Designed by Monroe Wheeler and printed in the types of Didot by Ducros et Colas of Paris. The illustrations have been printed using the collotype process by Daniel Jacomet. One page foreword by the Publisher. Endpapers foxed as usual from glue used in covers.

560. (Harrison of Paris) Dostoevsky, Fyodor. GENTLE SPIRIT, A FANTASTIC STORY. Translated from the Russian by Con stance Garnett with Frontispiece and Tailpiece by Christian Bérard. N.P.: Harrison of Paris, 1931, 8vo., cloth, slipcase with paper cover label. 85 pages. $ 75.00
Limited to 570 numbered copies. Being the eighth production of the press. (Ransom no.8). Set in 10–point Stempel-Baskerville and printed by L.C. Wittich at Darmstadt, Germany. Very fine copy.

561. (Harrison of Paris) Harte, Bret. THE WILD WEST. Paris: Harrison of Paris, (1930), 8vo., cloth, slipcase. (vi), 187, (3) pages. $ 65.00
Printed in an edition limited to 840 numbered copies on Montgolfier Freres Annonay paper. This is the second title from this publisher, printed by R. Coulouma at Argenteuil under the direction of H. Barthelemy. Eight water-color drawings by Pierre Fallke, stencil-colored by E. Charpentier in Paris. Stories include *The Outcasts of Poker Flat, Mr. Thompson's Prodigal, A Monte Flat Pastoral, Tennessee's Partner, and Mliss*. Spine darkened, with 2 small tears near middle edge.

562. (Harrison of Paris) Merimee, Prosper. CARMEN AND LETTERS FROM SPAIN, NEWLY TRANSLATED. With ten Monochrome water-colours by Maurice Barraud. N.P.: Harrison of Paris, 1931, square 8vo., boards, top edge gilt, slipcase. (viii), 175 pages. $ 75.00
Limited to 665 numbered copies of which this is one of the 595 to be printed on Rives pure-rag vellum. The sixth production of the press. (Ransom no.6). Printed in 12-point monotype Fournier by Aimé Jourde in Paris. The illustrations have been stencil-colored by Eugène Charpentier. A very fine copy.

563. (Harrison of Paris) OFFERINGS FOR THE PERSON OF TASTE WHO HAS EVERYTHING (ELSE). New York: Harrison of Paris, n.d. (circa 1933), folio, broadside. $ 5.00
With descriptions of four books available from the press including Katherine Anne Porter's *French Song-Book*. Printed on gray paper with red ink and containing two illustrations.

564. (Harrison of Paris) Porter, Katherine Anne. HACIENDA. New York: Harrison of Paris, (1934), 8vo., cloth, top edge gilt, slipcase, paper cover label. 81 pages. $ 125.00
Limited to 895 copies printed on Arnold's English pure-rag paper. (Ransom no.13 - the last book of the press). Designed by Monroe Wheeler and printed in linotype Baskerville italic. A first edition of the work of Porter (Schwartz A item). Ahearn mentions copies with page 52 not canceled but this copy has a cancelled page 52. Very fine copy with prospectus present.

565. (Harrison of Paris) PUBLICATIONS OF HARRISON OF PARIS. Paris: Harrison of Paris, n.d. (circa 1930), small 8vo., self paper wrappers. 8 pages printed French fold. $ 15.00
The first publisher's catalogue issued by this private press. Four pages on the philosophy of the press and four pages describing the four upcoming publications of the press.

566. (Hart Press) Powell, Thomas Reed. CONSTITUTIONAL METAPHORS, A REVIEW OF JAMES M. BECK'S "THE CONSTITUTION OF THE UNITED STATES." (Berkeley: Hart Press, 1941), 8vo., stiff paper wrappers. (ii), 5+(1) pages. $ 20.00
Printed in an edition limited to 100 copies, hand-set at The Hart Press, Berkeley. Originally published in the *New Republic*, February 11, 1925. X-Lib, wear to extremities. Previous owner's name on front flyleaf.

567. (Hawthorn House) Kirk, Richard R. FIRST EDITIONS. Glen Rock: Walter Klinefelter, 1933, 16mo., marbled paper wrappers. (36) pages. $ 35.00
First edition, limited to 220 copies printed by Edmund B. Thompson at Hawthorn House. A collection of verse about books.

568. (Hawthorn House) PRINTER'S COMMON-PLACE BOOK. Windham: Hawthorn House, (1937), 12mo., leather-backed boards. 24 pages. $ 75.00
Limited to 350 numbered copies printed by Edmund B. Thompson at his private press. Presentation from Thompson to Frank Rea Sloan Jr. on free endpaper dated 1937 and with Sloan's bookplate. Wear at spine ends and along hinge.

569. (Hawthorn House) Thompson, Edmund B. BOOKS FROM HAWTHORN HOUSE, 1938. (Windham, CT): Hawthorn House, 1938, 16mo., cord-tied stiff paper wrappers. (8 pages). $ 10.00

"Each book is printed on a fine rag paper from type set by hand, with decorative binding in boards." The brief list of titles includes "A Visit from St. Nicholas," with decorations by Valenti Angelo, and "Battle of the Frogs," illustrated by Ray Holden.

570. (Hawthorn House) Thompson, Edmund B. HAWTHORN HOUSE....A RECORD OF THE FIRST FIVE YEARS. (Windham, CT): Hawthorn House, (1938), large 8vo., stiff wrappers with label pasted on front cover. unpaginated (8). $ 55.00

Printed in an edition limited to 38 special numbered copies on Worthy Signature paper. A bibliography of the first thirty-three books printed at Hawthorn House, and articles printed for *The Colophon*, a book collector's quarterly. Illustrated with figures and title pages from previous books.

571. (Hawthorn House) [THREE PROSECTUSES ISSUED BY HAWTHORN HOUSE]. Three prospectuses issued by Hawthorn House, Windham, Connecticut announcing their hand-printed books. For the group:. $ 25.00

Includes prospectuses for Margaret Fuller's *The Complete History of the Deluge*, Edmund Thompson's *Maps of Conneticut*, and a general list describing a number of books. With printing in color.

572. (Hawthorn Press) Farmer, Geoffrey. PRIVATE PRESSES AND AUSTRALIA, WITH A CHECK-LIST. Melbourne: The Hawthorn Press, (1972), small 8vo., cloth, dust jacket. (x), 68 pages. $ 95.00

First edition limited to 450. John Kirtley's first private press was the beginning, followed by Perce Green's "Green Press," then George Hassell of Adelaide. Farmer attempts to identify the presses and types used by each private press and gives a bibliography of each press. Signed by John Gartner, the printer.

573. (Hawthornden Press) Drummond, William. A CYPRESS GROVE. (London): Hawthornden Press, 1919, small 8vo., quarter cloth with paper-covered boards, paper cover label. xvii, 17-78 pages. $ 35.00

Printed in an edition limited to 1000 numbered copies by Charles R. Butler at the Hawthornden Press and published by Chas. J. Sawyer, London. With frontis portrait of Drummond from 1766 engraving tipped-in. William Drummond (1585–1649) is considered a master of the sonnet form, but *A Cypress Grove* , appearing in 1623, is the first of his prose works and the only one published in his life time. Introduction and notes by Samuel Clegg. Label from the library of Will Ransom on back pastedown.

574. (Haymarket Press) BOOK OF TOBIT AND THE HISTORY OF SUSANNA REPRINTED FROM THE REVISED. London: The Haymarket Press, 1929, small 4to., original limp vellum lettered in gilt with cloth ties. xiv, 48 pages. $ 850.00

Printed in an edition limited to 100 numbered copies. Reprinted from the revised version of the Apocrypha with an introduction by Dr. Montague R. James. The Book of Tobit is one of the best stories of the old world and the earliest date that can be assigned to it is 350 BC, and the latest 170 BC It was written in Egypt and the original language was Hebrew. It is illustrated with four full color semi-erotic drawings by W. Russell Flint which are tipped-in.

575. (Heavenly Monkey) CHARLES VAN SANDWYK, AN INTERIM BIBLIOGRAPHY 1983 TO 2000. Vancouver: Heavenly Monkey, (2000), small 8vo., paper wrappers with a French wrap. (18) pages. $ 100.00

First edition. Printed in an edition limited to 50 numbered and signed copies. This is the first publication by the Heavenly Monkey Press which is run by Rollin Millroy, formerly the proprietor of the Alone Press. It is a bibliography of Sandwyk's 17 books, in which the artist has compiled along with Milroy. His etchings explored the worlds of fairies and animals in a style reminiscent of Rackham and Dulac. It is illustrated with two of Van Sandwyk's original copperplate etchings and a facsimile of his first book the miniature "Little People." It includes an introduction by Van Sandwyk along with his signature.

576. (Herity Press) Lieberman, J. Ben. THE WHYS AND THEREFORES OF A CHAPPEL. (White Plains): The Herity Press, 1961, 12mo., stiff paper wrappers. 16 pages. $ 20.00
Limited to 500 copies. This book answers questions for potential Chappel members, which is a club or society of private press proprietors or personal printers which live close enough together to meet.

577. (Heron Press) Ellenport, Samuel B. ESSAY ON THE DEVELOPMENT & USAGE OF BRASS PLATE DIES INCLUDING A CATALOGUE RAISONNE FROM THE COLLECTION OF THE HARCOURT BINDERY. Boston: Harcourt Bindery, 1980, large 4to., cloth, leather spine label. 32 pages of text followed by 99 plates with accompanying notes, (7) pages, two full-color plates tipped in. $ 125.00
S-K 7414. An excellent account of a method of hand-binding where the design is pressed on the book from a single brass plate in one procedure. Ellenport writes about the historical development of this method and provides plates of the brass dies used by the Harcourt Bindery. Finely printed at the Heron Press.

578. (Heyeck Press) Cady, Frank. POEMS ON A WHITE PAGE. Woodside, CA: The Heyeck Press, (1982), oblong 8vo., paper wrappers. (24) pages. $ 20.00
Privately printed and limited to 400 copies. Sixteen poems from the Flowering Quince Poetry Series: Number Four, written by Frank Cady. Drawings by Carole Romans.

579. (Heyeck Press) Mayes, Frances. THE BOOK OF SUMMER. Woodside, CA: The Heyeck Press, (1995), large 4to., marbled silk covered boards, slipcase. 61, (3) pages.
$ 295.00
One of an edition of 90 copies, numbered and signed by the author. A large, inviting book of poetry, as warm in design as the summers in Tuscany the author celebrates. Illustrated by Corinne Okada, bound by BookLab in silk, hand marbled in a stone pattern of ochre, gray, russet and white by Robin Heyeck, the book's designer and printer. Printed on dampened handmade Barcham Green Cambersand, uncut at fore and foot edges, with 16 point Centaur and Arrighi type.

580. (High House Press) Shenstone, William. TWENTY SONGS OF WILLIAM SHENSTONE. Shaftesbury: High House Press, 1926, 8vo., quarter cloth with decorated paper boards, paper cover label. (ii), 36, (2) pages. $ 65.00
Printed in an edition limited to 192 numbered copies. Slim volume of typical mid-eighteenth century poetry illustrated with decorations by Philip Ainsworth. Owner's bookplate on front pastedown and signature on front endpaper.

581. (Hill Press) Heaver Jr., Stephen. SOME ARABESQUE COMBINATION ORNAMENTS, WITH A BRIEF INTRODUCTION. Baltimore: The Hill Press, 1994, 8vo., self paper wrappers. (8) pages. $ 8.00
Printed letterpress by Heaver at his Hill Press. Short introduction followed by chronological list and illustrations of ornaments. With a bibliography of reference sources.

582. (Hill Press) Lincoln, Abraham. TWO SPEECHES OF ABRAHAM LINCOLN. Baltimore: The Hill Press, (2000), small 8vo., paper wrappers. (8) pages. $ 25.00
Printed in an edition limited to 90 copies by Steven Heaver at his Hill Press. This contains two speeches given by Abraham Lincoln, the first titled 'Note for a Law Lecture,' written about July 1, 1850, and the second titled 'Address of Farewell,' given at Springfield, Illinois, February 1861, before he moved to Washington. Each copy was printed in a single impression on an 1865 Albion handpress on undampened Zerkall Vellum.

583. (Hoffman, Richard J.) CHRISTMAS GREETINGS 1977. Van Nuys, CA: Richard J. Hoffman, 1977, broadside (9 X 6 inches), stiff paper. $ 15.00
Ruth and Richard Hoffman chose a verse by David Goodman with a surrounding design printed in magenta ink for their 1977 holiday greeting. A Christmas letter on mustard color paper that accompanied the card bears a handwritten greeting to the Dahlstroms.

584. (Hoffman, Richard J.) Cobden-Sanderson, T.J. THE IDEAL BOOK OR BOOK BEAUTIFUL. Los Angeles: Los Angeles State College, 1963, 4to., quarter-cloth with paper-covered boards. (vi), 9, (3). $ 65.00
Printed in an edition limited to 100 numbered copies under the direction of Richard J. Hoffman as a project by some members of the Senior Graphic Arts Class at Los Angeles State College. Professor Richard J. Hoffman "suggested the text and contributed most generously of his time and knowledge." Chapters include *The Ideal Book, Calligraphy, Typography, Illustration,* and *The Book Beautiful.* Originally published by the author at the Doves Press in 1901. Corners lightly bumped and small tear at top of front free endpaper.

585. (Hoffman, Richard J.) Crane, Frank. THE CRAFTSMAN'S CREED. Van Nuys, CA.: (Richard Hoffman), 1978, 12mo., stiff paper wrappers. (iv), 9, (3) pages. $ 25.00
Issue by Richard J. Hoffman as a keepsake for friends who met at his retirement party, June 4, 1978. Goudy Modern types on Urabec-Hoffman hand made paper. In original envelope with appreciation by Hoffman printed on front.

586. (Hoffman, Richard J.) DECORATIVE DIVERTISSEMENT. Van Nuys, CA: Richard J. Hoffman, 1980, 8vo., cloth-backed decorated paper covered boards. 103, (3) pages. $ 135.00
Limited to 150 copies. A book of typographic ornaments, some printed in color, with a supplement to an earlier printed book owned by Hoffman demonstrating type specimens. Each ornament and specimen is identified. Also contains a six page introduction by this excellent California pressman. Bookplate on free endpaper.

587. (Hoffman, Richard J.) Kohn, Jacob. BOOKS AND PEOPLE. Los Angeles: Richard J. Hoffman, 1951, 12mo., paper wrappers. 17 pages. $ 10.00
Typophile Monograph 34. Printed by Richard J. Hoffman. An address on books given to the Library Friends of the Krakowski Memorial Library in Pasadena.

588. (Hoffman, Richard J.) Lence, Karen V. A HISTORY OF THE WESTERN BOOKS EXHIBITION; IF THEY'VE GOT TO FLAP, LET THEM FLAP SPLENDIDLY. Los Angeles: The Rounce & Coffin Club, 1978, small 8vo., quarter cloth, decorated paper-covered boards. 94 (2) pages. $ 45.00
Printed by Richard J. Hoffman in an edition limited to 250 copies. A history of one of the most famous American regional book exhibits, the Western Books Exhibition, from its creation in 1939 into the 1970s. The basis for the book was the minute records, scrapbooks, publications and files of the Exhibition's sponsor, the Rounce & Coffin Club; interviews with Richard J. Hoffman, Muir Dawson, Grant Dahlstrom and other members were also part of the author's research. An important work on the artistry of bookmaking. Includes notes, list of jurors, catalogues and sources.

589. (Hoffman, Richard J.) Lyman, William Whittingham. POEMS IN THREE MOODS. Los Angeles: Published by the author, 1948, small 4to., quarter cloth with paper covered boards. viii, 44, (2) pages. $ 45.00
Designed and printed by Richard J. Hoffman at the College Press: Los Angeles City College. Type composed by Leon H. Gottlieb. Poems about *October in Napa Valley, My Friend of Dream, My Love Walks Forth, Mist Dance,* etc. Ink inscription in ink on front free endpaper. Worn at extremities, with small tear at top of spine.

590. (Hoffman, Richard J.) Moes, Robert J. THE LIFE AND TIMES OF "DR." JAMES STOKES. Los Angeles: (Zamorano and Roxburghe Clubs), 1982, 8vo., stiff paper wrappers. 21, (3) pages. $ 15.00
Printed by Richard J. Hoffman, Van Nuys, Ca. This is the third in a series of essays relating to California medical history and written as a keepsake for the 16th biennial joint meeting of the Zamorano Club of Los Angeles and the Roxburghe Club of San Francisco, October, 1982. Illustration.

591. (Hoffman, Richard J.) Moes, Robert J. MANUEL QUIJANO AND WANING SPAIN. Los Angeles: (Zamorano and Roxburghe Clubs), 1984, 8vo., stiff paper wrappers. 26, (6) pages. $ 15.00
Printed by Richard J. Hoffman, Van Nuys, Ca. Issued as the fourth in a series of essays relating to California's medical history and written as a keepsake for the 17th biennial joint meeting of the Zamorano Club of Los Angeles and the Roxburghe Club of San Francisco, October, 1984. With map of Manuel Quijano's route to missions and presidios.

592. (Hoffman, Richard J.) Moes, Robert J. THE ZAMORANO PRESS AND THE BOTICA, CALIFORNIA'S FIRST MEDICAL BOOK. Los Angeles: The Zamorano Club, 1988, small 4to., dark brown cloth spine with lighter woven cloth covered boards on which is printed a reproduction of the Ramage Press. 23, (3) pages. $ 65.00
Limited to 300 copies. A history of the first medical book printed in California, the Botica General De Los Remedios Esperimentados. This book was printed by California's first printer, Agustín Vicente Zamorano on a Ramage wooden press imported from Boston in 1834. With a woodcut showing a Ramage Press, a facsimile of Zamorano's signature and printing and design by Richard J. Hoffman. With a facsimile of the pamphlet reproduced from one of two known copies loosely inserted in a pocket in the front.

593. (Hoffman, Richard J.) Powell, Gertrude Eliza Clark. LOOKING BACK AND REMEMBERING. Tucson: privately printed, 1987, small 8vo., cloth. 85+(1) pages. $ 45.00
Printed by Richard J. Hoffman, Van Nuys, California, and bound by Roswell Bookbinding, Phoenix, Arizona. An Autobiographical Sketch by the author (1870–1957) with a Prologue and an Epilogue by Lawrence Clark Powell. Photographs.

594. (Hoffman, Richard J.) Powell, Lawrence Clark. LE MONDE PASSE, LA FIGURE DE CE MONDE PASSE, A REMEMBRANCE OF DUNCAN BRENT. Van Nuys, CA: Lawrence Clark Powell, 1983, small 8vo., cloth. 81, (3) pages. $ 45.00
Privately printed for Lawrence Clark Powell by Richard J. Hoffman, Van Nuys, CA, and bound in Phoenix, AZ by Roswell Bookbinding. A memoir and commentary on Duncan Brent's correspondence with the author, who was University Librarian at UCLA from 1944 to 1961. Photographs. With a Best Wishes card from the author laid in.

595. (Hoffman, Richard J.) Powell, Lawrence Clark. SUSANNA'S SECRET OR THE LOST MOZART LETTERS. Tucson: Press of the Mesquite Harpsichord, 1981, 8vo., two-toned cloth covered boards. 53+(1) pages. $ 65.00
First edition. Intended as a chamber production with period sets, costumes and music by Mozart and Hayden, this imaginative work is one man's view of the relationships between Mozart, his father, the composer, Franz Josef Hayden, and the soprano, Anna Selina Storace. Title page is printed in red and black with a decorative green border that is repeated at the beginning of each scene. Printed by Richard J. Hoffman. Author's presentation card loosely inserted.

596. (Hoffman, Richard J.) Powell, Lawrence Clark. WINTER CROSSING 1952, TRAVEL NOTES FROM A BYGONE ERA. N.P.: n.p., (1986), oblong 12mo., quarter cloth. (25) pages. $ 45.00
Log describing Powell's book travels across the country by train. Designed by Ward Ritchie and printed by Richard J. Hoffman for the writer. Illustrated with railroad ornaments.

597. (Hoffman, Richard J.) Slocum, Edwin H. SLOCUM HISTORY, A RESUME OF THE GENERATIONS WHO FOLLOWED FROM JAMES SLOCUM, BEING PRINCIPALLLY THE ANCESTRY, AND LIVES, OF JOHN B. AND OLIVE H. SLOCUM AND DESCENDANTS, IN GENERATIONS NINE THROUGH TWELVE. Van Nuys, CA: (Privately printed), 1975, 8vo., cloth. 204, (2) pages. $ 25.00
Designed and printed by Richard J. Hoffman, with an appreciation by the author. A genealogy, "chronological in its unfolding, a beginning is included as well as some coverage from generation one through the thirteenth."

598. (Hoffman, Richard J.) SOME OBSERVATIONS ON BOOK DESIGN. Van Nuys, CA: Richard J. Hoffman, 1986, small 4to., cloth-backed decorated paper covered boards. 18, (2) pages. $ 55.00
First edition. Printed letterpress and with a three color title pages. Illustrated.

599. (Hoffman, Richard J.) Todd, Edwin M. REFLECTIONS THROUGH A MURKY CRYSTAL. Pasadena, CA: (Richard J. Hoffman), 1986, 8vo., paper covered boards. xvi, 126 pages. $ 45.00
Printed in an edition limited to 1000 signed copies. Richard J. Hoffman enthusiastically employed a different type face and a large, harmonizing decorative initial in red or blue for each of the chapters in this book of serious, contemplative essays by the American physician and intellectual. Presentation copy signed in ink by author on portrait frontispiece. Cover soiled.

600. (Hoffman, Richard J.) WHEN A PRINTER PLAYS, A SHOWING OF PRINTER'S FLEURONS ARRANGED IN ARABESQUE PATTERNS. Van Nuys, CA: Richard J. Hoffman, 1987, 4to., cloth-backed decorated paper over boards. 55 pages. $ 275.00
Limited to 200 numbered and signed copies. Printed by letterpress and bound by Bela Blau of Los Angeles. The culmination of three years work resulted in this magnificent production. It handsomely displays, in two or more colors a tremendous variety of ornaments including designs by Garamond, Bruce Rogers, Bradley, etc. Alongside the examples are reprinted a number of interesting typographical essays on Printer's Flowers and Ornaments. Included are essays by Stanley Morrison, Beatrice Warde, W.A. Dwiggins and Francis Meynell.

601. (Hudson Press) Thomajan, P.K. THE BEARDED LADY OF BALD MOUNTAIN. (Houston: Hudson Press, 1963), 8vo., burlap covered boards, wood veneer cover label. (18) pages. $ 60.00
Printed in an edition limited to 100 numbered copies signed by the author and publisher. Hand set in Goudy Kennerly on Speckle Text paper. Two typed poems signed by the author laid in. With illustrations by William Hogarth.

602. (Imprenta Glorias) Bachardy, Don. THE PORTRAIT BY THE ARTIST. Los Angeles: Imprenta Glorias, 1997, 4to., orange paper covered boards, exposed spine sewing, clear plexi-glass slipcase. (vi), 15, (11) leaves. $ 600.00
Limited to 30 numbered copies. This book, the seventh book from Imprenta Glorias, contains an essay on self-portraiture followed by two self-portraits by Bachardy. The essay discusses the influence that writer Christopher Isherwood had on Bachardy's work. The design, embellishment, and printing of the book are by Gloria Stuart. Six Sitter's thoughts in pocket inside back cover. Hand-set by Stuart in Goudy 30 and Bernard's Tango typeface and printed on Hahnemuhle and Thai Unryu papers. The binding is by Allwyn O'Mara. Pages unopened. Signed below the colophon by Don Bachardy and Gloria Stuart.

603. (Imprenta Glorias) Cameron, James. THE 70TH ANNUAL ACADEMY AWARDS. Los Angeles: Imprenta Glorias, 1999, miniature book (3″ x 2.5″), accordion style gold cloth boards, ribbon ties, clear Plexiglas slipcase. Unpaginated (20 pages).

$ 175.00

Limited to 30 copies of which this is one of twelve for sale. This book contains James Cameron's speech on receiving the Academy Award for Best Picture of 1997, for "Titanic." Signed by both Cameron and Gloria Stuart, who co-starred in the film as well as designed the book. The type is Verona, and the paper is blue Fabriano. The book is designed, hand illustrated, and typeset by Stuart. It is printed by John Robinson and bound by Allwyn O'Mara.

604. (Imprenta Glorias) EVE VENUS AND OTHERS. Los Angeles: Imprenta Glorias, 1990, oblong small 4to., batik paper covered clamshell box, Plexiglas slipcase. Unpaginated.

$ 1,500.00

Limited in an edition of 24 numbered copies. This book contains quotations from a number of authors, such as John Keats, Sappho, and Charles Baudelaire, each illustrated with a mildly erotic handpainted and collage drawing. Each illustration is interspersed with prints of various vegetation and mirror images of the drawings that add another dimension of representation. Printed and illustrated by Gloria Stuart on a variety of papers including Somerset Satin, Unryu, Kanzesui, Momi, and Echizen Washi. With an original collage/watercolor entitled Sappho Ascendant inset into the lower lid of the binding. The binding was executed by D'Ambrosio. Title page calligraphy by Judy Detrick and decorative initials by Marie Balle. Signed by Gloria Stuart.

605. (Imprenta Glorias) Isherwood, Christopher. COMMONPLACE BOOK: BEING SOME QUOTATIONS CHRISTOPHER ISHERWOOD GATHERED AND RECORDED DURING HIS LIFETIME. Los Angeles: Imprenta Glorias, 1993, oblong 8vo., Beauvais patterned cloth, clear plexi-glass slipcase. Unpaginated (33 leaves).

$ 400.00

Limited to 20 numbered copies. This book, the sixth publication from the Imprenta Glorias, collects the favorite quotations of Anglo-American novelist and playwright Christopher Isherwood. With a preface and a portrait by Don Bachardy. The book's design, collage, and printing are by Gloria Stuart. Set in Verona type and printed on Hayle, Natsume, Kozo, and Unryu handmade papers. The title page and four of the quotations are printed on Kozo and mounted on blue paper in a window opening.

606. (Imprenta Glorias) Stuart, Gloria. BOATING WITH BOGART. Los Angeles: Imprenta Glorias, 1993, miniature book (3″ x 2″), paper covered boards, paper spine label. Unpaginated (26 leaves). $ 250.00

Limited to 100 numbered copies. In this book Gloria Stuart tells her story of going boating with Humphrey Bogart in 1938. Printed by Robin Price. Composition by Bieler Press. Embellishments by Davie Dicker. With a Humphrey Bogart United States postal stamp laid in. Signed by Gloria Stuart and Ward Ritchie.

607. (Imprint Society) Longus. DAPHNIS AND CHLOE. Barre, MA: Imprint Society, 1972, 8vo., quarter leather with paper-covered boards, slipcase. 152, (2) pages.

$ 55.00

Printed in an edition limited to 1950 numbered copies, of which this is out of series. Translated by Christopher Collins. Designed and produced in Switzerland by Max Caflisch. Fabag of Winterthur printed the text in Van Dijck Roman typeface on Zerkall paper and reproduced 16 of the 17 aquatints in three colors. The Swiss graphic artist, Felix Hoffmann, created the illustrations especially for this edition-- after a trip to the Greek Isles--and the frontispiece has been struck directly from the copperplate.

608. (Imprint Society) Thomas, Isaiah. HISTORY OF PRINTING IN AMERICA, WITH A BIOGRAPHY OF PRINTERS & AN ACCOUNT OF NEWSPAPERS. Edited by Marcus A. McCorison from the Second Edition. Barre, MA: Imprint Society, 1970, thick 8vo., cloth, slipcase. xxii, 650, (2) pages. $125.00
Reprint, with rearrangements, of the second edition of 1876. (S-K for binding references). Limited to 1950 numbered copies. With an original page from the first edition of 1810 tipped-in. Bookplate.

609. (Incline Press) Eastman, Bert. HELEN BINYON'S TIGER. Oldham: Incline Press, 2000, square 8vo., decorated paper wrappers with a paper cover label. (10) pages. $15.00

Printed in an edition limited to 100 numbered copies. This is the sixth New Year Booklet published by the Incline Press, which features Helen Binyon's Chinese shadow tiger one of the shadow puppets she uses in her shows. It includes two illustration of the tiger, one being a line drawing and the other a print in yellow, brown and white.

610. (Incline Press) FORTY SHEETS TO THE WIND. Oldham: Incline Press, 1999, tall 4to., portfolio bound in half cloth with paper covered boards, paper covered slipcase with a paper spine label. The portfolio contains approximately 60 broadsides and an accompanying booklet of (ii), 15, (3) pages. $180.00
Printed in an edition limited to 150 numbered sets. A portfolio of letterpress printed broadsides each set in different types. Designed as type specimens these sheets demonstrate the different faces in use and the different faces held by the Incline Press. The accompanying booklet discusses the production of the specimens and the history of the individual types employed. Various sample papers have been tipped-in throughout the text. The text also contains descriptions of the woodcuts, the design, and papers used. Many of the individual broadsides pay homage to the great names of printing and book design, such as "Verses Written to the Sound of Fire Engines" by Beatrice Warde, "The Birdcatcher," by Ralph Hodgson, "Little Fishes" by Bruce Rogers, "Some Papers Are Not Used," by Fred Goudy, and more. Many of the broadsides are printed upon colored papers and included illustrative vignettes. An unusual and remarkable collection.

611. (Incline Press) Graham, Robert. PLAYING GERSHWIN. N.P.: Incline Press, 1997, tall thin 8vo., paper wrappers. (iv), 10 pages. $60.00
Printed in an edition limited to 200 numbered copies signed by the author. This is the first of occasional series of short stories by modern authors, this one including 14 stories by Robert Graham. It is illustrated with hand-coloured lino-cuts by Peter Allen.

612. (Incline Press) INCLINE PRESS ILLUSTRATED BOOKS. Oldham: The Incline Press, 1998, broadside 21 x 14 inches. $25.00
Issued in commemoration of Oak Knoll Fest 1998. Printed in two colors with a Vandercook proofing press on dampened Zerkall paper.

613. (Incline Press) MARCO'S ANIMAL ALPHABET. Oldham: Incline Press, 2000, folio, blue buckram spine, patterned paper covered boards. Unpaginated (31 leaves). $285.00

Limited to 160 numbered copies. This book contains 27 original prints by Enid Marx. These 27 linocuts were completed in 1979, but were never formally editioned. Each is accompanied by a piece of doggerel verse by Marco (the artists name at the Royal College of Art). With colour scheme by Peter Allen. With an introduction by Graham Moss that tells the story of these prints setting them in the general context of Enid Marx's work. Set in 24pt. Scotch types (roman and italic) and hand printed on Fabriano Artistico paper.

614. (Incline Press) Marx, Enid. SOME BIRDS & BEASTS AND THEIR FEASTS. Oldham: Incline Press, 1997, 12mo., stiff paper wrappers. (ii), 26, (2) numbered leaves.
$ 30.00

Printed in an edition limited to 350 copies. An alphabet of wood engravings in which Enid Marx cut the wood blocks from which these pictures have been printed, and the block used to make the pattern paper. The fancy alphabet is called Fry's Ornamented, the Roman and Italic alphabet is Verona and the words are in Baskerville.

615. (Incline Press) Moss, Graham. AT INCLINE PRESS. Oldham: Incline Press, 2000, large 12mo., quarter cloth, with marbled paper covered boards, paper cover label. (16) pages.
$ 25.00

Printed in an edition limited to 100 copies. A brief illustrated history for the Oxford Guild of Printers' Millennium Project. The press mark used on the front cover is the work of the calligrapher David Young, 1993, and the illustration of the feather on the frontispiece is by Enid Marx. It is illustrated with wood-engravings by artists Elizabeth Friedlander, Brigid Holdworth, Jo Spaul, Lovat Fraser, Anna Ravenscroft, Ann Muir, Sybella Stiles, and John R. Smith.

616. (Incline Press) Paucker, Pauline. NEW BORDERS: THE WORKING LIFE OF ELIZABETH FRIEDLANDER. Oldham: Incline Press, 1998, 4to., three-quarter buckram, with boards covered in a patterned paper with a Friedlander Curwen design, slipcase. (iii), 92 pages, with 80 additional leaves of plates.
$ 225.00

Limited to 325 copies in this edition, signed by the author. The typographer and designer Elisabeth Friedlander (née Friedländer) designed the typeface Elisabeth for Bauer and is also known for her Mono-type and Linotype ornaments, and her patterns for Curwen papers. Born to a cultured German Jewish family in 1903, she studied design and typography with E.R. Weiss, and later did calligraphy for the Ullstein journal "Die Dame," in addition to the Bauer commission. Politics forced her to leave Germany for Italy in 1936, where she worked for Mondadori and Editoriale Domus, but Mussolini's Italy was no long-term haven, and in 1939 Friedlander came to England, where she became a successful free-lance designer after the war, producing calligraphy, bookplate and masthead designs, devices, ornaments, and patterned paper designs for the Curwen Press. This biography of Elisabeth Friedlander, based on her own work books, letters, various documents, and the testimony of friends and acquaintances, includes eighty plates and an additional twenty-three illustrations of her work in the text. Some items illustrated are: reproductions of calligraphy from Die Dame, specimens of Elisabeth type, settings of Monotype and Linotype borders by her, reproductions of work done for Mondadori and later for Penguin, fifteen paper patterns for Curwen, examples of freelance and agency advertising work, etc.

617. (Incline Press) Paul, Elliot. MONSIEUR DORLAN, RELIEUR. (Oldham, England): Incline Press, 1995, 12mo., single folded sheet laid in stiff paper wrappers. (8) pages.
$ 15.00

Issued as an Incline Press keepsake at the 21st Anniversary Conference of the Society of Bookbinders, Manchester, June, 1995. Machine setting in 12 pt Monotype Caslon and hand set in Verona & printed on his Arab treadle press by Graham Moss.

618. (Incline Press) PRESS MARKS. Oldham: Incline Press, 1998, small 8vo., paper wrappers with a small paper cover label. iv, 17+(1) pages.
$ 25.00

Printed in an edition limited to 350 numbered copies of which this is one of 150 that were offered for sale. This is the fourth Incline Press New Year Booklet, which depicts and describes twenty press marks used by contemporary presses. The text and press marks have been contributed by the printers themselves. Includes illustrations of each mark and a brief statement about each press.

619. (Incline Press) Tegetmieir, Denis. CORRESPONDENCE OF 1953 CONCERN-ING THE BOOK THE SEVEN DEADLY VIRTUES. Oldham: Incline Press, 1999, 4to., quarter cloth, marbled paper covered boards, paper cover label. (20) pages with one additional tipped-in notice in the back. $ 70.00

Printed in an edition limited to 120 numbered copies. A series of letters between the book collector Stanley Scott and Eric Gill and Denis Tegetmier concerning their 1934 book *The Seven Deadly Virtues*. Mr. Scott had managed to acquire two copies numbered copy 7 and was inquiring about this had happened. Printed on Zerkall paper with newly commissioned illustrations by Romey Brough.

620. (Inky Parrot Press) Brown, Marian. BATH NIGHT; THE CHAINED TREE. N.P.: Inky Parrot Press, 1983, 8vo., paper-covered boards, paper label on front cover, decorated endpapers. 3-36 pages. $ 75.00

Limited to 225 numbered copies, including 35 with hand-colored illustrations, of which latter group this is one. Signed by author and illustrator on colophon. Two short stories of somewhat opposing tendency: Carrie (Bath Night) learns to repay generosity with generosity, while Suzie (Chained Tree) learns that even pediatric patients play games of deceit and domination. Twenty-five drawings, most of them colored.

621. (Inky Parrot Press) Colverson, Tom and Dennis Hall (editors). A CATALOGUE OF FINE PRESS PRINTERS IN THE BRITISH ISLES. Oxford: The Inky Parrot Press, 1986, small 4to., stiff paper wrappers. Not paginated. $ 25.00

Limited to 1050 copies. Lists and describes 167 private presses, and 22 trade stands. Well illustrated with engravings from many of the presses.

622. (Inky Parrot Press) Cullingford, Cedric. INCONSTANT VISITORS. N.P. (but Headington, Oxford): The Inky Parrot Press, 1983, tall small 4to., sewn, stiff paper wrappers, french fold, paper label on cover. (22) pages. $ 45.00

Limited to 106 numbered copies, signed by author on colophon. Ten poems by C. Cullingford with 3 large linocuts and several vignettes (including cover label) by Cathy Gue. The poet perceives the muse of poetry, who seems to be staying in a place rather like London. Cover label lightly soiled.

623. (Insel-Verlag) Kessler, Harry Graf. TAGEBUCHER 1918–1937. Frankfurt am Main: Insel-Verlag, (1961), small 8vo., cloth. 799+(1) pages. $ 45.00

First edition. The diary of Harry Graf Kessler, the German diplomat, is reproduced here. Kessler was both an author and private pressman. Among his books is *Nationality* from 1921. Wolfgang Pfeiffer-Belli provides an introduction. Black and white portrait of Kessler at front. Includes index. In German. Inscriptions in ink on front and rear free endpaper.

624. (Italian Fine Printing) AL FAUSTO RITORNO DALLA GERMANIA DI PIO VI PONTEFICE MASSIMO. Perugia: Presso Carlo Baduel, 1782, small 4to., contemporary patterned paper wrappers. (ii), xxii, (ii), 154 pages. $ 850.00

An attractive festival book commemorating the return of Pius VI from a visit to Germany. The engraved title page was beautifully designed by Antonio Stefanucci and engraved by Raimondo Fauci, and the engraved frontispiece was designed by Petrus Labruzzi and engraved by Camillus Tinti. The decorative tail-piece is also by Stefanucci and Faucci. Carlo Baduel of Perugia printed the beautiful title page, the portrait, and the endpiece. Very nicely printed with a decorative border. Spine covering worn.

625. (Italian Fine Printing) Gennari, Giuseppe. TO SUA ECCELLENZA IL SIGNOR CAVALIERE ALVISE PISANI NEL GIORNO DEL SUO SOLENNE INGRESSO ALL DIGNITA DI PROCCURATORE DI S. MARCO ORAZIONI. Padova: Nella Stamperia del Seminario, 1796, 4to., original decorated wrappers. 27 pages.

$ 1,100.00

An excellent copy of a privately printed 'gratulatorie,' singing the praises of both the Republic of Venice and his excellence Alvise Pisani. This is printed at the Seminary Press in Padova and is an excellent example of the work produced by monastery print shops which existed throughout Italy during the 18th century. The engraved frontispiece is by Vitalba, and is also illustrated with a title page vignette, and an engraved head and tailpiece.

626. (Italian Fine Printing) Valaressi, Alysi. TERMINDANDO GLRIOSAMENTE IL REGGIMENTO DI PADOVA SUA ECCELLENZA IL N.H CONTE PIETRO MANIN CANTO. N.P.: n.p., n.d. (circa 1780), 4to., original marbled paper wrappers. xvi pages.

$ 750.00

First edition. An unusual and rare poem dedicated to Pietro Manin at the end of his tenure as governor of the city and province of Padova. It is beautifully illustrated with an architectual title-page and a wonderful engraved vignette showing the animal world responding to the sunrise. The engraved frontispiece and the two vignettes are of a primitive but effecting style. Covers faded.

627. (Janus Press) Cate, Phillip Dennis and Sinclair Hamilton Hitching. CLAIRE VAN VLIET: PRINTMAKER AND PRINTER, A SELECTION OF PRINTS AND ILLUSTRATED BOOKS FROM THE JANUS PRESS AT THE RUTGERS UNIVERSITY ART GALLERY, 1978. New Brunswick, NJ.: Rutgers University Art Gallery, 1978, 12mo., stiff paper wrappers. 6 pages.

$ 15.00

Printed in an edition limited to 600 by Claire Van Vliet at The Janus Press for The Rutgers University Art Gallery (Fine, 1975-80, p.51).

628. (Janus Press) Cortese, James. WHAT THE OWL SAID. Newark, Vermont: Janus Press, 1979, 4to., printed Belgian linen covered boards by James Bicknell, paper spine label. (ii), 26 (2). Page 8 is misnumbered as page 7.

$ 225.00

Limited to 165 numbered copies. (Fine, p. 46). 19 linoleum cut illustrations and 1 linocut decoration by Claire Van Vliet, printed in blue, yellow, sap green, and white. Titles printed in black and ochre, text in black, ochre and brown.

629. (Janus Press) Johnson, W.R. LILAC WIND. Newark (VT): The Janus Press / Brookston (IN): Twinrocker Handmade Paper Mill, 1983, 4to. (folded), accordion folded sheet with top edge irregularly shaped, and 7 folds and 8 panels (61 inches wide and of varying height (about 2. 5 to 11.75 inches), cloth-covered clamshell with paper spine label. Seven panels printed/decorated one side, one panel printed/ decorated on both sides (second side is title page), i.e. 9 pages.

$ 600.00

Limited to 150 numbered copies. R.E. Fine: The Janus Press 1981–1990, p.39. Three poems of W.R. Johnson printed on a 60+ inch sheet (formed from two smaller sheets joined together). "The three short Lilac Wind poems...are printed directly on an elaborately shaped folding paperwork that evokes Van Vliet's northern Vermont winters: the rounded snow-covered field below a cloudy sky at dusk that surrounds a full, round moon of ice-green, a color quite specific to Vermont's winter landscape. One handles and views the setting simultaneously with reading the poems"- Fine: op. cit, p.25. A paperpulp book, or pulp-painting, with titles and text in deep blue printed on paperwork from white, blue, grey and violet pulps, and a relief printed moon in light green.

630. (Janus Press) Levertov, Denise. BATTERERS. Vermont: Janus Press, 1996, 12″ x 15″ and folds out to 44″ wide, sewn into binders board and freestanding wooden cradle, buckram covered slipcase. 12 pages. $ 750.00

Limited to 100 copies, signed by the author and both artists. A powerful poem of concern for the Earth and women. The imagery in the wooden cover/frame is clay paper made by Kathryn Lipke Vigesaa and each one is unique. The cover frame is constructed so that it is freestanding on all four sides and so the art work can also be viewed in four directions. The poem is printed on a fold out landscape paperwork that was pulp painted on both sides of the sheet by Claire Van Vliet at MacGregor-Vinzani in Whiting, Maine.

631. (Janus Press) Lohf, Kenneth. SEASONS. SEVEN POEMS WITH A COLOR RELIEF PRINT BY CLAIRE VAN VLIET. Newark, VT: The Janus Press, 1981, large 12mo., quarter red Scholco cloth with dyed Japanese paper covered boards (24) pages. $ 125.00

First edition, limited to 150 numbered copies signed by the author and artist. (Fine, 35) Seven poems by Kenneth Lohf, former librarian of Rare Books and Manuscripts at Columbia University and past president of the Grolier Club, are presented here in Trump Mediaeval Italic on old Fabriano paper. Titles are printed in red and black. Includes a French folded linocut by Catherine Hall, who also dyed the Japanese paper on the cover. Set and printed by Nancy Reid.

632. (Janus Press) Meynell, Kate. EAT BOOK. Vermont: Janus Press, 1990, 4to., vellum spine, boards plastered with acrylic and wrapped in a rumpled linen napkin. 26 pages. $ 350.00

Printed in an edition limited to 150 numbered copies, signed by the author and illustrator. A sardonic poem with six sepia duotone still life prints of cherries, sausages, and white bread, made with Susan Johanknecht who lettered the text, made eight reliefs of various kitchen utensils, and designed the binding. With recipes written out by Alix Meynell.

633. (Janus Press) O'Callaghan, Julie. WELL-HEELED. Vermont: Gefn Janus Unlimited, 1998, 4″ x 7″, french-fold accordion book in Thai gold-threaded burgundy paper wrappers, white box. 16 pages. $ 15.00

Facsimile printed at the Stinehour Press of this artist book that was originally published in 1985 in an edition of 30 copies. This edition is unlimited with the first printing being 1000 copies. This poem is a satirical monologue from the point-of-view of a shoe addict. The 1985 original edition was handprinted and included lithographs with rubber stamped text and images drawn by Susan Johanknecht at Central School of Art in London in an edition of thirty copies. This edition, printed by offset is housed in a white box with a variety of sleeves including gold, silver, hot pink, and blue suede.

634. (Jonathan Edwards College Press) Edwards, Jonathan. OF INSECTS. New Haven: The Jonathan Edwards College Press, 1974, 8vo., cloth, paper spine label. (25) pages. $ 85.00

Limited to 100 numbered copies; this copy is lettered. Handsomely printed book with wood-engravings by Lance Hidy and George Shakespear. The text is from an essay based on Edward's scientific observations while at Yale. Preface by Wallace E. Anderson.

635. (Jones, George W.) Vergil, Publius Maro. THE GEORGICS OF VERGIL. London: George W. Jones, 1931, small 4to., quarter cloth with paper-covered boards. xxviii, 128, (2) pages. $ 85.00

Printed in an edition limited to 500 copies on specially made paper. Set in Linotype Estienne by its designer, George W. Jones (1860–1942), at *The Sign of the Dolphin* in Gough Square, Fleet Street, London. Translated by R. D. Blackmore, author of *Lorna Doone*. With an introduction by R.S. Conway and woodcut illustrations by Edward Carrick. This edition of the Georgics was issued on the two thousandth anniversary of Vergil's birth on a farm in the Po Valley of Northern Italy. Corners very slightly bumped and minor soiling to back cover.

636. (Jones, George W.) DeCasseres, Benjamin. ANATHEMA! LITANIES OF NEGATION. New York: Gotham Book Mart, 1928, 8vo., paper-covered boards. xii,44+(1)pages. $ 22.50

Printed in an edition of 1250 copies. Numbered and signed by the author. Foreword praising the work of this iconoclastic poet and essayist by Eugene O'Neill. Set in Granjon Old Face type and finely designed by George W. Jones. Printed at Stratford Press from typography arranged by S.A. Jacobs. Printed on Navarre paper bound in Fabriano. Pages deckled, many unopened. Two erratum slips inserted.

637. (Jones, George W.) ROBERT GRANJON, SIXTEENTH CENTURY TYPE FOUNDER AND PRINTER. Brooklyn: Mergenthaler Linotype Co., 1931, 4to., parchment-backed marbled paper covered boards, slipcase. (18) pages. $ 85.00

First edition thus, limited to 400 copies. Eight pages of text and four pages showing the complete range of Granjon type available from this linotype company. Printed by George W. Jones at The Sign of the Dolphin in London on Kelmscott paper. Slipcase is partially broken.

638. (Jones, George W.) Sachs, Hans. A TRUE DESCRIPTION OF ALL TRADES. Brooklyn: Mergenthaler Linotype Co., 1930, large 12mo., marbled paper-covered boards. 19 (3) pages. $ 25.00

Printed by George W. Jones in an edition limited to four hundred copies in Linotype Granjon on Kelmscott hand-made paper. Verse translated by A.F. Johnson. Originally published in Frankfort in 1568 as a collection of woodcuts illustrating all manner of trades and professions, accompanied by doggerel verses written by the popular Nuremberg poet, Hans Sachs. Six of the original 114 sketches by Jobst Amman are selected here that deal with the art of printing. The processes of paper-making and the various tools used in book-binding are portrayed in accurate detail.

639. (Juniper Press) Cade, Phillip J. HISTORY OF THE SAMUEL STEPHENS & WICKERSHAM QUOIN CO., INC. Winchester, MA: The Juniper Press, 1984, small 8vo., paper wrappers. (vi), 16, (2) pages. $ 17.50

Limited Edition Number 26. A brief history of the start of the Samuel Stephens & Wickersham Quoin Co. Included are illustrations and prices from his "Catalogue" from which he sold cabinets, cases, and galleys.

ONE OF 45 COPIES

640. Kelly, Rob Roy. AMERICAN WOOD TYPES 1828–1900, COLLECTED, CATALOGUED AND PRINTED BY ROB ROY KELLY. N.P.: n.p., 1964, folio, stiff paper covers with plastic comb binding, loose sheets, cloth-covered clamshell with paper label on front. (12) pages, with 97 broadsides (22.5675 x 17.5 inches / 57.2 x 44.4 cm), and 3 smaller sheets. $ 3,000.00

Limited to 45 numbered copies. If one accepts that there is a tension in typographic aesthetics between the functions of letters as signifiers and their quality as objects of appreciation in themselves, then large to very large display letters such as those here add an element of paradox: Their purpose (to get attention) and sheer size practically force the reader/viewer to consider the non-signifying or aesthetic aspect of the letters, even as they are used for communication of urgent, specific messages (advertising, announcements, etc.) for which letters are only a means to an end. Nineteenth-century large, ornamental wood faces represent one approach to resolving this difficulty, but, unfortunately, one rarely sees such letters in their larger sizes and appearing, as was originally intended, against a broadside-sized background! This scarce set of wood type specimens, printed by R.R. Kelly from his collection of American wood types "obtained from both rural and urban print shops located primarily in the Midwest," displays 137 large wood type faces and ornaments and borders properly, on broadside sheets (97). Specimens are alphabets (including lower case when available) and figures (when available). Some also include words or strings of letters. In one or two cases only a few letters were available. Compositions of letters vary and may incorporate cuts (in wood) of borders or other decorations. Several faces have their own backgrounds. Two sheets contain only decorations. Printing is mostly black, but with a fair amount of red-and-black. Impressions are usually crisp and uniformly inked. Where inking is uneven we assume that this has to do with the condition of the types used. The introductory brochure (same size as the broadsides), provides a basic classification of 19th-century display faces as applicable to wood types, discusses their manufacture and manufacturers, and reproduces the signatures or trademarks placed by some manufacturers on their types. A sheet-by-sheet catalogue of faces follows this. Entries identify each face by name, maker (if known), general category, and date of introduction (when known), and may note limitations in the Kelly collection (only upper-case, lacks figures, etc.) and/or include annotations. A small-size reproduction of a few letters may accompany the entry. Some of the material in the introduction was previously published elsewhere. Accompanying the above are several smaller sheets with much later decorative designs using letters in the style of 19th-cent. wood type. We assume that these were inserted as examples of 20th-century use or misuse of 19th-century wood type faces. The broadsides have no tears or creases. This copy has a number of photographs showing wood type being made loosely inserted along with ephemeral material concerning wood type.

641. (Kelly-Winterton Press) Pope, Alexander. THE PUZZLING OF THE GRAMMARIAN. New Rochelle, NY: James L. Weil Publisher, 2000, large 12mo., quarter cloth with decorated paper covered boards, paper spine label. (14) pages. $ 48.00
Printed in an edition limited to 60 copies. This text is based on the 1743 edition of The Iliad of Homer translated by Alexander Pope, and was printed to celebrate the 205th birthday of John Keats.

642. (Kelmscott Press) Cockerel, Sidney (editor). SOME GERMAN WOODCUTS OF THE FIFTEENTH CENTURY. (Hammersmith: The Kelmscott Press, 1897, 4to., original quarter linen with blue paper covered boards. xii, 36+(1) pages. $ 3,000.00
Printed in an edition limited to 233 copies of which this from a series of 225 copies printed on paper. (Cockerel 49, Peterson A49, Walsdorf 49) The thirty-five reproductions of woodcuts printed on twenty-three leaves (rectos only) were taken from books that were in the library of William Morris. He chose twenty-nine of them to illustrate a catalogue of his library, which was to have been annotated by him and printed at the Kelmscott Press. The other six were prepared for his article "On the Artistic Qualities of the Woodcut Books of Ulm and Augsburg in the Fifteenth Century" (Bibliographica I (1895), pp. 437-455), part of which is reprinted as an introduction to this book. The process blocks (with one exception) were prepared by Walker & Boutall. Finely printed in red and black in Morris's Golden type. One six-line woodcut initial. Appendices include a catalogue of the collection of fifteenth century books in William Morris' library by S.C. Cockerell. Corners lightly bumped.

643. (Kelmscott Press) de Vioragine, Jacobus. [LEAF FROM THE GOLDEN LEGEND]. (Hammersmith: Kelmscott Press, 1892), small 4to., single folded sheet. pages 913-914, 927-928. $ 45.00
This page was taken from volume III of The Golden Legend which was translated by William Caxton, edited by Frederick S. Ellis and printed by William Morris in 1892 at the Kelmscott Press. (Peterson A7) Golden type with four decorative initials.

644. (Kelmscott Press) Keats, John. POEMS OF JOHN KEATS. Hammersmith: The Kelmscott Press, 1894, 8vo., original limp vellum with silk ties, spine lettered in gilt. (vi), 384+(1) pages. $ 3,750.00
Printed in an edition limited to 307 copies of which this is one of 300 copies printed on paper. (Cockerel 24, Peterson A24, Walsdorf 24). Finely printed in red and black in Morris's Golden type, this has been one of the most sought after of all the smaller Kelmscott Press books. Ornamented throughout the text with wood-engraved initial letters and foliate borders.

645. (Kelmscott Press) LIST, 1 DECEMBER 1893. Hammersmith: The Kelmscott Press, 1893, small 8vo., self paper wrappers. (8) pages. $ 65.00
First edition. An announcement of books by the Kelmscott Press. (Peterson C12) Printed in two colors using Golden, Troy, and Chaucer types. Books already printed include Godefrey of Boloyne, Cavendish's Life of Wolsey, and Sidonia the Sorceress, with The Chroncyles of Syr John Froissart, Beowulf and the Story of the Glittering Plain in the press. Lightly glued to mat board.

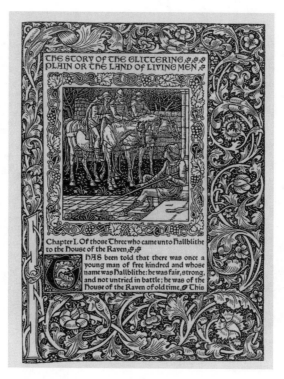

Item 646

646. (Kelmscott Press) Morris, William. THE STORY OF THE GLITTERING PLAIN. Hammersmith: Kelmscott Press, 1891, small 8vo., publisher's original stiff vellum with washleather ties, spine lettered in gilt. cloth slipcase. (ii), 188 pages.

$ 5,000.00

Printed in an edition limited to 206 copies of which this is one of 200 copies printed on paper. (Cockerell 1, Peterson A1, Walsdorf 1) This has also been called The Land of Living Men or the Acre of the Undying. "This book was set up from Nos. 81-4 of the *English Illustrated Magazine,* in which it first appeared; some of the chapter headings were re-arranged, and a few small corrections were made in the text. A trial page, the first printed at the Press, was struck off on January 31, 1891, but the first sheet was not printed until about a month later. The border was designed in January of the same year, and engraved by W.H. Hooper. This was the only book with washleather ties. All the other vellum-bound books have silk ties, except Shelley's *Poems* and *Hand and Soul,* which have no ties" (Cockerell, in Sparling). "Morris approached Walter Crane about illustrating it, 'but,' as Crane later recalled, 'he was so eager to get his first book out that he could not wait for the pictures, and so the *Glittering Plain* first appeared simply with his own initials and ornaments.' Hence in 1894 Morris produced another edition of the book (see A22)-the only K[elmscott] P[ress] title to be printed twice-with illustrations by Crane" (Peterson). Finely printed in Golden type with a decorative woodcut border on the title page designed and engraved by W.H. Hooper. Ornamented with six and ten line smaller initial letters throughout the text. Previous owner's ink signature, dated April 1891, on front pastedown.

Item 647

647. (Kelmscott Press) Morris, William. OF THE FRIENDSHIP OF AMIS AND AMILE. Hammersmith: Kelmscott Press, 1894, 12mo., original publisher's quarter cloth with blue paper covered boards. (iv), 67+(1) pages. $ 1,150.00

Printed in an edition limited to 515 copies of which this is one of 500 copies printed on paper. (Cockerel 23, Peterson A23, Walsdorf 23). A note which appeared in the announcement of this book stated "This tale dates from about the same period as that of KING FLORUS, and its literary & historical value is equally high." With a beautiful woodcut as the spread title page, woodcut initial letters and printing in red and black. Covers spotted. Internally fine.

648. (Kenmore Press) Peters, Robert. IKAGNAK. THE NORTH WIND WITH DR. KANE IN THE ARCTIC. Pasadena: Kenmore Press, 1978, large 8vo., cloth. (xv), 65, (5) pages. $ 85.00

First edition, limited to 100 numbered copies signed by Peters and the illustrator Steven Chayt. This book continues Peters interest in writing poetry in the guise of famous historical figures. His subject here, Dr. Elisha Kent Kane, was a popular American hero who explored the Arctic. Peters explains his intentions in a preface. At rear is an experimental paper, made at the press, containing flowers picked at Kane's tomb. Illustrated with etchings by Chayt .The book is printed on Frankfurt Rough, a moldmade paper from Germany.

649. (Kindle Press) Scott, Walter. TWO DROVERS, A SHORT STORY. Westwood, NJ: The Kindle Press, 1971, 8vo., half cloth over boards, slipcase. (vi), x, 35+(1) pages. $ 40.00

Limited to 680 numbered copies signed by Coleman Parsons. Printed on handmade paper by Meriden Gravure. A reprint of the best known Scott short story. Spine faded.

650. (Kingsport Press) Angle, Paul M. and Earl Schenck Miers (editors). THE AMERI-CAN FAMILY, AN ALBUM OF A SELF-RELIANT PEOPLE. Kingsport, TN: Kingsport Press, 1963, large 8vo., quarter cloth, paste paper covered boards, slipcase. 88, (4) pages. $ 30.00

Printed as a Keepsake in an edition limited to 1250 copies. Designed by Stefan Salter, with illustrations by Fritz Kredel. Printed on Fairfield Opaque paper. "In the pages that follow are a description of a house raising, tilling the soil, a corn husking, threshing and household chores, the place of the hired girl, courtship and marriage, religion and holidays--a fair sampling of the moments that gave to the Ameri-can family its special splendor."

651. (Kit-Cat Press) Pine, Edward. LAST THINGS AND OTHER POEMS. Bushey: Kit-Cat Press, 1962, large 12mo., paper wrappers. (22) pages. $ 15.00

Privately printed. A collection of poems by Edward Pine. Covers soiled with corners bumped.

652. (Kitemaug Press) Nosredna, Knarf. SAINT ARITHMETICUS. Spartanburg, SC: Kitemaug Press, 1967, miniature book (2 1/8 x 1 7/8 inches), stiff paper wrappers, dust jacket. (20) pages. $ 20.00

Limited to an edition of 500 copies. Tiny tale of the "patron saint of school children" printed in Van Son's Windmill Brown on a Kelsey 3 x 5 Excelsior hand press. Tipped in frontispiece lino-cut with tissue guard.

653. (Konglomerati Press) Chatfield, Hale. LITTLE FICTIONS, LOVING LIES. Gulfport, FL: Konglomerati Press, 1981, small 8vo., two-toned cloth, paper spine and cover labels. 59+(1) pages. $ 25.00

Printed in an edition limited to 1000 copies. This collection of short fiction by the American poet and au-thor is highlighted by black line illustrations on yellow backgrounds by Jeanne Meinke. Printed on Mo-hawk Superfine text paper, the book was hand set in Kennerly Old Style types cast by Barbara Russ and Richard Mathews who also designed, printed and bound it.

654. (Konglomerati Press) KONGLOMERATI [VOL.V, NO.3 / VOL.V, NO.4 / VOL.VI, NO.1], A COLLECTION OF EIGHT BOOKS. Gulfport, FL: The Kon-glomerati Press, (1976–1980), stiff paper wrappers, loose sheets in a portfolio, and paper covered boards. variously paginated. $ 100.00

A collection of the following works by the Konglomerati Press: Konglomerati Vol.V, No.3 and Vol.V, No.4: A collection of poetry by a variety of authors. Illustrated with occasional tipped-in black and white illustrations by various artists. Bound in stiff paper wrappers. Konglomerati Vol.VI, No.1: A collection of poetry by various authors, unbound in a stiff paper portfolio. Type printed in black decorated with or-ange printed patterns. The Seasons: Phelps Greenfield edition. From the American chapbook collection of the University of South Florida Library. A brief poetical description of each of the four seasons. Illus-trated with five brown prints. Bound in stiff paper wrappers. Cinderella, or the Little Glass Slipper: sec-ond edition. The classic tale of Cinderella retold in poetic style. Illustrated with black and white restored prints. Printed on gold-colored paper and bound in stiff paper wrappers. Spirit Hand by Robert Stern: First edition. The poetry of Robert Stern illustrated with black and white drawings by Kit Hirshberg. Bound in brown paper covered boards. Time and Other Birds by Mary Shumway: First edition. A collec-tion of poetry by Mary Shumway, illustrated with black and white Chinese calligraphy by Margaret Rigg, including one tipped-in frontispiece. Bound in stiff paper wrappers. The Stop Book by David Shevin: First edition, limited to 500 copies. A collection of poems by David Shevin. Illustrations consist of a collection of stamps inserted in a tipped-in envelope, to be placed by the reader within borders on ap-propriate pages. Bound with light brown paper covered boards. Minor, general wear. Three of the works have small white price tags stuck on front free endpapers or markings were tags have been removed.

655. (Konglomerati Press) Shumway, Mary. TIME AND OTHER BIRDS. Gulfport, FL: Konglomerati, 1976, large 12mo., stiff paper wrappers. (35) pages. $ 25.00

First edition of 300 copies designed and printed by Barbara Russ and Richard Mathews at Konglomerati Press. An elegant little chap-book with sixteen previously published poems by Shumway. Five original Chinese style calligraphy images by Margaret Rigg, artist and publisher of Possum Press. Line blocks of original calligraphy handprinted on a Vandercook proof press. Booklet handset in Kennerly types and printed on a Chandler and Price platen press. Korean Mulberry papers hand sewn, then glued into Tweedweave covers.

656. (Kutenai Press) Kemble, John. SPECIMEN OF AN ETYMOLOGICAL DICTIONARY ATTRIBUTED TO JOHN MITCHELL KEMBLE. . St Paul: Rulon-Miller Books, 1990, 8vo., cloth, paper spine label, slipcase. 61 pages. $ 495.00
Limited to 100 copies. Kemble was the foremost philologist of his day, and this text is taken from the recently discovered eight page manuscript which was dated 1830, three years before his edition of Beowulf. No trace of the actual dictionary itself is known, but this specimen is a fitting tribute to Kemble's work in etymology. Printed by hand under the direction of Gerald Lange in two colors on handmade Umbria Bianco paper by Emily Mason Strayer of the Kutenai Press. Photographic facsimile of the original text tipped in. An example of fine American book production.

657. (Laboratory Press) Flanner, Hildegarde. THAT ENDETH NEVER, A GIFT, CHRISTMAS 1921. Pittsburgh: Laboratory Press, 1926, large 12mo., loose sheets. title-page, 8 pages unopened and 1 page as illustration. $ 25.00
Envelope of trial-sheets for a book that was not published. Pen and ink illustration by Porter Garnett as last page. Garnett was founder of the Press, which was part of the printing department at the Carnegie Institute of Technology.

658. (Lakeside Press) THE CAXTON CLUB 1965 YEARBOOK. Chicago: Caxton Club, 1965, large 12mo., cloth. 110, (2) pages. $ 17.50
Printed for the Caxton Club by the Lakeside Press in an edition limited to 500 copies and covering the period from 1958 to 1965. With officers, committees, constitution, report of officers, publications from 1896 to 1964, meetings, and list of members. Memo from the Caxton Club to a member loosely inserted.

659. (Lakeside Press) Hayes, James. ROMAN LETTER, A STUDY OF NOTABLE GRAVEN AND WRITTEN FORMS FROM TWENTY CENTURIES. Chicago: Lakeside Press, 1951, small 4to., later cloth with original paper wrappers bound-in. 54, (2) pages. $ 25.00
With 58 figures in the text demonstrating the formation and design of the Roman letter.

660. (Lakeside Press) Labaree, Leonard W. and Whitfield J. Bell, Jr. MR. FRANKLIN, A SELECTION FROM HIS PERSONAL LETTERS. New Haven: Yale University Press, 1956, 4to., cloth-backed decorated boards. xxii, 61 pages. $ 37.50
First edition. Printed by the Lakeside Press. Rubbed along edges.

661. (Lakeside Press) Legler, Henry Eduard. OF MUCH LOVE AND SOME KNOWLEDGE OF BOOKS. Chicago: The Caxton Club, 1912, small 8vo., parchment-backed boards, slipcase. 47, (3) pages. $ 65.00
First edition, limited to 357 copies. Essays on collecting. With ornamental title page and other decorations in the book engraved from designs by Frederick William Gookin. Printed at the Lakeside Press. Slipcase is broken. Covers slightly age darkened.

662. (Lakeside Press) Mackaye, Percy. THE MYSTERY OF HAMLET, KING OF DENMARK, OR WHAT WE WILL, A TETRALOGY. New York: Bond Wheelwright Co., 1950, large 4to., polished buckram, top edge gilt, others uncut, slipcase. xvii+(i), 69+(1), 710, (2) pages with 6 additional leaves. $ 350.00
Limited edition of 357 numbered copies, signed by the author (p.xi) and by the book designer, Raymond Da Boll (colophon), with a reproduced photograph of the author's wife, Marion Morse MacKaye (1872–1939) tipped in (p.xi). Percy MacKaye (1875–1956), son of the actor Steele MacKaye, was a poet and playwright active in the earlier part of the 20th century. According to the author (p.655), the four plays are to be understood as parts III-VI of a "hepatology" related to Hamlet themes. Plays are in blank

verse with a few musical interpolations (words and music by author). In addition, there are a prelude, interludes between the plays, and a musical "postlude," followed by the afterword, a commentary, notes, a bibliography of MacKaye's publications, and other matter. The book was designed by Raymond Da Boll, who also provided the calligraphy, and printed at the Lakeside Press. Gilt-stamped decoration on covers with gilt-stamped lettering on spine.

663. (Lakeside Press) ROD FOR THE BACK OF THE BINDER, SOME CONSIDERATIONS OF BINDING WITH REFERENCE TO THE IDEALS OF THE LAKESIDE PRESS. Chicago: The Lakeside Press, 1928, 4to., cloth, leather cover label. 32 pages. $ 45.00
S-K 6997. With 16 plates and 29 figures in the text.

664. (Lakeside Press) Wroth, Lawrence C. D.B. UPDIKE, A GREAT PRINTER. Chicago: Lakeside Press, 1942, 12mo., paper wrappers. 13 pages. $ 15.00
First separate appearance; first appeared in the New York Herald Tribune.

665. (Leadenhalle Press) Roscoe, Mr. THE BUTTERFLY'S BALL AND THE GRASSHOPPER'S FEAST, A FACSIMILE REPRODUCTION OF THE EDITION OF 1808. London: Griffith and Farran, 1883, 8vo., original polished buckram, top edge gilt, fore edge deckled. variously paginated. $ 125.00
A facsimile reproduction of the edition of 1808. In the early 1800's, a series of children's books printed as *Harris's Cabinet* was extremely popular. Charles Welsh took the first four titles, "The Butterfly's Ball," "The Peacock at Home," "The Elephant's Ball" and "The Lion's Masquerade," and issued this volume in 1883. He hoped readers from the end of the century would be as charmed by the works as those from the beginning of the century were. Black and white engravings illustrate each of the stories. Minor wear to head and tail of spine, some spots on cover, foxing throughout.

666. (Lee Priory Press) SPECIMEN OF THE ORIGINAL WOODCUTS. Canterbury: H. Ward, 1834, 17" x 21" broadside. $ 275.00
A collection of over 50 woodcuts, "engraved for the purpose of illustrating the several works from the Lee Priory Press," printed on one broadside. Presumably this has been removed from, or was issued in conjunction with, the auction catalogue issued by W. Sharp at Lee Priory on August 11, 1834 (Pollard p.196). The center of this print identifies this as representing lot 1029. Sir Egerton Brydges founded the Lee Priory Press in 1813 and produced nearly 45 books before its closing in 1822. This collection of woodcuts, printed in 1834, contains specimens from several different books. Slight separation at crease, one edge torn with minor loss affecting four smaller wood engravings.

667. (Legacy Press) Baker, Cathleen A. and John DePol. ENDGRAIN DESIGNS AND REPETITIONS: THE PATTERN PAPERS OF JOHN DEPOL. Tuscaloosa, AL: The Legacy Press, 2000, large 8vo., quarter cloth, patterned paper covered boards. 154+(1), followed by 5 tipped in specimens, (1) pages. $ 295.00
Limited to 115 numbered copies, signed by both authors. This book contains 117 wood engraved designs by John DePol that were originally used to create patterned papers. These images are reproduced as originally conceived by DePol in beautiful black and white. Accompanying these images is an autobiographical sketch, an essay on the history of black & white patterns, the publication history of the images and patterns, and a bibliography. Also includes five tipped-in color specimens of published pattern papers. Set in Diotima type and hand-printed in black and red on Mohawk Superfine Ultrawhite Smooth paper from polymer plates.

668. (Libanus Press) Kinglake, Alexander William. PORTRAIT OF LADY HESTER. Engraved by Robert Gibbings. Wiltshire, England: Libanus Press, 1987, tall thin 8vo., quarter cloth, patterned paper covered boards. 31+(1) pages. $ 125.00
Limited to 300 numbered copies. Printed from Alexander William Kinglake's Eothen. Lady Hester, born in 1776, was the eldest daughter of the third Earl of Stanhope, inventor of the iron printing press, and William Pitt's niece, with whom she lived for many years and ran his household. Pitt said of her: "I let

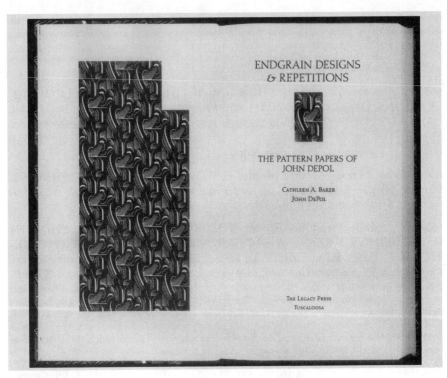

her do as she pleases; for if she were resolved to cheat the devil she could do it." Wood engravings by Robert Gibbings, originally commissioned in 1940 for the Kynoch Press but stopped from publication when a bomb hit its paper warehouse. Printed in 12 pt Bodoni italic on damped B F K Rives rag paper.

669. (Limited Editions Club) Addison, Joseph, Richard Steele and Eustace Budgell. SIR ROGER DE COVERLEY PAPERS. FROM THE SPECTATOR, LONDON: 1711–1712. With Some Prefatory Notes by W.M. Thackeray, and Illustrations Drawn for this Edition by Gordon Ross. New York: The Limited Editions Club, 1945, 8vo., padded fabric covers, slipcase. xxviii, 198, (2) pages. $ 75.00
Limited to 1500 numbered copies signed by Ross. Printed at the Aldus Printers with design by Richard Ellis.

670. (Limited Editions Club) Addison, Joseph. SPECTATOR ESSAYS BY JOSEPH ADDISON, RICHARD STEELE AND OTHERS. Selected, Edited, and Introduced by Robert Halsband and Illustrated by Lynton Lamb. New York: The Limited Editions Club, 1970, 4to., cloth, leather spine label, slipcase. xvi, 302 pages. $ 100.00
Limited to 1500 numbered copies signed by Lamb. Printed at the Curwen Press with hand-coloring at the studio of Walter Fischer.

671. (Limited Editions Club) Aeschylus. THE ORESTEIA. Translated from the Greek by E.D.A. Morshead. With an Introduction by Rex Warner. Illustrated by Michael Ayrton. New York: The Limited Editions Club, 1961, 4to., quarter leather over cloth, cloth spine label, slipcase. (xviii), 177, (3) pages. $ 65.00

Limited to 1500 numbered copies and signed by Ayrton. Designed by Adrian Wilson and printed at the Press of A. Colish. Front hinge is rubbed with the beginning of a crack.

672. (Limited Editions Club) Alain-Fournier. THE WANDERER (LE GRAND MEAULNES). Translated from the French by Francoise Delisle with an Introduction by Henri Peyre and illustrations by Dignimont. New York: The Limited Editions Club, 1958, tall 8vo., cloth, paper spine label, slipcase. xxx, 232, (4) pages. $ 65.00

Limited to 1500 numbered copies signed by Dignimont. Printed at the Thistle Press by Clarke & Way and designed by Jean Garcia. Illustrations colored by hand in the Studio of Walter Fischer of New York.

673. (Limited Editions Club) Alarcon, Pedro Antonio De. THREE-CORNERED HAT, THE TRUE HISTORY OF AN AFFAIR CURRENT IN CERTAIN TALES AND BALLADS. Now translated out of the Spanish by Martin Armstrong, with an Introduction by Gerald Brenan, & illustrated by Roger Duvoisin. New York: The Limited Editions Club, 1959, small 4to., cloth-backed boards, slipcase. xxii, 154, (2) pages.
$ 47.50

Limited to 1500 numbered copies signed by the Duvoisin. Printed by the Plantin Press of Saul and Lillian Marks.

674. (Limited Editions Club) Aristophanes. THE BIRDS. With an Introduction by Dudley Fitts and Illustrations by Marian Parry. New York: The Limited Editions Club, 1959, 4to., quarter leather, outer wrap-around cover, slipcase. xii, 52, (4) pages printed French fold. $ 75.00

Limited to 1500 numbered copies signed by Parry. Printed at The Thistle Press with color work done by Bert Clarke.

675. (Limited Editions Club) Aristotle. POLITICS & POETICS. Translated by Benjamin Jowett and S.H. Butcher with an Introduction by Horace M. Kallen and Portraits by Leonard Baskin. New York: The Limited Editions Club, 1964, small 4to., cloth, slipcase. xxvi, 331, (3) pages. $ 100.00

Limited to 1500 numbered copies and signed by Baskin. Printed at the Stinehour Press.

676. (Limited Editions Club) Arnold, Edwin. LIGHT OF ASIA, BEING THE LIFE AND TEACHING OF GAUTAMA, PRINCE OF INDIA AND FOUNDER OF BUDDHISM. With an introduction by Melford E. Spiro and illustrations by Ayres Houghtelling. Avon, CT: The Limited Editions Club, 1976, 4to., pictorial woven cloth, leather spine label, slipcase. xxiv, 193, (3) pages. $ 55.00

Limited to 2000 numbered copies signed by Houghtelling. Printed at the Press of A. Colish with typographic design by Frank Lieberman. Filled with color plates.

677. (Limited Editions Club) Austen, Jane. NORTHANGER ABBEY. With an Introduction by Sylvia Townsend Warner & Illustrations by Clarke Hutton. N.P.: The Limited Editions Club by The Garamond Press, 1971, tall 8vo., striped cloth, leather spine label, slipcase. xiv, 210, (4) pages. $ 100.00

Limited to 1500 numbered copies signed by Hutton. Designed by Richard Ellis.

678. (Limited Editions Club) Bacon, Francis. ESSAYES OR COUNSELS CIVILL & MORALL. New York: The Limited Editions Club, 1944, 4to., cloth-backed decorated paper covered boards, clamshell case. xii, 190, (2) pages. $ 150.00
Limited to 1500 numbered copies signed by the designer, Bruce Rogers. With an introduction by Christopher Morley and a postscript by A.S.W. Rosenbach. Printed by William E. Rudge's Sons. Still preserved in glassine wrapper.

679. (Limited Editions Club) Balzac, Honore De. EUGENIE GRANDET. Translated from the French by Ellen Marriage with an Introduction by Richard Aldington and illustrations by Rene Ben Sussan. New York: The Limited Editions Club, 1960, tall 8vo., cloth, two leather wrap-around labels, slipcase. xx, 271, (3) pages. $ 85.00
Limited to 1500 numbered copies signed by Sussan. Designed by Francis Meynell and printed at the Curwen Press. Hand-colored in the studio of Walter Fischer of New York.

680. (Limited Editions Club) Balzac, Honore De. OLD GORIOT. Translated from the French by Ellen Marriage with an Introduction by Francois Mauriac and illustrations by Rene Ben Sussan. New York: The Limited Editions Club, 1948, tall 8vo., quarter leather over marbled paper covered boards, slipcase. xviii, 316, (2) pages. $ 85.00
Limited to 1500 numbered copies signed by Sussan. Designed by Francis Meynell and printed at The Curwen Press. Illustrations printed by Georges Duval and colored in the Atelier Beaufume in Paris. Bookplate.

681. (Limited Editions Club) Beckford, William. VATHEK: AN ARABIAN TALE. Translated by Herbert Grimsditch. Decorated and Illuminated by Valenti Angelo. New York: The Limited Editions Club, 1945, 12mo., full leather stamped in gilt with a Angelo design, slipcase. xii, 135+(1) pages. $ 125.00
Limited to 1500 numbered copies signed by the illustrator, Valenti Angelo. (Angelo Biblio. p.64). Printed by the Aldus Printers under the direction of A.G. Hoffman. Title page and endpaper designs, ten borders, and nine illustrations in color and gold by Angelo. Box is broken with wear along edges; book is in very fine condition.

682. (Limited Editions Club) Bedier, Joseph. ROMANCE OF TRISTAN & ISEULT AS RETOLD BY JOSEPH BEDIER. Translated from the French by Hilaire Belloc and Paul Rosenfeld. With an Introduction by Padraic Colum and Illustrations by Serge Ivanoff. New York: The Limited Editions Club, 1960, small 4to., leather-backed boards, slipcase. xvi, 172, (2) pages. $ 45.00
Limited to 1500 numbered copies signed by Ivanoff. Printed at the Thistle Press. Leather spine age darkened with some cracking.

683. (Limited Editions Club) Bennett, Arnold. OLD WIVES' TALE. Two volumes. New York: The Limited Editions Club, 1941, thick 4to., cloth-backed decorated boards, dust jackets, slipcase. xxx,348; (viii),349-729,(3) pages. $ 150.00
Limited to 1500 numbered copies signed by John Austen, the illustrator. Contains a preface by Bennett and an Introduction by Frank Swinnerton. Printed at the University Press. Well preserved set.

684. (Limited Editions Club) Beyle, Marie-Henri. CHARTERHOUSE OF PARMA. The Translation by Lady Mary Loyd. Revised by Robert Cantwell, the Preface by Honore de Balzac and Illustrations by Rafaello Busoni. New York: The Limited Editions Club, 1955, small 4to., cloth-backed boards, slipcase. xx, 392, (2) pages. $ 65.00
Limited to 1500 numbered copies and signed by Busoni.

685. (Limited Editions Club) Bierce, Ambrose. MONK AND THE HANGMAN'S DAUGHTER. Translated from the German of Richard Voss by Gustav Adolf Danziger and adapted by Ambrose Bierce. With an Introduction by Maurice Valency and Illustrations by Michel Ciry. New York: The Limited Editions Club, 1967, small 4to., woven cloth, board wrapper, slipcase. xv, 80, (4) pages. $ 65.00
Limited to 1500 numbered copies and signed by the illustrator.

686. (Limited Editions Club) Bligh, William. VOYAGE TO THE SOUTH SEAS, UNDERTAKEN BY COMMAND OF HIS MAJESTY FOR THE CONVEYING THE BREAD-FRUIT TREE TO THE WEST INDIES IN HIS MAJESTY'S SHIP BOUNTY ... INCLUDING AN ACCOUNT OF THE MUTINY ON BOARD. Introduced by Alan Villiers and Illustrated With watercolours and drawings by Geoffrey C. Ingleton. N.P.: The Limited Editions Club, 1975, 4to., cloth, leather spine label, slipcase. xix, 150, (2) pages. $ 150.00
Limited to 2000 numbered copies signed by both Ingleton and the designer, Douglas A. Dunstan. Printed at the Griffin Press of South Australia. Newsletter loosely inserted.

687. (Limited Editions Club) Boccaccio, Giovanni. DECAMERON. Newly Translated from the Italian by Frances Winwar with an Introduction by Burton Rascoe. Two volumes. New York: The Limited Editions Club, 1930, 4to., cloth, leather spine labels. xiv,200; 201- 382,(4) pages. $ 185.00
Limited to 1500 numbered copies signed by the illustrator, T.M. Cleland. Printed at the Press of A. Colish. This is the seventh production of the Club. The slipcase is worn along edges.

688. (Limited Editions Club) BOOK OF ECCLESIASTES, IN THE REVISED KING JAMES VERSION. With an Introduction by Kenneth Rexroth and Illustrations by Edgar Miller. New York: The Limited Editions Club, 1968, 4to., full stamped calf, slipcase. ix, 53, (3) pages. $ 125.00
Limited to 1500 numbered copies signed by Miller. Printed at the Thistle Press with typographic design by David Way. Well preserved copy with Monthly letter loosely inserted.

689. (Limited Editions Club) BOOK OF THE PROPHET ISAIAH IN THE KING JAMES VERSION WITH WATER COLORS BY CHAIM GROSS. Introduction by Franklin H. Littell. New York: The Limited Editions Club, 1979, 4to., quarter leather, slipcase. xii, 121, (3) pages. $ 150.00
Limited to 2000 numbered copies signed by Gross and Littell. Printed at the Press of A. Colish and designed by Bert Clarke. Spine slightly age yellowed.

690. (Limited Editions Club) Browning, Robert. RING AND THE BOOK. With an Introduction by Edward Dowden. Illustrated with Engravings by Carl Schultheiss. Two volumes. New York: The Limited Editions Club, 1949, quarter red leather, slipcase. xxiv,340; (vi),341-690,(4) pages. $ 95.00
Limited to 1500 numbered copies signed by Schultheiss.

691. (Limited Editions Club) Bulwer-Lytton, Edward George. LAST DAYS OF POMPEII. With an Introduction by Edgar Johnson & Illustrations by Kurt Craemer. New York: The Limited Editions Club, 1956, small 4to., cloth, slipcase. xxi, 512, (4) pages. $ 125.00
Limited to 1500 numbered copies and signed by Craemer and Mardersteig. Printed at the Officina Bodoni in Verona. The plain paper dust jacket is not present. Slipcase soiled.

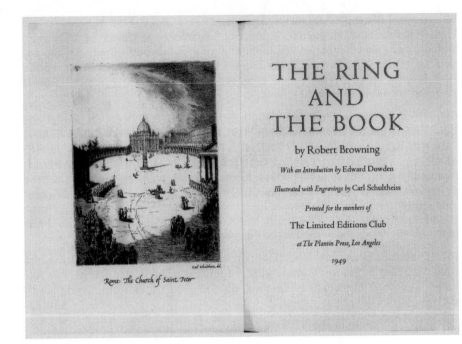

THE RING
AND
THE BOOK

by Robert Browning

With an Introduction by Edward Dowden

Illustrated with Engravings by Carl Schultheiss

Printed for the members of

The Limited Editions Club

at The Plantin Press, Los Angeles

1949

Rome. The Church of Saint Peter

Item 690

692. (Limited Editions Club) Cabell, James Branch. JURGEN, A COMEDY OF JUS-
TICE. With an Introduction by Edward Wagenknecht. Illustrations by Virgil Burnett.
Westport, CT: The Limited Editions Club, (1976), tall 8vo., cloth, slipcase. xviii, 290, (4)
pages. $ 60.00
Limited to 2000 numbered copies signed by Burnett. Hand-colored via the stencil process at the Atelier
Walter Fischer of New York City. Printed at The Stinehour Press and designed by Ted Gensamer.

693. (Limited Editions Club) Carlyle, Thomas. FRENCH REVOLUTION: A HIS-
TORY. With an Introduction by Cecil Brown and Illustrations by Bernard Lamotte.
New York: The Limited Editions Club, 1956, tall 8vo., quarter leather, slipcase. xviii, 629,
(3) pages. $ 75.00
Limited to 1500 copies signed by Lamotte. Printed by Peter Beilenson with illustrations reproduced in
collotype.

694. (Limited Editions Club) Carpentier, Alejo. KINGDOM OF THIS WORLD. N.P.:
The Limited Editions Club, n.d. (but 1988), folio, half morocco, with cloth covered
boards, slipcase. xiv, 104, (2) pages. $ 650.00
Letterpress printed in an edition limited to 750 numbered copies of which this is copy 7 signed by the illustrator Roberto Juarez and author of the introduction John Hersey. Richly illustrated with original
etchings printed on hand-made Japanese tissue. Hand sewn and bound by Carol Joyce. Printed in Monotype Jansen designed by Bruce Rogers. Includes the Limited Editions Club Letter which serves as the
prospectus.

695. (Limited Editions Club) Casanova, De Seingalt. MEMOIRS OF JACQUES CASANOVA DE SEINGALT, 1725–1798. Now fully annotated for the first time in English. The Memoirs and Notes translated by Arthur Machen & introduced by Havelock Ellis. Eight volumes. New York: The Limited Editions Club, 1940, cloth-backed decorated paper covered boards, contained in two slipcases. $ 200.00
Limited to 1500 numbered copies. Printed by R. & R. Clark of Edinburgh under the typographic direction of Francis Meynell.

696. (Limited Editions Club) Cervantes, Miguel De. DON QUIXOTE, THE INGENIOUS GENTLEMAN OF LA MANCHA. The Translation by John Ormsby. With a New Introduction by Irwin Edman and the Illustrations by Edy Legrand. Two volumes. New York: The Limited Editions Club, 1950, 4to., cloth-backed marbled paper covered boards, leather spine label, slipcase. 348; (ii),349-682,(2) pages. $ 135.00
Limited to 1500 numbered copies. Printed at the Imprenta Nuevo Mundo in Mexico City on paper produced by the Curtis Paper Co.. Illustrations reproduced by Georges Duval of Paris with colors applied by Fernand Mourlot. Slipcase shows wear along edges.

697. (Limited Editions Club) Collins, Wilkie. MOONSTONE. With an Introduction by Vincent Starrett. Illustrated by Dignimont. New York: The Limited Editions Club, 1959, tall 8vo., cloth, slipcase. xix, 464, (2) pages. $ 85.00
Limited to 1500 numbered copies and signed by the illustrator. Designed by John Dreyfus.

698. (Limited Editions Club) Collins, Wilkie. WOMAN IN WHITE. With an Introduction by Vincent Starrett. Illustrated by Leonard Rosoman. New York: The Limited Editions Club, 1964, tall 8vo., cloth-backed boards, slipcase. xvi, 534, (2) pages. $ 65.00
Limited to 1500 numbered copies and signed by Rosoman. Printed at the Elm Tree Press of Woodstock, Vermont. Spine slightly faded.

699. (Limited Editions Club) Confucius. ANALECTS OF CONFUCIUS. Translated from the Chinese, with an Introduction and Notes, by Lionel Giles. Illustrated with Paintings by Tseng Yu-Ho. New York: The Limited Editions Club, 1970, tall 8vo., woven cloth, paper spine label, cord-tied folding box. xxxii, 131, (3) pages. $ 125.00
Limited to 1500 numbered copies signed by Yu-Ho. Designed and printed by Saul and Lillian Marks at the Plantin Press.

700. (Limited Editions Club) Congreve, William. WAY OF THE WORLD, COMEDY IN FIVE ACTS. With Illustrations by T.M. Cleland and an Introduction by Louis Kronenberger. New York: The Limited Editions Club, 1959, small 8vo., patterned cloth, slipcase. xxiv, 108, (2) pages. $ 65.00
Limited to 1500 numbered copies and signed by Cleland. Colored by hand in the Studio of Walter Fischer in New York. Printed at the Press of A. Colish.

701. (Limited Editions Club) Conrad, Joseph. NIGGER OF THE NARCISSUS. With an Introduction by Howard Mumford Jones and Illustrations by Millard Sheets. N.P.: The Limited Editions Club, 1965, tall 8vo., quarter leather, slipcase. xx, 161, (3) pages.
$ 125.00
Limited to 1500 numbered copies signed by Sheets. Printed at The Ward Ritchie Press in Los Angeles and designed by Ritchie.

702. (Limited Editions Club) Conrad, Joseph. NOSTROMO, A TALE OF THE SEABOARD. With an Introduction by Rupert Croft-Cooke and Illustrations by Lima de Freitas. New York: The Limited Editions Club, 1961, 4to., woven cloth over cloth, paper spine label, slipcase. xxiii, 376, (2) pages. $ 150.00
Limited to 1500 numbered copies signed by de Freitas. Designed by Adrian Wilson and printed by Taylor & Taylor.

703. (Limited Editions Club) Conrad, Joseph. OUTCAST OF THE ISLANDS. With an Introduction by Clifton Fadiman and Illustrations by Robert Shore. Avon, CT: The Limited Editions Club, 1975, small 4to., cloth, slipcase. xii, 212, (2) pages. $ 65.00
Limited to 2000 numbered copies signed by Shore. Designed by John O.C. McCrillis and printed at The Stinehour Press.

704. (Limited Editions Club) Conrad, Joseph. YOUTH - TYPHOON - THE END OF THE TETHER. With an Introduction by Leo Gurko and Illustrations by Robert Shore. N.P.: The Limited Editions Club, 1972, small 4to., quarter leather, slipcase. xvi, 251, (3) pages. $ 85.00
Limited to 1500 numbered copies signed by the illustrator and also by the designer-printer, Ward Ritchie. Printed at the Ward Ritchie Press of Los Angeles.

705. (Limited Editions Club) Cooper, James Fenimore. DEERSLAYER, OR: THE FIRST WAR-PATH. With an Introduction by John T. Winterich and Illustrations by Edward A. Wilson. New York: The Limited Editions Club, 1961, thick 8vo., leather-backed boards, paper spine label, slipcase. xiv, 510, (4) pages. $ 95.00
Limited to 1500 numbered copies signed by the Wilson. With illustrations colored by hand in the studio of Walter Fischer.

706. (Limited Editions Club) Cooper, James Fenimore. PATHFINDER. New York: The Limited Editions Club, 1965, 8vo., cloth-backed boards, slipcase. xvi, 474, (2) pages.
$ 65.00
Limited to 1500 numbered copies signed by Powers. Designed and printed at The Stinehour Press.

707. (Limited Editions Club) Cooper, James Fenimore. PILOT. Introduction by John T. Winterich and Illustrated with Woodcuts by Robert M. Quackenbush. New York: The Limited Editions Club, 1968, small 4to., two-toned cloth, slipcase. xvi, 357, (3) pages.
$ 65.00
Limited to 1500 numbered copies signed by the illustrator. Six page introduction by Winterich.

708. (Limited Editions Club) Cooper, James Fenimore. SPY, A TALE OF THE NEUTRAL GROUND. With Illustrations by Henry C. Pitz and an Introduction by John T. Winterich. New York: The Limited Editions Club, 1963, thick 8vo., cloth, leather spine label, slipcase. xx, 406, (2) pages. $ 65.00
Limited to 1500 numbered copies signed by Pitz. With illustrations hand colored in the studio of Walter Fischer of New York. Printed at the Press of A. Colish.

709. (Limited Editions Club) Cowley, Malcolm. EXILE'S RETURN, A LITERARY ODYSSEY OF THE 1920s. Illustrated with Contemporary Photographs. Introduction by Leon Edel. New York: The Limited Editions Club, 1981, 8vo., cloth-backed boards, slipcase. xxii, 281, (3) pages. $ 200.00
Limited to 2,000 numbered copies signed by Cowley and the photographer, Berenice Abbott. With Monthly Letter loosely inserted.

710. (Limited Editions Club) Dana, Richard Henry. TWO YEARS BEFORE THE MAST, A PERSONAL NARRATIVE OF LIFE AT SEA. With an Introduction by William McFee. Illustrated with engravings in color by Hans Alexander Mueller. New York: The Limited Editions Club, 1947, tall thick 8vo., cloth, leather spine label, slipcase. xx, 351+(1) pages. $ 95.00
Limited to 1500 numbered copies signed by Mueller. Designed by Richard W. Ellis. Spine slightly age yellowed.

711. (Limited Editions Club) Darwin, Charles. DESCENT OF MAN AND SELEC- TION IN RELATION TO SEX. With a Preface by Ashley Montagu and Drawings by Fritz Kredel. N.P.: The Limited Editions Club, 1971, 4to., quarter leather, slipcase. xx, 362, (3) pages. $ 125.00
Limited to 1500 numbered copies signed by Kredel. Printed at the Griffin Press of Adelaide, South Aus- tralia.

712. (Limited Editions Club) De Maupassant, Guy. BEL-AMI. With an Introduction by Alex Waugh & Illustrations by Bernard Lamotte. New York: The Limited Editions Club, 1968, small 4to., cloth, slipcase. xii, 266, (2) pages. $ 65.00
Limited to 1500 numbered copies and signed by Lamotte. Printed at the Press of A. Colish.

713. (Limited Editions Club) De Maupassant, Guy. TALES OF GUY DE MAUPAS- SANT, 1850–1893. The Translations by Lafcadio Hearn and others chosen & with an Introduction by Justin O'Brien. The Illustrations from Water-Colours by Gunter Bohmer. New York: The Limited Editions Club, 1963, thick 8vo., cloth, slipcase. xii, 472, (2) pages. $ 80.00
Limited to 1500 numbered copies signed by Bohmer. Printed at the Curwen Press with typography by Francis Meynell. Spine slightly faded.

714. (Limited Editions Club) De Maupassant, Guy. WOMAN'S LIFE. Translated from the French by Marjorie Laurie; with an introduction by Edmond Jaloux, and illustra- tions by Edy Legrand. New York: The Limited Editions Club, 1952, tall 8vo., white pigskin spine over marbled paper covered boards, leather spine label, slipcase. xiv, 216, (2) pages. $ 65.00
Limited to 1500 numbered copies signed by Legrand. Produced using the typographic plans "originally prepared by Sir Francis Meynell for the edition published by the Nonesuch Press." Printed at the March- banks Press and colors applied by hand in the Studio of Walter Fischer. Pigskin spine shows small tear at top along front hinge.

715. (Limited Editions Club) Defoe, Daniel. FORTUNES AND MISFORTUNES OF THE FAMOUS MOLL FLANDERS. With Illustrations by Reginald Marsh. New York: The Limited Editions Club, 1954, 8vo., cloth, slipcase. xv, 353, (3) pages. $ 95.00
Limited to 1500 numbered copies signed by Marsh. Printed by Peter Beilenson and colored by stencil at the studio of Martha Berrien.

716. (Limited Editions Club) Defoe, Daniel. JOURNAL OF THE PLAGUE YEAR, &C. Now newly Introduced to the Public by Mr. James Sutherland, ... and Embellish'd with notable Illustrations by Signor Domenico Gnoli, of Rome. Bloomfield: The Limit- ed Editions Club, 1968, tall 8vo., woven cloth, leather spine label, slipcase. xx, 270, (4) pages. $ 75.00
Limited to 1500 numbered copies signed by Gnoli. Designed by Richard Ellis.

717. (Limited Editions Club) Defoe, Daniel. ROXANA, THE FORTUNATE MIS-TRESS. With an Introduction by James Sutherland and Woodcuts by Bernd Kroeber. Avon, CT: The Limited Editions Club, 1976, 4to., two-toned cloth, slipcase. xiv, 256, (2) pages. $ 60.00
Limited to 2000 numbered copies signed by Kroeber. Designed by Adrian Wilson and printed by The Stinehour Press.

718. (Limited Editions Club) Dickens, Charles. AMERICAN NOTES FOR GENER-AL CIRCULATION. With an Introduction by Angus Wilson. Illustrations by Raymond F. Houlihan. Avon, CT: The Limited Editions Club, 1975, 8vo., quarter leather, leather spine label, slipcase. xviii, 272, (2) pages. $ 65.00
Limited to 2000 numbered copies signed by Houlihan. Designed by Joseph Blumenthal.

719. (Limited Editions Club) Dickens, Charles. DEALINGS WITH THE FIRM OF DOMBEY AND SON, WHOLESALE, RETAIL, AND FOR EXPORTATION. With Illustrations by Henry C. Pitz. Introduction by John T. Winterich. Two volumes. New York: The Limited Editions Club, 1957, 8vo., cloth, paper spine labels, slipcase. xvi,396; (x),397-798,(2) pages. $ 85.00
Limited to 1500 numbered copies signed by Pitz. Printed and designed by Peter Beilenson with color plates reproduced by George C. Miller. Spines faded as usual. Slipcase cracked.

720. (Limited Editions Club) Dickens, Charles. HARD TIMES FOR THESE TIMES. Illustrated by Charles Raymond. Introduction by John T. Winterich. New York: The Limited Editions Club, 1966, 8vo., half cloth over boards, paper spine label, slipcase. xiv, 279, (3) pages. $ 75.00
Limited to 1500 numbered copies signed by Raymond. Designed by Joseph Blumenthal and printed at The Spiral Press.

721. (Limited Editions Club) Dickens, Charles. SHORT STORIES OF CHARLES DICKENS. Selected and Introduced by Walter Allen. Illustrated by Edward Ardizzone. New York: The Limited Editions Club, 1971, 8vo., quarter cloth over marbled paper covered boards, slipcase. xx, 423, (3) pages. $ 100.00
Limited to 1500 numbered copies signed by Ardizzone and the designer, Joseph Blumenthal. Printed at The Spiral Press.

722. (Limited Editions Club) Dill, Francis P. and Porter Garnett. IDEAL BOOK, TWO ESSAYS. New York: The Limited Editions Club, 1932, 12mo., boards, paper cover label. 42 pages. $ 20.00
Second printing, limited to 500 copies. This second printing was for the AIGA members. Minor wear at spine ends.

723. (Limited Editions Club) DOLPHIN, A JOURNAL OF THE MAKING OF BOOKS. Numbers 1-4, a total of six volumes (all published). New York: Limited Editions Club, 1933, 35, 38, 40–41, 4to., cloth. (viii),363,(18); 329,(20); xvi,507,(34); 104,(20); 109-232,(16); 233-312,(14) pages. $ 650.00
Limitations vary from 1200 to 2000 copies. An extremely important series of books devoted to all aspects of fine book production. Part one of volume four is an ex library copy with markings.

724. (Limited Editions Club) Dostoevsky, Fyodor. THE HOUSE OF THE DEAD. Translated from the Russian by Constance Garnett. Foreword by Boris Shagin. Wood engravings by Fritz Eichenberg. New York: The Limited Editions Club, 1982, tall 8vo., cloth, slipcase. xxiii, 360, (4) pages. $ 185.00

Limited to 2000 numbered copies signed by Eichenberg and Michael Bixler who set the type with wood-engravings printed by Daniel Keleher at the Wild Carrott Letterpress.

725. (Limited Editions Club) Doughty, Charles M. TRAVELS IN ARABIA DESER-TA. The Text as Abridged and Arranged by Edward Garnett, with a Prefatory note by Mr. Garnett, a General Introduction by T.E. Lawrence, and Illustrations by Edy Legrand. New York: The Limited Editions Club, 1953, tall 8vo., wrap-around cloth binding with flap. xxi, 455+(1) pages. $ 95.00

Limited to 1500 numbered copies. Printed at the Garamond Press with printing by Irvin Silvers. Illustrations reproduced in collotype by Arthur Jaffe in New York.

726. (Limited Editions Club) Dreiser, Theodore. AN AMERICAN TRAGEDY. With an Introduction by Harry Hansen and with Illustrations by Reginald Marsh. New York: The Limited Editions Club, 1954, thick tall 8vo., cloth, slipcase. xii, 556, (2) pages.
$ 100.00

Limited to 1500 numbered copies. This copy was not signed by Marsh as he died shortly before the book was published. Printed at The George Grady Press.

727. (Limited Editions Club) Du Maurier, George. PETER IBBETSON. With a Preface by Daphne du Maurier. Illustrated by the Author. New York: The Limited Editions Club, 1963, small 4to., leather-backed boards, slipcase. xviii, 344, (2) pages. $ 65.00

Limited to 1600 numbered copies. With the illustrations taken from the originals in the Pierpont Morgan Library. Typography by George Salter. Slipcase has small damaged spot along edge.

728. (Limited Editions Club) Dumas, Alexandre. BLACK TULIP A ROMANCE. Translated by S.J. Adair Fitz-gerald with an introduction by Ben Ray Redman. New York: The Limited Editions Club, 1951, 8vo., full leather, top edge gilt, slipcase. xxiv, 326, (2) pages. $ 95.00

Limited to 1500 numbered copies signed by Frans Lammers, the illustrator, and Jan Van Krimpen, the designer. Printed by Jon. Enschedé en Zonen in Haarlem, Holland. Spine darkened as usual with this title. Wear along edges of slipcase.

729. (Limited Editions Club) Dumas, Alexandre. CAMILLE, LA DAME AUX CAMELIAS. Illustrated by Bernard Lamotte. The Authorized Translation into English by Edmund Gosse with an Introduction by Andre Maurois, a Prefatory Letter from the Author and A Memoir of Marie Duplessis by Jules Janin. New York: The Limited Editions Club, 1955, small 4to., cloth, slipcase. xxiv, 231+(1) pages. $ 75.00

Limited to 1500 numbered copies signed by Lamotte. Printed at the Garamond Press with collotypes by Arthur Jaffe of New York. Bookplate. Well preserved copy.

730. (Limited Editions Club) Dumas, Alexandre. MAN IN THE IRON MASK. With Hand-colored illustrations by Edy Legrand and an Introduction by Andre Maurois. New York: The Limited Editions Club, 1965, tall 8vo., cloth, slipcase. xvi, 430, (2) pages.
$ 75.00

Limited to 1500 numbered copies and signed by Legrand. Printed by Edna Beilenson.

731. (Limited Editions Club) Dumas, Alexandre. MARGUERITE DE VALOIS. With Hand-Colored Illustrations by Edy Legrand and an Introduction by Henri Peyre. New York: The Limited Editions Club, 1969, tall 8vo., cloth, slipcase. xix, 338 pages. $ 65.00
Limited to 1500 numbered copies and signed by Legrand. Printed at the Sign of the Stone Book and hand-colored in the studio of Walter Fischer.

732. (Limited Editions Club) Dumas, Alexandre. TWENTY YEARS AFTER. With Hand-colored Illustrations by Edy Legrand and an Introduction by Ben Ray Redman. New York: The Limited Editions Club, 1958, tall 8vo., cloth, top edge gilt, slipcase. xiv, 496, (2) pages. $ 65.00
Limited to 1500 numbered copies and signed by Legrand. Designed by Peter Beilenson.

733. (Limited Editions Club) Eliot, George. MILL ON THE FLOSS. With an introduction by David Daiches. Illustrated with paintings by Wray Manning. New York: The Limited Editions Club, 1963, thick 8vo., cloth, leather spine label, slipcase. xviii, 472, (2) pages. $ 65.00
Limited to 1500 numbered copies signed by Manning. Printed by Edna Beilenson.

734. (Limited Editions Club) Eliot, George. SILAS MARNER, THE WEAVER OF RAVELOE. With an Introduction by John T. Winterich. Illustrated with Lithographs by Lynton Lamb. New York: The Limited Editions Club, 1953, 8vo., quarter leather over decorated paper covered boards, slipcase. xv, 246, (2) pages. $ 65.00
Limited to 1500 numbered copies signed by Lamb. Designed by Hans Schmoller and printed by James Shand at The Shenval Press. Illustrations drawn on stone and printed at The Curwen Press. Slipcase partially broken.

735. (Limited Editions Club) Fielding, Henry. HISTORY OF THE LIFE OF THE LATE MR. JONATHAN WILD THE GREAT. With Illustrations by T.M. Cleland. New York: The Limited Editions Club, 1943, tall 8vo., cloth-backed marbled paper covered boards, paper spine label. xviii, 231, (3) pages. $ 45.00
Limited to 1500 numbered copies signed by Cleland. Printed at the Marchbanks Press with the coloring of the illustrations done by hand stenciling in the studio of Charlize Brakely.

736. (Limited Editions Club) Fielding, Henry. HISTORY OF TOM JONES, A FOUNDLING. With Illustrations by T.M. Cleland and an Introduction by Louis Kronenberger. Two volumes. New York: The Limited Editions Club, 1952, tall 8vo., cloth, paper spine labels, slipcase. xviii,362; (vi),363-782 pages. $ 125.00
Limited to 1500 numbered copies signed by Cleland. Printed on Curtis paper with color plates by Deberny & Peignot and color printing by Lucien Delaporte. Minor slipcase wear.

737. (Limited Editions Club) Finney, Charles G. CIRCUS OF DR. LAO. New York: The Limited Editions Club, 1982, 4to., patterned cloth covered boards, cloth covered slipcase. (iv), vi, (ii), 122, (4) pages. $ 600.00
Printed in an edition limited to 2000 numbered copies signed by the designer and illustrator, Claire Van Vliet of the Janus Press. (Bibliography no.528). Includes a new introduction by Edward Hoagland. Illustrated with relief etchings and printed at the Stinehour Press in three colors. Newsletter laid-in.

738. (Limited Editions Club) Flaubert, Gustave. SALAMMBO. With an Introduction by Jusin O'Brien. Illustrated by Edward Bawden. New York: The Limited Editions Club, 1960, thick 4to., cloth, slipcase. xi, 316, (4) pages. $ 125.00
Limited to 1500 numbered copies signed by Bawden. Printed at the Cambridge University Press.

739. (Limited Editions Club) Flaubert, Gustave. THREE TALES BY GUSTAVE FLAUBERT. With an Introduction by Guy de Maupassant and Illustrated by May Neama. New York: The Limited Editions Club, 1978, small 4to., cloth-backed decorated paper covered boards, slipcase. xx, 132, (2) pages. $ 65.00
Limited to 1500 numbered copies signed by Neama. Printed at the Press of A. Colish with design by Bert Clarke.

740. (Limited Editions Club) FOUR GOSPELS, THE GOSPEL ACCORDING TO S. MATTHEW. With Decorations by E.R. Weiss and an Introduction by Ernest Sutherland Bates. New York: The Limited Editions Club, 1932, small 4to., parchment-backed boards. 237, (3) pages. $ 95.00
Limited to 1500 numbered copies signed by Weiss. Printed in Germany by Poeschel & Trepte. Beautifully produced book. No slipcase present. Bookplate.

741. (Limited Editions Club) France, Anatole. CRAINQUEBILLE. Newly Translated, with an Introduction, by Jacques LeClercq and Illustrated by Bernard Lamotte. New York: The Limited Editions Club, 1949, 4to., woven cloth, slipcase. xvi, 69, (3) pages. $ 65.00
Limited to 1500 numbered copies and signed by the illustrator.

742. (Limited Editions Club) France, Anatole. PENGUIN ISLAND. Translated from the French by A.W. Evans; with an Introduction by Carl Van Doren, a Preface by the Author, and Drawings by Malcolm Cameron. New York: The Limited Editions Club, 1947, tall 8vo., parchment- backed decorated paper covered boards, slipcase. xvi, 324, (2) pages. $ 50.00
Limited to 1500 numbered copies signed by Cameron. Printed at the Aldus Printers with design by Joseph Blumenthal. Bookplate on front pastedown.

743. (Limited Editions Club) France, Anatole. REVOLT OF THE ANGELS. The translation by Mrs. Wilfrid Jackson with an Introduction by Desmond MacCarthy and Illustrations by Pierre Watrin. New York: Limited Editions Club, 1953, small 4to., cloth, slipcase. $ 55.00
Limited to 1500 copies. Printed at the Plantin Press in Los Angeles. Name in ink, else fine.

744. (Limited Editions Club) Frazer, James George. GOLDEN BOUGH, A STUDY IN MAGIC AND RELIGION. With an introduction by Stanley Edgar Hyman and illustrations by James Lewicki. Two volumes. New York: The Limited Editions Club, 1970, thick small 4to., two-toned cloth, slipcase. xxiii,430; xii,431-884,(2) pages. $ 135.00
Limited to 1500 numbered copies signed by Lewicki. Printed at the Sign of the Stone Book with design by Charles E. Skaggs.

745. (Limited Editions Club) FRITHIOF'S SAGA. Translated into English Verse by Henry Wadsworth Longfellow, ... and the general Introduction by Bayard Taylor. Illustrated with drawings by Eric Palmquist. New York: Limited Editions Club, 1953, small 4to., cloth-backed boards, slipcase. $ 55.00
Limited to 1500 copies signed by Palmquist. Printed in Stockholm by the Royal Printing House.

746. (Limited Editions Club) Galsworthy, John. MAN OF PROPERTY. With an Introduction by Evelyn Waugh. Illustrations by Charles Mozley. New York: The Limited Editions Club, 1964, small 4to., cloth, slipcase. x, 285+(1) pages. $ 65.00
Limited to 1500 numbered copies signed by the Mozley. Printed at the Press of A. Colish with design by John Dreyfus.

747. (Limited Editions Club) Gautier, Theophile. MADEMOISELLE DE MAUPIN. With the Preface by the Author, an Introduction for the Modern Reader by Jacques Barzun and hand-colored illustrations by Andre Dugo. New York: The Limited Editions Club, 1943, small 4to., quarter leather over boards, cloth spine label, slipcase. xlvi, 299, (3) pages. $ 85.00
Limited to 1000 numbered copies bound and signed by Duyo. Designed by George Salter. The illustrations were lithographed by The Duenewald Printing Corporation with the colors applied by hand in the studio of Charlize Brakely. Slipcase spotted.

748. (Limited Editions Club) Goethe, Johann Wolfgang von. WILHELM MEISTER'S APPRENTICESHIP THE THOMAS CARLYLE TRANSLATION. With a new Introduction by Franz Schoenberner and Illustrations by William Sharp. New York: The Limited Editions Club, 1959, small 4to., cloth, slipcase. xxvii, 567, (3) pages. $ 75.00
Limited to 1500 numbered copies and signed by Sharp. Designed by Stefan Salter.

749. (Limited Editions Club) Gogol, Nikolai. OVERCOAT. THE GOVERNMENT INSPECTOR. In the Constance Garnett translation. With an introduction by Alfred Kazin and engravings by Saul Field. Westport, CT: The Limited Editions Club, 1976, 8vo., cloth, slipcase. xvi, 187, (3) pages. $ 65.00
Limited to 2000 numbered copies signed by Field. Designed by Charles E. Skaggs and printed by The Meriden Gravure Company.

750. (Limited Editions Club) Grass, Gunter. THE FLOUNDER. New York: Limited Editions Club, 1985, oblong small 4to., eelskin backing with cloth-covered boards, paper labels on covers, cloth-covered slipcase. xiii, (iii), 156; 159-326; 329-530 pages. $ 520.00
Limited to 1,000 numbered copies. History as a series of individual biographies and meals? Along with a talkative magical fish who doesn't want to be eaten (one recognizes, of course, the Grimm fairy tale). Men catch food, women prepare it, or at least in this novel, whose apparently everlasting fisherman protagonist keeps meeting the same persuasive, well-informed fish, while his apparently equally immortal wife appears again and again in different manifestations, in many guises but always as a cook, though, unlike him, lacking a personal memory of human history. In the "present" cycle, however, the flounder has been caught by three lesbians fishing in the Baltic and brought to trial before a radical feminist tribunal for having "served the male cause in an advisory capacity since the late Neolithic, well knowing that his advice redounded to the detriment of the female sex..." p.163. With the author's excellent illustrations.

751. (Limited Editions Club) Graves, Robert. POEMS. New York: The Limited Editions Club, 1980, 8vo., cloth-backed decorated paper covered boards, slipcase. xx, 144, (2) pages. $ 95.00
Limited to 2,000 numbered copies signed by the illustrator, Paul Hogarth and the designer, Freeman Keith. Printed at the Stinehour Press.

752. (Limited Editions Club) Hardy, Thomas. FAR FROM THE MADDING CROWD. New York: The Limited Editions Club, 1958, thick 8vo., quarter leather over pictorial paper covered boards, slipcase. xxi, 400, (4) pages. $ 135.00
Limited to 1500 numbered copies signed by Parker. Printed at the Cambridge University Press. With separate plate loosely inserted. Very minor rubbing of spine at each end.

753. (Limited Editions Club) Hardy, Thomas. MAYOR OF CASTERBRIDGE. Illustrated with Wood Engravings by Agnes Miller Parker. Introduction by Frank Swinnerton. New York: The Limited Editions Club, 1964, thick 8vo., quarter leather, slipcase. xvi, 317, (3) pages. $ 175.00
Limited to 1500 numbered copies signed by Parker. Printed at The Thistle Press.

754. (Limited Editions Club) Hardy, Thomas. TESS OF THE D'URBERVILLES, A PURE WOMAN, FAITHFULLY PRESENTED. Introduction by Robert Cantwell. Illustrated with Wood Engravings by Agnes Miller Parker. New York: The Limited Editions Club, 1956, thick 8vo., cloth, leather spine label, slipcase. xvi, 447, (3) pages.
$ 135.00

Limited to 1500 numbered copies signed by Parker. Printed at the George Grady Press. Bookplate.

755. (Limited Editions Club) Harris, Joel Chandler. UNCLE REMUS: HIS SONGS AND HIS SAYINGS. With a Foreword by Marc Connelly and Woodcuts by Seong Moy. New York: The Limited Editions Club, 1957, small 4to., woven cloth, paper spine label, slipcase. xviii, 158, (2) pages.
$ 125.00

Limited to 1500 numbered copies and signed by Moy. Designed by Robert L. Dothard and printed by Clarke & Way at The Thistle Press. Slipcase age yellowed. Bookplate.

756. (Limited Editions Club) Hawthorne, Nathaniel. TWICE-TOLD TALES, SELECTED AND INTRODUCED BY WALLACE STEGNER. New York: The Limited Editions Club, 1966, small 4to., cloth, leather spine label, slipcase. xv, 411 pages.
$ 100.00

Limited to 1500 numbered copies signed by Valenti Angelo, the illustrator of this title. Stegner chose 11 stories from "Twice-Told Tales," 8 from "Mosses from an Old Manse," 4 from "The Snow Image" and 1 not in any collection. Printed at the Stinehour Press with design by Lewis F. White. Some fading of slipcase.

757. (Limited Editions Club) Heine, Heinrich. POEMS OF HEINRICH HEINE. Selected and Translated, with an Introduction, by Louis Untermeyer and Illustrated by Fritz Kredel. New York: The Limited Editions Club, 1957, 8vo., leather-backed paste paper covered boards, slipcase. liv, 297+(1) pages.
$ 125.00

Limited to 1500 numbered copies signed by Kredel. Designed by Georg Salter and printed by Clarke & Way at the Thistle Press. The color illustrations were produced in the studio of Walter Fischer. Bookplate.

758. (Limited Editions Club) Holmes, Oliver Wendell. AUTOCRAT OF THE BREAKFAST-TABLE. With an Introduction by Van Wyck Brooks and Illustrations by R.J. Holden. New York: The Limited Editions Club, 1955, small 4to., cloth, leather spine label, slipcase. xviii, 280, (4) pages.
$ 65.00

Limited to 1500 numbered copies and signed by Holden. Designed by Carl Purington Rollins and printed at Yale University Press. Spine of book is age darkened. Head of spine slightly bumped.

759. (Limited Editions Club) Hope, Anthony. PRISONER OF ZENDA. With an Introduction by S.C. Roberts. Illustrated by Donald Spencer. New York: The Limited Editions Club, (1966), small 4to., quarter leather, slipcase. xviii, 188, (2) pages.
$ 65.00

Limited to 1500 numbered copies signed by Spencer. Designed by J. Martin Kupfer.

760. (Limited Editions Club) Howells, William Dean. RISE OF SILAS LAPHAM. With an Introduction by Henry Steele Commager and Illustrations by Mimi Korach. New York: The Limited Editions Club, 1961, tall 8vo., cloth, slipcase. xiii, 365, (3) pages.
$ 65.00

Limited to 1500 numbered copies signed by Korach. Designed by Richard Ellis. Slipcase shows minor fading.

761. (Limited Editions Club) Hughes, Richard. INNOCENT VOYAGE. Illustrated with Lithographs in Color by Lynd Ward and with an Introduction by Louis Unter-meyer. New York: The Limited Editions Club, 1944, tall 8vo., full leather, outer board cover, slipcase. viii, 221, (3) pages. $ 85.00
Limited to 1500 numbered copies signed by Ward.

762. (Limited Editions Club) Hugo, Victor. NOTRE-DAME DE PARIS. Translated by Jessie Haynes with the Illustrations by Bernard Lamotte and an introduction by Justin O'Brien. New York: The Limited Editions Club, 1955, small 4to., cloth, leather spine label, slipcase. xvii, 331, (3) pages. $ 75.00
Limited to 1500 numbered copies and signed by the illustrator. Composition by Joh. Enschedé en Zonen in Haarlem under the direction of Jan van Krimpen. Printed at the George Grady Press.

763. (Limited Editions Club) Hugo, Victor. TOILERS OF THE SEA. In the Translation by Isabel F. Hapgood and with an Introduction by Matthew Josephson. Illustrated with Wood-Engravings by Tranquillo Marangoni. New York: The Limited Editions Club, 1960, thick small 4to., cloth-backed boards, dust jacket, slipcase. $ 135.00
Limited to 1500 numbered copies signed by the illustrator. Printed at the Officina Bodoni by Giovanni Mardersteig. Spine of jacket is age yellowed as usual.

764. (Limited Editions Club) Ibsen, Henrik. PEER GYNT. Translated, with an Intro-duction by William and Charles Archer. Illustrated by Per Krohg. New York: The Lim-ited Editions Club, 1955, small 4to., cloth-backed decorated paper covered boards, slip-case. xviii, 314, (3), xix-xxiv pages. $ 75.00
Limited to 1500 numbered copies signed by Krohg. Printed in Oslo on special paper made for this edi-tion. Slipcase rubbed with wear along edges.

765. (Limited Editions Club) Irving, Washington. ALHAMBRA. With an Introduction by Angel Flores and Illustrated by Lima de Freitas. New York: The Limited Editions Club, 1969, small 4to., woven cloth, leather spine label, slipcase. xiii, 304, (2) pages.
                                                                          $ 75.00
Limited to 1500 numbered copies signed by de Freitas. Printed by the Press of A. Colish.

766. (Limited Editions Club) Jackson, Helen Hunt. RAMONA A STORY. With an In-troduction by J. Frank Dobie and Illustrations by Everett Gee Jackson. Los Angeles: The Limited Editions Club, 1959, small 4to., woven cloth, paper spine label, slipcase. xx, 428, (2) pages. $ 65.00
Limited to 1500 numbered copies and signed by the illustrator. Printed at the Plantin Press in Los An-geles.

767. (Limited Editions Club) James, Henry. AMBASSADORS. With Illustrations by Leslie Saalburg and a Preface by the Author. New York: The Limited Editions Club, 1963, tall 8vo., two-toned cloth, slipcase. xx, 384, (2) pages. $ 65.00
Limited to 1500 numbered copies and signed by the illustrator. Printed by the Garamond Press under the direction of Richard Ellis.

768. (Limited Editions Club) James, Henry. DAISY MILLER. Introduction by John Holloway. Illustrations by Gustave Nebel. New York: The Limited Editions Club, 1969, small 8vo., full leather, top edge gilt, slipcase. xviii, 92, (2) pages. $ 95.00
Limited to 1500 numbered copies signed by Nebel. Printed at the Cambridge University Press with de-sign by Will Carter.

769. (Limited Editions Club) James, Henry. PORTRAIT OF A LADY. Illustrations by Colleen Browning. Introduction by R.W. Stallman. New York: The Limited Editions Club, 1967, thick 8vo., cloth- backed marbled paper covered boards, slipcase. xiv, 516, (4) pages. $ 85.00
Limited to 1500 numbered copies signed by the Browning. Printed at the Garamond Press and designed by Peter Oldenburg.

770. (Limited Editions Club) James, Henry. TURN OF THE SCREW. With an Introduction by Carl Van Doren & Illustrations by Mariette Lydis. New York: The Limited Editions Club, 1949, small 4to., cloth, slipcase. xvi, 145, (3) pages. $ 75.00
Limited to 1500 numbered copies. Printed by Saul and Lillian Marks at The Plantin Press. Illustrations were printed in gravure by The Photogravure & Color Company of New York. Slipcase rubbed.

771. (Limited Editions Club) Jerome, Jerome K. THREE MEN IN A BOAT, TO SAY NOTHING OF THE DOG! With an Introduction by Stella Gibbons and drawings by John Griffiths. N.P.: The Limited Editions Club, 1975, oblong 4to., cloth, slipcase. xv, 174, (2) pages. $ 75.00
Limited to 2000 numbered copies signed by Griffiths. Printed by W.S. Cowell Ltd. of Ipswich, England, with design by John Lewis.

772. (Limited Editions Club) JOURNALS AND OTHER DOCUMENTS ON THE LIFE AND VOYAGES OF CHRISTOPHER COLUMBUS. Translated and Edited by Samuel Eliot Morison. Illustrated by Lima de Freitas. New York: The Limited Editions Club, 1963, 4to., cloth, leather spine label, cameo of Columbus on front cover, slipcase. xvi, 417, (3) pages. $ 175.00
Limited to 1500 numbered copies signed by de Freitas. Designed by Lewis F. White. Morison has gone back to the original source documents for his translations.

773. (Limited Editions Club) KING JAMES VERSION OF THE HOLY BIBLE, CONTAINING THE OLD AND THE NEW TESTAMENT TOGETHER WITH THE APOCRYPHA, TRANSLATED OUT OF THE ORIGINAL TONGUES IN THE YEAR 1611. Five volumes. New York: The Limited Editions Club, 1935, 8vo., blue cloth stamped in gilt, all edges gilt, enclosed in two slipcases. xlviii,406; (iv),407-954; (iv),955–1662,(2); (vi),1663-2074; (vi),2075-2576 pages. $ 165.00
Limited to 1500 numbered copies. Designed by George Macy and printed at the Yale University Press under the direction of George T. Bailey. Slipcases rubbed with wear along edges. Bookplate in each volume.

774. (Limited Editions Club) Kingsley, Charles. WESTWARD HO! Two volumes. New York: The Limited Editions Club, 1947, small 4to., cloth-backed boards, slipcase. (xvi),292; (viii),293-576,(3) pages. $ 75.00
Limited to 1500 numbered copies signed by the illustrator, Edward Wilson. With an Introduction by John Winterich. With colors applied by hand. Bookplate in each volume. Very well preserved set.

775. (Limited Editions Club) Kipling, Rudyard. TALES OF EAST AND WEST. Selected by Bernard Bergonzi and Illustrated by Charles Raymond. Avon, CT: The Limited Editions Club, 1973, small 4to., cloth, slipcase. xiii, 375, (3) pages. $ 75.00
Limited to 1500 numbered copies signed by Raymond. Printed at The Connecticut Printers with design by Frank Lieberman. Small bookplate on front pastedown.

776. (Limited Editions Club) Landor, Walter Savage. IMAGINARY CONVERSA-
TIONS. Selected & Introduced by R.H. Boothroyd. New York: The Limited Editions
Club, 1936, tall 8vo., cloth, dust jacket, slipcase. xiv, 303, (3) pages. $ 100.00
Limited to 1500 numbered copies and signed by the printer, Hans Mardersteig. Printed at his Officina
Bodoni in Verona. Jacket has small spot along spine.

777. (Limited Editions Club) Lawrence, D.H. SONS AND LOVERS. With an Introduction by Robert Gorham Davis and Illustrations by Sheila Robinson. Avon, CT: The
Limited Editions Club, 1975, thick 8vo., woven cloth, paper spine label, slipcase. xiv, 443,
(3) pages. $ 85.00
Limited to 2000 numbered copies signed by Robinson. Designed by Bert Clarke and printed at the Press
of A. Colish.

778. (Limited Editions Club) Le Gallienne, Richard. PHILOSOPHY OF LIMITED
EDITIONS. N.P.: (Helen and George Macy, 1933), 8vo., full blue calf stamped in gilt.
10, (2) pages printed French fold. $ 150.00
Limited to 100 copies. Set by hand by Helen Macy in a new type by Frederic Goudy. Chipped at head of
spine. Very scarce. Issued in a trade edition by the Limited Editions Club.

779. (Limited Editions Club) Lesage, Alain-Rene. ADVENTURES OF GIL BLAS DE
SANTILLANE. Translated by Tobias Smollett. Introduction by J.B. Priestley. Illustrations by John Austen. Two volumes. New York: The Limited Editions Club, 1937, small
4to., two-toned cloth, dust jackets, slipcase. xxvi,330; xii,33 pages. $ 150.00
Limited to 1500 numbered copies signed by Austen. Printed at the OUP under the direction of John
Johnson. With colored illustrations throughout. Slight yellowing of spines of jackets and wear to slipcase.

780. (Limited Editions Club) Livy. THE HISTORY OF EARLY ROME. Translated by
Aubrey de Selincourt. Illustrated by Raffaele Scorzelli. New York: The Limited Editions
Club, 1970, thick small 4to., cloth-backed patterned paper covered boards, slipcase. xviii,
499, (3) pages. $ 150.00
Limited to 1500 numbered copies signed by Scorzelli and by Giovanni Mardersteig, the designer and
printer. Printed at the Stamperia Valdonega with design at the Officina Bodoni.

781. (Limited Editions Club) London, Jack. CALL OF THE WILD. With an introduction by Pierre Berton and illustrations by Henry Varnum Poor. New York: The Limited
Editions Club, 1960, small 4to., thick green patterned cloth with matching slipcase,
leather spine label. xv, 158, (2) pages. $ 85.00
Limited to 1500 numbered copies signed by Poor. Printed at the Ward Ritchie Press. Patterned cloth is
worn in two small places along front hinge.

782. (Limited Editions Club) Lucretius. DE RERUM NATURA, OF THE NATURE
OF THINGS. Translated into English verse by William Ellery Leonard with an Intro-
duction by Charles E. Bennett, illustrated with wood-engravings by Paul Landacre. New
York: The Limited Editions Club, 1957, 8vo., full leather, slipcase. xx, 317, (3) pages.
                                                                                                $ 135.00
Limited to 1500 numbered copies signed by Landacre. Designed by Ward Ritchie and printed by The
Ward Ritchie Press. Newsletter loosely inserted. Hinges cracked in plates.

783. (Limited Editions Club) Manzoni, Alessandro. PROMESSI SPOSI (THE
BETHROTHED). The 1844 translation revised and with an Introduction by Ronald H.
Boothroyd. Illustrated with the designs of Francesco Gonin engraved for this Edition by

Bruno Bramanti. New York: The Limited Editions Club, 1951, 4to., cloth-backed decorated paper covered boards, paper spine label, dust jacket, slipcase. xiv, 676, (4) pages.
$ 175.00
Limited to 1500 numbered copies and signed by the engraver, Bruno Bramanti and the printer, Giovanni Mardersteig. Printed at the Officina Bodoni. Bookplate.

784. (Limited Editions Club) Marlowe, Christopher. FOUR PLAYS. Edited with an Introduction by Havelock Ellis. Copperplate Engravings by Albert Decaris. New York: The Limited Editions Club, 1966, 4to., quarter leather over cloth, slipcase. xviii, 280, (3) pages.
$ 85.00
Limited to 1500 numbered copies and signed by Decaris. Printed at The Thistle Press of New York with design by Adrian Wilson and devices by Fritz Kredel. Beautifully designed and printed. Slipcase faded.

785. (Limited Editions Club) Meredith, George. SHAVING OF SHAGPAT. With a Preface by Sir Francis Meredith Meynell and Illustrations by Honore Guilbeau. Designed and Decorated by W.A. Dwiggins. New York: The Limited Editions Club, 1955, 8vo., half- leather over marbled boards, slipcase.
$ 65.00
Limited to 1500 copies signed by Guilbeau. Some rubbing of spine. Bookplate.

786. (Limited Editions Club) Milton, John. THE MASQUE OF COMUS. Illustrated with Water-Colors by Edward Dulac. With a Preface by Mark Van Doren & The Airs by Henry Lawes with a Preface by Hubert Foss. (New York): The Limited Editions Club, 1954, small 4to., parchment backed marbled paper covered boards, slipcase. (vi), 57, (17) pages.
$ 125.00
Limited to 1500 numbered copies. Not signed by Dulac as he died shortly after finishing the illustrations. Bookplate.

787. (Limited Editions Club) Moliere. TARTUFFE & THE WOULD-BE GENTLE-MAN. Translated by H. Baker and J. Miller. With an Introduction by Henri Peyre and Illustrations by Serge Ivanoff. New York: The Limited Editions Club, 1963, small 4to., cloth, slipcase. xvi, 197, (3) pages.
$ 75.00
Limited to 1500 numbered copies and signed by the illustrator. Printed at the Thistle Press.

788. (Limited Editions Club) Morier, J.J. ADVENTURES OF HAJJI BABA OF IS-PAHAN. With a Preface by Sir Walter Scott and Illustrations by Honore Guilbeau. Two volumes. New York: The Limited Editions Club, 1947, 8vo., quarter leather over pictorial paper covered boards, slipcase. lii,233; x,233-498,(2) pages.
$ 95.00
Limited to 1500 numbered copies signed by Guilbeau. Designed and decorated by W.A. Dwiggins and printed by the Aldus Printers. Printed in red, black and blue throughout and with colorful decorated title pages by Dwiggins. Minor wear to leather spine. Bookplate. Newsletter loosely inserted.

789. (Limited Editions Club) Nietzsche, Friedrich. THUS SPAKE ZARATHUSTRA. Translated from the German by Thomas Common. With an Introduction by Henry David Aiken and Decorations by Arnold Bank. New York: The Limited Editions Club, 1964, small 4to., quarter parchment over cloth, slipcase. xx, 316, (2) pages.
$ 100.00
Limited to 1500 numbered copies. Designed by Adrian Wilson.

790. (Limited Editions Club) O'Neill, Eugene. AH, WILDERNESS! With an Introduction by Walter Kerr and Illustrations by Shannon Stirnweis. New York: The Limited Editions Club, 1972, small 4to., cloth-backed boards, paper spine label, slipcase. 161, (3) pages.
$ 85.00
Limited to 1500 numbered copies signed by Stirnweis. Designed by Adrian Wilson and printed at Mackenzie & Harris under the direction of Clifford Burke.

791. (Limited Editions Club) Ovid. THE ART OF LOVE. Translated by B.P. Moore. Illustrated by Eric Fraser. N.P.: The Limited Editions Club, 1971, 8vo., full parchment, slipcase. xii, 117, (3) pages. $ 75.00

Limited to 1500 numbered copies signed by Fraser. Printed at the Press of A. Colish with design by Robert L. Dothard.

792. (Limited Editions Club) Petrarch. THE SONNETS OF PETRARCH. In the Original Italian, Together with English Translations Selected and Edited with an Introduction by Thomas G. Bergin. Illustrated with Drawings by Aldo Salvadori. N.P.: Printed for the Limited Editions Club at the Stamperia Valdonega, 1965, 4to., quarter leather, dust jacket, slipcase. xix, 369, (3) pages. $ 200.00

Limited to 1500 numbered copies signed by both Giovanni Mardersteig and Salvadori. Very fine copy.

793. (Limited Editions Club) Petronius. SATYRICON OF PETRONIUS. The Translation by William Burnaby, revised for the present edition, with an introduction, by Gilbert Bagnani and illustrated by Antonio Sotomayor. New York: The Limited Editions Club, 1964, small 4to., parchment-backed cloth, slipcase. xxiii, 246, (2) pages. $ 65.00

Limited to 1500 numbered copies and signed by the illustrator. Printed at the Press of A. Colish.

794. (Limited Editions Club) Plato. LYSIS, OR FRIENDSHIP, THE SYMPOSIUM PHAEDRUS. Translated from the Greek, with Introductory Analyses, by Benjamin Jowett. With a Preface by Whitney J. Oates and Illustrations by Eugene Karlin. New York: The Limited Editions Club, 1968, tall 8vo., quarter vellum over boards, leather spine label, slipcase. xviii, 208, (2) pages. $ 85.00

Limited to 1500 numbered copies signed by Karlin. Printed at the Press of A. Colish and designed by Robert Dothard.

795. (Limited Editions Club) Porter, William Sidney. STORIES OF O. HENRY. Chosen & Introduced by Harry Hansen. Illustrated by John Groth. New York: The Limited Editions Club, 1965, small 4to., patterned cloth, slipcase. xvi, 366, (2) pages. $ 75.00

Limited to 1500 numbered copies signed by Groth. Printed at The Lane Press.

796. (Limited Editions Club) Prescott, William Hickling. HISTORY OF THE CONQUEST OF PERU 1524–1550. Mexico City: Limited Editions Club, 1957, small folio, bound in full tree calf with red leather spine labels stamped in gold, slip case. (xxxvi), 253 pages. $ 125.00

Printed in an edition limited to 1500 numbered copies. (Bibliography no.275). Printed at the Imprenta Nuevo Mondo in Mexico City by Harry Black, with 30 color drawings by Everett Gee Jackson, and signed by both. Designed as a companion volume to Diaz del Castillo's *The Discovery and Conquest of Mexico*, also printed in Mexico. Title page printed in brown and black with a color drawing by Jackson. Introduction by Samuel Eliot Morison. Spine age darkened with some wear. Slipcase rubbed.

797. (Limited Editions Club) Pushkin, Alexander. CAPTAIN'S DAUGHTER & OTHER STORIES. With an Introduction by Kathryn Feuer and Illustrations by Charles Mozley. New York: The Limited Editions Club, 1971, 4to., cloth, slipcase. xv, 227, (3) pages. $ 75.00

Limited to 1500 numbered copies signed by Mozley. Designed by Mozley and printed by the Westerham Press in Kent.

798. (Limited Editions Club) Pushkin, Alexander. GOLDEN COCKEREL FROM THE TALE BY ALEXANDER PUSHKIN. ILLUSTRATED BY EDMUND DULAC. New York: The Limited Editions Club, n.d. (1949), 4to., cloth with outer board cover and slipcase. 41, (3) pages. $ 150.00

Limited to 1500 numbered copies signed by Dulac. Filled with color illustrations and ornaments. Printed at the Fanfare Press of London under the direction of Ernest Ingham. Slipcase faded. Some spotting of front and back pastedowns and top edge of endpapers.

799. (Limited Editions Club) QUARTO-MILLENARY, THE FIRST 250 PUBLICATIONS AND THE FIRST 25 YEARS 1929 - 1954 OF THE LIMITED EDITIONS CLUB; A CRITIQUE, A CONSPECTUS, A BIBLIOGRAPHY, INDEXES. New York: The Limited Editions Club, 1959, 4to., quarter black calf over red cloth, red leather spine label, black leather cameo device in front cover, slipcase. 295 pages. $ 275.00

Limited to 2250 numbered copies. Many illustrations, including quite a few in color. Slipcase cracked along hinges.

800. (Limited Editions Club) Raspe, Rudolph and Others. SINGULAR ADVENTURES OF BARON MUNCHAUSEN. A Definitive Text edited, with an introduction by John Carswell and Illustrated by Fritz Kredel. New York: The Limited Editions Club, 1952, 8vo., quarter leather over marbled paper covered boards, slipcase. xli, 175+(1) pages. $ 100.00

Limited to 1500 numbered copies signed by Kredel. Printed at the Marchbanks Press with typography by George Salter. All hand-colored illustrations. Spine label of slipcase spotted.

801. (Limited Editions Club) Reade, Charles. CLOISTER AND THE HEARTH, A TALE OF THE MIDDLE AGES. With an Introduction by Hendrik Willem Van Loon and Illustrations in Photogravure by Lynd Ward. Two volumes. New York: The Limited Editions Club, 1932, tall 8vo., patterned cloth, slipcase. xv,367; (iv),367-745,(3) pages
. $ 120.00

Limited to 1500 numbered copies and signed by Ward. Printed and designed at The Press of A. Colish. No jackets. Slipcase is soiled with some spotting. Much better condition than usually found.

802. (Limited Editions Club) Robert, Maurice and Frederic Warde. CODE FOR THE COLLECTOR OF BEAUTIFUL BOOKS. New York: Limited Editions Club, 1936, 4to., cloth-backed decorated boards, paper spine label. xiv, 56 pages. $ 15.00

Wear along edges and covers rubbed and spotted. Bookplate.

803. (Limited Editions Club) Rostand, Edmond. CYRANO DE BERGERAC, A HEROIC COMEDY IN 5 ACTS. In a New English Version by Louis Untermeyer with Illustrations drawn by Pierre Brissaud. New York: The Limited Editions Club, 1954, small 4to., cloth, leather spine label, slipcase. xviii, 210, (2) pages. $ 85.00

Limited to 1500 numbered copies and signed by Brissaud. Printed by the Marchbanks Press. Colored by the stencil process in the studio of Walter Fischer of New York. Bookplate.

804. (Limited Editions Club) Rousseau, Jean-Jacques. CONFESSIONS OF JEAN-JACQUES ROUSSEAU THE ANONYMOUS TRANSLATION INTO ENGLISH OF 1783 & 1790. Revised and Completed by A.S.B. Glover, with a New Introduction by Mr. Glover. Illustrations by William Sharp. New York: The Limited Editions Club, 1955, tall 8vo., leather-backed boards, slipcase. xviii, 635, (3) pages. $ 65.00

Limited to 1500 numbered copies and signed by Sharp. Designed and printed by Peter Beilenson. Some rubbing along front hinge.

805. (Limited Editions Club) RUSSIAN FOLK TALES. Selected and Edited by Albert B. Lord. Illustrated by Teje Etchemendy. New York: The Limited Editions Club, 1970, small 4to., two-toned cloth, slipcase. xx, 196, (4) pages. $ 65.00
Limited to 1500 numbered copies signed by Etchemendy. Designed by Adrian Wilson.

806. (Limited Editions Club) Schiller, Johann Christoph Friedrich Von. WILLIAM TELL. Translated from the German in the Meter of the Original by Theodore Martin. With an Introductory Essay by Thomas Carlyle. Illustrated by Charles Hug. Zurich: Limited Editions Club, 1951, small 4to., cloth-backed boards, slipcase. 164 pages.
$ 95.00
Limited to 1500 numbered copies signed by Hug. Printed by Fretz Brothers in Zurich with typography by W. Dietheim. The illustrations are lithographs.

807. (Limited Editions Club) Schreiner, Olive. STORY OF AN AFRICAN FARM. With an Introduction by Isak Dinesen and Illustrations by Paul Hogarth. New York: The Limited Editions Club, 1961, small 4to., cloth, slipcase. xx, 259, (3) pages. $ 95.00
Limited to 1500 numbered copies signed by Hogarth. Printed at The Westerham Press with typography by Hans Schmoller. Lithography by The Curwen Press.

808. (Limited Editions Club) Scott, Walter. IVANHOE. Illustrated by Edward A. Wilson. Two volumes. New York: The Limited Editions Club, 1951, 8vo., cloth, slipcase.
$ 125.00
Limited to 1500 numbered copies, signed by Wilson. With Wilson's illustrations hand-colored through stencils in the studio of Walter Fischer.

809. (Limited Editions Club) Scott, Walter. TALISMAN. With an introduction by Thomas Caldecott Chubb and Illustrations by Federico Castellon. Ipswich: The Limited Editions Club, 1968, small 4to., quarter black calf over red cloth, top edge gilt, slipcase. xxx, 370 pages. $ 75.00
Limited to 1500 numbered copies and signed by the illustrator. Printed by W.S. Cowell with typography by John Lewis. Minor rubbing at spine ends.

810. (Limited Editions Club) SERMON ON THE MOUNT. With an Introduction, Parallel Texts, and Commentaries by Rowan A. Greer. New York: The Limited Editions Club, 1977, 4to., quarter leather over marbled paper covered boards, slipcase. (viii), 87, (3) pages printed French fold. $ 95.00
Limited to 1600 numbered copies. Designed by John Dreyfus with engravings by Leo Wyatt printed in red. Printed at the University Press under the direction of Vivian Ridler.

811. (Limited Editions Club) Shakespeare, William. COMEDIES, HISTORIES & TRAGEDIES OF WILLIAM SHAKESPEARE (37 volumes). With SHAKE-SPEARE, A REVIEW AND A PREVIEW. With THE POEMS OF WILLIAM SHAKESPEARE (Two volumes). With A SHAKESPEARE COMMENTARY. With TEN YEARS AND WILLIAM SHAKESPEARE (original leather). Forty two volumes. New York: The Limited Editions Club, 1939–1941, 4to., cloth-backed decorated boards, top edges gilt with COMMENTARIES in publisher's binding. $ 850.00
Limited to 1950 copies except for the *Poems* which is limited to 1500 numbered copies signed by Bruce Rogers. Overall design of this classic in book design and illustration was in the hands of Bruce Rogers. Each of the 37 volumes of Plays is illustrated by a different illustrator. The impressive list includes Eric Gill, Arthur Rackham, Gordon Ross, Edy Legrand, John Austen, Robert Gibbings, Fritz Kredel, Barnett Freedman, Edward Bawden, Gordon Craig, Frank Brangwyn, Valenti Angelo, Edward Wilson and Agnes Miller Parker. The text for this edition was edited by Herbert Farjeon who went back to the original ap-

pearances of the First Folio and Quarto Editions for punctuation and capitalization yet did correct obvious errors. All spines are spotted. The leather binding on the *Ten Years* is worn with small pieces missing. The *Poems* is in the original slipcase.

812. (Limited Editions Club) Shakespeare, William. LIFE OF KING HENRY V. The Arden Text, edited by Herbert Arthur Evans; with a general introduction by Mr. Evans and a special prefatory note by Mark Van Doren; illustrated with paintings by Fritz Kredel. New York: The Limited Editions Club, 1951, 4to., cloth, slipcase. xxi, 157+(1) pages. $ 125.00
Limited to 1500 numbered copies. With tipped-in color plates. Slipcase spotted.

813. (Limited Editions Club) Shaw, George Bernard. MAN AND SUPERMAN. Introduction by Lewis Casson. Illustrated by Charles Mozley. Two volumes. New York: The Limited Editions Club, 1962, 4to., two-toned cloth and a separate 8vo. volume bound in stiff paper wrappers, enclosed in a specially made slipcase. xl,137,(3); 63 pages. $ 95.00
Limited to 1500 numbered copies signed by Mozley. The second volume contains a reprint of Shaw's "The Revolutionist's Handbook & Pocket Companion." Printed by A. Colish under the direction of John Dreyfus.

814. (Limited Editions Club) Shaw, George Bernard. PYGMALION AND CANDIDA. With an Introduction by Alan Strachan and Illustrations by Clarke Hutton. Avon, CT: The Limited Editions Club, 1974, 4to., half cloth over pictorial paper covered boards, leather spine label, slipcase. xvi, 169, (3) pages. $ 65.00
Limited to 2000 numbered copies signed by Hutton. Printed at the Stinehour Press with typographic design by John Dreyfus.

815. (Limited Editions Club) Shaw, George Bernard. TWO PLAYS FOR PURITANS. New York: The Limited Editions Club, 1966, 4to., quarter leather with red decorated cloth, slipcase. xxxiv, 215, (2) pages. $ 65.00
Limited to 1500 numbered copies signed by Him. Printed at the Sign of the Stone Brook to the typographic plans of George Him who was also the illustrator. Hand colored at the studio of Walter Fischer. The two plays are "The Devil's Disciple" and "Caesar and Cleopatra" with a long preface by George Bernard Shaw who takes the opportunity to castigate the British theatre.

816. (Limited Editions Club) Sheridan, Richard Brinsley. RIVALS, A COMEDY. With an Introduction by John Mason Brown and Illustrations by Rene Ben Sussan. New York: The Limited Editions Club, 1953, tall 8vo., cloth, slipcase. $ 65.00
Limited to 1500 numbered copies signed by Sussan. Printed at the Curwen Press by Oliver Simon with copper engravings hand-colored in Paris. Spine of slipcase faded.

817. (Limited Editions Club) Sienkiewicz, Henryk. QUO VADIS? Translated from the Polish by Jeremiah Curtin with an Introduction by Harold Lamb and Illustrations by Salvatore Fiume. New York: The Limited Editions Club, 1959, small 4to., cloth, dust jacket, slipcase. xiii, 594, (4) pages. $ 135.00
Limited to 1500 numbered copies and signed by the illustrator and the printer. Printed by Mardersteig at his Officina Bodoni in Verona. Spine of jacket is age darkened as is common.

818. (Limited Editions Club) Smollett, Tobias. ADVENTURES OF PEREGRINE PICKLE, IN WHICH IS INCLUDED MEMOIRS OF A LADY OF QUALITY. With an Introduction by G.K. Chesterton and Illustrations by John Austen. Two volumes. New York: The Limited Editions Club, 1936, 4to., cloth, dust jackets, slipcase.
$ 150.00

Limited to 1500 numbered copies and signed by the illustrator. Printed at the Oxford University Press. Slipcase shows light rubbing.

819. (Limited Editions Club) Southey, Robert. CHRONICLE OF THE CID. Translated from the Spanish by Robert Southey with an Introduction by A.S. Pritchett and Illustrations by Rene Ben Sussan. New York: The Limited Editions Club, 1958, small 4to., cloth, leather spine label, slipcase. xxxvi, 196, (2) pages. $ 55.00

Limited to 1500 numbered copies and signed by Sussan. Printed in Haarlen by Joh. Enschedé. Rubbed at head of spine. Bookplate.

820. (Limited Editions Club) Spenser, Edmund. FAERIE QUEENE, DISPOSED INTO TWELVE BOOKES FASHIONING XII MORALL VERTUES. With an Introduction by John Hayward, Decorations Drawn by John Austen and Illustrations engraved in wood by Agnes Miller Parker. Two volumes. New York: Limited Editions Club, 1953, thick 4to., cloth, dust jackets, slipcase. xvi,512; (viii),513-992,(2) pages. $ 200.00

Limited to 1500 numbered copies signed by Parker. Printed at Oxford University Press. Excellent example of English book production. Jacket spines are faded with some spotting.

821. (Limited Editions Club) Stevenson, Robert Louis. BEACH OF FALESA. With an Introduction by J.C. Furnas and illustrations by Millard Sheets. New York: The Limited Editions Club, 1956, 4to., cloth-backed boards, slipcase. xviii, 113, (3) pages. $ 85.00

Limited to 1500 numbered copies signed by Sheets. Printed by The Ward Ritchie Press in Los Angeles. Slipcase soiled.

822. (Limited Editions Club) Stevenson, Robert Louis. MASTER OF BALLANTRAE. With an Introduction by G.B. Stern and with color lithographs by Lynd Ward. New York: The Limited Editions Club, 1965, small 4to., plaid cloth, leather spine label, slipcase. xix, 303, (3) pages. $ 95.00

Limited to 1500 numbered copies signed by Ward and printed at The Press of A. Colish.

823. (Limited Editions Club) Stevenson, Robert Louis. NEW ARABIAN NIGHTS. With an introduction by Norman H. Strouse and Illustrations by Clarke Hutton. Avon, CT: The Limited Editions Club, 1976, small 4to., cloth, slipcase. xv, 246, (2) pages.
$ 55.00

Limited to 2000 numbered copies signed by Hutton. Designed by Eugene M. Ettenberg and printed at The Garamond Press.

824. (Limited Editions Club) Stevenson, Robert Louis. STRANGE CASE OF DR. JEKYLL AND MR. HYDE. Introduction by John Mason Brown. Illustrations by Edward A. Wilson. New York: The Limited Editions Club, 1952, small 4to., quarter leather, slipcase. xv, 123+(1) pages. $ 65.00

Limited to 1500 numbered copies and signed by Wilson. Printed by the Marchbanks Press with the lithographs printed by George C. Miller. Rubbed at spine ends.

825. (Limited Editions Club) Stevenson, Robert Louis. TRAVELS WITH A DON-KEY. With a Prefatory Letter from the author, an Introduction by Andre Chamson and Illustrations by Roger Duvoisin. New York: The Limited Editions Club, 1957, 8vo., woven cloth, paper cover and spine labels, slipcase. xxii, 152, (4) pages. $ 65.00
Limited to 1500 numbered copies signed by Duvoisin. With the illustrations hand-colored in the studios of Walter Fischer. Printed by Saul and Lillian Marks at the Plantin Press. Spine slightly faded.

826. (Limited Editions Club) Stevenson, Robert Louis. TWO MEDIAEVAL TALES. New York: The Limited Editions Club, 1930, square 8vo., full leather stamped in blind. xviii, 67, (5) pages. $ 95.00
Limited to 1500 numbered copies and signed by the illustrator, C.B. Falls. With an introduction by Clay-ton Hamilton. The sixth production of the LEC. Printed by the Marchbanks Press and filled with color illustrations and initials. Lacks slipcase. Well preserved copy.

827. (Limited Editions Club) Surtees, R.S. JAUNTS AND JOLLITIES OF THAT RENOWNED SPORTING CITIZEN MR. JOHN JORROCKS OF ST. BOTOLPH LANE AND GREAT CORAM STREET. With Illustrations in Water-color by Gordon Ross and an Introduction by A. Edward Newton. New York: The Lim-ited Editions Club, 1932, tall 8vo., gilt decorated brown cloth, top edge gilt, slipcase. xviii, 219 pages and 10 illustrations. $ 100.00
Limited to 1500 numbered copies signed by Ross. Printed by D.B. Updike at his Merrymount Press. With a six page introduction by Newton. Slipcase bumped and rubbed. Monthly Letter loosely inserted.

828. (Limited Editions Club) Tarkington, Booth. MONSIEUR BEAUCAIRE. Illus-trated and Decorated by T.M. Cleland and with a preface by J. Donald Adams. New York: The Limited Editions Club, 1961, 8vo., woven cloth, spine label, half slipcase, slipcase.
          $ 55.00
Limited to 1500 numbered copies signed by Cleland. Printed at the Press of A. Colish.

829. (Limited Editions Club) TEN YEARS AND WILLIAM SHAKESPEARE, A SURVEY OF THE PUBLISHING ACTIVITIES OF THE LIMITED EDITIONS CLUB FROM OCTOBER 1929 TO OCTOBER 1940. N.P.: The Limited Editions Club, (1940), 4to., leather. 82 pages. $ 15.00
Contains "The Book as Literature" by John T. Winterich, a bibliography and index by Will Ransom and other articles. The leather bound version of this booklet. Crudely repaired with green fabric tape along spine and all edges. Internally very good.

830. (Limited Editions Club) Thackeray, William Makepeace. HISTORY OF HENRY ESMOND, ESQ. A COLONEL IN THE SERVICE OF HER MAJESTY Q. ANNE. With a new introduction by Laura Benet and illustrations by Edward Ardiz-zone. N.P.: The Limited Editions Club, 1956, tall 8vo., woven cloth, leather spine label, slipcase. xxi, 441, (3) pages. $ 95.00
Limited to 1500 numbered copies signed by Ardizzone. Hand-colored in the studio of Walter Fischer.

831. (Limited Editions Club) Thackeray, William Makepeace. HISTORY OF PEN-DENNIS, HIS FORTUNES AND MISFORTUNES, HIS FRIENDS AND HIS GREATEST ENEMY. With an Introduction by Robert Cantwell and with illustrations by Charles W. Stewart. Two volumes. New York: The Limited Editions Club, 1961, thick 8vo., embossed cloth, slipcase. xx,366; x,348,(2) pages. $ 85.00
Limited to 1500 numbered copies signed by Stewart. Printed by W.S. Cowell Ltd. with typography by John Lewis.

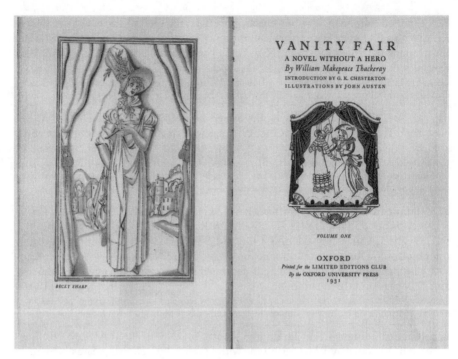

832. (Limited Editions Club) Thackeray, William Makepeace. ROSE AND THE RING. With the Marginal Glosses by Michael Angelo Titmarsh and the Illustrations drawn by Fritz Kredel with the Considerable Assistance of Mr. M.A. Titmarsh. New York: The Limited Editions Club, 1942, 4to., cloth, outer folder, slipcase. xvi, 119+(1) pages. $ 76.00
Limited to 1500 numbered copies. Designed by George Macy and printed at the Press of A. Colish. Plates colored by hand at the studio of Charlize Brakely. Bookplate.

833. (Limited Editions Club) Thackeray, William Makepeace. VANITY FAIR, A NOVEL WITHOUT A HERO. Introduction by G.K. Chesterton. Illustrations by John Austen. Two volumes. New York: The Limited Editions Club, 1931, thick small 4to., quarter cloth with patterned paper covered boards, matching dust jackets with paper cover and spine labels, slipcase. xx,366; viii,367-772,(2) pages. $ 175.00
Limited to 1500 numbered copies signed by Austen. Printed by the Oxford University Press under the direction of John Johnson. Top of slipcase partially detached. Bookplate in each volume.

834. (Limited Editions Club) Thackeray, William Makepeace. NEWCOMES, MEM-OIRS OF A MOST RESPECTABLE FAMILY EDITED BY ARTHUR PENDEN-NIS ESQ. With an Introduction by Angela Thirkell and with illustrations by Edward Ardizzone. New York: The Limited Editions Club, 1954, tall 8vo., cloth, slipcase. xxii,352; vii,353- 742,(2) pages. $ 125.00
Limited to 1500 numbered copies signed by Ardizzone. Printed at Cambridge University Press and hand-colored through stencils by Maud Johnson.

835. (Limited Editions Club) Thoreau, Henry David. CAPE COD. With an Introduction by Joseph Wood Krutch and Illustrations by R.J. Holden. New York: The Limited Editions Club, 1968, small 4to., pictorial boards, slipcase. xiv, 215, (3) pages. $ 100.00
Limited to 1500 numbered copies signed by Holden. Designed by Fred Anthoensen and printed at The Anthoensen Press.

836. (Limited Editions Club) Tolstoy, Leo. RESURRECTION, A NOVEL IN THREE PARTS. The Translation by Leo Wiener revised and edited for this Edition by F.D. Reeve. With an Introduction by Ernest J. Simmons and Illustrated with Wood Engravings by Fritz Eichenberg. New York: The Limited Editions Club, 1963, small 4to., cloth, slipcase. xviii, 403+(1) pages. $ 125.00
Limited to 1500 numbered copies signed by Fritz Eichenberg. This copy is not numbered but is one of the 35 copies produced for presentation and labeled "S.P." where the number is inserted. Printed at the Spiral Press by Joseph Blumenthal. With Monthly Letter loosely inserted.

837. (Limited Editions Club) Trollope, Anthony. BARCHESTER TOWERS. An Introduction by Angela Thirkell. Illustrated by Fritz Kredel. New York: The Limited Editions Club, 1958, thick 8vo., quarter leather over decorated paper covered boards, slipcase. xviii, 563, (3) pages. $ 95.00
Limited to 1500 numbered copies signed by Kredel. Printed by Peter Beilenson with Kredel's drawings hand-colored in the studio of Walter Fischer of New York. Designed by Richard Ellis. Some wear at top of front hinge.

838. (Limited Editions Club) Trollope, Anthony. WARDEN. An Introduction by Angela Thirkell and Illustrations by Fritz Kredel. New York: The Limited Editions Club, (1955), 8vo., cloth-backed boards, slipcase. xx, 261, (3) pages. $ 85.00
Limited to 1500 numbered copies signed by Kredel. Designed by Richard Ellis and printed at The Marchbanks Press. The Centennial Edition. Bookplate.

839. (Limited Editions Club) Twain, Mark. THE PRINCE AND THE PAUPER. With an Introduction by Edward Wagenknecht and Illustrations by Clarke Hutton. New York: The Limited Editions Club, 1964, tall 8vo., quarter blue suede over cloth, slipcase. 221, (3) pages. $ 125.00
Limited to 1500 numbered copies signed by Hutton. Printed by the Westerham Press.

840. (Limited Editions Club) Twain, Mark. PUDD'NHEAD WILSON. With an Introduction by Edward Wagenknecht. Illustrated by John Groth. Avon, CT: The Limited Editions Club, 1974, small 4to., pictorial cloth, leather spine label, slipcase. xvi, 164, (4) pages. $ 95.00
Limited to 2000 numbered copies signed by Groth. Designed by Roderick Stinehour and printed at the Stinehour Press. Accompanied by PUDD'NHEAD WILSON'S CALENDAR which is also inserted in the slipcase.

841. (Limited Editions Club) Twain, Mark. TRAMP ABROAD. Illustrated by David Knight and including several pictures made by the author of this book without outside help. With an Introduction by Edward Wagenknecht. New York: The Limited Editions Club, (1968), 8vo., cloth-backed marbled paper covered boards with cloth tips, slipcase. xviii, 395+(1) pages. $ 95.00
Limited to 1500 numbered copies signed by Knight. Designed by Eugene M. Ettenberg.

842. (Limited Editions Club) Verne, Jules. FROM THE EARTH TO THE MOON AND AROUND THE MOON. Introduction by Jean Jules-Verne. Illustrations by Robert Shore. Two volumes. New York: The Limited Editions Club, 1970, tall 8vo., cloth-backed boards, slipcase. xxi,206; (x),207-425,(3) pages. $ 75.00
Limited to 1500 numbered copies signed by Shore. Designed by Ted Gensamer.

843. (Limited Editions Club) Virgil. AENEID, TRANSLATED BY JOHN DRYDEN. Illustrated by Carolotta Petrina. New York: The Limited Editions Club, 1944, 4to., quarter leather with woven cloth covered boards, clamshell box. lxviii, 397, (3) pages.
$ 125.00
Limited to 1100 copies signed by the illustrator. Printed by E.L. Hildreth & Co with the illustrations printed by The Photogravure & Color Co. of New York. Bookplate. Note that the limitation was smaller than normal because of the war years.

844. (Limited Editions Club) Virgil. GEORGICS. Translated into English verse by John Dryden. New York: The Limited Editions Club, 1952, 4to., cloth-backed decorated boards, dust jacket, slipcase. xvi, 154, (4) pages. $ 200.00
Limited to 1500 numbered copies signed by Giovanni Mardersteig, the printer, and Bruno Bramanti, the illustrator. With an introduction by George F. Whicher. Printed at the Officina Bodoni. Top of jacket chipped.

845. (Limited Editions Club) Virgil. THE ECLOGUES PUBLIUS VIRGILIUS MARO. Translated into English verse by C.S. Calverley. With an Introduction by Moses Hadas and drawings by Vertes. New York: The Limited Editions Club, 1960, 4to., cloth, slipcase. xxvii, 96, (2) pages. $ 95.00
Limited to 1500 numbered copies signed by Vertes. Printed at the Press of A. Colish and designed by George Salter.

846. (Limited Editions Club) Voltaire, Francois Marie Arouet. CANDIDE OR OPTI-MISM. Translated by Richard Aldington with an Introduction by Anatole Broyard & Illustrations by May Neama. New York: The Limited Editions Club, 1973, small 4to., leather-backed boards, slipcase. xv, 123, (3) pages. $ 75.00
Limited to 1500 numbered copies and signed by Neama. Arranged by Richard Ellis.

847. (Limited Editions Club) Von Grimmelshausen, Johann Jakob Christoffel. AD-VENTURES OF SIMPLICISSIMUS. In a New Translation by John P. Spielman. Illustrated with Wood Engravings by Fritz Eichenberg. New York: The Limited Editions Club, 1981, 4to., cloth, slipcase. xxxviii, 319, (5) pages. $ 125.00
Limited to 2000 numbered copies and signed by Eichenberg. Beautifully illustrated.

848. (Limited Editions Club) Wallace, Lew. BEN-HUR, A TALE OF THE CHRIST. With an Introduction by Ben Ray Redman and Illustrations by Joe Mugnaini. New York: The Limited Editions Club, 1960, small 4to., quarter leather, leather cover label, slipcase. xxii, 486, (2) pages. $ 75.00
Limited to 1500 numbered copies and signed by the illustrator. Designed by John Fass. Top of slipcase is bumped.

849. (Limited Editions Club) Walpole, Horace. CASTLE OF OTRANTO, A GOTH-IC STORY. New York: The Limited Editions Club, 1975, 4to., quarter-leather over patterned boards, slipcase. xxvii, 100 pages. $ 75.00
Limited to 2000 numbered copies and signed by W.S. Lewis. Designed by Ruari McLean and printed at the Westerham Press in Kent, England, by Rowley Atterbury. The illustrations were reproduced from the originals by the Meriden Gravure Company. Lewis wrote the introduction.

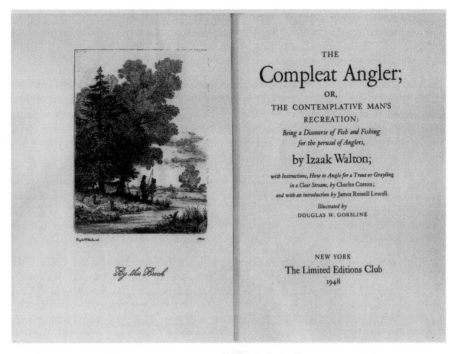

THE

Compleat Angler;

OR,

THE CONTEMPLATIVE MAN'S
RECREATION:

*Being a Discourse of Fish and Fishing
for the perusal of Anglers,*

by Izaak Walton;

*with Instructions, How to Angle for a Trout or Grayling
in a Clear Stream, by Charles Cotton;
and with an introduction by James Russell Lowell.*

Illustrated by
DOUGLAS W. GORSLINE

NEW YORK
The Limited Editions Club
1948

Item 850

850. (Limited Editions Club) Walton, Izaak. COMPLEAT ANGLER; OR, THE CONTEMPLATIVE MAN'S RECREATION BEING A DISCOURSE OF FISH AND FISHING FOR THE PERUSAL OF ANGLERS. With Instructions, How to Angle for a Trout or Grayling in a Clear Stream, by Charles Cotton; and with an Introduction by James Russell Lowell. Illustrated by Douglas W. Gorsline. New York: The Limited Editions Club, 1948, 4to., parchment-backed boards, slipcase. xlii, 317+(1) pages. $ 200.00
Limited to 1500 numbered copies signed by Gorsline.

851. (Limited Editions Club) Wells, H.G. INVISIBLE MAN. Illustrated by Charles Mozley. The Introduction by Bernard Bergonzi. New York: The Limited Editions Club, 1967, small 4to., cloth, slipcase. xx, 164, (2) pages. $ 65.00
Limited to 1500 copies and signed by the illustrator. Printed at the Press of A. Colish with design by Francis Meynell and color printing at the Stellar Press.

852. (Limited Editions Club) Wells, H.G. TONO-BUNGAY. With an Introduction by Norman H. Strouse & Illustrated by Lynton Lamb. New York: The Limited Editions Club, 1960, tall 8vo., cloth, paper spine label. xiii, 395, (3) pages. $ 85.00
Limited to 1500 numbered copies signed by Lamb. Printed at the Thistle Press with design by Bert Clarke.

853. (Limited Editions Club) Wharton, Edith. HOUSE OF MIRTH. With an Introduction by Arthur Mizener and illustrations by Lily Harmon. N.P.: The Limited Editions Club, 1975, thick 8vo., two- toned cloth, slipcase. xiv, 294, (2) pages. $ 75.00
Limited to 2000 numbered copies signed by Harmon. Designed by Philip Grushkin.

854. (Limited Editions Club) Whittier, John Greenleaf. POEMS OF JOHN GREENLEAF WHITTIER. Selected and Edited with a Commentary by Louis Untermeyer and Illustrated with pencil drawings by R.J. Holden. New York: The Limited Editions Club, 1945, large 8vo., full leather, slipcase. xx, 333, (3) pages. $ 85.00
Limited to 1500 numbered copies signed by Holden. Minor wear at spine ends.

855. (Limited Editions Club) Wilde, Oscar. SHORT STORIES OF OSCAR WILDE. With an Introduction by Robert Gorham Davis and Illustrations from Paintings by James Hill. New York: The Limited Editions Club, 1968, small 4to., cloth, slipcase. xviii, 313, (3) pages. $ 95.00
Limited to 1500 numbered copies signed by Hill. Printed at The Lane Press of Burlington, Vermont under the design of Robert L. Dothard.

856. (Limited Editions Club) Wister, Owen. VIRGINIAN, A HORSEMAN OF THE PLAINS. With an Introduction by Struthers Burt and Illustrations by William Moyers. New York: The Limited Editions Club, 1951, tall 8vo., cloth, leather spine and cover labels, slipcase. xxiv, 437+(1) pages. $ 85.00
Limited to 1500 numbered copies signed by Moyers. Printed by Saul and Lillian Marks at The Plantin Press. Bookplate.

857. (Limited Editions Club) WONDERFUL ADVENTURES OF PAUL BUNYAN. Now Retold by Louis Untermeyer, Together with Illustrations by Everett Gee Jackson. New York: The Limited Editions Club, 1945, 8vo., quarter leather over boards, board wrap-around protective cover, slipcase. (x), 131, (5) pages. $ 65.00
Limited to 1500 numbered copies signed by Jackson. Printed at the Aldus Printers with typographic design by Richard Ellis. Bookplate.

858. (Limited Editions Club) Wordsworth, William. POEMS OF WILLIAM WORDSWORTH. Selected, Edited, and Introduced by Jonathan Wordsworth. Illustrated by John O'Connor. N.P.: Printed for The Limited Editions Club at the University Printing House, Cambridge, 1973, tall 8vo., half-leather over cloth, slipcase. xviii, 259, (3) pages. $ 125.00
Limited to 2000 numbered copies signed by O'Connor. Designed by John Dreyfus and printed by Brooke Crutchley.

859. (Limited Editions Club) Wroth, Lawrence C. (editor). HISTORY OF THE PRINTED BOOK, BEING THE THIRD NUMBER OF THE DOLPHIN. New York: Limited Editions Club, 1938, thick 4to., cloth. xv, 507, (35) pages. $ 250.00
Limited to 1800 copies. Major sections on: 1. The Origin and Development by Fuhrmann, Lehmann-Haupt, Rath, Johnson, Stillwell, Beilenson, and Grannis; 2. The Printing House by Rollins, Pottinger, Hunter, Chapman; 3. Adornment of the Book by Hofer and McCarthy and 4. A Summary of Printing History by Winship. Excellent production. Information on paper. Covers rubbed.

860. (Limited Editions Club) Wyss, Johann. SWISS FAMILY ROBINSON. Illustrated with Engravings by David Gentleman and Introduced by Robert Cushman Murphy. New York: The Limited Editions Club, 1963, thick small 4to., quarter cloth with woven cloth covers, leather spine label, slipcase. xvi, 356 pages. $ 100.00
Limited to 1500 numbered copies signed by Gentleman. Printed by W.S. Cowell Ltd. with typography by Will Carter. Spine has some spotting around label.

861. (Limited Editions Club) Xenophon. ANABASIS OF XENOPHON. In the Translation by Henry G. Dakyns with an Introduction by Robert Payne, Illustrated with Woodcuts by A. Tassos. New York: The Limited Editions Club, 1969, 4to., cloth, slipcase. 269, (5) pages. $ 100.00
Limited to 1500 numbered copies and signed by Tassos. Printed in Greece by the Aspioti-Elka Graphic Arts Inc. Excellent woodcuts.

862. (Lipton, Ethan B.) Stern, Norton B. and William M. Kramer. MORRIS L. GOODMAN, THE FIRST AMERICAN COUNCILMAN OF THE CITY OF LOS ANGELES. Los Angeles: (Ethan B. Lipton), 1981, large 12mo., quarter cloth, paper-covered boards. (iv), 31, (3) pages. $ 30.00
Printed and designed by Ethan B. Lipton in an edition of 300 copies to celebrate the Los Angeles Bicentennial. With a card laid in noting the book in the 1982 Western Books Exhibition of the Rounce & Coffin Club. Morris Goodman was the only member of the seven-member Los Angeles City Council sworn in July 3, 1850 who had not been a Mexican citizen previous to statehood.

863. (Little Press) Lucie-Smith, Edward. THE LITTLE PRESS MOVEMENT IN ENGLAND AND AMERICA. London: Turret Books-Publishers, 1968, small 8vo., stiff paper wrappers. (32) pages. $ 17.50
First edition. catalogue for a Little Press exhibition held at The American Embassy in April and May, 1968. Lists 73 items printed by small presses after World War II, with four black and white plates of reproductions from the works.

864. (Lord John Press) Rothenberg, Jerome. VIENNA BLOOD. N.P.: (Lord John Press), n.d. (but 1979), large 8vo., stiff paper wrappers, cord tied. (14) pages. $ 45.00
Limited to edition of 30 numbered copies. Gleaned from the off-prints of *Out of the West* which featured the works of Rothenberg and four other poets. Signed by the author in ink on the first page.

865. (Los Angeles Club of Printing House Craftsmen) Clary, William W. B. FRANKLIN, PRINTER & PUBLISHER. Los Angeles: The Los Angeles Club of Printing House Craftsmen, 1935, large 8vo., quarter cloth with paper-covered boards. xi, (iii), 95+(1) pages. $ 50.00
Limited to 250 copies. Originally delivered as an address before the Los Angeles Club of Printing House Craftsmen at its annual Franklin dinner. Also containing *An Account of his Friendship with William Strahan, M.P., as well as Numerous Curious Anecdotes of Printing, not Generally Known, etc.* Deckled paper made by Dard Hunter. Spine chipped, some pieces missing, outer hinges loose. With two illustrations, a facsimile of Franklin's letter to Strahan, July 5, 1775, and a title page of the Laws of the Province of Pennsylvania, 1742.

866. (Lyceum Press) Powell, Lawrence Clark. SOME WRITING ABOUT LOS ANGELES. (Los Angeles): Stone & Lorson, 1992, large 12mo., stiff wrappers, paper cover label. (ii), 8, (4) pages. $ 65.00
Printed in an edition limited "to about 120 copies," signed by the author, designed and printed by Wm. Erik Voss and hand-coloured by Carmen Voss at the Lyceum Press. A survey of the best novels associated with Los Angeles, including *The Boosters* by Mark Lee Luther, written in 1923, and considered by

Powell to be the first debunking novel about the Angel City. "Long since out of print and very hard to come by, *The Boosters* deserves reprinting." Lawrence Clark Powell was a long-time head librarian at UCLA.

867. (Marble Hill Press) Reed, Talbot Baines. OLD & NEW FASHIONS IN TYPOGRAPHY. New York: The Marble Hill Press, (1965), 4to., stiff paper wrappers. 22, (2) pages. $ 25.00

A keepsake edition, limited to 100 copies for private distribution. A reprint of a paper read before The Society of Arts in London, April 16, 1890, taken from the Vol. I, No. 3, 1920 issue of "Ars Tyographica." Printed by George Sas from handset De Roos and Jessen types in black, with margin titles in ochre. Sewn into a pale green cover, front fore edge dark green, deckle, with title in ochre, using dark green cord. Bumped.

868. (Marchbanks Press) Banning, Kendall. THE GREAT ADVENTURE. New York: Marchbanks Press, 1926, small 8vo., quarter cloth, paper covered boards. 44 pages. $ 20.00

First edition. A book of poems. "For life itself is but an *Interlude*; a brief adventure of the soul between the miracles of *Birth* and *Death*." Bookplate of John DePol on front pastedown.

869. (Marchbanks Press) ALBERT A. BOYDEN, APRIL 10, 1875–MAY 2, 1925. New York: Privately printed, 1926, 12mo., cloth-backed boards. (viii), 135 pages. $ 20.00

Printed at the Marchbanks Press. Boyden worked at McClure. This booklet has contributions by Edna Ferber, Booth Tarkington, John H. Finley and others. Covers slightly spotted.

870. (Marchbanks Press) Cleland, T.M. HARSH WORDS. Newark: The Carteret Book Club, 1940, 12mo., boards, paper cover label. 34 pages. $ 35.00

First edition, limited to 200 numbered copies printed by The Marchbanks Press of New York. On design.

871. (Marchbanks Press) Falls, G.B. STORY OF THE BIRTH OF JESUS CHRIST ACCORDING TO THE GOSPELS OF SAINT MATTHEW AND SAINT LUKE. New York: Marchbanks Press, 1929, square 4to., paper covered boards decorated in gilt. (32) pages. $ 275.00

Printed in an edition limited to 1000 copies. The story of the birth of Jesus Christ designed by G. B. Falls with 8 full page drawings and smaller drawings in black and white with gilt decorated capitals. A stunning and unusual book with very decorative cover, bold illustrations by Fall and calligraphic text throughout.

872. (Marchbanks Press) Holmes, Oliver Wendell. ON LENDING A PUNCH-BOWL. New York: Privately printed, 1920, small 8vo., paper, silver colored boards, paper spine label, fore and bottom edges deckled. (22) pages. $ 20.00

Limited to 300 copies printed for Thomas Nast Fairbanks by the Marchbanks Press. Short ballad recounting some of the celebrations shared around the brim of an old silver punchbowl represented in the black and white frontispiece illustration. John DePol bookplate on front pastedown, typed description of book pasted to front free endpaper. Silver badly rubbed, edges worn and scraped, small red and white paper label pasted on spine near bottom.

873. (Marchbanks Press) Lehmann-Haupt, Hellmut. TERRIBLE GUSTAVE DORE. New York: The Marchbanks Press, 1943, small 4to., cloth, paper cover label. 48 pages. $ 45.00

First edition. Well illustrated sketch of Dore. Also includes a list of books about him.

874. (Marchbanks Press) Melcher, Frederic G. ON BECOMING ACQUAINTED WITH BOOKS. N.P.: Privately printed, 1962, 12mo., marbled paper covers, paper cover label. 13, (3) pages. $ 20.00

Limited to 550 copies and printed by the Marchbanks Press. Early autobiography by Melcher describing his life with books up to his first job, that of working for Lauriat's as a bookseller. Offset from marbled paper on title page.

875. (Marchbanks Press) SOME OF THE MANY THINGS WE PRINT. New York: Marchbanks Press, n.d., tall thin broadside folded twice. $ 17.50

Sale brochure in which the Marchbanks Press describes all of the different kinds of printing they do. Printed in black and red.

876. (Marchbanks Press) Sternheim, Carl. FAIRFAX. New York: Knopf, (1923), 8vo., quarter vellum with paper-covered boards, slipcase. (vi), 66, (2) pages. $ 35.00

First American edition, printed for Knopf by the Marchbanks Press under the supervision of Frederic W. Goudy, who is also responsible for designing the type, and limited to 950 numbered copies. Translated from the German by Alfred B. Kuttner. A story about Europe after World War I. Some fading on boards. Top of slipcase broken.

877. (Marchbanks Press) Warde, Beatrice. PRINTING SHOULD BE INVISIBLE. New York: The Marchbanks Press, (1937), 12mo., paper wrappers, paper cover label. 12 pages. $ 17.50

An address delivered by Warde before the British Typographers' Guild at St. Bride's Institute.

878. (Marion Press) BOOKS AND LETTERS COLLECTED BY WILLIAM HARRIS ARNOLD. New York: The Marion Press, 1901, small 4to., paper wrappers. xv, 125 pages. $ 25.00

Limited to 1500 copies. (McKay no.5285). Filled with the forgeries that Wise has supplied to Arnold over the years. Wrappers detached and chipped.

879. (Marion Press) Brown, Frances Swan. VERSES BY FRANCES SWAN BROWN. New York: The Marion Press, 1911, small 8vo., blue paper covered boards. frontispiece, 44 pages. $ 45.00

First edition, second printing. "Probably" printed in an edition of 200 copies on Japan vellum, signed by the author. (Larrimore no.125b). A collection of 37 poems written by the young Frances Swan Brown while a student at Spence School. Decorated with large initial Pabst old-style roman capitals printed in various colors. Frontispiece facsimile of a drawing of Miss Brown.

880. (Marion Press) PAPERS READ BEFORE THE NOVEL CLUB OF CLEVELAND. Cleveland: Published by the Club, 1899, small 8vo., original cloth. xx, 108, (2) pages. $ 50.00

Printed in an edition limited to 250 numbered copies. (Larremore no. 30). A collection of essays on novels read by members of the Club, which was organized according to Professor Moulton's book, "Five Years of Novel Reading." This is the first book bound by the Marion Press. Top of spine and corners slightly bumped.

881. (Marion Press) CATALOGUE OF A COLLECTION OF THE BOOKS OF ROBERT LOUIS STEVENSON IN THE LIBRARY OF GEORGE M. WILLIAMSON. Jamaica, NY: The Marion Press, 1901, small 4to., cloth, slipcase. (96) pages and tipped-in plate showing a portrait of Stevenson. $ 65.00

Limited to 150 numbered copies printed by this private press. With an introduction by Williamson followed by descriptions and illustrations of 115 items. Slipcase worn. Spine slightly faded.

882. (Maverick Press) Emmons, Earl H. A BROOKPLATE FOR BRUCE ROGERS. New York: Maverick Press, 1936, 16mo., self paper wrappers. (4) pages. $ 45.00
Limited to 100 copies produced as item nine of the Maverick Press. With a tipped-in bookplate that Emmons designed for Rogers, a small photograph of Rogers and a bookplate designed by Rogers. Bookplate loose. Paperclip mark on back cover.

883. (Maverick Press) Goudy, Fred T. SON OF A GOUDY, AN OPEN LETTER TO FREDERIC W. GOUDY FROM HIS NEAREST KIN AND SEVEREST CRITIC. N.P.: (Privately printed for Goudy at The Maverick Press, 1938), small 8vo., stiff paper wrappers. (10) pages. $ 20.00
Produced as a Keepsake for the 35th Anniversary of the Village Press.

884. (Mayflower Press) Low, Will H. STEVENSON AND MARGARITA. New Rochelle, NY: Mayflower Press, 1922, 8vo., quarter cloth with paper covered boards. (ii), 20, (2) pages. $ 45.00
Printed in an edition limited to 200 copies. Set into type by Charles P. Adams. Anecdotes about the author's friendship with Stevenson, his liking for cigarettes, and their mutual preference for Margarita, a blend *of good Virginia, a little Turkish, and a trace of Perique*. Bookplate of Herman Abromson (in homage to Christopher Morley) on front pastedown. Etched portrait of Stevenson by Arthur H. Hosking as frontis, but missing copy "pulled on large paper" for framing mentioned on colophon.

885. (Mayflower Press) Moore, T. Sturge. TRAGIC MOTHERS. London: Grant Richards, 1920, small 8vo., quarter cloth with illustrated paper-covered boards. 63+(1) pages. $ 40.00
First edition, printed at the Mayflower Press, Plymouth, England by William Brendon and Son. Three one-act plays with an author's Note: "My friend Mr. W.B. Yeats asked me to try my hand, having himself achieved brilliant success, in this new form of drama, independent of stage and scenery and suitable for chamber presentation. The idea had come to him while reading about the Japanese Noh plays." Some chipping on spine, with a few small spots.

886. (McCallister, Bruce) IN HONOR OF RUFUS BERNHARD VON KLEINSMID ON HIS TENTH ANNIVERSARY AS PRESIDENT OF THE UNIVERSITY OF SOUTHERN CALIFORNIA (1921–1931). (Los Angeles: University of Southern California), 1931, small 4to., stiff wrappers. (8) pages. $ 17.50
Printed for the University of Southern California by Bruce McCallister. "Testimonials of respect, affection, and gratitude celebrating a decade of pre-eminent development in higher education."

887. (Menhaden Press) Vanzetti, Bartolomeo. THE VANZETTI BOOK. Two volumes. (Pierre, SD: Menhaden, 1983), 12 mo., stiff paper wrappers. 27); (12) pages. $ 35.00
Printed in an edition of 50 copies. This booklet, handsomely printed by Menhaden Press during the tenure of Fred Hegeman, contains ten quotations from letters written by Vanzetti during his incarceration in a Boston prison from the time of his 1920 murder conviction until his execution. Printed with wide margins on Fabriano Roma from Emerson types, it also includes a woodcut by noted artist Sarah Chamberlain.

888. (Mermaid Press) CARRIERS' ADDRESSES. N.P.: The Mermaid Press, n.d., 12mo., stiff paper wrappers. (8) pages. $ 15.00
Printed by Fridolf Johnson at his private press for The Uncommomplace Book of the New York Chappel of Private Presses. Introduction followed by reprints of two 18th century American broadsides issued by Newspaper carriers.

889. (Merrymount Press) Baker, Alfred L. THE HIGHER CITIZENSHIP, TWO ADDRESSES. Chicago: Privately Printed, 1927, large 12mo., half cloth with marbled paper-covered boards. 41, (3) pages. $ 20.00
Privately printed for the author by D.B. Updike at The Merrymount Press, Boston, in an edition limited to 750 copies, of which this is one of 500 on regular paper (Smith, 653). Typeset in Lutetia, initial letters printed in red. Includes talk originally given in 1910, *The Stake of the Business Man in Conservation*, at the Second National Conservation Congress. Foxing on most pages, extremities slightly worn.

890. (Merrymount Press) Browning, Robert. RABBI BEN EZRA. New York: Crowell, 1902, large 12mo., cloth. (vi), 50, (2) pages. $ 25.00
Composition and electrotype plates by D.B. Updike at the Merrymount Press, Boston, set in Clarendon type (Smith, 120).

891. (Merrymount Press) CATALOGUE OF AN EXHIBITION ILLUSTRATING THE VARIED INTEREST OF BOOK BUYERS 1450–1600. Boston: Club of Odd Volumes, 1922, small 8vo., paper wrappers. Not paginated. $ 17.50
Printed by D.B. Updike at his Merrymount Press. (Smith p.216). Lists 79 books and accompanied each listing with a note on the printer. Front cover partially detached.

892. (Merrymount Press) CENTURY MEMORIALS, 1943. New York: (Century Club), 1944, small 8vo., cloth. 93+(1) pages. $ 20.00
Printed for the Century Club by D.B. Updike at the Merrymount Press, Boston. Brief eulogies of club members who died in 1943, including Steven Vincent Benet, Pierpont Morgan, and Lt. Tom La Farge, whose cutter foundered in an ice storm off the coast of Newfoundland while returning from a "difficult and very valuable work in the North Atlantic area."

893. (Merrymount Press) Chew, Beverly. ESSAYS & VERSES ABOUT BOOKS. New York: privately printed, 1926, 8vo., cloth-backed boards. xiv, 108 pages with 20 illustrations. $ 95.00
First edition, limited to 275 copies printed by D. B. Updike at the Merrymount Press. (Hart no. 220). Chew, though not a wealthy man, formed an excellent collection and was renowned for his love of books. Was a founding member of the Grolier Club. Small spot on back cover. Bookplate announcing that "This is one of the Fifty Books of 1927." This bookplate has discolored the free endpaper.

894. (Merrymount Press) A DESCRIPTION OF THE MERRYMOUNT PRESS, 232 SUMMER STREET, BOSTON, 1893–1917. Boston: Merrymount Press, 1917, large 12mo., stiff paper wrappers. 24 pages. $ 25.00
Second impression, revised. Brief history of the Merrymount Press, begun by D.B. Updike in 1893, with descriptions and photographs of its physical plant, including the ante-room, reception room, library, composing room, proof-reader's room, press room, etc. Wrappers detached and torn, laid in white cardboard portfolio, previous owner's name on inside front cover.

895. (Merrymount Press) Field, Eugene. TWO POEMS BY EUGENE FIELD, REPRODUCED FROM THE ORIGINAL MSS. (Boston): W.K. Bixby, (1922), large 8vo., quarter cloth with paper covered boards. (8) leaves. $ 75.00
Privately printed for W.K. Bixby in an edition limited to two hundred and fifty copies by D.B. Updike at The Merrymount Press in Old Style type (Smith, 554). Manuscript with corrections for *Seein' Things at Night* and *To M.L. Gray*. Mr. Gray was the guardian of Eugene and Roswell Field and a "splendid type of the sturdy, honest old New Englander (W.K. Bixby, Note)."

896. (Merrymount Press) Genung, John Franklin. STEVENSON'S ATTITUDE TO LIFE: WITH READINGS FROM HIS ESSAYS AND LETTERS. New York: Thomas Y. Crowell, 1901, large 12mo., cloth. (vi), 43+(1) pages. $55.00

Printed by D.B. Updike at his Merrymount Press. (Smith, 96). Set in Clarendon type and rubricated throughout. Originally given as a talk, with substantial quotations from Stevenson's writings.

897. (Merrymount Press) Greenough, Ruth Hornblower. CHESTER NOYES GREE-NOUGH, AN ACCOUNT OF HIS LIFE AS TEACHER, DEAN. Cambridge: Merrymount Press, 1940, 8vo., cloth. xvi, 336 pages. $75.00

First edition. An account of Greenough's life written by his wife. He was Dean of Harvard College and a noted book collector. With a frontispiece of Greenough's library building in color executed by Rudolph Ruzicka.

898. (Merrymount Press) Hardy, Thomas. OLD MRS. CHUNDLE, A SHORT STORY. New York: Crosby Gaige, 1929, small 8vo., quarter cloth, decorated paper-covered boards. (vi), 26, (4) pages. $95.00

First edition, posthumously printed in an edition limited to 755 copies, of which this is one of 700 numbered copies for sale, printed in Janson type on Zanders hand-made paper by D.B. Updike at the Merrymount Press in Boston and distributed by Random House (Smith, 683). This story--written circa 1880–1890 was probably intended to be included in *Life's Little Ironies* or *Wessex Tales*. Pages uncut, slightly rubbed at extremities.

899. (Merrymount Press) Heller, Helen West. WOODCUTS U.S.A. With an introduction by John Taylor Arms. New York: Oxford University Press, 1947, oblong 12mo., decorated paper wrappers. (40) pages. $30.00

Printed by D.B. Updike at his Merrymount Press. Contains 16 reproductions of Heller's woodcuts.

900. (Merrymount Press) Huntington, Rev. William Reed. THE KING'S CUP-BEARER, A SERMON IN MEMORY OF THE REV. E. WINCHESTER DON-ALD. Boston: Printed for Trinity Church, 1905, large 12mo., quarter cloth with paper covered boards. (vi), 22, (2) pages. $20.00

Printed for Trinity Church by D.B. Updike at the Merrymount Press, Boston. (Smith, 230). Preached on the Sunday next before Advent, November 20, 1904. Set in Mountjoye type, with portrait as frontis. Some wear to extremities.

901. (Merrymount Press) Johnson, Merle. AMERICAN FIRST EDITIONS, BIBLI-OGRAPHIC CHECK LISTS OF THE WORKS OF ONE HUNDRED AND FIVE AMERICAN AUTHORS. New York: R.R. Bowker Co., 1929, 8vo., cloth, paper spine label, top edge gilt. viii, 242 pages. $60.00

First edition, limited to 1000 copies. Printed by D.B. Updike at his Merrymount Press. The first edition of this landmark bibliographical reference tool.

902. (Merrymount Press) A LAST WILL, WILLISTON FISH. Boston: Alfred Bartlett, (1908), small 8vo., boards. 18 pages. $25.00

Printed by the Merrymount Press. Loosely inserted is a four page notice from Stella and Jacob Blanck commenting on this pamphlet and sent out with their Holiday wishes.

903. (Merrymount Press) MERRYMOUNT PRESS, BOSTON (ESTABLISHED 1893). Boston: Merrymount Press, n.d., small 4to., paper wrappers. 25+(1) pages. $22.50

With bibliographical information.

904. (Merrymount Press) Raymond, Thomas L. STEPHEN CRANE. Newark: The Carteret Book Club, 1923, small 8vo., cloth backed decorated paper covered boards, leather spine label, original glassine wrapper. ix, 43, (3) pages. $ 75.00
Limited to 250 numbered copies printed by D.B. Updike at his Merrymount Press. A very fine, unopened copy.

905. (Merrymount Press) Rist, John. DEPOSITIO CORNUTI TYPOGRAPHICI, THAT IS A COMICAL OR MIRTHFUL PLAY. New York: The Grolier Club, 1911, 8vo., half cloth over boards, slipcase. viii, 38 pages. $ 65.00
Limited to 250 copies printed by D. B. Updike at the Merrymount Press. This play, taken from the 1654 version of John Rist and translated by the English typographic historian William Blades, was originally performed by printers' apprentices upon entering into the workman category. The Grolier Club members performed the play at a 1909 meeting. Wear at spine extremities.

906. (Merrymount Press) Sedgwick, Henry Dwight. PRO VITA MONASTICA, AN ESSAY IN DEFENCE OF THE CONTEMPLATIVE VIRTUES. Boston: Atlantic Monthly Press, 1923, small 8vo., cloth. xviii, 164 pages. $ 30.00
First edition, printed by D.B. Updike at the Merrymount Press, Boston, set in Caslon type (Smith, 583). The author had previously written a *Life of Marcus Aurelius* and *Italy in the Thirteenth Century*. "My thesis then is, that the fate of Christianity lies in its power to recover, and make use of, those resources of the spirit from which in earlier times it drew innocence, peace, serenity, and joy (chapter 1)." Slight wear to extremities, former owner's address label on front free endpaper, bookseller's tag on rear pastedown.

907. (Merrymount Press) Updike, D.B. SOME ASPECTS OF PRINTING OLD AND NEW. New Haven: William Rudge, 1941, tall 8vo., cloth. (vi), 74 pages. $ 65.00
First edition. Printed by Updike at the Merrymount Press. Collection of papers including one on Gutenberg, Modern Typography, American University Presses, etc. Sol Hess's copy with his bookplate.

908. (Merrymount Press) Stevenson, Robert Louis. A CHRISTMAS SERMON. New York: Charles Scribner's Sons, 1900, large 12mo., quarter cloth with paper-covered boards. (iv), 23, (3) pages. $ 45.00
First separate edition (Cutler, 143). Printed for Scribner by D.B. Updike at The Merrymount Press, Boston. Gift inscription in ink on front free endpaper.

909. (Merrymount Press) Taylor, Henry H. PLAN OF PRINTING INSTRUCTION FOR PUBLIC SCHOOLS. New York: John Day, 1927, 12mo., cloth, paper spine label. xxii, 36 pages, 1 fold-out plate. $ 25.00
Printed at the Merrymount Press. Label chipped.

910. (Merrymount Press) Thoreau, Henry David. FRIENDSHIP. New York: Thomas Y. Crowell, (1906), large 12mo., silk covered boards, cover gilt stamped, top edges gilt, fore edges deckled. 56 pages. $ 45.00
First edition. A self-contained gem, this essay was originally part of the book, *A Week on the Concord and Merrimack Rivers*. Printed in black with red title and ornament on title page and red title shoulder note on each page by D.B. Updike at the Merrymount Press in Boston. (Updike, no.270). Portrait of the author as frontispiece. Minor discoloration to cloth.

911. (Merrymount Press) Updike, D.B. EXAMPLES OF PRINTING BY D.B. UPDIKE, THE MERRYMOUNT PRESS, FROM THE COLLECTION MADE BY MAX FARRAND. Pasadena: Huntington Library, 1935, large 12mo., stiff paper wrappers. unpaginated, but 4 pages. $ 15.00
Printed for the Huntington Library by Roland Baughman in an edition limited to 200 copies. A catalogue of twenty-five books.

912. (Merrymount Press) Zelie, John Sheridan. BILL PRATT, THE SAW-BUCK PHILOSOPHER. Williamstown: n.p., 1895, 8vo., cloth-backed boards, paper spine label. ix, 121 pages. $ 45.00

An early Merrymount Press printing (Smith no.13). With a highly decorative title page. Very good copy.

913. (Merrymount Press) Zelie, John Sheridan. BILL PRATT, THE SAW-BUCK PHILOSOPHER. Williamstown: n.p., (1915), 8vo., cloth-backed boards, paper spine label. ix, (i), 156, (4) pages. $ 45.00

A new edition of the original 1895 Merrymount Press printing (Smith no.13). With a highly decorative title page. This new edition contains material not in the first edition and was also printed at the Merrymount Press (Smith & Bianchi 427). Covers rubbed.

914. (Merrythought Press) Cron, B.S. THE RECENT OWNERS OF THE GOLDEN PSALTER. London: The Merrythought Press, 1963, small 8vo., stiff paper wrappers, paper title label. Unpaginated. $ 25.00

Limited to 124 copies. Traces the ownership of the twelfth-century illuminated Psalter known as The Golden Psalter from its ownership by Richard Heber in the early 1830s. It was owned by several famous collectors, including William Morris, before it was given by Sir Sydney Cockerell to Mr. Cron in 1956. The color frontispiece shows, in original size, the beginning of Psalm 52.

915. (Midnight Paper Sales) Hautman, Pete. BAD BEAT, WITH JOE CROW'S RULES FOR POKER AND LIFE. N.P.: Midnight Paper Sales, 1998, 12mo., cloth backing with decorated paper-covered boards, paper spine label, paper-covered slipcase with paper label on front. (iv), 42, (4) pages. $ 135.00

Limited to 200 numbered copies, signed on colophon by author and illustrator. Tuesday night at Zink's Club 34, not exactly a hang-out of the rich and famous, and the few regulars present (apart from those at the card game upstairs or too far gone for rational discourse) discuss sure bets of the past which turned out not to be sure at all. To which are appended Joe Crow's eminently practical rules: "Walk away from bad hands early," "When your mind is elsewhere, go there," "Bad beats only happen to good players," and many more. With 5 colored wood engravings by Gaylord Schanilec, who also did the colored label on the slipcase and the decoration of the cover papers. Set, printed and bound by Schanilec.

916. (Midnight Paper Sales) HUNGRY MIDNIGHT 4. (Stockholm, WI): Midnight Paper Sales, 2000, folio, cloth portfolio with paper spine label, contains title broadside and six other broadsides. 7 leaves. $ 150.00

Limited to 30 numbered sets. Printed for the occasion of readings at the Hungry Mind Bookstore, each of the six broadsides loosely inserted in this portfolio is limited to either 90 or 120 copies and signed by the author. Poetry and essays by Edwidge Danticat, James Galvin, Tawni O'Dell, Carl H. Klaus, Ha Jin and Patricia Hampl are presented. Illustrated with wood engravings in various colors by Gaylord Shanilec.

917. (Midnight Paper Sales) Logue, Mary. HOUSE IN THE COUNTRY. With wood engravings by Gaylord Schanilec. Minneapolis, MN: Midnight Paper Sales, 1994, 8vo., quarter cloth with brocaded cloth sides, paper spine label. 62, (4) pages. $ 220.00

Limited to 250 numbered copies and signed by the author and printer. The author, a writer by profession, buys a second home in Stockholm, Minnesota. This relates stories of the fix up and the developing fondness for her old and decrepit home. Accompanied by four spectacular full color woodcuts by Schanilec. Hand printed.

918. (Midnight Paper Sales) McNear, Suzanne. EXCERPTS FROM A WISCONSIN CHILDHOOD. N.P.: Midnight Paper Sales, 1997, small 8vo., quarter cloth, marbled paper covered boards, paper spine label, slipcase. (4), 17, (3) pages. $ 130.00

Limited to 120 copies hand-set, printed and bound by Ruth Raich and Gaylord Schanilec. Finely printed on heavy cream stock, deckle edges, illustrated in color from wood engravings by Gaylord Schanilec. Slipcase and quarter binding in navy cloth, with blue-green, tan and brown marbled cover sheets made for the edition by Angela Liguori. Signed by the author and illustrator.

919. (Midnight Paper Sales) Schanilec, Gaylord. EMERSON G. WULLING, PRINTER FOR PLEASURE. N.P.: Midnight Paper Sales, (2000), large 4to., quarter cloth with paper decorated paper covered boards, slipcase with cloth edges. 71, (4) pages. $ 445.00

Printed in an edition limited to 166 numbered and signed copies. A history and bibliography of Emerson Wulling's Sumac Press. The text for the history was transcribed from the tapes from two interviews with Wulling in 1995 and 1996, conducted by Schanilec, along with a visit with the Wullings by Rob Rulon-Miller in 1999. Wulling was a professor by day and printer by night, and owned a library which included fine and interesting printing from all periods and continents. The bibliography of the Sumac Press describes well over 200 publications. Finely printed by Gaylord Schanilec and contains illustrated tipped-in specimens of Wulling's printing, 25 with color wood engravings by Schanilec, as well as other color illustrations throughout. Introduction by Robert Rulon-Miller. The definitive work on Wulling's printing.

920. (Midnight Paper Sales) Schanilec, Gaylord. Y TWO K, A CHRONOLOGICAL MISCELLANY OF IMAGES ENGRAVED IN WOOD. Stockholm, WI: Midnight Paper Sales, 1999, large 8vo., quarter cloth with decorated paper covered boards and paper spine label. (26) pages. $ 132.00

First edition, limited to 99 copies, numbered and signed by the author. A great survey of Schanelec's work with seven black and white, and three color wood-engravings all printed from the original blocks. Includes works from *Offcuts, Chanticleer of the Wilderness, The Other Miller, Why We Live With Animals, My Town, Letter to an Imaginary Friend, Return of the Private,* and *Keepsakes*. Printed on Mohawk Superfine high finish paper with Vergatona Buff laid paper, both now discontinued. Bound in black quarter cloth with paper covered boards. Title page printed in three colors.

921. (Minnesota Outdoors Press) Arey, Richard Fred. WATERFALLS OF THE MISSISSIPPI. The Story of Eight Waterfalls Found in Saint Paul & Minneapolis, Descendants of the Late, Great River Warren Falls, and the Only Waterfalls along the Entire Mississippi River. St. Paul: Minnesota Outdoors Press, 1998, tall large 8vo., cloth, leather spine label, paper and cloth covered slipcase with large paper cover label. (viii), 72, (4) pages, with 1 additional leaf (foldout map). $ 350.00

Limited to 226 lettered or numbered copies, including 200 numbered in cloth, of which this is one. The geologic and more recent history of the eight falls in or along the Mississippi River gorge between St. Paul and Minnesota, beginning with an account of the formation of this gorge and the falls as a consequence of the last Ice Age. This is followed by a discussion of each waterfall accompanied by a 3- to 5-color print of a wood engraving depicting that waterfall by Gaylord Schanilec. Two of these are two-page prints. With a bibliography and a foldout map of the area drawn by the author. One of the prints is also used as a label on the front of the slipcase, and a part of this print is reproduced as a gilt stamping on the front cover of the book. Fore- and bottom edges rough-cut.

922. (Mosher Press) Lang, Andrew. AUCASSIN & NICOLETE. Portland, ME: Thomas B. Mosher, 1922, tall 12mo., two-toned paper-covered boards, paper spine label, slipcase. xxii, 66 pages. $ 25.00

Limited to 925 copies, the ninth edition (Bishop 10.9). Slipcase spotted.

923. (Mosher Press) Leith, W. Compton. SIRENICA. Portland, ME: Mosher, 1915, large 12mo., paper covered boards. xvi, 142, (2). $ 40.00

Printed by Thomas Bird Mosher in an edition limited to 450 numbered copies (Bishop 356, Hatch, 623). Introduction by William Marion Reedy.

924. (Mosher Press) Mosher, Thomas Bird. THE MOSHER BOOKS A LIST OF BELLES LETTRES ISSUED IN LIMITED EDITIONS BY THOMAS BIRD MOSHER AT XLV EXCHANGE STREET PORTLAND MAINE MDCCCXCI::MDCCCXVI. Portland, ME: Thomas Bird Mosher, 1916, small 8vo., paper wrappers. 64 pages. $ 19.00

Twenty-fourth catalogue. (Bishop no. 260) Arranged by series and then by author, this 1916 catalogue of Mosher publications includes a descriptive summary for titles still in print, a listing of the contents of each of the twenty volumes of *The Bibelot*, and an index. Last page and back wrapper creased, wrappers foxed, detached and partially split.

925. (Mosher Press) Thompson, Francis. THE HOUND OF HEAVEN. Portland, ME: Thomas B. Mosher, 1908, square 12mo., paper-covered boards, paper spine and cover labels, slipcase, fore and bottom edges uncut. x, 12, (2) pages. $ 20.00

First edition; printed in an edition limited to 925. (Hatch & Nash no.442.) No.1 in the Golden Text series. Wear to slipcase.

926. (Mosher Press) Thompson, Francis. THE HOUND OF HEAVEN. Portland, ME: Thomas Bird Mosher, 1926, square 12mo., quarter cloth with pattern paper boards, paper cover label. vii, (ii), 15, (3) pages. $ 27.50

Sixth edition limited to 925 copies. (Bishop no.FL114) Very popular inspirational poem from the early twentieth century. Printed on Van Gelder hand-made paper. First volume in the Golden Text series. Slight wear to bottom edge.

927. (Mosher Press) Whitman, Walt. LEAVES OF GRASS, FACSIMILE EDITION OF THE 1855 TEXT. Portland, ME: Thomas Bird Mosher and William Francis Gable, 1920, small 4to., embossed cloth. (ii), 14, (4) pages. $ 20.00

Second impression limited to 500 copies. (Bishop no. 192.1) Introduction, Emerson letter and Traubel memorial are loose in original boards; frontispiece and facsimile pages are missing. Wear to corners and to head and tail of spine.

928. (Mosher Press) Whittier, John G. SNOW-BOUND, A WINTER IDYLL. Portland, ME: Thomas B. Mosher, 1911, square 12mo., marble paper covered boards, paper spine and cover labels, top edges uncut. vi, 42, (2) pages. $ 25.00

One of 200 copies bound in marbled paper boards from an edition limited to 925 printed on hand-made Van Gelder paper. (Hatch & Nash no.540, Bishop no.358) Lovely version of a much-loved classic praising the beauty of winter in New England. As number seven in the Golden Text series, the title page is ruled with a large decorative red initial. Rear pastedown offset.

929. (Mountain House Press) Hunter, Dard. OLD PAPERMAKING. Chillicothe, Ohio: Private Press of Dard Hunter, 1923, small 4to., original green paper covered boards with parchment spine and tips, original mailing box with paper cover label. (iv), 112, (4) pages and nine leaves mounted with paper samples. $ 4,000.00

First edition of the author's first book on papermaking, limited to 200 numbered copies signed by Hunter. With a mounted frontispiece showing Dard Hunter's papermill, tipped-in facsimiles and illustrations in the text. Some yellowing of free endpaper in front otherwise a very well preserved copy.

930. (Mountain House Press) Hunter, Dard. PRIMITIVE PAPERMAKING, AN ACCOUNT OF A MEXICAN SOJOURN AND OF A VOYAGE TO THE PACIFIC ISLANDS IN SEARCH OF INFORMATION, IMPLEMENTS, AND

SPECIMENS RELATING TO THE MAKING & DECORATING OF BARK-PAPER. Chillicothe: Mountain House Press, 1927, folio, signatures loosely inserted in three-quarter cloth portfolio with cloth ties as issued, paper cover label. 48 pages.

$ 9,500.00

Limited to 200 numbered and signed copies. (Schlosser 34). With a frontispiece showing Hunter's Mountain House reproduced from a lithograph executed in 1852, 35 line illustrations, one of which is in color, 10 photographs, 31 specimens of bark paper and 2 specimens of mulberry bark. This was Hunter's third book on paper and the first to deal with non-European papermaking. His autobiography (chapter vi) describes the lengthy sea voyage that he took in 1926 to gather material for this book. His itinerary included Tahiti, the Cook Islands, the Fiji Islands in which he discovered tapa still being produced, Tonga where he gathered many samples and then on to Hawaii. Hunter hand-printed this book in the type that he had designed and cast. Hunter states that though he priced this book at$75.00, a price which he thought exorbitant, "the edition was exhausted with one month. I was still further encouraged." Minor smudging of front cover. Bookplate.

931. (Mt. Tam Press) A REPRINT OF THE TAYLOR & TAYLOR IMPRINT FOR THE WINTER MCMXVI-VII. San Raphael, CA: Mt. Tam Press, 1988, 8vo., paper wrappers, dust jacket, paper cover label. xii, 21, (3) pages. $ 35.00

One of an edition of three hundred copies printed for friends of Mt. Tam Press, collectors and libraries. A reprint of the Taylor & Taylor Imprint for 1916–17, redesigned in a stylistically compatible piece to serve as a keepsake for those interested in fine printing. Two pages of the original are reproduced in facsimile and to size. Printed on Mohawk Letterpress Text, with Fabriano cover stock.

933. (Museum Press) ADDRESSES GIVEN AT THE OPENING OF THE EXHI-BITION. New York: Pierpont Morgan Library, 1939, 8vo., cloth. (viii), 27, (3) pages.

$ 30.00

First edition. Keepsake No.58 issued by the A.I.G.A.. On the printing of the Museum Press under the direction of Henry Watson Kent. Contains essays by Updike, Rollins, Ivins, Rogers and Kent.

934. (Naiman Press) AMERICAN DECORATIVE PAPERMAKERS, THE WORK & SPECIMENS OF TWELVE CRAFT ARTISTS. N.P.: Busyhaus Publications, (1983), oblong 8vo., half leather over cloth. 65, (3) pages. $ 300.00

First edition, one of the 200 numbered copies bound in half leather by the Harcourt Bindery. A study of marbling with an introduction by Don Guyot, essays and tipped-in specimens by 10 marblers, technical notes, and a bibliography of the subject. Finely printed at the Naiman Press. Includes a wood egraving by Michael McCurdy.

935. (Nash, John Henry) CATALOGUE, DR. OTTO VOLLBEHER COLLEC-TION OF AMERICANA VETUSTISSIMA. San Francisco: Printed by John Henry Nash, 1935, large 8vo., paper wrappers. (ii), 14 pages. $ 30.00

Printed in an edition limited to 500 copies. (O'Day pg.90) A catalogue for the exhibition of Americana Vetustissima, a collection belonging to Dr. Otto Vollbehr, that was never before displayed in America. All items were printed prior to 1550 and 24 are described here. The back cover has a section at the top that is faded. Covers crinkled around part of the edges.

936. (Nash, John Henry) Dare, Helen, et al. TRIBUTES TO ANNE BREMER. Two volumes. San Francisco: Printed for Albert M. Bender by John Henry Nash, 1927, large 12mo., paper covered boards with a paper covered slipcase and a paper spine label on books and slipcase. (viii), (vii),31; (x), 31 pages. $ 65.00

Printed in an edition limited to 150 copies. (Nash Printings 53) These poems are tributes to the memory of the great artist Anne Bremer, which are sincere expressions of grief at her death and tributes to her gifts as an artist by a group of distinguished California writers. Slightly faded on slipcase.

937. (Nash, John Henry) Harte, Bret. THE HEATHEN CHINEE, PLAIN LAN-
GUAGE FROM TRUTHFUL JAMES (TABLE MOUNTAIN, 1870). San Francis-
co: John Henry Nash, 1924, folio, black and tan German batik covered boards. (15)
leaves. $ 200.00
Printed in an edition limited to 255 numbered copies (O'Day, pp. 35-36). Includes an Introduction by Ina
Coolbrith, A fellow-worker with Bret Harte on the Overland Monthly; and a Note concerning the history of the manuscript by J.C. Rowell of the University of Ca. Library; a Bibliography with Notes by
Robert Ernest Cowan, Librarian of the William Andrews Clark, Jr. Library; and The Printer's Page by
John Henry Nash. In addition to its typographical importance this presentation of Harte's poem com-
bines several of the most illustrious names in California literature. Coolbrith's narrative of her association with Harte on the Overland Monthly includes reminiscences of such rare spirits as Joaquin Miller,
Mark Twain, and Charles Warren Stoddard. Frontispiece as 5 facsimile leaves of the original manuscript
of "The Heathen Chinee" originally tipped in and sewn, but presently detached. Text of the poem printed in black, with large initial printed in green. Frontis, title and text pages within ornamental borders and
rule designs printed in orange. Garamond roman and italic type on Simili Japan paper. Back flyleaf discolored from previously laid in paper, small pieces missing from head and tail of spine, right bottom edge
of front cover, and middle edge of back.

938. (Nash, John Henry) O'Day, Edward F. AN APPRECIATION OF JAMES
WOOD COFFROTH, MDCCCXXIX--MDCCCLXXII, WRITTEN FOR HIS
SON JAMES W.COFFROTH. San Francisco: John Henry Nash, 1926, 4to., quarter
vellum with marbled boards, top edges uncut, leather spine label, slipcase. vii, (i), 65, [3]
pages. $ 85.00
Limited to 250 numbered copies for private distribution. (O'Day, 50). Born in Franklin, Pennsylvania in
1829, James Wood Coffroth moved to California in 1850 where he eventually became an influential
newspaper owner, lawyer and state senator. With vivid glimpses of his turbulent early days in Sonora
and Sacramento during the Gold Rush, this biography also examines the role he played in the titanic political struggles that characterized politics in California. His promising career was cut short by his un-
timely death in 1872. Frontispiece portrait, borders and decorated title page by William H. Wilke. Letter
signed by J.W. Coffroth loosely inserted. Printed by John Nash.

939. (New York Chappel) ANY NUMBER CAN PRINT. New York: New York Chappel, 1960, small 8vo., printed folder containing 20 separately printed pieces of ephemera
printed by different private presses in the New York area. $ 45.00
Limited to not more than 142 copies as one of the contributions contains that limitation.

940. (New York Chappel) SECOND UNCOMMONPLACE BOOK OF THE NEW
YORK CHAPPEL. New York: n.p., 1961, tall 12mo., cloth, paper cover label. 8 sepa-
rately printed contributions bound in one. $ 65.00
Limited to 200 copies. Includes the work of the Gladhand Press, The Grimalkin Press, The Herity Press,
The Mermaid Press, The Ron Press, The Serendipity Press, The Press of the Iron Horse and the Private
Press of the Haywoods.

941. (Nonesuch Press) BODKIN PERMITTING, BEING THE PROSPECTUS
AND RETROSPECTUS FOR 1929 OF THE NONESUCH PRESS. (London):
Nonesuch Press, 1929, large 12mo., marbled stiff paper wrappers, paper cover label.
27+(1) pages. $ 15.00
The Nonesuch Press began to have its books distributed in the United States by Random House in 1927.
(Dreyfus, P18). Foreword by Sir Francis Meynell, with prospectus of books for 1929 and retrospectus of
Nonesuch unlimited editions to follow. Printed by the Westminster Press.

THESEUS
ROMULUS
LYCURGUS
NUMA POMPILIUS
SOLON
PUBLICOLA
THEMISTOCLES
FURIUS CAMILLUS
PERICLES
FABIUS MAXIMUS
ALCIBIADES
CORIOLANUS

The Lives of the Noble

GRECIANS & ROMANES

COMPARED TOGETHER BY THAT GRAVE
LEARNED PHILOSOPHER AND
HISTORIOGRAPHER

PLUTARKE

OF CHÆRONEA

*

TRANSLATED OUT OF GREEKE INTO FRENCH BY JAMES
AMYOT: AND OUT OF FRENCH INTO ENGLISHE BY
THOMAS NORTH: THE ILLUSTRATIONS BY T. L. POULTON:
WITH THE FIFTEEN SUPPLEMENTARY LIVES OF 1603
THE NONESUCH PRESS · LONDON · MCMXXIX

Item 944

942. (Nonesuch Press) de Maisse, Andre Hurault. DE MAISSE, A JOURNAL OF ALL THAT WAS ACCOMPLISHED BY MONSIEUR DE MAISSE, AMBASSADOR IN ENGLAND FROM KING HENRI IV TO QUEEN ELIZABETH ANNO DOMINI 1597. London: Nonesuch Press, 1931, 8vo., cloth, dust jacket. xviii, 146 pages. $ 75.00

Printed in an unlimited edition by R. & R. Clark on machine made cream laid paper with the Nonesuch watermark, set in Monotype Scotch Roman (Dreyfus, 77). Translated from the French and edited with an introduction by G. B. Harrison and R. A. Jones. The *Journal* had never before been printed in full, either in French or English. De Maisse kept a full and entertaining diary of contemporary life at the Court of Queen Elizabeth, providing many details about famous people "in a period of which every scrap is of interest." Wear to dust jacket.

943. (Nonesuch Press) Hotson, J. Leslie. THE DEATH OF CHRISTOPHER MARLOWE. London: The Nonesuch Press, 1925, 8vo., brown buckram stamped in gilt. 76 pages. $ 125.00

First impression, with the canceled title page. (Dreyfus no.22) Includes a presentation from the author on the front free endpaper and the bookplate of the presentee on the front pastedown. "It contains the first publication of original documents (discovered at the Public Record Office) connected with the death of Marlowe. "Finely printed with several illustrations and a fold out frontispiece.

944. (Nonesuch Press) Plutarch. THE LIVES OF THE NOBLE GRECIANS & ROMANES COMPARED TOGETHER BY THAT GRAVE LEARNED PHILOSOPHER AND HISTORIOGRAPHER PLUTARKE OF CHAERONEA. Five vol-

umes. London: The Nonesuch Press, 1929–1930, 4to., polished buckram, paper spine labels, top edge gilt. (iii),xxviii,(iv),431+(1); (ix),442,(2); (ix), 454,(2); (ix),482,(2); (ix),410,(2) pages. $ 400.00

Printed in an edition limited 1050 numbered copies. (Dreyfus no.63). Each volume includes several full pages illustrations by T.L. Poulton, lithographed at the Curwen Press. The Plutarke of Chaeronea who lived 46–120 A.D., a great historiographer of his time, writes about the lives of noble Grecians and Romans, such as Theseus, Romulus, Lycurgus, Numa Pompilius, Solon, Phocion, Cimon, Nicias, Alexander, Julius Caesar, Pompeius, Demetrius, Cicero and many more. It has been translated out of Greek into French by James Amyot, and out of French into English by Thomas North. North's translation first appeared in 1579 and it is this text that makes up this edition. There are spare paper spine labels tipped in on the back pastedown. Back cover of volume II has some bubbling to the cloth. The spine label on Volume V is very slightly chipped.

945. (Nonesuch Press) Tennyson, Alfred Lord. IN MEMORIAM. London: The Nonesuch Press, 1933, small 4to., boards covered with Italian black and gold printed paper, printed paper spine label, slipcase. (iv), xxiv), 145, (7) pages. $ 225.00

Limited to 1,875 copies. (Dreyfus no.91). Printed on Van Gelder mould-made paper in italic with Granjon ornaments printed in terra cotta. Issued on the 100th anniversary of the death of Arthur Hallam, for whom the poem was written. Edited and with an introduction by John Sparrow.

946. (Nova Press) Barlow, William P., Jr. A PLAYLET FOR WATER SKIERS, (IN ONE ACTLET). Piedmont, CA: Nova Press, 1961, 1964, small 8vo., paper-covered boards. volume I, vi, 12 (2) pages; volume II, vi, 16 (2) pages. $ 45.00

Two volumes, issued separately in 1961 and 1964, limited to 220 and 250 copies each, as annual Christmas productions of the Nova Press. "For a number of years I have been distributing Christmas booklets regularly dealing with printing or book collecting. This has been a bit unfair to my water skiing friends, who have been regularly mystified by them" (preface). Some creases on covers of volume II. and a little soiling to endpapers of each.

947. (Nut Quad Press) Rollins, Carl Purlington. THE ORDEAL OF WILLIAM MORRIS. (San Fernando, CA): Roxburghe Club of San Francisco and Zamorano Club of Los Angeles, (1996), 8vo., stiff paper wrappers. (16) pages. $ 25.00

Printed letterpress in an edition of 150 copies and issued as a keepsake to the attending members of the Roxburghe Club of San Francisco and the Zamorano Club of Los Angeles at their joint meeting in San Francisco, October 26-27, 1996. Printed on Somerset Mouldmade paper using Golden type designed by William Morris for his Kelmscott Press. A 1934 address by the author at Yale University, on the 100th Anniversary of William Morris's birth, and here reprinted on the 100th Anniversary of his death.

948. (Occasional Works) Cone, Claribel. ALICE DERAIN. Woodside, CA: Occasional Works, 1984, 8vo., stiff wrappers, paper cover label. (vi), 10, (2) pages. $ 45.00

Printed in an edition limited to 250 signed numbered copies. Designed by Ann Rosener. Hand-set in Monotype Bembo on 100 percent Arches Text paper. With five tipped-in paintings by the author--oil and pastel on paper--photographed by Leo Holub and reproduced in color by Mastercraft Press. Fiction with Gertrude Stein as a character.

949. (Occidental College Library Press) Hornby, C.H. St John. SUBIACO, A LETTER FROM C.H. ST. JOHN HORNBY TO ROBERT GEORGE COLLIER PROCTOR. (Los Angeles: Roxburghe and Zamorano Clubs, 1982), 12mo., stiff paper wrappers. (4) pages. $ 20.00

Printed by Tyrus G. Harmsen at the Occidental College Library Press in an edition limited to 150 copies for members of the Roxburghe and Zamorano Clubs, on the occasion of their joint meeting, October 9–10, 1982. Prefatory note by Harmsen and typed letter signed by him loosely laid in. The Subiaco was modelled after the first type of Sweynheym and Pannartz, with which they had printed three books in 1465.

950. (Officina Bodoni) Barduzzi, Bernardino. LETTER IN PRAISE OF VERONA (1489). In the original Latin text with an English translation by Betty Radice. Verona: Officina Bodoni, 1974, tall 8vo., quarter vellum with blue Roma paper sides with woodcut pattern in white, top edge gilt, slipcase. 55, (3) pages. $ 625.00
Limited to 150 numbered copies. (Schmoller 190). Printed on Pescia mould-made paper by Giovanni Mardersteig at the Officina Bodoni in yellow, red and black. Postscript by Giovanni Mardersteig translated into English by Hans Schmoller. Reprint and translation of one of the rarest of Italian incunabula, Barduzzi's letter to Giovanni Nesi, printed in 1489 by Paulus Fridenperger, Verona's last 15th century printer. This version contains the little known decorations added by Felice Feliciano which were used for the first reprint of the 1489 edition. Feliciano was, according to Mardersteig, one of the most important Italian calligraphers of his day. A number of examples of his work are reproduced here along with a short biographical sketch by Mardersteig. Prospectus loosely inserted.

951. (Officina Bodoni) Feliciano, Felice. IPPOLITO E LIONORA, FROM A MANUSCRIPT OF FELICE FELICIANO IN THE HARVARD COLLEGE LIBRARY. Cambridge: Harvard College, 1970, tall 8vo., full vellum-colored Linson boards, top edge gilt, slipcase. 117, (3) pages. $ 650.00
Limited to 200 numbered copies. (Schmoller 166). Printed on Magnani mould-made paper by Giovanni Mardersteig at the Officina Bodoni. A facsimile of a novella written out by hand by the 15th century Italian calligrapher, Felice Feliciano. Has a preface by Philip Hofer, a transcription of the story with commentary and notes by Franco Riva, an English translation and bibliography by Martin Faigel and an essay on Feliciano by Mardersteig.

952. (Officina Bodoni) Keats, John. TO CHARLES COWDEN CLARKE. New Rochelle, NY: James L. Weil Publishers, 1989, large 8vo., paper wrappers, cord-tied. (10) pages. $ 175.00
Printed in an edition limited to fifty keepsake copies. A poem written by John Keats to his friend Charles Cowden Clarke. This edition was handset in a variant of the Dante type and printed on the Officina Bodoni handpress by Martino Mardersteig on Magnani handmade paper. Slightly soiled and faded on covers.

953. (Officina Bodoni) Le Grand, Frederic. EPITRE AU MARQUIS D'ARGENS DU 23 SEPTEMBRE 1757. Montagnola: Officinae Bodoni, 1924, 4to., quarter vellum with Putois marble-paper sides, plain paper dust jacket and fragments of slipcase. 22, (2) pages. $ 950.00
Printed in an edition limited to 225 copies. (Officina Bodini 10) The Epitre au Marquis d'Argens, which King Eberhard wrote at Erfurt on 23 September 1757, belongs to the most critical period of his life, after his defeat at Kolin. The news of the death of his mother caused him mental anguish, and again and again he thought of suicide. These thoughts and their justification formed the content of this verse-letter to his French friend. His escape into verse-making in those months helped him to overcome his grief. Original French text with German verse. Dust jacket chipped and yellowed. Very unusual to find in such excellent condition with paper protective jacket still intact.

954. (Officina Bodoni) Mardersteig, Giovanni. ON G.B. BODONI'S TYPE FACES. Verona: Officina Bodoni, 1968, tall 8vo., stiff green paper wrappers. 34 pages. $ 275.00
Limited to 200 copies and printed as a Keepsake for Gallery 303. (Schmoller no.157). Biographical information on Bodoni and the types of his used by Mardersteig followed by various type specimens.

955. (Officina Bodoni) NEWLY DISCOVERED TREATISE ON CLASSIC LETTER DESIGN. Paris: At the Sign of the Pegasus, 1927, 8vo., quarter vellum with paper covered boards. 81, (3) pages. $ 750.00
First edition, printed by Giovanni Mardersteig at his Officina Bodoni in an edition limited to 350 copies of which only 300 were offered for sale. (Mardersteig, no.21). Introduction by Stanley Morison. The original publication, which is the first printed treatise on the construction of Roman capital letters, is in-

Item 956

cluded here in facsimile. The original text and type specimens are reproduced in collotype by Albert Frisch of Berlin on mould-made paper. Original text also translated into English. This is the last book printed by Mardersteig in Mantagnola, Switzerland, before his move to Verona, Italy. Slight darkening of spine. Chip out of one corner.

956. (Officina Bodoni) OFFICINA BODONI, THE OPERATION OF A HAND-PRESS DURING THE FIRST SIX YEARS OF ITS WORK. Paris and New York: Editiones Officinae Bodoni, 1929, 4to., cloth with decoration in gilt on front cover and gilt lettering on spine, top edge gilt, others uncu, dust jacket. 80, (2) pages. $ 1,250.00
First edition, limited to 500 copies (Schmoller no.32). The English language edition of a book that was also published in German and Italian. This bibliography and history of the press covers the years 1923 to 1929. The first section describes how a book is made at the press and is accompanied by 12 woodcuts by Frans Masereel. This is followed by descriptions of the books and occasional publications and a look at the various printer's devices used. Offset from flaps of dust jacket. Unusual to find so well preserved.

957. (Officina Bodoni) PASTONCHI, A SPECIMEN OF A NEW LETTER FOR USE ON THE "MONOTYPE" London: The Lanston Monotype Corporation, (1928), small 4to., half vellum with marbled paper covered boards, remnants of slipcase. 65, (5) pages. $ 650.00

Printed in an edition limited to 200 copies on special Fabriono paper by Mardersteig at his Officina Bodoni. (Officina Bodoni 25). A trade edition was also issued by is not bound in quarter vellum and printed on special paper. An English specimen of a new type-face is designed by Eduardo Cotti under the direction of Francesco Pastonchi. Various specimen booklets of various sizes bound in. Introduction by Giovanni Mardersteig. Moderate internal foxing.

958. (Officina Bodoni) Plato. CRITO, A SOCRATIC DIALOGUE BY PLATO. Paris: The Pleiad, 1926, 8vo., marbled paper-covered boards, slipcase. 37+(1) pages.
$ 500.00

Printed in an edition limited to 475 numbered copies. (Officina Bodoni no.16). Printed under the supervision of Frederic Warde and the first use of this type face. Well preserved copy.

959. (Officina Bodoni) SAYINGS OF THE SEVEN SAGES OF GREECE. Verona: Officina Bodoni, 1976, tall 8vo., quarter vellum with grey Ingres paper sides with terracotta geometric pattern, top edge gilt, slipcase. 87, (3) pages. $ 675.00

Limited to 160 numbered copies. (Schmoller no.196). "Original Greek text, edited with a translation into English by Betty Radice from the version of Joannes Stobaeus." Contains sayings by Cleobulus, Solon, Chilon, Thales, Pittacus, Bias and Periander printed in black on a terracotta background resembling that found on Greek vases. Mardersteig has written a note on the history of the text and the development of early Greek letter forms up to the time of Pericles and has included a heliogravure reproduction of a marble inscription. The text letters of the sayings were developed by Mardersteig from the marble inscription of the decree in honor of Oeniades. This book is well produced and also sheds light on Mardersteig's work with letterforms. Explanatory leaflet loosely inserted.

960. (Officina Pragensis) STARA PRAHA/ PRVNI CAST. Prague: Officina Pragensis, 1935, portfolio with stiff paper boards. (vi), 12 prints. $ 3,500.00

Limited to 70 numbered copies. Twelve original lithographs signed and dated by the Czech "master of the book arts" Hugo Steiner-Prag. Each lithograph is taken directly from the stone and shows a dramatic scene from the city of Prague. These lithographs, completed in Steiner-Prag's prime, are a great example of his work as a book illustrator. Working in Europe and the United States throughout the first half of the twentieth century, Steiner-Prag designed 412 books and illustrated 65 others (including many for the Limited Editions Club). This collection was the first item to be published by his Officina Pragensis in 1935 but was not released for sale on the booksellers market. Instead, only 70 copies were printed: 20 for the author and 50 for patrons of the Officina Pragensis. This copy is one of the 50 printed exclusively for Steiner-Prag's patrons and contains a handwritten inscription to Jindricha Waldesa on the title-page. The titles of the lithographs are listed on the half-title page.

961. (Ogham Press) Tompkins, Willis. "FOR GOD AND CUTHBERT," A BRIEF ACCOUNT OF THE LINDISFARNE GOSPELS, WITH A REPRODUCTION FROM THE GOSPEL ACCORDING TO SAINT LUKE. New York: Ogham Press, (1952), large 12mo., stiff paper wrappers. (12) pages. $ 20.00

With specimen of writing from the Lindisfarne Gospels and line engravings by J. Leith Roseman. Christmas greeting from author laid in along with *Manifesto* from the Ogham Press announcing that it will be called by various names, "according to circumstances and mood."

962. (Old School Press) CHISWICK PRESS TYPE SPECIMEN BOOK (SAMPLE PAGES). Buckland Dinham, England: Old School Press, 1984, narrow 8vo., stapled stiff paper wrappers. (16 pages). $ 20.00

Printed in an edition limited to 100 numbered copies. Sample pages of initial letters, borders & ornaments, etc., extracted from the Chiswick Press type specimen book of 142 leaves and issued as a Christmas keepsake for friends, December, 1984. Most of these examples were designed by Mary Byfield, or

Item 960

Charlotte and Elizabeth Whittingham. A presentation copy from the bookseller, Tony Appleton, who compiled *A Handlist of The Writings of Stanley Morison,* and also wrote the introductory copy to this booklet.

963. (Old School Press) Burnett, David. CHESIL BEACH. Bath: The Old School Press, 1997, small 4to., quarter cloth with paper covered boards. (15) pages.　　　$ 95.00
Printed in an edition limited to 225 numbered and signed copies. Presentation copy, "For Michael and Frances with best wishes from David. 18th November, 1997." This is third in a series of six books of work by British poets published by The Old School Press, this one featuring David Burnett. It is illustrated with a wood-engraving by Christopher Wormell. Signed by Burnett and Wormell.

964. (Old School Press) Post, Desmond. ANTIGONE. Bath: Old School Press, 1996, small 4to., quarter cloth with paper covered boards. (30) pages.　　　$ 75.00
First edition, limited to 112 numbered copies, signed by the author and illustrator of which this is one of 100 bound in quarter yellow cloth with boards covered by a hand-made Larroque paper, pink with white speckles. A poem based the tragic story of Antigone, the daughter of Oedipus, King of Thebes. Text hand-set in Perpetua and printed on Zerkall mould-made paper. Illustrated with five woodcuts by Inger Lawrance, printed from the original cherry blocks.

965. (Old Stile Press) BENEDICITE OMNIA OPERA. Llandogo: Old Stile Press, 1987, small 4to., quarter cloth with decorated paper covered boards, with all edges in gilt, stored in a cloth slipcase with paper covered sides. (60) pages. $ 135.00
Printed in an edition limited to 225 numbered and signed copies. (Harrop pg. 60). This is the first book which has been designed consciously as a whole, with each page opening being designed separately and not relying on the page before or after. Alyson MacNeill cut the images for the pages of this book and for its bindings. Signed by the artist, MacNeill.

966. (Old Stile Press) Brothers Grimm. FAITHFUL JOHN. (Monmouthshire): The Old Stile Press, (1988), tall 8vo., quarter cloth with printed paper boards, cloth slipcase, paper cover label. $ 125.00
Printed in an edition limited to 220 numbered and artists signed copies. Finely illustrated throughout by Harry Brockway with marginal wood engravings that grace every page. The Brothers Grimm story tells of three ravens haunt the attempts of a young prince to court a beautiful princess. Translated by Lucy Crane.

967. (Old Stile Press) CHESTER MIRACLE PLAYS, ABRAHAM AND ISAAC. (Monmouthshire): The Old Stile Press, (1999), oblong 4to., paper covered boards. (41) french fold pages. $ 110.00
Printed in an edition limited to 220 numbered and signed copies. Elaborately illustrated with full page expressively rendered woodcuts by J. Martin Pitts. Each illustration in addition to visually narrating the story neatly incorporates the original text. This interpretation of the story of Abraham and Isaac is that of the Chester cycle of miracle plays. This is one of the earliest written in the first half of the fourteenth century.

968. (Old Stile Press) Fryer, Katherine. BEFORE THE WAR AND LONG AGO. Llandogo: The Old Stile Press, 2000, oblong 8vo., decorated paper covered boards, glassine dust jacket. (37) pages. $ 125.00
Printed in an edition limited to 100 numbered and signed copies. A selection of wood engravings and linocuts with reminiscences by Fryer. Nicholas McDowall discusses in the preface his study of the wood-engraved blocks, linocuts and some proofs by Fryer, who lost her engraving tools during a bombing raid in the Second World War. The bombing and other disruptions took their toll on the blocks and many images exist now only in the form of a single proof. This book reproduces a number of these images as line blocks and one can get a hint at least of what would have come from the original wood. The majority are printed from the original blocks, wood or lino. A signed impression of a wood engraving "With the Swans, Christchurch," engraved by Fryer in 1999 is loosely inserted. Signed by the artist.

969. (Old Stile Press) Gwilym, Dafydd Ap. HOUSES OF LEAVES. Llandogo: Old Stile Press, 1993, large 8vo., cloth spine, Abbey Mills laid paper covered boards, blue cloth slipcase. 62 pages. $ 110.00
Limited to 250 numbered copies, signed by the artist. (Harrop 92). A selection of poems by Dafydd ap Gwilym, a poet generally considered one of the greatest figures in Welsh literature. Illustrated with 30 line drawings by John Elwyn reproduced from lineblocks and printed in grey. Garamond type set by Bill Hughes. Printed on Zerkall cream mouldmade paper on a FAG Control 900 press.

970. (Old Stile Press) Hughes, Ted. EARTH DANCES. (Llandogo): The Old Stile Press, (1995), 4to., onion paper covered boards. Cloth covered slipcase. 43, (4) pages. $ 325.00
Printed in an edition limited to 250 numbered an signed copies. R. J. Lloyd, painter and printmaker has made a selection of poems, on the subject of landscape, written by poet Ted Hughes for this collaboration. A series of wonderfully decorative linocut images have been interwoven with poems on text pages while others take full pages. The poems have been hand-set by Nicolas McDowall on mould-made text paper. Illustrations are printed directly from the lino on four different kinds of fibrous handmade paper (incorporating nettle, alkanet, Japanese knotweed and iris) each hand made by Frances McDowall.

971. (Old Stile Press) Lear, Edward. TWO NONSENSE STORIES. Llandogo: Old Stile Press, 1990, small 4to., red cloth spine, Old Dutch Ingres two toned paper covered boards, black sprinkled edges, black cloth slipcase. 72 pages. $ 95.00

Limited to 206 numbered copies. (Harrop 74). This book includes Lear's "The Story of the Four Little Children Who Went Round the World" and "The History of the Seven Families of the Lake Pipple-Pop-ple." Illustrated with images by Gillian Martin. Set in artist's drawn alphabet by Frances McDowall, made into computer typeface by Nicolas McDowall. Printed on T.H. Saunders mouldmade paper on a Victoria platen press. Pen and ink drawings and text printed from polymer blocks made by the printer. Signed by the artist.

972. (Old Stile Press) THE SEAFARER. Llandogo, Gwent: The Old Stile Press, 1988, small oblong 8vo., stitched, stiff paper wrappers, orihon folds, in folder (thin fiberboard with flaps inside buckram- covered limp boards) with cloth tape ties. (44) pages.
$ 110.00

Limited to 240 numbered copies. Signed on colophon by illustrator and translator. An Anglo-Saxon poem almost certainly written down and "revised" by Christian monks, using this pagan Germanic art and its themes for Christian purposes: The Seafarer, an exile, recounts the harshness of his travels ("wild were the waves") but expresses joy in voyaging ("my mind roams with the waves") while lamenting the passing of earthly glories ("kings and kaisers and gold-giving lords / are no longer as they were") and advises the listener to seek other glories. Each should strive to "win the praise of those living / after him ... / with daring deeds on earth against the malice / of the fiends, against the devil, so that / the children of men may later honour him / and his fame live afterwards with the angels." (Modern English text by Kevin Crossley-Holland.) The 40+ woodcuts by Inger Lawrance printed in one or two colors are mini-mally representational, often suggesting natural phenomena in a cryptic way, particularly wind and water. The orihon binding (sheets folded at the outer edge-a style of manuscript binding) and the stitch-ing with black ribbon give the book a kind of archaic style. The book is well protected in its folder tied with wide cloth tape.

973. (Old Stile Press) Skelton, Robin. LENS OF CRYSTAL. Monmouthshire: The Old Stile Press, (1996), small 4to., printed paper covered boards, paper covered slipcase. un-paginated. $ 160.00

Printed in an edition limited to 250 numbered copies signed by the poet and artist. Robin Skelton ex-plores the beautiful and ingenious verse forms of medieval Wales, developed from the sixth century on-wards. He writes poetry of intense beauty and Sara Philpott responds to them with elaborate linocut im-ages. Printed in red and black throughout.

974. (Old Stile Press) Wilde, Oscar. THE BALLAD OF READING GAOL. Llandogo, near Monmouth, Gwent: The Old Stile Press, 1994, large 8vo., paper-covered boards, top edge darkly stained, other edges roughly trimmed, two silk place markers, paper-cov-ered slipcase. 46 pages. $ 140.00

Limited to 225 copies, signed by artist on colophon. One of Oscar Wilde's last works, published anony-mously in 1898, one year after his release from prison, and based on his experiences there: A bitter, dark ballad of the prison-life and (scheduled) death of a condemned murderer ("He looked upon the garish day / with such a wistful eye; / The man had killed the thing he loved / And so he had to die.") Eight somber wood engravings by Garrick Palmer accompany the text; elements of these engravings are also used (in black and gray) for the design on the paper cover of the heavy slipcase, the boards of which are thicker than the book (giving the impression of "imprisoning" the book).

975. (Old Stile Press) Williams, Eric. LAND. Llandogo: The Old Stile Press, (1996) ob-long 4to., printed paper covered boards with cloth covered slipcase and paper label cover. 46 pages. $ 210.00

Printed in an edition limited to 240 numbered and signed copies. Finely illustrated with fourteen wood engravings of the English landscape by Garrick Palmer. These striking images illustrate a selection of poems chosen by Eric Williams. Finely printed on Zerkall mould-made paper.

976. (Oliphant Press) Roth, Henry. NATURE'S FIRST GREEN. New York: Targ Editions, 1979, narrow 8vo., cloth, dust jacket. (12) pages. $75.00
Printed in an edition limited to 350 signed and numbered copies. Written by the author of the classic novel, *Call It Sleep,* this brief reminiscence about Roth's days as an assistant to a movie projectionist was created to provide the editor, William Targ, with "something very special" to begin Targ Editions. Roth often said that it was due to Targ that he began to write seriously again. Designed and printed by Ronald Gordon at The Oliphant Press with the title page illustration by Marc Hinkley.

977. (Out of Sorts Press) THE TYPE LOUSE. Larchmont (NY): Out of Sorts Press, 1974, 12mo., stapled, stiff paper wrappers. (12) pages. $17.50
Limited to 250 copies, "printed...for the Typocrafters and APA." Strange insects interfere with typesetting at a religious press, cause printer to loose job. Selection from: A Treasury of American Folklore (Crown Publishers).

978. (Overbrook Press) Acheson, Dean Gooderham. ADDRESSES ON THE OCCASION OF THE PRESENTATION OF THE WOODROW WILSON AWARD FOR DISTINGUISHED SERVICE TO DEAN GOODERHAM ACHESON. Stamford: The Overbrook Press, n.d. (circa 1954), tall 8vo., paper wrappers. 38, (2) pages. $15.00
No limitation. Not in Cahoon.

979. (Overbrook Press) Adams, Frederick B. RADICAL LITERATURE IN AMERICA, TO WHICH IS APPENDED A CATALOGUE OF AN EXHIBITION HELD AT THE GROLIER CLUB IN NEW YORK CITY. Stamford: Overbrook Press, 1939, small 4to., cloth, slipcase. 61, (5) pages. $100.00
First edition, limited to 650 copies. With excellent annotated descriptions of books important in the field. Some illustrations and foldout plates. Some spotting and damage to slipcase.

980. (Overbrook Press) Bennett, Arnold. LOVE AFFAIR. Stamford, CT: The Overbrook Press, 1965, 8vo., paper wrappers, paper cover label. (8) pages. $25.00
Printed in an edition of 400 copies and includes an illustrated two-color title page.

981. (Overbrook Press) Chiang Kai-Shek, Madame. ADDRESSES DELIVERED BEFORE THE HOUSE OF REPRESENTATIVES AND THE SENATE OF THE UNITED STATES, FEBRUARY 18, 1943. Stamford: Overbrook Press, 1943, large 8vo., black paper covered boards, with paper cover label. 15+(1) pages. $45.00
Printed in an edition limited to 600 copies (Cahoon, pp. 38-39). Printed as a tribute to Mme. Chiang Kai-shek, with color decorations by Rudolph Ruzicka.

982. (Overbrook Press) Cleland, T.M. PROGRESS IN THE GRAPHIC ARTS AN ADDRESS DELIVERED AT THE NEWBERRY LIBRARY IN CHICAGO ... ON THE OCCASION OF THE OPENING OF AN EXHIBITION OF THE AUTHOR'S WORKS. Stamford: The Overbrook Press, 1949, 8vo., paper wrappers, paper cover label. 32 pages. $35.00
First edition, limited to 1000 copies. With errata slip and Christmas greeting loosely inserted.

983. (Overbrook Press) Fulbright, Senator J.W. THE PRICE OF EMPIRE. Stamford: Overbrook Press, 1967, 8vo., stiff paper wrappers. (ii), 14, (4) pages. $15.00
Limited to one thousand copies. An address delivered at a special meeting sponsored by the American Bar Association. "The war in Vietnam is poisoning and brutalizing our domestic life...and the Great Society has become a sick society...the price of empire is America's soul and that price is too high." Card laid in from the publisher with Season's Greetings.

984. (Overbrook Press) Gotlieb, Howard B. MR. SEYMOUR AS CURATOR OF THE HOUSE COLLECTION. Stamford: Overbrook Press, 1964, large 12mo., stiff paper wrappers. 8, (4) pages. $ 20.00

Printed in an edition limited to 200 copies. Personal reminiscence of Charles Seymour (1885–1963) as Curator of the Edward M. House Collection in the Yale Library. Mr. Seymour had previously been a diplomat at the Paris Peace Conference after World War I, and Yale's president in 1937.

985. (Overbrook Press) THE ISSUE, A STATEMENT OF THE BRITISH VIEW. Stamford: Overbrook Press, 1940, large 12mo., buff paper covers with printed label pasted on upper cover. 40 pages. $ 15.00

Printed in an edition limited to 500 copies printed on W & A All Rag Paper (Cahoon, p.27) An "honest attempt to state what an Englishman believes to at stake in this tragic struggle." Explicit mentioning of outrages in Prague and the deportation of intellectuals and Jews to concentration camps. Reprinted by the Overbrook Press as a "contribution to our own thinking about a question which finds us increasingly perplexed and concerned."

986. (Overbrook Press) JAMES HARVEY ROGERS (1886–1939), IN MEMORIAM. Stamford: Overbrook Press, 1940, 8vo., cloth. (xi), 34 (2) pages. $ 30.00

Limited to 450 copies. Includes essay "James Harvey Rogers as an Economist," by Walt W. Rostow, selected bibliography, and engraved portrait as frontis. "Ex-Libris John DePol" bookplate on front pastedown. (Cahoon, p. 24).

987. (Overbrook Press) Lassalle, Ferdinand. UNE PAGE D'AMOUR DE FERDINAND LASSALLE, RECIT, CORRESPONDANCE, CONFESSIONS. Stamford: Overbrook Press, 1959, 8vo., cloth. (viii), 86, (2) pages. $ 75.00

Printed in an edition limited to 250 copies, handset in Caslon Old Face type and printed on Arches paper (Cahoon, p.90). Originally published in 1878, this book "purports to contain the letters addressed by Lassalle to a young Russian girl with whom he fell desperately in love while taking the cure at Aix-la-Chapelle in the autumn of 1860 (Introductory Note)." With seasons greetings card from Frank & Helen Altschul laid in.

988. (Overbrook Press) Lehman, Irving. IRVING LEHMAN, MEMORIAL CEREMONIES HELD AT OPENING SESSION OF THE COURT OF APPEALS, ALBANY, N.Y., OCTOBER 23, 1945. Stamford: Overbrook Press, 1946, large 12mo., stiff paper wrappers. 22, (2) pages. $ 15.00

Printed in an edition limited to 1000 copies in two colors on Glenbourne Deckle Edge Text paper (Cahoon, p.48). Addresses by Joseph M. Proskauer, Charles B. Sears, Nathaniel L. Goldstein and John T. Loughran. Handset in Caslon Old Face type.

989. (Overbrook Press) Luce, Clare Boothe. LITTLE ROCK AND THE MUSCOVITE MOON, CHALLENGES TO AMERICA'S LEADERSHIP. Stamford: Overbrook Press, 1957, 8vo., stiff paper wrappers. (ii), 13, (3) pages. $ 15.00

Printed in an edition limited to 1000 copies (Cahoon, p.79), A speech delivered at the Alfred E. Smith Memorial Dinner, New York City, October 17, 1957. Card from Frank Altschul, publisher of The Overbrook Press laid in.

990. (Overbrook Press) Malgaigne, Joseph Francois. CONSEILS POUR LE CHOIX D'UNE BIBLIOTHEQUE ECRITS POUR UNE JEUNE FILLE. N.P.: The Overbrook Press, 1936, 12mo., cloth spine, paper over boards, paper spine label. (viii), 22 pages. $ 65.00

Limited to 250 copies. Printed in black with a blue line border. Short introduction followed by the reprint of this 19th century essay written on forming a library. Greeting card from Frank Altschul, the printer, loosely inserted.

991. (Overbrook Press) Malik, Charles. WAR AND PEACE, A STATEMENT MADE BEFORE THE POLITICAL COMMITTEE OF THE GENERAL ASSEMBLY, NOVEMBER 23, 1949. Stamford: Overbrook Press, (1950), 8vo., cloth with gold lettering. (2), 44, (2) pages. $ 25.00

Limited to 1000 copies. The author was Lebanon's chief delegate to the United Nations and provides an analysis of the Soviet challenge. Introduction by Frank Altschul. Ex-Libris John DePol bookplate.

992. (Overbrook Press) Malik, Charles. WAR AND PEACE, A STATEMENT MADE BEFORE THE POLITICAL COMMITTEE OF THE GENERAL ASSEMBLY, NOVEMBER 23, 1949. Stamford: Overbrook Press, (1950), 8vo., cloth. 44, (2) pages. $ 20.00

Printed in an edition limited to 1000 copies (Cahoon, p.63). The author was Lebanon's Ambassador to the United States and its Delegate to the United Nations. The book is a contemporary analysis of the nature of the Soviet challenge. Card laid in "With the compliments of Frank Altschul," publisher of the Overbrook Press. John DePol bookplate on front pastedown.

993. (Overbrook Press) Tinker, Chauncey B. & Carl P. Rollins. ADDRESSES COMMEMORATING THE ONE HUNDREDTH ANNIVERSARY OF THE BIRTH OF WILLIAM MORRIS DELIVERED BEFORE THE YALE LIBRARY ASSOCIATES IN THE STERLING MEMORIAL LIBRARY. N.P.: The Overbrook Press, (1935), large 8vo., cloth, paper spine and cover labels, top edge gilt. (vi), 33 pages. $ 85.00

Limited to 450 copies. The border on the title page was designed by Valenti Angelo and the woodcut initials in blue were drawn by Anna Simons. Preface by Wilmarth Lewis. An early Overbrook Press production. Spine faded. Bookplate on front pastedown with offset from glue used.

994. (Overbrook Press) SAM A. LEWISOHN (1884–1951). Stamford: Overbrook Press, 1951, 8vo., stiff paper wrappers. 50, (2) pages. $ 15.00

Printed in an edition limited to 2100 copies in paper wrappers for the family and friends of Sam A. Lewisohn, a prominent New York businessman, art collector, and philanthropist (Cahoon, p.67). Memorial tributes, gravure portrait.

995. (Overbrook Press) Savile, George. LADY'S NEW-YEAR'S-GIFT, OR: ADVICE TO A DAUGHTER FROM THE MISCELLANIES OF GEORGE SAVILE, LORD MARQUESS OF HALIFAX. FIRST PRINTED FOR MATTHEW GILLYFLOWER: LONDON 1700. Stamford, CT: The Overbrook Press, 1934, small 8vo., boards, top edge gilt, slipcase. (vi), 107, (3) pages. $ 85.00

Limited to 300 copies. (Cahoon p.5 - the fourth production of the press). With a drawing by Valenti Angelo on the title page. (Angelo Biblio. p.53). Design and composition by Margaret B. Evans and presswork by John F. MacNamara.

996. (Overbrook Press) Seaman, William E. Rabbi. GEORGE. JOANNA. JAMES OAKES, IN MEMORIAM. Stamford: Overbrook Press, 1966, small 8vo., stiff paper wrappers. (iv), 7+(1) pages. $ 15.00

Printed in a limited edition for the family and friends of George, Joanna, and James Oakes. Remarks by Rabbi E. William Seaman, Washington Hebrew Congregation, Washington, D.C., January 8, 1965. Family photo as frontis.

997. (Overbrook Press) Seymour, Charles. WOODROW WILSON IN PERSPEC-TIVE. Stamford: Overbrook Press, 1956, 8vo., stiff paper wrappers. 21, (3) pages.

$ 15.00

Printed in an edition limited to 1000 copies by Frank Altschul at the Overbrook Press (Cahoon, p.77). Handset in Caslon Old Face type and printed on Bethany paper. Reprinted from *Foreign Affairs*. The author was President Emeritus of Yale University.

998. (Overbrook Press) SOVIET-AMERICAN RELATIONS. Stamford: Overbrook Press, 1946, 8vo., stiff paper wrappers. 17, (3) pages. $ 15.00

Printed in an edition limited to 1000 copies "for the convenience of the Delegates to the Assembly of the United Nations" by the Federal Council of the Churches of Christ in America. (Cahoon, p.50).Handset in Centaur and Arrighi types and printed in two colors on Ragston Wove paper.

999. (Overbrook Press) A SPECIMAN BOOK OF TYPES, ORNAMENTS AND MISCELLANY. Stamford, CT: Overbrook Press, 1948, large 8vo., quarter cloth, printed paper covered boards, paper spine label. (iv), 77+(1) leaves. $ 1,500.00

Printed in an edition limited to only fifty copies (Cahoon, p.57). Handset in various types, borders, rules, ornaments, etc., and printed in various colors on English Curfew Handmade paper. Includes large display faces in addition to ornaments, chess symbols, and color and black and white woodcuts by Rudolf Ruzicka and Valenti Angelo.

1000. (Overbrook Press) Streeter, Edward. ADDRESS DELIVERED AT THE DIN-NER FOR NEW MEMBERS OF THE CENTURY ASSOCIATION, OCTOBER 5, 1961. Stamford: The Century Association, 1962, large 12mo., stiff paper wrappers with paper cover label. (ii), 11, (3) pages. $ 10.00

Printed in an edition limited to 2500 copies by the Overbrook Press, for members of The Century Association. Anecdotes and information, including the advice, that since members are forbidden to talk about business, to "follow the policy of discussing only topics of which they are completely ignorant." Covers lightly soiled.

1001. (Overbrook Press) Thompson, Dorothy. IN SUPPORT OF THE PRESIDENT. Stamford, CT: The Overbrook Press, 1945, 12mo., boards, paper cover label. 29+(1) pages. $ 15.00

Limited to 1500 copies. (Cahoon p.44).

1002. (Overbrook Press) TYPES, BORDERS, RULES & DEVICES OF THE PRESS ARRANGED AS A KEEPSAKE. Stamford, CT: The Overbrook Press, 1934, 16mo., marbled paper covered boards, paper cover label. (24) pages. $ 350.00

Limited to 150 copies. (Ransom, Selected Checklist, no.1). Designed and hand-set at Frank Altschul's private press and printed in five colors. With a printed notice by the publisher loosely inserted.

1003. (Overbrook Press) Vincent, George Edgar (eulogy). GEORGE EDGAR VIN-CENT, ADDRESSES DELIVERED AT THE MEMORIAL SERVICES HELD ON MAY 19, 1941. Stamford: Overbrook Press, 1941, small 8vo., cloth. (vi), 54, (2) pages. $ 35.00

Printed in an edition limited to 350 copies (Cahoon, p.32). Eulogies and memorial tributes to an early member of Chautauqua, and former president of the University of Minnesota and the Rockefeller Foundation, with an address by John D. Rockefeller, Jr. Gravure portrait as frontis. Bookplate of John DePol. Some glue staining on endpapers near inner hinges.

1004. (Overbrook Press) Warren, Earl. THE BLESSINGS OF LIBERTY. Stamford: Overbrook Press, 1955, 8vo., blue stiff paper covers. 13, (3) pages. $ 17.50
Printed in an edition limited to 750 copies in two colors on Early American paper (Cahoon, p.76). Reprinted from an address delivered at the Second Century Convocation of Washington University, St. Louis, Mo., February 19, 1955. Handset in Lutetia type.

1005. (Overbrook Press) White, Alain et. al. A SKETCHBOOK OF AMERICAN CHESS PROBLEMATISTS. Two Volumes. Stamford: Overbrook Press, 1942, 12mo., cloth, slipcase. (iv),138; (iv),163,(3) pages. $ 300.00
Printed in an edition limited to 250 copies (Cahoon, p.34). Compiled by Alain White, Edgar W. Allen and Burney M. Marshall. Set in Linotype Fairfield and handset Lutetia types with chess diagrams. Printed in two colors on Winterbourne Tinted Laid paper. Selected as one of the Fifty Books of the Year by the American Institute of Graphic Arts. Ex-Libris John DePol bookplate on front pastedown

1006. (Overbrook Press) Wilde, Oscar. THE HAPPY PRINCE AND OTHER TALES. Stamford: The Overbrook Press, 1936, small 8vo., cloth-backed decorated paper covered boards, slipcase. (vi), 82, (4) pages. $ 350.00
Printed in an edition limited to 250 copies. (Cahoon p.9). With six full page wood engravings in two colors by Rudolph Ruzicka who has also designed the book. Well preserved copy. Bookplate of John DePol.

1007. (Overbrook Press) Wilkie, Wendell Lewis. OCCASIONAL ADDRESSES AND ARTICLES, TO WHICH ARE PREFIXED BIOGRAPHICAL SKETCHES. Stamford: Overbrook Press, 1940, large 8vo., cloth. (ix), ix, 394 pages. $ 35.00
Printed in an edition limited to 1000 copies (Cahoon, p. 27). Reprints of talks and magazine articles from "Fortune," "The North American Review," "New Republic," etc. Gravure portrait as frontispiece. Linotype set in Janson type, printed on W & A All Rag paper. John DePol bookplate on front pastedown

1008. (Overbrook Press) Wilson, Woodrow. CABINET GOVERNMENT IN THE UNITED STATES. Stamford: Overbrook Press, 1947, 8vo., green paper covered boards with paper cover label. xii, (ii), 30, (2) pages. $ 25.00
Limited to 1000 copies and printed for the Woodrow Wilson Foundation. (Cahoon p.56). Introduction by Thomas K. Finletter. " Ex-Libris John DePol" bookplate on front pastedown.

1009. (Overbrook Press) Zilboorg, Gregory. I WON'T APOLOGIZE, TWO LETTERS BY DR. GREGORY ZILBOORG. Stamford: Overbrook Press, 1938, large 12mo., stiff paper wrappers with an overall pattern designed by Valenti Angelo. (iv), 22, (4). $ 20.00
Limited to 500 copies set in Electra and printed on French fold Japanese paper (Cahoon, p.18). The beginning of the first letter states that "Jew-baiting is becoming brazen here in America," and concludes that "the warning may not be passed over heedlessly," in Hitler's Germany or elsewhere.

1010. (Oyez Press) Everson, William (Brother Antoninus). THE LAST CRUSADE. N.P.: Oyez, (1969), small folio, quarter vellum with cloth covered boards. (vi), 25, (i) pages. $ 250.00
Printed in an edition limited to 165 numbered and signed copies. Designed and printed by Graham Mackintosh. Printed in red and black on Arches paper, bound by Jack Gray. XIVth century heraldic device on title page printed in red. A lovely book.

1011. (Oyez Press) Everson, William. RIVER-ROOT, A SYZGY FOR THE BICENTENNIAL OF THESE STATES. Berkley: Oyez Press, 1976, 4to., quarter leather with decorated paper covered boards. 50, (3) pages. $ 225.00
Printed in an edition limited to 250 numbered and signed copies. A collection of poems by William Everson. Illustrations are by Patrick Kennedy and the design is by Thomas Whitridge. Includes an afterword by the author.

[173]

1012. (Pandora Press) Campion, Thomas. THE MAN OF LIFE UPRIGHT. Leicester: Pandora Press, 1962, small 8vo., stiff paper wrappers. (12) pages. $ 55.00
Printed in an edition limited to 130 numbered copies. A poem by Campion which is illustrated with six woodcuts by Rigby Graham.

1013. (Paul Elder & Company) Jordan, David Starr. ERIC'S BOOK OF BEASTS. San Francisco: Paul Elder, (1912), large 12mo., quarter cloth with paper covered boards. (ii), 112 (4) pages. $ 45.00
First edition. Printed by Paul Elder on a Tomoye Press. Designed by John Swart, with decorations by Jean Oliver. The original fifty-four watercolors by the author rendered in black and white by Shimada Sekko. A few pages uncut and some others torn at edges but all plates intact.

1014. (Paulinus Press) Braybrooke, Neville. FOUR POEMS FOR CHRISTMAS. Marlborough: Paulinus Press, 1986, small 4to., stiff paper wrappers, cord-tied. (20) pages. $ 45.00
Limited edition of 250 numbered copies. Signed by author and engraver on colophon. Four poems: "Sheep," "Joseph Speaks," "Mary Speaks," and "The Wise Men," together with a brief essay on Joseph, "The Forgotten Man." Poems had previously appeared elsewhere.

1015. (Peacock Press) Richardson, Ernest Cushing. SOME OLD EGYPTIAN LI-BRARIANS. Berkeley: Peacock Press, 1964, 12mo., paper wrappers. (x), 94 pages. $ 15.00
Reissue of the 1911 first edition. The author sites various sources in Egyptian writings to describe the library as it existed in ancient Egypt.

1016. (Peacock Press) Shores, Louis. AROUND THE LIBRARY WORLD IN 76 DAYS AN ESSAY IN COMPARATIVE LIBRARIANSHIP. Berkeley: Peacock Press, 1967, 12mo., paper wrappers. 28 pages. $ 15.00
First edition. Recounts his round-the-world tour of libraries.

1017. (Peacock Press) Thompson, Lawrence S. BIBLIOKLEPTOMANIA. Berkeley: Peacock Press, 1968, small 4to., paper wrappers. 40 pages. $ 25.00
First separate appearance. The history of book theft. Covers faded.

1018. (Peacock Press) Thompson, Lawrence S. INCURABLE MANIA. Berkeley: Pea-cock Press, 1966, 12mo., paper wrappers. 24 pages. $ 15.00
First edition. Autobiography of a book collector.

1019. (Penmaen Press) Connellan, Leo. CROSSING AMERICA. Lincoln, MA: Pen-maen Press, (1976), 8vo., cloth. (38) pages. $ 45.00
Printed in an edition limited to 200 numbered copies signed by the author. Hand-printed by Michael McCurdy, Scott-Martin Kosofsky and Sidney Licht. The title-page wood engraving and the type-setting are by Michael McCurdy. Original binding design by Robert Hauser.

1020. (Penmaen Press) Csoori, Sandor. MEMORY OF SNOW. Great Barrington, (MA): Penmaen Press, (1983), 8vo., cloth, dust jacket. 67, (3) pages. $ 45.00
Printed in an edition limited to 750 copies of which this is one of 200 copies bound i boards. Includes a woodcut of the author by Michael McCurdy.

1021. (Penmaen Press) Peich, Michael. A FIRST TEN: A PENMAEN BIBLIOGRA-PHY. Lincoln (MA): Penmaen Press, 1978, 8vo., cloth, cloth-covered slipcase. ix, (iii), 34, (2), xiii [sic], (4) pages, with 16 additional pages of plates. $ 125.00
The special edition, limited to 100 numbered copies and signed the six participants. This edition contains an extra plate inserted in a folder which is one of 100 numbered copies signed by McCurdy. Descriptive bibliography of the productions of the Penmaen Press. With an introduction by Peich, an afterword by the wood engraver and owner of the Press, Michael McCurdy, and four chapters: Books (12 entries), Broadsides (8 entries), Ephemera (14), and Plates (16 pages with 25 illustrations, including 4 photographs). Book entries give complete collations and describe various editions. Title page and chapter openings have wood engravings by Michael McCurdy. With half-title page and colophon devices (engraver unidentified). Spine and slipcase faded. The folder containing the extra plate is also faded. Prospectus loosely inserted.

1022. (Penmiel Press) Burrett, Edward. TRIBUTE TO DIANA BLOOMFIELD, A POT-POURRI OF HER WOOD ENGRAVINGS AND DRAWINGS. Esher, Surrey: Penmiel Press, 1985, 8vo., cloth, plain stiff paper slipcase. 27, (3) pages. $ 85.00
Limited to 150 copies; signed by E. Burrett. Sixty-plus engravings and drawings by the English engraver, D. Bloomfield: Sketches, bookplates, vignettes, text illustrations, head- and tail pieces, and other designs. Mostly smaller pieces. With a preface by E. Burrett of Penmiel Press, who also designed and printed the book, and brief postscript by Bloomfield. Endpapers reproduce a monograph design, and the cover illustration is a gilt-stamped reproduction from a Bloomfield drawing. In Monotype Baskerville, offset.

1023. (Pennyroyal Press) Moser, Barry. THE HOLY BIBLE. Two volumes. West Hatfield, Massachusetts: Pennroyal Caxton Press, 1999, folio, full vellum over boards, each volume housed in a cloth clam shell case with a paper spine label. The title is stamped in gilt on the front board and spine.   (xiv),187+(1),(vi),247+(1),(vi)109,(9); (x),197,(3),(viii),234,(14) pages. $ 10,000.00
Printed in an edition limited to 425 copies, this being one of 400 copies printed on Zerkall Bible paper. The Pennyroyal Caxton Bible follows Frederick H. A. Scrivener's 1873 critical edition of the Cambridge Paragraph Bible of the Authorized English Version. Volume one contains the first three sections, the Pentateuch, the Historical Books, and the Poetical Books. Volume two contains sections four and five, the Prophets and the Books of the New Testament. Moser has cut over 235 stunning illustrations which have been executed in a new engraving medium called Resingrave, a cast, white polymer resin, and are printed directly from the blocks. This is the first edition of twentieth century in which both the Old and the New Testaments are illustrated by a single artist. The paper is Zerkall Bible, which was manufactured especially for this project and it bears the unique watermark of the Pennyroyal Caxton Press. The type is Matthew Carter's Galliard and the composition is by Bradley Hutchinson of Texas, one of the finest letterpress printers in America. Titles and versal letters are set in Matthew Carter's Mantinia, a typeface based on inscriptional forms used by the Italian Renaissance painter Andrea Mantegna. Three display words have been designed by letter cutter, John Benson, especially for this project. A magnificent production, this book ranks among the greatest achievements of twentieth-century fine bookmaking because of its attention to detail, artwork and typography.

1024. (Pennyroyal Press) PENNYROYAL, A CHECKLIST OF BOOKS, POSTERS AND BROADSIDES FROM PENNYROYAL PRESS 1969 TO 1986. With a Listing of Miscellaneous Books and Broadsides Illustrated with Original Art for other Publishers. West Hatfield (MA): Pennyroyal Press, 1986, 8vo., stiff paper wrappers. (58) pages, 1 sheet. $ 25.00
Listing of 48 books published by Pennyroyal from 1969-86, 83 posters and broadsides printed by them, and 18 items "illustrated with original art for other publishers." Introduction gives history of press.

1025. (Pentagram Press) Tarachow, Michael. GLINT ORNAMENTS AT WORK AND PLAY. Minneapolis, MN: Pentagram Press, 2001, small 4to., Japanese linen portfolio, leather cover label. 13 leaves, 2 cards with envelopes. $ 225.00
Printed in an edition limited to 42 sets. Using only two decorative fleurons designed by Dr. David Bethel and released by Monotype under the family name of Glint, Tarachow designed and printed this collection of small broadsides that showcase the ornament's versatility. With quotes about printing from Bruce Rogers, Eric Gill, Richard Hoffman, Leonard Bahr, Emerson G. Wulling and Carl Dair, and literary exerpts from Bethel, Larry Fahnoe, Lew Welch, Clifford Burke, Charles Olson, and William Blake, each example provides a unique combination of paper, ornaments and text. Japanese papers, mouldmade French and Italian sheets and domestic machine made papers were all used. A few Pentagram Holiday cards that feature the Glints are also included.

1026. (Periwinkle Press) A.E. [George Russell]. A GOLD STANDARD FOR LITERATURE. Norton, MA: Periwinkle Press, 1939, 8vo., pattern paper covered boards. (14) pages. $ 45.00
Limited to edition of 200 signed copies. This excerpt from *The Living Touch* presents George Russell's thoughts on the need to stem the proliferation of books with nothing "important" to say. Hand printed on Highclere English handmade paper with three small blue illustrations decorating the text.

1027. (Periwinkle Press) Burton, Katherine. ANDREW CARNEGIE,... SOMETHING OF THE FAIRY TALE... (Norton: Periwinkle Press, 1939), 12mo., boards. (16) pages. $ 45.00
First edition, limited to 200 copies printed by hand on handmade paper. Number 5 of the Bibliolatrous Series. Scarce biographical sketch of this American book collector.

1028. (Periwinkle Press) Burton, Katherine. HENRY CLAY FOLGER, "... FOR I AM AN AMERICAN". (Norton: Periwinkle Press, 1939), 12mo., boards. (16) pages. $ 45.00
First edition, limited to 200 copies printed by hand on handmade paper. Number 7 of the Bibliolatrous Series. Scarce biographical sketch of this American book collector who formed a superb Shakespeare collection.

1029. (Periwinkle Press) Burton, Katherine. HENRY E. HUNTINGTON, "THIS LIBRARY WILL TELL THE STORY". Norton: Periwinkle Press, 1939, 12mo., boards. (16) pages. $ 45.00
First edition, limited to 200 copies printed by hand on handmade paper. Number 6 of the Bibliolatrous Series. Scarce biographical sketch of this American book collector and friend of Rosenbach.

1030. (Periwinkle Press) Burton, Katherine. SIR JOHN COTTON "... FOR PUBLIC USE AND ADVANTAGE." Norton: Periwinkle Press, 1939, 12mo., boards. (16) pages. $ 45.00
First edition, limited to 150 copies printed by hand on handmade paper. Number 3 of the Bibliolatrous Series. Scarce biographical sketch of this book collector, the grandson of Sir Robert Cotton. Scarce.

1031. (Periwinkle Press) Burton, Katherine. ST. COLUMBA, "TO EVERY COW HER CALF..." (Norton: Periwinkle Press, 1938), 12mo., boards. (12) pages. $ 45.00
First edition, limited to 150 copies printed by hand on handmade paper. Number 1 of the Bibliolatrous Series. Scarce biographical sketch of the patron Saint of book collectors according to the author.

1032. (Perpetua Press) Austin, William. THE POEMS OF WILLIAM AUSTIN. Oxford: Perpetua Press, (1983), small 4to., quarter cloth with paper-covered boards, slipcase. xvi, 31+(1) pages. $ 95.00

Printed in an edition limited to 150 numbered copies, hand-set in 18pt. Bembo, printed on Old Mill paper wove from the Cartiera Fedrigoni, Verona, Italy, by Vivian Ridler, and signed by her and Anne Ridler. Edited with an introduction by Anne Ridler. William Austin (1587–1634) published nothing in his lifetime, although he did send copies of his poems to his friends. His nine extant poems were published by his widow in the year following his death and quickly sold out--probably limited to 1500 copies, according to the custom of the times. Some spotting to spine.

1033. (Peter Pauper Press) Baudelaire, Charles. FLOWERS OF EVIL. Mount Vernon, NY: Peter Pauper Press, (1958), large 12mo., pictorial paper covered boards. (ii), 61+(1) pages. $ 15.00

First edition. (Remembering Peter, p. 69) Translated by Jacques LeClercq one hundred years after they were first published, the poems presented here were taken from the complete text of *Les Fleurs du Mal*, or *Flowers of Evil*. While Baudelaire's poetic genius can only be hinted at in translation, his interpretation of the anguish of the human dilemma still shines through. Two-color woodcuts by Jeff Hill.

1034. (Peter Pauper Press) Haas, Irvin. BRUCE ROGERS: A BIBLIOGRAPHY, HITHERTO UNRECORDED WORK 1889–1925. COMPLETE WORK, 1925–1936. With a Letter of Introduction by Beatrice Warde. Mount Vernon, NY: Peter Pauper Press, 1936, 8vo., cloth, paper spine label. viii, 72, (2) pages. $ 75.00

First edition, limited to 425 copies. Booklabel of Leonard F. Bahr. Errata slip loosely inserted.

1035. (Peter Pauper Press) Kipling, Rudyard. BARRACK-ROOM BALLADS & DEPARTMENTAL DITTIES. Mount Vernon, NY: Peter Pauper Press, n.d. (but 1948), small 8vo., paper covered boards. 78 pages. $ 45.00

Decorated by Fritz Kredel. inscription in ink on front free endpaper. John DePol bookplate on front pastedown. Small tear at top of slipcase.

1036. (Peter Pauper Press) THE LOVE LETTERS OF HENRY VIII TO ANNE BOLYNE. Mount Vernon: Peter Pauper Press, n.d. (but 1937), small 8vo., decorated paper covered boards, paper spine and cover labels, top edge stained red. 57+(1) pages. $ 20.00

Printed in an edition limited to 1,450 copies. (Recalling Peter, p. 52) Portraits by John Rudolph of King Henry and Queen Anne bring life to these letters that document the fleeting passion of a king. Paul Noble Banks bookplate detached from front pastedown and loosely inserted. Spine chipped, cover worn.

1037. (Peter Pauper Press) POOR RICHARD'S ALMANACK. Mount Vernon: Peter Pauper Press, (1987), 8vo., boards, dust jacket. (80) pages. $ 25.00

Special gift book issued by Blackwell North America. Illustrated with a number of woodcuts printed in brown ink.

1038. (Peter Pauper Press) Ramsey, Betty Jo (editor). THE LITTLE BOOK OF FAMOUS INSULTS. Mount Vernon, NY: Peter Pauper Press, (1964), large 12mo., paper-covered boards, dust jacket. 60 pages. $ 17.50

Illustrated by Fritz Kredel. Include's Winston Churchill's description of Clement Atlee as "A sheep in sheep's clothing."

1039. (Peter Pauper Press) Stiles, Henry Reed. BUNDLING; ITS ORIGINS, PROGRESS AND DECLINE IN AMERICA. Mount Vernon, NY: Peter Pauper Press, n.d. (but 1937), 8vo., later full leather, leather spine label. 88, (2) pages. $ 35.00
First edition. (Recalling Peter, p. 52) Written in 1871 and "reprinted for the enlightenment of the present generation," this is a spirited look at the origin, practice and decline of a decidedly non-Puritanical custom in New England. Wood cuts by Herb Roth printed in maroon. Label of Clement Samford, Bookbinder, glued to rear pastedown. Cover discolored and slightly rubbed at edges and back of spine.

1040. (Pickering, William) ARISTOPHANES. A METRICAL VERSION OF THE ACHARNIANS THE KNIGHTS AND THE BIRDS IN THE LAST OF WHICH A VEIN OF PECULIAR HUMOUR AND CHARACTER IS FOR THE FIRST TIME DETECTED AND DEVELOPED. London: William Pickering, 1840, 4to., original limp blue cloth with original paper spine label. variously paginated. $ 325.00
First edition thus, translated by John Hookham Frere. Not described by Keynes. A note in pencil which is loosely inserted states that only a few copies of this book were printed for private distribution amongst the translator's friends with a few copies being given to Pickering for sale. A metrical version of the Acharnians The Knights and The Birds, in which a vein of peculiar humor and character is for the first time detected and developed. Dicaeopolis is the principal character in this play who is driven from his house and property to take shelter in the city. His whole thoughts are occupied with regret for the comforts he has lost, and with wishes for a speedy peace. Translated by John Hookham Frere. Slight marginal water stain on title and several other leaves but generally well preserved. The paper spine label is worn and chipped. Some splitting on spine.

1041. (Pickering Press) A COMMONPLACE BOOK. Madison, NJ: Fairleigh Dickinson University, 1982, small 8vo., paper wrappers. Unpaginated. $ 25.00
A small pamphlet, consisting of six leaves sewn into a paper wrapper, with quotes from various sources "Set in various types by divers hands with mild guidance from John Anderson." Appears to be a project done by a class in fine printing taught by John Anderson of Pickering Press.

1042. (Pickering Press) Fraser, James. INTRODUCTORY COMMENT TO THE PUBLICATION OF A FACSIMILE EDITION OF HUGO STEINER-PRAG'S MANUSCRIPT BOOK, RUND UM PARIZKA 28. Madison, NJ: The Florham-Madison Campus Library, Farleigh Dickinson University, 1987, 8vo., stiff paper wrappers. 13+(1) pages. $ 20.00
Designed, hand-set, and printed by John Anderson at the Pickering Press in an edition limited to 200 copies (Anderson, pp.73-4). Issued for the opening of an exhibition marking this important collection's addition to the library. Illustration.

1043. (Pickering Press) Fraser, James H. EARLY PRINTING IN MORRISTOWN, NEW JERSEY. Morristown, NJ: The Joint Free Library of Morristown and Morristown Township, 1970, large 8vo., loosely inserted in stiff paper wrappers. 30 (2) pages. $ 25.00
First edition. Printed by John Anderson at the Pickering Press. Lists 57 items with occasional illustrations. Introduction and compiling by James H. Fraser. Includes frontispiece of an early imprint.

1044. (Pickering Press) Gill, Eric. THE PROCRUSTEAN BED. Philadephia: The Pickering Press, 1957, small 8vo., paper wrappers, paper cover label. (14) pages. unopened copy. $ 55.00
Describes the process in which printers create a neat appearance of printed pages. The Pickering Pattern paper engraved in wood by John DePol. The engraving facing the title page was also cut in wood by John DePol.

1045. (Pickering Press) [LOT OF 18 PIECES OF EPHEMERA FROM THE PICK-ERING PRESS]. Philadelphia: Pickering Press. $ 35.00

A lot of ephemera printed by John Anderson at his Pickering Press (1947–1987), based mostly in Philadelphia and Maple Shade, NJ. The lot of 18 pieces contains many commercial brochures, as well as a label for *Anderson's Party Whisky*, a selection from *The Complete Angler* issued as a keepsake for Juniata College, and 2 leaves of colored wood engravings signed by John DePol of *The Falls at Deepende*.

1046. (Pickering Press) NEW FACES. Maple Shade: Pickering Press, n.d., 16mo., paper covers. 4 panel fold out. $ 17.50

The first showing of much of the typographic material exhibited in Philadelphia. Examples of designs from this press.

1047. (Pickering Press) Rushmore, Arthur W. F.W.G., A TRIBUTE TO FREDERIC WILLIAM GOUDY, 1865–1947. (Philadelphia): Pickering Press, 1952), 8vo., stiff paper wrappers. 3 pages in French fold. $ 20.00

Printed by John Anderson at the Pickering Press, in an edition limited to 100 copies (Anderson, page 56). Type set by the author in Goudy Medieval in French fold. This text was written shortly after Goudy's death as a "spontaneous, personal tribute to an old friend. It was never intended for publication and only recently has Mr. Rushmore been persuaded to permit its issuance in this form." Small crease at right front cover.

1048. (Pinch-Penny Press) Anderson, Frank J. PRIVATE PRESSES IN THE SOUTHEASTERN UNITED STATES. Starkville: The Pinch-Penny Press, 1972, small 8vo., paper wrappers. 43 pages. $ 25.00

First edition, one of 1000 copies. A listing of presses in the area with brief biographical histories of each.

1049. (Plain Wrapper Press) Rummonds, Richard-Gabriel. EPHEMERA., PLAIN WRAPPER PRESS. Verona: Plain Wrapper Press, 1970–1987, various sizes, gathered in a folio sized cloth clamshell box with a red leather spine label. variously paginated. $ 350.00

Approximately 35 pieces of ephemera including book prospectuses, catalogues of books in-print, order forms, several small booklets, cards, keepsakes, small broadsides, etc. Many are finely printed on a variety of colored papers. Many items contain illustrations printed from the blocks or plates.

1050. (Plain Wrapper Press) Santucci, Luigi. THE WOMAN WITH HER MOUTH OPEN. (Verona): Plain Wrappers Press, (1980), 4to., full unbleached limp vellum over boards with calf tapes at spine and calf ties at fore edge, chemise with gilt-stamped matching vellum spine, slipcase. 43, (2) pages. $ 750.00

First edition, limited to 110 press copies signed by author and artist. (Smyth 26). A short story in Italian, with an English translation, about a pregnant woman whose child speaks to her. Includes a three page color screen print by Emilio Tadini. Printed on "GF" handmade wove paper with handset Enschedé Spectrum using a Washington handpress in black and orange. Bound at the press by Carol Joyce. Yellow Van Heek-Scholco Brillianta cloth endpapers.

1051. (Plantin Press) Adler, Patricia. POEMS AND SONGS. Los Angeles: Plantin Press, 1969, 8vo., quarter cloth with pattern paper boards, paper spine label. (vi), 37, (3) pages. $ 65.00

Printed in an edition limited to 325 copies printed by Saul and Lillian Marks at the Plantin Press. Slim volume of contemporary poetry. Presentation copy signed in ink on front free endpaper with several pieces of correspondence laid in.

1052. (Plantin Press) Barrett, Edna Dueringer. MRS. COLLETTI AND OTHER POEMS. Los Angeles: Suttonhouse, (1936), small 8vo., cloth. (vi), 79+(1) pages.

$ 35.00

Printed and bound by Saul Marks at the Plantin Press in an edition limited to 500 copies. Illustrated by Henry Shire, with decorated binding and endpapers.

1053. (Plantin Press) Carpenter, Edwin H. (Editor). A SIXTEENTH CENTURY MEXICAN BROADSIDE FROM THE COLLECTION OF EMILIO VALTON. Los Angeles: Plantin Press, 1965, 4to., quarter buckram with paper covered boards, paper spine label. (ii), 14 pages. $ 45.00

Printed in an edition limited to 140 copies printed by Saul & Lillian Marks at the Plantin Press, for Dawson's Book Shop, Los Angeles. Described, with a Checklist, by Edwin H. Carpenter. Printing was introduced into Mexico from Spain in the later years of the sixteenth century and are classified as American incunabula. The broadsides in Valton's collection were mostly legal forms required by the Spanish bureaucracy and the business transactions of ordinary citizens. This copy was probably a press overrun and lacks the broadside otherwise laid in. Still, a nice copy of a work by a distinguished printer on handmade paper.

1054. (Plantin Press) NICOLAUS COPERNICUS, 1473–1973, HIS REVOLUTIONS AND HIS REVOLUTION. Bethlehem, PA: Lehigh University, 1973, 4to., stiff paper wrappers. (iv), 49+(1) pages. $ 25.00

Beautifully printed exhibition catalogue. Limited to 1500 copies printed by Saul and Lillian Marks at the Plantin Press. Foreword by James D. Mack and catalogue and historical essay by Seymour L. Chapin.

1055. (Plantin Press) Corwin, Norman. PRAYER FOR THE '70s. Los Angeles: Plantin Press, (1972), small 4to., patterned paper covered boards, paper spine and cover labels. (12) pages. $ 75.00

Edition of 100 copies printed for Joyce Reed Rosenberg by Saul and Lillian Marks. This contemporary prayer was printed in black with a red ornament on the title page and red capitals scattered throughout the text. Front cover has four abrasions to front cover

1056. (Plantin Press) Crispin, Angela. GOLD TREASURES AND OTHER POEMS. Los Angeles: Plantin Press, 1966, small 8vo., quarter buckram with handmade paper-covered boards, paper cover label. (vi), 69+(1) pages. $ 25.00

A collection of 69 poems printed by Saul Marks at the Plantin Press. Some of the poems previously appeared in The American Bard, The American Poet, Authors and Artists of America, The Muse, etc.

1057. (Plantin Press) Crotty, Homer D. GLIMPSES OF DON QUIXOTE & LA MANCHA. Los Angeles: Plantin Press, 1963, large 8vo., quarter cloth with marbled paper covered boards, paper spine label. xviii (vi), 42, (4) pages. $ 45.00

Printed in an edition of 250 copies for the Zamorano Club (Marks, 43-43), with an Introductory Essay by Walter Fitzwilliam Starkie. The author's travels in the early 1960's following the footsteps of Don Quixote and Sancho Panza, from Seville to La Mancha. "I am sure there must be many Don Quixotes remaining in Spain, but their presence is far from obtrusive. On the other hand, the number of Sancho Panzas is beyond count." Illustrated with photographs, decorations, and facsimiles of early printings. Some offsetting on pastedowns.

1058. (Plantin Press) Digby, Kenelme. SR. KENELME DIGBYES HONOUR MAINTAINED BY A MOST COURAGIOUS COMBAT WHICH HE FOUGHT WITH THE LORD MOUNT LE ROS, WHO BY BASE AND SLANDEROUS WORDS REVILED OUR KING. Los Angeles: (K. Garth Huston, 1970), large 12mo., stiff paper wrappers. (ii), 7, (3) pages. $ 22.50
Printed for K. Garth Huston by Saul & Lillian Marks at the Plantin Press in an edition limited to 150 copies. An essay about this book which was originally printed in London in 1641, only four copies are known to exist. With reproduction of the woodcut from the title page of a copy in the British Museum.

1059. (Plantin Press) Cobden-Sanderson T.J. Dreyfus, John (editor). FOUR LECTURES BY T.J. COBDEN-SANDERSON. San Francisco: The Book Club of California, 1974, 4to., cloth backed boards, paper label on the spine. xi, 105+(1) pages. $ 175.00
S-K 5544. Printed in an edition limited to 450 copies printed by Saul and Lillian Marks at the Plantin Press. Contains and introductory essay on Cobden-Sanderson's life, with details of his American pupils, and his lectures in the United States in 1907. Illustrated.

1060. (Plantin Press) FRA GIOVANNI'S GREETING OF 1513 A.D. PRINTED FOR FRIENDS OF A.T. BRUGGER: CHRISTMAS 1965. N.P.: n.p., 1965, 8 3/4 x 6 inches, self paper wrappers. [4] pages. $ 17.50
First edition. Single folded leaf printed in red and black with engraved illustration. Small blemish to front cover, edges faded.

1061. (Plantin Press) Frierman, Jay D. (editor). THE NATALIE WOOD COLLECTION OF PRE-COLUMBIAN CERAMICS FROM CHUPICUARO, GUANAJUATO, MEXICO. Los Angeles: UCLA Museum & Laboratories of Ethnic Arts & Technology, 1969, small 4to., cloth, paper spine and cover label. xvi, 92, (4) pages.
                    $ 75.00
Limited to two hundred copies in special binding printed for Dawson's Bookshop, Los Angeles, by Saul & Lillian Marks, The Plantin Press. Number 1 in the series of Occasional Papers issued by the museum. Photographs of each figure by staff photographer William Doherty. Monograph studies by Muriel Porter Weaver, et.al., with a photographic catalogue of the collection and an inventory of the burials excavated at Chupicuaro in 1946-7, with maps.

1062. (Plantin Press) GRAPHIC ARTS COLLECTION, UCLA ART RENTAL PROGRAM. Los Angeles: University of California, 1965, large 8vo., stiff paper wrappers. (20) pages. $ 17.50
First edition. Catalogue of prints available to UCLA students to provide them with the experience of daily living with original works of art. Cover illustration is a 1913 woodcut by Erich Heckel.

1063. (Plantin Press) Heifetz, Milton D. THE AESTHETIC PRINCIPLE. Los Angeles: The Plantin Press, 1966, large 8vo., paper wrappers. (ii), 15+(1) pages. $ 15.00
First edition. This essay first appeared in the Summer, 1966 issue of the *Art Journal* of the College Art Association of America.

1064. (Plantin Press) Hilton, William Hayes. SKETCHES IN THE SOUTHWEST AND MEXICO 1858–1877. Los Angeles: Plantin Press, 1963, large oblong 12mo., buckram spine with paper-covered boards. ix, (52) pages. $ 45.00
First edition. Printed for Dawson's Book Shop by Saul Marks at the Plantin Press. Introduction and notes by Carey S. Bliss. Twenty-five reproductions taken from the collection of Hilton's drawings on file at the Huntington Library, San Marino, California. Hilton was a soldier, miner, cattle drover, and rancher, who, as a diversion for himself and his friends sketched many western scenes often described but rarely pictured, throughout Texas, Mexico, Arizona and California from 1858 to 1877 and possibly later. The

drawings illustrate trips on the Butterfield Overland Stage in 1858 and 1859; mining, prospecting and hunting in Arizona and California about 1862-64; Hilton's career in Mexico, 1862–1869, and sketches around Monterey, San Francisco and Northern California between 1870 and 1877.

1065. (Plantin Press) AN INTRODUCTION TO THE DEPARTMENT OF SPE-CIAL COLLECTIONS AT THE STANFORD UNIVERSITY LIBRARIES. Stanford, CA: (Stanford University), 1973, large 8vo., paper wrappers, cord tied. 24, (2) pages. $ 15.00
First edition. Describes ten various rare and special collections that are maintained at the Stanford University Library.

1066. (Plantin Press) Kessler, Jascha. WHATEVER LOVE DECLARES. Los Angeles: Plantin Press, 1969, 8vo., cloth-backed boards, paper spine label. (viii), 59, (3) pages. $ 35.00
Printed in an edition limited to 500 copies by Saul & Lillian Marks at the Plantin Press. Poems mostly reprinted from periodicals here and abroad, includes *Satires, Elegies,* and *Invocations*

1067. (Plantin Press) Marks, Saul and Lillian. HOLIDAY GREETING AND GOOD WISHES FOR THE NEW YEAR. Los Angeles: Plantin Press, 1964, small 4to., stiff paper wrappers. (4) pages. $ 20.00
Holiday greeting card containing foldout leaf of lavishly-detailed woodcut, *Ornamental Design with Satyr & Nymph,* by German Northern Renaissance engraver Hans Sebald Beham (1500–1550).

1068. (Plantin Press) Meadows, Don. BAJA CALIFORNIA, 1533–1950 A BIBLIO-HISTORY. Los Angeles: Glen Dawson, 1951, large 12mo., pictorial cloth. (ii), 32, (4) pages. $ 25.00
First edition, printed by Saul and Lillian Marks at the Plantin Press. The sixty titles selected for this small volume provide a "detailed history of conditions and affairs in the Long arm of Mexico from the time of its discovery to 1950." Publisher's card signed for presentation loosely inserted. Number Four in the Early California Travels Series. Cover silverfished.

1069. (Plantin Press) Nethery, Wallace. ELIANA AMERICANA. Los Angeles: The Plantin Press, 1971, large 12mo., quarter cloth with paper covered boards, and a gold stamped label. (ii), 42 pages. $ 35.00
Printed in an edition of 350 copies. An account of Charles Lamb's transatlantic reputation and publishing history, from the pirates' earliest raids, to the appearance of Final Memorials with its revelation, fourteen years after his death. Indexed.

1070. (Plantin Press) Nunis, Doyce B.(Ed.). SAINT STANISLAW, BISHOP OF KRAKÓW IN COMMEMORATION OF THE 900TH ANNIVERSARY OF HIS MARTYRDOM IN 1079. Santa Barbara, CA: Saint Stanislaw Publications Committee, 1979, small 4to., cloth, dust jacket. 83, (4) pages. $ 15.00
First edition. The life of the patron saint of Poland, published under auspices of the California Chapter of the Polish American Historical Association. Dedicated to His Holiness, Pope John Paul II, with a foreword by His Eminence John Cardinal Krol, Archbishop of Philadelphia. Printed by the Plantin Press.

1071. (Plantin Press) Osler, Sir William. SIR KENELM DIGBY'S POWDER OF SYMPATHY. Los Angeles: Plantin Press, 1972, large 12mo., paper covered boards, dust jacket. xiv, (vi), 33, (3) pages. $ 35.00
First edition, printed by Saul Marks at the Plantin Press. An Unfinished Essay by Sir William Osler. Introduction and Notes by K. Garth Huston, M.D. Based on a talk given by Osler before the Johns Hopkins Historical Club on November 12, 1900. Digby's book was first published in 1658 and chiefly de-

scribed a salve to heal wounds suffered in battle, along with the influence of suggestion, and wrapping it from the air. With facsimiles of original title page, Osler's manuscript, and portrait of Digby printed in 1621.

1072. (Plantin Press) Ovid. THE CREATION AND THE FOUR AGES. (Los Angeles: The Plantin Press, 1971), large 8vo., paper wrappers, cord tied. (12) pages. $ 25.00
First edition. Printed for friends of Saul and Lillian Marks, this pamphlet is highlighted with a blue ornament and section titles and two red initial capitals.

1073. (Plantin Press) Plantin, Christophe. LE BONHEUR DE CE MONDE. Los Angeles: University of California, 1971, small 4to., single leaf. single leaf. $ 25.00
Sonnet composed by founder of original Plantin Press in Antwerp and printed on a single leaf of handmade paper for members of the Renaissance Conference of Southern California. Printed in Aldine Bembo types on Albion handpress of Bibliographical Printing Chapel, School of Library Service, UCLA. Typography by Plantin Press.

1074. (Plantin Press) [PLANTIN PRESS EPHEMERA]. (Los Angeles: Plantin Press), 1967 - 1977, variously sized. variously paginated. $ 35.00
Collection of 12 broadsides, book prospectuses, and catalogs, all finely printed on handmade paper with printer's ornaments and illustrations. Sizes range from miniature prospectus for Robert Louis Stevenson's *Prayers Written at Vailima* to small 4to. sample from *A Tribute to Elmer Belt* exhibition catalog.

1075. (Plantin Press) Schedel, Hartmann. SARMATIA, THE EARLY POLISH KINGDOM, TRANSLATED, WITH INTRODUCTION AND NOTES, BY BOGDEN DERESIEWICZ. Los Angeles: The Plantin Press, 1976, large 8vo., buckram, paper spine label. 48, (2) pages. $ 175.00
Limited to 350 numbered copies and signed by the translator on the colophon. The Nuremberg physician and humanist, Hartmann Schedel (1440–1514) wrote the Liber Cronicarum (the so-called "Nuremberg Chronicle") from 1491 to 1493, in which year it was printed in Nuremberg by Anton Koberger. Schedel's section on "Sarmatia" (i.e. Poland) is based on printed sources (many from his own library) and probably on information obtained from various informants. This translation by B. Deresiewicz has 5 parts: "The Early Polish Kingdom," "St. Stanislaw," "Krakow," "Lübeck" (which, for publishing reasons, appeared with the "Sarmatia" material in Schedel's work), and "Nysa," each with notes by the translator. Five of the original woodcuts by Michael Wohlgemut (to whom Dürer was apprenticed) and Wilhelm Pleydenwurff are reproduced. The front cover has a gilt-stamped decoration (about 2x2 in.). Decorated endpapers.

1076. (Plantin Press) Serra, Fray Junípero. TURNING THE TIDE, A LETTER WRITTEN BY FRAY JUNÍPERO SERRA, O.F.M. THAT SUSTAINED SPAINISH COLONIZATION OF ALTA CALIFORNIA. Los Angeles: The Zamorano Club, 1970, large 8vo., stiff paper wrappers. (viii), 6, 11, (3) pages. $ 75.00
Limited to an edition of 150 copies. Reproduced for the first time in facsimile, this letter from Father Junípero Serra strongly encouraged the continuing support of the Mexican viceroy for the port of San Blas in 1773. Translated by Antonine Tibesar, O.F.M., this keepsake was printed by Saul and Lillian Marks at the Plantin Press to commemorate the 1970 joint meeting in Los Angeles of the Roxburghe Club and the Zamorano Club.

1077. (Plantin Press) Steinitz, Kate T. PIERRE-JEAN MARIETTE & LE COMTE DE CAYLUS AND THEIR CONCEPT OF LEONARD DA VINCI IN THE EIGHTEENTH CENTURY. Los Angeles: Zeitlin & Ver Brugge, 1974, 8vo., quarter cloth, paper over board, paper spine label. 39+(1) pages. $ 55.00
Limited to 500 copies printed by Saul and Lillian Marks at their Plantin Press. Gives a description of the lives of Mariette and Caylus with a catalogue describing relevant items in the Mariette collection.

1078. (Plantin Press) STUDIES FOR A NATIVITY AND THE 'MONA LISA CARTOON' WITH DRAWINGS AFTER LEONARDO FROM THE ELMER BELT LIBRARY OF VINCIANA. Los Angeles: University of California, 1973, small 4to., stiff paper wrappers. 49, (3) pages. $ 25.00
First printing, issued as publication number 6 by the UCLA Center for Medieval and Renaissance Studies, and printed by Saul & Lillian Marks at the Plantin Press. An exhibition in honour of Elmer Belt, M.D. on the occasion of his eightieth birthday. catalogue and introduction by Carlo Pedretti. Belt was a prominent collector of Vinciana and donated the entirety to UCLA. Illustrated with drawings by Leonardo.

1079. (Plantin Press) Turner, Justin G. THE THIRTEENTH AMENDMENT AND THE EMANCIPATION PROCLAMATION. Los Angeles: The Plantin Press, 1971, small 8vo., stiff paper wrappers. (iv), 17+(1) pages. $ 17.50
First edition. Turner explains the ramifications of Lincoln's Emancipation Proclamation in 1863 and how it led to the passing and ratification of the Thirteenth Amendment to the U.S. Constitution.

1080. (Plantin Press) VELVETS EAST AND WEST FROM THE 14TH TO THE 20TH CENTURY. (Los Angeles: Los Angeles County Museum of Art), 1966, large 8vo., stiff pictorial paper wrappers. 63+(1) pages. $ 25.00
First edition. Catalogue from an exhibition held at the Lytton Gallery from March to May 1966. Assembled from the Textiles and Costumes Section of the Los Angeles County Museum of Art, the display showcased the wide variety of fabric and treatments produced over seven centuries on the looms of weavers of this luxurious cloth. Black and white photographs. Printed by the Plantin Press.

1081. (Plantin Press) Vogler, Richard A. (editor). GRAPHIC ARTS RENTAL PROGRAM. Los Angeles: University of California, Los Angeles, 1970, 8vo., stiff wrappers. viii (ii), (30) pages. $ 15.00
Printed by Saul & Lillian Marks at the Plantin Press, Los Angeles. A catalogue of 161 prints, with introduction describing the principal graphic processes and a few of the practices of printmaking. Cover by Roy Lichtenstein, with frontispiece and two illustrations in text.

1082. (Plantin Press) Waltz, Nathan. SPECIMEN OF CUBEO INDIAN BARK CLOTH. Los Angeles: Dawson's Bookshop, 1969, 8vo., stiff paper wrappers. (iv), 4 pages. $ 75.00
Limited to only 80 copies and printed by Saul and Lillian Marks at the Plantin Press. A short history of bark cloth or tapa. Tipped-in is a large specimen of the cloth. Scarce.

1083. (Plantin Press) Weber, Francis J. EL PUEBLO DE NUESTRA SENORA DE LOS ANGELES, AN INQUIRY INTO EARLY APPELLATIONS. Los Angeles: (Roman Catholic Archdiocese of Los Angeles), 1968, small 8vo., quarter cloth with paper-covered boards, paper spine label. (vi), 17+(1) pages. $ 35.00
Printed in an edition limited to 250 copies by Saul Marks at the Plantin Press. With color print of Nathaniel Currier's depiction of La Reina de los Angeles, executed sometime prior to his affiliation with James Merritt Ives in 1857.

1084. (Plantin Press) Weber, Rev. Francis J. THE RARE BOOK, SOME OBJECTIVE CRITERIA. Los Angeles: (Roxburghe-Zamorano Clubs), 1971, 8vo., stiff paper wrappers. (8) pages. $ 25.00
Printed in an edition limited to 240 signed and numbered copies for the Roxburghe-Zamorano meeting by Saul Marks at the Plantin Press, Los Angeles. Reprinted from Coranto, Vol. VII, no. 1, 1971.

1085. (Plantin Press) Zamorano, Don Agustín Vicente. THE HAND OF ZAMORANO, A FACSIMILE REPRODUCTION OF A MANUSCRIPT ON THE CALIFORNIAS IN 1829, WRITTEN BY DON AGUSTÍN VICENTE ZAMORANO,

AS SECRETARY TO GOVERNOR JOSÉ MARÍA DE ECHEANDIA, TRANS-
LATED BY ARNULFO D. TREJO AND ROLAND D. HUSSEY, WITH A PREF-
ACE BY GEORGE L. HARDING. Los Angeles: The Zamorano Club, 1956, 4to., stiff
paper wrappers. (iv), 5, (11) pages. $ 85.00
Printed in an edition limited to 250 copies published as a memento of the third joint meeting of the
Zamorano Club of Los Angeles and the Roxburghe Club of San Francisco. Facsimile reproduction of a
document prepared and written by provincial secretary Zamorano and signed by Governor Echeandia
stating the organization of the military and civil governments of Baja and Alta California as of September 22, 1829. Introduction by Lawrence Clark Powell, University of California librarian, who discovered
the original in a Clark Memorial Library vault. Contents first listed in English, then followed by Spanish facsimiles. Printed on simulated parchment by Saul and Lillian Marks of the Plantin Press.

1086. (Plough Press) Docker, Frances. JOHN PAAS & JAMES COOK, PROVIN-
CIAL BOOKBINDING IN THE EIGHTEEN THIRTIES. Leicestershire: The
Plough Press, 1978, square 8vo., cloth. 26 pages and 10 plates. $ 65.00
S-K 5553. First edition, limited to 200 numbered copies. A study of bookbinding and murder in England.
Along with telling this interesting story, there are reproductions of a binder's trade card, various en-
graved brass ornaments, tools, and numerous illustrations concerning the murder taken from contem-
porary sources.

1087. (Plough Press) Lalande, Jme. De. ART OF MAKING PAPER TAKEN FROM
THE UNIVERSAL MAGAZINE OF KNOWLEDGE AND PLEASURE. Lough-
borough: Plough Press, (1978), 8vo., cloth. 31 pages., 6 plates, 5 of which are foldouts.
$ 75.00
Limited to 200 copies. Reprint of the 1762-63 English edition. Lalande's essay is considered to be the earliest important work on the history of the production of paper. The article was not known in an English
translation until Wakeman at the Plough Press discovered this article in the Universal Magazine.

1088. (Plough Press) Loys Le Roi. ON PRINTING. Loughborough: The Plough Press,
1974, 12mo., stiff paper wrappers, cord-tied. 8, (4) pages. $ 40.00
Limited to 120 copies. One of a series of pamphlets on printing issued by The Plough Press as part of a
series entitled Artes Typographicae. This essay originally appeared in Paris in 1576 and was translated
into English by Robert Ashley and published in 1594.

1089. (Plough Press) McKay, Barry. PATTERNS AND PIGMENTS IN ENGLISH
MARBLED PAPER - AN ACCOUNT OF THE ORIGINS, SOURCES AND
DOCUMENTARY LITERATURE TO 1881. Oxford: The Plough Press, (1988), 4to.,
cloth over marbled paper covered boards. 93, (3) pages with 8 original eighteenth and
nineteenth century classic marbling samples and 6 contemporary interpretations by
Payhembury Marbled Paper. $ 300.00
First edition limited to 160 copies. This important work traces the spread of marbling to Europe during
the fifteenth century, taking into account the eleventh century Japanese suminigashi technique. It
reprints in full two major seventeenth century technical descriptions on marbling by Evelyn and
Kircher and an account of the mid-eighteenth century technique by Robert Dossie. There are notes on
the pigments employed by these marblers and contemporary recipes. Printed by Letterpress at The September Press on Zerkall Elfenbien Halbmatt paper.

1090. (Plough Press) Morris, Ann. PRIVATE PRESS IN LEICESTERSHIRE.
Loughborough: The Plough Press, (1976), small 4to., paper wrappers. (iv), 55 pages.
$ 30.00
One of 500 copies. Being a brief history and biography of 23 private presses that have been established
in the Loughborough and Leicestershire area of England, with complete checklists of their productions.
The presses include, the Twelve by Eight Press of John Mason, the Brewhouse Press, the Plough Press
and others. Covers slightly faded.

1091. (Plough Press) Wakeman, Geoffrey and Graham Pollard. FUNCTIONAL DE-
VELOPMENTS IN BOOKBINDING. New Castle, DE and Kidlington, England: The
Plough Press, 1993, 8vo., cloth, leather spine label. 96 pages and containing six tipped-
in handmade facsimile samples of cloth bindings and 31 other illustrations in black and
white. $ 300.00

Limited to 180 numbered copies of which this is one of the 125 cloth bound copies. Printed by hand by
Paul Wakeman, the son of Geoffrey Wakeman, at the Plough Press. Three separate essays which provide
a fascinating study of English trade binding from the sixteenth century to the mid-nineteenth century.
In "Illustrations of English Trade Bindings of the Seventeenth and Eighteenth Centuries," Geoffrey
Wakeman describes what an ordinary book of the period looked like. Pollard's essay "Changes in the
Style of Bookbinding, 1550–1830" originally appeared in "The Library" in 1956. The third article is
again by Wakeman and is entitled "Bookbinding Styles in the Loughborough and Ashby-de-la-Zouch
Parish Libraries." This article is based on illustrated slide lectures Wakeman gave while teaching at
Loughborough and was meant to demonstrate to students the changes in binding style over the period
covered in Pollard's article. These slides are reproduced as plates which are contained in a pocket in the
back of the book.

1092. (Plough Press) Wakeman, Geoffrey. NINETEENTH CENTURY TRADE
BINDING. Two volumes. Oxford: The Plough Press, 1983, 4to., cloth, paper spine labels, slipcase. 46, (2) pages in first volume; second is a cloth folder containing one sheet
with seven specimens of different types of leather pasted on, another sheet with nine
specimens of cloth pasted on, a four page section with 71 reproductions of cloth rub-
bings being the Winterbottom designs and a specimen of brass type that would be used
by a bookbinder. $ 385.00

Limited to 152 numbered copies and out of print before publication; this copy out of series. Another fine
Plough Press on a subject area which has become increasingly important. Wakeman discusses the materials and machinery used in trade binding in both cloth and leather and has 27 illustrations from contemporary sources to aid the text. The book is hand-printed in two colors on mould made paper.

1093. (Plough Press) Wakeman, Geoffrey. VICTORIAN COLOUR PRINTING.
Loughborough: The Plough Press, 1981, 4to., leather spine, marbled paper over boards.
35, (5) pages, 8 plates, with accompanying text, rear pocket containing prints. $ 650.00

Limited to 150 copies. Wakeman has written a precise and detailed essay on the technical aspects of producing colored illustrations in 19th century England. This is accompanied by 16 textual illustrations of
type equipment used and patented by the various printers, and 8 original plates showing different techniques discussed in the book: Baxter's Process, Knight's Patent, Chromolithography, Relief Printing, etc.
In a rear pocket are examples of printed ephemera and a set of proofs printed by Wakeman from an original set of blocks used to print the separate colors. Important.

1094. (Porpoise Press) Fergusson, Robert. SCOTS POEMS. Edinburgh: Porpoise
Press, 1925, small 8vo., paper covered boards, paper cover label. xii, 92, (2) pages.
                                                                                                                $ 65.00

Printed in an edition limited to 550 numbered copies on mould-made paper, of which 500 copies are for
sale (Ransom, page 385)."Faithfully re-printed from *The Weekly Magazine* and the editions of 1773 and
1779." Fergusson's "talent for versification in the Scots dialect has been exceeded by none--equalled by
few." Printed in Great Britain at the Kynoch Press. Textual note by Bruce Dickins, mentioning that no
glossary is added, but "the reader may be referred to the Reverend Alexander Warrack's *Scots Dialect
Dictionary* published in 1911." Robert Burns' immediate predecessor and acknowledged by him as such.

1095. (Possum Press) Wilder, Amos N. IMAGINING THE REAL. St. Petersburg, FL: Possum Press, 1978, 8vo., stiff paper wrappers. 56, (2) pages. $ 25.00
Printed in an edition limited to 350 copies, with the text set in Janson and the illustrations made from zinc blocks and printed on Carnival Vellum text papers. The author served in the American Ambulance Field Service in France in 1916, served as Albert Schweitzer's secretary at Oxford in 1922, taught at Harvard (1954-62) and was the brother of Thornton Wilder. A book of essays, poetry, and an oral interview with the publisher.

1096. (Prairie Press) Cheever, Lawrence Oakley. EDWARD A. WILSON, BOOK IL-LUSTRATOR A BIOGRAPHICAL SKETCH, TOGETHER WITH A CHECK-LIST OF HIS WORK. Muscatine: Prairie Press, 1941, 8vo., stiff paper wrappers. (24) pages. $ 65.00
First edition, limited to 220 copies printed at this private press. Contains colored reproductions of some of Wilson's work.

1097. (Prairie Press) Klinefelter, Walter. A SMALL DISPLAY OF OLD MAPS AND PLANS. Iowa City: Prairie Press, (1962), 12mo., quarter cloth with label pasted on spine and paper-covered boards, dust jacket. 80 (4) pages. $ 67.50
Printed in an edition limited to 550 copies. Designed and printed by Carroll Coleman, hand-set in Bulmer on Alexandra paper. A collection of postage stamp designs that reproduce or call to mind "maps from the days of exploration and discovery, and plans that were drawn for the establishment of towns and the building of fortifications." United States 3 cent stamp commemorating Fort Ticonderoga (1955) tipped in as frontispiece.

1098. (Prairie Press) PROGRAMME FOR TCHAIKOVSKY'S FIFTH SYMPHO-NY. Iowa City: Prairie Press, 1970, 8vo., quarter cloth, with marbled paper covered boards, publisher's original plain white dust jacket. 31, (5) pages. $ 125.00
Printed in an edition limited to 300 numbered and signed by Frank Egler copies. (Cheever 168). A manuscript by Warren Goeffrey Kenfield, Paris, early 1888, along with a history of the work by Egler. The typographical ornaments are printed in blue on a special mould-made paper imported from Holland. Dust jacket slightly soiled.

1099. (Prairie Press) Twain, Mark. MARK TWAIN'S FIRST STORY. N.P.: Prairie Press, n.d.(1952), small 8vo., stiff paper wrappers. 22, (2) pages. $ 30.00
Second printing. Presentation from editor on front blank. A brief early story by Twain, published in 1852 in a Boston magazine, with a lengthy introduction by Franklin J. Meine. Title page illustration (unattributed) repeated on front cover.

1100. (Pratt Adlib Press) MIME: THE ART OF ETIENNE DECROUX. Brooklyn: Pratt Adlib Press, 1965, large 4to., stiff paper wrappers, cloth slipcase, paper spine label. Unpaginated. $ 55.00
Limited to 1000 numbered copies, signed by the illustrator. Keepsake No. 8 in a series issued by this press, based on lectures mimed by Etienne Decroux, text based on notes taken by Fritz Eichenberg, and printed in hand set Garamond on french fold Curtis Colophon paper. Illustrations printed from hand-etched zinc relief plates executed by Ronald Schwerin. Slipcase is worn but book itself is fine. Bookplate of John DePol.

1101. (Pratt Adlib Press) Sargeant, Winthrop. HUMILITY CONCENTRATION & GUSTO. Brooklyn: The Pratt Adlib Press, 1960, 4to., paper wrappers. 22 pages. $ 25.00
Printed in an edition limited to 300 numbered copies under the direction of Fritz Eichenberg. This is second in a series of publications of the Pratt Ad Lib Press. A profile of Moore, who was regarded as America's greatest woman poets. It is illustrated with original woodcuts by Richard Bennett. Darkened around the edges and along the spine, corners bumped.

1102. (Press At Colorado College) Reeve, F.D. NIGHTWAY. N.P.: The Press at Colorado College, (1987), tall thin 8vo., two toned cloth. (37) pages. $ 75.00
Printed in an edition limited to 100 numbered copies this being the press proof. A poem which present the imaginary performance of the Navajo nine day personal ceremony of purification. It was designed, composed, printed and bound by six students at Colorado College. It was printed on Arches Text paper, with five sizes of monotype Bembo and a Vandercook Universal III. Spot on front cover with the top of the spine slightly rubbed.

1103. (Press of A. Colish) Bennett, Arnold. NINETEENTH CENTURY ENGLISH PRINTING OFFICE AS DESCRIBED BY ARNOLD BENNETT IN HIS NOVEL CLAYHANGER. New York: The Typophiles, 1985, 8vo., stiff paper wrappers. 24 pages. $ 15.00
Limited to 480 copies. Designed by Abe Lerner and printed by the Press of A. Colish. Typograph Monograph, New Series, Number 2.

1104. (Press of A. Colish) BERT CLARKE - TYPOGRAPHER, A CATALOGUE OF AN EXHIBITION OF SELECTED WORKS WITH AN INTRODUCTION BY JOHN DREYFUS & CATALOGUE NOTES BY MR. CLARKE. New York: The New York Public Library, 1987, 8vo., stiff paper wrappers. 44, (42) pages. $ 20.00
Text followed by plates showing the typographical design work by Clarke. Printed by the Press of A. Colish.

1105. (Press of A. Colish) CHRISTMAS VERSE. New York: Oxford University Press, 1945, 12mo., decorated paper wrappers. vii, 34, (2) pages. $ 15.00
Monograph number 16 issued by the Typophiles, one of 350 copies. Designed by John Begg, printed by the press of A. Colish and with calligraphy by Arnold Bank.

1106. (Press of A. Colish) Hutner, Martin. DANIEL BERKELEY UPDIKE AND THE BRITISH CONNECTION. New York: The Typophiles, 1988, 8vo., stiff paper wrappers. 20,(4) pages; 10 plates. $ 45.00
Limited to 350 copies printed at the Press of A. Colish with design by Jerry Kelly. New Series Number 5 of the Typophile Monographs. Introduction by Abe Lerner. Considerable information on William Morris. Presentation from the author to John DePol on colophon page. With DePol's bookplate and signature.

1107. (Press of A. Colish) Mayor, A. Hyatt. ARTISTS & ANATOMISTS. N.P.: Artist's Limited Edition in Association with the Metropolitan Museum of Art, (1984), 4to., cloth, dust jacket. (vi), 132, (2) pages. $ 45.00
The interrelation of art and anatomy from ancient times to the present. 91 illustrations in the text. Printed at A. Colish with design by Bert Clarke and title page lettering by Jerry Kelly.

1108. (Press of A. Colish) Mayor, A. Hyatt. SELECTED WRITINGS AND A BIBLIOGRAPHY. New York: Metropolitan Museum of Art, (1983), 8vo., cloth. 194, (2) pages. $ 20.00
First edition, limited to 2000 letterpress copies printed at the Press of A. Colish. A bibliography and anthology of articles of Hyatt Mayor (1901–1980) was curator of prints at the Metropolitan Museum of Art from 1946 to his retirement in 1966, and the author of more than 200 articles and reviews and 9 books, including *Prints & People: A Social History of Printed Pictures*, 1971. Illustrated. Bookplate of John DePol on front pastedown.

1109. (Press of A. Colish) Shapiro, S.R. 85, MAY 14, 1955. N.P.: Printed by A. Colish for Bruce Rogers and his friends, 1955, small 4to., self paper wrappers. (4) pages.
$ 30.00

Limited to 85 copies. A poem about Rogers written by Shapiro and arranged in type by Colish. Printed on the special handmade paper produced for Colish and containing the joint watermark of Rogers and Colish. Printed on the first page only. Some wrinkling.

1110. (Press of A. Colish) Sterne, Laurence. THE ACT OF CHARITY, AN EXCERPT OF TWO CHAPTERS FROM A SENTIMENTAL JOURNEY THROUGH FRANCE & ITALY BY MR. YORICK. New York: Linweave Limited Editions, 1933, 4to., stiff paper wrappers. (6 pages).
$ 17.50

Printed at the Press of A. Colish, with an illustration by T.M. Cleland, on Linweave Milano, Plaza Gray paper. With promotional sample describing Linweave papers and envelopes as insert.

1111. (Press of A. Colish) Williams, Gordon R. FANTASY IN A WOOD-BLOCK OR WHAT OCCURRED WHEN JOHN JAMES AUDUBON, THE NATURAL-IST, VISITED WITH THOMAS BEWICK, THE WOOD-ENGRAVER, IN THE YEAR 1827. Chicago: The Caxton Club, 1972, 8vo., cloth-backed marbled paper covered boards, paper spine label. (iv), 18 pages.
$ 75.00

First edition, limited to 500 copies, and produced for the Club by A. Colish. With a description of their meeting and the Bewick woodblock they examined. The actual block was used by R. Hunter Middleton to produce a print which is mounted in this book.

1112. (Press of Appletree Alley) Feldman, Irving. ALL OF US HERE. Lewisberg, PA: Bucknell University & The Press of Appletree Alley, 1990, tall 8vo., quarter cloth with printed paper covered boards. 57+(1) pages.
$ 200.00

Printed in an edition limited to 145 numbered copies signed by the author and illustrator. Finely illustrated with five full page woodcut illustrations by george Zoretich. Issued as part of The Bucknell University Fine Editions: A Series in Contemporary Poetry. The series logo was engraved by John Depol and appears on the first printed page. This copy Bears John DePol's bookplate on the front pastedown and his signature on the first printed leaf.

1113. (Press of the Bald Eagle) FIRST BIRTHDAY BOOK; 33 LD BALDY EAGLE MARKS BY ARTIST-DESIGNER FRIENDS OF BALDY FOR WHIMSY AND OTHER FORMS OF EPHEMERA. Westmoreland Hills, MD: LD's Press of the Bald Eagle, 1960, small 8vo., paper wrappers. 72 pages.
$ 20.00

First edition, published after Douglas's death. The designers represented in the book include Harry Carter, Warren Chappel, Fritz Eichenberg, John Fass and Edward Wilson.

1114. (Press of The Good Mountain) Howells, William Dean. COUNTRY PRINTER, EXCERPTS FROM AN ESSAY WRITTEN IN 1896. Rochester: The Press of the Good Mountain, 1967, 12mo., boards, paper cover label. (viii), 12, (2) pages.
$ 55.00

Limited to 100 copies. Handset by Dennis Grastorf. Presentation from the printer. Spine slightly faded.

1115. (Press of the Iron Horse) DePol, John. THE SEASONS OR, LIFE IN THE COUNTRY. Flushing: (Press of the Iron Horse), 1953, small 12mo., paper wrappers, cord tied, paper cover label, fore edge deckled. (ii), 5, (3) pages.
$ 35.00

Printed in an edition limited to 350 copies. A short story engraved on wood by John DePol, this tiny volume only consists of five woodcut illustrations that silently tell a tale of life in the country. A smaller engraving accompanies the colophon. The title page and the table of contents are printed in two colors.

1116. (Press of the Nightowl) Agner, Dwight. BOOKS OF WAD, A BIBLIOGRA-PHY OF THE BOOKS DESIGNED BY W.A. DWIGGINS. With a Foreword by Alexander Lawson. Baton Rouge: Press of the Nightowl, 1974, small 4to., half cloth over marbled paper covered boards. xii, 88 pages. $ 250.00
First edition, limited to 206 numbered copies. With ornamentation printed in different colored inks. Introduction by Lawson and preface by the author.

1117. (Press of the Nightowl) Garrett, Charlotte. PRESENCES. Baton Rouge: Press of the Nightowl, 1977, 12mo., stiff paper wrappers. 29, (3). $ 17.50
Printed by Dwight Agner in an edition limited to 200 numbered copies, of which this is one of 80 copies printed on Warren Old Style paper with Curtis Tweedweave wrappers. Handset in Eric Gill's Joanna type. Poetry.

1118. (Press of The Nightowl) Lawson, Alexander. COMPOSITOR AS ARTIST, CRAFTSMAN, AND TRADESMAN. Athens, Georgia: The Press of the Nightowl, 1990, 8vo., cloth. (iv), 36 pages. $ 40.00
First edition, limited to 350 numbered copies of which this is one of the trade copies bound thus. An interesting essay illustrated with wood engravings by Joseph Sanders.

1119. (Press of the Nightowl) Zachert, Martha Jane K. FINE PRINTING IN GEOR-GIA, 1950²–1990. SIX PRIZE-WINNING PRIVATE PRESSES. Athens: The Press of the Nightowl, (1995), 8vo., cloth, paper cover label. xiv, 141, (3) pages. $ 65.00
First edition, limited to 340 copies. Histories and bibliographies of the following presses: The Ashantilly Press, The Pigeonhole Press, The Tinhorn Press, The Beehive Press, The Press of the Nightowl, and The Hillside Press. A.L.s. from Dwight Agner, owner of the Press of the Nightowl, loosely inserted.

1120. (Press of the Three Bears) Millward, Mr. and Mrs. Russell & Edna Boyden Mill-ward. TYPE BOOK, TYPE FACES, ORNAMENTS, BORDERS & FLEURETTES. Washington, D.C.: Press of the Three Bears, n.d. but circa 1955, small 8vo., cord-tied stiff paper wrappers. (24) pages. $ 35.00
Press proof of the publisher's first attempt at a type book, noted as such on sheet loosely laid in, with signature. *A Small Hobby Printery Owned and Operated Without Profit ... In The Interest of Educational Projects*. Signature of book illustrator John DePol, the previous owner, on inside front cover.

1121. (Press of the Three Bears) Goudy, Frederic W. TYPE SPEAKS. Washington, DC: The Press of the Three Bears, 1938, 16mo., stiff paper wrappers, cord- tied. (6) pages. $ 15.00
Limited to 275 copies. Printed by this private press as a Keepsake for the Pilgrimage to Deepdene in celebration of the 35th Anniversary of the Village Press.

1122. (Press of the Woolly Whale) Angell, Norman. PATRIOTISM VERSUS WEL-FARE: AN EXTRACT FROM "THE UNSEEN ASSASSINS". New York: Press of the Woolly Whale, 1932, small 8vo., cloth-backed boards. ix, 32, (2) pages. $ 55.00
Bibliography no.32. Being the fifth Armistice Day issue. The title page is printed in black and light blue on gray T.J. paper. Minor rubbing.

1123. (Press of the Woolly Whale) Cary, Melbert. MISSING GUTENBERG WOOD BLOCKS. New York: Press of the Woolly Whale, 1940, 8vo., cloth-backed boards. (16) pages, 20 wood blocks with accompanying text on 20 leaves. $ 75.00
An elaborate spoof on the invention of printing issued as a Christmas greeting on the 500th Anniversary of the birth of printing.

1124. (Press of The Woolly Whale) Emmons, Earl H. CHAPEAU IMMORTEL. New York: The Press of the Woolly Whale, 1928, broadside (15 x 20 inches).　　$45.00
The first publication of Melbert Cary's Press of the Woolly Whale, limited to 350 copies. Printed on Kelmscott handmade paper in Goudy Newstyle. A humorous poem about an old hat worn by Frederic W. Goudy with a drawing by Herb Roth.

1125. (Press of The Woolly Whale) Goudy, Fred W. and Will H. Ransom. VILLAGE PRESS. (New York: Press of the Whooly Whale, 1938), 8vo., self paper wrappers. (4) pages.　　$20.00
Facsimile of a type specimen circular, the first piece of printing issued by The Village Press. Prepared for participants in the Pilgrimage to Deepdene, July 23, 1938, in celebration of the thirty-fifth anniversary of the press. *This is the first showing of a new type designed by Mr. Goudy for the exclusive use of the Village Press.* Logo on front cover.

1126. (Press of The Woolly Whale) Rollins, Carl Purlington. THIS HOUSE OF HAVOC. New York: American Institute of Graphic Arts, 1941, 8vo., paper wrappers, cord-tied. (16) pages.　　$15.00
This essay was printed by the Press of the Woolly Whale to celebrate Mr. Rollins' receiving the Medal of the AIGA. Covers faded and with chip out along spine at top.

1127. (Press of The Woolly Whale) SOME NEW LIGHT ON THE GENESIS OF THE AMPERSAND. New York: Prepared for the Typophiles by The Press of the Woolly Whale, (1936), 16mo., paper wrappers, cord-tied. (16) pages.　　$20.00
No.36 in the PWW bibliography. Originally printed as a signature for a Typophile volume on the ampersand, and now issued as a separate publication. Printed in black, green and red. Covers detached.

1128. (Press of the Woolly Whale) Wroth, Lawrence C. OATH OF A FREEMAN. WITH A HISTORICAL STUDY AND A NOTE ON THE STEPHEN DAYE PRESS BY MELBERT B. CARY, JR. New York: Press of The Woolly Whale, 1939, small 8vo., cloth, paper cover label. (16) pages with a double spread page facsimile of the Daye printing.　　$35.00
Study of the first known printing in America. With a notice from the A.I.G.A. indicating that this book is Keepsake No.60 issued by the Association. Some wear at head of spine.

1129. (Press on Washington Street) RIGHT THOUGHTS ON PRINTING IN AN AGE WHEN THE PRINTERS NEED CORRECTING. New York: Press on Washington Street, 1972, 8vo., stiff paper wrappers. (16) pages.　　$17.50
Printed in an edition limited to 125 copies prepared for the Typophiles.

1130. (Previous Parrot Press) Graham, Rigby. WOODCUTS AND WORDS, WITH SOME THOUGHTS ON CUTTING. And an introduction by Michael Bown. Hanborough: The Previous Parrot Press, 1994, small 4to., patterned paper covered boards. 52, (4) pages. Accompanied by a separate portfolio of four woodcuts and all enclosed in a slipcase.　　$185.00
First edition, limited to 242 copies of which 48 have the extra portfolio of plates. This is one of these special copies. Signed by Graham and Bown. Phototypeset by Bookmarque and printed litho on Zerkell mould-made paper. Illustrated.

1131. (Price, Robin) Gilgun, John. THE DOOLEY POEMS. Los Angeles, CA: Robin Price, 1991, 4to., quarter cloth with printed paper boards, top and fore edges cut, bottom edges slightly deckled. (26) pages. $ 125.00
First edition, limited to 150 copies numbered and signed by the author. A collection of thoughtful poems by Gilgun, shaped from time spent on Doodley's farm in Missouri. Hand-set in 16 point Nicolas Jenson, printed in black and green on Gutenberg Laid paper. Bound in quarter green cloth with ivory colored paper boards with a multi-colored monoprint by Robin Price.

1132. (Primavera Press) Jones, Louise Seymour. WHO LOVES A GARDEN. Primavera Press, 1934, 8vo., paper-covered boards, dust jacket. 195+(1) pages. $ 45.00
Designed by Ward Ritchie and printed in an edition limited to 500 copies (Ritchie, 71). Inscribed by the author on half-title page. Flower initials designed by Marie Balle. A book of short essays and marginalia on gardens, "written in a style reminiscent of Burton's *Anatomy of Melancholy*. Gift inscription on front free endpaper. Clipping about book laid in. Dust jacket worn at extremities.

1133. (Primavera Press) Ruthhven, Madeleine. SUMMER DENIAL AND OTHER POEMS. Los Angeles: The Primavera Press, 1932, large 8vo., paper covered boards, paper cover label, dust jacket. 65, (2) pages. $ 85.00
First edition, limited to 304 copies. Signed by author on cover's paper label and presentation dated 1957 on the free endpaper. This collection of poems by American writer Madeleine Ruthven was designed by Grace Marion Brown and printed by Ward Ritchie of the Primavera Press. Includes seven poems by Ruthven. Light foxing to initial and terminal leaves. Dust jacket torn at top and bottom of spine with pieces missing. Cover lightly rubbed.

1134. (Primavera Press) Van Wyck, William. THE SINISTER SHEPARD. A TRANSLATION OF GIROLAMO FRACASTORO'S SYPHILIDIS SIVE DE MORBO GALLICO LIBRI TRES. Los Angeles: The Primavera Press, 1934, 8vo., cloth with paper label. xxii, (ii), 85, (3) pages. $ 75.00
First edition, limited to 1000 copies. (Hart 13, Ritchie 71). A translation of this important work on the germ theory of infection by Fracastoro. This poem, originally printed in Rome 1531, gave Syphillis its name and recognized its venereal cause. The introduction is a translation of an article by Dr. Albert Garrigues that appeared in *Æsculape* in 1925. Illustrated in black & white. Printed by Ward Ritchie. later pencil inscription on front endpaper.

1135. (Printing Office at High Loft) Heckscher, August. LETTER FROM A MAINE ISLAND. (Seal Harbor, ME): The Printing Office at High Loft, (1977), 8vo., stiff paper wrappers. (28) pages. $ 75.00
Printed in an edition limited to 80 copies on Nideggen paper. Decorations by Philip H. Heckscher, printed from the original blocks. Type set by the Penmaen Press, binding by Gray Parrot.

1136. (Printing Office at High Loft) Heckscher, August. THE SILENCE OF CHRISTMAS. (Seal Harbor, ME: High Loft, 1983), 12mo., decorated stiff paper wrappers. 9, (3) pages. $ 30.00
Printed in an edition limited to 150 copies. Best Wishes card laid in signed by the author, and the nameplate of book designer Abe Lerner on inside front cover. Reprinted from *The Christian Science Monitor*.

1137. (The Printing Office of Philip Reed) Browning, Elizabeth Barrett. SONNETS FROM THE PORTUGUESE. Chicago, IL: The Printing Office of Philip Reed, n.d., large 12mo., quarter cloth with pattern paper boards. (iv), XLIV, (2) pages. $ 55.00
First edition. Lovely little volume of Browning's classic love sonnets. Some pages uncut, slight wear to tail of spine.

1138. (Private Press of a Yankee Ink Dauber) Hamsun, Knut. THE CALL OF LIFE. Ellington, CT: Private Press of a Yankee Ink Dauber, (1962), Miniature books (2 1/2 x 2 inches), quarter cloth, marbled paper boards. (40) pages printed French-fold. $ 15.00
Printed in an edition limited to 350 numbered copies signed by the Yankee Ink Dauber, Frederick B. MacMahon. A short story taken from the 1929 publication, *Told in Norway*. Back inside hinge broken.

1139. (Private Press of a Yankee Ink Dauber) Wilde, Oscar. THE SELFISH GIANT. (Ellington, CT: Private Press of a Yankee Ink Dauber, n.d.), miniature book (2 3/4 x 2 1/4 inches), leather, paper spine and cover labels. (26) pages printed French-fold. $ 35.00
Limited to 120 numbered copies signed by the Yankee Ink Dauber, Frederick B. MacMahon. A message in miniature complete with moral. Hand-set in Cheltenham Oldstyle and printed directly from the type.

1140. (Private Press of Frederic Brewer) Williams, William Carlos. DEAR EZ: LET-TERS FROM WILLIAM CARLOS WILLIAMS TO EZRA POUND. Blooming-ton: Private Press of Frederic Brewer, (1985), 8vo., cloth with marbled paper covered boards, dust jacket. (54) pages. $ 45.00
Limited to 203 numbered copies. Commentary and notes by Mary Ellen Solt. Published for The Friends of the Lilly Library. Seven letters from 1946–1951 are reproduced, during Pound's incarceration at St. Elizabeth Hospital. John DePol bookplate and signature.

1141. (Private Press of Oliver A. Wallace) Morley, Christopher. OUTWARD BOUND. Grand Rapids: The Private Press of Oliver A. Wallace, 1924, 8vo., decorated paper-cov-ered boards, label on front cover. 16 pages, with one additional leaf with plate. $ 50.00
Limited to 377 numbered copies. Private press reprint of a Morley article which originally appeared in the NY Evening Post in 1923. (Lee no.41). One of Morley's maritime writings: The sailing ship Tusitalia is towed from its berth to the mouth of Lower New York Bay, hoists sails, and departs over the horizon. The plate is a tipped-in print, somewhat retouched, of a photograph of the ship taken by Morley, possi-bly from the tugboat. There are page decorations and an illuminated initial using various nautical mo-tifs, along with a tailpiece (all unattributed). Per colophon, book two of the "Oliver Press." Rubbed along edges and spine.

1142. (Private Press of The Indiana Kid) Weygand, James Lamar. THIRD BOOK OF PRESSMARKS GATHERED FROM AMERICA'S PRIVATE PRESSES AND FROM OTHERS NOT SO PRIVATE. Nappanee, IN: Private Press of the Indiana Kid, 1962, small 8vo., cloth. 100, (6) pages. $ 125.00
Limited to about 250 copies. Reproductions of the press marks of 86 private presses in color with short historical discussion of the press. This third volume also contains the index to the first two volumes. In-cludes the Bird & Bull Press of Henry Morris, the Grabhorn Press, the Village Press, the Crabgrass Press and the Colt Press. Loosely inserted is printed slip issued by Weygand with copies of this book.

1143. (Private Press of The Indiana Kid) Weygand, James Lamar. THE TIGHTWADS GUIDE TO GOLD STAMPING. Nappanee, IN: Private Press of the Indiana Kidd, 1972, 8vo., quarter cloth, decorated paper over boards. 22, (2) pages. $ 135.00
Limited to 150 copies. Printed on Grapes paper handmade by the author/printer. Describes how Wey-gand went about gold stamping, without spending a great deal of money on expensive equipment. He also gives a list of suppliers for materials needed. Spine slightly faded.

1144. (Private Press) OAK KNOLL FEST 1995. cloth portfolio with paper cover label containing 17 10″ x 15″ letterpress printed posters issued in celebration of Oak Knoll Fest 1995 held in New Castle on October 7th. $ 225.00
Issued in only 65 sets of which 46 are for sale. Each private press printer was given the same text to in-corporate in a poster celebrating this private press book fair. They added their own design concepts and illustrations and chose their own type and paper. Posters were included by the following participants: Alembic Press, Ascensius Press, Bird & Bull Press, Bowne & Co., Caliban Press, Campbell-Logan

The Geography of Home

40 Original Prints by Elizabeth Sanchez, Gary Young and Gene Holtan. Text by Gary Young.

Published by Quadqpress, Santa Cruz, California.

Item 1149

Bindery (printed by Pentagram Press), John DePol (printed by Pentagram Press), Larkspur Press, Midnight Paper Sales, The Old Stile Press, Out of the Woods Press, Pentagram Press, Perpetua Press, Previous Parrot Press, Stephen Heaver, Stone House Press and Whittington Press. With some stunning uses of color.

1145. (Profile Press) ALMANAC FOR THE YEAR 1946. New York: The Profile Press, n.d. (circa 1946), 8vo., stiff paper wrappers with a hand-made paper dust jacket that includes a cameo cut-out revealing a two-color press logo. Unpaginated. $20.00
Printed on two kinds of paper. Includes for each month a calendar, reproductions of famous works of art, and quotes from famous writers.

1146. (Profile Press) PROFILE PRESS PRESENTS THE ALPHABET IN SUNDRY APPLICATIONS. New York: The Profile Press, n.d., 12mo., paper wrappers. 103 pages. $25.00
Being a commonplace book announcing the Press's inception. A very attractive display of the Press's types and designs. Covers soiled. Name and date in ink on free endpaper.

1147. (Protean Press) Loux, Stephanie. OH MOTHER AND OTHER POEMS. San Francisco: Protean Press, (1991), small 8vo., cloth, paper spine label. (36) pages. $75.00
Printed by Terry Horrigan at the Protean press in an edition limited to 70 numbered copies, signed by the author, on Mohawk Letterpress paper using various sizes of Spectrum type. Title-page calligraphy by Ann Miller. The photoengraved illustrations are from line drawings by Rik Olson. Selected by the Rounce & Coffin Club in Los Angeles as one of the Western Books of 1992, with their card laid in.

1148. (Purgatory Pie Press) Smith, Esther K. (editor). POSTCARDS IV (PORTFO-LIO). New York: Purgatory Pie Press, 1985, 12mo., postcards loosely inserted in portfolio. $ 45.00

Portfolio of twelve postcards printed in a series limited to 200 numbered sets and issued as Purgatory's *The Twelve Days of Christmas*. Each card is designed by a different artist and signed by them and the printer on the back. Very colorful and distinctive cards, mostly linocuts, printed on a Vandercook letter-press by Dikko Faust

1149. (Quadqpress) Young, Gary. THE GEOGRAPHY OF HOME. Santa Cruz, CA: Quadqpress, (1987), oblong 8vo., gray handmade paper over boards housed in a red-wood box with protective lining. (v), 92 pages. $ 900.00

Limited to 60 numbered copies, signed by the author, artist, and designer. 40 original prints were produced using a variety of relief methods at each press. The cover and end sheets were handmade by La Papeterie St-Armand in Montreal. Includes prospectus, illustrated notecard invitation to an exhibition of the prints in the Santa Cruz Art Center, and an original presentation letter and sketch to Muir and Glen Dawson, signed by the publisher, Gene Holtan.

1150. (Quercus Press) Grabhorn, Edwin. SOME REMARKS ON THE PRINTED BOOK. San Mateo, CA: Quercus Press, 1948, 8vo., paper covered boards, paper cover label. (6) pages. $ 100.00

Reprinted from the October 18,1948 issue of the San Francisco Chronicle Fiesta edition, on a hand press in December, 1948. Discusses the printer's part in the creation of the book.

1151. (Raccoon Press) Dougan, Olive C. SHADOWS AND OTHER POEMS. Arcadia, CA: Raccoon Press, 1963, small 8vo., stiff paper wrappers. (34) pages. $ 20.00

Printed in an edition of 250 copies for private distribution only by Carol Cockel at the Raccoon Press. A handsomely produced selection of nine moody and haunting poems, two reprinted from *The Poetry Review*. This collection appeared after the author's death and was edited by her husband, Robert Ormes Dougan, librarian at the Huntingdon Library and Art Gallery. Erratum slip inserted before colophon. Printed double-spaced with wide margins on Rives paper.

1152. (Ram Press) Sitwell, Osbert. INTRODUCTION TO THE CATALOGUE OF THE FRICK COLLECTION. New York: The Frick Art Reference Library, 1949, 8vo., stiff paper wrappers, cord-tied. 12, (4), pages. $ 20.00

Reprinted from the catalogue by Robert Haas at The Ram Press. An introductory essay to the catalogue of the Henry Clay Frick collection.

1153. (Rampant Lions Press) Carter, Will. CARTER'S CAPS. Cambridge: Rampant Lions Press, 1982, oblong 8vo., paper wrappers. (viii), (54) pages. $ 35.00

Limited to 550 copies. This book shows the alphabet in capital letters as cut by Will Carter. Carter includes a 3 page commentary and notes on each letter.

1154. (Rampant Lions Press) Ewart, Gavin. A CLUSTER OF CLERIHEWS. Leamington Spa: Sixth Chamber Press, 1985, oblong 12mo., quarter cloth with decorated paper covered boards, paper cover label. (24) pages. $ 85.00

Printed in an edition limited to 175 numbered and signed copies and 26 lettered copies, this being one of the numbered copies. (Rampant Lions Press, under 1985, 1st book). A collection of 15 clerihews by Ewart, along with one more which is anonymous remembered from the 1930's in Cambridge. It was designed and printed by Sebastian Carter and hand-set in Walbaum and Bodoni. Signed by the author.

1155. (Rampant Lions Press) Franklin, Colin. POETS OF THE DANIEL PRESS. Cambridge: Rampant Lions Press, 1988, large 8vo., quarter morocco, paper-covered boards, slipcase, edges roughly trimmed. 94, (2) pages. $ 250.00

Limited edition of 45 variously numbered copies, including 30 bound in quarter leather and printed on handmade paper. Numbered in Roman numerals. A precursor of the private press movement, the Daniel Press was established by C.H.O. Daniel (1836–1919) and operated by him at Oxford, where he eventually became Provost of Worcester College. Unlike many successors, the Daniel Press published first (& usually only) editions of works, i.e. current literature, mostly by persons associated with Oxford and/or known to Daniel. Among Daniel Press authors were various poets little-known or forgotten today, justly or otherwise. After an introduction discussing the Daniel Press, C. Franklin presents 10 poets, with brief biographical/critical introductions and comments, and texts of various poems, entire or in excerpts: Robert Bridges, Richard Watson Dixon, Mary Coleridge (great-niece of S.T.C.), Ethel Kate Wedgwood [sic], Alice Buckton, Margaret L. Woods, Herbert Warren, Laurence Binyon, F.W. Bourdillon, and Henry Patmore.

1156. (Rampant Lions Press) Franklin, Colin. PRINTING AND THE MIND OF MORRIS. Cambridge: Rampant Lions Press, 1986, 8vo., cloth-backed boards, paper cover label. 58, (2) pages. $ 125.00

Limited to 450 numbered copies printed on Hahnemuhle mould-made paper of which 400 are for sale. An essay on William Morris and the Kelmscott Press paralleling his "typographic decoration and literary elaboration of style he chose for his prose romances."

1157. (Rampant Lions Press) Hodgart, Matthew (editor). VANITY OF HUMAN WISHES, THE TENTH SATIRE OF JUVENAL IMITATED BY SAMUEL JOHNSON. Cambridge: Rampant Lions Press, 1984, 4to., quarter cloth, with decorated paper covered boards in a paper covered slipcase. 34, (4) pages with 8 pages of plates.
                    $ 375.00

Printed in an edition limited to 200 copies, this being one of the 188 regular copies. (Rampant Lions Press 1984, 5th book listed). A witty meditation on the difficulties of being human by Johnson, which is based on the Tenth Satire of Juvenal. He finished writing it in 1748 and it was first published in 1749, but he revised the poem several times. It is illustrated with 8 etchings by Denis Tegetmeier, which were printed in Paris. The text has been edited and introduced by Matthew Hodgart. It was designed and printed by Will Carter at the Rampant Lions Press, hand-set in Monotype Bembo and printed on Hodgkinson's mould-made paper.

1158. (Rampant Lions Press) Lascelles, Mary. THE ADVERSARIES AND OTHER POEMS. Cambridge: Rampant Lions Press, (1971), large 8vo., quarter cloth with decorated paper-covered boards. 56, (2) pages. $ 100.00

Printed in an edition limited to 150 copies designed and printed by Will and Sebastian Carter at the Rampant Lions Press, Cambridge (Carter, checklist). Features characteristic of all Rampant Lions work, from its first book in 1934 are--"a general acceptance of the classical tradition of typography as practiced by Bruce Rogers, Francis Meynell and their peers but (as with them) realized in a personal way (Crutchley, page 8)."

1159. (Rampant Lions Press) Piper, David. SHADES, AN ESSAY ON ENGLISH PORTRAIT SILHOUETTES. New York: Chilmark Press, (1970), small 4to., quarter cloth with decorated paper covered boards. 64 pages. $ 50.00

Printed in an edition limited to 500 numbered copies. Designed by Sebastian Carter, and printed by him and Will Carter at the Rampant Lions Press, Cambridge, in 14 point Monotype Octavian designed by David Kindersley and Will Carter on St. Paul's Cray rag paper. With thirty-six illustrations, including a hollow-cut silhouette, purported to be of Jane Austen, that was found pasted on the flyleaf of a volume of the second edition of *Mansfield Park* with the contemporary words "L'Aimable Jane" inscribed on it. A survey of this art during its heydays from the mid seventeenth to mid eighteenth centuries, with selected bibliography.

1160. (Rampant Lions Press) Postgate, Raymond (editor). THE AGAMEMNON OF AESCHYLUS. Cambridge: The Rampant Lions Press, 1969, large 8vo., terra cotta cloth, blocked spine label. (ii), 141 pages. $ 95.00
Limited to 500 copies of which this is one of 250 signed by the editor. (Carter 36). This book reproduces the original Greek text of Aeschylus' "Agamemnon" and includes an introduction, a commentary, and a translation into modern English prose by the editor. "Agamemnon," the first part of Aeschylus' Oresteia, was first produced in 458 B.C., in Athens, during the archonship of Philocles. Printed on Hollingsworth wove paper, machine-set in Porson Greek and 11pt Baskerville with commentary in 8pt Baskerville.

1161. (Rampant Lions Press) PRINTER'S DOZEN, ELEVEN SPREADS FROM UNREALISED BOOKS DESIGNED AND PRINTED AT THE RAMPANT LIONS PRESS BY SEBASTIAN CARTER. Cambridge: Rampant Lions Press, (1993), small 4to., quarter cloth over marbled paper covered boards, leather spine label, slipcase. Not paginated. $ 350.00
Limited to 211 copies of which this is one of the 200 copies bound thus. Seven page introduction by Carter in which he discusses design and the histories of these unpublished books. This is followed by the 11 sections of the books which are printed on handmade paper in different colors.

1162. (Rampant Lions Press) Reed, Henry. LESSONS OF THE WAR. New York: Chilmark Press, 1970, 4to., quarter oatmeal canvas, patterned paper covered boards. 35, (2) pages. $ 95.00
Limited to 420 numbered copies, fifth Clover Hill Edition. (Carter 38). Five war poems by Henry Reed "designed and printed for the Clover Hill Editions by Will and Sebastian Carter at the Rampant Lions Press, Cambridge, England on mould-made paper from Wookey Hole Mill and bound by Wigmore Bindery." Machine-set in 14d Walbaum.

1163. (Rampant Lions Press) Skinner, Martyn. OLD RECTORY OR THE INTER-VIEW. Cambridge: Rampant Lions Press, (1970), small 4to., paper covered boards with a paper cover label. (vi), 21, (2) pages. $ 145.00
Printed in an edition limited to 300 copies. (Rampant Lions Press 39). This is the first in a series of three books containing poems published from 1970 to 1978. This volume is the prologue, the session was published in 1973 and the epilogue was published in 1978. Old Rectory is an ambitious exercise in that difficult and unfashionable genre, the long philosophical poem. Presentation from Skinner on half-title to "O.V.O." dated 1970. Also inserted is a postcard from Sinner dated 1970 and referring to this book.

1164. (Rampant Lions Press) Skinner, Martyn. OLD RECTORY OR THE INTER-VIEW. THE SESSION IN SEVEN SCENES. Cambridge: Rampant Lions Press, (1973), small 4to., paper covered boards with a paper cover label, fore edges deckled. (vi), 54, (2) pages. $ 135.00
Printed in an edition limited to 200 copies. (Rampant Lions Press 39). This is the second in a series of three books containing poems published from 1970 to 1978. This volume follows that of The Prologue printed in 1970. The Epilogue is the third book, published in 1978. The Session is an ambitious exercise in that difficult and unfashionable genre, the long philosophical poem.

1165. (Rampant Lions Press) Smart, Christopher. SONG TO DAVID. EDITED BY J.B. BROADBENT. Cambridge: Rampant Lions Press, (1960), 4to., creme colored board spine with patterned paper covered panels, dust jacket. xxi, 40 pages. $ 75.00
Limited to 600 numbered copies. Designed by Will Carter and printed at his private press. With a frontispiece drawn by Lynton Lamb. Printed in two colors.

1166. (Rampant Lions Press) Sparrow, John. LAPIDARIA SEPTIMA. Cambridge: Rampant Lions Press, 1975, small 4to., stiff paper wrappers with paper dust jacket. (36) pages. $ 65.00

The seventh in a series of books produced by Sparrow in which he reproduces Latin inscriptions found in churches from around the world. Printed at the Rampant Lions Press on heavy paper and containing a title and colophon designed by Reynolds Stone and printed in red ink.

1167. (Rampant Lions Press) Sparrow, John. LAPIDARIA OCTAVA. Cambridge: Rampant Lions Press, 1981, small 4to., stiff paper wrappers with paper dust jacket. (36) pages. $ 65.00

The eighth in a series of books produced by Sparrow in which he reproduces Latin inscriptions found in churches from around the world. Printed at the Rampant Lions Press on heavy paper and containing a title and colophon designed by Reynolds Stone and printed in red ink.

1168. (Ransom, Will) Dalton, Power. STAR POLLEN. Chicago: Private Press of Will Ransom: Maker of Books, 1922, small 8vo., cloth, paper spine label, slipcase. 66, (2) pages. $ 75.00

The second publication of this private press, limited to 259 numbered copies. Printed on Tuscany handmade paper. With the bookplate of Edmund Gress. Slipcase is broken; book is in very fine condition.

1169. (Ransom, Will) Pickard, William John. SPIDER PHAETON AND OTHER STORIES. Chicago: Will Ransom, 1924, small 8vo., cloth-backed boards, paper spine label. 163, (3) pages. $ 25.00

First edition. One of the specially designed book published by Will Ransom, the private press enthusiast.

1170. (Rara Avis Press) Schulz, Bruno. BIRDS. Madison: The Rara Avis Press, 1980, tall 8vo., cloth, paper spine label. (20) pages. $ 75.00

Limited to 150 numbered copies signed by the printer, Christine Bertelson. Translated from the Polish by Celina Wieniewska and with five illustrations by Janet Morgan.

1171. (Rasselas Press) Maugham, William Somerset. THE LETTERS OF WILLIAM SOMERSET MAUGHAM TO LADY JULIET DUFF. Pacific Palisades, CA: Rasselas Press, 1982, large 8vo., cloth, paper spine and cover label. xx (iv), 81, (5) pages.
$ 45.00

Printed as a first edition of correspondence of W. Somerset Maugham and limited to 300 numbered copies of which this copy is out of series. Printed letterpress by Patrick Reagh. This is the first collection of Maugham's correspondence to be published, consisting of 92 letters and 14 postcards, from 1935 to 1962, "disclosing an aspect of Maugham's personality not generally known--that of a kind, affectionate, and considerate friend (introduction)." Edited and with an introduction by Loren R. Rothschild. Pen and ink drawing of Maugham as frontispiece.

1172. (Rather Press) JANE GRABHORN, PRINTER. Oakland, CA: The Rather Press, n.d., miniature book (2 3/4 x 2 1/4 inches), cloth. 25+(1) pages. $ 65.00

Limited to 150 numbered copies. An excerpt from *Thanks, Jane* which Lois and Clif Rather published as a memorial to Jane Grabhorn, this is only the second miniature book produced by the Rather Press. Printed on Warren's Olde Style paper in Centaur type with Arrighi titling.

1173. (Rather Press) POEMS FOR PRINTERS. Oakland: The Rather Press, (1970), square 8vo., paper wrappers. (20) pages. $ 55.00

Printed in an edition limited to 105 copies. (Rather Press pg 6). A collection of poems or jingles about printing gathered from old printing manuals. The illustrations by Lois Rather are assembled from a mixed accumulation of printer's ornaments as her first typesetting lesson, which form pictures, borders and decorations.

1174. (Rather Press) Rather, Clifton and Lois. FINE POINTS: A PRINTERS' MIS-
CELLANY. Oakland: The Rather Press, 1977, 8vo., stiff paper wrappers. 17, (3) pages.
$ 30.00

A gathering of sayings from important printers concerning various aspects of private press printing. Inscribed by Cliff Rather on front cover.

1175. (Rather Press) Rather, Clifton and Lois. HERE'S HOW, AN AUTOBIOGRA-
PHY, PART II. Oakland, CA: Rather Press, (1970), small 8vo., quarter cloth with paper
covered boards. (vi), 128 pages. $ 75.00

Printed in an edition limited to 72 copies, this copy being signed by both authors on front free endpaper.
Printed in 14-point Cloister Bold in roman and italic, with " titles and inserts from various fonts on
hand, all hand set and printed on the faithful ancient muscle-powered Sigwalt." The authors printed
their first book in 1965 by building a flat-bed wooden press using a hard maple rolling pin. List of books
from the Rather Press includes *Household Hints for Hippie Housewives* and *Limerick Calendar for
1969.* Illustrated with photographs. Wrinkling along front inside hinge.

1176. (Rather Press) Rather, Clifton. A JUG OF WINE, A WATERBED, AND
WOW! Oakland, CA: The Rather Press, (1971), small 8vo., quarter cloth, pictorial
paper covered boards. (iv), 47+(1) pages. $ 65.00

Limited to edition of 80 copies. This collection of essays was written in Clif Rather's own inimitable style
then typeset, printed on papers left over from past projects and bound by his own hand. Signed by Clif
and Lois Rather on front free endpaper.

1177. (Rather Press) Rather, Clifton. PRINTER'S PROGRESS. Oakland: The Rather
Press, (1972), square 8vo., stiff paper wrappers. 20, (4) pages. $ 35.00

Printed in an edition limited to 200 copies. Clif Rather of the Rather Press gives a short history of the
press and discusses some of the problems he has had through the years.

1178. (Rather Press) Rather, Lois. BOHEMIANS TO HIPPIES: WAVES OF RE-
BELLION. Oakland: Rather Press, 1977, large 8vo., quarter cloth with paper-covered
boards. 165, (3) pages. $ 75.00

Printed in an edition limited to 150 numbered copies, designed, hand-set, hand-sewn and cased by Clif
and Lois Rather, in 14-point Spectrum roman and italic, on Curtis Tweedweave paper. Color woodcut ,
Smoking Nude , by Glenn Wessels as frontispiece. Chapters describing bohemian life in San Francisco
from Bret Harte and Adah Menken to Allen Ginsberg and William Everson.

1179. (Rather Press) Rather, Lois. BOOKS AND SOCIETIES. Oakland: Rather Press,
(1971), square 8vo., cloth. (iv), 88, (4) pages. $ 65.00

First edition, limited to 137 copies. Ten chapters on the relation of the book and society. Emphasis on
book clubs, unions, typography, etc. Handset and printed by the Rathers at their private press.

1180. (Rather Press) Rather, Lois. DUMSMUIR HOUSE. Oakland: Rather Press,
(1982), large 8vo., quarter cloth with paper-covered boards. 75 (3) pages. $ 65.00

Printed in an edition limited to 100 numbered copies. Researched, written, designed, hand-set in Bembo
type printed on Tweedweave paper, hand-sewn and cased by Clif and Lois Rather. Illustrated with wood
engravings by Stanley H. Cohen. Continues the authors series of books dealing with California history.
Dunsmuir House is a thirty-seven room mansion built in the San Leandro section of Oakland in 1899
"by a wealthy alcoholic playboy for his long-time mistress." Some fading to covers.

1181. (Rather Press) Rather, Lois. LIFE WITH SAMMI. Oakland: Rather Press,
(1970), small 8vo., quarter cloth with paper-covered boards. 22 pages. $ 55.00

Printed in an edition limited to 80 copies in 18-point Goudy Thirty, with thanks to Lawton Kennedy "for
the paper." Reminiscences by the author of her seal-point cat, *Samantha from Siam.* With decorations
and memorial photograph.

1182. (Rather Press) Rather, Lois. LOTTA'S FOUNTAIN. Oakland, CA: Rather Press, 1979, large 8vo., quarter cloth with pictorial paper covered boards, fore edge deckled. 99+(1) pages. $ 75.00

Limited edition of 150 numbered copies. Signed by Lois and Clif Rather, this is the story of Lotta Crabtree whose early days as an entertainer during the California Gold Rush led to her immense popularity as the darling of the American stage. Her success in the play, "Zip; or Pointe of Light," inspired her to donate a lighthouse shaped fountain to the city of San Francisco in 1875. There are both blue and black and white illustrations throughout with two tipped-in photos. Index. Minor foxing to preliminary leaves.

1183. (Rather Press) Rather, Lois. MISS KATE: KATE DOUGLAS WIGGIN IN SAN FRANCISCO. Oakland: The Rather Press, 1980, tall 8vo., cloth-backed decorated boards. 91 pages. $ 85.00

First edition, limited to 150 numbered copies "researched, written, designed, hand-set, hand-sewn and cased by Clif and Lois Rather."

1184. (Rather Press) Rather, Lois. OUR FRIEND LAWTON. Oakland, CA: Rather Press, 1987, large 8vo., self paper wrappers, cord tied. (12) pages. $ 25.00

First edition. Loving tribute to Lawton Kennedy and the impact he had on Lois and Clif Rather as they worked to improve the operations of the Rather Press. Signed by the author in ink on the front cover with a handwritten note loosely laid in.

1185. (Rather Press) Rather, Lois. REMEMBERING ADRIAN. Oakland, CA: Rather Press, 1989, small 8vo., paper wrappers, cord tied. (ii), 17, (3) pages. $ 55.00

Limited to edition of 40 copies. Loving memorial to Adrian Wilson by Lois Rather which includes mention of some of the antics of the Moxon Chappel of which they and their spouses were members from 1973-78. Inscribed on the cover by the author.

1186. (Rather Press) Rather, Lois. SAFE FOR DEMOCRACY. Oakland: Rather Press, 1987, large 8vo., stiff paper wrappers. (28) pages. $ 25.00

Printed in an edition limited to 60 copies and signed by the author on front cover. Handset in 14-point Bembo and "printed on a small hand-lever table model Sigwalt Press" on Curtis Tweedweave. The author's diaries from the age of eleven in World War I, relating her reactions and those of a small mid-Western town (Streeter, Illinois).

1187. (Rather Press) Rather, Lois. SAMMI — MARCH 1976. (Oakland: Rather Press, 1976), small 8vo., decorated paper wrappers, cord tied. (12) pages. $ 20.00

Printed in an edition limited to 150 copies. Poem in honor of the eighteenth birthday of Sammi, the well-loved seal-point cat of Lois and Clif Rather. Illustrated with a linocut.

1188. (Rather Press) Rather, Lois. SAN FRANCISCO'S FIRST PRINTERS PRESS. Oakland: Rather Press, (1970), 8vo., stiff paper wrappers. 26, (2) pages. $ 75.00

Printed in an edition limited to 60 numbered copies. "Printed , not by Elbert Hubbard or Lawton Kennedy, but by Clif Rather" (colophon).

1189. (Rather Press) TEN YEARS OF THE RATHER PRESS A BIBLIOGRAPHY 1968–1978. N.P.: Rather Press, (1978), large 8vo., stiff paper wrappers. (16) pages. $ 35.00

Limited to an edition of 200 copies. Annotated listing of the titles produced during the first ten years of the Rather Press, "a purely private press, not operated for profit, the vehicle of the whims of its partners, Clif and Lois Rather." Illustrated throughout with black and white illustrations and decorations from their publications. Front cover creased.

1190. (Rather Press) THANKS, JANE - JANE BISSELL GRABHORN 1911–1973. Oakland, CA: The Rather Press, 1974, 8vo., paper wrappers, cord tied. (24) pages. $ 35.00
Limited to 149 copies. Lois and Clif Rather published this selection of her letters as a memorial to Jane Grabhorn. The charming and generous spirit of this talented printer shine through her letters written to the Rathers in 1970.

1191. (Reagh, Patrick) Bidwell, John (editor). BIBLIOPHILE'S LOS ANGELES, ESSAYS FOR THE INTERNATIONAL ASSOCIATION OF BIBLIOPHILES ON THE OCCASION OF ITS XIVTH CONGRESS. Los Angeles: University of California, 1985, 8vo., cloth-backed boards, paper spine label. x, 186, (2) pages. $ 100.00
Limited to 350 copies. Foreword by Robert Vosper followed by eight essays on collecting and books by Robert Rosenthal, Tyrus G. Harmsen, Richard H. Rouse, Charles L. Heiskell, Ward Ritchie, Ruth E. Fine, and Alan Jutzi. Printed by Patrick Reagh.

1192. (Reagh, Patrick) Lange, Gerald W., Ed. CORANTO, JOURNAL OF THE FRIENDS OF THE LIBRARIES, UNIVERSITY OF SOUTHERN CALIFORNIA. N.P.: University of Southern California, 1988, 8vo., stiff paper wrappers. 47 pages. $ 15.00
Issue No. 24. A revival of the dormant journal, no.23 having been published in 1985. In this issue four authors reminisce over southern California's rich tradition of fine printing, examine its present state and explore future possibilities. Articles by guest editor Lange, Ward Ritchie, Sandra D. Kirschenbaum, Tyrus G. Harmsen. Lange designed this issue and it was letterpress printed by Patrick Reagh at his shop in Glendale, CA.

1193. (Reagh, Patrick) Powell, Lawrence Clark. THE ROAD TO SWARTHMOOR. Tucson: Privately printed, 1996, 8vo., handmade paper wrappers, paper cover label. (viii), 13, (5) pages. $ 45.00
First edition, privately issued by the author on his 90th birthday. An autobiographical sketch. Designed by Vance Gerry and printed by Patrick Reagh. Signed by Powell on the title page.

1194. (Reagh, Patrick) Powell, Lawrence Clark. Z TO A. TRAVEL NOTES FROM ILLYRIA TO CAMBRIA. 1966. Tucson: (Lawrence Powell), 1990, 8vo., stiff paper wrappers. (viii), 12, (2) pages. $ 25.00
Remembrances of Powell's travels in Zagreb, Dubrovnik and Aberystwyth where he gave speeches on library related topics. A keepsake for the 20th biennial meeting of the Roxburghe and Zamorano clubs in Los Angeles, 1990. Illustrated. Printed by Patrick Reagh and bound by Bela Blau.

1195. (Reagh, Patrick) Ritchie, Ward. FINE PRINTERS, THE NEW GENERATION IN SOUTHERN CALIFORNIA. Sacramento: California State Library Foundation, 1988, 8vo., paper wrappers. 25, (3) pages, with 2 additional leaves of illustrations.
                                                                             $ 35.00
Printed by Patrick Reagh (one of the printers discussed) in an edition limited to 1000 copies.

1196. (Reagh, Patrick) Ritchie, Ward. FINE PRINTING, THE LOS ANGELES TRADITION. Washington: Library of Congress, 1987, small 8vo., stiff paper wrappers. viii, 65, (3) pages. $ 25.00
A lecture by Ward Ritchie, pioneer bookman and printer of southern California, sponsored by the Center for the Book in the Library of Congress. Designed by Scott Freutel, printed by Patrick Reagh in an edition of 1500 copies, bound by Cardoza-James. Illustrated.

1197. (Reagh, Patrick) Rubovits, Norma. MARBLED VIGNETTES. Los Angeles: Dawson's Book Shop, 1992, small 4to., cloth. (iv), 8 pages. $ 150.00

Limited to 135 copies printed letterpress by Patrick Reagh on Arches Text Wove. A conversation between Muir Dawson and Norma Rubovits on marbling accompanied by one marbled vignette as a frontispiece mounted under a window mat.

1198. (Reagh, Patrick) Rubovits, Norma. MARBLED VIGNETTES. Los Angeles: Dawson's Book Shop, 1992, small 4to., cloth loosely inserted in a matching imported fabric covered clamshell case containing the text volume and 5 matted examples of marbled vignettes. (iv), 8 pages. $ 750.00

Limited to 135 numbered and signed copies printed letterpress by Patrick Reagh on Arches Text Wove; this is one of 35 sets accompanied by the extra examples and inserted in case. A conversation between Muir Dawson and Norma Rubovits on marbling accompanied by one marbled vignette as a frontispiece mounted under a window mat. Each of the vignettes are single marbled sheets and not a cut out from a larger sheet. Each vignette is unique in size, color and design and have been signed by Rubovits.

1199. (Reagh, Patrick) Thrower, Norman J.W. LEAF FROM THE MERCATOR-HONDIUS WORLD ATLAS, EDITION OF 1619, WITH AN ESSAY BY NORMAN J.W. THROWER. Fullerton, CA: Stone & Lorson Publishers, 1985, folio, quarter vellum over boards, slipcase. (viii), 23, (3) pages. $ 495.00

Limited to 115 numbered copies printed by Patrick Reagh with design by Vance Gerry. "The first leaf book to incorporate a double page, 18 x 22 inch map ...." The leaf is a beautiful example of map production and is hand-colored.

1200. (Reagh, Patrick) Tufts, Kingsley. CONCEPTS AND IMPRESSIONS. (Los Angeles): Privately printed, 1989, 8vo., cloth. x,105, (3) pages. $ 55.00

Printed in an edition limited to 250 numbered copies signed by the author. Designed by Kingsley Tufts in collaboration with William and Victoria Dailey and printed letterpress in Baskerville types on Rivas paper by Patrick Reagh. A book of poetry.

1201. (Reagh, Patrick) Tufts, Kingsley. FRAGMENTS AND CONSEQUENCES. (Los Angeles): Privately printed, 1990, 8vo., cloth. x, 115, (3) pages. $ 55.00

Printed in an edition limited to 250 numbered copies signed by the author. Designed by Kingsley Tufts in collaboration with William and Victoria Dailey and printed letterpress in Baskerville types on Rivas paper by Patrick Reagh. Gift card from the author to a Library laid in. Poetry.

1202. (Reagh, Patrick) Lailá, Majnun. THE RED GULL PRESS AND TWINROCKER HANDMADE PAPER ARE PLEASED TO ANNOUNCE THE PUBLICATION OF A BOOK OF TRANSLATIONS OF POEMS BY A SEVENTH-CENTURY ARAB POET MAJNUN LAILÁ. (Hitchin, England: Red Gull Press, 1985), large 8vo., stiff paper wrappers. (6) pages with one leaf bound-in. $ 20.00

Prospectus printed in an edition of 300 copies for *Poems* by Majnun Haila, the seventh-century Arab poet whose work and legend has strongly influenced Sufi diction and thought. Both the prospectus and the *Poems* it announces were produced by Michael Gullick at his Red Gull Press. One of the 125 copies with a reject leaf from the book bound in as a sample of the abaca fibre paper made by Kathryn and Howard Clark of Twinrocker Handmade Paper.

1203. (Red Howler Press) Moyer, David M. ARTIFICIAL HORIZONS. Lebanon, PA: Red Howler Press, 1990, tall 4to., stiff paper wrappers, bound in Japanese fashion. (36) pages. $ 125.00

Printed in an edition limited to only 50 signed and numbered copies. Includes a preface by Robert Troxell. Contains seven original wood-engravings by David Moyer, each signed and numbered. Wood-engravings printed from endgrain maple blocks on Okawara Japanese paper.

1204. (Red Howler Press) Moyer, David M. TOWERS. Lebanon, PA: Red Howler Press, 1992, 4to., stiff paper wrappers, bound in the Japanese. (32) pages. $ 135.00

Printed in an edition limited to only 50 numbered and signed copies. Includes six original wood engravings from maple blocks each being numbered and signed by the artist, David Moyer. Introduction by Gretchen Heinze. A imagined tour of the towers where scientists work, as inspired by Francis Bacon's *The New Atlantis*.

1205. (Red Hydra Press) Baker, Cathleen A. BY HIS OWN LABOR, THE BIOGRAPHY OF DARD HUNTER. Two volumes. Northport, AL: Red Hydra Press, 2000, small 4to., quarter green leather and printed pattern paper covered boards by Gray Parrot, cloth clamshell box, paper spine label. 368 pages. $ 1,800.00

Printed letterpress in an edition limited to 155 numbered and signed copies of which only 125 copies are offered for sale. A new authorized biography of Dard Hunter based largely upon the manuscript archive in preserved in Hunter's Mountain House. A passionate yet critical study of Dard Hunter's life with a moving account of the trials, successes, and legacy of this larger-than-life artist. Hunter's many accomplishments are described in a descriptive bibliography of his design work for the Roycroft shops and his own limited edition books. This is followed by a description of his Paper-making moulds and watermarks. Finely illustrated with 124 plates with some in black and white and some in color. They depict various illustrations from books, original drawings, and family photos. Includes a two-color wood engraved frontispiece portrait of Hunter by John DePol printed from the original blocks. Finely printed on dampened handmade paper created especially for this project by Twinrocker. Indexed. This is sure to be a major addition to the reference literature available on Dard Hunter.

1206. (Red Mountain Editions) Beecher, John. TO LIVE AND DIE IN DIXIE & OTHER POEMS. Birmingham: Red Mountain Editions, (1966), 8vo., cloth, paper spine label, dust jacket. 93 (3) pages. $ 65.00

First edition. Book design and block prints by Barbara Beecher. Forty-seven poems on a wide variety of themes. The opening poem, *In Egypt Land*, is a dramatic narrative of a black sharecroppers' revolt in Alabama (1932). Of this poem John Howard Griffin, author of *Black Like Me*, says: "I have read John Beecher's *In Egypt Land* so often that it has become part of my own conscience. It is a great work, timeless and contemporary and somehow growing from the very earth that Beecher knows so well and loves so poignantly." John Beecher was a great-great-nephew of Henry Ward Beecher and Harriet Beecher Stowe. Inscribed by author on front free endpaper.

1207. (Redcoat Press) Lamb, Charles. GRACE BEFORE MEAT, AN ESSAY OF ELIA. Westport: The Redcoat Press, 1952, 12mo., cloth-backed boards. (vi), 25, (3) pages. $ 35.00

Limited to 210 copies. Two page preface by the printer followed by the reprint of this short essay. Printed by hand with ornaments in red.

1208. (Redcoat Press) Smith, Alexander. ON THE IMPORTANCE OF A MAN TO HIMSELF. Westport, CT: The Redcoat Press, 1946, 12mo., cloth- backed marbled paper covered boards. (iv), 32, (4) pages. $ 65.00

Limited to 160 copies printed on "The Spur" handmade paper. (Ransom 22; PPNYP p.255).

1209. (Riccardi Press) London, O.R. KING WHO KNEW NOT FEAR, A TALE OF OTHER DAYS. London: Philip Lee Warner, Publisher to the Medici Society, 1912, 8vo., half-cloth over boards. 30, (6) pages. $ 45.00

Limited to 530 numbered copies. The first book printed in Riccardi 11-point face. (Tompkinson p.150). The Riccardi Press Booklets, No.1.Spine age darkened. and rubbed along edges.

1210. (Riccardi Press) Purser, Louis Claude. APULEI PSYCHE ET CUPIDO. London: Medici Society, 1913, 8vo., quarter cloth, paper-covered boards. (viii), 41, (2) pages.

$ 45.00

Printed in an edition limited to 525 numbered copies. From the series, *Scriptorum Classicorum Bibliotheca Riccardiana*, published by the Medici Society, founded by publisher Philip Lee Warner. Roman author Lucius Apuleius (125? - 175?) greatly influenced the beginnings of western prose fiction, and this untranslated version of his *Cupid and Psyche* was edited by renowned classics scholar Purser. Printed by Riccardi Press on hand-made paper. Bookplate of Jacob Hammer and booksellers tag on front pastedown. Library stamp on front free endpaper, pocket removed from rear pastedown.

1211. (Ritchie, Ward) Grayson, Charles. THE SPORTSMAN'S HORNBOOK. New York: Random House, 1933, 8vo., quarter leather with paper covered boards, two raised bands. xiii, (i), 169, (3) pages. $ 125.00

Limited to edition of 500 copies. A loosely inserted Random House Fall and Winter 1933–1934 CATALOGUE describes this volume as "an anthology of sporting verse from Greek times to yesterday's newspapers." Selections include Henry Van Dyke on fishing, Virgil on boxing, Chaucer on the hunt and Christopher Morley on swimming. Designed by Ward Ritchie with illustrations by Ernest Smythe. Head of spine, paper on cover chipped.

1212. (Ritchie, Ward) Agnew, Franklin H. THE LAY OF A SUMMER'S DAY, OR LOVE IS "MIGHTIER THAN ALL." Los Angeles: Faun Press, 1933, large 12mo., quarter cloth with decorated paper-covered boards, dust jacket. 48, (2) pages. $ 45.00

Designed and printed for the Faun Press by Ward Ritchie, in an edition limited to 100 copies (Ritchie, p.70). Poetry on Love and Religion. Dust jacket chipped with pieces missing from spine.

1213. (Ritchie, Ward) Anderson, Gregg. WORK OF THE MERRYMOUNT PRESS AND ITS FOUNDER DANIEL BERKELEY UPDIKE (1860–1941), AN EXHIBITION PREPARED BY GREGG ANDERSON. San Marino: The Huntington Library, 1942, small 8vo., paper wrappers. (ii), 35, (3) pages. $ 20.00

Printed at the Ward Ritchie Press.

1214. (Ritchie, Ward) Barr, William P. THE PAGEANT OF MAN'S REDEMPTION, AN INTERPRETATION OF THE CHOPINEAUX TAPESTRY. Los Angeles: (Mrs. Edward Lawrence Doheny), 1948, 8vo., cloth, paper cover label. 28, (2) pages.

$ 95.00

Printed in an edition limited to 100 numbered copies by Anderson & Ritchie, designed by Joseph Simon, and selected by the Rounce and Coffin Club as one of the Western Books of 1948 (Ritchie, 98). Inscribed by the publisher (Estelle Doheny, 1948) on the front free endpaper. The tapestry was woven in 1784 "with a center medallion of the Crucifixion after the painting by Rubens." In 1948 it was acquired by Estelle Doheny, who placed it in its permanent home in the Laurence Doheny Memorial Library, in St. John's Seminary, Camarillo, California. With color print of the tapestry as frontispiece.

1215. (Ritchie, Ward) Baughman, Roland and Robert Schad. GREAT BOOKS IN GREAT EDITIONS, AN EXHIBITION COMMEMORATING THE 500TH ANNIVESARY OF THE INVENTION OF PRINTING. San Marino: The Huntington Library, 1940, square 8vo., self paper wrappers. 48 pages. $ 15.00

Printed by the Ward Ritchie Press. Illustrated.

1216. (Ritchie, Ward) Beck, Melissa. TYPOGRAPHIC BOOKPLATES OF WARD RITCHIE. With a Foreword by Ward Ritchie. Santa Monica, CA: Kenneth Karmiole, 1990, 8vo., cloth-backed paper over boards. Not paginated. $ 55.00

First edition, limited to 300 copies. Contains an illustration and brief description of each of the 90 bookplates designed by this California printer.

1217. (Ritchie, Ward) COPYBOOK FROM THE HAND OF AGUSTIN V. ZAMORANO. With text by George L. Harding, Roby Wentz, and Ray Nash. Los Angeles: The Zamorano Club, 1974, small 4to., cloth. (xviii) page followed by 7 leaves of facsimile. $ 95.00
Limited to 250 copies printed by Ward Ritchie for the Zamorano Club. A facsimile of this early 19th century copybook prepared by Zamorano for his friend Don Ignacio Coronel, Los Angeles' first school teacher. Covers slightly rubbed.

1218. (Ritchie, Ward) Cowan, Robert Ernest. 1850–1870 FORGOTTEN CHARACTERS OF OLD SAN FRANCISCO. (Los Angeles): Ward Ritchie Press, 1938, small 8vo., stiff paper wrappers. 65, (2) pages. $ 35.00
Printed in an edition of 500 copies, of which 25 were reserved for members of the Rounce and Coffin Club. Historian Cowan, the great bibliographer of California, portrays flamboyant old San Francisco eccentrics, such as Emperor Norton and Philo Jacoby, in an entertaining style with a wealth of contemporary detail. Book designed by Ward Ritchie and selected as one of the Western books (Ritchie, p. 77). Contains eight illustrations: photos and facsimiles. Wide margins; text printed in black; headpiece and ornaments with red.

1219. (Ritchie, Ward) Hard, Frederick. IF MUSIC & SWEET POETRY AGREE. Los Angeles: The Ward Ritchie Press, 1954, 8vo., paper wrappers. 31, (2) pages. $ 15.00
Printed in an edition limited to 400 copies. (Warde Ritchie Press pg 112). Presentation copy 'For Phil Hanna with warm regards, Frederick Hard." An address before the Sunset Club on Monday, November 22, 1954. Covers faded.

1220. (Ritchie, Ward) Hathaway, Louise. THE ENCHANTED HOUR. San Francisco: John J. Newbegin, (1970), small 8vo., cloth, paper cover and spine labels. ix, (i), 129+(1) pages. $ 30.00
Printed in an edition limited to 500 copies. (Warde Ritchie pg 84). The established facts and legends surrounding a historic locket which Hathaway spotted in a jewelry store. Covers slightly faded.

1221. (Ritchie, Ward) Jeffers, Robinson. STARS. Pasadena: Flame Press, 1930, large 12mo., stiff paper wrappers. 3+(1) pages. $ 750.00
First edition, second printing, one of 110 copies printed by Ward Ritchie on March 10, 1930, "with the kind permission of Mr. Robinson Jeffers (Harmsen, *Lilienthal Jeffers Collection*, p. 23)." The first printing was limited to 80 copies, in black boards, but only 15 or so were bound and distributed, according to the printer. The Flame Press was the first press name used by Ward Ritchie, inspired by a Rockwell Kent engraving he had seen in Jake Zeitlin's bookstore in Los Angeles. The design was of a reclining man with an arm upraised against a background of a huge flame. Pages uncut.

1222. (Ritchie, Ward) Ritchie, Ward. JOHN GUTENBERG, 1440–1940, A FANCIFUL STORY OF THE 15TH CENTURY. Los Angeles: Ward Ritchie Press, 1940, 8vo., stiff paper wrappers. 49, (3) pages. $ 20.00
First edition, limited to 300 copies. A spoof relating the history of John Gutenberg. Indentation mark on front cover and first blank

1223. (Ritchie, Ward) Jones, Louise Seymour. HAVE PATIENCE LITTLE SAINT, A GARDENER'S CRUSADE. Los Angeles: Ward Ritchie Press, (1941), 8vo., paper-covered boards, dust jacket. x, 154 pages. $ 45.00
Designed and printed by Ward Ritchie (Ritchie, p.85). Inscribed by the author on half-title page. The final volume in "A Garden Trilogy, following *Who Loves a Garden (1935)* and *Put a Feather in Your Hat* (1938). Dust jacket in two pieces with part of spine lacking.

1224. (Ritchie, Ward) Jones, Louise Seymour. PUT A FEATHER IN YOUR HAT, LIGHT GARDEN READING. Los Angeles: The Ward Ritchie Press, (1938), 8vo., quarter cloth with paper-covered boards, paper spine label. 150 pages. $ 45.00
Designed by Ward Ritchie (Ritchie, p.77). Short essays and poems, Signed by the author on the half title.

1225. (Ritchie, Ward) KELMSCOTT, DOVES AND ASHENDENE, THE PRIVATE PRESS CREDOS. With an Introduction by Will Ransom. New York: The Typophiles, 1952, tall 12mo., cloth. vi, 197+(1) pages. $ 65.00
Limited to 700 copies of which this is one of the 400 printed for the Typophiles as Chapbook 27. Reprints articles by Frederic Goudy, William Morris, S.C. Cockerell, T.J. Cobden-Sanderson, Alfred W. Pollard, Edward Johnston and C.H. StJ. Hornby. Contains a note on this book by Paul A. Bennett. Designed by Ward Ritchie and printed by Anderson - Ritchie. Covers slightly faded.

1226. (Ritchie, Ward) Keran, Don W. (compiler). DAVID W. DAVIES: A BIBLIOGRAPHY. Fullerton, CA: Orangerie Press, California State University, 1973, small 8vo., stiff paper wrappers. 39+(1) pages. $ 15.00
A bibliography of the writings of David W. Davies, scholar, librarian, and founder of the Orangerie Press. With entertaining annotations by DWD, a biographical sketch, and several affectionate essays by friends and colleagues. Printed by Ward Ritchie at the Castle Press.

1227. (Ritchie, Ward) Kindersley, David. MR ERIC GILL. Los Angeles: Warde Ritchie Press, 1967, 12mo., stiff paper wrappers. 26 pages. $ 25.00
Crease in front cover.

1228. (Ritchie, Ward) Latimore, Sarah Briggs and Grace Clark Haskell. ARTHUR RACKHAM, A BIBLIOGRAPHY. Los Angeles: Suttonhouse, 1936, 8vo., cloth-backed boards, slipcase. xiv, 111+(1) pages. $ 425.00
First edition, limited to 550 numbered copies. Printed by the Ward Ritchie Press. With many illustrations including a full color reproduction of a scene from IMAGINA as the frontispiece. Very scarce in first edition.

1229. (Ritchie, Ward) Leitch, Flavia Gaines. PRAYING THROUGH. Los Angeles: Pilot Press, (1932), large 12mo., cloth. (ii), 68 pages. $ 35.00
Designed by Ward Ritchie. "The world needs men and women, today, who can pray through for suffering humanity." Minor chipping on spine. Previous owner's name in pencil on front free endpaper.

1230. (Ritchie, Ward) McCloy, Elizabeth Johnston. OCCIDENTAL COLLEGE LIBRARY, AN APPRECIATION OF THE FOUNDERS AND DONORS. Los Angeles: Occidental College, 1953. $ 15.00
Handsomely printed on handmade paper by Anderson & Ritchie at The Ward Ritchie Press. An acknowledgement of gifts recently given to the library, as well as homage to founders and friends who contributed books, financial help and support in the past.

1231. (Ritchie, Ward) Morley, Christopher. THE GUTENBERG ADDRESS. Los Angeles: Ward Ritchie Press, 1942, tall 8vo., stapled, self paper wrappers. (8) pages. $ 25.00
Limited to 2,000 copies. Essay on books, war and Nazis, with a proposed "Gutenberg Address" ("Twenty-five score years ago, a German workman brought forth a new idea, conceived in...(etc)." A Morley parody without parasitic intent. With 2-color cover illustration.

1232. (Ritchie, Ward) Nee, Elaine Castle. LETTERS & NOTES, VOLUME I. Los Angeles: Ward Ritchie Press, 1953, 8vo., quarter cloth with illustrated paper covered boards paper spine label, dust jacket. xxii, 499, (31) pages. $ 65.00
Diary entries from Los Angeles in the early 1930's, letters, essays on Virginia Wolf, reading the American classics, and conversations with a drug store clerk. Many photographs and 2 prints by Laura van Pappelendam. Light foxing on front cover and endpapers.

1233. (Ritchie, Ward) Parkes, Dow. NIDUS, A DRAMATIC POEM IN THREE VOICES. Los Angeles: Ward Ritchie Press, (1950), 8vo., paper-covered boards. (ii), 44, (4) pages. $ 75.00
Printed in an edition limited to 100 copies, handset in Bembo on Strathmore Pastelle paper. Designed by Ward Ritchie, with typesetting by the author, and the presswork by Joseph Simon. Thirty additional copies were printed for presentation to members of the Rounce & Coffin Club. Selected as one of the Western Books for 1950 (Ritchie, 101).

1234. (Ritchie, Ward) Pitwood, James Beattie. THE SLOUGH OF DESPOND FROM A POEM. (Pasadena: Ward Ritchie), 1929, 8vo., self paper wrappers. (4) pages. $ 20.00
First edition. (Ritchie p. 127) First stanza of a poem written by Ritchie under one of his pen names and printed by him at the Frank Wiggins Trade School.

1235. (Ritchie, Ward) Ritchie, Ward. A PRINTER'S SALUTE TO ENGLAND ON AMERICA'S BICENTENNIAL. London: Wynken de Worde Society, 1976, 8vo., stiff paper wrappers. (ii), 16 pages. $ 20.00
Printed at the Curwen Press on paper donated by Grosvenor Chater & Co, with typography by Banks and Miles. A talk given at the Wynken de Worde Society International Meeting at Stationer's Hall, London, on 15 July, 1976. Discusses Ritchie's visit to England in 1931, with his anecdotes about Francis Meynell of the Nonesuch Press, Richard Cobden-Sanderson, John Johnson at the Oxford University Press, Bruce Rogers, Robert Graves and Laura Riding at their Seizen Press in Palma, Mallorca, and others. Photograph of Ritchie as frontispiece.

1236. (Ritchie, Ward) Ritchie, Ward. WARD RITCHIE PRESS AND ANDERSON, RITCHIE, AND SIMON. With a Foreword by Lawrence Clark Powell. Los Angeles: Ward Ritchie Press, 1961, small 8vo., cloth, paper spine label. x, 156, (2) pages. $ 60.00
First edition, limited to 1300 copies of which this is one of 1000 of the trade edition. A bibliography of books designed and printed by Ritchie. With a number of title page reproductions.

1237. (Ritchie, Ward) Rosenberg, Betty. CHECKLIST OF THE PUBLISHED WRITINGS OF LAWRENCE CLARK POWELL. Foreword by W.W. Robinson. Los Angeles: University of California, 1966, 8vo., stiff paper wrappers. 96, (2) pages. $ 25.00
Printed by the Ward Ritchie Press.

1238. (Ritchie, Ward) Ruud, Gudrun. BRIDE OF THE WIND. Los Angeles: (Ward Ritchie Press), 1937, small 8vo., quarter cloth, paper covered boards, paper spine label, deckled fore edge. (x), 48, (2) pages with five leaves of illustrations. $ 65.00
Limited to 275 copies printed for the author. Small volume of poetry with black and white illustrations by Agnes Schubert. Presentation copy signed in ink by the author on front free endpaper. Spine label worn.

1239. (Ritchie, Ward) Smith, George Smedley. INTERVALLUM. (Los Angeles): Anderson & Ritchie: The Ward Ritchie Press, (1948), large 8vo., quarter cloth with paper covered boards, paper spine label. (30) French fold pages. $ 75.00
Printed in an edition limited to 58 copies (Ritchie, page 98). Designed by Fred Reid and set by hand in Centaur and Arrighi types. A book of eighteen poems. Selected as one of the Western books of 1948.

1240. (Ritchie, Ward) Ritchie, Ward. A TALE OF TWO BOOKS. Los Angeles: Printed by Richard J. Hoffman, n.d. (circa 1985), 8vo., stiff paper wrappers. 26, (2) pages.
$ 35.00

First edition. Ritchie provides a behind-the-scenes look at his work with Merle Armitage and Alfred Young Fisher on two separate occasions. Introduction by Charles Heiskell, president of the Book Collectors of Los Angeles.

1241. (Ritchie, Ward) Ritchie, Ward. VARIATIONS AND QUOTATIONS. Laguna Beach: Ward Ritchie, 1990, 8vo., half cloth over sculptured boards, diagonally positioned printed paper label. (iv), (34), (2) pages.
$ 475.00

First edition, limited to 50 copies signed by Ward Ritchie. An interesting production from this great designer and printer. Contains one line quotes from a variety of famous people including Lawrence Clark Powell, Ernest Hemingway, and William Addison Dwiggins. Each is complimented by an abstract illustration of blocks and squares printed in a variety of colors.

1242. (Ritchie, Ward) Ritchie, Ward. YEARS TOUCHED WITH MEMORIES. With a Foreword by Lawrence Clark Powell. Clifton: Bookman Publications, Inc., (1992), 8vo., cloth-backed boards. (viii), 171 pages.
$ 38.00

First edition. The autobiography of this legendary California bookman. He recalls his private press work, his friends Lawrence Clark Powell, Jake Zeitlin, Paul Landacre, Robinson Jeffers, W.A. Dwiggins and many others. Illustrated.

1243. (Riva, Franco) Carducci, Giosue. PER IL TRANSPORTO DELLE RELIQUIE DI UGO FOSFOLO IN SANTA CROCE. Poiano, Italy: Franco Riva, 1978, folio, cloth covered boards. (8) pages.
$ 150.00

Finely letterpress printed by Franco Riva on his handpress in an edition limited to 100 numbered copies. Printed on handmade specially watermarked paper with Riva's press device. Riva was a scholar of Italian printing and a sometime collaborator with Giovanni Mardersteig to which the design of this item pays homage. The text is a poem about the relics of St. Foscolo which were transferred in 1871 from England to the church of Santa Croce in Florence. Finely printed in the manner of Officina Bodoni. Covers show some soiling.

1244. (Robert Reid & Takao Tanabe) Claudet, F.G. GOLD, ITS PROPERTIES, MODES OF EXTRACTION, VALUE, &C. Vancouver, Canada: Robert Reid & Takao Tanabe, 1958, 8vo., one quarter oasis niger with leather spine label and marbled paper covered boards. 44+(4) pages.
$ 195.00

Printed in an edition limited to 275 numbered copies. First published in 1871. Introduction by Neal Harlow. Includes tipped in facsimile of the original title cover.

SEVEN SIGNED WOOD ENGRAVINGS AND A WATERCOLOR BY JOHN O'CONNOR

1245. (Rocket Press) O'Connor, John. ARIEL AND MIRANDA, SEVEN WOOD ENGRAVINGS BY...INSPIRED BY SHAKESPEARE' S "THE TEMPEST". Blewbury, Oxfordshire: The Rocket Press, n.d.(1992), folio, clamshell case with paper labels, folded sheet, sheets mounted in stiff board folders. (4) pages, 8 folders. $ 1,350.00

Printed in an edition limited to 65 numbered sets, of which this is one of 20 which include an original watercolor. John S. O'Connor (1913-) was a student of Eric Ravilious, John Nash and others at the Royal Academy of Art in the mid-30's. His own works began to appear in the late 30's, some of them in the publications of the Golden Cockerell Press. Since that time, Mr. O'Connor has produced paintings, watercolors, lithographs, and engravings in various media. Peppin and Micklethwait (Dictionary of British Book Illustrators, 1983, p.218) describe his wood engravings as "strikingly decorative in the tradition of Eric Ravilious, with tonal and textural contrast achieved through a wide variety of tooling." Hamilton (Wood Engraving and the Woodcut in England c1890–1990, 1994, p.150) characterizes O'Connor's work (his landscapes) as "strong edges, deep shadows and dramatic contrasts of light and dark" which give "a sense of rhythm and pattern to the image." Garrett (History of British Wood Engraving, 1978, p.222) regards O'Connor's engraving style as in the "Ravilious manner," which he has just described (p.221) as "illustrative, decorative and dominated by intricate pattern and texture." In his introduction to this set, Mr. O'Connor discusses his interest in Shakespeare's The Tempest and provides the rationale for these engravings: "I like to consider the years previous to the brief action of the play. The "sprite" close to his master and to Miranda the child: and I suggest the boy and girl would have enjoyed each other's company in the manner of brother and sister. He would be a little wild; she enclosed in that strangely mature innocence that is written into Miranda. Shy at first, the two children would play in streams, collect herbs..." etc. There are nine illustrations: the seven signed and numbered (with regard to copy) engravings, a similarly signed watercolor on the same theme but not precisely copying any of the engravings, and a small (3x4 in.) unsigned engraving affixed to the front of the clamshell case. Figures (Ariel and Miranda, or Ariel alone) are variously posed, each partially outlined by a pure white area roughly approximating their forms. Two prints are in black, yellow, and white; the rest are black-and-white. Sizes (other than the case illustration) are roughly 4x6 or 6x8 inches. Cutouts in fronts of folders frame the pictures when the folders are closed. Accompanied by a folded folio sheet with title and Mr. O'Connor's introduction and signed by the artist (verso of the title page), with the annotation "92," presumably the date of publication. The interior lining of the clamshell case is printed with a repeated motif taken from one of the engravings. Printed at the Rocket Press.

1246. (Rogers, Bruce) Aldrich, Thomas Bailey. A BOOK OF SONGS AND SONNETS SELECTED FROM THE POEMS OF THOMAS BAILEY ALDRICH. (Boston: Houghton, Mifflin), 1906, large 12mo., paper-covered boards. 113+(1) pages. $ 60.00

Printed in an edition limited to 430 numbered copies at the Riverside Press, Boston, for Houghton, Mifflin, designed and typeset by Bruce Rogers (Warde, 70). Aldrich (1836–1907) was editor of the *Atlantic Monthly*, author of stories such as *The Story of a Bad Boy*, and several volumes of poetry. Minor wear to head and tail of spine. Previous owner's bookplate on front pastedown.

1247. (Rogers, Bruce) Beatty, John W. RELATION OF ART TO NATURE. New York: William Edwin Rudge, 1922, 8vo., cloth-backed boards. (xviii), 71, (11) pages. $ 50.00

First edition, limited to 950 copies. designed by Bruce Rogers. (Warde no.163). Rubbed along bottom of front cover.

1248. (Rogers, Bruce) Carlyle, Thomas. JOCELIN OF BRAKELOND. New York: William Edwin Rudge, 1923, large 12mo., cloth. (xii), 157, (3) pages. $ 60.00

Printed from Caslon monotype by Bruce Rogers at the press of William Edwin Rudge, Mount Vernon, NY, in an edition limited to 510 numbered copies (Warde, 168). Introduction by Patrick Kearney. An account of monastic life in twelfth century England based on a contemporary manuscript and included with commentary as part of Carlyle's book *Past and Present*, printed in 1843. Pages uncut.

1249. (Rogers, Bruce) Conrad, Joseph. TREMOLINO. New York: Philip C. Duschnes, 1942, small 8vo., boards, slipcase. (iv), 59, (3) pages. $ 175.00

Limited to 1000 copies and designed by Bruce Rogers. Printed at the Press of A. Colish with colored woodcuts by E.A. Wilson who has signed the colophon page. With a presentation from Bruce Rogers dated 1942 on second blank page. Accompanied by a folder showing that this copy came from the library of Will Ransom. The folder has the four page prospectus mounted along with Ransom's bookplate which describes this acquisition. Bookplate on front pastedown which has come loose and exposed the glue marks underneath it.

1250. (Rogers, Bruce) Cooke, George Willis. BIBLIOGRAPHY OF JAMES RUSSELL LOWELL. Boston: Houghton Mifflin and Co., 1906, 8vo., cloth, paper spine label. xii, 208 pages. $ 40.00

First edition, limited to 530 numbered copies. Designed by Bruce Rogers. Front hinge partially split. With bookplate of private book-collecting club's library. Prospectus mounted to back pastedown.

1251. (Rogers, Bruce) Forrester, Alfred Henry. A FEW WORDS ABOUT PIPES, SMOKING & TOBACCO. New York: New York Public Library, 1947, small 8vo., quarter cloth with paper-covered boards. xii, 91+(1) pages. $ 55.00

Designed by Bruce Rogers and printed by A. Colish, New York in an edition limited to 500 copies (Blumenthal, pp.178-9). Text throughout set in Cochin italic. Publications No. 1 from the New York Public Library Arents Tobacco Collection. An unpublished manuscript, circa 1840, written and profusely illustrated by Alfred Henry Forrester (1804–1872), well-known in his day as "Alfred Crowquill, " an English caricaturist and author.

1252. (Rogers, Bruce) Freeman, John. THE RED PATH AND THE WOUNDED BIRD. Cambridge: Dunster House, 1921, large 8vo., quarter cloth with paper covered boards, paper cover label. (viii), 30, (2) pages. $ 150.00

Printed in an edition limited to 450 this being one of the 50 which are numbered and signed. (Warde no.148, Updike no.297). Two poems by John Freeman. Designed by Bruce Rogers. Corners show wear. Minor foxing.

1253. (Rogers, Bruce) Gargaz, Pierre-Andre. PROJECT OF UNIVERSAL AND PERPETUAL PEACE. New York: George Simpson Eddy, 1922, 12mo., cloth-backed boards, paper spine label, slipcase. (vi), vi, 25, 25, 47, 47, 4, ix pages. $ 85.00

Limited to 1250 copies designed by Bruce Rogers (Warde 159) and printed by William Edwin Rudge. First edition reprinted along with an English version, with an introduction and typographical note by Eddy. Label chipped; slipcase rubbed. Presentation from Rogers "To W. van R. Whitall from Bruce Rogers, 7 Nov. 1923." With Whitall's leather bookplate. Wear at head of spine and bumped. Slipcase coming apart.

1254. (Rogers, Bruce) Guralnik, David B. MAKING OF A NEW DICTIONARY. Cleveland: The World Publishing Co., (1953), 8vo., paper wrappers. (ii), 26 pages.
$ 15.00

The story of the making of Webster's New World Dictionary. This booklet was arranged by Bruce Rogers. Front cover spotted.

1255. (Rogers, Bruce) Hergesheimer, Joseph. THE PRESBYTERIAN CHILD. New York: Knopf, 1923, 8vo., quarter cloth , with decorated paper covered boards, paper spine label, slipcase. 65, (3) pages. $ 45.00

Printed in an edition limited to 950 numbered copies at the press of William Edwin Rudge, Mount Vernon, NY and signed by the author (Warde, 169). Designed and printed by Bruce Rogers on Monotype Scotch Roman. The author's childhood memoirs. Slipcase repaired with cloth tape.

1256. (Rogers, Bruce) THE HISTORY OF OLIVER AND ARTHUR. (Boston: Houghton, Mifflin and Company, 1903), small 4to., quarter linen with linen corners, dark green textured paper sides, paper spine label, slipcase. (xvi), cviii, (iv) pages.
$ 350.00

Number 162 of 330 copies printed at the Riverside Press, Cambridge. (Warde 39; Work of Bruce Rogers 95; Blumenthal p.17). This book is an excellent example of Bruce Rogers' allusive style (where he designed the book in a style appropriate to the period in which it was written.) In this case, Rogers has chosen to illustrate the book with woodcuts, evocative of the period, placed in the text. The book is printed in two columns with the Priory Text font. This is one of three books Rogers did in black-letter for the Riverside Press. Chapter headings, major initial letters, and page numbers are printed in red. The title page is printed with red swash lettering and a woodcut in black. The colophon is also printed in red with Bruce Rogers' initials and a classic thistle design. This is the first English translation of the tale originally written in French in 1511. The tale is of interest in its own right, and doubly so because it apparently is based on the same tale as William Morris' The Friendship of Amis and Amile. Extra spine label tipped in. Inscribed on endpaper to E.R. H(oadley) from W.K. B(ixby) Dec. 25th, 1910. Light wear to slipcase. Book has minor soiling in places. Bookplate. Newspaper review of this book and bookseller's description loosely inserted (which caused minor yellowing of endpaper).

1257. (Rogers, Bruce) Ibycus, Alcman Sappho. POEMS OF ALCMAN SAPPHO IBYCUS. New York: Alfred A. Knopf, 1945, 8vo., creme colored cloth with designs in gilt decorating corners, top edge gilt. Not paginated. $ 40.00
Limited to 950 copies printed for Knopf by A. Colish and with designs in a second color by Bruce Rogers. Translated from the Greek by Olga Marx and Ernst Morwitz with Greek and English texts facing each other. Lengthy introduction. Ink inscription on free endpaper which someone has described in pencil as "presentation from Philip Hofer to Caroline Newton.

1258. (Rogers, Bruce) Lang, Andrew. THIRD IDYLL OF THEOCRITUS. Translated from the Greek by Andrew Lang. New York: Museum Books, 1928, small 4to., paper wrappers. (9) pages. $ 55.00
Limited to 375 copies. (Haas no.144). With a water-color illustration by Bryson Burroughs. A scarce Rogers item, very attractive and uncommon for Rogers in format and design. Chipped around edges.

1259. (Rogers, Bruce) Moore, George. PERONNIK THE FOOL. Mount Vernon: William Edwin Rudge, 1926, 8vo., decorated cloth with paper spine label. (vi), 68, (2) pages. $ 95.00
Limited to 785 copies printed by William Edwin Rudge Press. (Warde 130). Designed by Bruce Rogers and including an interesting colophon printed in black and red incorporating his initials.

1260. (Rogers, Bruce) Moore, T. Sturge. RODERIGO OF BIVAR. New York: William Edwin Rudge, 1925, 8vo., cloth-backed decorated paper covered boards, paper spine label. 51, (3) pages. $ 45.00
Limited to 525 copies. Designed by Bruce Rogers (Haas 113) and printed in Italian Old-style with an ornament in red on the title page. Covers slightly soiled.

1261. (Rogers, Bruce) Morley, John. EDMUND BURKE, A HISTORICAL STUDY. New York: Alfred A. Knopf, 1924, 8vo., cloth. (xvi), 255+(1) pages. $ 65.00
Printed in an edition limited to 780 numbered copies at the press of William Edwin Rudge, Mount Vernon, NY (Warde, 181). Typography by Bruce Rogers. Foreword by Harold J. Laski. With chapters on the English Constitution, Issues of the Time, American Independence, Economical Reform, Ireland and India, his Characteristics, and the French Revolution. Small snag at top of front hinge and part of front cover above title creased and bent.

1262. (Rogers, Bruce) Murdock, Harold. EARL PERCY DINES ABROAD, A BOSWELLIAN EPISODE. Boston: Houghton Mifflin, 1924, large 8vo., cloth, paper spine label, slipcase. xii, 46 pages, 10 plates. $ 85.00
Printed in an edition limited to 550 numbered copies (Warde, 79). Handsomely printed and illustrated by Riverside Press. From 1896–1911 renowned book designer and typographer Bruce Rogers was in charge of its limited editions department, where he not only designed and printed fine books but also designed typefaces that became Riverside hallmarks. This book, penned by eminent historian Murdock, narrates the spirited conversation at an actual dinner party given in London in April 1778 by General Pasquale Paoli in honor of Earl Percy. Among the other guests was James Boswell. A section of informative notes follows the text. Includes ten plates with black and white illustrations, among which are facsimiles and one fold-out map. Most pages unopened. Some wear to slipcase.

1263. (Rogers, Bruce) Norton, Charles Eliot. DIVINE COMEDY OF DANTE ALIGHIERI. New York: Bruce Rogers & The Press of A. Colish, 1954, 8vo., paper wrappers. (8) pages. $ 25.00
Prospectus for this folio edition of Dante with Bruce Roger's illustrations from Botticelli's original drawings. The folio was to be limited to 300 copies. Presentation "For 'Uncle Bob' Leslie from the author of this opus. S.R. Shapiro."

1264. (Rogers, Bruce) Plutarch. A CONSOLATORIE LETTER OR DISCOURSE SENT BY PLUTARCH OF CHAERONEA UNTO HIS OWNE WIFE AS TOUCHING THE DEATH OF HER AND HIS DAUGHTER. Boston: Houghton Mifflin and Co., 1905, 8vo., cloth-backed boards, paper spine label. 31, (3) pages. $ 85.00
Limited to 375 numbered copies. Designed by Bruce Rogers and with his mark in the colophon. Includes a four page prospectus loosely inserted which features a reset title which differs from the actual one used in the book. (Warde no.54) . Rubbed around edges.

1265. (Rogers, Bruce) Rogers, Bruce. [POSTCARD AND LETTER WRITTEN TO MARTHA ANDERSON]. N.P.: n.p., 1939, 1941, 3 1/2" x 5 1/4"; 5 1/2" x 9". $ 50.00
Postcard signed B.R. and stamped April 3, 1939 that Rogers sent to Martha Anderson while he was staying in Nassau, the Bahamas. Also a handwritten letter signed "Bruce Rogers" and dated July 3, 1941 that he mailed to her from his home in New Fairfield, Connecticut.

1266. (Rogers, Bruce) Ronsard, Pierre de. SONGS & SONNETS OF PIERRE DE RONSARD, GENTLEMAN OF VENDOMOIS. Boston: Houghton Mifflin, 1903, large 12mo., paper-covered boards, paper spine label. xxxvi, 137+(1) pages. $ 55.00
Printed in an edition limited to 425 numbered copies by Bruce Rogers at the Riverside Press, Cambridge (Warde, 37). Selected and translated into English verse by Curtis Hidden Page, with an introductory essay & notes. Ronsard (1524–1585) was the best known of a group of poets known as the Pleiade and devoted to revivifying the French language. Some scratches on spine, wear to extremities.

1267. (Rogers, Bruce) Sargent, George H. AMY LOWELL, A MOSAIC. New York: William Edwin Rudge, 1926, 8vo., cloth-backed decorated paper covered boards. (vi), 28, (2) pages. $ 25.00
First edition, limited to 450 copies. (Warde & Haas no. 132) With a checklist of Lowell's writing. Bookplates removed and endpapers spotted. One page with tear.

1268. (Rogers, Bruce) SELECTION OF BOOKS FROM THE LIBRARY OF THE LATE JOHN WILLIAMS WHITE. Cambridge: Dunster House Bookshop, March 1921, small 8vo., paper wrappers. 12 pages. $ 15.00
catalogue no.6 issued by this firm. Printed at William Edwin Rudge and designed by Bruce Rogers (Warde 150) with his mark in the colophon.

1269. (Rogers, Bruce) Shakespeare, William. LOVE'S LABOUR'S LOST. Cambridge: Cambridge University, 1962, 12mo., cloth in dust jacket. (iv), 121+(1) pages. $ 15.00
Issued as a volume in the Cambridge Pocket Shakespeare, edited by John Dover Wilson, with glossary. The basic design is that produced by Bruce Rogers for the *New Shakespeare* (1923). An attractively printed and bound small volume.

1270. (Rogers, Bruce) Slater, John Rothwell. PRINTING AND THE RENAIS-SANCE, A PAPER READ BEFORE THE FORTNIGHTLY CLUB OF ROCHESTER, NEW YORK. New York: William Edwin Rudge, 1921, 8vo., boards, paper spine label. 36 pages. $ 65.00
First edition, limited to 600 copies. Designed by Bruce Rogers (Warde 149). Wear at spine ends. Much better condition than usually found.

Item 1272

1271. (Rogers, Bruce) Southey, Robert. JOURNAL OF A TOUR IN THE NETHER-LANDS IN THE AUTUMN OF 1815. Boston: Houghton, Mifflin, 1902, small 8vo., quarter cloth with marbled paper covered boards. (vi), 273, (3) pages. $ 40.00
Designed and printed in an edition limited to 519 numbered copies by Bruce Rogers at the Riverside Press, Cambridge. (Warde,30). "The MS. was bought at Keswick in 1864, by a well-known North Country banker and antiquarian of the day and is now for the first time published." One of the first trips to Holland by an Englishman after the fall of Napoleon, with many anecdotes and details. Some spotting on spine.

1272. (Rogers, Bruce) Tory, Geofroy. CHAMP FLEURY. BY GEOFROY TORY. TRANSLATED INTO ENGLISH AND ANNOTATED B Y GEORGE B. IVES. New York: The Grolier Club, 1927, 4to., quarter parchment with decorated paper covered boards. (ii), xxiii, 208, (2) pages. $ 650.00
First edition thus, limited to 390 copies. Designed by Bruce Rogers and printed by William Edwin Rudge. English translation of this landmark 16th century book on the formation of letters presented in a beautiful illustrated format by Bruce Rogers. This is one of the most important examples of the design work of Rogers. Parchment spine is soiled; tips are bumped.

[213]

1273. (Rogers, Bruce) Vincent, Leon H. THE FRENCH ACADEMY. Cambridge: Houghton, Mifflin, (1901), large 12mo., cloth. (viii), 159+(1) pages. $ 25.00
Designed by Bruce Rogers and printed at the Riverside Press. Title-page adapted from an engraved title by Moreau-le-jeune (Haas, 33). Brief history of the French Academy from its beginnings as a literary society in the Hotel de Rambouillet in the early 1600's.Bookplate of previous owner on front pastedown. Some wear at extremities.

1274. (Rogers, Bruce) Walsh, Richard J. KIDD: A MORAL OPUSCULE. The Verses (sic) by Richard J. Walsh. Illustrations (sick) by George Illian. New York: William Edwin Rudge, 1922, boards, paper cover label. (22) pages. $ 50.00
First edition. (Warde 161). Illustrations colored by hand. "Executed (hung up) at the Printing House of Billo Rudge" with Fred Goudy as Typothetic Designer, Bertha Goudy as Compositrice Extraordinaire, Bruce Rogers as Lay-out Man, Frank S. Goerke as Lock- up Man, Edith Diehl as Book Bindress, etc. Covers and endpapers are stained. Book has a new cloth spine. However, this copy is inscribed by Bertha Goudy on free endpaper. A good candidate for rebinding.

1275. (Rogers, Bruce) BOMBED BUT UNBEATEN, EXCERPTS FROM THE WAR COMMENTARY OF … WARDE. New York: The Typophiles, 1941, tall 12mo., cloth-backed decorated paper covered boards. xviii, 102 pages. $ 65.00
First edition, limited to 850 numbered copies. With an editorial note by Paul Standard and an appreciation by D.B. Updike. Designed by Bruce Rogers. Chap Book Five issued by the Typophiles. With the bookplate of John DePol.

1276. (Rogers, Bruce) Wendell, Barrett (translator). THE HISTORY OF THE TRANSLATION OF THE BLESSED MARTYRS OF CHRIST, MARCELLINUS AND PETER. Cambridge: Harvard University Press, 1926, 8vo., cloth, paper spine label. (vi), 114, (2) pages. $ 75.00
Printed in an edition limited to 500 copies with typography by Bruce Rogers (Haas, 123). Translated by Barrett Wendell. Originally written by Eginhard, circa 800, whose wife Emma was said to be Charlemagne's daughter, offers a vivid glimpse of life in the ninth century. Some wear to extremities.

1277. (Rogers, Bruce) Wolfe, Humbert. SILVER CAT AND OTHER POEMS. New York: William Edwin Rudge, 1928, 8vo., boards, paper spine label, dust jacket. (32) pages. $ 125.00
Limited to 780 copies printed on Strathmore Artlaid paper. Designed by Bruce Rogers (Haas 151). Printed in Granjon type with title page having a cat in silver and silver borders. Jacket is chipped with wear at spine ends.

1278. (Rogers, Bruce) Vincent, Leon H. BIBLIOTAPH AND OTHER PEOPLE. Boston: Houghton Mifflin and Co., 1899, 8vo., original cloth. 234 pages. $ 35.00
Chapters on the writings of John Keats, Thomas Hardy, Robert L. Stevenson and three chapters on the bibliotaph. Designed by Bruce Rogers. Bookplate.

1279. (Rosemary Press) Burrage, Charles Dana. THE ECONOMIC FUTURE DURING THE CONTINUANCE OF THE WAR AND AFTER ITS TERMINATION. N.P.: Rosemary Press, (1922), 8vo., stiff paper wrappers. 24 pages. $ 25.00
Printed as a Rosemary Press Brochure for the use of the members of The Chile Club, being A Prize Essay (second prize) written for *Commerce and Finance*, December 6, 1916. Bookplate of Will Ransom, dated 7/23/49 pasted on inside of back wrapper.

1280. (Roycrofters) SOME BOOKS FOR SALE AT OUR SHOP. East Aurora, NY: Roycrofters, (1899), small 8vo., paper wrappers. 23+(1) pages. $ 65.00

A list of books made by the Roycrofters in 1899. Includes an article about the owners and the beautiful workmanship at the shop, which appeared in the Buffalo Times. A photograph of a sculpture of Elbert Hubbard, by Saint Gerome-Roycroft loosely inserted.

1281. (Rudge, William Edwin) Bliss, Edgar S. HERE, THERE AND EVERYWHERE, AN INFORMAL ACCOUNT OF INCIDENTS, PEOPLE AND PLACES. Springfield, Ma.: Privately printed for the author, 1931, large 8vo., paper-covered boards. 55+(1) pages. $ 30.00

Printed for the author in an edition limited to 500 copies by William Edwin Rudge on Worthy Hand and Arrows Paper. Anecdotes from the author's trips to the Orient, starting when he graduated from college in 1888. Bookplate of Sol Hess on front pastedown. Head of spine chipped.

1282. (Rudge, William Edwin) Cooper, James Fenimore. THE SPY, A TALE OF THE NEUTRAL GROUND. New York: Bowling Green Press, 1929, 12mo., cloth. xxxv,(v),310; (viii),328; (viii),339,(3) pages. $ 75.00

Printed in an edition limited to 1000 numbered copies by William Edwin Rudge at his Bowling Green Press in New York (Ransom, p.222). Typography and design by Frederic Warde. Twelve color plates printed by offset process in Germany, from pastels by William H. Cotton. With a general introduction by Henry Seidel Canby. Bookplate of previous owner on front pastedown endpaper of each volume. Some fading on spine and top separated on slipcase.

1283. (Rudge, William Edwin) Howell, James. CERTAIN LETTERS OF JAMES HOWELL SELECTED FROM THE FAMILIAR LETTERS AS FIRST PUBLISHED BETWEEN 1645 & 1655. New York: William Edwin Rudge, 1928, 8vo., half cloth over boards, top edge gilt, slipcase. (xiv), 85 pages. $ 75.00

Limited to 1000 copies. Completed as a course project for a course taught by Frederic Goudy with typography suggested by him and binding by Edith Diehl. Introduction by Guy Holt. Signed by Goudy on the half-title. Slipcase has been repaired with linen tape.

1284. (Rudge, William Edwin) Longfellow, Henry Wadsworth. THE LEAP OF ROUSHAN BEG. New York: William Edwin Rudge, 1931, large 8vo., cloth. (xiv), 37+(1) pages. $ 25.00

Printed in an edition limited to 500 copies by William Edwin Rudge at Mount Vernon, New York, with typography by Frederic Warde. A complete facsimile, edited with an introduction and notes by Arthur Christy. "To the reader who cares for out-of-the-way items and the study of sources, this poem will always prove fascinating, for through it Longfellow is seen in an entirely new light. He stands out as the founder of a distinct type of English-Oriental poetry in America." Facsimile of original manuscript printed above text. Wear at extremities, fading and a few stains on covers.

1285. (Rudge, William Edwin) Lounsbury, Charles. HIS WILL. (Mount Vernon, NY): William Edwin Rudge, (1916), 8vo., two toned paper-covered boards. (10) pages.

$ 30.00

Printed in an edition limited to two hundred copies "in the shop of William Edwin Rudge for his friends," Christmas, 1916. With a Tribute by H.H. McClure, noting that the author was confined in an insane asylum for years, and died there. John DePol bookplate on front pastedown. Some soiling to boards and inner gutter.

1286. (Rudge, William Edwin) Moore, George. THE MAKING OF AN IMMOR-
TAL, A PLAY IN ONE ACT. New York: Bowling Green Press, 1927, large 12mo.,
paper-covered boards. (ii), 59+(1) pages. $ 25.00
Printed at the printing house of William Edwin Rudge, Mount Vernon, NY, in an edition limited to 1240
numbered copies signed by the author. Set in the gardens of the Palace at Whitehall in October, 1599, and
includes dialogue with Queen Elizabeth, Shakespeare, and Francis Bacon. Extremities worn and piece
chipped off near head of spine. Previous owner's signature on front free endpaper.

1287. (Rudge, William Edwin) Nevins, Allan. JOB OF THE MONTH, A SIGNA-
TURE FROM "THE HISTORY OF THE BANK OF NEW YORK & TRUST
COMPANY." New York: William E. Rudge's Sons, (1934), small 4to., stiff paper wrap-
pers. unpaginated, but 16 pages. $ 20.00
Extracts from Nevin's book, issued as a promotional booklet for Rudge, who call the reader's attention
to The Illustrations, The Baskerville type page, and The privately-watermarked, permanent paper.

1288. (Rudge, William Edwin) THE PRINTING HOUSE OF WILLIAM EDWIN
RUDGE. New York: Printing House of William Edwin Rudge, (1933), 12mo., cord-tied
stiff paper wrappers. (16) pages. $ 17.50
Promotional pamphlet with list of Rudge books selected each year from 1923–1932 by the American Institute of Graphic Arts for its annual exhibition of Fifty Books of the Year. "The total number of Rudge
books exceeds the total number of books selected from any other one printer." Bookplate of John DePol
pasted on inside front cover.

1289. (Rudge, William Edwin) QUARTO CLUB PAPERS, 1928–1929. New York:
The Quarto Club, 1930, 8vo., cloth-backed marbled paper covered boards, top edge gilt,
slipcase. (x), 120 pages. $ 75.00
Limited to 140 numbered copies. Handsomely printed by William Rudge with typography by Frederic
Warde. This third book of essays by this club of book collectors includes "An Adventure in Americana"
by Elmer Adler, "Travels in Arabia Deserts" by Solomon Lowenstein, and "Some Famous Prison Books"
by Holstein. Worn slipcase.

1290. (Rudge, William Edwin) Scott, Temple. GOUDY, AN ADDRESS BY TEMPLE
SCOTT AT A MEETING OF THE AIGA. N.P.: Privately Printed for the author by
Edwin Rudge, (1923), small 8vo., boards, paper cover label. (ii), 13 pages. $ 35.00
Limited to 400 copies.

1291. (Rudge, William Edwin) Guedalla, Philip. BONNET AND SHAWL, AN
ALBUM. New York: Crosby Gaige, 1928, small 8vo., quarter cloth with marbled paper
covered boards. 200, (2) pages. $ 35.00
Printed in an edition limited to 571 numbered copies, signed by the author. Printed by William Edwin
Rudge, at Mount Vernon, N. Y. and designed by Frederic Warde. Studies of nine Victorian women, including Jane Welsh Carlyle, Catherine Gladstone, Mary Ann Disraeli, Emily Tennyson, Sophia Swinburne, and Emily Palmerston.

1292. (Rudge, William Edwin) Horgan, Paul. FROM THE ROYAL CITY OF THE
HOLY FAITH OF ST. FRANCIS OF ASSISI. Santa Fe, NM: Villagra Bookshop,
1936, 8vo., cloth. 27+(1) pages. $ 125.00
Printed by The Rydal Press in 1936. Being five accounts of Life in that place: The Captain General, 1690;
The Evening Air, 1730; Triumphal Entry, 1780 ; Bittersweet Waltz, 1846; and Frock Coats & the Law,
1878. These sketches of early Santa Fe first appeared in The Yale Review, 1933, and include tasteful anecdotes about Billy the Kid and General Lew Wallace, author of Ben Hur, who was Governor of the Terri-
tory in the late 1870's. The Kid was heard to remark that "I intend to ride into the plaza at Santa Fe, hitch
my horse in front of the Palace, and put a bullet through Lew Wallace." Illustrated Villagra bookshop
label on back pastedown.

1293. (Samson Press) Grierson, H.J.C. THE FLUTE. Warlingham: Samson Press, 1931, large 8vo., quarter cloth with decorated paper covered boards, top edge gilt. 36, (2) pages. $195.00

Limited to 120 numbered copies. (Ransom, Selected Check-List p.268) The third book of the press. Printed by hand by J.M. Shelmerdine and Flora Grierson at their Samson Press. Operations of the press began in 1931, but were interrupted when the press was burnt out in 1936, and again stopped by the war. Activity was resumed in 1946. This is a collection of poetry with some translations from J.M. de Heredia, P.C. Hooft, Joost van den Vondel, and P.C. Boutens. It was printed in Caslon Old Face. Presentation copy "Olga from the Sampson Press" on the free endpaper. The edges of the pages are soiled.

1294. (Samurai Press) Gibson, Wilfred Wilson. THE STONEFOLDS. London: The Samurai Press, 1907, small 8vo., paper covered boards. (viii), 32, (4) pages. $95.00
First edition, limited to 500 copies. (Woolmer VII). A short verse play by Wilfred Wilson Gibson, a British poet who drew his inspiration from the workday life of ordinary provincial families, that exploits the ideals of contemporary Georgian life. Hand-printed by Arthur K. Sabin. The paper spine label called for by Woolmer seems never to have been applied to this copy. Minor fading to spine.

1295. (Samurai Press) Gibson, Wilfrid Wilson. ON THE THRESHOLD. (London: Samurai Press, 1907), small 8vo., grey paper covered boards. (vi), 33, (1) pages. $95.00
Printed in an edition limited to 500 copies (Woolmer, pp. 12–13). Contains 3 one-act plays, described by the publisher as "Dramatic Poems dealing with modern life. Hand-printed by Arthur K. Sabin. Includes laid in prospectus of other works by the author and others on back pastedown endpaper.

1296. (Santa Susana Press) Corwin, Norman. GREATER THAN THE BOMB. N.P.: California State University, Northridge Libraries, 1981, large 8vo., cloth, paper spine label. (x), 37, (5) pages. $65.00
Printed in an edition limited to 300 numbered copies and signed by the author. The first publication in English of a play broadcast internationally on the radio in 1950 and read by Richard Basehart, Charles Boyer, Joan Crawford, and others. Originally entitled *Document A/777*, it became the Universal Declaration of Human Rights, Adopted and Proclaimed by the General Assembly of the United Nations. This is the third publication of the California Master Series from California State University, Northridge Libraries, edited by Norman Tanis. Designed and printed by Patrick Reagh and Vance Gerry for the Santa Susana Press.

1297. (Santa Susana Press) Emboden, William A. JEAN COCTEAU AND THE ILLUSTRATED PRESS. Northridge, CA: Santa Susana Press, 1990, large 4to., quarter leather, buckram boards and slipcase. (viii), 29 (5) pages. $300.00
Limited to 226 numbered copies signed by the author of which this is one of 101 regular copies. Thirteen lithographs, in color and black and white, reproduced from the Severin Wunderman Museum.

1298. (Santa Susana Press) Tanis, Norman, Dennis Bakewell, Don Read. LYNTON R. KISTLER, PRINTER-LITHOGRAPHER, A DESCRIPTION OF THE BOOKS HE HAS PRINTED DURING THE YEARS FROM 1927 THROUGH 1974. Northridge: Santa Susana Press, 1976, 12mo., cloth backed boards. (ii), 30 pages. $45.00

Limited to 150 copies. Signed by Kistler, Bohne and Tanis. With a two page introduction by Jake Zeitlin. With an inscription on half-title by Tanis.

1299. (Santa Susana Press) Moore, Brian. TWO STORIES. Santa Susana Press, 1978, large 12mo., quarter cloth with paper covered boards. 58, (2) pages. $45.00
First edition, limited to 326 of which this copy is signed but out of series. Issued as the first of the California Master Series by California State University and Northridge Libraries. Printed by The Plantin Press, edited by Norman Tanis. "The characters in this work are meant to be real. References to persons living and dead are intended."

1300. (Santa Susana Press) Ritchie, Ward. A BOWL OF QUINCE. (Pasadena, CA): Santa Susana Press, 1977, large 8vo., cloth. (vi), 21, (3) pages. $ 95.00
Designed and printed in an edition limited to 199 numbered copies by Grant Dahlstrom at his press in Pasadena, California. The text is set in Linotype Janson and printed on Curtis Rag paper. Illustrated by Irving Block and signed by him and Ward Ritchie on the colophon. "A half century ago Ward Ritchie was Peter Lum Quince, an aspiring poet who turned into a printer, making books which he hoped were beautiful. Here we have resurrected some of those poems of his youth, which we hope also may be considered beautiful, along with the fitting illustrations by Irving Block (prefatory note by Norman E. Tanis)."

1301. (Scripps College Press) EXAMPLES OF PRINTING DESIGNED BY STUDENTS AT THE SCRIPPS COLLEGE PRESS 1946–1971. N.P.: Privately printed, n.d., small 8vo., cloth. (ii), 119, (3) pages. $ 75.00
Limited to 200 copies and printed by Patrick Reagh. Short history followed by displays of printing.

1302. (Scripps College Press) [LOT OF 14 PIECES OF EPHEMERA FROM SCRIPPS COLLEGE PRESS]. Claremont, CA: Scripps College Press. $ 50.00
Lot of ephemera from Scripps College Press, from the late 1980's, mostly invitations and brochures to lectures and exhibits on the Book Arts. Includes 1977 booklet on Founders Day Events, 1948 pamphlet on the Ida Rust MacPherson Collection on Women's History in the Scripps College Library, printed by the Ward Ritchie Press, and a keepsake hand-printed by Christine Bertelson, Master Printer at the Scripps College Press, of a recipe for *Turkey Marka*. The Scripps College Press was established in 1941, when the graduating class commissioned Frederic W. Goudy to design a proprietary type that would capture the essence of the college. A few duplicate items.

1303. (Scripps College Press) Maryatt, Kitty, Et.Al. (editors). LIVRE DES LIVRES. (San Francisco): Scripps College Press, 1993, small 4to, loose signatures gathered in stiff paper wrappers, cloth chimese, cloth slipcase. Unpaginated. $ 250.00
Printed in an edition limited to 60 numbered copies. Produced by Scripps College typography students and Kitty Maryatt , in the French livre de peintre tradition of a collaborative book where the publisher assembles a famous modern author, celebrated artist and fine printer; the materials are first quality, the style grandiose and the format large. It is traditionally issued in sheets and taken to a binder after purchase for a fine leather binding. The twist on this is to issue a book in its final form, hand-painted with original prints inside the French fold. "In the grand scheme of bookish tradition, there is the livre d'artiste, the livre de peintre, and now the livre des livres." Each student selected poetry or prose concerning art, obtained permission to use the material , and designed and signed a folded print. The whole is printed on a luxurious French paper, gray Rives B F K, because they "wanted to paint the pages to shine with iridescence like the F.-L. Schmied books," and printed on a Vandercook Universal III. Authors featured include Lawrence Ferlinghetti, Diane Wakoski, John Fowles, and Rena Rosenwasser.

1304. (Scripps College Press) Scripps, Ellen Browning. A SAMPLING FROM TRAVEL LETTERS, 1881–1883. Claremont, CA: Scripps College Press, (1973), large 12mo., self paper wrappers. 41, (3) pages. $ 15.00
First edition, printed by Anderson, Ritchie & Simon, and designed by Ward Ritchie. Letters selected from columns originally printed in the *Detroit-Evening News,* each averaging ten typewritten pages. The author's brothers founded the Scripps-Howard newspaper chain, and she was the founder and benefactor of Scripps College in 1931.

1305. (Shady Tree Press) THE RAPA RAPID READER, THE SECOND CHILDHOOD EDITION. (Melrose, MA): Shady Tree Press, 1963, miniature book (3.25 x 2.375 inches), stiff paper wrappers. (20) pages. $ 20.00
Printed in an edition of 100 copies. Printed from handset types and bound by Ernie Rapa at his Shady Tree Press. Twelve woodcut initials for each of the 12 months, each in a printed frame with text underneath. Printed in colors.

1306. (Shakespeare Head Press) Caxton, William (translator). OVYDE: HYS BOOKE OF METHAMORPHOSE. Oxford: Basil Blackwell, 1923, 4to., quarter cloth, paper covered boards, paper spine label, printed paper dust jacket. xl, 189, (2) pages. $ 350.00 Limited to 375 numbered copies. (Ransom 32). Books X-XV of Ovid's Metamorphosis, translated by William Caxton; newly printed from the manuscript in the Pepysian Library at Magdalene College, Cambridge. The Shakespeare Head Press, established in Stratford by Arthur Henry Bullen in 1904 for the express purpose of printing an edition of Shakespeare in the Bard's hometown, was acquired after Bullen's death in 1920 by Basil Blackwell of Oxford, who appointed the distinguished scholar and print-er Bernard Newdigate (1869–1944) as typographer. Glaister says that this book is the first strictly limit-ed edition issued by the press under these new circumstances. Edited by Stephen Gaselee and H.F.B. Brett-Smith. With introductions by both editors. Printed on Batchelor's Kelmscott hand-made paper. Prospectus laid in. Spine of dust jacket slightly age darkened. Well preserved copy.

1307. (Shakespeare Head Press) Clapperton, R.H. PAPER, AN HISTORICAL AC-COUNT OF ITS MAKING BY HAND FROM THE EARLIEST TIMES DOWN TO THE PRESENT DAY. Oxford: Printed at The Shakespeare Head Press, 1934, folio, original half blue morocco over cloth, top edge gilt, others uncut. xvi, 158 pages.
$ 1,850.00
First edition, limited to only 250 numbered copies. (Schlosser no.70). Grannis states (in "Some Recent Books about Paper") "In R.H. Clapperton's historical account of hand-made paper we have an authori-tative, painstaking and luxurious volume, the like of which has not been seen before, I think, in any Eng-lish production on paper. Printed on handmade paper produced by J. Barcham Green & Son at the Hayle Mill. Includes 12 chapters on the beginning of papermaking in 12 locations throughout the world in-cluding China, Japan, France, England and America. Contains over 50 large plates and two plates show-ing watermarks and a one page bibliography. Well preserved copy.

1308. (Shakespeare Head Press) Sleigh, Herbert. THE NOVEMBER DAWN. Strat-ford-Upon-Avon: Shakespeare Head Press, 1923, large 12mo., quarter cloth with deco-rated paper covered boards, paper cover label, fore and bottom edges uncut. 29+(1) pages. $ 45.00
First edition. A short poem in dialogue form. The Shakespeare Head Press, founded by A.H. Bullen in 1904, was bought by Sir Basil Blackwell in 1920, who hired Bernard Newdigate as designer. "It became one of the most mature and sophisticated of the private presses, producing works in the grand manner that are a pleasure to read and examine--the close-set page well leaded, large sizes on the title pages, and absolute blackness on the white page (Franklin,149)."

1309. (Shakespeare Head Press) Tatius, Achilles. THE LOVES OF CLITOPHON AND LEUCIPPE. Oxford: Basil Blackwell, 1923, 4to., quarter cloth, paper covered boards, paper spine label, printed paper dust jacket. xxxi, (ix), 152, (5) pages. $ 150.00 Limited to 498 numbered copies. (Ransom 29x). This book contains the Greek prose romance by Tatius translated from the Greek by William Burton; reprinted for the first time from a copy, now unique, printed by Thomas Creede in 1597. This romance, a typical adventure story of love triumphing over in-numerable obstacles- shipwrecks, tortures, abductions, and attacks by pirates, influenced the develop-ment of the novel centuries later. Includes a facsimile of the original title page with title: "The most de-lectable and pleasant history of Clitiphon and Leucippe." Edited by Stephen Gaselee and H.F.B. Brett-Smith. With a historical introduction by Gaselee and an essay on the translator by Brett-Smith. Printed on Batchelor's Kelmscott handmade paper. One corner bumped, dust jacket worn with pieces missing.

1310. (Sherwin Beach Press) Lenehan, Michael. ESSENCE OF BEEING. Chicago: The Sherwin Beach Press, 1992, large 4to., two-tone cloth, dust jacket. (vi), 45+(1) pages.
$ 300.00
Limited to 200 numbered copies. An account of two beekeepers, with some history and explanations of beekeeping. Six full-page illustrations by Alice Brown-Wagner, who also set most of the pages, with "bee" fleurons and decorated initials by Albert Richardson. Set in Cooper Oldstyle and printed on Fab-riano Roma. The plain dust jacket is blind-stamped with a honeycomb pattern. Prospectus laid in.

1311. (Sherwin Beach Press) Trow, George W.S. WITHIN THE CONTEXT OF NO CONTEXT. Chicago: Sherwin Beach Press, 1992, 8vo., black Japanese rayon cloth over boards with paper spine and cover label. Bound by Trisha Hammer. 110 pages. $ 340.00
Printed in an edition limited to 200 copies. A reissue of the original 1978 New Yorker essay with a new introduction by the author. Four new illustrations have been added to this edition by Howard Coale. A poetic and original essay exploring the role of television in American life.

1312. (Sherwin Beach Press) Twain, Mark. THE INNOCENTS ABROAD. Two volumes. Chicago: Sherwin Beach Press, 1998, small 4to., each volume bound in a non-adhesive binding with exposed spine sewing consisting of 7 black double raised cords attached to hard covers wrapped in red cloth, both volumes are enclosed in a black-and-white linen-covered hard-case wrapper with black leather straps over brass studs, created by Trisha. 445 pages plus 20 pages of illustrations. $ 1,250.00
Printed in an edition limited to 200 copies. One of Mark Twain's most exciting non-fiction works written in 1867. He writes about his experiences while traveling abroad, and his feelings about foreign countries and their people. Heather McAdams' 14 cartoon illustrations (7 single panels and 7 spreads) illustrate tourism through time.

1313. (Shoe String Press) Martin, Samuel Rev. EPISTLE IN VERSE OCCASIONED BY THE DEATH OF JAMES BOSWELL, ESQUIRE, OF AUCHINLECK. Hamden, CT: Shoe String Press, 1952, large 8vo., stiff paper wrappers. x, 17, (3) pages.
                                                                                    $ 20.00
A reproduction of the first edition printed in Edinburgh in 1795, with an introductory note by Robert F. Metzdorf, Curator of Manuscripts, Yale University Library. This is the first time the Epistle has been republished in its entirety.

1314. (Sign of the Blue-Behinded Ape) Franklin, Benjamin. A LETTER BY DR. FRANKLIN TO THE ROYAL ACADEMY OF BRUSSELS. New York: At the Sign of the Blue-Behinded Ape, 1929, large 12mo., paper covered boards. xv, (2) pages.
                                                                                    $ 35.00
First edition, limited to 1000 copies. A letter credited to Benjamin Franklin in which he rebukes the Brussels Academy for having rejected his discovery by writing of a more "practical" discovery--a cure for flatulence. With an illustration by Bewick. An introduction from the press is given.

1315. (Sign of the Blue-Behinded Ape) AN IMMORAL ANTHOLOGY. N.P.: Blue-Behinded Ape, 1933, large 8vo., quarter cloth with decorated paper covered boards, paper spine label. 130, (8) pages. $ 95.00
Printed in an edition limited to 290 copies by Peter Beilenson at the Walpole Printing Office. Erotic poetry by Herrick, Suckling, Donne, de la Fontaine, the Earl of Rochester, Keats, Campion, etc. With appropriate line drawings and decorations by Andre Durenceau. Signature of Frederic J. Farrell on title page.

1316. (Signet Press) Dickens, Charles. PUBLIC DINNERS. Greenock, Scotland: The Signet Press, 1962, 8vo., paper covered boards. 16, (2) pages. $ 75.00
Hand set and printed in a edition limited to 120 numbered copies, each signed by the printer Thomas Rae at his Signet Press. Text by Dickens is drawn from his SKETCHES OF BOZ. Title page printed in two colors, initial letter printed in blue.

1317. (Signet Press) Freebairn, James (Translator). THE DEATH OF MARY QUEEN OF SCOTS, FROM THE LIFE OF MARY STEWART QUEEN OF SCOTLAND AND FRANCE WRITTEN ORIGINALLY IN FRENCH. Greenock, Scotland: Signet Press, 1960, large 12mo., pictorial paper covered boards. (24) pages. $ 65.00
Limited to edition of about 100 copies. First printed at Edinburgh in 1725, this volume detailing the last days of the Queen of Scotland, was set by hand in American Uncial types, printed on Zerkall mould made paper and hand bound by Thomas Rae in 1960. Woodcut frontispiece portrait by David Chambers. Printed in red and black letters.

1318. (Signet Press) Munro, James (editor). JAMES WATSON'S PREFACE TO THE HISTORY OF PRINTING, 1713. Greenock, Scotland: The Signet Press, 1963, 8vo., boards, clear plastic wrapper. xiii, 35 pages. $ 55.00
Limited to 250 copies designed, printed and bound by Thomas Rae at The Signet Press. The HISTORY OF PRINTING by Watson was the first account of printing in Scotland. Contains two fold-out facsimiles of the title page and ornaments used in the original book. Front cover spotted.

1319. (Signet Press) Rae, Thomas (editor). SOME NOTES ON WOOD ENGRAVING BY THOMAS BEWICK, SELECTED FROM HIS 'MEMOIR'. Greenock, Scotland: The Signet Press, 1961, tall 12mo., stiff paper wrappers. 20, vi, (ii) pages. $ 30.00
First edition thus, limited to 370 numbered copies. With reproductions of Bewick woodcuts throughout.

1320. (Signet Press) Rae, Thomas and Geoffrey Handley-Taylor. BOOK OF THE PRIVATE PRESS, A CHECK-LIST. Greenock, Scotland: The Signet Press, 1958, 8vo., paper wrappers. xvi, 48 pages. $ 25.00
Limited to 750 numbered copies. Details of over 240 private presses all over the world are given.

1321. (Signet Press) Seymour, William Kean. THE FIRST CHILDERMAS. Greenock (Scotland): The Signet Press, 1959, large 8vo., paper-covered boards. (ii), 37, (3) pages. $ 75.00
Limited to 350 numbered copies, including 50 in this binding and signed by author. A short play following the tradition of plays for religious occasions but with a modern concern for motivation; here, Herod's murder of the Innocents. The title page illustration (in red), repeated on the front cover, is a redrawing of an "old woodcut" (unidentified). Scene designations printed in red. Designed, set and printed by Thomas Rae. Some soiling of covers, with irregular light browning on front.

1322. (Silver Buckle Press) CALENDAR OF ORNAMENTAL MATERIAL FROM THE COLLECTION OF SILVER BUCKLE PRESS. Madison: University of Wisconsin-Madison Libraries, 1988, large 12mo., paper wrappers. (60) pages. $ 100.00
Printed in an edition limited to 65 numbered copies. This calendar of ornamental material from the collection of the Silver Buckle Press is a specimen book that displays the Press's diverse collection of turn of the century printer's ornaments. A total of fifteen ornamental compositions were set from a variety of decorative and border fonts. The universal calendar, usable in any year, has three pages of numbered grids per month and a section for names, addresses and phone numbers. It was printed on letterpress on T.H. Saunders mould made paper and bound with a laced-on paper case structure designed by Bill Anthony.

1323. (Slide Mountain Press) McFee, William. REFLECTIONS OF MARSYAS. Gaylorsville: The Slide Mountain Press, 1933, large 8vo., paper covered boards with a paper wrap around spine and cover label. 85, (2) pages, some unopened. $ 75.00
First edition. Printed in an edition limited to 300 copies. Signed by author. A collection of poems by McFee, which begins with a brief explanation of each. Also an introduction by the author. Slightly yellowed.

1324. (Southworth-Anthoensen Press) Anthoensen, Fred. JOHN BELL TYPE ITS LOSS AND REDISCOVERY. With a Type-facsimile of John Bell's first Type Specimen, 1788. Portland, ME: Southworth-Anthoensen Press (But Printed by The Meriden Gravure Co. in 1965 for the Heritage of the Graphic Arts)., 1939, 8vo., paper wrappers. 20, (8) pages. $ 25.00
Limited to 250 copies.

1325. (Southworth-Anthoensen Press) BOOKBINDING IN AMERICA, THREE ESSAYS. Portland, ME: The Southworth-Anthoensen Press, 1941, 8vo., cloth-backed paste paper covered boards, slipcase. xix, 293 pages. $ 115.00
S-K 129. First edition. (Brenni 1217). Contains Early American Bookbinding by Hand by Hannah French, The Rise of American Edition Binding by Joseph W. Rogers and On the Rebinding of Old Books by Hellmut Lehmann-Haupt. An important reference book. Covers rubbed especially the slipcase.

1326. (Southworth-Anthoensen Press) CATALOGUE OF THE COLLECTION OF SAMUEL BUTLER IN THE CHAPIN LIBRARY WILLIAMS COLLEGE. Portland, ME: The Southworth-Anthoensen Press, 1945, 8vo., cloth. 35 pages. $ 12.50
Frontispiece portrait by Charles Gogin.

1327. (Southworth-Anthoensen Press) Klinefelter, Walter. CHRISTMAS BOOKS. With A BIBLIOGRAPHICAL CHECK-LIST OF CHRISTMAS BOOKS With MORE CHRISTMAS BOOKS. Introduction by Wilbur Macey Stone. Index by Will Ransom. Three volumes. Portland, ME: Southworth-Anthoensen Press, 1936, 1937, 1938, small 8vo., first two are cloth-backed boards, third is cloth. The first volume was the only one issued in a box - the box is present. xxiv,(iv); xxiv,114,(4); ix,77,(3) pages. $ 225.00
Complete set; second volume limited to 1500 copies; third volume limited to 500 copies. Includes the works of A. Edward Newton among others. Bookplate in each volume. Very fine set.

1328. (Southworth-Anthoensen Press) Osborne, Lucy Eugenia. SHORT-TITLE LIST, THE CHAPIN LIBRARY WILLIAMS COLLEGE. Portland, ME: Southworth-Anthoensen Press, 1939, 4to., blue cloth, top edge gilt. viii, 595 pages. $ 65.00
First edition, limited to 500 copies. A catalogue of one of the finest rare book libraries in the country.

1329. (Southworth-Anthoensen Press) TYPES AND BOOKMAKING CONTAINING NOTES ON THE BOOKS PRINTED AT THE SOUTHWORTH-ANTHOENSEN PRESS. BY FRED ANTHOENSEN. AND A BIBLIOGRAPHICAL CATALOGUE BY RUTH A. CHAPLIN. WITH SPECIMENS OF ITS WORK, TYPES, BORDERS. Portland, ME: Southworth- Anthoensen Press, 1943, tall 8vo., cloth, leather spine label, slipcase. x, 170, (4) pages. $ 250.00
Limited to 500 copies. 265 books fully described bibliographically with some tipped-in title pages and other illustrations. A delightful specimen book from one of the best of America's presses. Loosely inserted is brochure entitled "A Review of 'Type and Bookmaking' by Lawrence C. Wroth."

1330. (Southworth-Anthoensen Press) Weber, Carl J. THOMAS HARDY IN MAINE. Portland, ME: The Southworth-Anthoensen Press, 1942, 8vo., paper covered boards. (iv), 20, (4) pages. $ 45.00
Limited to 425 copies printed as Keepsake No.16 issued by this press. Illustrated.

1331. (Southworth-Anthoensen Press) Wroth, Lawrence C. COLONIAL PRINTER. Portland, ME: The Southworth-Anthoensen Press, 1938, tall 8vo., cloth, top edge gilt, slipcase. xxiv, 368 pages. $ 125.00

Second edition, revised, limited to 1500 copies. With chapters on the first presses, the Colonial printing house, ink, type, bookbinding, etc. With illustrations. Bookplate removed from front pastedown.

1332. (Southworth-Anthoensen Press) Wroth, Lawrence C. COLONIAL PRINTING PRESS, A CHAPTER FROM THE COLONIAL PRINTER. Portland, ME: Southworth-Anthoensen Press, 1938, 8vo., stiff paper wrappers. (vi), 22, (4) pages. $ 17.50

Printed as a Keepsake for the convention of the International Assoc. of Printing House Craftsmen. Contains 8 full page plates. Minor cover soiling.

1333. (Southworth-Anthoensen Press) Wroth, Lawrence C. REVIEW OF TYPES AND BOOKMAKING. Portland, ME: The Southworth-Anthoensen Press, 1943, 8vo., paper wrappers. 4 pages. $ 10.00

Reprint of the review of this type specimen book.

1334. (Southworth Press) Dyer, Isaac Watson. BIBLIOGRAPHY OF THOMAS CARLYLE'S WRITINGS. Portland, ME: The Southworth Press, 1928, 8vo., cloth. xiv, 587 pages. $ 100.00

First edition, limited to 600 copies. The definitive bibliography to date. Well printed. Covers rubbed. With a booklabel indicating that this copy came from the library of Percy Muir.

1335. (Southworth Press) Rosenbach, A.S.W. EARLY AMERICAN CHILDREN'S BOOKS. With Bibliographical Descriptions of the Books in His Private Collection. Portland, ME: Southworth Press, 1933, thick 4to., full blue pigskin stamped in blind on covers and gilt stamped on spine, five raised bands, top edge gilt, others uncut, slipcase with paper label. lix, 354, (4) pages. $ 1,750.00

First edition, one of 88 copies signed by Rosenbach (this being No.LVI) and printed on Zerkall Halle papers. Rosenbach inherited his uncle's library of early American children's books and spent many years of his life adding rarities to it. This magnificent volume summarizes this effort with detailed descriptions of the books and over 100 illustrations. The collection was given to the Free Library of Philadelphia en masse. Covers rubbed along hinges and bands.

1336. (Spiral Press) Adams, Frederick B, Jr. TO RUSSIA WITH FROST. Boston: The Club of Odd Volumes, 1963, 8vo., quarter cloth with paper-covered boards in slipcase. (ii), 41(3). $ 125.00

Printed in an edition limited to 500 copies, designed by Joseph Blumenthal and printed at The Spiral Press, New York. The photographs taken in Russia, including the frontispiece, are by James Brilliant Wood engravings by Thomas W. Nason, printed from the original blocks. An expanded account of a talk given at the monthly meeting of the Club of Odd Volumes on March 20, 1963. The trip originated as a result of an invitation to visit the Soviet Union extended to Frost by Soviet Ambassador Dobrynin at a dinner party, where they got along so well that, as Frost put it, he didn't know who was fooling whom. With a great presentation on the colophon page "For Abe and Kit with affection Joe Spiral (sic). Cream Hollow June 1981."

1337. (Spiral Press) BR MARKS & REMARKS, THE MARKS BY BRUCE ROGERS, ET AL. THE REMARKS BY HIS FRIENDS ... New York: The Typophiles, 1946, 12mo., cloth. (x), 150 pages. $ 60.00

First edition, one of 805 numbered copies. Designed by Joseph Blumenthal and printed at the Spiral Press. Remarks by Kent, Bowles, Rollins, Pottinger, Morley, Hendrickson and Warde. Minor rubbing at spine ends.

1338. (Spiral Press) Duval, Elizabeth W. T.E. LAWRENCE, A BIBLIOGRAPHY. New York: Arrow Editions, (1938), 8vo., cloth-backed boards, paper spine label, slipcase. (ii), 96 pages. $ 125.00
First edition, limited to 500 copies printed at the Spiral Press.

1339. (Spiral Press) MAURICE SERLE KAPLAN, 1908–1951. N.P.: n.p., n.d., 12mo., self paper wrappers. (4) pages. $ 5.00
Monograph 33. Printed by the Spiral Press.

1340. (Spiral Press) REQUIEM FOR VICTOR HAMMER. N.P.: n.p., (1967), tall 8vo., boards, paper cover label. (18) pages. $ 185.00
Limited to 250 copies printed at The Spiral Press of New York. Includes various readings concerning Victor Hammer made by Raymond McLain at the Burial Service. Loosely inserted is a small printed note on this memorial tribute by R. Hunter Middleton and printed in one of Hammer's uncials.

1341. (Spiral Press) Seligmann, Herbert J. IN MEMORY OF LILIAS, COLLECTED POEMS OF HERBERT J. SELIGMANN, 1919–1964. (New York: Spiral Press, 1964), 8vo., cloth. (ii), 100, (4) pages. $ 45.00
Printed by the Spiral Press in an edition limited to 200 copies. Chosen from previous editions of two hundred copies each printed in 1930 and 1932, and from the author's notebooks. Poems issued to "commemorate the spirit" of the author's wife, Lilias Hazewell MacLane, many have to do with Cape Split, Addison, Maine, "A place she loved, where her grandmother had been born."

1342. (Stamperia Valdonega) Bumgardner, George. NOVELLE CINQUE, TALES FROM THE VENETO. Illustrated with facsimiles from the 16th century manuscript. Translated, edited, and annotated by George H. Bumgardner. Barre, MA: Imprint Society, 1974, tall 8vo., cloth-backed boards, slipcase, paper cover label. 143, (3) pages.
$ 65.00
Limited to 1950 copies; this copy is out of series. Translated into English for the first time from the manuscript in the Beinecke Library at Yale and designed and printed by Martino Mardersteig at the Stamperia Valdonega in Verona. With illustrations in color. Small spot on slipcase where label was removed.

1343. (Stamperia Valdonega) Campbell, Sandy. B, TWENTY-NINE LETTERS FROM COCONUT GROVE. Verona: Stamperia Valdonega, 1974, tall 8vo., stiff paper wrappers. 59, (3) pages. $ 55.00
Limited to 300 copies. Printed by Martino Mardersteig at the Stamperia Valdonega in Verona. A collection of letters written by Campbell to Donald Windham during 1956 describing the production of a play under Tennessee Williams in which Tallulah Bankhead acted.

1344. (Stamperia Valdonega) Campion, Thomas. SELECTED SONGS OF THOMAS CAMPION. Boston: David Godine, 1973, small 4to, quarter gilt ruled cloth with marbled paper covered boards, slipcase. 161, (3) pages. $ 200.00
Limited to 250 numbered copies. Selected and prefaced by W.H. Auden. Introduction by John Hollander. Designed, set and printed under the supervision of Martino Mardersteig at the Stamperia Valdonega in Verona, Italy. The calligraphy for the score is by Edith McKeon Abbott. Title page designed by Leo Wyatt.

1345. (Stamperia Valdonega) Dreyfus, John. INTO PRINT, SELECTED WRITINGS ON PRINTING HISTORY, TYPOGRAPHY AND BOOK PRODUCTION. Boston: David R. Godine, (1995), 8vo., cloth. x, 339 +(1) pages. $ 75.00
First edition. A compilation of writings on many aspects of printing and book design, chosen by the author. The topics are varied, and include eighteenth-& nineteenth-century studies, private presses, type design and manufacture, exhibitions and speculations. In an interesting chapter on twentieth-century typographers, the author discusses Stanley Morrison, Eric Gill, Bruce Rogers and several other well

known printers. Illustrated with photographs and facsimiles. Handlist of the author's writings, notes and references, index. Finely printed at the Stamperia Valdonega in Verona under the supervision of Martino Mardersteig.

1346. (Stamperia Valdonega) Mardersteig, Giovanni. DIE EINZIGARTIGE CHRONIK EINER INKUNABEL: PETRUS MAUFERS DRUCK DES AVICENNA, KOMMENTARS VON GENTILE DA FOLIGNO, PADUA 1477. Verona: Stamperia Valdonega, 1967, large 8vo., paper-covered boards, plain paper dust jacket. (ii), 30, (4)pages. $ 250.00
Printed in an edition of 250 copies. A history of how Petrus Maufer undertook to print da Foligno's commentaries on the third book of Avicenna's *Canondi Medicina.*, a monumental tome of over 1,000 two-column pages. Insights on Maufer's decisions as to the actual printing of the *Commentary* and his financial dealings to complete the project. Text printed in "Dante" type designed by Mardersteig. Three plates included. Note card loosely inserted signed by Mardersteig. Minor wear to jacket.

1347. (Stamperia Valdonega) François, N. (de Neufchâteau). CONSEILS D'UN PÈRE À SON FILS IMITÉS DES VERS QUE MURET A ÉCRITS EN LATIN POUR L'USAGE DE SON NEVEU. Verona: n.p., 1969, small 8vo., cloth, paper slipcase. (vi), 46, (2) pages. $ 65.00
Printed in an edition limited to 500 signed copies by Martino Mardersteig at the Stamperia Valdonega. Revised and reprinted from the 1801 edition produced by Giambattista Bodoni. The renowned humanist scholar Marc Antoine Muret (1526–1585) composed the book's original Latin verses, and in 1796 they appeared with their French, Italian and German.

1348. (Stamperia Valdonega) Petrarch. FRANCESCO PETRARCA, LETTERA A GIOVANNI ANCHISEO (LO INCARICA DI PROCUR ARGLI LIBRI). Minano: Stamperia Valdonega di Verona, 1967, 8vo., stiff paper wrappers, slipcase. 37 pages. $ 75.00
A reprint of a letter from Petrarch to Giovanni of Incisa commissioning him to search for books. Translated into English by Betty Radice.

1349. (Stamperia Valdonega) Schmoller, Hans. TWO TITANS, MARDERSTEIG AND TSCHICHOLD, A STUDY IN CONTRASTS. New York: The Typophiles, 1990, 12mo., cloth, dust jacket. 77 pages. $ 27.50
Typophile Chap Book 59, limited to 1100 copies. Designed by Abe Lerner and printed by Martino Mardersteig at The Stamperia Valdonega, Verona. Based on a slide lecture delivered by the author at the Center for the Book in the Library of Congress. A fascinating comparison of the lives of these two great designers. Well illustrated.

1350. (Stamperia Valdonega) Wasson, R. Gordon. HALL CARBINE AFFAIR, AN ESSAY IN HISTORIOGRAPHY. Danbury: Privately printed, 1971, 4to., quarter blue morocco over blue cloth, top edge gilt, slipcase. xvi, 249 pages. $ 250.00
Limited to 276 copies. Designed by Mardersteig and printed at the Stamperia Valdonega in Verona on Pescia handmade paper. The book is an exhaustive study of the sale of defective carbines to the United States Army by J.P. Morgan in 1861 at the start of the Civil War. Very fine condition.

1351. (Stamperia Valdonega) Whitmarsh, Esther. RONDO. Verona: Stamperia Valdonega, 1986, large 12mo., paper-covered boards. 53,(3) pages. $ 45.00
Printed in an edition limited to 50 copies. A group of poems. Printed on Magnani paper from Centaur type at the Stamperia Valdonega. Covers slightly soiled.

1352. (Stamperia Valdonega) HISTORICAL ARCHIVES. Milano: Banca Commerciale Italiana, (1988), 8vo., stiff paper wrappers. (32) pages. $ 15.00
An overview of how the BCI set up its Historical Archives and how it plans to make its documentary assets available to researchers. Handsomely designed and printed by the Stamperia Valdonega of Verona. Contains facsimiles and illustrations, some in striking color.

1353. (Stamperia Valdonega) Rabaiotti, Renato (editor). HORAE BIBLIOGRAPHICAE CANTABRIGIENSES. A FACSIMILE OF DIBDIN'S CAMBRIDGE NOTEBOOK 1823 WITH READINGS FROM THE LIBRARY COMPANION 1824. With an introduction by Renato Rabaiotti. New Castle, DE: Oak Knoll Books, 1989, 8vo., quarter leather with acetate dust jacket, slipcase. 79, (2) pages. $ 185.00
First edition, limited to 250 copies. Printed by Martino Mardersteig at the Stamperia Valdonega, Verona on Magnani mould-made paper. A hitherto unpublished notebook reproduced in facsimile and accompanied by corresponding readings from the 1824 first edition of the *Library Companion*. It contains Dibdin's comments on books, manuscripts and prints examined by him in the University, Pepys, St. John's College and Trinity College libraries. The introduction by the editor, Renato Rabaiotti, describes the events surrounding Dibdin's life in the 1820's and places the notebook in the perspective of Dibdin's career. There is also a current finding-list of the books, manuscripts and prints Dibdin examined, compiled by David McKitterick. A fine production of one surviving testament of Dibdin's ambition to publish a Tour of England.

1354. (Stamperia Valdonega) O'More, Haven. SACRIFICIAL BONE INSCRIPTIONS. Millerton: Sadev, (1987), large 8vo., cloth, dust jacket. not paginated. $ 45.00
First edition. Printed in an edition limited to 750 copies by Martino Mardersteig at the Stamperia Valdonega. A collection of poetry that deals with sacrifice as the primary operational necessity for human beings.

1355. (Stamperia Valdonega) Rhodes, Dennis E. (editor). BOOKBINDINGS & OTHER BIBLIOPHILY. Verona: Edizioni Valdonega, 1994, 8vo., cloth, dust jacket. 368 pages. $ 125.00
First edition. For over forty years, Anthony Hobson has occupied a commanding position in the world of books. Succeeding his father, G. D. Hobson, the great historian of bookbinding, as head of Sotheby's book department, he ran it for some twenty years with equal commercial skill and scholarly learning. Since then, he has established an independent reputation with a series of studies of bookbinding and the history of books generally concerning subjects in renaissance Italy. On the occasion of his seventieth birthday, a group of his friends decided to honor his achievements with a collection of essays. Twelve contributors have provided essays on bookbinding and the history of books. The subjects range from great collectors like Grolier, Mahieu, Anne de Montmorency, to bookbinding techniques and the book trade. In geographical scope there are essays on Ethiopic bookbinding, the Visconti Library at Milan, and British book collectors in Italy. The book has been edited by Dennis Rhodes who has also compiled a bibliography of Anthony Hobson's writings. This book is itself a notable contribution to the history of books, bookbinding, and the book trade. It celebrates the achievements of a life devoted to these subjects. SALES RIGHTS: Available in North & South America from Oak Knoll Books. Available outside North & South America from Edizioni Valdonega.

1356. (Stanbrook Abbey Press) Kendall, Katharine. THE INTERIOR CASTLE. Worcester: Stanbrook Abbey Press, 1968, 8vo., quarter blue Liberty silk, silver-grey Japanese wood-veneer paper covered boards, gold blocked, blue Canson Ingres paper covered and lined drop-back box. (vi), 13, (3) pages. $ 225.00
Limited to 310 copies of which 275 were for sale. (Butcher A19). "Katherine Kendall (1883–1966) was best known as a violinist and leader of the Kendall String Quartet. She "began to express herself in her later years through the medium of poetry." At her death in 1966, she bequeathed this, her longest poem, to her friend Margaret Alexander, who here supplies an introductory note and the hand-drawn initials. Hand-set in Cancelleresca Bastarda in 20 point Romulus Open Capitals printed on damped W.S. Hodgkinson white wove handmade paper.

Item 1356

1357. (Stanton Press) Strabo, Walafrid. HORTULUS OR THE LITTLE GARDEN. Middlesex: The Stanton Press, (1923), small 4to., quarter cloth with decorated paper covered boards, paper cover label. 38, (4) pages. $ 125.00
First edition. (Ransom pg. 426). Printed in an edition limited to 132 numbered copies. The is the first time this story has been done into English verse from the Latin by R.S. Lambert, and was made from the text of Duemmler published in the Monumenta Germaniae Historia in 1884. It is decorated with woodcuts by Elinor Lambert. The covers are slightly soiled and chipped around the edges and the corners are slightly bumped. Private library stamp is on the front free endpaper and the pages are slightly yellowed.

1358. (Stellar Press) Ryder, John. THE JUST SHAPING OF THE LATE TWENTI-ETH-CENTURY BOOK. Brighton: Stellar Press, 1982, large 12mo., paper wrappers. (18) pages. $ 35.00
Printed for Christmas 1982 in an edition of 125 copies for Tony Appleton at the Stellar Press. Signed and numbered by the author. An essay examining how printed English has developed and attained its distinct legibility. Includes typography illustrations; some red print; one folding leaf of plates. Inscribed underneath colophon: "for Abe [Lerner] & Kit [Currie] from Tony & Patsy."

1359. (Still Point Press) Lowman, Al. REMEMBERING CARL HERTZOG, A TEXAS PRINTER AND HIS BOOKS. Dallas, TX: Still Point Press, (1985), 4to., quarter cloth with paper covered boards and a paper spine label in a paper covered slip-case. (iv), 46, (4) pages. $ 150.00
Printed in an edition limited to 300 numbered copies. Al Lowman recounts personal experiences with the late Carl Hertzog, and provides insight into the characteristics which contributed to the achievements of the legendary El Paso printer, designer, and typographer. It includes thirty-six black and white illustra-

tions of Hertzog's best know work. It was set in Monotype Centaur, a fine contemporary typeface created by Bruce Rogers, and printed on Frankfurt cream paper. Prospectus loosely inserted. A one-half inch piece is missing from spine of slipcase.

1360. (Oliphant Press) Auchincloss, Kenneth. MAGNIFICENT OBSESSION, THE PRINTING OF THE BOSWELL PAPERS. New York: The Typophiles, 1995, tall 8vo., stiff red paper wrappers, cord-tied. 23+(1) pages. $ 25.00
Typophiles Monograph - New Series Number 13. The story of the printing of the Boswell papers owned by Lt. Colonel Ralph Heyward Isham by Bruce Rogers. Limited to 800 copies printed at The Stinehour Press with design by Abraham Brewster at the Oliphant Press. Distributed for the Typophiles by Oak Knoll Press.

A LEAF BOOK

1361. (Stinehour Press) Barker, Nicolas. ALDUS MANUTIUS AND THE DEVELOPMENT OF GREEK SCRIPT & TYPE IN THE FIFTEENTH CENTURY. With Original Leaves from the First Aldine editions of Aristotle, 1497; Crastonus' Dictionarium Graecum, 1497; Euripides, 1503; and the Septuagint, 1518. Sandy Hook: Chiswick Book Shop, 1985, small 4to., cloth, slipcase. $ 750.00
Limited to 200 copies. With new text by Barker, 50 illustrations and four leaves showing four different Greek Aldine types. Printed and bound at Meriden-Stinehour. Prospectus loosely inserted. Slipcase spotted.

1362. (Stinehour Press) Lasner, Mark Samuels. SELECTIVE CHECKLIST OF THE PUBLISHED WORK OF AUBREY BEARDSLEY. Boston: Thomas G. Boss Fine Books, 1995, 8vo., cloth, dust jacket. 128 pages. $ 75.00
First edition. Well printed by the Stinehour Press. A new Beardsley reference book which "resolves longstanding ambiguities, corrects oft-repeated errors, and provides a wealth of new information." 224 items described in detail and well indexed. Includes a section on Beardsley forgeries.

1363. (Stinehour Press) Bianchi, Daniel B. MERRYMOUNT PRESS, A CENTENARY KEEPSAKE. Bridgewater, CT: Distributed by The Stinehour Press, 1993, tall 8vo., cloth. (vi), 24, (2) pages followed by 55 pages of illustrations and a colophon page.
$ 200.00

Limited to 200 numbered copies signed by Bianchi. This is a keepsake volume issued to celebrate the 100th anniversary of the founding of the press. The historical introduction is followed by many illustrations and also includes some tipped-in examples of actual printing done by the press and a swatch of the leather imported from England to bind the 1928 Book of Common Prayer. Beautifully printed at The Stinehour Press.

1364. (Stinehour Press) Blumenthal, Joseph. TYPOGRAPHIC YEARS, A PRINTER'S JOURNEY THROUGH A HALF-CENTURY. New York: The Grolier Club, (1982), 8vo., cloth-backed decorated paper covered boards, slipcase. viii, 153, (3) pages.
$ 125.00

First edition, one of 300 numbered copies signed by Blumenthal and issued thus for the Grolier Club. Illustrated autobiography by this book designer. With information on The Spiral Press. Printed by the Stinehour Press.

1365. (Stinehour Press) Chaucer, Geoffrey. THE CANTERBURY TALES, THE NEW ELLESMERE CHAUCER MONOCHROMATIC FACSIMILE (OF HUNTINGTON LIBRARY MS EL 26 C 9). San Marino, CA: Huntington Library, 1997, large folio, cloth. 484 pages. $ 275.00

Edition limited to 1000 copies. Edited by Daniel Woodward and Martin Stevens, this full-sized mono-chromatic facsimile conveys the trim, texture and decoration of the original Ellesmere manuscript pages. The frontispiece, a copy of the page that begins the Knight's Tale, is reproduced in color. Elegant-ly printed by the Stinehour Press of Lunenberg, VT from the same transparencies used to create the full-color facsimile edition.

1366. (Stinehour Press) David, Ismar. THE BOOK OF JONAH. Southbury, CT: Chiswick Book Shop, 1991, 4to., cloth. xiii, 17 pages. $ 150.00

Limited to 350 copies signed by David. Printed in three colors by the Meriden-Stinehour Press on An-ders' Elephant Hide and Mohawk Superfine Text papers. With introduction by Chaim Potok. David's il-lustrations and calligraphy enhance the story of Jonah which is told both in English and Hebrew. A beau-tiful volume. With the bookplate of John DePol and a card loosely inserted in which the Cohen's have in-dicated this was a gift to him.

1367. (Stinehour Press) Duschnes, Philip C. BRUCE ROGERS, A GENTLE MAN FROM INDIANA. N.P.: Privately printed for Duschnes at the Stinehour Press, 1965, 8vo., stiff paper wrappers. 25 pages. $ 25.00

Limited to 750 copies.

1368. (Stinehour Press) EARLY CHILDREN'S BOOKS AND THEIR ILLUS-TRATION. New York: The Pierpont Morgan Library, (1975), 4to., cloth, dust jacket. xxx, 263 pages. $ 125.00

First edition. Printed at the Stinehour Press. With many illustrations including some in color. Detailed descriptions of over 200 items. Contributions by Charles Ryskamp, Gerald Gottlieb and J.H. Plumb. Jacket chipped.

1369. (Stinehour Press) Fahy, Conor. PRINTING A BOOK AT VERONA IN 1622, THE ACCOUNT BOOK OF FRANCESCO CALZO LARI. Edited with an Intro-duction by Conor Fahy. Paris: Fondation Custodia, 1993, 8vo., cloth, dust jacket. (8), 171, (25) pages. $ 75.00

This book is an account of the production details concerning the printing and distribution of the *Musaeum Francisci Calceolarii*, a large illustrated volume containing a Latin description by two Veronese doctors, Benedetto Ceruti and Andrea Chiocco, of some of the Calzolari family's natural his-tory collection. The *Musaeum* was published in 1622 with 800 folio pages and 45 line engravings and is described as the most complex and ambitious piece of book production to emerge from the small Veronese printing industry in the first 30 years of the 17th century. This account book that describes the Calzolari collection is an important and fascinating document of the early Italian printing industry. It provides a unique general view, from the inside, of the preparation, printing and distribution of a sub-stantial volume, produced in one of the many provincial centres of Italian printing. By the seventeenth century, Italy was no longer at the cutting edge of development in European printing, but its historic role as a centre of cultural and artistic pre-eminence had endowed it with a wealth of material which still per-mitted original initiatives like the *Musaeum*. The *Musaeum* is a large folio volume with numerous line engravings. This account book has been transcribed by Conor Fahy, a leading authority on Italian print-ing, and is here published for the first time with a lengthy introduction. The volume also contains a pho-tographic reproduction of the *Musaeum*, an Italian-English glossary and extensive appendices and in-dexes. This book was chosen by the American Institute of Graphic Arts as one of the Fifty Books of 1993, has been printed and bound by the Stinehour Press of Lunenberg, Vermont and contains 58 plates.

1370. (Stinehour Press) Foot, Mirjam M. HENRY DAVIS GIFT, A COLLECTION OF BOOKBINDINGS. VOLUME II A CATALOGUE OF NORTH-EURO-PEAN BINDINGS. London: The British Library, (1983), small 4to., cloth with leather spine label. 368 pages. $ 200.00

S-K 1241. First edition. Covers bindings made in the British Isles, the Netherlands (including Belgium), Germany, Austria and Denmark. There are 368 entries with excellent bibliographical notes on each binding and the binders who executed them. Each entry has an accompanying illustration, many occupying a full page. An excellent reference work, finely printed by The Stinehour Press.

1371. (Stinehour Press) GROLIER CLUB, 1884–1984, ITS LIBRARY, EXHIBITIONS, & PUBLICATIONS. New York: The Grolier Club, 1984, 4to., cloth, slipcase. 258, (2) pages. $ 200.00

First edition, limited to 600 copies. Printed by the Stinehour Press with plates by Meriden Gravure. Collection of essays on the club followed by a bibliography of all publications.

1372. (Stinehour Press) Harvard, Stephen. ORNAMENTAL INITIALS THE WOODCUT INITIALS OF CHRISTOPHER PLANTIN, A COMPLETE CATALOGUE. New York: American Friends of the Plantin-Moretus Museum, 1974, 4to., cloth-backed boards, dust jacket. xiii, 26 pages followed by the plates. $ 150.00

A study of what is perhaps the best collection of early ornamental letters. Nearly 60 lots are fully described and documented. This book is printed at the Stinehour Press. Jacket chipped at top of spine.

1373. (Stinehour Press) Hitchings, Sinclair. THE STINEHOUR PRESS, NOTES ON ITS FIRST FIVE YEARS. Lunenburg, VT: (Stinehour Press), 1957, small 8vo., stiff paper wrappers. 47+(1) pages. $ 25.00

With a selective list of printing, a gathering of sample pages, and drawings by John R. Nash (Farrell, 62). The Stinehour Press published some of its own titles in limited editions, but mostly served as a printer for such clients as Dartmouth College, The Fogg Art Museum, The Boston Museum of Fine Arts, The Pierpont Morgan Library, and other private presses. Bookplate of John DePol on inside of front wrapper.

1374. (Stinehour Press) Kipling, Rudyard. A BALLAD OF BITTERNESS. Syracuse, NY: Syracuse University Library Associates, 1983, 12mo., stiff paper wrappers. (10) pages. $ 17.50

Printed at the Stinehour Press, Lunenburg , VT., in an edition limited to 400 copies. This is the earliest manuscript in the Syracuse University Kipling Collection, written in 1883 as a Christmas greeting home, when he was seventeen. Small card loosely laid in folder bound in before text, with ms. in Kipling's handwriting. John DePol's signature on inside of wrapper and his bookplate on front pastedown.

1375. (Stinehour Press) Lang, H. Jack. ROWFANT MANUSCRIPTS. With an Introduction by Herman W. Liebert. Cleveland: The Rowfant Club, (1978), tall 8vo., cloth-backed boards. ix, 65, (3) pages. $ 75.00

Limited to 400 numbered copies finely printed by the Stinehour Press. With a number of reproductions of important manuscripts in this book collecting club's library, including a Dickens letter, material relating to Locker-Lampson and a full page portrait of Conrad.

1376. (Stinehour Press) Lathem, Edward Connery. RUDOLPH RUZICKA: SPEAKING REMINISCENTLY. New York: The Grolier Club, 1986, 8vo., cloth-backed boards. 150, (30) pages. $ 55.00

Limited to 750 copies. Printed by Meriden-Stinehour and designed by Roderick Stinehour. With a chronology of his life and reproductions of a number of his illustrations. Contains an index which is of real help in tracking down his friendships with various other typographers such as Dwiggins and his many jobs for the Grolier Club.

1377. (Stinehour Press) Lerner, Abe. DESIGNING A BOOK. New York: The Ty-pophiles, 1993, small 8vo., paper wrappers. (16) pages. $ 27.50
Printed in an edition limited to 800 copies printed at the Stinehour Press. Typophile Monograph, New Series, No. 10. Abe Lerner discuss the making of the Typophile Chap Books Bibliography. With the sig-nature of John DePol on the inside front cover.

1378. (Stinehour Press) Mansbridge, Georgia. BRUCE ROGERS: AMERICAN TY-POGRAPHER. New York: The Typophiles, 1997, small 8vo., cloth. xiii, 95, (3) pages.
                                                                                        $ 85.00
Limited to 500 copies. Short biography of Bruce Rogers (1870–1957), a reprint of the 1965 Master's The-sis by Mansbridge, who was acquainted with Mr. Rogers during the last decade or so of his life. (Facing the title page is a photo of the author and Mr. Rogers.) There is no discussion of books designed by Mr. Rogers, but a concluding chapter quotes various comments, positive and negative, by others on the work of Rogers. Concludes with notes, primary and secondary bibliographies (not updated since the original publication). Printed at the Stinehour Press. Bruce Rogers' colophon device is gilt-stamped on the front cover. Distributed for the Typophiles by Oak Knoll Press.

1379. (Stinehour Press) Norman, Haskell F. ONE HUNDRED BOOKS FAMOUS IN MEDICINE. Catalogue Edited by Hope Mayo. New York: The Grolier Club, 1995, small 4to., cloth, leather spine label, slipcase. xlii, 390, (4) pages. $ 250.00
Limited to 1500 copies. Designed by Jerry Kelly and printed at The Stinehour Press. Full bibliographical descriptions and excellent annotations accompany at least one illustration each for the 100 titles select-ed. Some plates in color. This book accompanies the Grolier Club's other 100 book checklists for science, English literature and American literature.

1380. (Stinehour Press) Melanson, John. A COLLECTION OF WOOD ENGRAV-INGS BY JOHN MELANSON. Lunenburg, VT: Stinehour Press, (1963), 8vo., stiff paper wrappers. unpaginated, with 17 leaves of wood engravings. $ 125.00
Printed in an edition of 50 copies. (Farrell, p.38) Seventeen wood engravings cut for The Stinehour Press during the years 1959 to 1963 from the original blocks on handmade Hosho. Bookplate of John DePol on inside front wrapper.

1381. (Stinehour Press) Nash, Ray and Roderick D. Stinehour (editors). PRINTING & GRAPHIC ARTS. 38 issues, the complete set. Lunenburg, VT: The Stinehour Press, 1953, 8vo., stiff paper wrappers. $ 350.00
Excellent articles on the history of early American typefounders, bibliographies of type specimen books, early Canadian printing, earliest American color printing, etc. This set is very difficult to find complete.

1382. (Stinehour Press) OFFICINA BODONI & THE STAMPERIA VALDONE-GA, AN EXHIBITION MARKING THE 100TH ANNIVERSAY OF THE BIRTH OF GIOVANNI MARDERSTEIG. New York: The Grolier Club, 1992, small 8vo., stiff paper wrappers. 29, (3) pages. $ 15.00
Printed at The Stinehour Press and designed by Jerry Kelly who wrote the introduction and curated the exhibition. Foreword by Kenneth A. Lohf, President of the Grolier Club.

1383. (Stinehour Press) PRINTING AT THE WHITTINGTON PRESS, 1972–1994, AN EXHIBTIION. With Remarks by John Randle, John Dreyfus & Mark Batty. N.P.: International Typeface Corporation and The Grolier Club, 1994, 8vo., stiff paper wrappers. 63+(1) pages. $ 30.00
Limited to 2,500 copies printed by letterpress at the Stinehour Press with design by Jerry Kelly. This is one of 250 copies signed by Randle on the title page. A well annotated exhibition catalogue describing the production of the Whittington Press. Includes illustrations.

1384. (Stinehour Press) Sherman, Stuart C. THE VOICE OF THE WHALEMAN, WITH AN ACCOUNT OF NICHOLSON WHALING COLLE. Providence, RI: Providence Public Library (printed by the Stinehour Press), 1965, large 8vo., two-tone cloth, dust jacket. 219 pages. $ 45.00

836 manuscript logbooks, journals and account books spanning the years between 1762–1922 from the Nicholson Whaling Collection at the Providence Public Library, with an account of the collection, an explanation of logbooks and journals, and a discussion of "whaling records as a source of history." Twenty illustrations. A few pencil marks; dust jacket missing some pieces, lightly soiled.

1385. (Stinehour Press) THINKING IN SCRIPT, A LETTER OF THANKS FROM EDWARD JOHNSTON TO PAUL STANDARD, 26 APRIL - 5 MAY 1944. With an Introduction by Mark Argetsinger. Rochester: Rochester Institute of Technology, n.d. (1995), small 4to., stiff paper wrappers. 51+(1) pages. $ 30.00

Limited to 1000 copies and printed at the Stinehour Press with design by Jerry Kelly. Standard raised funds to help Johnston and received in return a beautiful 8 page letter. This letter is reproduced in facsimile along with text describing this episode. Foreword by David Pankow.

1386. (Stinehour Press) Tzara, Tristan. CINEMA CALENDRIER DU COEUR ABSTRAIT - MAISONS. Ann Arbor, MI: Thomas Press, n.d. (1982?), small 4to., paper-covered boards, strip (3.25 x 23 in.) wrapped around cover, translucent protector, folded sheet loosely inserted, paper-covered slipcase. (38) pages, with 6 additional pages in the brochure and 19 additional leaves of woodcuts. $ 95.00

Limited to 1,000 copies. Facsimile edition of the original 1920 edition (itself limited to 150 copies) of two groupings of Dadaist poetry by T. Tzara (1896–1963), generally regarded as the founder of the Dada movement, with 19 woodcuts by the Dadaist and later surrealist artist Hans Arp (1887–1966). A folded sheet (dated 1982) with English translation of the text by Mary Ann Caws is loosely inserted. The letterpress printing was done by the Stinehour Press.

1387. (Stinehour Press) Voet, Leon. MAKING OF BOOKS IN THE RENAISSANCE AS TOLD BY THE ARCHIVES OF THE PLANTIN-MORETUS MUSEUM. N.P.: American Friends of the Plantin-Moretus Museum, (1966), 8vo., stiff paper wrappers. pp.33-62, (2) pages. $ 35.00

Limited to 200 copies printed on better paper by The Stinehour Press. The article first appeared in P&GA, Volume X, No.2.

1388. (Stinehour Press) Zweig, Stefan. THE MEANING AND BEAUTY OF AUTOGRAPHS. New York: Lion Heart Autographs, 1995, large 12mo., stiff paper wrappers. 22, (2) pages. $ 17.50

Printed in an edition limited to 500 numbered copies in Hermann Zapf's Renaissance Roman type on Simpson Teton paper at the Stinehour Press. Designed by Jerry Kelly. Translated by David H. Lowenherz with a photograph of Zweig as frontis and three others in text taken on his American tour in 1938.

1389. (Stone House Press) Digby, John. INCANTATIONS. Roslyn, NY: Stone House Press, 1987, 8vo., cloth. 71+(1) pages. $ 75.00

Printed in an edition limited to 215 numbered copies signed by the author and printer, of which 190 were for sale (Brody, 87.1). Designed by George Laws, typeset in Monotype Poliphilus and Blado Italic, and printed by hand at the Stone House Press by M.A. Gelfand and Jim Ricciardi on Mohawk Superfine paper. *Incantations* "represents the author's most deliberate integration of his work as a poet and collagist, centering on a vision of essential unity in nature from the viewpoint of primitive man." With an Introduction by Anna Balakian. " Prospectus and Seasons Greetings card from the publisher laid in.

1390. (Stone House Press) Krapf, Norbert (editor). UNDER OPEN SKY, POETS ON WILLIAM CULLEN BRYANT. Illustrated by John DePol. New York: The Stone House Press, 1986, 8vo., quarter cloth with patterned papers over boards. xv, 109 pages.
$ 95.00

Limited to 185 signed and numbered copies, of which 140 copies are for sale. Contains essays and poems about Bryant by twenty present day American poets. Illustrated with 17 DePol wood engravings. With prospectus and a Christmas card from Gelfand loosely inserted.

1391. (Stone House Press) Liebaers, Herman. BOOKS OVER BOMBS, IFLA IN MOSCOW, AUGUST 1991. A FOOTNOTE. Roslyn: The Stone House Press, 1995, 8vo., stiff paper wrappers. 21 pages.
$ 30.00

Limited to 200 numbered copies. Biographical introduction by George Wickes and wood engraving by John DePol. Liebaers was President of the IFLA (International Federation of Library Associations.

1392. (Stone House Press) Meyer, Gerard Previn. RENEWALS, SELECTED POEMS AND TRANSLATIONS. Roslyn Harbor, NY: Stone House Press, 1982, 8vo., cloth, dust jacket. (x), 100, (2) pages.
$ 95.00

Printed in an edition limited to 140 copies, of which this is one of 125 which is numbered & signed (Brody, 82.1). Presentation copy to Abe Lerner signed by the author and the publisher, Morris Gelfand. Handset in Kennerley & Goudy Open types and printed by hand on Ragston paper by M.A. Gelfand. Minor wear to dust jacket

1393. (Stourton Press) Swinburne, Algernon Charles. HIDE-AND-SEEK. London: The Stourton Press, 1975, 4to., half brown calf, cloth, top edge gilt. 14, (3) pages.
$ 95.00

Edition limited to two hundred and fifty numbered copies. This book contains the first printing of a poem composed by Swinburne during his undergraduate days at Oxford University. Cast, set, and printed by Fairfax Hall on Joseph Batchelor's Kelmscott hand-made paper in the Aries types designed for the Stourton Press by Eric Gill. With a foreword and note by John S. Mayfield. Leather on spine and along hinges shows wear. Prospectus loosely inserted.

1394. (Stratford Press) THE CONSTITUTION OF THE UNITED STATES OF AMERICA. Cincinnati: The Stratford Press, (1945), 4to., cloth, slipcase. 44, (2) pages.
$ 35.00

Printed directly from type at the private press of Elmer Gleason.

1395. (Sumac Press) Davis, Richard Harding. HOW STEPHEN CRANE TOOK JUANA DIAS. With a Prefatory Note by John T. Winterich. La Crosse: Sumac Press, 1976, 8vo., paper wrappers. (16) pages.
$ 20.00
Limited to 300 copies. Minor spotting of front cover.

1396. (Sumac Press) Klinefelter, Walter. FURTHER DISPLAY OF OLD MAPS & PLANS. La Crosse: Sumac Press, 1969, 8vo., cloth, dust jacket. Not paginated. $ 45.00
Limited to 300 copies. The second in a series of books that describe stamps that use cartography in their design. Top of jacket chipped.

1397. (Sumac Press) Klinefelter, Walter. THIRD DISPLAY OF OLD MAPS AND PLANS. La Crosse: Sumac Press, 1973, 8vo., cloth, dust jacket. Not paginated. $ 45.00
Limited to 300 copies. One stamp mounted.

1398. (Sumac Press) Klinefelter, Walter. FOURTH DISPLAY OF OLD MAPS & PLANS, STUDIES IN POSTAL CARTOGRAPHY. La Crosse: Sumac Press, 1978, 8vo., cloth, dust jacket. 67 pages. $ 35.00
Limited to 300 copies. The 4th in a series of books about stamps that use cartography in their design. Each illustration of a stamp is accompanied by a discussion of the map used and the explorers who first made it.

1399. (Sumac Press) Klinefelter, Walter. WALTER KLINEFELTER BIBLIO-LIST. LaCrosse: Sumac Press, 1976, 8vo., wrappers with signatures loosely inserted. 12 pages.
                                                                                $ 30.00
Limited to 295 copies printed by hand by Emerson Wulling. With some title page facsimiles. Corners bumped.

1400. (Sumac Press) Phelps, Fred Totten. CHECKLIST OF PRIVATE PRINTINGS. La Crosse: The Sumac Press, 1977, 8vo., stiff paper wrappers. (20) pages. $ 25.00
Limited to 270 copies printed by Emerson Wulling. Introduction followed by bibliographical descriptions of 28 items printed by Phelps, many at his Voyageur Press.

1401. (Sumac Press) Wulling, Emerson G. COMP'S-EYE VIEW OF FOOTNOTES. La Crosse: Sumac Press, 1953, 12mo., stiff paper wrappers. 18, (2) pages. $ 25.00
First edition, limited to 450 copies. A private pressman looks at the typographical problems of footnote arrangement. In mailing envelope from the press (which has left a small mark on front cover.

1402. (Sumac Press) Wulling, Emerson G. COMP'S-EYE VIEW OF PAPER. La Crosse: The Sumac Press, 1971, 12mo., paste paper covers. (12) pages. $ 25.00
Limited to about 174 copies printed by Wulling at his private press.

1403. (Sumac Press) Wulling, Emerson G. COMP'S-EYE VIEW OF WILDER BENTLEY AND THE ARCHETYPE PRESS. La Crosse: Sumac Press, 1983, 8vo., stiff paper wrappers. (18) pages. $ 55.00
Limited to 300 copies. Well printed and with some illustrations in red. With small broadside concerning this gift loosely inserted as is a one page T.L.s. from Emerson Wulling dated 1983 to "Cheney" with comments on this booklet and other typographic matters.

1404. (Sumac Press) Wulling, Emerson G. J. JOHNSON, TYP., ODDMENTS FROM HIS TYPOGRAPHIA, OR THE PRINTERS' INSTRUCTOR, WITH AN ORIGINAL LEAF THEREFROM. La Crosse: Sumac Press, 1967, 12mo., cloth. (24) pages. $ 60.00
Printed in an edition limited to 396 copies; designed, set and printed by Emerson G. Wulling at his private press. Fine.

1405. (Swamp Press) CHAPBOOKS, PERIODICAL ISSUES, CATALOGUES AND EPHEMERA FROM THE SWAMP PRESS, 1973–1989. Sixty-three items. Oneonta (NY) / Amherst (MA): The Swamp Press, 1973-89, miniature book to 4to.; sewn, stitched or stapled; in stiff paper wrappers, paper-covered boards, or (1) quarter leather or (2) cloth, with various additional loose or folded loose sheets and 1 scroll. Various paginations (up to about 40 maximum). $ 450.00
Diverse materials from a small-press publisher of contemporary poetry and fiction, including probably the first American publication in English of a volume of poetry by the German poet Reiner Kunze. The Swamp Press was started, per publisher's statement on a colophon, in Oneonta, NY in 1976 (however: one of the Swamp Press imprints here has a copyright date of 1973), by E. Rayher and J. Mish, originally for the purpose of publishing "Tightrope," a small press magazine for poetry, fiction, and artistic illustration. The Press soon began to publish "chapbooks" in addition to the magazine. In the early 1980's, Rayher and the Swamp Press moved to Massachusetts, while Mish remained in Oneonta and started the

Serpent and Eagle Press. Included in this collection are seven issues of "Tightrope," numbers 7–10 and 12–14, dated from 1978 to 1989 (one undated). Three of these are explicitly designated limited editions. The issues contain mostly poetry and illustrations, with some prose fiction and a few photos. Bindings are mostly sewn or stitched, but one issue consists of loose sheets held together by a metal rivet. One issue has a triangular shape. There are, in addition, twenty-eight titles of "chapbooks" (booklets and brochures, one scroll, one folded sheet), including two produced by the Swamp Press for the Nocturnal Canary Press, and one printed for the Coal for Eye Press. Four titles are present in two versions, making a total of 32 "items." There are also three duplicates, which we have not included in our "item" count. Most of these are poetry, mostly with illustrations. Two items are a translation (in 2 different editions) of a 1972 volume of poems by the German poet Reiner Kunze (b.1933); per introduction, this is the first American publication (in English) of one of Kunze's poetry collections. A few books are prose fiction with illustrations. One poetry item is a long vertical paper strip with illustrative material printed on paper stock, overlain by a second strip of semitransparent tissue on which the text is printed, both strips rolled up in a scroll encased in a clear plastic box. Illustrations include etchings, woodcuts, linocuts, drawings, scratchboard prints, etc. Twenty-eight "items" have an explicit limited edition statement, twelve are numbered, and six are signed by the author and/or illustrator. "Chapbook" authors are: P. Cox, M. David, D. Donovan, M. Dudley, B. Egyedi, A. Fulton, A. Glaze, L. Gorman, E. Kaplan, R. Kunze, F. Lindsay, P.W. Lyles, J. Mish, W.S. New, M. Newell, P. O'Neill, K. Poppino, E. Rayher, S. Ruhl, L. Spina, C. Stone, and J. Suarez. A number of the books have illustrations by Jon Vlakos. 15 ephemera are included: bookmarks, cards, prospectuses and other matter, along with 4 Swamp Press catalogues, priced and from the 1980's (one undated), with duplicate copies of 3 of these, and 4 novelty items in the form of miniature books. Lastly, there is a book of poetry/illustrations from "Xerox Sutra Editions," which seems to have no connection to the Swamp Press except that its author also published with the Swamp Press. Items are in very good condition. The stitching of one issue of "Tightrope" has come undone; several covers show light soiling.

1406. (Swann Press) Collard, Lorna Keeling. ROSEMARY. FOUR SONNETS. Leeds: Swann Press, 1926, large 12mo., gilt stamped cloth. unpaginated. $ 85.00
First edition, limited to 25 numbered copies signed by Lorna Collard and illustrator Joyce Collard. Four sonnets about remembrance and reading. Illustrated with three original prints.

1407. (Symposium Press) Cunningham, J.V. LET THY WORDS BE FEW. Los Angeles: Symposium Press, 1986, 8vo., cloth, paper spine label. (viii), 17, (5) pages. $ 65.00
Designed and printed by Patrick Reagh for the Symposium Press in an edition limited to 350 numbered copies, of which 285 were for sale. This copy is numbered and noted as review copy on colophon. Type set in 13 point Bembo on 80-lb. Mohawk Superfine paper. Hand-bound by Bela Blau. Poems and epigrams. Prospectus laid in.

1408. (Tamalpais Press) Harding, George L. CHARLES A. MURDOCK, PRINTER & CITIZEN OF SAN FRANCISCO: AN APPRAISAL. Berkeley: Tamalpais Press, 1973, 8vo., cloth. x, 83, (3) pages. $ 85.00
Limited to 310 copies printed by Roger Levenson at the Tamalpais Press. Biography of the "earliest printer of taste in the far-west." Illustrated. Signed by Harding and Levenson on front free endpaper. Prospectus loosely inserted.

1409. (Tamalpais Press) Olmsted, Duncan H. BARTOLOMEUS ZANNI, PRINTER AT VENICE 1486–1518 AND AT PORTESE 1489-90. Together with a Leaf from Jacobus de Voragine's LEGENDARIO DE SANCTI, Printed by Zanni at Venice, 1503. Berkeley: Tamalpais Press, 1962, 4to., paper wrappers. (6) pages. $ 125.00
Limited to 135 numbered copies. A monograph compiled from various sources about Bartolomeus Zanni, one of the 150 printers practicing the trade in Venice in the 1500's.

1410. (Taylor & Taylor) Laurie, Annie. MY NEIGHBOR HAS GONE ON A LONG JOURNEY AND I DID NOT SAY GOOD-BY. San Francisco: 1917, large 12mo., quarter cloth with paper-covered boards. 12, (2) pages. $ 35.00

Reprinted by Taylor & Taylor from *The San Francisco Call* of October 23, 1917. "My neighbor has gone away--on a long, long journey. I wish I had had a chance to say goodbye to her across the garden wall--before she went." Illustrated with three small tipped in illustrations of the neighbor's garden and the view they shared from their homes on Telegraph Hill.

1411. (Taylor & Taylor) Taylor, Edward Dewitt. THIS MEMORIED DAY. THESE VERSES, WRITTEN TO MY WIFE MARIE GRIFFITH TAYLOR IN CELE-BRATION OF OUR FIFTIETH WEDDING ANNIVERSAY FEBRUARY 4, 1943, ARE PRESENTED TO HER WITH MY DEEPEST AFFECTION. San Francisco: Taylor & Taylor, 1943, small 4to., paper-covered boards. 13 pages printed on rectos only. $ 55.00

Printed in an edition limited to 75 copies, this copy being a presentation copy, signed by author on front free endpaper. Taylor & Taylor was a firm which did fine printing in San Francisco in the earlier part of the 20th century (John Nash was a partner from 1911 to 1916). The Taylor's were also active in the Book Club of California. Covers and pastedowns of this copy are unevenly browned, with the covers also somewhat soiled & with several small stains.

1412. (Taylor & Taylor) Taylor, Edward Robeson. FROM A WINDOW ON RUSS-IAN HILL, SAN FRANCISCO WITH MESSRS TAYLOR & TAYLOR'S CHRISTMAS GREETINGS TO THE FRIENDS OF THEIR PRESS, MCMXVI. (San Francisco: Taylor & Taylor, 1916), 8vo., paper wrappers. (4) pages. $ 25.00

Printed in an edition of 500 copies by Taylor and Taylor, acknowledged as one of turn-of-the century California's premier fine printing houses (Barr, p.140). Noted California poet Taylor composed the son-net, printed on the inside verso of the french-fold card. Tipped in photo by western photographer W.E. Dassonville on inside recto. Red, blue and green printer's ornaments. Hand-made paper.

1413. (Plain Wrapper Press) PLAIN WRAPPER PRESS, 1966–1988, AN ILLUS-TRATED BIBLIOGRAPHY OF THE WORK OF RICHARD-GABRIEL RUM-MONDS. With Bibliographical Descriptions by Elaine Smyth and a Foreword by Decherd Turner. Austin, TX: W. Thomas Taylor, 1993, small 4to., stiff paper wrappers. 74, (2) pages. $ 45.00

Limited to 340 copies. Designed and printed by Bradley Hutchinson at the printing office of W. Thomas Taylor with Monotype Dante set by Michael and Winifred Bixler and photographs in color by Carring-ton Weems.

1414. (Taylor, W. Thomas) Tyler, Ron. AUDUBON'S GREAT NATIONAL WORK, THE ROYAL OCTAVO EDITION OF THE BIRDS OF AMERICA (WITH: ORIGINAL PLATES FROM THE FIRST AND SECOND EDITIONS OF THE BIRDS OF AMERICA, WITH THE ORIGINAL TEXT DESCRIBING THE BIRD DEPICTED [BROCHURE]). Austin, TX: W. Thomas Taylor, 1993, small 4to., quarter cloth, paper-covered boards, clamshell case (with sewn brochure, tall large 8vo., in stiff paper wrappers). xvii, (iii), 213, (3) pages (brochure: (6) pages, 2 additional leaves of plates). $ 550.00

Limited to 225 unnumbered copies. John James Audubon (1785–1851) published the large folio edition of The Birds of America, with engraved plates, in England from 1826 to 1838. This edition met with ap-proval among artists and scientists, but was too expensive to reach a wide audience, nor did Audubon de-rive much income from it. He therefore brought out a royal octavo version with additional materials (1st ed. 1839–1844), published in the U.S. with lithographic plates; this version made Audubon the familiar figure which he still is today. Audubon, whose understanding of business and publishing had improved by then, also earned enough to become reasonably well-off. The author gives an account of the publication of the folio, followed by a lengthier account of the production of the octavo from the folio and the publication history of the octavo, covering, among other things, the production of the plates, their characteristics, Audubon's co-workers, differences from the folio edition and among the various editions of the octavo, along with Audubon's relations with publishers and his own marketing efforts. A concluding chapter discusses Audubon's works in the context of Romanticism. The book has 67 illustrations, including 34 showing plates & variants in color. The 2 plates in the brochure belonging to this copy show the "Shore Lark." With tables (printing history of 1st ed., subscriber list, etc.), appendix, notes, bibliography, and index. A patterned paper in shades of green covers the boards, and the case is covered in the same fabric used in the binding. A book for those interested in Audubon, American art of the mid–19th century, or 19th-century American publishing.

1415. (Taylor, W. Thomas) Blumenthal, Joseph. BRUCE ROGERS, A LIFE IN LETTERS 1870–1957. With a foreword by John Dreyfus. Austin, TX: W. Thomas Taylor, (1989), small 4to., cloth. xvii, 215 pages. $ 95.00
First edition, limited to 2000 copies. A biography of Rogers by an acknowledged expert in the field. Designed and printed at the press of W. Thomas Taylor with plates produced at The Press of A. Colish. Has 57 plates printed with a number in two colors.

1416. (Taylor, W. Thomas) Blumenthal, Joseph. BRUCE ROGERS, A LIFE IN LETTERS 1870–1957. With a foreword by John Dreyfus. Austin, TX: W. Thomas Taylor, (1989), small 4to., stiff paper wrappers. xvii, 215 pages. $ 30.00
First edition, limited to 2000 copies; this is one of the paper bound copies. Bruce Rogers is without doubt the most important figure in 20th-century American bookmaking. Though there is extensive and diverse literature devoted to his work, all of it has been fragmentary, focusing on one aspect or another of his career that has spanned over 50 productive years. This work provides a definitive account of Rogers and his books. The narrative is woven together with a rich selection from Rogers' correspondence and the text is well-illustrated throughout with examples of Rogers' work. The biography of Rogers has been written by Joseph Blumenthal, an acknowledged expert in the field. Designed and printed at the press of W. Thomas Taylor with plates produced at The Press of A. Colish. Has 57 plates printed with a number in two colors.

1417. (Taylor, W. Thomas) Blumenthal, Joseph. ROBERT FROST AND HIS PRINTERS. Austin, TX: W. Thomas Taylor, (1985), tall 8vo., cloth, slipcase. xi, 105+(1) pages. $ 45.00
First edition, limited to 1000 copies. Printed letterpress by A. Colish with 31 pages of illustrations produced at the Meriden Gravure Company. Blumenthal writes about the printing details of over 30 of Frost's books including ones designed or printed by Mosher, Ruzicka, Dwiggins, Dahlstrom, Ritchie, Beilenson, and Hunter.

1418. (Taylor, W. Thomas) Breslauer, B.H. COUNT HEINRICH IV ZU CASTELL, A GERMAN RENAISSANCE BOOK COLLECTOR AND THE BINDINGS MADE FOR HIM DURING HIS STUDENT YEARS IN ORLEANS, PARIS, AND BOLOGNA. Austin, TX: W. Thomas Taylor, 1987, folio, Fabriano paper over boards. 38 pages. $ 165.00
Limited to 190 copies. A history of this 16th century library which has survived virtually intact to the present day and descriptions of the French and Italian bindings on the books. Five color plates including four of bindings. Printed in Monotype Centaur and Arrighi on Johannot mouldmade paper. Covers slightly rubbed.

1419. (Taylor, W. Thomas) Duncan, Harry. DOORS OF PERCEPTION, ESSAYS IN BOOK TYPOGRAPHY. Austin, TX: W. Thomas Taylor, 1983, 8vo., quarter Niger goatskin with leather tips and paste paper over boards by C. Blinn. (ii), 99, (3) pages.
$ 200.00

First edition, limited to 325 copies and signed by Duncan. Designed by Carol J. Blinn at her Warwick Press. Essays on The Cummington Press, The Technology of Hand Printing, The Art of the Printed Book, My Master Victor Hammer and The Permanence of Books.

1420. (Taylor, W. Thomas) Duncan, Harry. DOORS OF PERCEPTION, ESSAYS IN BOOK TYPOGRAPHY. Austin, TX: W. Thomas Taylor, 1987, 8vo., stiff paper wrappers. (ii), 99, (3) pages.
$ 16.50

Second printing, reprinted from the first edition which was limited to only 325 copies. Five provocative essays describe Duncan's ideal in his own life and explores its implications for today's hand-printer and for future generations interested in typography and printing. This popular book contains essays on the Cummington Press, The Technology of Hand Printing, The Art of the Printed Book, My Master Victor Hammer and The Permanence of Books.

1421. (Taylor, W. Thomas) A GARLAND FOR HARRY DUNCAN. Austin, TX: W. Thomas Taylor, 1989, large 8vo., quarter leather with cloth covered boards. (10), 96, (9) pages.
$ 125.00

Printed in an edition limited to 500 copies. Contributions from fifty-eight poets on the occasion of the fiftieth anniversary of the Cummington Press. Some of the poets are Stephen Berg, Warren Slesinger, Gerald Stern, Jane Greer and others. Illustrated with a drawing by Keith Achepohl.

1422. (Taylor, W. Thomas) Fine, Ruth E. PRINTERS' CHOICE, CATALOGUE OF AN EXHIBITION HELD AT THE GROLIER CLUB NEW YORK, DECEMBER 19, 1978 - FEBRUARY 3, 1979. A SELECTION OF AMERICAN PRESS BOOKS, 1968–1978. Bibliographical Descriptions and Notes by W. Thomas Taylor. Austin, TX: W. Thomas Taylor, 1983, small folio, cloth, paper spine label. xviii, 67, (3) pages.
$ 400.00

Limited to 325 numbered copies printed and designed by David Holman at the Wind River Press. Includes descriptions of 41 American presses. Many of the presses contributed an example of their printing which has been tipped-in. Some of the presses represented are the Adagio Press, the Allen Press, Bird & Bull Press (with an example of their printing), Cummington Press, Gehenna Press, Janus Press, the Press of the Nightowl, etc.

1423. (Taylor, W. Thomas) Gauffecourt, Jean-Vincent Capronnier De. TRAITE DE LA RELIEURE DES LIVRES. A Bilingual Treatise on Bookbinding Translated from the French by Claude Benaiteau. With an Introduction by John P. Chalmers. Edited by Elaine B. Smyth. Austin, TX: W. Thomas Taylor, 1987, tall 8vo., quarter red leather over boards, leather spine label. 130, (4) pages.
$ 185.00

Limited to 300 copies of which this is one of 40 copies bound thus and printed letterpress on Gampi Torinoko. A reprint of the very scarce first separately issued French bookbinding manual, printed by its author in 1763. Translated into English and with a long introduction giving background information on the author and the manual. Well printed by W. Thomas Taylor.

1424. (Taylor, W. Thomas) Middleton, Christopher. RAZZMATAZZ. Austin, TX: W. Thomas Taylor, 1976, large 8vo., stiff paper wrappers. iv, 9, (3) pages.
$ 35.00

Printed in an edition limited to 250 numbered and signed copies. A poem by Middleton. Designed and printed by Gregory Holman.

1425. (Taylor, W. Thomas) Pollard, Alfred W. ITALIAN BOOK ILLUSTRATIONS AND EARLY PRINTING, A CATALOGUE. London: Bernard Quaritch, 1914. (But Austin: W. Thomas Taylor, 1994), small 4to., cloth, paper spine label. xiii, 255 pages.
$185.00

Reprint of the 1914 first edition, limited to about 250 copies. Full bibliographical descriptions of many important 16th and 15th century Italian books. Illustrated.

1426. (Taylor, W. Thomas) Roberts, Verne L. & Ivy Trent. BIBLIOTHECA MECHANICA. New York: Jonathan A. Hill, (1991), 4to., cloth-backed decorated boards. xiv, 391 pages.
$260.00

Trade edition, limited to 1,000 copies. Bibliography of the private library of Verne Roberts, which contains about 1200 items in the fields of mechanics, biomechanics and the history of technology in the 15th, 16th and 17th centuries. Contains extensive descriptions of the books and authors document the development of ideas in science and technology. Some of the items in the collection are very rare. Contains 50 illustrations. Designed and produced by W. Thomas Taylor.

1427. (Taylor, W. Thomas) Schreiber, Fred. SIMON DE COLINES, AN ANNOTATED CATALOGUE OF 230 EXAMPLES OF HIS PRESS 1520–1546. Provo: Friends of the Brigham Young University Library, 1995, small 4to., cloth, paper spine label. lxxxiv, 242, (4) pages.
$150.00

First edition, limited to 750 copies. The first true Renaissance printer, Colines worked with the finest French book decorators and type designers to transform the French book. By using the format pioneered by Aldus Manutius, his press (1520–1546) published reasonably priced "pocket" classics, making them affordable by students and popularizing italic and cursive types in France. Colines holds the distinction of having prepared the first critical text of the Greek New Testament, the first printed in France. He produced the earliest accented Greek type in France, fifteen years prior to the Grecs du Roi. In 1528, de Colines introduced an elegant cursive, derived from Arrighi, followed by a smaller italic based on the Aldine. The 230 books described in this work, one-third of Colines' actual production, illustrate de Colines' types, ornamental initials, printer devices and title borders. A catalogue of the books published and facsimiles of two of Colines' publisher catalogues are also included. Designed by W. Thomas Taylor. Illustrated.

1428. (Taylor, W. Thomas) Taylor, W. Thomas. TEXFAKE, AN ACCOUNT OF THE THEFT AND FORGERY OF EARLY TEXAS PRINTED DOCUMENTS. Austin, TX: W. Thomas Taylor, 1991, tall 8vo., cloth backed boards. xix, 159 pages. $39.95

First edition. With an introduction by Larry McMurtry. Describes the history and impact of various forged Texas documents. Mr. Taylor, who was instrumental in uncovering the forgeries, includes his own evidence which made him suspect forgery. The forged and original documents are described in detail and includes an up-to-date census of each document, as well as plates which illustrate differences between the genuine document and the fake. Also gives an account of the related looting and reselling of items belonging to Texas libraries. An in-depth and readable book.

1429. (Taylor, W. Thomas) Turner, Decherd. RHEMES NEW TESTAMENT, BEING A FULL AND PARTICULAR ACCOUNT OF THE ORIGINS, PRINTING, AND SUBSEQUENT INFLUENCES OF THE FIRST ROMAN CATHOLIC NEW TESTAMENT IN ENGLISH ... ACCOMPANIED BY A LEAF FROM THE ORIGINAL EDITION, AND OTHER PROFITABLE ILLUSTRATIONS. San Francisco: The Book Club of California, 1990, small 4to., quarter red goatskin over Fabriano paper covered boards, plain paper dust jacket. (vi), 37, (3) pages. $210.00

Limited to 395 copies printed by W. Thomas Taylor. The leaf was taken from an imperfect copy of the first edition of 1582. Bookplate.

1430. (Taylor, W. Thomas) Wilson, Adrian. TWO AGAINST THE TIDE A CON-SCIENTIOUS OBJECTOR IN WORLD WAR II, SELECTED LETTERS, 1941–1948. Edited and with commentary by Joyce Lancester Wilson. Austin, TX: W. Thomas Taylor, 1990, 8vo., cloth, paper spine label. xii, 198, (2) pages. $ 25.00
Limited to 850 copies and printed from Monotype Ehrhardt at the press of W. Thomas Taylor. Adrian Wilson (1923–1988) was internationally known as a designer and printer of fine books. During his career, he produced over 200 titles, authored a standard text, *The Design of Books*, for his field, wrote two important scholarly books on early printing and manuscripts and inspired the friendship of a wide circle of fellow bibliophiles around the world. Less well-known is that Wilson was a conscientious objector during the Second World War, and that he learned the rudiments of printing in a work camp at Waldport, Oregon, to which he was assigned. When Wilson left home to attend Wesleyan University in September 1941, he began to write long, intimate letters to his parents, almost daily, describing his life at college, his growing involvement with pacifists there and his struggle to decide on a course of action. These letters are now published for the first time here in this work designed by Jerry Kelly and printed from Monotype Ehrhardt at the Press of W. Thomas Taylor.

1431. (Taylor, W. Thomas) WORK & PLAY OF ADRIAN WILSON, A BIBLIOG-RAPHY WITH COMMENTARY. Edited by Joyce Lancester Wilson. Austin, TX: W. Thomas Taylor, 1983, folio, quarter bound in oasis morocco dyed to match the Tuscany Red ink used in the text, Dutch linen sides stamped with Wilson's type-juggler device. 158, (2) pages. $ 600.00
Limited to 325 numbered copies (though the bibliography states 350 copies). Adrian Wilson (1923–1988) was internationally known as a designer and printer of fine books. This beautifully produced bibliography contains a biographical introduction and illustrates 196 items produced by Wilson, each accompanied by lengthy comments by Wilson himself concerning the printing of each book and other pertinent facts. Printed by hand on handmade paper by Adrian Wilson and containing many tipped-in specimens of his work, some of the specimens are actual pages, often in color, from these books. A beautifully produced book.

1432. (Tenfingers Press) PROVERBIS ON MUSYE FROM THE GARET AT THE NEW LODGE IN THE PARK OF LEKINGFELDE. Los Angeles: Tenfingers, 1962, 12mo., paper-covered boards. (24) pages. $ 100.00
Printed in an edition of 100 copies and signed by Frank J. Thomas of Tenfingers Press. The first typographic version of the *Proverbis on Musyke*, verses taken from a manuscript discovered in the title's Garet at the New Lodge and now housed in the British Museum. Printed by Thomas on his handpress in Bembo and Narrow Bembo on Warren Olde Style paper. Wood and lino-cut illustrations also by Thomas, as is the frontispiece photograph. Includes a booklet with three "proverbis."

1433. (Tenfingers Press) Thomas, Frank J. TYPOGRAPHIC CURIOSA, AN UN-PREMEDITATED ASSEMBLAGE DONE AT THE 10 FINGERS PRESS. (Los Angeles: Tenfingers Press), 1964, small 12mo., stiff paper wrappers. (10) pages and 5 illustrations. $ 25.00
Printed in an edition limited to 150 numbered copies on Strathmore Grandee paper from handset types. With various designs in color printed or pasted on pages facing text.

1434. (Tern Press) Best, Thomas. A CONCISE TREATISE ON THE ART OF AN-GLING. N.P.: The Tern Press, 1992, large 8vo., quarter cloth with patterned paper covered boards, paper cover and spine labels. (76) pages. $ 125.00
Printed in an edition limited to 175 numbered and signed copies. Taken from actual experience of Thomas Best who describes the various methods of the art of angling. Included are descriptions of fish, the making and choosing of rods, lines, hooks, baits used and fly-fishing. Text reprinted from the edition of 1787. Newly illustrated with etchings by Nicholas Parry.

1435. (Tern Press) Burghah, Ed. PROVIDENCE IMPROVED. (Market Drayton): Tern Press, (1993), tall 8vo., paper covered boards with paper spine and cover label. unpaginated. $ 100.00

Printed in an edition limited to 200 signed and numbered copies. This diary is one of Cheshire's rarest written works, it provides us with a unique look into a violent and bloody English Civil War. Newly illustrated by Nicholas Parry with 19 relief etchings.

1436. (Tern Press) Clare, John. DON JUAN. Market Drayton: Tern Press, (1998), 12mo., decorated paper covered boards. (58) pages. $ 60.00

Printed in an edition limited to 100 numbered and signed copies by the Tern Press. The poem Don Juan by John Clare which criticizes woman, marriage, fashion, etc., is illustrated with 15 prints by Nicholas Parry. Printed on Rivioli paper.

1437. (Tern Press) Clare, John. THE HUE & CRY, A TALE OF THE TIMES. (Market Drayton: Tern Press, (1990), small 4to., decorated cloth, paper cover and spine labels. (42) pages. $ 140.00

Printed in an edition limited to 125 numbered and signed copies. A fine press edition of the historical satire which has been edited by Eric Robinson. It includes 15 beautiful woodcut illustrations by Nicholas Parry. It was also printed and bound in a gold pictorial cloth by Nicholas and Mary Parry. Signed by Nicholas Parry.

1438. (Tern Press) Clare, John. THE FLITTING. Market Drayton: The Tern Press, (1991), oblong 12mo., quarter cloth, with paper covered boards, paper spine label. (56) pages. $ 70.00

Printed in an edition limited to 100 signed and numbered copies. Clare writes this poems about flitting in the spring of 1832, to a new cottage, and the loss of friendships and the difficulties in leaving the woods. This poem is one of the powerful Clare ever wrote. It is printed on T.H. Saunders paper from a variety of ancient sources of Caslon type with prints of combined techniques. Edited by Eric Robinson. Illustrated, printed, bound and signed by Nicholas and Mary Parry.

1439. (Tern Press) Griffiths, Bill (editor). THE LAND CEREMONIES CHARM. Market Drayton: The Tern Press, 1985, large 8vo., paper covered boards, paper cover label. (3) pages. $ 50.00

Printed in an edition limited to 185 numbered and signed copies. This text was originally written on the last pages of an M.S. containing a verse life of Christ in Old Saxon (The Heliand), thought to have been written down in the first quarter of the eleventh century. Photos of the text were taken from the British Library (MS. Cotton Caligula A VII), and have been translated and edited by Bill Griffiths. The Early English script, has been illustrated and bound by Mary Parry. Signed by Bill Griffiths and Mary Parry.

1440. (Tern Press) Griffiths, Bill. THE GOAT SECRET. N.P.: Tern Press, 2000, large 8vo., stiff paper wrappers. (12) pages. $ 35.00

A legend about Kaldi, a goat-herder in ancient times in the Yemen, and the discoverer of coffee. Illustrated with lithographs by Nicholas Parry.

1441. (Tern Press) Grubb, David. COUNTRY ALPHABET. Market Drayton, England: Tern Press, 1998, oblong 12mo., quarter cloth, paper spine label, printed paper covered boards. (32) pages. $ 75.00

Printed in an edition limited to only 95 numbered copies. The latest edition of Mary Parry's lovely hand colored alphabet books. Each letter is on its own page and bears a short passage of text and its own hand colored illustration. Printed in Garamond on Zerkall Antik paper.

1442. (Tern Press) Halsey, Alan. EPITAPHS & VARIATIONS. Market Drayton: The Tern Press, 1990, large 8vo., quarter cloth with decorated paper covered boards, paper cover label. (24) pages. $ 40.00
Printed in an edition limited to 75 numbered and signed copies. Etched lino prints by Nicholas Parry. Signed by the Parry's and Alan Halsey.

1443. (Tern Press) THE HISTORY OF SUSANNA. Market Drayton: The Tern Press, 1990, large 8vo., decorated cloth, paper cover and spine labels. (20) pages. $ 60.00
Printed in an edition limited 185 numbered and signed copies. A story of a woman from biblical times. It is illustrated with five erotic etched linoprints on Views of the Rhine paper by Nicholas Parry. It was printed and bound by Nicholas and Mary Parry and signed by both.

1444. (Tern Press) Jefferies, Richard. THOUGHTS ON THE MIGRATION OF BIRDS. Market Drayton: Tern Press, 1999, 4to., quarter cloth with pastepaper covered boards and paper spine and cover labels. (40) pages. $ 180.00
First edition. Limited to 95 numbered copies printed at the Tern Press by Nicholas and Mary Parry and signed by both. Includes 17 beautiful, full page lithograph prints of birds by Nicholas Parry. Each bird is printed in a shade of brown, green, gray, or black. Set in 22 point Caslon and printed on Arches paper. Bound in yellow cloth and brick red pastepaper decorated with waved lines.

1445. (Tern Press) Jones, Robert Gerallt. BARDSEY: A FORTNIGHT'S JOURNAL TRANSLATED FROM THE ORIGINAL WELSH BY THE AUTHOR. Market Drayton: Tern Press, 1976, 4to., full pigskin. Unpaginated (70 pages). $ 375.00
Limited to 50 numbered copies. This book contains the author's journal from his two week visit to the island of Bardsey. Printed in 16D on 18pt. Univers medium on Medway handmade paper at the Tern Press. With fifteen lino cut illustrations by Nicholas Parry. Signed by Robert Gerallt Jones and Nicholas Parry. Frontispiece.

1446. (Tern Press) LOVE WILL FIND A WAY OUT. Market Drayton: Tern Press, (1998), folio, paper covered boards, paper cover and spine labels. (18) pages. $ 230.00
Printed in an edition limited to ninety numbered and signed copies. This was taken from Percy's *Reliques of Ancient English Poetry*. It is illustrated with seven full lithograph prints in three colors by Nicholas Parry. It has been printed on T.H. Saunders paper. Signed by Nicholas and Mary Parry.

1447. (Tern Press) Pennar, Meirion. CAD GODDAU: THE BATTLE OF THE TREES. Market Drayton: Tern Press, (1992), small 4to., paper covered boards, paper cover and spine labels. (48) pages. $ 50.00
Printed in an edition limited to 90 numbered and signed copies. An expression of ancient beliefs of the Brythons with regard to life, to nature, to the individual soul. In Wales the change of the seasons was depicted as a combat between two assailants and in this poem the battle is between trees and grass and the contestants of Winter. It has been translated by Meirion Pennar and illustrated with lino-cuts by Nicholas Parry. Signed by Nicholas and Mary Parry.

1448. (Tern Press) Perryman, K.A. CALL OF THE CUCKOO. Market Drayton, England: Tern Press, (1997), small 4to., patterned cloth covered boards, paper spine and cover label. (22) pages. $ 75.00
Printed in an edition limited to 100 numbered copies signed by the proprietors of the press Nicholas and Mary Parry. Letterpress printed on T.H. Saunders paper and illustrated with seven wood engravings. Text comprises individual poems about the buzzard, sparrow, cuckoo, kestrel, thrush, and dove.

1449. (Tern Press) Summers, Susan. CROWN OF FLOWERS. Market Drayton, Shropshire, England: The Tern Press, 1997, square 12mo., cloth. (32) pages. $ 75.00
Printed in an edition limited to 150 numbered copies signed by the printers Mary and Nicholas Parry. A lovely alphabet book with hand colored illustrations by Mary Parry.

1450. (Tern Press) VERSES FROM THE PSALMS BOOK I. (Market Drayton): The Tern Press, (1983), large 12mo., quarter cloth with paper covered boards. unpaginated.
$ 50.00

Printed in an edition limited to 175 numbered and signed copies. Dramatically illustrated with large wood engravings by Nicholas Parry that fill nearly every page. The revised version Psalms are marked off into five books. This is Book I which was probably put together by David or Solomon and formed the original Psalter, B.C. 1015.

1451. (Tern Press) VERSES FROM THE PSALMS BOOK II. Market Drayton: The Tern Press, (1986), small 8vo., quarter cloth, with printed paper covered boards. (36) pages.
$ 50.00

Printed in an edition limited to 175 numbered and signed copies. Dramatically illustrated with wood engravings by Nicholas Parry that fill nearly every page. Contains verses 42 to 72 from The Psalms Book II.

1452. (The Press in the Gatehouse) Mylan, Milan J. FOUR POEMS. Los Angeles: The Press in the Gatehouse, 1969, small 8vo., cord-tied stiff paper wrappers. 11+(1) pages.
$ 20.00

With a preface by William E. Conway, librarian of the Clark Library, Los Angeles. A presentation copy from the author, signed on the front flyleaf.

1453. (Thistle Press) Kraus, Hans P. SIR FRANCIS DRAKE, A PICTORIAL BIOG-RAPHY. With an Historical Introduction by Lt. Commander David W. Waters & Richard Boulind and a detailed Catalogue of the Author's Collection. Amsterdam: N. Israel, 1970, folio, cloth. viii, 236, (2) pages.
$ 200.00

First edition, finely letterpress printed at the Thistle Press. Full bibliographical descriptions of 60 manuscripts, printed books and maps and views. Well illustrated.

1454. (Thomas, Peter and Donna) COLLECTION OF PAPER, SAMPLES FROM HAND PAPERMILLS IN THE UNITED STATES OF AMERICA. Santa Cruz: Peter & Donna Thomas, 1993, small 4to., quarter brown Oasis Morocco with handmade paper covered boards, paper outer wrapper which is ribbon-tied. Three preliminary leaves printed on paper handmade by Thomas followed by 27 four page signatures of handmade paper made by different American papermakers. The second leaf of each of these signatures contains a letterpress printed statement from the producer of the paper for that section.
$ 550.00

Limited to 195 copies of which 158 are for sale. An interesting display of the work of some of the premier hand-papermakers practicing in the United States today.

1455. (Thomas, Peter and Donna) COLLECTION OF PAPER, SAMPLES FROM HAND PAPERMILLS IN THE UNITED STATES OF AMERICA. Santa Cruz: Peter & Donna Thomas, 1993, small 4to., full leather brown Oasis Morocco leather with handmade paper covered boards, cloth-covered slipcase. Three preliminary leaves printed on paper handmade by Thomas followed by 27 four page signatures of handmade paper made by different American papermakers. The second leaf of each of these signatures contains a letterpress printed statement from the producer of the paper for that section. Special edition has seven additional paper samples sewn in after the colophon.
$ 950.00

Limited to 25 copies. An interesting display of the work of some of the premier hand-papermakers practicing in the United States today. Prospectus loosely inserted.

1456. (Thomas, Peter and Donna) Graham, Rigby. YOU CAN'T MAKE PAPER FROM A LOOFA. Santa Cruz: Peter & Donna Thomas, 1991, 8vo., stiff handmade paper covers, cord-tied. (ii), 27, (3) pages. $ 50.00

Second edition, corrected. Limited to 50 numbered copies. The illustrations in this book were taken from Mason's 12 x 8 PAPERS, a book produced in 1958. Designed, printed and bound by the Thomases.

1457. (Thomas, Peter and Donna) Saroyan, William. SAROYAN. Santa Cruz: Peter and Donna Thomas, 1991, miniature book (2.25 x 3 inches), paper covered boards. Unpaginated. $ 25.00

Limited to 150 numbered copies. Printed and bound by Peter and Donna Taylor, using paper they made from rag, Russian hemp rope, abaca, cotton and other stray fibers. This unusual miniature consists of a quotation from Saroyan, "Love of paper is the most important thing," reproduced in watermarks, bound folded and uncut, with leaves of paper in light plum color echoing the cover and endpapers, bound between the folds to accent the watermarking. Illustrated with a US postage stamp pasted in, commemorating the author.

1458. (Thomas, Peter and Donna) START MAKING PAPER EVERYONE! (Santa Cruz: The Good Book Press, 1986), tall 12mo., cloth, paper cover label. 8 leaves. $ 75.00

Limited to 18 numbered copies. Produced on hand-made paper made by the two Thomas children with the help of their father and hand- lettered by Donna Thomas in different colored inks.

1459. (Thomas, Peter and Donna) Thomas, Peter. BIKUPAN, THE STORY OF A TRIP TO VISIT A HAND PAPER MILL IN SWEDEN, WITH A BIT OF HISTORY ADDED IN FOR GOOD MEASURE. Santa Cruz: Peter & Donna Thomas, 1992, small 4to., quarter blue leather over marbled paper covered boards, slipcase. (viii), 13, (3) pages. $ 165.00

Limited to 119 numbered copies printed by hand by Peter and Donna Thomas on paper handmade by Peter using white and black rags with blue pigment. Thomas visited the Lessebo mill in Sweden, a mill which had first started manufacturing paper in 1693. In addition to describing what he found there, Thomas gives a history of papermaking in Sweden. Tipped-in are six samples of paper from Lessebo, one made in 1990 and the rest during various times in the 20th century.

1460. (Thumbprint Press) Holme, Frank. FIRST GOUDY CARTOON. Forest Hills: Thumbprint Press, 1938, tall 12mo., self paper wrappers. (4) pages. $ 10.00

Printed as a Keepsake for the 35th anniversary of the Village Press.

1461. (Tideline Press) Baatz, Ronald. ALL THE DAYS ARE. Tannersville: Tide Line Press, (1974), small 8vo., stiff paper wrappers cord tied. 20 pages printed french fold. $ 35.00

Privately printed and limited to 140 copies. A collection of poems by Ronald Baatz. Printed on Linweave Mardi Gras.

1462. (Tideline Press) Crane, George. POEMS FROM THE NOVEL. N.P.: Tideline Press, 1976, large 8vo., paper wrappers. not paginated. $ 50.00

Printed in an edition limited to 75 numbered and signed copies. These poems from the novel have been designed and printed by Leonard Seastone. Goudy Oldstyle was used on dampened Gutenberg Laid. It includes a blind embossed sheet which was never bound in but inserted as a broadside.

1463. (Tideline Press) Seastone, Leonard. NORTH SIDE OF MOUNTAIN, SOUTH SIDE OF STREAM, POEMS. Tannersville (NY): Tideline Press, 1975, 4to., sewn, stiff paper wrappers. (7) leaves. $ 45.00

Limited to 100 numbered copies. Seastone wrote, designed and printed this book of 5 poems, set in Garamond Italic with Curtis cover papers. Title page woodcut vignette is also by the author.

1464. (Tideline Press) Seastone, Leonard. RIP'S LAKE. Tannerville, NY: The Tideline Press, 1982, square 12mo., paper wrappers. (4) pages printed French fold. $25.00
Limited to 50 numbered copies signed by Seastone and handset and printed on Fabriano papers.

1465. (Tideline Press) Seastone, Leonard. A SOLO IN THE CHOIR. N.P.: The Tideline Press, n.d., paper folder containing 25 separately printed broadsides, some being foldouts. $35.00
Limited to 100 numbered copies. The entire text is printed with hand cut blocks. Introduction by Loyd Haberly.

1466. (Tideline Press) Seastone, Leonard. SONG OF SUSAN, A FAIRY TALE. Tannersville, NY: Tideline Press, 1977, oblong 12mo., paper wrappers. 7 leaves. $65.00
Limited to 26 lettered copies signed by Seastone. Printed by hand on a Washington hand-press.

1467. (Tideline Press) Skinner, Douglas Reid. DREAMS FROM A WORLD PLACE. N.P.: Tideline Press, 1979, small 8vo., stiff paper wrappers. (10) leaves. $75.00
Limited to 33 copies, of which probably none were originally intended for sale. Signed by author on colophon. Six poems.

1468. (Tideline Press) Wild, Peter. PIONEERS. Tannersville: Tideline Press, 1976, 8vo., paper wrappers. (22) pages. $35.00
Privately printed and limited to 50 numbered copies. A collection of poems by Peter Wild about pioneers. Printed on dampened Ingres mouldmade papers. Illustrations are by Elaine Scull, and designed, wood engraved and printed by Leonard Seastone. Signed by author and artists. Corner bumped.

1469. (Tiger Press) Harmsen, Tyrus G.(editor). SIR MUIRHEAD BONE, ILLUS-TRATOR. Los Angeles: Occidental College, 1990, 8vo., stiff paper wrappers. (12) pages. $15.00
Handlist of an Exhibition at the Mary Norton Clapp Library, Occidental College, from February 16-April 5, 1990. A publication of the school's Book Arts Program, printed by the editor at the Tiger Press. Sir Muirhead Bone (1876–1953) is considered one of the outstanding draughtsman and etchers of the early twentieth century. Illustrations.

1470. (Tiger Press) Harmsen, Tyrus G. FORTY YEARS OF BOOK COLLECTING. Los Angeles: Tiger Press, 1985, 12mo., stiff paper wrappers. (24) pages. $25.00
Printed in an edition limited to one hundred and fifty copies for members of the Rounce & Coffin Club and friends of the author. A talk given at a meeting of the Rounce and Coffin Club in 1982, and first printed for members of the Zamorano Club in *Hoja Volante*, 1984. Text set in Linotype Caledonia by Richard J. Hoffman and display set in Perpetua by the author.

1471. (Tiger Press) OBSERVATIONS ON READING. Los Angeles: The Book Arts Program of Occidental College, 1989, 8vo., cord-tied stiff paper wrappers. (10) pages. $25.00
Printed in an edition limited to fifty copies by the students in Letterpress Printing at the Tiger Press. A brief anthology, with each page set in a different type by a class member. Invitation to a lecture by book designer John Dreyfus and a card *With the compliments of* Tyrus G. Harmsen laid in.

1472. (Tinhorn Press) Ellis, Gene. POEM ON A FRAGMENT OF A LOVE LETTER FOUND IN A SAVANNAH CEMETERY, 1974. Atlanta: Tinhorn Press, 1979, large 12mo., cord-tied stiff paper wrappers. (12) pages. $17.50
Printed in an edition limited to two hundred copies in handset ATF Bulmer. The ornate initials are from a Savannah printing house of the eighteen-fifties. Card *With Compliments of the Printer* tipped in.

1473. (Tommasini) COLLECTION OF A.R. TOMMASINI CHRISTMAS BOOKS. Berkeley: A.R. Tommasini, (1948–1982), small 12mo. Variously paginated.
$ 550.00

First editions. This is a complete set of A.R. Tommasini Christmas books from 1948 through 1982. These small volumes were printed yearly for friends of the press. The books generally dealt with book arts topics: "What "Did Gutenberg Invent?," "The Story of Paper Told Briefly Once Again" "A Belated Tribute to Printers," etc. In 1977, Tommasini printed "Tommy's 30," a review of all books until then and in 1978 he issued "XXX Plus One" which includes a list of all the owners with complete sets of his Christmas keepsakes. The present collector, Joseph Baxley, is included in the list. Many include a Christmas greeting loosely inserted. Also included is the correspondence between Baxley and Tommasini. Most preserved in their original mailing envelopes.

1474. (Toothpaste Press) Hanson, Jim. REASONS FOR THE SKY. West Branch, IA: Toothpaste Press, 1979, large 12mo., stiff paper wrappers. (18) pages. $ 15.00

Designed and printed by Allan Kornblum in an edition limited to 900 copies, using a 10x15 hand-fed platen press. Handset in Plantin and Libra types on Ingres-Fabriano paper. Some of these poems have previously appeared in *The Denver Post, The 432 Review,* and *Out There.*

1475. (Toothpaste Press) Mikolowski, Ken. LITTLE MYSTERIES. West Branch: The Toothpaste Press, 1979, 12mo., stiff paper wrappers. (20) pages. $ 17.50

Second printing of 2,000 copies. A collection of mystery poems by Ken Mikolowski, with illustrations by Ann Mikolowski.

1476. (Torch Press) Allison, Young E. OLD MUSIC MASTER, A SMALL TOWN CHRISTMAS MEMORY. Introduction by J. Christian Bay. Cedar Rapids: Privately Printed for the Friends of the Torch Press, 1956, small 8vo., cloth-backed boards, paper spine label. 32 pages. $ 25.00

Limited to 400 copies. With a long historical sketch of Allison.

1477. (Torch Press) Bay, J. Christian (editor). WHERE DID YOU GET THAT HAT? A SYMPOSIUM BY YOUNG E. ALLISON, MEREDITH NICHOLSON, WILLIAM FORTUNE AND HARRY S. NEW. Cedar Rapids: Privately printed for the Friends of the Torch Press, 1945, small 8vo., cloth-backed boards, paper cover label. 46 pages. $ 25.00

Limited to 400 copies. Reprints of the humorous letters concerning Allison's hat.

1478. (Torch Press) Bay, J. Christian. HANDFUL OF WESTERN BOOKS. Chicago: Privately printed at the Torch Press, 1935, small 8vo., cloth-backed boards, paper label. 44 pages. $ 95.00

First edition, limited to 350 copies. The first of a series of three books written by Bay describing the best western books. Some soiling.

1479. (Torch Press) Bay, J. Christian. SECOND HANDFUL OF WESTERN BOOKS. Chicago: Privately printed at the Torch Press, 1936, small 8vo., cloth-backed boards, paper label. 56 pages. $ 95.00

First edition, limited to 400 copies.

1480. (Torch Press) Bay, J. Christian. IN THE HOUSE OF MEMORIES (TABLE TALK). Cedar Rapids: Privately printed for the Friends of the Torch Press, 1946, small 8vo., cloth-backed boards, paper cover label. 37 pages. $ 25.00

Limited to 400 copies. Biographical sketch of A. St. John Adcock followed by reprints of part of his book entitled, *The Booklover's London.*

1481. (Torch Press) Bay, J. Christian. JOURNEYS AND VOYAGES TO NATURE. Cedar Rapids: The Torch Press, 1950, small 8vo., cloth-backed boards, paper cover label. 67 pages. $ 45.00
Limited to 400 copies. Very fine copy in original glassine wrapper.

1482. (Torch Press) Brewer, Luther A. LEIGH HUNT AND CHARLES DICKENS, THE SKIMPOLE CARICATURE. Cedar Rapids: The Torch Press, 1930, large 8vo., quarter cloth with paper covered boards. 36 pages. $ 65.00
First edition. Printed in an edition limited 300 copies. An account of Brewer's collection of Leigh Hunt first editions, manuscripts, letters, and general Huntiana, and the relationship between Hunt and Dickens. Spotting on covers.

1483. (Torch Press) Brewer, Luther A. LOVE OF BOOKS WITH A REPRINT OF LEIGH HUNT'S ESSAY ON "MY BOOKS". Cedar Rapids: Privately printed for the Friends of Luther Albertus and Elinore Taylor Brewer, 1923, small 8vo., parchment-backed boards. 38, (2) pages. $ 75.00
Limited to 300 copies. Brewer on his favorite subject, Leigh Hunt.

1484. (Torch Press) Foster, Thomas Henry. BEADLES, BIBLES & BIBLIOPHILES. N.P.: Privately Printed for the Friends of May and Harry Foster at the Torch Press, 1948, 8vo., quarter cloth, paper over boards, paper label on spine and cover. 48 pages, 7 plates.
$ 65.00
No limitation given. Includes chapters on the "Shakespeare" folio, John Milton and William Morris. Scuff mark on top of front cover.

1485. (Torch Press) 1953. GOD SPEEDE THE PLOUGH (1601), FACSIMILE REPRINT. Introduction by J. Christian Bay. Cedar Rapids: Privately Printed for the Friends of the Torch Press, 1953, small 8vo., cloth-backed boards, paper spine label. 30, (16) pages. $ 25.00
Limited to 400 copies. Reprint, with historical information added by Bay, of this early treatise on agriculture.

1486. (Torch Press) Holberg, Ludvig. VIRTUES AND FAULTS OF SOME EUROPEAN NATIONS (1743). Now Leniently Translated by J. Christian Bay, with an Introduction. Cedar Rapids: Privately Printed for the Friends of the Torch Press, 1958, small 8vo., cloth-backed boards, paper spine label. 52 pages. $ 25.00
Limited to 350 copies. Bay translated this essay from his native Danish tongue in his 87th year.

1487. (Torch Press) Seymour, George Steele (editor). BOOKFELLOW POETRY ANNUAL 1938. Chicago: The Bookfellows, 1938, small 8vo., cloth. Frontispiece, 190 pages. $ 30.00
First edition, limited to 490 copies printed by the Torch Press. Contains a dedication from W.A. Burr, author of "Ravishment" and "Roundel," two poems appearing in the book, on front free endpaper. Formerly appearing under the name *A Bookfellow Anthology*, this is the first publication of the new series given the name *The Bookfellow Poetry Annual* begun by request after the old work was discontinued for a year. Contains a black and white frontispiece of Josephine Hancock Logan to whom the work was dedicated for her gift of prize money, to be known as the Frank Granger Logan Memorial prize in memory of her husband, for the best poem appearing each year. Some pages unopened.

1488. (Tower Press) Millet, Kate. ELEGY FOR SITA. (New York: Targ Editions, 1979), oblong 4to., cloth-covered boards, dust jacket. 106, (6) pages. $ 95.00
First edition limited to 350 copies and signed by author. Number 5 of the Targ Editions, published in Greenwich Village. Written after her companion's suicide as a follow-up to Millett's 1977 autobiographical work, *Sita.*. Prose elegies, erotic drawings, book design by Millett. A splendid work of poetic

expression as well as a beautifully produced volume, printed on 80 lb. Artemis Ivory deckle edge by Tower Press, New York. Spine gold-stamped. Typeset in Tiffany and Baskerville by Waterfall Graphics. Prospectus laid-in.

1489. (Tragara Press) Lyon, Lilian Bowes. UNCOLLECTED POEMS. Edinburgh: The Tragara Press, 1981, small 8vo., marbled paper wrappers, paper cover label. (16) pages.
$ 75.00

Limited to 95 numbered copies printed on Barcham Green hand-made paper and printed by Alan Anderson at the Tragara Press. First appearance of three of these poems.

1490. (Tragara Press) SCEPTIC, PERHAPS, CARRIES THE MATTER TOO FAR. From The Sceptic by David Hume. Edinburgh: The Tragara Press, 1973, (16.25 x 9.5 inches), broadside.
$ 17.50
Folded.

1491. (Tragara Press) Weeks, Donald. FREDERICK WILLIAM ROLFE, CHRISTCHURCH, AND THE ARTIST. Edinburgh: The Tragara Press, 1980, 8vo., stiff paper wrappers, paper cover label. 27, (3) pages.
$ 75.00
Limited to 120 numbered copies set in Baskerville and printed on Abbey Mills paper. First separate appearances of these three book reviews by Rolfe.

1492. (Trianon Press) Blake, William. VISIONS OF THE DAUGHTERS OF ALBION. N.P.: Trianon Press, n.d., folio, quarter leather with decorated paper covered boards with a paper covered slipcase. unpaginated.
$ 750.00
Printed in an edition limited 446 numbered copies; this copy is out of series. This is one of the simpler symbolic poems executed by Blake in Illuminated Printing. The theme is in effect, partly a protest against the sexual morals of the day. The eleven plates are almost constant in their arrangement and the colouring is also relatively uniform, flat water-colour washes being used in the majority. The illuminated pages were reproduced in Paris by Trianon Press in the workshops of Messrs. Hourdebaigt and Crampe by collotype and stencil. Text printed by Imprimerie Desgrandchamps with binding by Mansell of London.

1493. (Trianon Press) Blake, William. JERUSALEM. London: The Trianon Press for the William Blake Trust, n.d. (circa 1950), large 4to., cloth with a paper covered clamshell box, with cloth spine. variously paginated.
$ 1,850.00
Printed in an edition limited to 516 copies of which 250 are numbered, this being a numbered copy. Jerusalem was the last of Blake's great epic poems which he began about 1804 and did not complete before 1818. This is a facsimile in color of the unique copy owned by Colonel William Stirling, which is bound in four fascicles each of twenty five plates. The reproduction has been made by Daniel Jacomet et Cie, Paris. The etched base has now been reproduced by collotype by the Trianon Press in orange and the prints have then been colored by hand by a stenciling process, so the final results has the closest possible resemblance to Blake's original plates. There are 4 full page illustrations which required an average of forty-four applications of water colors. Fifty-on have some text with designs filling half the page or more, and forty-five have text with small marginal decorations only of varying degrees of significance. Introduction followed by Preludium by Joseph Wicksteed and Bibliographical Statement by Geoffrey Keynes. The clamshell box is worn along edges.

1494. (Trianon Press) Blake, William. JERUSALEM, THE EMANATION OF THE GIANT ALBION. London: Published by The Trianon Press for The William Blake Trust, 1974, 4to., quarter leather, marbled paper over boards, slipcase. 25, (23) pages.
$ 650.00
Limited to 558 copies, this being one of 500 copies bound thus. Facsimile of the original (from Lord Cunliffe's copy) and the trial proofs (from Mr. Kerrison Preston), with commentary by Geoffrey Keynes. Plates produced by the Trianon Press under the direction of Arnold Fawcus. Printed on Arches pure rag paper made to match the paper used by Blake, each page is watermarked with Blake's monogram. Beau-

tifully reproduces Blake's account of Albion (Man), continually torn between the forces of imagination and religion. With an additional eight illustrations. Printed by the Imprimerie Darantiere, Dijon; binding by Reliural, Paris; and the hand-made slipcase by Adine, Paris.

1495. (Trianon Press) Blake, William. MILTON, A POEM. Chateau de Boissia: Trianon Press, 1967, small 4to., quarter leather with marbled paper covered boards, top edge gilt, marbled paper covered slipcase. 50 leaves of plates, (18) pages. $ 850.00
Printed in an edition of 426 numbered copies, of which this is one of 380. This is a facsimile of William Blake's, Milton, A Poem from the original copy in the collection of Lessing Rosenwald in the Library of Congress. Finely printed by the Trianon Press in collotype with additional hand stencil on Arches pure rag paper made to match the paper used by Blake. Each page is watermarked with Blake's monogram. The facsimile is followed by a bibliographical history by Geoffrey Keynes.

1496. (Trianon Press) Blake, William. ALL RELIGIONS ARE ONE. London: The Trianon Press for the William Blake Trust, 1970, 4to., half green leather over marbled paper covered boards, slipcase. 10 leaves of facsimile followed by (8) pages. $ 285.00
Limited to 662 numbered copies. Reproduction of the original Blake book issued in about 1784 that is in the Huntington Library. Has text by Geoffrey Keynes. Produced and published under the supervision of Arnold Fawcus of the Trianon Press. The reproductions of the plates were done in color using the collotype process with some coloring added by hand. Printed by the Imprimerie Darantiere, Dijon; binding by Engel, Malakoff, and the hand-made slipcase by Aldine, Paris. Spine slightly faded.

1497. (Trianon Press) Blake, William. AMERICA, A PROPHECY. Paris: The Trianon Press, 1963, 4to., half blue morocco, marbled paper covered boards, top edge gilt, slipcase. $ 750.00
Limited to 526 numbered copies. A full color reproduction of Blake's interesting conception of America originally executed in 1793. With a five page discussion of the book by Geoffrey Keynes.

1498. (Trianon Press) Blake, William. THE BOOK OF AHANIA. London: Published by The Trianon Press for The William Blake Trust, 1973, 4to., quarter leather, marbled paper over boards, slipcase. (15) pages. $ 275.00
Limited to 808 copies, this being one of 750 copies bound thus. Facsimile of the original with commentary of Geoffrey Keynes. Reproduces the copy owned by Lessing Rosenwald at the Library of Congress, the only known complete copy along with the original frontispiece which was owned by Geoffrey Keynes. Printed on Arches pure rag paper made to match the paper used by Blake. Reproduces Blake's illustrations and manuscript of 1795, one of the last of Blake's series of Illuminated Books written while he was living in Lambeth. Printed by the Imprimerie Darantiere, Dijon; binding by Reliural, Paris; and hand-made slipcase by Aldine, Paris. A beautiful production.

1499. (Trianon Press) Blake, William. THE BOOK OF LOS. London: The Trianon Press, 1976, 4to., quarter tan morocco with hand marbled paper covered boards, matching slipcase covered in marbled paper. Unpaginated. $ 285.00
Printed in an edition limited to 538 numbered copies. (Julie Fawcus 1976.) One of Arnold Fawcus's collotype reproductions of the original works of William Blake commissioned by the William Blake Trust. Reproduced from the unique copy in the British Library. Printed on Arches pure rag paper made to match the paper used by Blake. Printed by Imprimerie Darantiere, Dijon; binding by Reliural, Paris; hand-made slipcase by Armbruster, Paris. Minor scuff to spine.

ONE OF 32 COPIES

1500. (Trianon Press) Blake, William. THE BOOK OF LOS. London: The Trianon Press, 1976, 4to, full tan morocco, matching slipcase covered in marbled paper. Unpaginated. $ 900.00
Printed in an edition limited to 538 numbered copies of which this is one of 32 copies numbered in Roman numerals and bound thus. (Julie Fawcus 1976.) These special copies are bound in full morocco and contain a set of plates showing the progressive stages of the collotype and hand-stencil process, a

guide sheet and stencil and an actual copper plate. One of Arnold Fawcus's collotype reproductions of the original works of William Blake commissioned by the William Blake Trust. Reproduced from the unique copy in the British Library. Printed on Arches pure rag paper made to match the paper used by Blake. Printed by Imprimerie Darantiere, Dijon; binding by Reliural, Paris; hand-made slipcase by Armbruster, Paris.

1501. (Trianon Press) EXHIBITION OF THE ILLUMINATED BOOKS OF WILLIAM BLAKE, POET, PRINTER, PROPHET, ARRANGED BY THE WILLIAM BLAKE TRUST. A Commemorative Handbook with a study by Geoffrey Keynes and a foreword by Lessing J. Rosenwald. N.P.: William Blake Trust, (1964), small 4to., stiff paper wrappers. 56 pages. $ 55.00
With numerous plates reproduced in color by the Trianon Press of Paris. Covers soiled.

1502. (Trianon Press) Blake, William. THERE IS NO NATURAL RELIGION. Two volumes. London: Published by the Trianon Press for The William Blake Trust, 1971, 4to. and small 8vo., half leather over marbled paper covered boards, enclosed in a slipcase. Not paginated. $ 450.00
Limited to 616 numbered copies. The plates were reproduced from the Rosenwald copy at the Library of Congress and with additional material from the collection of Geoffrey Keynes. With the superb reproductions by the Trianon Press of Arnold Fawcus and with text printed on Arches pure rag paper made to match the paper used by Blake. Illustrations done in collotype and hand-stenciled. With editorial matter printed by the Imprimerie Darantiere, Dijon, the binding by Dval, Paris, and the hand-made slipcase by Aldine, Paris.

ONE OF 50 COPIES

1503. (Trianon Press) Blake, William. THERE IS NO NATURAL RELIGION. Two volumes. London: Published by the Trianon Press for The William Blake Trust, 1971, 4to. and small 8vo., full leather, enclosed in a marbled covered slipcase. Not paginated.
                                                                     $ 1,500.00
Printed in an edition limited to 616 numbered copies of which this copy is from a series of 50 copies bound in full morocco with an additional set of plates showing the progressive stages of the collotype and hand-stencil process. The plates were reproduced from the Rosenwald copy at the Library of Congress and with additional material from the collection of Geoffrey Keynes. With the superb reproductions by the Trianon Press of Arnold Fawcus and with text printed on Arches pure rag paper made to match the paper used by Blake. With editorial matter printed by the Imprimerie Darantiere, Dijon, the binding by Dval, Paris, and the hand-made slipcase by Aldine, Paris.

1504. (Trianon Press) Breil, Abbe Breuil. PHILIPP CAVE. London: Abbe Breuil Publications, (1957), large 4to., cloth, dust jacket. (ii), vi, 21, with 19 pages of plates including 1 double page. $ 110.00
First edition. Printed in an edition limited to 1,200 unnumbered copies. With the collaboration of Mary E. Boyle and Dr. E. R. Scherz, this is the second volume of a series recording this remarkable work. It reveals an interesting and little-known frieze in the Erongo region of South-West Africa. In addition to some unusual, early drawings of animals in white, it includes a 'Tall Man' which has been nicknamed the 'Pharaoh' by the Abbe and his companions. The original copies are reproduced in 31 plates by color collotype and hand stencil by the Trianon Press, and 30 photographs, reproduced by collotype.

1505. (Trianon Press) Breuil, Abbe Henri. ANIBIB & OMANDUMBA AND OTHER ERONGO SITES. Paris: The Calouste Gulbenkian Foundation, (1960), folio, cloth, dust jacket with a cardboard slipcase. (viii), 39 pages, with 42 pages of plates and 4 double pages of plates. $ 200.00
First edition. Printed in an edition limited to 800 unnumbered copies. This is the fourth volume in the series recording the work of the Abbe Breuil on the rock paintings of Southern Africa, with a collaboration of Mary E. Boyle and Dr. E. R. Scherz. It includes detailed explanatory notes by the Abbe on each

painting. Anibib and Omandumba, together with Springbokfontein, are neighboring properties in the Erongo mountain range of South-West Africa. It is illustrated with 80 plates, 72 figures and 55 photographs reproduced in monochrome collotype by the Trianon Press, with a further 17 photographs of sites in Omandumba West discovered after the Abbe's last visit in 1950.

1506. (Trianon Press) Breuil, Abbe Henri. THE TSISAB RAVINE AND OTHER BRANDBERG SITES. France: The Calouste Gulbenkian Foundation through Trianon Press, (1959), folio, cardboard slipcase. variously paginated. $ 200.00

First edition, limited to 1000 copies. The Tsisab Ravine in the Brandberg Mountain range of South-West Africa, which is the site of the famous 'White Lady of the Brandberg,' is also the site of a great number of painted rock shelters clustered together nearby. This volume is the outcome of the labors of Abbe Breuil and his companions who camped in the Tsisab Ravine in 1947 and again in 1948 in order to study the sites and to take tracings directly from the rock face. The Abbe's color copies are reproduced by the collotype and hand-stencil process in 77 plates, including one double-page, and are documented by 50 photographs reproduced in monochrome collotype, including two double-page photo-montages. It also includes introductory and topographical material, as well as a detailed description of the plates with the collaboration of Mary E. Boyle, Dr. E. R. Scherz and R. G. Strey.

1507. (Trianon Press) Breuil, Henri. SOUTHERN RHODESIA, THE DISTRICT OF FORT VICTORIA AND OTHER SITES. France: The Singer-Polignac Foundation with the Trianon Press, (1966), folio, cloth, dust jacket with a cardboard slipcase. Unpaginated. $ 450.00

First edition. Printed in an edition limited to 388 unnumbered copies. This is the fifth in the series about rock painting in South Africa with a collaboration of Mary E. Boyle and a foreword by Roger Heim. This volume describes two expeditions made by Abbe Breuil to Rhodesia, then Southern Rhodesia in 1948 and 1950. His study reveals affinities with the White Lady, and traces of immigrants from the north several thousand years before the white settlers of our own time. Most of the paintings here have never before been published and are largely unknown. Regions include Dandabari, Chamavara, Mbara, The Chibi Reserve, the White Rhino shelter and more. It is illustrated with 63 color plates, reproduced by the collotype and hand-stencil process by the Trianon Press, 19 photographs in monochrome collotype, and 3 line illustrations.

1508. (Trianon Press) Breuil, Henri. THE WHITE LADY OF THE BRANDBERG. Paris: The Trianon Press, (1966), folio, cloth, dust jacket. x, 31, (2), with 15 pages of plates including 3 double pages of plates. $ 125.00

First edition. Printed in an edition limited to 800 unnumbered copies. This is first in the series devoted to the Rock Paintings of Southern Africa and to record in print and color her most ancient archives, with a collaboration of Mary E. Boyle and Dr. E. R. Scherz. The rock painting which is the subject of this book is one of the most beautiful and enigmatic of them all, the White Lady of the Brandberg. The text includes Abbe Breuil's detailed description of the figures, and an account of his methods of copying rock art. Included are 22 color plates and 33 photographs printed at the Trianon Press.

1509. (Trianon Press) Keynes, Geoffrey. BLAKE'S ILLUSTRATIONS OF DANTE. London: The Trianon Press for the William Blake Trust, 1978, large oblong folio, quarter morocco with cloth covered boards, cloth covered slipcase. (37) pages. $ 600.00

Printed in an edition limited to 440 numbered copies. In the autumn of 1824, Blake's friend John Linnell, a young painter, suggested he might occupy himself with illustrating designs for Dante's Divine Comedy. Twenty-four years later Blake took up the idea with much enthusiasm and spent much of his last three years on the project. After Blake's death in August 1827 Linnell found himself in possession of seven more or less finished copperplate versions of subjects chosen by Blake. This facsimile edition contains reproductions of the seven engravings with their associated watercolor sketches. These have been finely printed in Paris at the workshops of the Trianon Press. Included is a detailed description of each plate. Bookplate on front pastedown.

Item 1509

1510. (Trianon Press) Fontaine, Jean De La. FABLES (CHOISIES). Los Angeles: William Andrews Clark, Jr., 1928, small 4to., quarter leather with paper covered boards, dust jacket. (36) pages. $ 125.00

Privately printed for William Andrews Clark, Jr. by Chester Troan, in an edition limited to 100 numbered copies. The text is from a very scarce edition printed in Bouillon, Belgium, in 1776, with eight plates by Bertin and Savart. The ornamental borders are by Clara Ortiz Troan. The text is written in old French, which accounts for the variant spelling of many words. Bookplate of previous owner on front pastedown.

1511. (Trovillion Private Press) Schauinger, Herman. BIBLIOGRAPHY OF TRO-VILLION PRIVATE PRESS OPERATED BY VIOLET & HAL TROVILLION AT THE SIGN OF THE SILVER HORSE. Herrin, IL: Trovillion Private Press, 1943, 8vo., cloth. viii, 49 pages. $ 95.00

Limited to 277 signed and numbered copies. Bookplate. Greetings notice loosely inserted.

1512. (Trovillion Private Press) Trovillion, Hal W. and Violet. AS A HOBBY A PRI-VATE PRESS. (Herrin, IL: Trovillion Private Press, 1941), 12mo., stiff paper wrappers. (16) pages. $ 20.00

Originally printed as an article in the *National Amateur Journalist* magazine, and republished by the authors "with a hope that it may bring encouragement to those who are searching for a happy hobby." With a check-list of thirty-three books printed by the Trovillion Private Press. Small smudge mark on back cover.

1513. (Trovillion Private Press) Trovillion, Hal W. and Violet. THE PRIVATE PRESS AS A DIVERSION. Herrin, IL: Trovillion Private Press, 1937, small 8vo., quarter cloth with decorated paper covered boards. viii, 81, (8) pages. $ 95.00

Printed in an edition limited to 147 numbered copies. The purpose of the this book was to preserve in permanent form the many sincere appreciations expressed by those who had enjoyed the books and brochures issued at Christmas intervals and sent out to friends as holiday greetings. Includes index to authors. Prospectus for other books of the press loosely inserted.

1514. (Turkey Press) Waldrop, Keith. THE QUEST FOR MOUNT MISERY AND OTHER STUDIES. Isla Vista, CA: Turkey Press, (1983), 8vo., paper covered boards. (24) pages. $ 20.00

Printed in an edition limited to 300 copies on Mohawk Superfine paper, set in Perpetua by Los Angeles Type Founders, and printed by Sandra Liddell Reese on a Vandercook 219. Cover and art by Harry Reese. All copies sewn and bound by hand. Twelve short prose pieces by the author of *The Space of Half an Hour* (Burning Deck, 1983) and *Wind Scales* (Treacle Press, 1976). Illustrated card from publisher laid in.

1515. (Twelve By Eight Press) Lubbock, J.G. ART AND THE SPIRITUAL LIFE. Leicester: Twelve-by-Eight Press, 1967, folio, decorated paper covered boards, top edge cut, fore and bottom edges uncut. 22 pages. $ 750.00

Printed in an edition limited to 150 copies signed by the author/artist. Magnificently illustrated with eight color plates, several of which span two pages. The plates were "hand printed by the artist at Waldringfield in Suffolk from copper plates worked by engraving, aquatint, soft ground, intaglio, relief and deep etching, with some additional colour from linoblocks." Designed by Will Carter and printed on hand made paper made by J. Barcham Green. Bound by John Mason and G.S. Percival.

1516. (Twelve By Eight Press) Mason, John. J.H. MASON, R.D.I., A SELECTION FROM THE NOTEBOOKS OF A SCHOLAR PRINTER MADE BY HIS SON JOHN MASON. Illustrated by Rigby Graham. N.P.: The Twelve by Eight Press, (1961), 8vo., stiff decorated paper covered boards. $ 40.00

First edition, signed by John Mason. Very fine copy.

1517. (Twelve By Eight Press) SOME PAPERS HAND MADE BY JOHN MASON. London: Maggs, 1959, 8vo., parchment-backed handmade paper covered boards with actual leafs inlaid in both covers, enclosed in cardboard box. 32 leaves.

$ 550.00

First edition, limited to 100 numbered copies signed by Mason. Short history of this papermaker followed by actual examples of paper produced during the period 1954 to 1959. Consists of heavy stock produced in different colors some of which contain illustrations and some of which contain leaf specimens, flowers, etc. Very fine copy in soiled box.

1518. (Twelve By Eight Press) Mason, John. MORE PAPERS HAND MADE BY JOHN MASON. Leicester: Twelve by Eight Press, 1960, 4to., parchment, protective wrap-around folder. Pages containing a line or two of explanation of different specimens intermixed with 42 hand-made paper specimens. $ 750.00

The paper specimens are printed with various designs and colors and include the work of Blair Hughes-Stanton, Stanbrook Abbey, Will Carter and Bernard Roberts. This is copy number "Variant 28" and has an tipped-in sheet on which is stated that this book was begun in 1958 but not completed until 1965. The sheet is signed, dated and the limitation number given. Most of these specimen books differ in the number of leaves present depending on when they were actually put together.

1519. (Typographeum) Risk, R.T. TYPOGRAPHEUM. Francestown, (New Hampshire: Typographeum), 1997, 8vo., cloth, paper spine label. 43, (2) pages. $ 50.00
Printed in an edition limited to 115 copies by the author. Includes essays on Gutenberg; Jenson; Aldus; the Samuel Stephens and Wickersham Quoin Company of Boston, printing equipment manufactures; and David Low, Bookseller.

1520. (Ulrich, Robert L.) Ulrich, R.L. THE GOBBOON, SOMETHING FROM ALMOST EVERYONE, THE QUARTERLY OF THE SOCIETY FOR THE PROMOTION OF INTELLECTUAL TYPOGRAPHY. (Cambridge City, IN: Robert L. Ulrich), 1975, small 8vo., stiff paper wrappers. unpaginated, but 46 pages. $ 25.00
The second issue of four of *The Gobboon*. A collection of letterpress "pages from long suffering friends, acquaintances and utter strangers for another *omnium gatherum*" from the publisher. Illustrations and type specimens.

1521. (Unica T) Mayröcker, Friederike. BRANCUSI "DER KUSZ" (KALKSTEIN). (Oberursel/Tanus: Unica T, 1994), tall narrow folio, three colored letterpress concertina, paper covered slipcase with lid. unpaginated. $ 290.00
First edition, limited to 50 numbered and signed copies. Text from Mayröcker and Goethe's *Faust* run in opposite directions. Goether's text can be read when holding the book horizontally and Mayröcker can be read vertically. Behind the text are photographs (20 in all) of kissing couples from Hollywood movies. The concertina arrangement is meant to remind one of a film strip. The photographs have been printed from polymer-clichés by Ines v. Ketelhodt. In German.

1522. (University of California Press) Deutsch, Monroe E. A TRIBUTE TO LUCY WARD STEBBINS AT A DINNER IN HER HONOR AT THE WOMEN'S FACULTY CLUB. Berkeley: (University of California Press), 1941, large 12mo., quarter cloth with marbled paper-covered boards, paper cover label. (ii), 9, (3) pages. $ 30.00
Printed in an edition limited to 50 copies in October, 1941. Remarks by the Provost about Lucy Ward Stebbins, a native Californian, who had just retired after twenty-eight years as Dean of Women at Berkeley.

1523. (University of California Press) Evans, Herbert M. and Dorothy A. Evans. A VISIT WITH G.B.S. Berkeley, CA: (University of California Press), 1947, large 12mo., quarter cloth with paper-covered boards. (viii), 18, (2) pages. $ 45.00
Printed in an edition limited to 250 copies by the University of California Press, of which this is one of sixty copies for members of the Roxburghe Club of San Francisco. An account by Evans (1882–1971), an American embryologist and discoverer of vitamin E, of a visit with Bernard Shaw at his house in Ayot St. Lawrence, near London, when the playwright was ninety. Photograph of Shaw as frontispiece. Presentation label of University of California Press to previous owner on front free endpaper and label with his name on front pastedown. Letter from manager of the Press folded and laid in.

1524. (University of California Press) Hart, Walter Morris. PARIS IN SEPTEMBER 1938. (Los Angeles: University of California Press, 1943), large 12mo., quarter cloth, paper covered boards. 15+(1) pages. $ 35.00
Printed in an edition limited to 60 copies. An address delivered before the Harvard Club of San Francisco, November 10, 1938.

1525. (University of California Press) Rogers, Bruce. BR TO FWG. Berkeley: University of California Press, 1940, 12mo., quarter vellum over marbled paper covered boards. 21, (3) pages. $ 35.00
First edition, limited to 350 copies. Reprints a letter from Rogers to Goudy written while Rogers was in Cambridge. Vellum spine soiled. Bookplate on free endpaper. Tip rubbed.

1526. (Untide Press) Everson, William. WAR ELEGIES. Waldport, Oregon: Untide Press, 1944, 8vo., stiff paper wrappers. (32) pages. $ 85.00

First edition, limited to 975 copies. The Untide Press presents this work in its first printed edition. Before this printing, the elegies were issued only in mimeographed form in 1943. A series of war poems illustrated by Kemper Nomland, Jr. Everson was a conscientious objector. Hand set in Goudy Light Oldstyle and Futura types. Printed in red and black on Linweave Early American.

1527. (Untide Press) Walker, John. ARMA VIRUMQUE CANO. Pasadena: The Untide Press, (1950), 8vo., stiff paper wrappers. (40) pages. $ 45.00

Printed in an edition limited to 500 copies. Designed with linoleum cut decorations by Kemper Nomland, Jr., hand-set in Bembo and Futura type on Kilmory Text paper. Poetry.

1528. (Uphill Press) Aldrich, Thomas Bailey. A LETTER: FROM THOMAS BAILEY ALDRICH TO BAYARD TAYLOR. Uphill Press, (1966), large 12mo., paper-covered boards, paper cover label. (ii), 9, (3) french fold pages. $ 45.00

Printed in an edition limited to 200 copies. The letter written in the Finger Lakes area at Auburn, New York, August 20, 1965, describes the author's row across a lake to an old house filled with "a collection of books that would make your eyes stare--shelf after shelf of rare old black-letter volumes, annotated and autographed by famous hands."

1529. (Uphill Press) Du Bellay, Joachim. SONNETS TRANSLATED FROM LES REGRETS. (New York: Uphill Press, 1972), 8vo., cord-tied stiff paper wrappers. (16) pages. $ 25.00

Printed in an edition limited to 110 copies. A presentation copy from the publisher, August Heckescher, to the book designer, Abe Lerner, signed on the colophon, and with a card laid in containing a further inscription. Translated by Heckescher, with an introductory note. *Les Regrets* was published in 1558, after the poet's three year stay in Rome.

1530. (Vale Press) Ricketts, Charles. CATALOGUE OF MR. SHANNON'S LITHOGRAPHS, WITH PREFATORY NOTE BY CHARLES RICKETTS. (London: E.J. Van Wisselingh at the Dutch Gallery Brook Street), n.d. (but 1902), small 8vo., blue paper covered boards. (xiv), 32, (xiv) pages. $ 500.00

Limited to 202 copies. (Ransom, Tomkinson, L'Art Ancien no.36). Printed on hand made paper with Vale Press watermark. Slight wear along joints and the usual offset to endpapers.

ONE OF 10 COPIES ON VELLUM

1531. (Vale Press) Rossetti, Dante Gabriel. HAND AND SOUL. London: The Vale Press, 1899, tall 12mo., full limp vellum with green ribbon ties. 45 pages. $ 3,000.00

Limited to 220 copies of which this is one of 10 copies printed on vellum. (*Bibliography* p.xxvii). The text was reprinted from the "Germ." Printed in red and black with initial woodcut borders of grapevines by Charles Ricketts. Original order form loosely inserted. Rossetti was one of Rickett's favorite authors.

1532. (Village Press) A NOVEL TYPE FOUNDERY, A DISSERTATION ON TYPE DESIGN AND THE VILLAGE TYPES TOGETHER WITH A SPECIMEN OF TYPES, BORDERS AND ORNAMENTS ETC. New York: The Village Press and Letter Foundery, 1914, small 8vo., stiff paper wrappers, cord tied. (16) pages. $ 85.00

First edition (Cary no. 96). CATALOGUE provides samples of the Forum and Kennerly types, and Village borders and page ornaments as designed and sold by Frederic W. Goudy in 1914. Signed by Goudy in ink on inside front cover. Cover soiled.

1533. (Village Press) Towne, Charles Hanson. TWO SINGERS. New York: William Edwin Rudge, 1928, 8vo., cloth-backed boards. (18) pages. $ 45.00
Limited to 350 copies printed at the Village Press by Frederic Goudy and set by Bertha Goudy. Each copy signed by the author.

1534. (Village Press) TYPOGRAPHICA: THE VILLAGE LETTER FOUNDRY & THE VILLAGE TYPES. Marlborough-on-Hudson: The Village Letter Foundery, 1926, 4to., stiff paper wrappers. 34 pages. $ 25.00
Cary no.175. Short history of the Village Letter Foundery followed by the priced type specimens. Covers split along hinge.

1535. (Village Square Press) AN EXCERPT FROM GOETHE'S FAUST. New York: Village Square Press, 1931, large 12mo., two tone paper covers. (viii), 12 pages. $ 95.00
Privately printed and limited to seventy copies. Signed by the designer F. L. Amberger. This book contains an Excerpt from Goethe's Faust, Part 1, Scene 2. Designed and illustrated hand-set in Weiss type. It has been hand-printed on Japan paper and hand bound. Covers age yellowed with rubbing.

1536. (Volk, Kurt H.) CHARTER OF THE UNITED NATIONS. New York: (Kurt H. Volk, 1948), 4to., quarter simulated leather and marbled paper-covered boards. 22, (6) pages. $ 35.00
Printed in an edition limited to 1000 numbered copies signed by the typographer. "This book was conceived by Kurt H. Volk, Typographer, and painstakingly executed in collaboration with Meyer Wagman, a member of the staff." With amendments and facsimile signatures of the American Delegation and leading members of other delegations. Previous owner's signature on front pastedown and part of Seasons Greetings card from Kurt Volk laid in. Rubbed at extremities, corners bumped.

1537. (Volk, Kurt H.) Hagedorn, Ivan H. KURT HANS VOLK, 1883–1962. N.P.: Privately printed, (1962), 4to., cloth, boxed. (14) pages and a photographic portrait.$ 50.00
Issued by Volk's heirs as a memorial volume; reprints Hagedorn's eulogy. Fine in slightly darkened box. Volk was a printer and book designer. Box shows wear. Loosely is a presentation card from the family. Bookplate and name in ink on front pastedown.

1538. (Volk, Kurt H.) Pisan, Christine De. OROYSON NOSTRE DAME, PRAYER TO OUR LADY. Foreword by Jean Misrahi. Translated by Jean Misrahi and Margaret Marks. New York: Kurt H. Volk, 1953, oblong 4to., cloth, slipcase. 26 pages. $ 45.00
First English translation. Conceived and printed by Kurt Volk. Each page of text contains the original French text printed in red beside the English translation printed in black with decorative ornaments separating the two. Nice example of Volk typography. Snag in top corner of slipcase.

1539. (Volk, Kurt H.) PROCEDINGS AND THE SIGNING OF THE NORTH ATLANTIC TREATY. (New York: United Nations, 1949), 4to., quarter simulated leather with marbled paper-covered boards. 25 (5) pages. $ 35.00
Printed in an edition limited to 1000 numbered copies signed by the Typographer. "This book was conceived by Kurt H. Volk, Typographer, and executed in collaboration with Meyer Wagman." With remarks by Harry S. Truman, Dean Acheson, Paul-Henri Spaak and others, the text of the North Atlantic Treaty, and facsimile signatures. Worn at extremities.

1540. (Volk, Kurt H.) Strope, Jeremy. SNOWFLAKE. New York: Kurt H. Volk, 1952, tall 8vo., silk covered boards. 12, (4) pages. $ 20.00
Beautifully printed on special paper, printed French fold. One of Volk's Christmas books. Wear at spine ends.

1541. (Volk, Kurt H.) UNDERSTANDING. New York: Kurt Volk, 1954, 8vo., half-leather over marbled paper covered boards, top edge gilt, slipcase. 52 pages. $ 25.00
Limited to 1000 copies. Interesting book design.

1542. (Volk, Kurt H.) USING TYPE CORRECTLY. New York: Kurt H. Volk, (1935), 8vo., cloth. 105 pages. $ 35.00

First edition. 42 pages of introductory material followed by specimens. Volk was one of the U.S.'s most famous printers - designers during this period.

1543. (Volk, Kurt H.) Whitman, Walt. FRAGMENTS FROM WALT WHITMAN, BEING A REARRANGEMENT OF SOME OF THE GREAT PASSAGES OF LEAVES OF GRASS WHICH PROVIDE A TALISMAN FOR THE ANCIENT TRUTHS OF MANKIND. New York: Kurt H. Volk, 1956, 8vo., quarter cloth with decorated paper covered boards. (iv), 90, (4). $ 35.00

Limited to an unspecified number of copies. "Conceived" by Kurt H. Volk, typographer, designed by Meyer Wagman and edited by John L. Davenport. Set in 10 point Janson with Caslon Oldstyle for the larger sizes. Engraving of Whitman at the age of 35 as frontis.

IN A PRESENTATION BINDING

1544. (Wall, Bernhardt) Barton, William Eleazar. ABRAHAM LINCOLN AMERI-CAN. Lime Rock, Connecticut: n.p., 1940, small 4to., stiff paper wrappers. (6), 7 etched leaves. $ 450.00

Second edition, limited to 100 copies and containing a new frontispiece not in the first edition. (Weber p.37). This copy is in a binding crafted by Wall for Doctor Martin Burge and has the following inscription on the front cover "To Doctor Martin H. Burge, His Book, Says Bernhardt Wall." The inscription is done in two colors in a calligraphic hand. Weber describes two other Wall titles, one on Robert E. Lee, and one on the California Missions, that had been inscribed to this same Doctor Burge. In one Wall credits Burge with encouraging him to do the miniature book on Lee. (Weber, p. 50). In all his publications, Wall wrote his own books and, using handmade paper, printed the text and illustrations for each page by hand from an etched plate. He then cut, folded, gathered, sewed, bound, lettered, and labeled them. The etchings in this volume reproduce an oration on Lincoln given at Springfield, Illinois in 1926 by Dr. William Barton, author of *The Lincoln of the Biographers* and *A Bibliography of Biographies of Abraham Lincoln*. The original edition of 30 copies was printed in 1931 (although Weber states that it too was limited to 100 copies). The text comprises 13 leaves of etchings finely printed on cream-colored handmade paper. Endsheets are made of taped-in acid free paper and bear a tipped facsimile letter on the third blank.

1545. (Walpole Press). ON MODERN GARDENING. New York: Young Books, 1931, large 12mo., quarter cloth with paper-covered boards, paper spine label, slipcase. x (ii), 80, (2) pages. $ 85.00

Printed at the Walpole Press in an edition limited to 325 copies, with a Preface and Bibliographical Note by W.S. Lewis. This essay was first published in 1780 by Strawberry Hill in volume four of the *Anecdotes of Painting in England*. "Horace Walpole's essay is a brief history of landscape gardening, from the First Garden to 'Capability' Brown. Since Sir Francis Bacon, the English trees and lawns had not secured so fashionable an advocate (Preface)." Four illustrations, including a *View from the great bedchamber at Strawberry-hill*, 1784.

1546. (Ward Ritchie Press) Jones, Louise Seymour. HUMAN SIDE OF BOOK-PLATES. N.P.: The Ward Ritchie Press, 1951, 8vo., cloth-backed boards. xiii, 158 pages. $ 65.00

First edition, the second printing of 1952. With an introduction by Lawrence Clark Powell. The story behind many collectors' bookplates. Includes four references to A. Edward Newton's bookplates.

1547. (Warwick Press) Kelleher, Jack (editor). DONALD HALL: A BIBLIOGRAPH-ICAL CHECKLIST. Easthampton, MA: Warwick Press, 2000, 8vo., cloth with a paper spine label. xi, (i), 78, (2) pages. $ 120.00

Printed in an edition limited to 550 copies, this being one of the 50 copies bound in cloth and signed by Hall and Jack Kelleher. A bibliographical checklist of the writings of Donald Hall, who spent five decades writing poems and prose. Along with writing every day he was also acting as editor, contributor, or trans-

volumes of prose or verse, making poems and writing prose and children's books, writing plays,
᷾ book describes over four hundred entries covering the wide variety of Hall's work in fourteen
᷾nt categories. Includes a foreword by Richard Wilbur.

1548. (Weather Bird Press) Bohne, Paul W. UNIQUE 1824 COLUMBIAN PRESS. Los Angeles: Weather Bird Press, 1974, 8vo., paper wrappers. (ii), 6 pages. $ 25.00
History of the purchase and restoration of this unique press.

1549. (Weather Bird Press) Fay, Elliot. SOME LETTERS CONCERNING D.H. LAWRENCE FROM MABEL DODGE LUHAN, DOROTHY BRETT AND FRIEDA LAWRENCE TO ELIOT FAY. Fallbrook: The Weather Bird Press, 1978, small 8vo., paste paper with paper label. (iv), 12, (3) pages. $ 75.00
First edition, limited to 200 copies. A series of letters to Elio Fay on the topic of D.H. Lawrence. Fay was a professor of romance languages and an author. The letters are commented on and a short introduction and biography are given.

1550. (Weather Bird Press) Gerry, Vance. L.A. TYPE, A CONCISE HISTORY. Pasadena: The Weather Bird Press, 2000, 8vo., cloth, dust jacket. 42 pages. $ 100.00
Printed in an edition limited to 100 copies. The history of Los Angeles Type Founders which was started in 1937 by Walter Gebhard and Arthur Neilsen when they started casting and setting type part time in Los Angeles. This work is based on a 1979 interview by the UCLA Oral History Program with Don Winter. It is illustrated in black and white and color examples of their work along with a color portrait of Gebhard tipped in on the frontispiece, and a Los Angeles Type Founders, Inc., specimen sheet is also tipped in.

1551. (Weather Bird Press) Gerry, Vance. SAN PASQUAL PRESS. WITH A FORE-WORD BY WARD RITCHIE. Fullbrook (CA): The Weather Bird Press, 1986, large 8vo., cloth, dust jacket. (xii), 27, (3) pages. $ 125.00
Limited to 150 copies. In 1936 and 1937, a printer with the improbable name of Business Printers produced several books which would qualify as fine printing, including 3 designed by Ward Ritchie. In 1938, the owner of Business Press, an insurance company (!) decided to start a trade publisher, the San Pasqual Press, devoted to quality publishing of western authors. The Press lasted only two years, until the death of the bibliophile president of the insurance co., but during that time published several dozen books, including one which became an AIGA Book of the Year in 1939. With illustrations of covers, title pages, etc. Includes a checklist of publications.

1552. (Weather Bird Press) Laden-Hardt, Rue. IN THE GARDEN. Pasadena: The Weather Bird Press, 1999, large 8vo., stiff paper wrappers, paper cover label, dust jacket. (25) french fold pages. $ 200.00
Printed in an edition limited to 50 copies. A collection of pochoir colored drawings of garden spots are accompanied by beautiful prose by Laden-Hardt. Stenciled by hand.

1553. (Weather Bird Press) Owen, Wilfred. SELECTED WAR POEMS OF WIL-FRED OWEN. Pasadena: Weather Bird Press, 1983, folio, quarter leatherette with green cloth, dust jacket. (34) pages. $ 200.00
Printed in an edition limited to 125 numbered copies printed letterpress signed by the illustrator. Designed by Vance Gerry. Finely printed on high quality Arches artists paper. Thirteen 2- color linocuts by Dale Barnhart. Some waterstaining on front cover and dust jacket. Minor chipping to jacket

1554. (Weather Bird Press) Quayles, Bunston. HEARTY FARE, A GENTLEMEN'S COOKERY BOOK. (Pasadena, CA): Weather Bird Press, 1990, large 12mo., quarter cloth with paper-covered boards, dust jacket. viii (ii), 35+(1) pages. $ 55.00
Printed in an edition limited to 150 copies. "The recipes in this book are to be considered inspirational rather than directive. May the reader find here something to content his heart." Fare includes *Los Angeles Stewed Chicken, Potato Hot Pot, Roast Beef Hash*, etc.

1555. (Weather Bird Press) Ritchie, Ward. A SOUTHLAND BOHEMIA. Pasadena: Vance Gerry: Pasadena, 1996, small 8vo., stiff paper wrappers, paper cover label. 24, (2) pages.
$ 20.00
A talk given by Ward Ritchie and Gloria Stuart at the Southwest Museum Library on October 1, 1995.

1556. (Weather Bird Press) Ritchie, Ward. A SOUTHLAND BOHEMIA, THE AR-ROYO SECO COLONY AS THE CENTURY BEGINS. Pasadena: Vance Gerry: Pasadena, 1996, small 8vo., cloth-backed boards, paper cover label. 24, (4) pages. $ 45.00
A talk given by Ward Ritchie and Gloria Stuart at the Southwest Museum Library on October 1, 1995. Introduction by Glen Dawson. With spread page full color map of Southland Bohemia as drawn by Ward Ritchie. Printed electrostatically with digital typesetting by Pall Bohne.

1557. (Weather Bird Press) Roscoe, William. THE BUTTERFLY'S BALL AND GRASSHOPPER'S FEAST. Pasadena, CA: Weather Bird Press, 1996, small 4to., pat-terned stiff paper wrappers, paper cover label, dust jacket. Unpaginated. $ 250.00
Limited to 50 copies bound by Mariana Blau. This is a delightful rendering of a poem first published in 1806 for the amusement of the author's young son. King George III then added to its popularity by hav-ing it set to music for his children. The illustrator, Vance Gerry, has embellished the text of this edition with sixteen large linoleum-cut block illustrations in black and white.

1558. (Weather Bird Press) Strehl, Dan (Editor). TID BITS FROM BOHEMIAN LIFE AS SEEN BY SAVARIN ST. SURE, FROM THE NEWSLETTER OF THE BOHEMIAN DISTRIBUTING COMPANY. Pasadena: The Weather Bird Press, 2001, 8vo., decorated paper covered limp boards, paper cover label. 22 pages. $ 35.00
Limited to 100 numbered copies. Five articles from the gastronomic gem, *Bohemian Life* are reprinted in this small volume. Originally appearing during World War II, these selections aimed to help readers remember there was still a way to enjoy oneself in spite of rationing and other constraints of the time.

1559. (Weather Bird Press) Surtees, R.S. JORROCKS' SCANTY BREAKFAST. Pasadena: The Weather Bird Press, 2000, small 8vo., stiff paper wrappers. (5) pages.
$ 20.00
Printed in an edition limited to "a few" copies. An excerpt taken from "Jorrocks' Jaunts & Jollities." There is one color drawing on the title page.

1560. (Weather Bird Press) Trefz, Val. SUPPLEMENT TO SAN PASQUAL PRESS. Pasadena: The Weather Bird Press, 1989, 8vo., paper wrappers. (12) pages. $ 15.00
This booklet is a supplement to San Pasqual Press which was published by Vance Gerry in 1986. It in-cludes additional information about the press provided by Val Trefz and Harvey Humphrey, with an up-date checklist, from 1936 to 1942.

1561. (Welch, Allen) Doyle, Esther M. WHERE THE HEART IS. (Huntingdon, PA): Juniata College, 1971, 8vo., stiff paper wrappers. (12) pages and 7 drawings. $ 15.00
Printed letterpress by Allen Welch, Mount Union, PA, in an unstated numbered edition, on Hamilton's Louvain Supreme text paper, with text type set in Linotype Fairfield. Issued as the fourth Juniata College keepsake published for friends of the college. Signed letter from the illustrator loosely laid in. With the bookplate of John DePol on inside of front cover.

1562. (Weygand, James Lamar) Weygand, James Lamar. THEY CALLED IT NAPPA-NEE. Nappanee, IN: James Lamar Weygand, (1945), 12mo., cloth, paper spine and cover label. (viii), 8, (4) pages.
$ 55.00
Designed, "imprinted" & bound by the author at Harmony Heaver Hall in an edition limited to 125 copies, "for his friends thruout the world." Discusses the origin of the town name, which seems to be the Ojibway Indian word for "flour," but translated by others as "mud-knee-deep."

1563. (White Rabbit Press) BIBLIOGRAPHY OF THE WHITE RABBIT PRESS. By the Compiler of the Auerbahn Press Bibliography. Berkeley: Poltroon Press, 1985, 8vo., cloth, dust jacket. 91, (3) pages. $ 55.00
Limited to 500 copies. Short history followed by a bibliography of the books and broadsides printed by this California press devoted to modern literature and poetry.

1564. (White Rhinoceros Press) Johnston, George Burke. [LOT OF TWELVE ITEMS FROM THE WHITE RHINOCEROS PRESS]. Blacksburg, VA: White Rhinoceros Press, 1965–1978. $ 45.00
Items included with a letter sent to a library director in response to a request for information. With specimen pages, title pages, three cord-tied pamphlets of poetry in stiff wrappers, a signed card of a poem *On The Death of J.R.R. Tolkien*, another one, also signed, on the *White Rhinoceros*, etc. "My press is a double hobby: the printing itself is a pleasure, and it gives me a way to distribute poems and other materials for which the Big World would find scant interest (from enclosed letter)."

1565. (Whittingham, Charles) Cowper, William. COWPER'S MINOR POEMS. London: printed by Charles Whittingham for John Sharpe, 1825, 12mo., full contemporary leather with gilt paneled boards, four raised bands, all edges gilt. vi, 7–108, iv, 5–108 pages in addition to four engraved plates. $ 75.00
First edition. A collection of poems by Cowper, in two parts. Contains 148 pieces including 36 translations from Vincent Bourne. Includes four black and white engraved illustrations. Foxing, mostly to plates and some endpapers. Slight wear to hinges. Spine slightly faded.

1566. (Whittington Press) AN ACROBATIC ALPHABET. Lower Marston Farm, Risbury: The Whittington Press, n.d., broadside, 21 x 15 inches. (1986) $ 45.00
Printed in an edition limited to 50 copies on Hoshi paper. A figurative alphabet designed of various acrobats wood-engraved by Barbara Crow. Foldmark on lower left hand corner of broadside.

1567. (Whittington Press) Allen, Perter. TRAVELS IN THE CEVENNES. Risbury, England: The Whittington Press, 1998, small 4to., decorated paper covered boards, wrap around paper label, top edge cut, fore and bottom edges deckled, slipcase. (56) pages. $ 220.00
Printed in an edition limited to 150 copies of which this is one of 100 numbered and signed copies. Written and stenciled with forty pochoir illustrations. Each illustration is in a sense an original, for the colors applied by pochoir consist of artists' watercolor applied through stencils directly to the paper, in this case by Peter Allen himself. The route that Robert Louis Stevenson described in his "Travels with a Donkey" a hundred years earlier has been retraced by Peter Allen over a period of years. Allen's diary extracts, and forty vividly colored pochoir illustrations, bring to life the rugged character of this little known "département" of southern France.

1568. (Whittington Press) Bidwell, John. FINE PAPERS AT THE OXFORD UNIVERSITY PRESS. A descriptive catalogue, with sample pieces of each of the papers. Lower Marston Farm, Risbury, Herefordshire: The Whittington Press, 1998, large 4to., half-buckram, slipcase. 120 pages. $ 475.00
Limited to 350 copies, including 300 in this binding. In 1986, the Oxford University Press moved its paper warehouse and sold to Whittington Press a large number of sheets of many different papers found in the old warehouse, leftovers from books printed at the OUP from about 1900 to 1970. Per prospectus, these papers represented "an extraordinary microcosm of the output of British (and some Continental) hand-made paper mills between those dates." Whittington set some of these papers aside for use in the present publication. The author, John Bidwell, curator of graphic arts at Princeton University, consulted the OUP archives to determine which book or books were printed with each paper. In this catalogue of forty hand- and mould-made papers, he identifies and gives a history of the mill which produced each paper, describes that paper, and notes the OUP books printed on that paper. For each paper, a sample, gen-

Items 1570 & 1571

erally a half- or quarter-page, is tipped in opposite its description. One of the rarest papers in the collection is Batchelor's Kelmscott, made originally to the specifications of William Morris. Printed in Centaur type on Zerkall mould-made paper.

1569. (Whittington Press) BOOKS COMING FROM THE WHITTINGTON PRES 1988, 1989, & 1990. Manor Farm: The Whittington Press, 1988, small 4to., paper wrappers. 15+(1) pages. $15.00
A catalogue of The Whittington Press's new books and books advertised in the 1986-87 catalogue with updated information. Printed by hand and illustrated with wood-engraving by John O'Connor and Richard Kennedy.

JUST PUBLISHED

1570. (Whittington Press) Butcher, David. BRITISH PRIVATE PRESS PROSPECTUSES, 1891-2001. (Risbury, Herefordshire): Whittington Press, (2001), small 4to., half-buckram with patterned paper covered boards, buckram and paper covered slipcase. xii, 147, (3) pages with 16 additional leaves of illustrations. $247.50
Printed in an edition limited to 260 numbered copies. The development of the private press in Britain during the twentieth century is traced through this collection of prospectuses that come from both famous and not so famous publishers. As the books they represent become rarer and more expensive, the prospectuses, which can offer fascinating clues to the development of the titles they promote, are becoming collectible items themselves. Frontispiece is a wood-engraving by Eric Ravilious for the cover of the Golden Cockerel Press' Autumn List 1931. Includes 16 colored plates and three facsimile prospectuses inserted in a pocket in the back board.

1571. (Whittington Press) Butcher, David. BRITISH PRIVATE PRESS PROSPEC-
TUSES, 1891-2001. Risbury, Herefordshire: Whittington Press, 2001, small 4to., half
leather with marbled paper covered boards with a portfolio, slipcase. xii, 147, (3) pages
with 16 additional leaves of illustrations. $ 865.00
Limited edition of 50 numbered copies, with an extra portfolio of original prospectuses that is not included in the regular edition. The development of the private press in Britain during the twentieth century is traced through this collection of prospectuses that come from both famous and not so famous
publishers. As the books they represent become rarer and more expensive, the prospectuses, which can
offer fascinating clues to the development of the titles they promote, are becoming collectible items
themselves. This edition contains a portfolio of rare original prospectuses that the Press has been collecting over the last 15 years. Frontispiece is a wood-engraving by Eric Ravilious for the cover of the
Golden Cockerel Press' Autumn List 1931. Includes 16 colored plates and three facsimile prospectuses in
the back board.

1572. (Whittington Press) Clare, John. FOLKS TELL ME THAT THE MAY'S IN
FLOWER. Lower Marston Farm, Risbury: The Whittington Press, 1992, broadside, 24
x 16 inches. $ 25.00
A poem by John Clare, with wood-engravings by Hellmuth Weissenborn, printed on the tenth anniversary of his death.

1573. (Whittington Press) Craig, Edward (editor). EDWARD GORDON CRAIG:
THE LAST EIGHT YEARS, 1958–1966. Letters from Ellen Gordon Craig. Edited
and with an Introduction by Edward Craig, & with two wood-engravings by John Craig.
Manor Farm: The Whittington Press, (1983), tall 8vo., quarter cloth with patterned
paper covered sides, paper spine label. (viii), 48, (3) pages. $ 145.00
Limited to 385 numbered copies signed by Edward Craig.

1574. (Whittington Press) David Butcher (compiler). WHITTINGTON PRESS, A
BIBLIOGRAPHY 1982-93. Lower Marston Farm: The Whittington Press, 1996,
folio, quarter buckram, paper covered boards, slipcase. (x), 179, (3) pages. $ 225.00
Edition of 380 copies, numbered, 244 bound thus. A catalogue raisonné of the works published by The
Whittington Press between 1982 and 1993 compiled by David Butcher, with an introduction and notes
by John Randle. Includes, with full limitations given, books published by The Whittington Press, titles
produced for other publishers, minor publications and ephemera, catalogues and prospectuses, posters
and broadsides. An appendix consisting of a checklist of books published from 1972 to 1981 is included,
along with indices to titles, and to names and subjects. Well illustrated with examples from various
works, many tipped-in samples of ephemera, MATRIX wrappers, marbled paper and more. Quarter
bound in green buckram with pochoir sides stenciled by John Thornton to a design by Miriam Macgregor, printed on Zerkall mould-made paper, slipcased in dark green paper covered board accented with
green buckram.

1575. (Whittington Press) DIARY OF AN APPLE TREE. Lower Marston Farm
(Herefordshire): Whittington Press, 1997, oblong 8vo., paper covered boards, slipcase.
(8) pages with 13 additional leaves of prints. $ 150.00
Limited edition of 385 copies, including 300 bound in printed pattern paper of which this copy is one. A
brief text is followed by thirteen original wood engravings depicting an apple tree and surroundings,
with a constantly varying sky in the background, through the progression of the seasons, from early
Spring through Summer, Fall and Winter, and back to Spring. The black-and-white prints are densely
detailed, with complex shadings and patterns, very few straight lines, and some slight exaggeration of
the size of the leaves. Size of prints is about 4.25″ x 5.75.″ The first print, March, is repeated at the end.

1576. (Whittington Press) FAGELPERSPEKTIV OVER THE WHITTINGTON PRESS. Lower Marston Farm, Risbury: Whittington Press, 1994, broadside, 16 x 24 inches. $ 25.00

A broadside showing the layout of the Whittington Press drawn by Miriam Macgregor, with a short history on the press.

1577. (Whittington Press) FIERY BEACON GALLERY PAINSWICK, GLOUCESTER, WILL HOLD AN EXHIBITION OF THE WORK OF NINE ARTISTS & A PRESS. Lower Marston Farm, Risbury: Whittington Press, 1989, broadside, 24 x 16 inches. $ 35.00

Printed in an edition limited to 200 copies. A broadside of the exhibition held at The Fiery Beacon Gallery in 1989 that featured nine artists who worked for the Whittington Press. Includes a wood-engraving by Hellmuth Weissenborn.

1578. (Whittington Press) Foden, Peter. THE FELL IMPERIAL QUARTO BOOK OF COMMON PRAYER. Lower Marston Farm, Risbury, Herefordshire: The Whittington Press, 1998, folio, half leather with printed paper-covered boards, top edge stained brown, slipcase in paper and buckram. (vi), 44, (2) pages with 7 additional leaves. $ 325.00

Limited to 200 numbered copies. In the early 20th century, the Oxford University Press decided that its large-size Book of Common Prayer, a mid–19th century design, was inferior to the Cambridge version and generally ill-suited for liturgical practice, and designed a new one, influenced by the private press movement and using 17th-century matrices in the possession of the Press, the "Fell" types, named after Dr. John Fell (1625–1686), who had bequeathed them to Oxford in 1686. Work on this "new," updated edition of the 1662 Book of Common Prayer was carried out in the years 1911–1914, during which time much of the book was printed, but the project was abandoned with few or no copies of the imperial quarto version completed at the beginning of World War I (a smaller Fell Prayer Book was, however, published), and a number of the imperial 4to. quires remained in the OUP Walton Street printing establishment until this was closed in 1989. At that time the quires came into the possession of the Whittington Press. In the early 90's, it was suggested that the Whittington Press might try to finish the printing of the book, and Fell types still at Oxford and at the St. Bride Printing Library were made available for this purpose. The author, formerly archivist at the OUP, describes the finding of these quires, the state of Oxford printing, particularly ecclesiastical printing, in the early 20th century, the history and design of the book, and the aftermath, with an afterword by John Randle of the Whittington Press on printing with Fell types. Two sheets (4 pages) of the original quires are bound in, along with two sheets (4 pages) of type facsimile using the Fell matrices by the Whittington Press, and another sheet showing a facsimile of the title page on one side and a facsimile of the Calendar on the other.

1579. (Whittington Press) HELLMUTH WEISSENBORN, ENGRAVER WITH AN AUTOBIOGRAPHICAL INTRODUCTION BY THE ARTIST. Andoversford: The Whittington Press, (1983), folio, cloth, paper cover and spine labels, slipcase. xvi, 68, (2) pages. $ 400.00

Limited to 260 numbered copies. Two page foreword by John Randle followed by a 6 page autobiography by Weissenborn with tipped-in photographs. The text is followed by a selection of over 2000 of his engravings printed in either black, blue or red. Weissenborn, before his death in 1982 at the age of 83, had 15 of his books printed by the Whittington Press.

1580. (Whittington Press) Kennedy, Olive. LETTERS FROM A PORTUGUESE NUN. Manor Farm: Whittington Press, (1986), small 4to., paper-covered boards with a paper-covered slipcase. (vi), iv, 36, (1) pages. $ 275.00

Printed in an edition limited to 235 numbered and signed author and illustrator. (Whittington 84) A series of five letters, probably from Mariana Alcaforada, a nun in the convent at Beja in southern Portugal, to the Comte de Chamilly, a French officer who served in the campaign which liberated Portugal from Spain in 1668. Includes line-block reproductions of eleven drawings by Richard Kennedy. Translated from the French and with an introduction by Olive Kennedy. Bound in light Hahnemuhle laid paper-covered boards, printed spine titling, frontispiece drawing repeated on the front. Headbands, top edge purple, with cream Ingres endpapers and a black Ingres paper-covered slipcase.

1581. (Whittington Press) Macgregor, Miriam. NEW CASTLE, A BRIEF EN-COUNTER. Risbury: The Whittington Press, 1998, 4to., decorated paper covered boards in a paper covered slipcase. (20) pages. $ 450.00
Printed in an edition limited to only 100 numbered and signed copies of which this is one of the 75 regular copies. A beautiful illustrated book on New Castle, Delaware. These images and words are the result of Miriam Macgregor's visit to Oak Knoll Fest in October 1998. The pochoir illustrations and cover are cut on stencils and watercolored by the artist. Includes a view of Oak Knoll Books at its previous location at 414 Delaware Street.

1582. (Whittington Press) Macgregor, Miriam. WINE FROM MY GARDEN. Risbury, Herefordshire: The Whittington Press, 2000, miniature book (2.25″ x 1.75″), cloth, paper covered slipcase. Unpaginated (32 pages). $ 85.00
Limited to 200 numbered copies of which this is one of 150 bound in cloth. Written and illustrated by Miriam Macgregor with 14 attractive hand-coloured wood engravings. This book follows the same miniature format as "Weeds In My Garden" (1986) and "Predators In My Garden" (1993) and gives a description of 12 fruits, flowers, and vegetables used to make wine. Co-published with Lorson's Books and Prints, California. Printed in 6 point Garamond on Zerkall paper. Signed by Miriam Macgregor.

ONE OF 50 COPIES

1583. (Whittington Press) Macgregor, Miriam. WINE FROM MY GARDEN. Risbury, Herefordshire: The Whittington Press, 2000, miniature book (2.25″ x 1.75″), full leather, silk covered solander box. (32) pages. $ 245.00
Limited to 200 numbered copies of which this is one of 50 special copies bound in full leather and containing a separate portfolio of prints. Written and illustrated by Miriam Macgregor with 14 attractive hand-coloured wood engravings. This book follows the same miniature format as "Weeds In My Garden" (1986) and "Predators In My Garden" (1993) and gives a description of 12 fruits, flowers, and vegetables used to make wine. Co-published with Lorson's Books and Prints, California. Printed in 6 point Garamond on Zerkall paper. Signed by Miriam Macgregor.

1584. (Whittington Press) MATRIX 2, A REVIEW FOR PRINTERS & BIBLIO-PHILES. Andoversford: The Whittington Press, 1993, small 4to., stiff paper wrappers. (iv), 122 pages. $ 300.00
Reprint of the first edition, limited to 475 numbered copies. Twenty-one chapters on various aspects of printing, private press, illustration and papermaking. Includes articles by Adrian Cunningham on Eric Gill, John Biggs on wood-engraving in Russia, James Mosely on Gill and the Golden Cockerel Type, John Randle on the Rampant Lions Press and many others.

SPECIAL EDITION

1585. (Whittington Press) MATRIX 7. Manor Farm: The Whittington Press, 1987, small 4to., quarter bound in leather with pattern paper covered sides. (viii), 166, (2) pages. Accompanied by a separate case in which is mounted a cassette recording a talk by Stanley Morison on Eric Gill. Both pieces are inserted in a slipcase. $ 550.00
Limited to 960 copies of which this is one of the 110 special copies done in this manner. Filled with tipped in plates and other illustrations. Articles by Cleverdon on Morison and Gill, Dreyfus on French Resistance Printing, Carter on Victor Hammer, Cave on Golden Cockerel, Mortimer on Ornamented Types, Thompson on Gordon Craig, Crutchley on the Shape of Books and many others.

1586. (Whittington Press) MATRIX 9. Manor Farm: The Whittington Press, 1989, small 4to., stiff paper wrappers. (viii), 200, (2) pages. $ 225.00

Limited to 925 copies of which this is one of the 820 copies of the trade edition bound thus. Filled with tipped in plates and other illustrations. This year's articles include Thoughts on Wood by Robert Gibbings, Notes on the Printing Methods of the Golden Cockerel Press by A. C. Cooper, Jan Tschichold and Chinese Woodblock Printing by Charles Antin and The Printing of the "Alice" Engravings by Jonathan Stephenson and many others.

SPECIAL EDITION

1587. (Whittington Press) MATRIX 9. Manor Farm: The Whittington Press, 1986, small 4to., quarter leather with marbled paper by Colleen Gryspeerdt over boards. With a reproduction of a "Letter to Colette" bound in cloth backed boards, all enclosed in a slipcase. (viii), 166, (2) pages. $ 550.00

Limited to 925 copies of which this is one of the 105 special copies bound thus and containing a bound reproduction of a "Letter to Colette." Filled with tipped in plates and other illustrations. This year's articles include Thoughts on Wood by Robert Gibbings, Notes on the Printing Methods of the Golden Cockerel Press by A. C. Cooper, Jan Tschichold and Chinese Woodblock Printing by Charles Antin and The Printing of the "Alice" Engravings by Jonathan Stephenson and many others.

1588. (Whittington Press) MATRIX 10. Manor Farm: The Whittington Press, 1990, small 4to., stiff paper wrappers. (viii), 237 pages. $ 250.00

Limited to 925 copies of which this is one of the 820 copies of the trade edition bound thus. Filled with tipped in plates and other illustrations. This year's articles include Berthold Wolpe, 1905-89 by Montague Shaw, Gerard Meynell and the Westminster Press by John Dreyfus, Stanley Morison and Jan van Krimpen by Sebastian Carter, and From a Cambridge Diary by Brooke Crutchley.

SPECIAL EDITION

1589. (Whittington Press) MATRIX 10. Manor Farm: The Whittington Press, 1990, small 4to., quarter leather, marbled paper over boards, slipcase. (viii), 237 pages.
$ 550.00

Limited to 925 copies of which this is one of the 105 copies of the special edition bound thus and containing a portfolio of separate prints and broadsides (in most cases signed) of: 1. The School Prints 2. Four autolithographs by Gordon Gunn 3.Two autolithographic leaves from Rena Gardiner's Workshop Press. 4.The Miller Farm - a colored wood-engraving by Gaylord Schanilec 5.Type broadside from Mark Arman's Workshop Press 6. A Book of Jugs, autolithographs by Alan Powers 7.The cover of Matrix 10, as printed with the cover of A Book of Jugs.

SPECIAL EDITION

1590. (Whittington Press) MATRIX 11. Manor Farm: Whittington Press, 1991, 4to., quarter leather, marbled paper over boards, in slipcase with separate bound copy of additional material. (v), 207, (14) pages. $ 600.00

Limited to 955 copies, this being one of 105 copies bound thus. Filled with tipped in plates, photographs and samples of private press items. Some of the articles in this issue are "Reynolds Stone and Cambridge" by Brooke Crutchley, "Stanley Morison and Jan van Krimpen, a Survey of their Correspondence" by Sebastian Carter, "On Preparing Designs for Monotype Faces" by Jan Van Krimpen and "Compton Marbling" by Solveig Stone. Also includes, in a separate bound volume, a copy of TWINS by John O'Connor, illustrated with two color engravings and is signed by the author.

1591. (Whittington Press) MATRIX 11. Herefordshire: Whittington Press, 1991, 4to., stiff decorated paper wrappers. (v), 207 pages. $ 250.00
Limited to 955 copies, this being one of 850 copies bound thus. Filled with tipped in plates, photographs and samples of private press items. Some of the articles in this issue are "Reynolds Stone and Cambridge" by Brooke Crutchley, "Stanley Morison and Jan van Krimpen, a Survey of their Correspondence" by Sebastian Carter, "On Preparing Designs for Monotype Faces" by Jan Van Krimpen and "Compton Marbling" by Solveig Stone. Bookplate on free endpaper.

1592. (Whittington Press) MATRIX 12. Herefordshire: Whittington Press, 1992, 4to., stiff decorated paper wrappers. (vi), 222 pages. $ 250.00
Limited to 925 copies, this being one of 825 copies bound thus. Filled with tipped in plates, photographs and samples of private press items. Some of the articles in this issue are "The Library of Emery Walker" by William Peterson, Simon Lawrence on The Fleece Press, Roderick Cave on the "Ceremonial Papers of the Chinese, Part One," "Dennis Cohen and the Cresset Press" by John Dreyfus, "The Types of Jan van Krimpen" by Sebastian Carter, "Chiyogami" by Tanya Schmoller and many others.

1593. (Whittington Press) MATRIX 13. Herefordshire: Whittington Press, 1993, 4to., stiff decorated paper wrappers. (vi), 234 pages. $ 275.00
Limited to 925 copies, this being one of 835 copies bound thus. Filled with tipped in plates, photographs and samples of private press items. Some of the articles in this issue are "Epinal's Imagerie - the Pochoir Image Factory of France" by Peter Allen, "The Vine Press, 1957–1963" by John Dreyfus, James Mosely on "The Caslon Type Foundry in 1902," and other articles on paper, printing, Richard Wood and the Talbot Press, James Guthrie and the Pear Press, etc.

1594. (Whittington Press) MATRIX 14. Herefordshire: Whittington Press, 1994, 4to., limp boards, dust jacket. (vi), 236, (2) pages. $ 250.00
Limited to 925 copies. Filled with tipped in plates, photographs and samples of private press items. Some of the articles in this issue are "One Day in Alpignano: a Visit to Alberto Tallone Editore" by Roderick Cave, "Edward Anthony Craig, Wood-Engraver" by L.M. Newman, Ruari McLean on "Stanley Morison's Handwriting," William Peterson on "Sydney Cockerell and the Kelmscott Press" and others by Joanna Selborne, Mike Hudson, John Dreyfus, Sebastian Carter and others.

1595. (Whittington Press) MATRIX 15. Herefordshire: Whittington Press, 1994, 4to., limp boards, dust jacket. (vi), 234, (2) pages. $ 250.00
Limited to 950 copies. Filled with tipped in plates, photographs and samples of private press items. Some of the articles in this issue are "Letters are Things: The Wood-engraved initials of Eric Gill" by Sebastian Carter, Fiona MacCarthy on William Morris, Ruari McLean on "Typography and Parsons," Ward Ritchie on "Paul Landacre and the Ward Ritchie Press, Henry Morris on his Bird & Bull Press, John Dreyfus on Fernand Baudin, and many others including an index to Matrix 11–15.

1596. (Whittington Press) MATRIX 16. Herefordshire: Whittington Press, 1996, 4to., limp boards, dust jacket. (vi), 203, (3) pages. $ 220.00
Limited to 925 copies. Filled with tipped in plates, photographs and samples of private press items. Some of the articles in this issue are "The Hammersmith Hot-house" by John Dreyfus, "Making a Visible Spirit" by Dan Carr, "Cave Paper" by Bridget O'Malley and Amanda Degener, "Borders designed by Edward Bawden" by Michael Johnson, "Weather Bird and Disney" by Vance Gerry, "The Wood engravings of Joan Hassall" by Ruari McLean, "David Kindersley" by Lottie Hoare, "The Story of a Book, Illustrations by Henri Matisse" by Albert Skira, "Merle Armitage" by Ward Ritchie and many others. Includes a review of press books published in 1995 by David Chambers.

1597. (Whittington Press) MATRIX 17. Herefordshire: Whittington Press, 1997, 4to., paper-covered limp boards, dust jacket. (vi), 195, (3) pages, with 42 additional pages and 2 additional leaves of plates and other materials. $ 250.00
Limited to 850, including 770 in "stiff covers" (limp boards). Some contents of this issue: Maureen Richardson on a papermaking tour of Japan (with 2 samples), John Dreyfus on Maximilien Vox, Hal Bishop on "Joan Ellis, a Lost Engraver from the Underwood School" (with reproductions of 8 wood en-

gravings), Adela Spindler Roatcap on Dadaist typography (with illustrations), Alan Dodson on Caslon, Jerry Kelly on the dust jacket designs of Hermann Zapf (with examples), Barbara Henry on Bowne & Co. Stationers at the New York Seaport Museum, 2 articles by Roderick Cave, a survey of 1996 private press books by David Chambers, and 7 book reviews. And more. With photographs and many pages of book design/typographic specimens (covers, text pages, alphabets, etc.). Several tipped in engravings.

1598. (Whittington Press) MATRIX 18. Herefordshire: Whittington Press, 1998, 4to., paper-covered limp boards, dust jacket. (vi), 236, (2) pages, with many additional pages of plates and other materials. $ 240.00
Limited to 825, including 745 in "stiff covers" (limp boards). Some contents of this issue: Ruari McLean on Jan Tschichold, WM Erik Voss on LA Type, David McKitterick on "The Fanfare Press" (with type specimens), Michael Johnson on "Bruce Rogers and The Rime of the Ancient Mariner," Martyn Ould and Martyn Thomas on "Researching the revival of the Fell Types," Roderick Cave on Chinese Ceremonial papers (with fold-out specimens), Sebastian Carter on Type for Books, a survey of 1997 private press books by David Chambers, and 8 book reviews. And more. With photographs and many pages of book design/typographic specimens (covers, text pages, alphabets, etc.). Several tipped in engravings.

1599. (Whittington Press) MATRIX 19. Herefordshire: Whittington Press, 1999, 4to., paper-covered limp boards, dust jacket. (vi), 246 pages, with many additional pages of plates and other materials. $ 225.00
Printed in an edition limited to 800 copies, this being one of 720 copies which are bound in stiff wrappers. This issue of the Matrix contains twenty-four articles including David Chambers on the Circle Press, Theo Rehak on the Kelmscott Press, John Dreyfus on American Proprietary Typefaces, John DePol on John Fass, John Dodson on German Type Specimens, Roderick Cave on Will Ranson and the Cunninghams, followed by 11 book reviews. Well illustrated with many tipped-in specimens printed on special papers, color plates, wood engravings printed on special paper, etc. Scholarly and finely printed.

1600. (Whittington Press) MATRIX 20. Herefordshire: Whittington Press, 2000, 4to., Korean hand made paper-covered limp boards, dust jacket. (vi), 234 pages, with numerous additional pages of plates and other materials. $ 225.00
Printed in an edition limited to 825 copies, this being one of 745 copies which are bound in stiff paper wrappers. This issue of Matrix contains twenty-four articles including "Tales from Bleeding Heart Yard," by Simon Lawrence, "New Borders: the Working Life of Elizabeth Friedlander," by Pauline Paucker, "Caslon Punches and Matrices," by Justin Howes, "Emerson Wulling, Printer for Pleasure," by Gaylord Schanilec, "Icones," by Leonard Baskin, "Private Press 1999, a Review," by David Chambers, "Printing and the Mind of Man," by Sebastian Carter and more. Well illustrated with many tipped-in specimens printed on special papers, color plates, wood engravings printed on special paper, etc. Scholarly and finely printed.

1601. (Whittington Press) MISCELLANY OF TYPE COMPILED AT WHITTINGTON. Andoversford, Gloucestershire: The Whittington Press, (1990), 4to., quarter cloth, printed paper over boards, slipcase. iv, (iv), 125, (2) pages. $ 450.00
First edition, limited to 530 numbered copies, of which this is one of the 460 trade copies bound thus. A magnificent type specimen book which has been designed to be enjoyed as much for its content as its typographical displays. The basis for this book is the large collection of monotype faces held by the press, which includes Bible Centaur and all the other monotype faces originally held by the Oxford University Press. Each one has been elegantly displayed in a variety of different sizes and a deliberate attempt has been made to show the rarely-seen larger sizes. The texts are extracts from books or articles published by the press and are accompanied by an original illustration. Printed in two colors throughout this is one of the finest private press books of the year and an inspiration to any typographer.

1602. (Whittington Press) O'Connor, Jeannie. WOOD-ENGRAVINGS OF JOHN O'CONNOR. Andoversford, Gloucestershire: The Whittington Press, (1989), 4to., cloth-backed boards, slipcase. (vi), 79, (5) pages. $ 225.00
First edition, limited to 400 numbered copies this being one of the 300 trade copies bound thus. Set in 14-pt Bell and printed by letterpress on Tosa Butten and Zerkall mould made paper. Bound by The Fine Bindery. A delightful story of this engraver's work and life. The illustrations are mainly printed from the original blocks and several are printed in two colors. Includes a bibliography of books with illustrations by O'Connor. An excellent production from this fine private press.

1603. (Whittington Press) O'Connor, John. PEOPLE & PLACES. Lower Marston Farm, England: The Whittington Press, 1999, small 8vo., quarter cloth with decorated paper covered boards. (16) pages followed by 36 leaves of plates. $ 60.00
Printed in an edition limited to 375 numbered copies set in Van Dijck type and printed at Whittington on Zerkall Rosa paper. A beautiful collection of 36 wood-cut engravings from John O'Conner's sixth decade of engraving. The engravings in this volume have been appearing in the magazine "Oldie" since 1992. They accompanied the regular and entertaining columns by Germaine Greer, who wrote of her personal battle with wild and domestic nature in a tooth-and-claw relationship. The engravings portray the English landscape, buildings and people. His sympathy with the English countryside and his knowledge of its architecture are evocatively demonstrated.

1604. (Whittington Press) O'Connor, John. KNIPTON, A LEICESTERSHIRE VILLAGE. With thirty-five wood-engravings by the artist. Risbury: The Whittington Press, (1996), small folio, cloth-backed boards, slipcase. (32) pages. $ 185.00
Limited to 200 numbered copies of which this is one of the 155 trade copies. Signed by O'Connor. With the woodcuts printed in different colors.

1605. (Whittington Press) Phipps, Howard. FURTHER INTERIORS. Lower Marston Farm: The Whittington Press, 1992, small 4to., stiff paper wrappers tied with ribbon, slipcase. 15+(1) pages. $ 175.00
Limited to 300 signed and numbered copies, this being one of 235 bound thus. Printed on Zerkall Rosa and Ingras papers using the original woodblocks. Contains 15 wood engravings of interiors, four of them printed in four and five colors. Phipps use of light and shadow gives the engravings an irresistible quality. A beautiful collection.

1606. (Whittington Press) POEMS FOR ALAN HANCOX. (Lower Marston, nr. Risbury: The Whittington Press, 1993), 4to., quarter cloth over decorated paper covered boards, top edge gilt. (42) pages. $ 100.00
Limited to 350 numbered copies. Biography of this bookseller, collector and friend of many authors followed by poems written in his honor by 18 authors including Seamus Heaney and Ted Hughes.

1607. (Whittington Press) PORTRAITS OF PRESSES. PHOTOGRAPHS BY SKI HARRISON OF FLEECE, GREGYNOG, I.M. IMPRIMIT, OLD STILE, RAMPANT LIONS, ROCKET, TERN, WHITTINGTON & CTD. Leominster: The Whittington Press, (1997), oblong small 4to., quarter cloth, patterned paper covered boards, slipcase. xii, 53+(1) pages and 35 leaves of photographs. Also present are tipped-in examples of the work of the presses. $ 300.00
Limited to 500 numbered copies, of which only 350 were offered for sale. A survey of contemporary British private presses with chapters on the Fleece Press, Gregynog Press, I.M. Imprimit, Old Stile, Rampant Lions, Rocket, Tern, Whittington, and CTD. Each press has a textual passage by the printer often giving some history and philosophy of the press, a specimen of work done by the press, and a series of finely produced photographic images by Ski Harrison. Introduction by John Randle. A wonderful survey of some of the best English private presses.

1608. (Whittington Press) Randle, Rosalind. ROSE'S AGA RECIPES. Andoversford: The Whittington Press, (1995), small 8vo., cloth, paper cover label. (24) pages. $ 25.00
Fifth edition, augmented and limited to 950 copies. Illustrated with linocuts by Judith Verity. A cookbook by the co-proprietor of the Whittington Press.

1609. (Whittington Press) Thomas, Edward & Helen Thomas. PERSONAL LET-TERS. Risbury, Herefordshire: The Whittington Press, 2000, 8vo., limp boards. (iv), iv, (2), 22, (3) pages. $ 55.00
Limited to 200 numbered copies. This book contains six letters exchanged by writers Edward and Helen Thomas during their twenty years together. The letters, mostly written around World War I, recount the struggles of finding literary work in London at the time. Set in Van Dijck type and printed on Zerkall paper. Includes six wood-engravings taken from a set of twelve entitled Country Scenes which Hellmuth Weissenborn engraved in 1950.

1610. (Whittington Press) Thomas, Helen. A VISIT TO WILLIAM MORRIS. Gloucestershire: The Whittington Press, (1979), large 8vo., paper wrappers, paper cover label. xii, (3) pages. $ 65.00
Printed in an edition limited to 500 copies signed by Myfanwy Thomas, who wrote the foreword. (Whittington no. 39). Thomas tells about her visit with William Morris in 1895 in her first essay which was published in the Times in 1963. The wood engraved frontispiece is taken from 'The Diary of Edward Thomas.' It is illustrated with three wood engravings by Hellmuth Weissenborn, and is printed in black, with the title and engravings in brown.

1611. (Whittington Press) Weissenborn, Helmuth. LONDON SCENES WOOD-ENGRAVINGS. Risbury, Herefordshire: Whittington Press, (2001), small 4to., paper covered boards tied with ribbon in the Japanese style, paper cover label, foredge uncut. (28) french fold pages. $ 50.00
Printed in an edition limited to 300 numbered copies. Includes ten wood engravings printed from the original blocks with a foreword by John Randle. Fascinated by the response of Londoners to the nightly bombings of their city, this series of prints captures the gritty essence of everyday life during WWII. Having already been interred on the Isle of Man as an enemy alien in 1940, Weissenborn risked being thought a spy to make his unforgettable sketches.

1612. (Whittington Press) THE WHITTINGTON PRESS. Lower Marston Farm, Risbury: The Whittington Press, 1984, broadside. 24 x 16 inches. $ 45.00
A brief history of the Whittington Press. Printed on Amatruda hand-made paper, with a wood engraving of Manor Farm by Miriam Macgregor.

1613. (Whittington Press) WHITTINGTON SUMMER SHOW. Lower Marston Farm, Risbury: Whittington Press, n.d., broadside, 15 by 10. 5 inches. $ 15.00
A broadside advertising the Whittington summer show. Wood-engraving by Hellmuth Weissenborn. Yellow ink has smudged somewhat.

1614. (Wilmac Press) McKenny, J. Wilson. PRINTING FOR FUN. San Mateo, CA: Wilmac Press, 1961, 12mo., paper wrappers. 8 leaves. $ 25.00
Printed in an edition limited to 137 copies. Members of the Moxon Chappel included the author, Ben Lieberman, Lewis Osborne, Robert Maines, Carroll Mahone, George Pfeiffer, Robert McMakin, and Alvin Badenhop. Additions and corrections tipped in on 4th leaf; some glue staining.

1615. (Wilson, Adrian) Wilson, Adrian. PRINTING FOR THEATER. San Francisco: Adrian Wilson, 1957, folio, cloth. (vi), 57, (2) pages. $ 1,500.00
Printed in an edition limited to 250 copies. Programs for 41 plays are bound in with 18 additional programs, announcement, etc. are laid in a pocket on the inside back cover. This is perhaps the first consecutive exploration of the materials of printing in the service of theater. Many artists of the programs, have attempted to distill the play into one fresh, essential image through linoleum blocks, wood engravings,

pen drawings, even photography. The original programs which are tipped into this book are from a theater group known as The Interplayers which appeared in plays such as Sartre's 'No Exit,' Chekhov's 'Boor,' and Eliot's 'Family Reunion.' The paper is handmade Tovil, a staunch British sheet, replete with ecclesiastical watermarks and deckle edges. The programs are made from papers such as novelty wrapping to handmade Fabriano and French wallpaper. The stalwart binding is composed of linen from Belgium, boards from the jute mines of India and glue from the finest Western stallions. Nuiko Haramaki's linoleum cuts decorate the flanks of the volume, as well as the title page and the chapter heads. Small split along front hinge of cover. Inside front hinge cracked. Two copies of the prospectus and what appears to be page proofs of part of the book loosely inserted. Scarce.

1616. (Wilson, Adrian) Meany, Andrée. LA CALIFORNIE. UNE MERVEILLEUSE AVENTURE. San Francisco: (Adrian Wilson), 1953, 8vo., later marbled paper covered boards, original front paper wrapper bound-in. (x), 62, (5) pages. $ 45.00
First edition, limited to 250 copies. (Wilson 31). A finely printed edition of California's history. Meany takes us from the Conquistadores to the French pioneers and then looks at California's Spanish and Mexican heritage. Preface by René Bellé. Typography by Mackenzie & Harris. This was their first use of the Van Dijck typeface, designed by Jan van Krimpen for Enschedé. Printed on Strathmore Pastelle paper. Nuiko Haramaki designed the linocut for the title page. Original stiff paper wrappers bound in. An Adrian Wilson publication.

1617. (Wilson, Adrian) Moore, Marianne. IDIOSYNCRASY & TECHNIQUE. Berkeley: University of California Press, 1958, large 12mo., paper wrappers, wrap around paper cover label. (vi), 28 pages. $ 60.00
First edition. Printed in an edition limited to 1000 copies. (Abbott A15, Wilson 62). Two lectures give by Marianne Moore in 1956 at the University of California as part of the inauguration of the Ewing Lectures. It was designed by Adrian Wilson.

1618. (Windhover Press) Hodges, Gregg. A MUSIC. Iowa City: The Windhover Press, 1990, large 8vo., stiff paper wrappers. (18) pages. $ 85.00
Printed in an edition limited to 225 copies (Berger 96). Six poems by Hodges. It is illustrated with woodcuts in two colors by Bridget O'Malley. It is finely printed from Romanee types on watermarked Johannat paper.

1619. (Windhover Press) Wright, Charles. XIONIA. N.P.: Windhover Press, The University of Iowa, (1990), 4to., quarter cloth, paper covered boards, paper spine label. 38, (4) pages. $ 225.00
Printed in an edition limited to 250 copies signed by the author. A collection of the author's poetry some of which had previously appeared in The New Yorker, The Paris Review, The New Republic and other periodicals. Interesting typographical arrangement printed from Joanna types on Iyo handmade, a Japanese paper, and Johannot, a French mouldmade paper.

1620. (Windsor Press) Fryer, Benjamin N. and James Johnson. BRUCE ROGERS AND THE FIGUREHEAD OF THE JOSEPH CONRAD. San Francisco: Windsor Press, 1938, small 4to., quarter cloth with paper-covered boards. (vi), 12, (2) pages.
$ 75.00
Printed in an edition limited to three hundred numbered copies by Cecil and James Johnson at their Windsor Press in San Francisco. Bruce Rogers was an illustrator and landscape artist before his career as a printer. In the thirties he visited Alan Villiers, the owner of the 203-ton ship *Joseph Conrad*, and agreed to carve a full-size figurehead. Photograph of the figurehead as frontispiece and others in text. Some offset on boards.

1621. (Windsor Press) Johnson, James Sydney. NOCTURNE IN ST. GAUDEN'S. San Francisco: Printed for The American Institute of Graphic Arts by The Windsor Press, 1929, 8vo., boards, paper cover label. 14, (2) pages. $ 40.00

Limited to 700 copies. (Ransom describes the first 20 books printed by this press but doesn't list this one for 1929 as that is the ending date of bibliography). With an original woodcut by Howard Simon and presswork by Lawton Kennedy. Prospectus loosely inserted.

1622. (Windsor Press) Stevenson, Robert Louis. A LODGING FOR THE NIGHT, A STORY OF FRANCIS VILLON. San Francisco: Windsor Press, 1926, small 12mo., quarter cloth with paper covered boards. viii, 27+(1) pages. $ 35.00

Printed by The Brothers Johnson, C.A. and J.S. for C.F. Benoit in an edition limited to 750 copies on Rye Mill hand-made paper "after which the type was distributed," (Ransom, 448). Foreword by James S. Johnson. Title page illustration by Julian A. Links.

SPECIAL EDITION

1623. (Wood Lea Press) Collins, Judith. OMEGA CUTS. Woodbridge, Suffolk: The Wood Lea Press, 1998, large 4to., quarter leather with decorated paper-covered boards, decorated endpapers, brochure, cloth-covered clamshell case. 148 pages. $ 650.00

Limited to 105 copies in this special edition which includes an extra pamphlet by Simon Lawrence of the Fleece Press. An illustrated catalogue of woodcuts from the Omega Workshop. Woodcuts enjoyed a revival as an artistic medium in the late 19th and early 20th centuries, and the artists--Roger Fry, Vanessa Bell, Duncan Grant, [Dora] Carrington, et al.--associated with the Workshop contributed a number of wood- and linocuts to Omega publications between about 1911 and 1921. This limited edition contains 206 illustrations, 165 of them reproductions of cuts by Fry and 12 others--all of those woodcuts known to exist from these artists (but not necessarily made for Omega), including 17 tipped-in reproductions in color. The catalogue itself is compiled by Jeremy Greenwood, who is a partner in the Wood Lea Press and has also compiled catalogues of the wood engravings of John and Paul Nash. Introduction is by Judith Collins, who wrote an earlier book on the Omega Workshops in 1984. Enclosed is also a brochure with 10 prints made directly from original blocks that are only in this special edition. Endpapers and cover paper are based on patterned papers of the Workshop.

1624. (Wood Lea Press) Collins, Judith. OMEGA CUTS. Woodbridge, Suffolk: The Wood Lea Press, 1998, large 4to., cloth, decorated endpapers, slipcase. 148 pages.
$ 250.00

Limited to 450 copies in this edition. An illustrated catalogue of woodcuts from the Omega Workshop. Woodcuts enjoyed a revival as an artistic medium in the late 19th and early 20th centuries, and the artists--Roger Fry, Vanessa Bell, Duncan Grant, [Dora] Carrington, et al.--associated with the Workshop contributed a number of wood- and linocuts to Omega publications between about 1911 and 1921. This limited edition contains 206 illustrations, 165 of them reproductions of woodcuts by Fry and 12 others--all those known to exist from these artists (and not necessarily made for Omega), including 17 tipped-in reproductions in color. The catalogue itself is compiled by Jeremy Greenwood, who is a partner in the Wood Lea Press and has also compiled catalogues of the wood engravings of John and Paul Nash. Introduction is by Judith Collins, who wrote an earlier book on the Omega Workshops in 1984. Endpapers are based on patterned papers of the Workshop.

1625. (Wood Lea Press) Greenwood, Jeremy. WOOD-ENGRAVINGS OF PAUL NASH. Woodbridge: The Wood Lea Press, 1997, 4to., quarter cloth with patterned paper over boards, cloth covered slipcase. 141, (3) pages. $ 175.00

First edition. Limited to 550 copies, 490 thus bound. Includes an introduction by Simon Brett, 100 wood-engravings, 5 pattern papers, and some little known etchings and engravings on copper. Printed by Smith Settle in Berthold Plantin and, for main headings, Adobe Sabon. Quarter bound in gray cloth, the binding paper being a facsimile of Curwen pattern paper no. 24 (G.100.) in white, black and dark yellow.

1626. (Woodside Press) THE TYPOPHILES PUBLISHING PROGRAM. New York: The Typophiles, 1999, 8vo., stiff paper wrappers, cord-tied. (ii), 17, (5) pages.

$ 25.00

Limited to 500 copies. Typophile Monograph, New Series - Number 15. Printed at the Woodside Press in the Brooklyn Navy Yard. Preface by Theo Rehak giving a history of the publishing program followed by a tribute to Morris Gelfand. With a wood engraving by John DePol on the title page. Distributed for the Typophiles by Oak Knoll Press.

1627. (Workshop Press) Arman, Mark. LETTERPRESS, PRINTERS' TYPES AND DECORATIONS, FIVE ARTICLES BY MARK ARMAN WHICH WERE IN-CLUDED IN THE WHITTINGTON PRESS ANNUAL PUBLICATION MA-TRIX BETWEEN 1987 & 1991. Thaxted Essex: The Workshop Press, (1993), tall 8vo., quarter leather, leather cover label. viii, 48 pages. $ 185.00

Limited to 110 signed and numbered copies of which this is one of a few copies bound thus (number "7" of run). Specimens are printed in various colors for variety and include some large foldout broadsides and tipped-in specimens.

1628. (Workshop Press) Arman, Mark. A SPECIMEN OF PRINTERS' FLOWERS, TYPES & DECORATIONS. Thaxted Essex: The Workshop Press, (1992), 8vo., quar-ter cloth, decorated paper over boards. vii, 34, (32) pages. $ 125.00

Limited to 180 signed and numbered copies. Presents over 370 printers' flowers and decorations, most of which have been accumulated from one private collection. The book is divided in two parts. Part one con-sists of short essays on the use and definition of printers' flowers and part two consists of the various specimens, with some of the larger specimens printed on bigger pages tipped in. Specimens are printed in various colors for variety.

1629. (Yellow Barn Press) Colebrook, Frank. WILLIAM MORRIS: MASTER-PRINTER, A LECTURE GIVEN ON THE EVENING OF NOVEMBER 27, 1896 TO STUDENTS OF THE PRINTING SCHOOL, ST. BRIDE FOUNDA-TION INSTITUTE IN LONDON. With an introduction by William S. Peterson. Council Bluffs, IA: Yellow Barn Press, (1989), 8vo., cloth, paper spine and cover labels. xii, 34, (2) pages. $ 325.00

Limited to 155 numbered copies. Printed by letterpress on Rives paper and engraved by John DePol. Re-produces a lecture which first appeared in *The Printing Times and Lithopgrapher* of November 1896. A fascinating lecture, excellently illustrated. Bookplate.

1630. (Yellow Barn Press) Coleman, Carroll D. THE PARSON/PRINTER OF LUSTLEIGH. Council Bluffs, IA: The Yellow Barn Press, 1999, large 12mo., quarter cloth with decorated paper covered boards and paper spine label. (20) pages. $ 39.00

First edition, limited to 130 numbered copies printed at the Yellow Barn Press. The true story of Printer William Davy and typesetter Molly Hole, of Devonshire. This story first appeared in Colophon in the fall of 1935. The author, Carroll Coleman, started the Typographic Laboratory and the School of Jour-nalism of the University of Iowa and after his resignation, in 1950, devoted all his time to the Prairie Press. Set in 13 point Monotype Poliphilus printed on Rives paper. Bound in a speckled copper-colored cloth with paper covered boards decorated with shimmering gold and copper over blue. Illustrated with four linocuts by Bill Jackson, including one frontispiece.

1631. (Yellow Barn Press) Garland, Hamlin. THE RETURN OF A PRIVATE. Council Bluffs (IA): Yellow Barn Press, 1998, large 8vo., quarter cloth, paper-covered boards, paper spine label. viii, 23, (2) pages. $ 59.00
Limited to 150 numbered copies, with three 2-color wood engravings by Gaylord Shanilec. One of the stories from Garland's Main-Travelled Road (first publ. 1891), with a title supplied by the publisher. Bitter, very understated satire: a penniless, ill Civil War veteran returns home to his impoverished farm and family to discover that years of danger and hardship do not earn him a single greeting or word of thanks from any except those who would welcome him in any case.

1632. (Yellow Barn Press) JULIAN SYMONS REMEMBERED, TRIBUTES FROM FRIENDS. COLLECTED BY JACK WALSDORF AND KATHLEEN SYMONS. Council Bluffs, IA: The Yellow Barn Press, (1996), 8vo., cloth-backed marbled paper covered boards, leather spine label. xi, 55, (3) pages. $ 60.00
Limited to 225 numbered copies. Includes 25 tributes including ones by Simon Brett, P.D. James, H.R.F. Keating, Alan Ross, George Sims and others. Printed by hand by Neil Shaver at his private press. A lovingly produced tribute.

1633. (Yellow Barn Press) Levy, Newman. SANDY MACPHERSON: BOOK COLLECTOR. Council Bluffs (IA): The Yellow Barn Press, 1998, large 12mo., quarter cloth, marbled paper-covered boards, paper spine labels. Frontispiece; (26) pages. $ 45.00
Limited to 150 numbered copies. A retelling and new setting, with 8 linocuts (including frontispiece) by Bill Jackson, of a tale which originally appeared in the Quarto Club Papers of 1928. Book collector MacPherson doesn't have to go to those overpriced auctions; he knows how to find the good stuff: a first edition Beowulf, genuine Assyrian love letters (also useful in construction work), the rare 1903 Philadelphia phone book.....and the mother of all presentation copies. Cover papers are marbling over a darkly gilt background. One and two-tone linocuts.

1634. (Yellow Barn Press) Lieberman, J. Ben. THE LIBERTY BELL ON THE KELMSCOTT GOUDY PRESS. With an Introduction by Jack Walsdorf and an Afterword by Jethro K. Lieberman. And the Story of the John DePol Wood Engraving of this Famous Press. Council Bluffs: The Yellow Barn Press, (1996), 8vo., quarter cloth with pattern paper covered boards (design by John DePol), paper spine label. vii, 22, (2) pages. $ 100.00
Limited to 215 numbered copies. Printed by hand by Neil Shaver at his Yellow Barn Press. The story of how the printing press that William Morris had used to print his famous "Chaucer" ended up in America. John DePol's copy with his bookplate and name in ink.

1635. (Yellow Barn Press) Shewring, Walter. LATE VERSES AND EARLIER WALTER SHEWRING. Illustrated by John DePol. Council Buffs, IA: The Yellow Barn Press, (1988), 8vo., quarter cloth with Curwen patterned paper over boards, paper spine label. (viii), 28 pages. $ 100.00
First edition, limited to 150 numbered copies. A collection of thoughtful and dramatic poems from this scholar and poet who was an early collaborator with Eric Gill. With the bookplate of John DePol. Prospectus loosely inserted.

1636. (Yellow Barn Press) Symons, Julian. DOES LITERATURE EXIST? Council Bluffs, IA: The Yellow Barn Press, (1993), 8vo., cloth-backed marbled paper covered boards, paper spine label. (vi), 17+(1) pages. $ 40.00
First edition, limited to 175 numbered copies. Printed by hand by Neil Shaver on a Vandercook. The first printing of Symon's Lurcy Lecture presented at Amherst College in March of 1992 in which he attacks deconstruction and its principal practitioners and comments on standards of judgement in literature.

1637. (Yellow Barn Press) Walsdorf, Jack. THE YELLOW BARN PRESS A HISTORY AND BIBLIOGRAPHY. Council Bluffs, IA: Yellow Barn Press, 2001, large 4to., quarter goat skin with John DePol pattern paper covered boards, leather spine label, cloth covered clamshell box with paper spine label. xvii, (ii),122, (2) pages with 22 color plates and two pages of black and white photographs. $ 400.00

First edition, limited to 175 numbered copies. This volume was lovingly compiled by Jack Walsdorf and includes bibliography, history and comments on each title printed by Neil Shaver. The color plates provide wonderful examples of the wide variety of books that have been produced with such care at the Yellow Barn Press since 1979. The book is enhanced with many wood engravings, some in color, by the master of that craft, John DePol, who did some of his best work for Yellow Barn. Photos, a sketch, a flyer and even a fabric sample are tipped in. Finely printed on Zerkall paper. Prospectus loosely inserted.

1638. (Yolla Bolly Press) REMEMBERING ALBERT SPERISEN. San Francisco: The Book Club of California, (1999), large 8vo., stiff paper wrappers. (24) pages. $ 15.00

Printed in an edition limited to 1100 copies at The Yolla Bolly Press. A keepsake in which nine friends remember Albert Sperisen, member of the Book Club of California, printer, artist, designer and book collector. Illustrated. Corners bent.

1639. (Zak, Eugène) Morand, René. LA PORTE LOURDE,POÈMES EN PROSE DE RENÉ MORAND. Paris: Galerie Zak, (1929), small 4to., stiff paper wrappers. (viii), 36,(3) pages; 9 plates. $ 250.00

Limited edition of 300 copies. Modernist prose poems illustrated with nine lithographs by Polish-born artist Eugene Zak,1884–1926. Finely printed on Arches wove paper, with large print, wide margins.

1640. (Zamorano Press) Bowen, William Alvin. GOSSIP FROM THE SIXTEENTH CENTURY. Los Angeles: The Zamorano Press, 1938, small 8vo., cloth. (xvi), 49, (1) pages. $ 45.00

Edition limited to 125 copies. Three plays written for the Zamorano Club by one of its members, the plots being imaginary conversations between Martin Luther and Dr. Eck, Erasmus and printer/publisher John Froben, and Pope Clement VII and Benvenuto Cellini; also a fictitious letter from Luther to his "rib," Katie. With a short bibliography of works by Mr. Bowen.

1641. Zapf, Hermann and John Dreyfus. CLASSICAL TYPOGRAPHY IN THE COMPUTER AGE. PAPERS PRESENTED AT A CLARK LIBRARY SEMINARY. Los Angeles: William Andrews Clark Memorial Library, 1991, 8vo., stiff paper wrappers. xv, 36 pages. $ 15.00

First edition. The essays contained in this book examine the recent developments in printing technology. These new developments have opened the field of graphic arts from political, social or economic constraints that once threatened freedom of the press and helped assure the supremacy of the trade. Bidwell's introduction is followed by two essays entitled "Letterpress Printing, Photocomposition, and Desktop Publishing" by Zapf and "Who is to Design Books Now That Computers are Making Books" by Dreyfus. Designed and printed at the Castle Press.

1642. (Zapf, Hermann) HERMANN ZAPF & HIS DESIGN PHILOSOPHY, SELECTED ARTICLES AND LECTURES OF CALLIGRAPHY AND CONTEMPORARY DEVELOPMENTS IN TYPE DESIGN, WITH ILLUSTRATIONS AND BIBLIOGRAPHICAL NOTES, AND A COMPLETE LIST OF HIS TYPEFACES. Chicago: Society of Typographic Arts, (1987), 4to., cloth, dust jacket. (ii), 254, (2) pages. $ 135.00

First edition. Filled with illustrations, often in color. Shows all 175 typefaces he designed including a number that have never been seen before. Jacket chipped with small tears.

Item 1643

1643. Zapf, Hermann. PEN AND GRAVER, ALPHABETS & PAGES OF CAL-
LIGRAPHY. With a Preface by Paul Standard. Cut in Metal by Augst Rosenberger.
New York: Museum Books, (1952), oblong 4to., parchment-backed boards. Not paginated. $475.00
First edition in English, limited to 2000 copies. Printed by D. Stempel on Italian Fabriano paper. A landmark in the history of calligraphy. The text is set in the Palatino type, designed for the foundry by the
author for use in the original German edition.

1644. Zapf, Hermann. TYPOGRAPHISCHE VARIATIONEN, 78 BUCHTITEL
UND TEXTSEITEN ALS GESTALTUNGSMOGLICHKEITEN DER TY-
POGRAPHIE UND BUCHGRAPHIK ENTWORFEN VON HERMANN
ZAPF. Frankfurt am Main: Leonhard Keller und Arthur Wetzig, 1963, 4to., paper cov-
ered boards, leather spine label. Not paginated. $290.00
The trade edition of the German printing of this famous book. Introduction in German by Georg Kurt
Schauer, in English by Paul Standard and in French by Charles Peignot. Set in 16 languages with the
types of D. Stempel "taken from the foundry's archives" and printed by Heinrich Egenolf. A magnificent
display of typography and type specimens printed in black with some part printed in an alternative color.
Enclosed in original mailing box. As new copy.

Books about Private Press and Fine Printing

1645. (Aldebrink Press) Seymour, Ralph Fletcher. SOME WENT THIS WAY, A FORTY YEAR PILGRIMAGE AMONG ARTISTS, BOOKMEN AND PRINTERS. Chicago: Privately printed, (1945), 8vo., cloth, dust jacket. 294 pages. $ 55.00
First edition. Includes the history of the Aldebrink Press, reminiscences of Copeland & Day, Way & Williams, etc. Jacket doesn't quite fit book as is true with all copies. Presentation from the author on half-title. Jacket has paper repair on back cover.

1646. (Anthoensen, Fred) Whitehill, Walter Muir. FRED ANTHOENSEN, A LECTURE. New York: The Composing Room, 1966, 8vo., cloth, box with paper label on front. 18 pages followed by a facsimile of a letter from Paul Standard. $ 75.00
First edition, limited to 385 copies. Issued as a Christmas book by the Anthoensen Press and with greetings loosely inserted. Box is faded.

1647. Archer, H. Richard and Ward Ritchie. MODERN FINE PRINTING. Los Angeles: William Andrews Clark Memorial Library, 1968, 8vo., paper wrappers. (iv), 44 pages. $ 20.00
Contains "The Private Press: Its Essence and Recrudescence" by Archer and "Tradition and the Printers of Southern California" by Ritche. Covers faded.

1648. (Archer, John) SAGITTARIUS: HIS BOOK, GATHERED FOR JOHN ARCHER BY HIS FRIENDS. New York: The Typophiles, 1951, tall 12mo., cloth. (x), 94 pages. $ 45.00
Limited to 640 copies; the 25th Chapbook issued by the Typophiles. Has a title page designed by Dwiggins, contributions by Warren Chappell, Bruce Rogers, Paul Bennett and others. Contains reproductions of Archer's design work.

1649. Badaracco, Claire Hoertz. TRADING WORDS; POETRY, TYPOGRAPHY AND ILLUSTRATED BOOKS IN THE MODERN LITERARY ECONOMY. Baltimore: Johns Hopkins University Press, 1995, 8vo., cloth, dust jacket. xiii, (iii), 259 pages. $ 37.00
First Edition. William Morris and mass advertising? Moby Dick and marketing goals? Russian revolutionaries and commercial art? Monotype sans serif and corporate identity? Designers and printers as celebrities? Case studies in literary, business, and cultural history, 1900–1940. This book "examines how theories of mass society first appeared as developments in the commercial sector; how artists, poets, writers, graphic designers, and illustrators contributed to the modern literary economy; how those in the publicity trades relied on an audience whose "childish faith" in words seemed nearly universal; and how the business imagination shaped certain ideas in twentieth-century culture." (author's preface). The case studies in "this volume illustrate that process where the meaning of a public text is negotiated, as it took place among aesthetic revolutionaries... the imagist poets...the new typographers at British Monotype...the printers of R.R. Donnelly's 'definitive' New American Books, and Macy's marketing of the 'Limited' Editions Club." (p.192) This book offers an interesting perspective on printing and typography, book design and illustration, and modernism and publishing during an era of great change.

1650. (Beaumont Press) Beaumont, Cyril W. FIRST SCORE. Bronxville: Nicholas T. Smith, (1980), 8vo., cloth, dust jacket. (xi), 96, (3) pages. $ 25.00
Reprint of the first edition, originally printed in 1927 and limited to 390 copies. The history of this press with bibliographical information on the first twenty books issued. With much on book production.

1651. Bigelow, Charles, Paul Hayden, and Linnea Gentry (Editors). FINE PRINT ON TYPE. THE BEST OF FINE PRINT MAGAZINE ON TYPE AND TYPOGRAPHY. San Francisco: Fine Print, 1988, 4to., cloth, dust-jacket. (viii), 148 pages. $ 45.00
First edition. An anthology of the most interesting and informative articles published in Fine Print under the title "On Type." Covers a wide range of topics from the sixteenth century to the present day.

1652. (Black Sun Press) Minkoff, George Robert. BIBLIOGRAPHY OF THE BLACK SUN PRESS. With an Introduction by Caresse Crosby. Great Neck: G.R. Minkoff, 1970, 4to., cloth. 60 pages. $ 45.00
First edition, limited to 1250 copies.

1653. (Bodoni) Schröder, Fritz. GIAMBATTISTA BODONI. EINE KULTURHIS-TORISCHE STUDIE. Berlin: Mergenthaler Setzmaschinen-Fabrik, 1938, large 12mo., quarter cloth with paper covered boards. 32 pages. $ 30.00
First edition. A study of Giambattista Bodoni and his importance to the development of typography. Schröder provides a short outline of his life. Illustrated in black & white. Bibliography at end. Printed with Korpus and Petit Bodoni. In German.

1654. (Book Club of California) Magee, David. BOOK CLUB OF CALIFORNIA, A CATALOGUE OF THE PUBLICATIONS KEEPSAKES & EPHEMERA OF-FERED FOR SALE BY DAVID MAGEE. San Francisco: David Magee, 1964, 8vo., paper wrappers. (46) pages. $ 20.00
The last page contains "Ode on the Great Magee Move" by Herman W. Liebert.

1655. BOOKWAYS. 1. . Austin, TX: W. Thomas Taylor, 1991, small 4to., stiff paper wrappers. 52 pages. $ 15.00
Articles by Harry Duncan and Tom Taylor and many reviews of fine press books.

1656. BOOKWAYS. 3. . Austin, TX: W. Thomas Taylor, 1992, small 4to., stiff paper wrappers. 52 pages. $ 15.00
With Decherd Turner on "A Perplexed Scene," an article by Alastair Johnston and many reviews of fine press books.

1657. BOOKWAYS. 5. . Austin, TX: W. Thomas Taylor, 1992, small 4to., stiff paper wrappers. 56 pages. $ 15.00
With special articles by Tom Taylor describing "Printing from Plastic" and by Frances Butler on "Pou-chois: A Late Twentieth Century Revisit."

1658. BOOKWAYS. 6. . Austin, TX: W. Thomas Taylor, 1993, small 4to., stiff paper wrappers. 56 pages. $ 15.00
With special articles by Richard Kuhta on the Cuala Press and Irish literature, Robert McPhillips on fine press poetry, a conversation with Pam Smith and a look at the private collection of Jerry Kelly.

1659. BOOKWAYS. 7. . Austin, TX: W. Thomas Taylor, 1993, small 4to., stiff paper wrappers. 68 pages. $ 15.00
With special articles by Tom Taylor giving a survey of American typefounders, a look at the private col-lection of Travis Beck, a description of the Barrois collection of printing ephemera and a history of the Providence Public Library by Philip J. Weimerskirch.

1660. BOOKWAYS. 8. . Austin, TX: W. Thomas Taylor, 1993, small 4to., stiff paper wrappers. 76 pages. $ 15.00
With special articles by Martin Antonetti on Italian private press printing, Colin Franklin on "Some Phrase-Books from Old Japan," a conversation with Dwight Agner and others.

1661. BOOKWAYS. 9. . Austin, TX: W. Thomas Taylor, 1993, small 4to., stiff paper wrappers. 72 pages. $ 15.00

With special articles by Gerald Lange on digital type foundries, a survey of American Hand Papermakers, a conversation with Lynne Avadenka, and a look at the private collection of Breon Mitchell.

1662. BOOKWAYS. 10. . Austin, TX: W. Thomas Taylor, 1994, small 4to., stiff paper wrappers. 60 pages. $ 15.00

Articles by Karl Young, Roger Burford Mason on the periodical "Albion," memoirs by Charles Antin, computer printing by Gerald Lange, conversations with Amos Paul Kennedy, Jr. and an interview with the collector, James Beall.

1663. BOOKWAYS. 11. . Austin, TX: W. Thomas Taylor, 1994, small 4to., stiff paper wrappers. 71 pages. $ 15.00

With special articles by fine printing in New Zealand by Alan Loney, private press printing in Australia by Jadwiga Jarvis and glimpses of collectors and libraries in New Zealand, New South Wales and Maori.

1664. BOOKWAYS. 12. . Austin, TX: W. Thomas Taylor, 1994, small 4to., stiff paper wrappers. 76 pages. $ 15.00

With five articles on book collecting stories by Nick Lyons, Linda Hardberger, Rose Glennon, Colin Franklin and Alastair Johnston and conversations with Felicia Rice and another on the bindings of Tim Ely.

1665. BOOKWAYS. 13 & 14. . Austin, TX: W. Thomas Taylor, 1995, small 4to., stiff paper wrappers. 112 pages. $ 20.00

Megan & Paul Benton on various printings of Leaves of Grass, "Words for Vincent Fitz Gerald: A Personal History" by Michael Feingold, articles on William Everson, William Rueter, Joanne Sonnichsen and personal recollections by Paul Hayden Duensing.

1666. (Bradley, Will H.) Bambace, Tony. WILL H. BRADLEY: HIS WORK, A BIBLIOGRAPHICAL GUIDE. New Castle, Delaware and Boston, Massachusetts: Oak Knoll Press and Thomas G. Boss Fine Books, 1995, 8vo., cloth. xxiii, 216 pages. $ 75.00

First edition. A giant in the design field, Will H. Bradley (1868–1962) became and is still widely regarded as one of the masters of book, magazine and graphic design during the Art Nouveau and Arts & Crafts periods. His typographic and illustrative work pushed the boundaries of these fields into new directions. In addition, his re-introduction and use of Caslon type heralded its popularity ad garnered reviewers' praise. Oak Knoll Press now publishes this title for those interested in the design of books, magazines and printed material of the period. The guide also includes 261 illustrations including his designer's marks to help identify his pieces for the art student or historian, art reference librarian and the Bradley collector, making this book an ideal source for such work. The guide itself includes a *Book Work* section containing three parts: one of 81 definite books of Bradley's own execution, one listing those exhibiting the Bradley stamp but with no confirming documentation and one listing those using his designs but were probably not produced by him. The remaining sections document magazine covers, advertisements, illustrations, posters and other works such as programs, catalogues, cards, bookplates, calendars and broadsides among many more examples of Bradley's work.

1667. (Bradley, Will H.) Bambace, Tony. WILL H. BRADLEY: HIS WORK, A BIBLIOGRAPHICAL GUIDE. New Castle, Delaware and Boston, Massachusetts: Oak Knoll Press and Thomas G. Boss Fine Books, 1995, 8vo., quarter leather with paste paper over boards, leather spine label. xxiii, 216 pages. Accompanied by original copies of

RUBÁIYÁT OF OMAR KHÁYYAM, THE ASTRONOMER-POET OF PER-
SIA and LAUNCELOT & THE LADIES, two books with designs by Bradley. All inserted in a cloth clamshell box with a leather spine label. $ 1,000.00
First edition. One of three extra-deluxe copies, signed and numbered by the author. The copy of
Launcelot & The Ladies is inscribed and signed by the author, Will Bradley. Bradley designed the lettering, binding, half title, title page, divisional title page and opening headpiece in this book. The binding
features yellow-green lettering on dark blue cloth. Books with Bradley presentations are quite uncommon.

1668. (Caflisch, Max) Zapf, Hermann et al. MAX CAFLISCH, TYPOGRAPHIA
PRACTICA. Hamburg: Maximilian-Gesellschaft, 1988, tall 4to., grey cloth stamped in
blind and in gilt, cardboard slipcase. 355, (3) pages. $ 175.00
First edition, limited to 1400 copies. An excellently produced new book devoted to the work of the Swiss
designer and type historian, Max Caflisch. Text in German. Contributions by Berlincourt, Bertheau,
Bosshard, Blum, Gschwend, Darrell Hyder (in English), Jager, Ramseger, Romano, Schmid, Stresow,
Unger, Willberg and Hermann Zapf. Filled with illustrations of Caflisch's work with some in color. Also
contains a bibliography.

1669. (Cambridge Christmas Books) Crutchley, Brooke. PRINTER'S CHRISTMAS
BOOKS. With a Foreword by Euan Phillips. London: St. Bride Printing Library, 1975,
square 8vo., stiff paper wrappers. 40 pages. $ 35.00
Reprint of the 1974 Cambridge Christmas Book which describes the other books in the series, a series
which started in 1930. With a number of illustrations.

1670. (Cambridge Christmas Books) Crutchley, Brooke. THE CAMBRIDGE
CHRISTMAS BOOKS. Brighton: (Tony Appleton), 1976, large 12mo., stiff paper
wrappers. (16) pages. $ 65.00
Printed in an edition of 220 signed and numbered copies. Crutchley was University printer at Cambridge
and oversaw the production of the Christmas Book series from its inception 1930 until its discontinuation in 1973. The text is taken from a talk he gave at St. Bride Printing Library in December 1975 at the
opening of an exhibition of the Christmas books. Designed and printed by Sebastian Carter at the Rampant Lions Press, Cambridge. Printed on hand-made Abbey Mills paper.

1671. (Cary, Melbert B. Jr.) THE MELBERT B. CARY, JR. GRAPHIC ARTS COL-
LECTION. Rochester, NY: Rochester institute of Technology School of Printing, n.d.,
slim 8vo., paper wrappers. 15+(1) pages. $ 10.00
A brief description of the important holdings of the Melbert B. Cary, Jr. Graphic Arts Collection in the
graphic arts complex of the Rochester Institute of Technology. In addition to works of historical interest,
many important private presses are represented, including the Press of the Woolly Whale, which Mr.
Cary founded. Illustrated in color.

A LEAF BOOK

1672. CATALOGUE OF AN EXHIBITION OF BOOKS ILLUSTRATING BRITISH
AND FOREIGN PRINTING, 1919 - 1929. London: British Museum, 1929, square 8vo.,
stiff paper wrappers. 57, (3) pages. $ 95.00
Well printed descriptions of the books of the exhibition. Contains seven tipped-in leaves from books
printed by such presses as the Shakespeare Head Press, the Golden Head Press, Bruce Rogers, and D.B.
Updike. Minor wear at spine ends.

1673. Cave, Roderick. PRIVATE PRESS. New York: R.R. Bowker Co., 1983, 4to., cloth,
dust jacket. xvi, 389 pages. $ 64.95
Second edition, revised and enlarged. This work is more than a chronicle for antiquarians, bibliophiles,
collectors, historians, and printing enthusiasts. Roderick Cave transcends a factual documentation of private press activities and brings to a full-bodied text the personal observations and insights of a 25-year

involvement with the private press phenomenon. This selective history spans the private press movement from the origin of printing to the most contemporary private presses. In this edition, Cave has revised the original from 1971 and has added a new chapter on private press printing in the United States and Great Britain from 1970 to 1983 and on private press activity in Canada, Australia, and New Zealand.

1674. (Clam Flat Press) Hawthorne, Roger. UNIQUE PRINT SHOP IS FOUND ON CAPE COD. Barnstable, MA: Harrison C. Kerr, 1964, 12mo., paper wrappers. 10 leaves.
$ 25.00

Third edition. Short article on Harrison C. Kerr's Clam Flat Press. Illustrated with artwork by Marsden Lore.

1675. Clay, Steven (Editor). WHEN WILL THE BOOK BE DONE? GRANARY'S BOOKS. New York: Granary Books, 2001, square 8vo., stiff paper wrappers. 207+(1) pages.
$ 40.00

First edition. Since 1985, Granary Books has brought together bookmakers, writers and artists to explore the relationship between the verbal and the visual. This volume provides a complete bibliography and description of nearly 100 titles pertaining to books, writing and publishing published by Granary. Each entry is annotated with quotes from the artists and writers, critical notes, bibliographic information and full color illustrations. Includes an introduction by Charles Bernstein, a chronological checklist and an index.

1676. (Corvinus Press) Nash, Paul W. and A.J. Flavell. THE CORVINUS PRESS, A HISTORY AND BIBLILOGRAPHY. (Aldershot, England): Scolar Press, (1994), 8vo., cloth, dust jacket. lvi, 245+(1) pages.
$ 80.00

First edition. The Corvinus Press was founded in 1936 by Viscount Carlow, and produced a number of books of typographic and literary importance before Carlow was killed in action in 1944. Carlow was a personal friend of T.E. Lawrence, and was invited to serve on one of the trusts set up to administer Lawrence's estate. This gave him access to Lawrence's unpublished works and inspired him with the idea of printing them himself as an appropriate memorial to his friend. This book provides a full description of all books printed by Lord Carlow as well as substantial appendices, giving details of ephemera, typefaces and papers, and a checklist of books from the Dropmore Press, which took over the stock and equipment of Corvinus in 1945.

1677. (Cranach Press) Schroder, Rudolf Alexander. CRANACH PRESS IN WEIMAR. N.P.: Cranach Press, n.d., 4to., self-paper wrappers. 14 pages. $ 35.00

A history and bibliography of the press. Decorated with woodcuts. This is an English translation of the 1931 Cranach Press edition done by Gallery 303 and John Dreyfus and Heide Gekeler.

1678. (Curwen Press) Gilmour, Pat. ARTISTS AT CURWEN, A CELEBRATION OF THE GIFT OF ARTISTS' PRINTS FROM THE CURWEN PRESS. London: The Tate Gallery, (1977), small 4to., cloth, dust jacket. 167 pages. $ 50.00

First edition. an extensive exhibition catalogue of the works of many artists associated with the Curwen Press and Studio including Paul Nash, John Piper and Henry Moore. The book is illustrated with 32 plates, many of which are in full color. Also has biographical sketches and checklists of the artists' work.

1679. (Curwen Press) Simon, Herbert. SONG AND WORDS, A HISTORY OF THE CURWEN PRESS. London: George Allen & Unwin Ltd., (1973), 8vo., cloth, dust jacket. (viii), 261 pages.
$ 65.00

First edition. History of this important publisher and containing information on Stanley Morison and Claud Lovat Fraser and a checklist of books printed at the Curwen Press.

1680. (Dahlstrom, Grant) Ritchie, Ward and Margot & H. Richard Archer. GRANT DAHLSTROM AT SEVENTY-FIVE (MORE TRIBUTES) BY WARD RITCHIE AND MARGOT & H. RICHARD ARCHER. Los Angeles: the New Ampersand Press, 1978, tall 8vo., paper wrappers. (vi), 6, (4) pages. $ 35.00
First edition, limited to 300 copies.

1681. (Dahlstrom, Grant) TYPOGRAPHY, BOOKS, & PRINTING BY GRANT DAHLSTROM. Los Angeles: University of California, 1946, 8vo., paper wrappers. (ii), 10 pages. $ 15.00
A catalogue for the exhibition held at the University of California in 1946, which featured books by Grant Dahlstrom. There are approximately 90 entries and it include an introduction by Jakob Zeitlin.

1682. (Daniel Press) Madan, F. DANIEL PRESS, MEMORIALS OF C.H.O. DANIEL WITH ADDENDA AND CORRIGENDA. London: Dawsons, (1974), 8vo., cloth. viii, 198, 12 pages and 15 plates. $ 38.00
Reprint of the 1921–1922 Oxford University Press edition. Part of the addenda is a complete descriptive bibliography of the press.

1683. Dematteis, Liliana. LIBRI D'ARTISTA IN ITALIA 1960–1998. Italy: Regione Piemonte, (1968), small 4to., stiff paper wrappers, dust jacket. 285+(1) pages. $ 40.00
First edition. An exhibition catalogue listing 2,928 Italian artists' books published between 1960 and 1998. Works are presented chronologically under artists' names listed in alphabetical order. Includes many black and white reproductions and an introduction, "Artists' Books, Historical Notes and Cultural Contexts," written in Italian and English.

1684. (Derrydale Press) DERRYDALE PRESS BOOKS. Long Valley, New Jersey: Calderwoods Books, n.d., small 8vo., stiff paper wrappers. (ii), 34 pages. $ 15.00
A catalogue of Derrydale Press books and other items which offers 213 books on hunting, fishing, shooting, and other sports. 21 other bibliographies, catalogue and miscellaneous items are also offered.

1685. (Dolmen Press) Miller, Liam (editor). BOOKS AND BOOKLETS PUBLISHED BY THE DOLMEN PRESS, DUBLIN, AUGUST, 1951--APRIL, 1971. (Dublin): Dolmen Press, 1971, 8vo., stiff paper wrappers. 40 pages. $ 35.00
A updated checklist issued to coincide with a retrospective exhibition of Dolmen Press books at Oxford University Press, London, printed in 14 point Pilgrim type (Miller, 178). The Dolmen Press was established in 1951 to publish Irish writers from their own country. The catalogue is arranged chronologically.

1686. (Doves Press) Bakker, Steven A. (editor). CATALOGUE ONE, A PROOFCOPY OF THE FIRST ITEM PRINTED AT THE DOVES PRESS, 1900. (Amsterdam): Antiquariaat De Zilverdistel, (1992), large 12mo., stiff paper wrappers. (vi), 29, (3). $ 15.00
The first full color catalogue of De Zilverdistel, printed in an edition of 850 copies, being just one item, the only known inscribed proofcopy of the first book by Thomas James Cobden-Sanderson, printed at the Doves Press in 1900. With a quotation from Sanderson's diary, a detailed description of the proofcopy, and the entire text of his article on bookbinding. Photographs and facsimiles as illustrations.

1687. (Doves Press) Nordlunde, C. Volmer. THOMAS JAMES COBDEN-SANDERSON, BOGBINDER OG BOGTRYKKER. Kobenhavn: Arnold Busck, 1957, tall 8vo., stiff paper wrappers. 79, (3) pages. $ 60.00
S-K 5511. Limited to 600 copies. With chapters on the Doves Bindery, the Doves Press, etc. and with various illustrations showing his work including a foldout plate.

1688. (Doves Press) Tidcombe, Marianne. DOVES BINDERY. London and New Castle, Delaware: The British Library and Oak Knoll Books, 1991, 4to., cloth. 490 pages. $ 185.00

First edition. This famous bindery was founded by T.J. Cobden-Sanderson in 1893 and over a period of 30 years it produced some of the finest bookbinding ever conceived. In its early years the bindery shared premises with William Morris's Kelmscott Press. The consequent collaboration resulted in a series of richly-decorated copies of the Kelmscott Chaucer. Later on the majority of the bindery's work was for the Doves Press, which Cobden-Sanderson founded with Emery Walker in 1900. Dr. Tidcombe's comprehensive work provides a detailed history of the Bindery and includes a complete catalogue of the books produced, over 120 of which are described in full and illustrated. The text is supported by indexes and appendices, including a discussion of fake bindings discovered by the author in collections all over the world. Well illustrated with over 200 black and white illustrations and 16 pages in color. Now out of print.

1689. Dreyfus, John. A LONDONER'S VIEW OF THREE LOS ANGELES PRINTER FRIENDS AND THEIR WORK: GRANT DAHLSTRON, SAUL MARKS, AND WARD RITCHIE. Los Angeles: Occidental College, 1990, 8vo., stiff paper wrappers. (iv), 37 pages. $ 15.00
Illustrated.

1690. Drucker, Johanna. FIGURING THE WORD, ESSAYS ON BOOKS, WRITING, AND VISUAL POETICS. New York: Granary Books, 1998, 8vo., stiff paper wrappers. xiv, 312 pages. $ 24.95
First edition. A collection of selected writings by Drucker which have been previously published in literary or scholarly journals from the early 1980's to the present. The essays are written in a variety of styles and in a variety of formats which reflect the many aspects of her work and thinking. Illustrated.

1691. Drucker, Johanna. THE CENTURY OF ARTISTS' BOOKS. New York: Granary Books, (1995), 8vo., cloth, dust jacket. xii, 377 pages. $ 35.00
First edition. Contains 200 halftone illustrations. Covers Russian Futurism and Surrealism to Fluxus, Conceptual art to Postmodernism.

1692. (Edizioni Dell'Elefante) EDIZIONI DELL'ELEFANTE 1964–1990, WORK OF THE ROMAN PUBLISHERS. Cambridge: Harvard College Library, (1990), oblong 8vo., paper wrappers, dust jacket. 20 pages. $ 15.00
Annotated exhibition catalogue describing 36 items. Creased.

1693. (Equinox Cooperative Press) Hart, Henry. RELEVANT MEMOIR, THE STORY OF THE EQUINOX COOPERATIVE PRESS. With a Foreword by Lynd Ward. New York: Three Mountains Press, 1977, 8vo., cloth, dust jacket. 111 pages including facsimiles of Ward drawings and a bibliography of the press. $ 25.00
First edition. At the very bottom of the Great Depression in the United States, a group of young men and women in and around the book business formed a cooperative corporation dedicated to publishing works of literary significance that commercially-minded publishers were neglecting, and to publishing such works in ways that enabled the graphic arts to illuminate as well as enhance an author's meaning. Such idealism usually withers as soon as it blossoms but the Equinox Cooperative Press succeeded, and the present memoir describes the participants in that valiant enterprise, their motives, the principles that guided them, their mode of work, the books they published, and the reasons they disbanded just when they were the most profitable.

1694. (Eragny Press) Pissarro, Lucien. NOTES ON THE ERAGNY PRESS. N.P.: Heritage Series, n.d., 8vo., paper wrappers. 8 pages. $ 15.00
Reprinted from an edition published by The Cambridge University Press. Illustrated.

1695. (Eragny Press) Urbanelli, Lora. BOOK ART OF LUCIEN PISSARRO, WITH A BIBLIOGRAPHIC LIST OF THE BOOKS OF THE ERAGNY PRESS 1894–1914. London: Moyer Bell, 1997, 8vo., quarter cloth with decorated paper covered boards, dust jacket. 127 pages with colophon. $ 29.95
First edition. Contains 62 pages of plates of wood-engraved illustrations along with 17 pages of color illustrations. This the most thorough introduction to the life and work of Lucien Pissaro, son of the Impressionist artist Camille Pissaro. This volume establishes Lucien Pissaro as a creator and entrepreneur in his own right. The bibliography is nothing more than a chronological list with a reproduction of a title page.

1696. Eshelman, Willliam R. (Editor). SOME CALIFORNIA PRINTERS AND THEIR CHAPELS, INSERTS FROM THE CALIFORNIA LIBRARIAN 1960–1963. N.P.: n.p., n.d. (circa 1993), large 8vo., 13 single folded sheets inserted in tri-fold paper portfolio with paper cover label. $ 75.00
The thirteen inserts taken from issues of the *California Librarian* form a short history of printing in California in the early 1960's. Designed to provide a discussion of the printer's work as well as an illustration of it, all of the samples except for the ones on Cheney, Stricker and Anderson were printed by the subjects. Includes a copy of an excerpt from a letter by Eshelman to the Stone House Press, July 8, 1993 detailing the project. Small tear to upper corner of portfolio.

1697. (Everson, William) WILLIAM EVERSON, A COLLECTION OF BOOKS & MANUSCRIPTS. Santa Barbara, CA: Joseph the Provider Books, (1987), 8vo., stiff paper wrappers. (x), 53+(1) pages. $ 10.00
First edition, limited to 500 copies, 100 of which are hardbound. With a foreword by Ralph B. Sipper and preface by William Everson. Story of Everson's life, his own philosophy plus a 222 item bibliography of his works.

1698. (Fendrick Gallery) Fendrick, Daniel. THE BOOK AS ART. Two volumes. Washington, D.C.: Fendrick Gallery, 1976; (1977), large 12mo.; small 8vo., stiff paper wrappers. (16); (18) pages. $ 15.00
Two catalogues for "Artists' Books" exhibitions held at the Fendrick Gallery. Volume I lists and describes works exhibited from January 12 - February 14, 1976. Volume II Catalogues works exhibited from February 15 - March 12, 1977. Leaflet with price quotes inserted in both Catalogues. Both volumes nicely illustrated with photographs by John Tennant. Depict designs by Buckminster Fuller and Barton Lidicé Benes, among many others.

1699. Fine, Ruth E. THE PATRICIA G. ENGLAND COLLECTION OF FINE PRESS AND ARTISTS BOOKS. Washington: National Gallery of Art, (2000), tall thin 4to., stiff paper wrappers. 88 pages. $ 24.95
A list of the books in the collection of Patricia England which consists of fine press and artist books which vary in range from Shakespearean drama to poetry by Pablo Neruda. It includes an interview with England by Ruth Fine, curator of modern prints and drawings of the National Gallery of Art. Lamia Doumato compiled annotated entries on each book and the text was edited by Ulrike Mills. It is illustrated in color with eleven selections from the collection. Index.

1700. FINE PRINT, A NEWSLETTER FOR THE ARTS OF THE BOOK. (Title changed to FINE PRINT, THE REVIEW FOR THE ARTS OF THE BOOK after volume II, no.1). Volume I, no.1 to Volume XVI, no.3, a complete set. San Francisco: Fine Print, 1975–1990, 4to., stiff paper wrappers. $ 575.00
Complete run of this periodical. Volume I,1 (1975) to Vol 16,3(1990) for a total of 63 issues Filled with information on the private press, printing and bookbinding.

1701. (Foulis, T.N.) Elfick, Ian and Paul Harris. T.N. FOULIS, THE HISTORY AND BIBLIOGRAPHY OF AN EDINBURGH PUBLISHING. New Castle, Delaware and London: Oak Knoll Press & Werner Shaw Ltd., 1998, small 8vo., cloth, dust jacket. 277 pages. $ 55.00

First edition. Operating from Edinburgh and London, the firm, T. N. Foulis, published more than 400 titles during the period 1904-25. The vast majority of their books were produced to the most exacting of standards. In recent times, the hallmarks of a Foulis book in the form of colored buckram bindings, tipped-in color plates, the elegant Auriol typeface and rose-watermarked paper have drawn collectors to these elegant volumes. Today, such features are virtually unheard of in a world of generally uniform book production. Once handled, any true bibliophile must find it difficult to put down a Foulis-produced book. From the handsome classics sturdily bound in buckram to the charming so-called envelope books developed in the first decade of the century developed essentially as gift books, the Foulis output is quite unique, and they are now being increasingly sought after. Although it is still relatively easy to obtain a handsomely produced copy of the publisher's bestselling, *Reminiscences of Scottish Life and Character* by Dean Ramose, well-preserved copies of the charming and fragile envelope books, many of them illustrated by artists of the caliber of Jessie M. King, W. Russell Flint, Frank Brangwyn, and F. Cayley Robinson, are now very difficult to find. The authors, both longstanding collectors of Foulis productions, have faced many complexities in preparing this history and bibliography. The publisher, Thomas Noble Foulis, is something of an enigma, born and raised in Edinburgh and dying in obscurity in Essex after the failure of the firm to which he devoted himself. Foulis listed many books which were never published in advertisements and catalogues. Those which were published appeared in many puzzling variants of bindings and formats, sometimes in different series from those announced and in very small editions. Descendants of Thomas Foulis have no records today of their now illustrious forbear. No official records or letter books of the firm survive. All these circumstances have contributed to painstaking detective work by the authors, both collectors and witnesses to all copies of the books listed in the bibliography. Illustrated. SALES RIGHTS: Available in North & South America from Oak Knoll Books. Available outside North & South America from Werner Shaw Ltd.

1702. Franklin, Colin. PRIVATE PRESSES. Chester Springs: Dufour, (1969), 8vo., cloth, dust jacket. 240 pages. $ 54.00

First U.S. edition. Discussion of the Daniel Press, Kelmscott Press, Ashendene, Essex House, Vale, Eragny, Doves, etc., with bibliographies.

1703. (Baskin, Leonard) Van Wingen, Peter M. CAPRICES, GROTESQUES & HOMAGES, LEONARD BASKIN AND THE GEHENNA PRESS (EXHIBITION CATALOG). Washington, DC: Library of Congress, (1994), small 4to., stapled stiff paper wrappers. unpaginated, but 12 pages. $ 15.00

A catalogue issued by the Library of Congress Rare Book and Special Collections Division for its 1994 exhibit on Leonard Baskin's career as a designer and printer of fine, limited edition books, started with the founding of the Gehenna Press in 1942 when he was a student at Yale. With an Exhibition checklist. Illustrations. Letter laid in from woman who attended the exhibit opening.

1704. (Gehenna Press) Brook, Stephen. BIBLIOGRAPHY OF THE GEHENNA PRESS, 1942–1975. Northampton: J.P. Dwyer, 1976, 8vo., cloth. xvi, 77, (3) pages.
                                                                              $ 85.00

Limited to 400 numbered copies. Biographical and bibliographical information.

1705. (Gehenna Press) GEHENNA PRESS, THE WORK OF FIFTY YEARS, 1942–1992, THE CATALOGUE OF AN EXHIBITION CURATED BY LISA UNGER BASKIN CONTAINING AN ASSESSMENT OF THE WORK OF THE PRESS BY COLIN FRANKLIN, A BIBLIOGRAPHY OF THE BOOKS OF THE GEHENNA PRESS BY HOSEA BASKIN & NOTES ON THE BOOKS BY

THE PRINTER, LEONARD BASKIN. Dallas and Northampton: The Bridwell Library & The Gehenna Press, (1992), small 4to., stiff paper wrappers. (ii), 238, (2) pages.
$50.00
Limited to 2000 copies. Filled with illustrations including a number in color. An excellent reference work for anyone interested in the privately printed book during the 20th century.

1706. (Gehenna Press) GEHENNA PRESS, THE WORK OF FIFTY YEARS, 1942–1992, THE CATALOGUE OF AN EXHIBITION CURATED BY LISA UNGER BASKIN CONTAINING AN ASSESSMENT OF THE WORK OF THE PRESS BY COLIN FRANKLIN, A BIBLIOGRAPHY OF THE BOOKS OF THE GEHENNA PRESS BY HOSEA BASKIN & NOTES ON THE BOOKS BY THE PRINTER, LEONARD BASKIN. Dallas and Northampton: The Bridwell Library & The Gehenna Press, (1992), small 4to., cloth, paper spine and cover labels. (ii), 238, (2) pages.
$125.00
Limited to 2000 copies, the hardbound version. Filled with illustrations including a number in color. An excellent reference work for anyone interested in the privately printed book during the 20th century.

1707. (German Printing) GERMAN FINE PRINTING 1948–1988. New York: The Grolier Club, 1992, 8vo., stiff paper wrappers. not paginated.
$25.00
Printed in an edition limited 1500 copies. A checklist of an exhibition held at The Grolier Club, December 18, 1991 to March 12, 1992, on German printing. It was printed by letterpress from Joseph Blumenthal's Emerson and Hermann Zapf's Hunt roman types at The Stinehour Press. Includes 130 entries and is illustrated. Distributed for the Typophiles by Oak Knoll Press.

1708. (Gill, Eric) Gill, Evan. ERIC GILL, A BIBLIOGRAPHY. Revised by D. Steven Corey and Julia Mackenzie. Winchester: St Paul's Bibliographies, 1991, 8vo., cloth, dust jacket. xv, 368 pages.
$60.00
It is fifty years since the death of Eric Gill (1882–1940) and yet the reputation of this remarkable artist and thinker continues to grow. Famous for his stone carving, wood engraving, type designs and writing, he has also found a wide appeal amongst a younger generation who are sympathetic to his outlook on life - to "make a cell of good living in the chaos of our world." Since the original bibliography by Gill's brother, Evan, was published in 1953, a great deal of new material has come to light in the fine collections built up in the USA and elsewhere in recent years, and this new edition is a complete revision of the original bibliography. It includes not only all the new discoveries but also the material published on Gill in the last thirty-eight years. The number of bibliographical entries has increased by over one third in this greatly expanded work. The book has been redesigned with advice from Gill's nephew, Christopher Skelton, placing greater emphasis on the illustrations which have been either retaken from the original editions or introduced as completely new ones of bibliographical interest.

1709. (Gill, Eric) Kindersley, David. MR ERIC GILL. New York: The Typophiles, 1967, 12mo., cloth. 26 pages.
$45.00
First edition, limited to 400 copies for the Typophiles out of the total edition. Chapbook 44.

1710. (Gill, Eric) Skelton, Christopher. ERIC GILL, THE ENGRAVINGS. Boston: Godine, (1990), thick 4to., cloth, dust jacket. 478 pages.
$75.00
Reprint of the edition designed by Skelton. Over 1000 engravings described and illustrated.

1711. (Gill, Eric) Speaight, Robert. LIFE OF ERIC GILL. London: Methuen & Co., (1966), 8vo., cloth, dust jacket. xviii, 323 pages.
$45.00
First Edition.

1712. (Gilliss, Walter) WALTER GILLISS, 1855–1925. New York: Douglas McMurtrie, 1925, 12mo., parchment wrappers. 30 pages. $ 40.00

Tributes to Gilliss issued as a Christmas greeting. Printed on Japan vellum. Slightly soiled cover, else fine.

1713. Gilliss, Walter. RECOLLECTIONS OF THE GILLISS PRESS AND ITS WORK DURING FIFTY YEARS 1869–1919. New York: The Grolier Club, 1926, 8vo., leather-backed boards, top edge gilt, others uncut. xxii, 134 pages. $ 70.00

First edition, limited to 300 copies and printed on hand-made paper. With 13 plates and 2 illustrations in the text. Contains a short-title list of the imprints of this famous press. Gilliss printed many of the fine productions of William Loring Andrews. Wear at top of spine and a few other places on spine.

1714. (Gogmagog Press) Chambers, David, Colin Franklin and Alan Tucker. MORRIS COX & THE GOGMAGOG PRESS. Pinner, Middlesex: Private Libraries Association, 1991, small 4to., cloth. 184 pages. $ 90.00

A tribute to the work of Morris Cox and his Gogmagog Press. Cox started his press, in 1957, as a means to present his own poetry and illustrations, in the meanwhile, creating some beautiful bindings and some highly individual techniques in printing. The text presents Cox's life and work, some of his poetry and illustrations and a lengthy and well annotated bibliography of the press. Well illustrated throughout, some in color. Available in North and South America; other areas from Private Library Association.

1715. (Grabhorn Press) CATALOGUE OF SOME FIVE HUNDRED EXAMPLES OF THE PRINTING OF EDWIN & ROBERT GRABHORN OFFERED FOR SALE AT THE BOOK SHOP OF DAVID MAGEE. San Francisco: David Magee, n.d., 4to., paper wrappers. xvi, 63 pages. $ 45.00

Contains the essay "Two Gentlemen from Indiana." Bumped at spine ends.

1716. (Grabhorn Press) CATALOGUE OF SOME FIVE HUNDRED EXAMPLES OF THE PRINTING OF EDWIN & ROBERT GRABHORN OFFERED FOR SALE AT THE BOOK SHOP OF DAVID MAGEE. San Francisco: David Magee, n.d., 4to., paper wrappers. xvi, 63 pages. $ 35.00

Contains the essay "Two Gentlemen from Indiana." Spine covering is damaged. Tape marks on endpapers.

1717. (Gregynog Press) Harrop, Dorothy. HISTORY OF THE GREGYNOG PRESS. Middlesex: Private Libraries Association, 1980, small 4to., cloth. xv, 266 pages. $ 85.00

First edition, one of 750 copies for sale out of a total edition of 2500. A history of the press and a revised bibliography of the forty-five books printed there. Many illustrations. Also includes a handlist of ephemera with 235 items described.

1718. (Gregynog Press) Hutchins, Michael. PRINTING AT GREGYNOG, ASPECTS OF A GREAT PRIVATE PRESS. Translated by David Jenkins. N.P.: Welsh Arts Council, 1976, small 4to., stiff paper wrappers. 39 pages. $ 25.00

Well illustrated guide to the exhibition. With text in Gaelic and English.

1719. (Gregynog Press) LIST TWO, THE GREGYNOG PRESS. Belgium: De Zilverdistel N.V. Rare Books, 1996, large 8vo., spiral bound with acetate front wrapper and paper back wrapper, (v), 15 pages. $ 10.00

First edition. Sales catalogue issued in March 1996 for Zilverdistel N.V. Rare Books. Lists 34 works published by the Gregynog Press plus four more from Gwasg Gregynog.

1720. (Hague & Gill) PRINTED BY HAGUE AND GILL, A CHECKLIST PRE-PARED IN CONJUNCTION WITH THE EXHIBIT "A RESPONSIBLE WORKMAN" OBSERVING ERIC GILL'S CENTENARY. N.P.: The Regents of the University of California, 1982, 8vo., stiff paper wrappers. 48 pages. $ 35.00

A checklist of Gill's works, posters and one-page job printings omitted, and a lengthy introduction by James Davis. With a list of works typeset by Hague and Gill but printed elsewhere, and a chronology. Illustrated with devices by Gill.

1721. (Hammer, Victor) Graves, Joseph. VICTOR HAMMER, CALLIGRAPHER, PUNCH-CUTTER, & PRINTER. Charlottesville: Bibliographical Society of the University of Virginia, 1954, 12mo., self paper wrappers. 12 pages. $ 7.50

A biographical sketch of this noted private pressman.

1722. (Hammer Creek Press) Cohen, Herman. CHECKLIST OF THE HAMMER CREEK PRESS. In Quarterly News Letter of the Book Club of California, Vol. XXVII, No.4, Fall 1962,. 8vo., stiff paper wrappers. pp.82- 88. $ 15.00

Descriptions of 56 items. Also has an article on the press by Jackson Burke.

1723. (Hoffman, Richard J.) CELEBRATING THE LIFE OF RICHARD J. HOFF-MAN, A BOOKMAN'S BOOKMAN, THE PRINTER, A PRACTICAL PRINT-ER, A BRIEF HISTORY. N.P.: n.p., n.d., 8vo., cloth. (iv), 57, (3) pages. $ 65.00

Limited to 400 copies printed letterpress. With contributions by Reverend Richard J. Bower, Ethan B. Lipton, Doyce B. Nunis, Ward Ritchie, Richard Docter and Clifford G. Dobson. A memorial to this noted printer and private pressman.

1724. (Hoffman, Richard J.) Lipton, Ethan B. (editor). RICHARD J. HOFFMAN: PRINTER AND TEACHER OF PRINTING. Los Angeles: California State University, 1978, 8vo., cloth-backed decorated paper covered boards, paper spine label. (xii), 140, (20) pages. $ 75.00

Limited to 400 copies. Tipped-in frontispiece portrait of Hoffman followed by articles and tributes by Ward Ritchie, Muir and Glen Dawson, Carey Bliss, Grant Dahlstrom and many others. With a bibliography of the works of this private pressman.

1725. (Hogarth Press) Luedeking, Leila and Michael Edmonds. LEONARD WOOLF: A BIBLIOGRAPHY. New Castle, Delaware and Winchester: Oak Knoll Books and St Paul's Bibliographies, 1992, 8vo., cloth. xvi, 296 pages. $ 78.00

First edition. The first volume in the Winchester Bibliographies of Twentieth Century Writers series. The full stature of Leonard Woolf can only be appreciated by an awareness of all his writings and of the influence he exerted in the first half of this century. His book, *International Government*, became one of the formative influences on the League of Nations; through his writings he became the architect of the Labour Party's often enlightened foreign policy between the Wars; through his literary editorship of the *New Statesman* and his founding of the *Political Quarterly*, his integrity and clear thinking were widely manifest. Woolf's excellent judgement as the publisher at the Hogarth Press was no better shown than by his early awareness of the importance of Freud's ideas, whose complete works were published by the Press in translation. This bibliography of all Woolf's publications will certainly increase our appreciation of his abilities both as a writer and thinker. There are four main sections to the bibliography: Books and Pamphlets, Contributions to Books and Pamphlets, Contributions to Periodicals (of which there are approx. 1,000), and Manuscript Collections. There is also a chronology of Woolf's life and main works plus three appendices on various aspects of his writing. *Leonard Woolf: A Bibliography* will be welcomed by the ever-increasing number of Bloomsbury Group collectors and enthusiasts, as well as librarians and scholars in the field of literature and political history.

1726. (Hogarth Press) Willis Jr, J.H. LEONARD AND VIRGINIA WOOLF AS PUBLISHERS: THE HOGARTH PRESS, 1917-41. Charlottesville: University Press of Virginia, (1992), thick 8vo., two toned cloth, dust jacket. xviii, 451 pages.
$ 35.00

First edition. Gives detailed financial information on specific books published by the press.

1727. (Hogarth Press) Woolmer, J. Howard. CHECKLIST OF THE HOGARTH PRESS, 1917–1938. With a Short History of the Press by Mary E. Gaither. Andes: Woolmer - Brotherson Ltd, 1976, 8vo., cloth, dust jacket. xi, 177 pages. $ 25.00
First edition. Much on Virginia and Leonard Woolf.

1728. Hubert, Renee Riese and Judd D. THE CUTTING EDGE OF READING: ARTISTS' BOOKS. New York: Granary Books, 1999, small 4to., leatherette, dust jacket. (vi), 266 pages. $ 55.00
First edition. This volume extends the work initiated by Renee Hubert in "Surrealism and the Book," (University of California Press, 1987), by focusing critical attention on recent and contemporary artists' books. The study begins with a chapter on "Transitions," which discusses the work of Pierre Alechinsky and Paolo Boni and others. It is illustrated throughout in black and white and includes a bibliography and index.

1729. (Hunter, Dard) Preissig, Vojtech. DEAR MR. HUNTER, THE LETTERS OF VOJTECH PREISSIG TO DARD HUNTER 1920 –1925. Buffalo: P22 Editions, 2000, small 8vo., stiff paper wrappers. x, (ii), 63, (3) pages. $ 14.95
First edition, limited to 1000 copies. A collection of letters from Vojtech Preissig, an accomplished Czech typographer, book designer, and artist who in the 1890's became involved in the book arts and especially in the "book beautiful" movement. Preissig began writing to Hunter in 1920 and 46 of these letters are included here. Illustrated.

1730. (Insel-Verlag) Brinks, John Dieter. VOM ORNAMENT ZUR LINIE, DER FRÜHE INSEL-VERLAG 1899 BIS 1924. 2. Berlin: Triton, 2000, 4to., linen-covered boards, both volumes enclosed in a linen slipcase. 391,(3) pages; 20 inserts in portfolio. $ 200.00
Printed in an edition of 2000 copies. Volume I of a series of three installments, not yet completed. Praised as "a masterpiece of book production" and "a product of enthusiasts" by critic Wilfried F.Schoeller, the book traces the early 20th-century history of the Insel publishing house. Insel earned its renown by turning book production into an art form as it printed the works of classic authors and gave a new generation of writers, such as Rainer Maria Rilke, their start. The editor Brinks reveals Insel's high aesthetic standards through sumptuous illustrations of its work. In all, there are 240 illustrations, seven of which are foldouts, many polychrome with three and four colors, and many with stunning gold print. One splendid example of the high-quality illustrations is the foldout of a series of classics, *The Thousand and One Nights* and the *Decameron*, the bindings designed by Marcus Behmer. The colors are so rich and the detail so striking that the reader almost feels he can touch and leaf through the deckled pages of the books shown. Another example depicted is that of Henry van de Velde's designs for the covers of Nietzsche's *Also Sprach Zarathustra*, as well as sample pages from the edition, both finely detailed with gold print. Text edited by Brinks with 17 essays contributed by him and 12 other specialists such as Juergen Suess, Marcus Haucke, and Suzanne Buchinger. Essays beautifully printed with wide margins and double-spaced on Gardapat paper in cursive Borgis White Antiqua. Outstanding documentation for the essays at the back of the book, as well as detailed indices for artwork and literary sources. Accompanying the book is a slim briefcase volume containing 12 facsimile resolution papers and 8 folder reproductions in their original format. Distributed for Triton in North America by Oak Knoll Press. In German.

1731. (Janus Press) Lehrer, Ruth Fine. JANUS PRESS 1955-75 CATALOGUE RAISONNE. Burlington: The University of Vermont, 1975, small 8vo., paper wrappers. 43 pages. $ 20.00
Originally published by the Private Library Associations, this edition contains new material. It was published in conjunction with an exhibition at the University.

1732. (Jones, George W.) CATALOGUE OF THE WELL-KNOWN COLLECTION OF RARE AND VALUABLE BOOKS ILLUSTRATING THE HISTORY OF PRINTING, FORMED BY GEORGE W. JONES. London: Sotheby & Co., 1936, tall 8vo., paper wrappers. (viii), 74 pages. $ 35.00
Some illustrations in the text but no plates. Sale catalogue of the books of this private pressman and typographer.

1733. (Kelmscott Press) Forman, H. Buxton. BOOKS OF WILLIAM MORRIS, DESCRIBED WITH SOME ACCOUNT OF HIS DOINGS IN LITERATURE AND IN THE ALLIED CRAFTS. New York: Burt Franklin, (1969), 8vo., cloth. xv, 224 pages. $ 65.00
Reprint of the 1897 first edition. A annotated bibliography.

1734. (Kelmscott Press) KELMSCOTT PRESS, WILLIAM MORRIS & HIS CIRCLE. Exeter, NH: The Colophon Book Shop, 1996, small 8vo., stiff paper wrappers with cloth taped-spine. 143+(1) pages. $ 10.00
Well printed sales catalogue describing the collection of John J. Walsdorf. With a one page preface by Walsdorf.

1735. (Kelmscott Press) Lawrence, David J (editor). KELMSCOTT PRESS & ITS LEGACY. Dallas, TX: Bridwell Library, 1996, small 8vo., stiff paper wrappers. (viii), 60, (2) pages. $ 15.00
First edition, limited to 500 copies. catalogue for an exhibition held to mark the 100th anniversary of the death of William Morris at the Bridwell Library at the Southern Methodist University in Dallas, Texas in 1996. Includes an introduction by curator Isaac M. Gewirtz followed by a checklist of the exhibition. Includes items relating to the Medieval Ideal, and the Kelmscott, Ashendene, Vale, Eragny, Essex, and Doves presses.

1736. (Kelmscott Press) Peterson, William S. KELMSCOTT PRESS, A HISTORY OF WILLIAM MORRIS'S. N.P.: University of California Press, 1991, thick 4to., cloth, dust jacket. xiv, 371+(1) pages. $ 125.00
First U.S. edition finely printed in two colors throughout at England's Alden Press. The best modern history of the Kelmscott press. Well illustrated and indexed.

1737. (Kelmscott Press) Ritchie, Ward and S. Dale Harris. WILLIAM MORRIS AND THE KELMSCOTT PRESS. (Palo Alto, CA: Stanford University Library, 1967), small 8vo., stiff paper wrappers. (8) pages. $ 10.00
Two essays printed on the occasion of the opening of the *William Morris Show* at the Stanford University Library, May 18, 1967. The label on the cover is a facsimile of William Morris' first Kelmscott Press mark which was originally cut in wood by him. Offset to label.

1738. (Kelmscott Press) Vallance, Aymer. WILLIAM MORRIS, HIS ART HIS WRITINGS AND HIS PUBLIC LIFE. London: Studio Editions, (1986), small 4to., cloth, dust jacket. xiv, 462 pages. $ 65.00
Reprint of the 1897 first edition. Scarce biography of this multi-faceted artist. Illustrated throughout, one in color. Also contains a chronological list of the printed works of William Morris, and a list of the publications of the Kelmscott Press.

1739. (Kelmscott Press) Walsdorf, John J. WILLIAM MORRIS IN PRIVATE PRESS AND LIMITED EDITIONS A DESCRIPTIVE BIBLIOGRAPHY OF BOOKS BY AND ABOUT WILLIAM MORRIS, 1891–1981. Foreword by Sir Basil Blackwell. Phoenix: Oryx Press, 1983, tall 8vo., cloth-backed boards, slipcase. xxvi, 602 pages. $ 125.00

First edition. 208 books bibliographical described. Also reprinted are priced copies of important auction catalogues and bookseller's catalogues listing Morris material including the 1956 Cockerell sale. Presentation from Walsdorf to John DePol on free endpaper and with DePol's bookplate. Postcard from Walsdorf loosely inserted.

1740. (Kelmscott Press) WILLIAM MORRIS AND THE KELMSCOTT PRESS AN EXHIBITION HELD IN THE LIBRARY OF BROWN UNIVERSITY. Providence, RI: Brown University Library, 1960, small 4to., paper wrappers. iii, 49 pages followed by 16 full page plates. $ 25.00

Important exhibition catalogue. Covers slightly faded.

1741. (Kelmscott Press) WORK OF WILLIAM MORRIS, AN EXHIBITION ARRANGED BY THE WILLIAM MORRIS SOCIETY. London: The Times Bookshop, (1962), square 8vo., paper wrappers. 75 pages. $ 30.00

Limited to 2000 copies. Illustrated.

1742. (Kelmscott Press) KELMSCOTT PRESS: 1891 TO 1898 A NOTE BY WILLIAM MORRIS ON HIS AIMS IN FOUNDING THE KELMSCOTT PRESS. A SHORT HISTORY AND DESCRIPTION OF THE KELMSCOTT PRESS. By S.C. Cockerell. New York: The Typophiles, 1984, small 8vo., self paper wrappers. 32 pages. $ 17.50

Facsimiles of both these histories. Illustrated.

1743. Kirshenbaum, Sandra. FIVE FINE PRINTERS: JACK STAUFFACHER, ADRIAN WILSON, RICHARD BIGUS, ANDREW HOYEM, WILLIAM EVERSON. N.P.: Library Associates, University Library, 1979, oblong 8vo., stiff paper wrappers. not paginated. $ 25.00

A unique collaboration at the University of California which presented a panel discussion featuring several well-known fine printers from California. It included an exhibition and a catalogue in which the printers represented the world of fine printing. Illustrated.

1744. Klima, Stefan. ARTISTS BOOKS: A CRITICAL SURVEY OF THE LITERATURE. New York: Granary Books, 1998, small 8vo., stiff paper wrappers. (ii), 110 pages. $ 17.95

First edition. The first published guide to writings on artists books. Included are five essays, with topics such as definition and identity, disputed origins, and current status, along with a carefully researched bibliography. This is an important reference tool for scholars, librarians, critics, collectors, and general readers.

1745. Kotin, David B. READER, LOVER OF BOOKS, LOVER OF HEAVEN, A CATALOGUE BASED ON AN EXHIBITION OF THE BOOK ARTS IN ONTARIO. Two volumes. Willowdale: North York Public Library, 1978, 1981, 8vo., stiff paper wrappers. 109,(3); 79,(3) pages. $ 30.00

With a checklist of Ontario private presses by Marilyn Rueter and an introduction by Douglas Lochhead.

1746. (Kynoch Press) Archer, Caroline. KYNOCH PRESS: THE ANATOMY OF A PRINTING HOUSE. New Castle, Delaware: Oak Knoll Press, 2000, large 8vo., cloth, dust jacket, ISBN: 1-58456-046-0. 240 pages with 68 b/w illustrations. $ 49.95
First edition. The history of the Kynoch Press that Caroline Archer offers is a result of exhaustive research, enriched by personal accounts from surviving staff which give a fascinating perspective on the half-century from 1930 to 1980. This work contains very detailed listings of the types held by the press at every period. Co-published with The British Library - North and South America selling rights. Available January 2001.

1747. Larsen, Poul Steen. CONTEMPORARY DANISH BOOK ART. HELGE ERNST - ILLUSTRATOR; POUL KRISTENS EN - PRINTER; OLE OLSEN - BOOKBINDER. Los Angeles: University of California, (1986), 4to., stiff paper wrappers. 44 pages. $ 25.00
Many illustrations in color.

1748. Lauf, Cornelia. ARTIST/AUTHOR COMTEMPORAY ARTISTS' BOOKS. New York: Distributed Art Publishers Inc. and the American Federation of Arts, (1998), square small 4to., paper covered boards, dust jacket. 183, (3) pages. $ 45.00
An catalogue from the first exhibition about books as an art form organized by The American Federation of Arts, in 1998 and 1999. It featured books that were authored by artist, and "bookworks," meaning artworks in book form. It includes essays about the art of the book by Cornelia Lauf, Glenn O'Brien, Clive Phillpot, Jane Rolo, and Brian Wallis along with and interview with Martha Wilson by Thomas Padon. It is illustrated with several black and white and color plates, and includes a bibliography and an index.

1749. (Lecuire, Pierre) LIBRI DI PIERRE LECUIRE. Florence: Di Centro, 1990, 8vo., stiff paper wrappers. 95 pages. $ 25.00
A catalogue for the exhibition of Pierre Lecuire's works held at the Biblioteca Nazionale Centrale di Firenze from March 14 to April 14, 1990. Lists 32 of Lecuire's books each accompanied by a full page reproduction of an illustration from that particular book. Includes bibliographical references and an index. With an introduction by Lucia Chimirri and a preface by Piero Bigongiari. All in Italian.

1750. Lieberman, Elizabeth Koller. CHECK-LOG OF PRIVATE PRESS NAMES. small 8vo., stiff paper wrappers. $ 10.00
Includes the following years in the series: 2. 1961 (2); 4. 1963 (2). A register of the private press names in use with date started. Price is per issue

1751. (Limited Editions Club) LIMITED EDITIONS CLUB 1990. New Castle, DE: Oak Knoll Books, n.d. (circa 1990), 8vo., paper wrappers. 36 pages. $ 7.50
An Oak Knoll catalogue entirely devoted to publications of the Limited Editions Club; 284 items.

1752. (Limited Editions Club) Meynell, Francis. ADDRESS BY SIR FRANCIS MEYNELL AT THE DEDICATION OF THE GEORGE MACY MEMORIAL COLLECTION OF BOOKS PUBLISHED BY THE LIMITED EDITIONS CLUB, WITH A LIST OF THE TITLES. New York: Columbia University, 1957, 8vo., stiff paper wrappers, paper cover label. 46 pages. $ 15.00
With notes by Bruce Rogers and Helen Macy at beginning of text.

1753. (Limited Editions Club) OAK KNOLL BOOKS CATALOGUE 111. New Castle, DE: Oak Knoll Books, n.d., 8vo., paper wrappers. 89 pages. $ 7.50
Catalogue no.111, including 85 books from the Limited Editions Club.

1754. (Limited Editions Club) OAK KNOLL BOOKS CATALOGUE 135. New Castle, DE: Oak Knoll Books, n.d., 8vo., paper wrappers. 93 pages. $ 7.50
Catalogue no.135, featuring nearly 250 books from the Limited Editions Club.

1755. LIVRES D'ARTISTES DE COLLECTIF GÉNÉRATION. (Paris): Générations A.F.A.A., (1991), 8vo., stiff paper wrappers. 95+(1) pages. $ 30.00
First edition. Gervais Jassaud has gathered together various artists from different cultures to collaborate on books. This enterprise, known as Collectif Génération, has been described as "the only publishing house in the field of artists' books to keep up with its epoch.." This book contains a series of essays devoted to their books. A list of publication from 1968–1976 is found at rear. Illustrated. In English and French.

1756. (Mardersteig, Giovanni) Hagelstange, Rudolf. BEISPIELHAFTES LEBENSWERK, LAUDATION AUF GIOVANNI MARDERSTEIG. Mainz: Gutenberg Gesellschaft, 1968, 8vo., stiff paper wrappers. 15+(1) pages. $ 17.50
Kleiner Druck no.83 issued by this printing museum.

1757. (Marion Press) Larremore, Thomas A. and Amy Hopkins Larremore. MARION PRESS, A SURVEY AND A CHECKLIST. Checklist by Joseph W. Rogers. New Castle, DE: Oak Knoll Books, 1981, 8vo., cloth, dust jacket. xxii, 271 pages. $ 35.00
Frank E. Hopkins set up a press in the attic of his "Red House" in Jamaica, New York in 1896 and named it after his daughter Marion. He printed the first announcement of his press a few months after the death of William Morris and continued printing until his own death in 1933. Unlike most of the founders of private presses in the 1890s, who drifted into printing from other fields, Hopkins was already well schooled in the practical aspects of the printing business. Forced to leave college for financial reasons after his father fell ill he found a job working for the De Vinne Press as a proofreader. The book designs that he subsequently created for De Vinne were among the finest produced by the firm and are generally considered those publications on which De Vinne's considerable reputation was built. Although Hopkins died in relative obscurity, his works remain as an example of the quality of fine printing in America at the turn of the century. Amy and Thomas Larremore, daughter and son-in-law of Frank E. Hopkins, have written a sensitive, in-depth account of his life including an even-handed evaluation of his typography and design work at the Marion Press. In addition Joseph W. Rogers has compiled a detailed, descriptive, bibliographical checklist of Hopkins work at the Marion Press. This fascinating study of a private press was originally published in a limited edition in 1943.

1758. (Marion Press) Larremore, Thomas A. and Amy Hopkins. MARION PRESS; A SURVEY AND A CHECKLIST. Checklist by Joseph W. Rogers. Jamaica, NY: Queens Borough Public Library, 1943, 8vo., cloth. xx, 272, (2) pages. $ 200.00
First edition, limited to 228 numbered copies. The Marion Press was founded by Frank Hopkins, former shop-foreman for Theodore DeVinne. A total of 197 items are described in detail in the book and a 173 page history of the press and the press movement is given which gives much information on turn of the century printing. Loosely inserted are two A.L.s from Larremore (14 pages) in which he discusses this book among other things.

1759. Marks, Lillian. ON PRINTING IN THE TRADITION. Sacramento: California State Library Foundation, 1989, small 8vo., sewn, stiff paper wrappers. (viii), 13, (3) pages. $ 25.00
This edition limited to 310 copies of which this is one of the 250 printed on Mohawk Superfine Paper. An essay on fine printing historical and contemporary by Lillian Marks, who with her husband Saul operated the Plantin Press. Printed on the California State Library's 1854 Albion which had earlier belonged to the Plantin Press. Woodcut title page vignette by E.D. Taylor.

1760. (Merrymount Press) Beckwitkh, Alice H.R.H. THE HUMANIST PRINTER, EXHIBITIONS & A CONFERENCE HONORING DANIEL BERKELEY UPDIKE'S MERRYMOUNT PRESS: 1893–1993. Providence, RI: American Printing History Association, 1993, large 8vo., stiff paper wrappers, paper cover label. 28 pages.
$ 10.00

Issued as an exhibition catalogue at the 18th Annual Conference of the American Printing History Association, 1993. Updike (1860–1941) is one of the most important American printers in this lineage, stressing scholarship, access, and clarity. Illustrated.

1761. (Merrymount Press) Bianchi, Daniel B. SOME RECOLLECTIONS OF THE MERRYMOUNT PRESS. (Berkeley): George L. Harding & Roger Levenson, 1976, small 8vo., cloth. xii, 26, (2) pages.
$ 65.00
Limited to 100 copies for sale. Information on D.B. Updike.

1762. (Merrymount Press) Kup, Karl. DANIEL BERKELEY UPDIKE AND THE MERRYMOUNT PRESS. New York: The AIGA, 1940, small 8vo., stiff paper wrappers. 56 pages.
$ 20.00
Limited to 1000 copies. With essays by Royal Cortissoz, David Pottinger, Lawrence Wroth, and Updike on the occasion of the exhibit. With decorations by Dwiggins, Cleland, Benson and others. Includes a checklist of Updike's work by Kark Kup.

1763. (Merrymount Press) UPDIKE: AMERICAN PRINTER AND HIS MERRYMOUNT PRESS. New York: The American Institute of Graphic Arts, 1947, 8vo., cloth, dust jacket. (ii), 156 pages followed by many plates reproducing titles pages of Merrymount Press books.
$ 50.00
First edition. Contains notes on the press and its work by Updike and numerous other articles on the press by Morison, Anderson, Cleland, Howe, Winship, Ruzicka, Pottinger and Rollins. Jacket chipped at spine ends and soiled.

1764. (Merrymount Press) Winship, George Parker. DANIEL BERKELEY UPDIKE AND THE MERRYMOUNT PRESS OF BOSTON MASSACHUSETTS, 1860–1894–1941. Rochester: The Printing House of Leo Hart, 1947, 8vo., cloth, dust jacket. xiv, 141 pages.
$ 40.00
First edition. Jacket chipped with small tears along edges.

1765. (Miniature Books) Bradbury, Robert C. ANTIQUE UNITED STATES MINIATURE BOOKS, 1690–1900. North Clarendon, VT: Microbibliophile, 2001, 8vo., cloth, dust jacket. viii, 357, (7) pages with 13 pages of illustrations. $ 75.00
Limited to an edition of 1000 copies. Provides bibliographic information on over 1,600 antique miniature books printed between 1690 and 1900, most of which are in the collections of the American Antiquarian Society in Worcester, Massachusetts and the Lilly Library at Indiana University in Bloomington, Indiana. It gives an overview of the development of the American book as reflected in its smallest examples as well as descriptions of more than 300 printers and publishers. In addition, a chronological list includes Bradbury numbers assigned to each title for reference purposes. The entire work is fully indexed by book titles, authors and publishers with more than 30 illustrations.

1766. (Miniature Books) Bradbury, Robert C. TWENTIETH CENTURY UNITED STATES MINIATURE BOOKS. North Clarendon, VT: Microbibliophile, 2000, 8vo., cloth, dust jacket. xv, 465+(1) pages with 16 pages of illustrations. $ 75.00
Limited to an edition of 1,000 copies. Provides bibliographic information on over 3,300 miniature books printed in the twentieth century starting with the author's private collection. It gives an overview of the development of miniature books as well as descriptions of more than 300 printers and publishers who create them. In addition, a numbered chronological list is included for reference purposes. The entire work is fully indexed by book titles, authors and publishers with nineteen black and white photographs.

1767. MODERN BRITISH AND AMERICAN PRIVATE PRESSS (1850–1965).
With a preface by D. T. Richnell. London: British Museum Publications, (1976), 8vo.,
cloth. (iii), 211 pages. $ 55.00
The most comprehensive bibliography on the subject. The presses are listed alphabetically with bibliographical annotations of the books they published which the British Library holds.

1768. (Morris, William) COLLECTOR'S CHOICE, THE JOHN J. WALSDORF
COLLECTION OF WILLIAM MORRIS IN PRIVATE PRESS AND LIMITED
EDITION, AN EXHIBITION. Washington: George Washington University Library,
1980, 8vo., stiff paper wrappers. 62 pages. $ 15.00
Well illustrated.

1769. (Mosher, Thomas Bird) Bishop, Philip R. THOMAS BIRD MOSHER, PIRATE
PRINCE OF PUBLISHERS. New Castle, Delaware and London: Oak Knoll Press &
The British Library, 1998, 4to., cloth. 552 pages. $ 125.00
First edition. This groundbreaking bibliography and biography describes the books published by Amer-
ican publisher, Thomas Bird Mosher, whose editions helped to convey England's literature and design to
the American public. "The Mosher Books" include works by authors such as William Morris, Oscar
Wilde, Fiona Macleod, Robert Louis Stevenson, Walter Pater, A. C. Swinburne, Dante Gabriel Rossetti,
George Meredith, Robert Browning, and George Gissing. By promoting these authors, Mosher acted as
a prime conduit in disseminating the more exotic literary fruits of the Aesthetic, Pre-Raphaelite, and
Arts & Crafts movements. This book also reveals the dramatic story behind the literary piracy slanders
brought against Mosher. His passion for little-known texts and literary gems often led Mosher to
reprint books without the author's permission, though he often did pay royalties. Mosher never techni-
cally broke any copyright laws, and authors like George Russell came to his defense and challenged their
own publishers to issue editions just as fine and affordable as Mosher's productions. Mosher's books
stimulated American interest, and many authors were delighted that their works were being beautifully produced and widely distributed. Mosher's books also introduced to an admiring public, the designs
of Morris, Rossetti, Blake, Ricketts, Housman, Mackmurdo, Pissarro, and Strang. The Mosher books exposed Americans to designs from the Vale, Eragny, Daniel, Chiswick, and Kelmscott presses. Well-
known binders also embellished Mosher productions with their best work. This book includes an introduction by Dr. William E. Fredeman, an 8-page full-color section, and over 200 illustrations. SALES
RIGHTS: Available outside the UK from Oak Knoll Books. Available in the UK from The British Library.

1770. (Nonesuch Press) Meynell, Dame Alix. FRANCIS MEYNELL OF THE
NONESUCH PRESS. Manchester, England: Manchester Polytechnic Library, 1979,
small 4to., stiff paper wrappers with tape spine. 17+(1) pages. $ 15.00
The Stanley Morison Memorial Lecture, given by Sir Francis Meynell's wife at the opening of an exhibit
on the Nonesuch Press, October 17, 1979. Many anecdotes and quotes from Meynell, including the story
of the statistician who was drowned in a lake, the *average* depth of which was...three inches. Covers
creased and somewhat soiled, with small tear.

1771. NORTH WEST BOOK ARTS, A BIMONTHLY JOURNAL OF THE
BOOK ARTS IN THE PACIFIC NORTHWEST. Volume I, Number 1 to Volume II,
no.3. The first 9 issues. Seattle, WA: TR Publishers, 1980–1982, 4to., stiff paper wrappers. $ 45.00
The first number is a photocopy. Illustrated.

1772. (Officina Bodoni) Barr, John. OFFICINA BODONI, MONTAGNOLA -
VERONA BOOKS PRINTED BY GIOVANNI MARDERSTEIG ON THE
HAND PRESS, 1923–1977. London: British Library, (1978), square 8vo., cloth, dust
jacket. 96 pages. $ 55.00
Well-illustrated and annotated catalogue.

1773. (Officina Bodoni) Mardersteig, Giovanni. OFFICINA BODONI, DAS WERK EINER HANDPRESSE, 1923–1977. Hamburg: Maximilian- Gesellschaft, (1979), small 4to., cloth, cardboard slipcase. lxi, 289, (3) pages. $ 250.00
First edition, one of 500 copies for Germany. The definitive bibliography of the press written by Mardersteig prior to his death.

1774. (Officina Bodoni) OFFICINA BODONI, VERONA, CATALOGUE OF BOOKS PRINTED ON THE HAND PRESS MXMXXIII - MXMLIV. London: British Museum, 1954, tall 8vo., stiff paper wrappers. ix, 34, (10) pages. $ 45.00
First edition, limited to 500 copies printed by the Stamperia Valdonega in Verona. Contains a five page introduction by Stanley Morison. Covers faded in places. Endpaper foxed.

1775. (Old Stile Press) Harrop, Dorothy. A OLD STILE PRESS IN THE TWENTI-ETH CENTURY, A BIBLIOGRAPHY 1979–1999. (Monmouthshire): Old Stile Press, (2000), small 4to., decorated paper covered boards. 135+(1) pages. $ 45.00
Printed in an edition limited to 1000 copies. A bibliography of The Old Stile Press that covers all material produced by this press from its beginning in 1979 to 1999. Each entry is accompanied with woodcut illustrations from the books. There are introductory essays by Dorothy Harrop, Frances McDowall, Nicolas McDowall and Peter Wakelin. Indexed.

1776. (Pazifische Presse) Jaeger, Roland. NEW WEIMAR ON THE PACIFIC, THE PAZIFISCHE PRESSE AND GERMAN EXILE PUBLISHING IN LOS ANGE-LES 1942-48. Translated from the German by Marion Philadelphia and edited by Victoria Dailey. Los Angeles: Victoria Dailey Publisher, 2000, 8vo., quarter cloth with pictorial paper covered boards, paper spine label. (ii), 87+(1) pages, with 10 additional pages of illustrations. $ 45.00
Limited to edition of 300 copies. The story of the Pazifische Press and the role it played in providing a voice in their native tongue to the German exiles living in Los Angeles during the Second World War. In the letter sent to prospective subscribers, the publishers, Ernst Gottleib and Felix Guggenheim, stated their intention to provide a few literary treasures that would still be enjoyed "when Hitler has long since become nothing more than a dark chapter in the book of history." While not a financial success, Pazifische did fill an historically significant niche until production was finally shut down in 1948. Includes a bibliography of the all of the eleven titles published.

1777. (Perishable Press) TWO DECADES OF HAMADY AND THE PERISH-ABLE PRESS LIMITED AN ANECDOTALLY ANNOTATED CHECK LIST FOR AN EXHIBITION AT GALLERY 210. (Mt. Horeb, Wisconsin: The Perishable Press, 1984), 4to., stiff paper wrappers. 128 pages and 32 illustrations. $ 55.00
With a preface by Hamady.

1778. (Plain Wrapper Press) PLAIN WRAPPER PRESS, 1966–1988, AN ILLUS-TRATED BIBLIOGRAPHY OF THE WORK OF RICHARD-GABRIEL RUM-MONDS. With Bibliographical Descriptions by Elaine Smyth and a Foreword by Decherd Turner. Austin, TX: W. Thomas Taylor, 1993, small 4to., stiff paper wrappers. 74, (2) pages. $ 45.00
Limited to 340 copies. Designed and printed by Bradley Hutchinson at the printing office of W. Thomas Taylor with Monotype Dante set by Michael and Winifred Bixler and photographs in color by Carrington Weems.

1779. (Press of The Woolly Whale) PRESS OF THE WOOLLY WHALE, CATA-LOGUE OF AN EXHIBITION OF BOOKS AND PRINTED PIECES FROM THE PRIVATE LIBRARY OF MELBERT B. CARY. Buffalo: The Phoenix Press, 1939, 8vo., stiff paper wrappers. (24) pages. $ 35.00
Limited to 300 copies. The most definitive checklist of the press's activities, listing 56 items with full descriptions.

1780. (Primavera Press) Hart, James D. & Ward Ritchie. INFLUENCES ON CALI-FORNIA PRINTING. Los Angeles: University of California, 1970, 8vo., stiff paper wrappers. 84 pages. $ 15.00
Contains a bibliography of the Primavera Press by J.M. Edelstein in addition to other information.

1781. (Printing) ART OF THE BOOK, WILLIAM MORRIS AND AFTER, 1892–1977. Cambridge: Fitzwilliam Museum, 1978, small 8vo., stiff paper wrappers. Not paginated but 106 items described. $ 15.00
Foreword by Michael Jaffe and preface by Brooke Crutchley.

1782. THE PRIVATE LIBRARY. Per issue: $ 5.00
Filled with information on book-collecting, private press books and other articles related to the book-collecting world. Individual issues as follows: 1st Series: Vol 7 1,2,3,4; Vol 8 2,3,4; 2nd Series: Vol 2 3; Vol 5 1,2,3,4; Vol 7 2; Vol 6 1,2,3; Vol 10 2,3; Fourth Series Vol 2 2, 4 2.

1783. (Private Press Books) Cave, Roderick & Thomas Rae. PRIVATE PRESS BOOKS. Various issues. Pinner: Private Library Association, 1959–1967, 8vo., stiff paper wrappers. Per issue: $ 20.00
Descriptions of modern private press books issued in each year. Have the following: 1959(5), 1960(4),1961(5), 1962(9), 1963(4), 1964(6), 1965(2), 1966(4), 1967, 1972, 1976, 1977, 1979(3), 1980(2), 1981–1984(3), 1985-86(8), 1987(2), 1988(5).

1784. (Private Press Books) PRIVATE PRESS BOOKS 1989. Pinner: Private Libraries Association, 1991, 8vo., paper wrappers. 72 pages. $ 30.00
Lists many books, by press, printed by private presses for the year of issue. Beautifully illustrated with illustrations from some of the entries.

1785. (Private Press Books) Kerrigan, Philip (editor). PRIVATE PRESS BOOKS 1990. Pinner: Private Libraries Association, 1992, 8vo., paper wrappers. 101 pages. $ 40.00
Lists 271 books, by press, printed by private presses for the year 1990. Beautifully illustrated with illustrations from some of the entries. Also includes a complete index for the period 1981 - 1990.

1786. (Private Press Books) Bolton, Claire and David (editors). PRIVATE PRESS BOOKS 1991. Pinner: Private Libraries Association, 1993, 8vo., paper wrappers. 78 pages. $ 40.00
Lists 298 books, by press, printed by private presses for the year 1991. Beautifully illustrated with illustrations from some of the entries.

1787. (Private Press) EIGHTY FROM THE EIGHTIES, A DECADE OF FINE PRINTING. New York: The New York Public Library, 1990, 8vo., paper wrappers. (8) pages. $ 15.00
Pamphlet to an exhibition of fine press books held at the New York Public Library between November 1990 and April 1991. Contains a statement by the curators of the exhibition Francis O. Mattson and Daniel J. Tierney, Jr., and includes a checklist of the 81 books, by 76 presses exhibited. Illustrates works by the Arion Press, Logan Elm Press, and Handpresse Gutsch.

1788. (Private Presses) CATALOG OF SPECIAL AND PRIVATE PRESSES IN THE RARE BOOK DIVISION THE RESEARCH LIBRARIES, THE NEW YORK PUBLIC LIBRARY. Two volumes. Boston: G.K. Hall, 1978, folio, cloth. xxi,657; (ii),629 pages. $ 450.00

With an introduction by Maud D. Cole. Reproductions of the card CATALOGUE descriptions of the holdings of this library. Includes famous 18th century presses up to the present along with the work of noted book designers. In all there are over 15,000 books and pamphlets described from over 1,200 presses. This set contains information not available elsewhere are many obscure presses.

1789. (Private Press) MORRIS - DRUCKE UND ANDERE MEISTERWERKE ENGLISCHER UND AMERIKANISCHER PRIVATPRESSEN. Mainz: Gutenberg- Museum, 1954, 8vo., stiff paper wrappers. 32 pages. $ 35.00

Exhibition of private press books and illustrators from England and America. Even has a section on the Roycroft Press.

1790. (Private Press) OAK KNOLL BOOKS CATALOGUE 175. New Castle, DE: Oak Knoll Books, n.d., 8vo., paper wrappers. 136 pages. $ 10.00

Catalogue no.175, devoted to fine printing and private press books. Includes 70 general books about fine printing and over 900 individual private press books.

1791. (Private Press) OAK KNOLL BOOKS CATALOGUE 188. New Castle, DE: Oak Knoll Books, n.d. (circa 1996), 8vo., paper wrappers. 129 pages. $ 10.00

catalogue no.188, featuring over 200 books from the 1996 Oak Knoll Fest. Includes a note on the festival and sketches of each of the 16 private presses featured.

1792. (Private Press) OAK KNOLL FEST 1995 A DAY OF BOOK ARTS. New Castle, DE: Oak Knoll Books, 1995, 8vo., paper wrappers. 29 pages. $ 10.00

A separately issued catalogue of the books present at the 1995 Oak Knoll Books private press fair. Includes a program of events and histories of the participating presses.

1793. (Private Press) PRINTER AND THE ARTIST A CATALOGUE OF PRIVATE PRESS BOOKS & ILLUSTRATED BOOKS FROM THE UNITED KINGDOM, EUROPE & AMERICA. London: Bertram Rota, 1974, 8vo., paper wrappers. 155 pages. $ 35.00

Being a sales catalogue of 1320 items from major and minor private presses with a great deal of information about the presses, both biographical and bibliographical.

1794. (Private Press) SANTA CRUZ PRINTERS' CHAPPEL EXHIBITION CATALOGUE OF LETTERPRESS PRINTING & BOOK ARTS. (Santa Cruz, CA): Printers' Chappel of Santa Cruz County, (1983), 8vo., stiff wrappers. (28) pages. $ 25.00

catalogue from a 1983 Exhibition of Santa Cruz letterpress printers. Includes Blackwells Press, Green Gables, Middle Earth Books, Moving Parts Press, Owl & Butterfly, Good Books, etc. With photographs of each printer in his or her shop and a facing page of commentary written by each. Folded exhibit poster and handwritten note from Nick Zachreson of Blackwells Press laid in.

1795. (Private Press) STAMPATORI TORCHI LIBRI, 1895–1996. Verona, Italy: Biblioteca Civica di Verona, 1996, 8vo., self paper wrappers. (16) pages. $ 10.00

First edition. An exhibition catalogue devoted to the history of fine printing with a large number of English and American examples. Annotated descriptions describe 31 items. Lists works by Plain Wrapper Press and Doves Press. Illustrated.

1796. Ransom, Will. PRIVATE PRESSES AND THEIR BOOKS. New York: R.R. Bowker Co., 1929, 8vo., cloth. 493 pages. $ 185.00

First edition, limited to 1200 copies printed by the Lakeside Press. 193 page history of private presses followed by bibliographies and biographies of many of the private presses. Small bump along top edge of front cover. Bookplate.

1797. Ransom, Will. SELECTIVE CHECK LISTS OF PRESS BOOKS. PART TWO. New York: Philip Duschnes, 1947, small 8vo., paper wrappers. pp.33-64. $ 20.00

One of the parts of Ransom's expansion of his private press bibliography. This part describes all the books designed by the Hawthorn House, The Prairie Press, The Hours Press, The Seizin Press and St. Dominic's Press.

1798. Ransom, Will. SELECTIVE CHECK LISTS OF PRESS BOOKS. PART THREE. New York: Philip Duschnes, 1946, small 8vo., paper wrappers. pp.65–100.
$ 25.00

One of the parts of Ransom's expansion of his private press bibliography. This part describes all the books printed by the Limited Editions Club and the Heritage Press.

1799. Ransom, Will. SELECTIVE CHECK LISTS OF PRESS BOOKS. PART SEVEN / EIGHT. New York: Philip Duschnes, 1947, small 8vo., paper wrappers. pp.221-284. $ 20.00

One of the parts of Ransom's expansion of his private press bibliography. This part describes all the books designed by W.A. Dwiggins, the Bremer Press, William Loring Andrews, the Redcoat Press, etc. With a note in red ink on the front cover.

1800. (Ricketts, Charles) Capelleveen, Paul Van. A NEW CHECKLIST OF BOOKS DESIGNED BY CHARLES RICKETTS AND CHARLES SHANNON. The Hague: Museum van het Boek/Museum Meermanno-Westreenianum, 1996, 8vo., paper wrappers. 69+(1) pages. $ 15.00

The book designers and illustrators, C. Ricketts (1866–1931) and C. Shannon (1863–1937), began to work together around 1888 and, in 1889, to publish the Dial, which ran to 1897. In 1889 or 1890 they made the acquaintance of Oscar Wilde and thereafter designed and illustrated some of his books, working for a time with the publisher John Lane. In 1894, they founded the Vale Press, which continued until 1904, producing, among other things, a 39-volume set of Shakespeare! After 1904, Ricketts continued to do work for other publishers, including one book for Nonesuch. This checklist lists 262 Ricketts and/or Shannon items in four sections, with 21 additional entries in two appendices (books projected but not published, and items falsely attributed to Ricketts). A typical entry indicates author, title, editor, publisher, month of publication, pagination and dimensions, color, no. of copies, form of issue (binding,etc.), printer and type, decorations and binders. With references, list of abbreviations, and index. Distributed for Museum van het Boek.

1801. Ricketts, Charles. DEFENCE OF THE REVIVAL OF PRINTING. New York: Battery Park Books, 1978, 8vo., cloth. (ii), 37 pages. $ 25.00

Reprint of the 1899 Ballantyne Press edition. With comments on the English private press revival.

1802. (Ritchie, Ward) Davies, David W. CONCISE ACCOUNT OF WARD RITCHIE HIS PRINTING & HIS BOOKS. Los Angeles: Dawson's Book Shop, 1984, 8vo., printed paper wrappers. ix, 55, (2) pages. $ 45.00

First edition, limited to 300 copies. Designed by Vance Gerry. A fascinating account of this great book designer and printer and containing a bibliography of books and articles by and about Ritchie. Well illustrated.

1803. Ritchie, Ward. OF BOOKMEN & PRINTERS, A GATHERING OF MEM-ORIES. With a foreword by Lawrence Clark Powell. Los Angeles: Dawson's Book Shop, 1989, 8vo., composite boards, slipcase. 189, (3) pages. $250.00

Limited to 500 copies of which this is one of 50 copies bound thus by D'Ambrosio and signed by Ritchie and Powell. Designed and written by the printer, Ward Ritchie, this work contains his reminiscences of book collectors, book artists, bookmen and printers. Some of these reminiscences are rewritten versions of previously published pieces. These stories include Los Angeles booksellers of the Great Depression and the formation of the Zamorano Club; bookseller Jake Zeitlin; artist and wood engraver Paul Landacre; eccentric book designer Merle Armitage; poet Robinson Jeffers; Jane Grabhorn's irreverent wit and whimsical creations, during her days at the Grabhorn Press; Ward's apprenticeship with Francois-Louis Schmied, the Parisian book printer and artist of the 1920's and 30's; music composer John Cage; C.H. St. John Hornby of the Ashendene Press; the former librarian and dean of the UCLA Library School, Lawrence Clark Powell, Ritchie's boyhood friend; and last but not least, the individuals and history of once wealthy and sophisticated Virginia City. The special binding consists of a two-tone front cover in relief, consisting of a cloth-covered board cut in the shape of an "R" over a paper-covered board.

1804. Ritchie, Ward. OF BOOKMEN & PRINTERS, A GATHERING OF MEM-ORIES. With a foreword by Lawrence Clark Powell. Los Angeles: Dawson's Book Shop, (1989), 8vo., cloth backed boards. 189 pages. $50.00

Limited to 500 copies. Designed and written by the great printer, Ward Ritchie, this work contains many reminiscences of book collectors, book artists, bookmen and printers many of which are notable and recognizable figures in the world of fine books. These stories include the Los Angeles booksellers of the Great Depression and the formation of the Zamorano Club, bookseller Jake Zeitlin, artist and wood engraver Paul Landacre, eccentric book designer Merle Armitage, poet Robinson Jeffers, Jane Grabhorn's irreverent wit and whimsical creations which colored her days at the Grabhorn Press; Ward's apprenticeship with Francois-Louis Schmied, the preeminent Parisian book printer and artist of the 1920s and 30's; music composer John Cage, C.H. St. John Hornby of the Ashendene Press, Ritchie's boyhood friend and former librarian and dean of the Library School at UCLA, Lawrence Clark Powell; and last of all, but not least, the individuals and colorful history of once wealthy and sophisticated Virginia City. Distributed for Dawson's Book Shop by Oak Knoll Press.

1805. (Ritchie, Ward) Powell, Lawrence Clark. THE WORK OF WARD RITCHIE, DESIGNER, PRINTER, POET. Tucson: Truepenny Books, 1997, small 8vo., stiff wrappers with paper cover label. 92, (2) pages. $30.00

Printed in an edition limited to 300 copies and signed by the author on the title-page. Designed by Vance Gerry, typesetting and printing by Commercial Printers, Tucson. Remarks by Ritchie's friend of ninety years on "his alter ego and his muses. "I sensed from the beginning that , as he became one of the best printers of our time, he was also a poet, from whom he created his alter ego, Peter Lum Quince. Few of us recognized why he had chosen this other being, who was, and was not, Ward Ritchie" (preface). Includes selections of poetry by "Quince" from 1930 to 1991.

1806. (Rogers, Bruce) BOUQUET FOR BR, A BIRTHDAY GARLAND GATH-ERED BY THE TYPOPHILES. New York: The Typophiles, 1950, tall 12mo., cloth-backed decorated boards. (76) pages. $50.00

First edition, limited to 600 copies of which 300 were set aside for Typophiles. Chapbook 24. Includes reproductions of some of Rogers' title pages, 6 photographs of Rogers and a number of calligraphic tributes by such designers as Arnold Bank, R. Hunter Middleton, George Salter, Paul Standard and others.

1807. (Rogers, Bruce) BR TODAY, A SELECTION OF HIS BOOKS, WITH COMMENTS. New York: The Grolier Club, 1982, 8vo., cloth-backed boards. xiv, 41, (3) pages. $45.00

Limited to 450 copies. Introduction by Herb Johnson followed by selected comments on 35 of Rogers' most important book designs.

1808. (Rogers, Bruce) LIST ONE, SOME WORK OF BRUCE ROGERS PART ONE: 1895–1914. Pittsford: Herbert H. Johnson, n.d., small 8vo., paper wrappers. (16) pages. $ 10.00

A catalogue by Herbert H. Johnson's book store offering 89 books designed by Bruce Rogers. A note to Dr. Shapiro from Helen Johnson is inserted. Name and address printed in ink on cover.

1809. Rogers, Bruce. PI, A HODGE-PODGE OF THE LETTERS, PAPERS AND ADDRESSES. Cleveland: The World Publishing Co., 1953, 8vo., cloth. x, 185, (3) pages. $ 35.00

First edition. Forty-four separate articles on typography and 36 plates reproducing some of the most interesting of Rogers' design work. Bump in outer edges of covers. Remnants of jacket loosely inserted.

1810. (Rogers, Bruce) Targ, William. MAKING OF THE BRUCE ROGERS WORLD BIBLE. Cleveland and New York: World Publishing Co., (1949), 4to., cloth, slipcase. 20, (22) pages. $ 40.00

First edition, limited to 1875 copies. With numerous photos of the making of this well designed Bible including reproductions of the decorations and initials used. Slipcase is tape repaired as it was split along hinges.

1811. (Rogers, Bruce) Warde, Frederic. BRUCE ROGERS, DESIGNER OF BOOKS. With a List of the Books Printed Under Mr. Roger's Supervision. Cambridge: Harvard University Press, 1926, 8vo., cloth, paper spine label. 75 pages of text followed by 15 plates. $ 65.00

First edition. This essay and bibliography originally appeared in the Fleuron although this book contains some alterations. Wear at spine ends.

1812. (Rogers, Bruce) Warde, Frederic. BRUCE ROGERS, DESIGNER OF BOOKS. With a List of the Books Printed Under Mr. Roger's Supervision. Cambridge: Harvard University Press, 1926, 8vo., cloth, paper spine label. 75 pages of text followed by 20 plates. $ 150.00

First edition, one of 210 copies bound in a different cloth from the trade edition and containing extra illustrations. This essay and bibliography originally appeared in the Fleuron although this book contains some alterations. Rogers has signed his name on the title page making it part of the title of the book. With the leather bookplate of Leroy Arthur Sugarman (which has caused offset on the free endpaper).

1813. (Rogers, Bruce) WORK OF BRUCE ROGERS, JACK OF ALL TRADES MASTER OF ONE: A CATALOGUE OF AN EXHIBITION ... WITH AN IN-TRODUCTION BY D.B. UPDIKE, A LETTER FROM JOHN T. Mc-CUTCHEON, AND AN ADDRESS BY MR. ROGERS. New York: Oxford University Press, 1939, 8vo., cloth, dust jacket. liv, 127 pages. $ 85.00

First edition. A bibliography of the design work. Inscribed by Rogers on the half-title. Jacket worn with tears and soiling. Original prospectus loosely inserted.

1814. Rothenberg, Jerome (editor). A BOOK OF THE BOOK. New York: Granary Books, 2000, large 8vo., cloth, dust jacket. xiii, (iii), pps.7-537, (5) pages. $ 44.95

First edition. A collection of works from over ninety writers, poets, painters, performers, scholars, critics, anthropologists and historians which show a wide range of discursive writings that deal with one or another aspect of the book and writing. It is illustrated throughout in black and white and features a full color fold out facsimile of the great Blaise Cendrars/Sonia Delaunay book of 1913, "La Prose du Transsiberien."

1815. (Rudge, William Edwin) Rudge, Frederick G. WILLIAM EDWIN RUDGE, A BRIEF ACCOUNT OF HIS LIFE AND WORK TOGETHER WIT H SOME NOTES ON HIS INFLUENCE ON AMERICAN PRINTING. 1937, 8vo., paper wrappers. (ii), 34 pages. $ 20.00

In PM, Vol.3, No.6, February, 1937. An account of this famous printer and printing house. Bruce Rogers designed the title page. Illustrated.

1816. Rummonds, Richard-Gabriel (Editor). TWO PRIVATE PRESSES FROM VERONA, OFFICINA CHIMÈREA - AMPERSAND. N.P.: n.p., n.d. (circa 2000), small 8vo., self paper wrappers. 16 pages. $ 15.00

First edition. An exhibition catalogue that focuses on the work of two small presses in Verona, Italy, Officina Chimèrea and Ampersand. Founded by Gino Castiglione and Alessandro Corubolo, Officina Chimèrea has produced forty-six books with the two partners assembling all the various elements for each project themselves. They have used an 1855 Albion handpress since 1968. Ten of their currently available works are described. Ampersand, the most recent private press to be established in Verona, was started by Alessandro Zanella in 1982. Although he has now expanded and uses some modern technology to create larger editions, Zanella still upholds the same meticulous standards that he employs for his handpress work. Information on eleven titles from Ampersand is included. Fourteen color illustrations are used to complement the entries.

1817. Rummonds, Richard-Gabriel. UN TIPOGRAFO FRA DUE CULTURE. Milano: Fondazione biblioteca di via Senato, 1999, oblong 8vo., stiff paper wrappers, printed paper dust jacket. 112, (3) pages. $ 46.95

A catalogue of the exhibition held in Milan, Fondazione biblioteca di via Senato, September 23-October 17, 1999. Thoroughly illustrated with color reproductions of pages from the books displayed. Includes a preface by Gino Castiglioni, an essay on Rummonds work by Michael Peich, bibliographical references, and a name index. All in Italian.

1818. (Samurai Press) Woolmer, J. Howard. SAMURAI PRESS, 1906–1909, A BIBLIOGRAPHY. Revere, PA: Woolmer - Brotherson Ltd., 1986, 8vo., cloth, dust jacket. xix, 70 pages. $ 35.00

First edition. Annotated bibliography of this 20th century British publisher founded by Maurice Browne with others. Each booklet has the title page illustrated. Presentation from the author on free endpaper.

1819. (Shakespeare Head Press) Sidgwick, Frank. FRANK SIDGWICK'S DIARY AND OTHER MATERIAL RELATING TO A.H. BULLEN & THE SHAKESPEARE HEAD PRESS AT STRTFORD-UPON-AVON. Oxford: Basil Blackwell, 1975, 8vo., cloth, dust jacket, top edge gilt. 90 pages, with a pocket at the rear of the book containing the 1904 announcement of the press, paper wrappers, 12mo., 16 pages.
$ 25.00

Limited to 1000 copies. A.H. Bullen established the Shakespeare Head Press in 1904 with his partner, Frank Sidgwick. Sidgwick kept a diary of his day-to-day activities during the first year of operation. This is now published along with other material. Jacket soiled.

1820. (Silver, Louis H.) PRESS BOOKS AND WORKS OF REFERENCE COLLECTED BY THE LATE LOUIS H. SILVER. New York: Parke-Bernet Galleries, 1965, 8vo., stiff paper wrappers. (vi), 32, (2) pages. $ 17.50

Auction catalogue for the November 16, 1965 sale of books collected by the late Louis H. Silver, with knock down prices written in margins. With books by the Ashendene, Doves, and Kelmscott Presses, the Gutenburg Bible Facsimile of 1913–14, and Charles Dickens' copy of *The Poetical Works of John Keats*.

1821. Smith, Keith. TWO HUNDRED BOOKS BY KEITH SMITH. New York: Keith Smith Books, 2000, 8vo., cloth, dust jacket. 335+(1) pages. $ 35.00

First edition. Printed in an edition limited to 1000 copies. An annotated bibliography of all of the books made by Smith, which range from artist books to poetry and textbooks to dictionaries. Most of his 150 one of a kind books are in his own collection. He has published over two dozen small edition artist books and book-length poems, and has compiled ten small dictionaries. The 200 books are represented by over 500 illustrations. Indexed.

1822. (St. Dominic's Press) Sewell, Brocard. CHECK-LIST OF BOOKS, PAM-PHLETS, BROADSHEETS, CATALOGUES, POSTERS, ETC. PRINTED BY H.D.C. PEPLER AT SAINT DOMINIC'S PRESS, DITCHLING, SUSSEX, BE-TWEEN THE YEARS A.1916 AND 1936 D. Ditchling: Ditchling Press, 1979, 8vo., paper wrappers. (viii), 43 pages. $ 35.00

First edition. The press is known for using many of Eric Gill's illustrations and devices.

1823. (Steiner-Prag, Hugo) Schlegel, Irene. HUGO STEINER-PRAG, SEIN LEBEN FUR DAS SCHONE BUCH. Memmingen: Edition Curt Visel, (1995), small 8vo., cloth, dust jacket. 227, (3) pages. $ 50.00

First edition. A new study of the work of this designer and illustrator. Steiner-Prag illustrated a number of the books for the Limited Editions Club in America and established a design school in New York upon his emigration to the United States in 1945. Illustrated.

1824. (Stinehour Press) Farrell, David. STINEHOUR PRESS, A BIBLIOGRAPHI-CAL CHECKLIST OF THE FIRST THIRTY YEARS. With an introduction by Roderick Stinehour. Vermont: Meriden-Stinehour Press, (1988), 8vo., cloth, dust jack-et. xxi, 300 pages. $ 60.00

First edition, limited to 1200 numbered copies. A checklist of the printed works produced by this fine press in the first thirty years. Contains an interesting introduction on the origins of the press and is well illustrated, with many of the title pages shown in two colors.

1825. (Stone & Kimball) Kramer, Sidney. HISTORY OF STONE & KIMBALL AND HERBERT S. STONE & CO WITH A BIBLIOGRAPHY OF THEIR PUBLICA-TIONS, 1893–1905. Preface by Frederic G. Melcher. Chicago: Norman Forgue, 1940, 8vo., cloth, slipcase. xxii, 380 pages. $ 200.00

First edition, one of the 500 to be printed on rag paper. Best book on the subject. Presentation from Kramer and Norman Forgue on the free endpaper.

1826. Thompson, Susan Otis. AMERICAN BOOK DESIGN AND WILLIAM MORRIS. New York: R.R. Bowker Co., 1977, 4to., cloth, dust jacket. xvii, 258 pages with 111 illustrations. $ 100.00

First edition. Traces the effect of men like Updike, Rogers, Goudy, Bradley, Cleland, Dwiggins, Ransom, Nash and Rollins on book production in America. This copy has an extra sheet bound in that has a print-ed presentation page reading "Presented to Paul N. Banks on the occasion of the May 17th, 1978 meet-ing of the Caxton Club with the appreciation of the members & guests whose signatures appear below.. (followed by the signatures of 31 members)."

1827. Tiessen, Wolfgang. SERVING AUTHOR AND READER. ABOUT THE DE-SIGN OF MY BOOKS. TYPHOPHILE MONOGRAPH NEW SERIES NO. 4. New York: The Typophiles, 1987, 8vo., stiff paper wrappers, dust jacket. 17+(1) pages plus 20 full-page plates. $ 8.50

First edition. Edited by Abe Lerner, President of The Typophiles. Translated from the German by Stefan B. Polter. Issued to contradict an unfavorable review of Tiessen's books in "Fine Print."

1828. (Trianon Press) Anderson, Emily. PURSUIT OF HAPPY RESULTS, BARRY SPANN AND THE MAKING OF TWENTY-SEVEN LANDSCAPES. With an Introductory Note by Nicolas Barker. Boston: Published for members of HOC VOLO, David Godine, 1991, 8vo., cloth, dust jacket. x, 104, (2) pages. $ 45.00
First edition. This book describes the collaboration between Barry Spann and Arnold Fawcus in producing this very special book for the Trianon Press in Paris. It reproduces the plates in 400–line screen duotone. With the bookplate of John DePol.

1829. (Unica T) UNICA T. ZEHN JAHRE KÜNSTLERBÜCHER. TEN YEARS OF ARTISTS' BOOKS. (Oberusel/Ts): Unica T, 1996, small 4to., paper covered boards. 227+(1) pages. $ 85.00
First edition. CATALOGUE for an exhibition of Unica T at the Museum für Kunsthandwerk in Frankfurt am Main. Unica T is a group of female book artists: Anija Harms, Doris Preussner, Uta Schneider, Ines v. Ketelhodt, and Ulrike Stoltz. Here, in English and German, several essays are devoted to their work and concerns. The richly illustrated CATALOGUE follows with biographies of each artist and numerous examples of their work (pictured in color). In English and German.

1830. Van der Bellen, Liana (editor). ARTISTS IN BOOKS, MADE IN CANADA IV. Ottawa: National Library of Canada, 1984, 8vo., stiff paper wrappers. (42) pages.
                    $ 15.00
Catalogue issued for the Artists in Books Exhibit, Made in Canada IV, at the National Library of Canada, from November 30, 1984 to March 24, 1985, in English and French. With color illustrations and description of each entry.

1831. Van der Bellen, Liana (editor). ARTISTS IN BOOKS, MADE IN CANADA V. Ottawa: National Library of Canada, 1987, small 4to., stiff paper wrappers. (50) pages.
                    $ 15.00
A catalogue issued with the Artists in Books exhibit at the National Library of Canada, October 14, 1987 to March 14, 1988. Contains 47 entries, mostly illustrated , with copy in French and English.

1832. Van Wingen, Peter M. PRIVATE PRESSES WITH PROPRIETARY TYPES. (Washington, D.C.): Library of Congress, n.d., small 8vo., stiff paper wrappers. unpaginated, but 11+(1) pages. $ 15.00
Issued for an exhibit at the Library of Congress, with a checklist of exhibited presses with proprietary types, from 1891 to World War II. Includes type specimens from the Ashendene, Caradoc, Doves, Eragny, Kelmscott, Gregynog, Grabhorn, Spiral, Village, and Cranach Presses, etc.

1833. (Village Press) Cary, Melbert B. BIBLIOGRAPHY OF THE VILLAGE PRESS. Including an Account of the Genesis of the Press by Frederick W. Goudy and a Portion of the 1903 Diary of Will Ransom, Co-Founder. New Castle, DE: Oak Knoll et al, 1981, 8vo., cloth, dust jacket. 220 pages. $ 35.00
This bibliography documents the career of the Village Press with meticulous detail and insight. In a short memoir at the beginning of this book Frederic W. Goudy gives an account of a printers life that is certain to be familiar to anyone who has experienced the "fun and fury" of a private press. The section from the diary of Will Ransom, co-founder of the press, gives some idea of the magnitude of the initial problems that were encountered. Despite these difficulties the press still produced books that were an able tribute to William Morris, in many ways Goudy's chief inspiration in book design. However the press was no mere imitation of the Kelmscott Press - in the years of its operation it forged a style that was distinctly Goudy's. Frederic W. Goudy was one of the most influential type designers of the twentieth century. His influence on advertising art and book design was considerable and he became an arbiter of typographic taste for an entire generation between the Wars. Part of the reason for this success lay with his practical knowledge of the problems of designer and printer. Much of this expertise was gained through the Village Press. This book was originally published in 1938 in a limited edition of only 260 copies.

1834. (Village Press) Cary, Melbert. VILLAGE PRESS, A RETROSPECTIVE EX-HIBITION 1903–1933. N.P.: The AIGA, 1933, 8vo., paper wrappers. 32 pages.

$ 20.00

With a note by Melbert Cary and a five page history by Will Ransom. Chipped along edges.

1835. Von Lucius, Wulf D. MAKING ARTIST BOOKS TODAY, A WORKSHOP IN POETENKILL, NY AUGUST 18TH-23RD, 1997. Stuttgart: Lucius and Lucius, 1998, 6 1/2" x 10 1/4", limp paper wrappers of handmade paper, collaged with news clippings and other ephemera. 121 pages. $ 50.00

Limited edition of 800 copies (plus 20 deluxe copies). A collection of personal statements from book artists which emerged out of the Poestenkill workshop for binders, librarians, collectors, typesetters, and other bibliophiles. The essays include: "The World of the Book: A World for the Book," (Hank Hine); "The Tactility of Artist Books" (Harry Reese); "Crossing Borders--the New Aesthetics in Artist Books" (Gunnar A. Kaldewey); "Artist Books in South America" (Luis Angel Parra); "Exhibiting Artist Books" (Mindell Dubansky); and "Collecting Contemporary Artist Books" (Wulf D. von Lucius). With 196 black-and-white illustrations, *Making Artist Books Today* is a wonderful reference book as well as a window into the state of the field at this time.

1836. (Way & Williams) Kraus, Joe W. HISTORY OF WAY & WILLIAMS WITH A BIBLIOGRAPHY OF THEIR PUBLICATIONS: 1895–1898. Philadelphia: George S. MacManus Co., 1984, square 8vo., cloth, paper cover label. xii, 111 pages.

$ 45.00

Limited to 500 copies and printed with the assistance of Henry Morris of the Bird & Bull Press. An important American private press. With a number of illustrations of title pages and book covers.

1837. Warren, Arthur. CHARLES WHITTINGHAMS PRINTERS. New York: The Grolier Club, 1896, tall 8vo., original half leather. (vi), 344 pages. $ 300.00

First and only edition, limited to 388 copies. (Hart no.112). History of the Chiswick Press, the most successful English printing House, and comparable only to the Didots of France. Well illustrated and printed on hand-made paper. Covers soiled and spine faded. Preliminary and endpages foxed.

1838. (Whittington Press) PRINTING AT THE WHITTINGTON PRESS, 1972–1994, AN EXHIBTIION. With Remarks by John Randle, John Dreyfus & Mark Batty. N.P.: International Typeface Corporation and The Grolier Club, 1994, 8vo., stiff paper wrappers. 63+(1) pages. $ 25.00

Limited to 2,500 copies printed by letterpress at the Stinehour Press with design by Jerry Kelly. A well annotated exhibition catalogue describing the production of the Whittington Press. Includes illustrations.